Abstract Automata

Peter H. Starke

ABSTRACT AUTOMATA

1972

NORTH-HOLLAND PUBLISHING COMPANY
AMSTERDAM · LONDON

AMERICAN ELSEVIER PUBLISHING COMPANY, INC-NEW YORK

Library of Congress Catalog Card Number 70-146193
ISBN North-Holland: 0720420520

This book is a translation of
ABSTRAKTE AUTOMATEN
Published by VEB Deutscher Verlag der Wissenschaften, Berlin 1969
Translated from the German by I. Shepherd

PUBLISHERS:
NORTH-HOLLAND PUBLISHING COMPANY – AMSTERDAM
NORTH-HOLLAND PUBLISHING COMPANY, LTD. – LONDON

SOLE DISTRIBUTORS FOR THE U.S.A. AND CANADA:
AMERICAN ELSEVIER PUBLISHING COMPANY, INC.
52 VANDERBILT AVENUE
NEW YORK, N. Y. 10017

Printed in Germany East

PREFACE

The aim of this book is to give a systematic presentation of the fundaments of the three main branches of abstract automata theory: deterministic, non-deterministic and stochastic automata. I was prompted to do this by the interest shown in a series of lectures and seminars on automata theory which I have given since 1965 at the Humboldt University, not only by students but also by members of various scientific and technical institutes.

In the following chapter I shall introduce the problems to be dealt with in this book, and motivate the three different notions of automata mentioned above. I have endeavored to facilitate the reader's work by giving rather complete proofs and by listing the most important symbols and terms used in the book in a preliminary chapter. The bibliography contains an exhaustive list of the works on automata theory published up until 1967, including publications on application and other problems which could not be developed here.

I am deeply indebted to Professors G. Asser (Greifswald), K. Schröter (Berlin), and H. Thiele (Berlin) for their helpful criticisms and suggestions and especially to the latter two for allowing me to present the second part of this book which consists of my own research, as my dissertation at the Humboldt University.

I also want to thank P. MünteferING and H.-J. Pohl for their help in reading the proofs and the VEB Deutscher Verlag der Wissenschaften for their kind cooperation.

Peter H. Starke

TABLE OF CONTENTS

INTRODUCTION

The theory of abstract automata is the mathematical investigation of digital cybernetical systems with respect to their most general system theoretical properties. In this chapter we shall explain what we mean by digital cybernetical systems and give their mathematical description. We shall mention the main problems considered in this book, as well as certain others which cannot be studied here in detail.

A *cybernetical system*, that is, one which receives, stores, processes and discharges information, is called *digital* if it works pulsewise, in separate steps in time.[1]) This kind of system works on a time scale consisting of a sequence of time intervals having at most their end points in common. Since these intervals do not overlap, the time scale is called *discrete*. In general it is built into the system itself (e.g., in all electronic digital computers), however it can also be superimposed on the system from outside. For our purposes it makes no difference which type of time scale is used.

Let us consider an arbitrary digital cybernetical system $\mathfrak{S}$. We enumerate the intervals in the time scale by the positive natural numbers in the order of their consecutive occurrence. Thus the number 1 is assigned to the first working interval of $\mathfrak{S}$ which begins when the system is switched on. The information received by $\mathfrak{S}$ from its environment is carried by a *signal* described by a time function x. Thus $x(t)$ is the value of the signal which appears in the input of $\mathfrak{S}$ in time t. Simultaneously, $\mathfrak{S}$ puts out a signal y which is the result of the information processing carried on by $\mathfrak{S}$; thus $y(t)$ is the signal value appearing in the output of $\mathfrak{S}$ in time t. The collection of the values of all quantities which are needed to describe how the system $\mathfrak{S}$ functions (into a vector, for example), is called the *state* z of $\mathfrak{S}$. Therefore, the state of $\mathfrak{S}$ is also a function of time. Let us consider the functioning of $\mathfrak{S}$ in the ith step, i.e., in the time interval $t_i \leqq t \leqq t'_i$ $(t_i < t'_i)$. The starting point for the work of $\mathfrak{S}$ in the ith step is its state at the beginning of this step, that is, the value $z(t_i)$. The partial result achieved in the previous steps is stored in this value. In the course of the ith step, the partial signal $x(t)$ appears in the input of $\mathfrak{S}$ for $t_i \leqq t \leqq t'_i$ and is processed in $\mathfrak{S}$. As a result the state takes the value $z(t'_i)$ at the end of the ith step (i.e.,

---

[1]) For the concept of a system and other fundamental concepts of Cybernetics mentioned in what follows cf. e.g. "Wörterbuch der Kybernetik" (Ed. G. Klaus), Dietz-Verlag, Berlin 1967.

in time t'_i). This value is stored until the time t_{i+1} when the step $i+1$ begins. Thus we always have $z(t'_i) = z(t_{i+1})$. In addition, in its output, $\mathfrak{S}$ generates the partial signal $y(t)$ for $t_i \leqq t \leqq t'_i$ during step i. The value $z(t_i)$ is called the *state of* $\mathfrak{S}$ *in step* i and accordingly the value $z(t'_i) = z(t_{i+1})$ is called the *state of* $\mathfrak{S}$ *in step* $i+1$. The time function $x(t)$ for $t_i \leqq t \leqq t'_i$ is called the *input signal of* $\mathfrak{S}$ *in step* i, and $y(t)$ for $t_i \leqq t \leqq t_i$ is called the *output signal of* $\mathfrak{S}$ *in step* i.

Obviously, an arbitrary information processing system $\mathfrak{S}$ can be considered as a digital system if we describe its functioning on a given time scale. Consequently the theory developed here can be applied to these systems. So far, however, this theory only has practical significance for systems working with *discrete* signals, that is, whose signal values can only carry information in separate moments of time. Without any loss of generality, we can assume that the input signal can carry information exactly once in every step.

If the system $\mathfrak{S}$ works with discrete signals, then the *input signal* x_i in step i does not mean a function $x(t)$ for $t_i \leqq t \leqq t'_i$, but the *signal value* $x(t^*_i)$ taken by the input signal at that precise time t^* of the ith step in which the input signal is carrying information. Accordingly, the *output signal* y_i of $\mathfrak{S}$ in step i is the unique information carrying *signal value* of the output signal $y(t)$. In practice most digital systems use discrete signals.

We shall next assume that the system $\mathfrak{S}$ works in a strongly *deterministic* way, independent of chance. This is an idealization which in the concrete construction of a real system can only be realized approximately, by means of additional control instruments. In this case the state z_{i+1} of $\mathfrak{S}$ in step $i+1$ depends only on the state z_i of $\mathfrak{S}$ in step i, and the input signal x_i received by $\mathfrak{S}$ in step i. One might think that the step number i could also influence the value of z_{i+1}. In this case, however, the step number must belong to the important quantities determining the way in which $\mathfrak{S}$ functions and thus, according to our definition, the information concerning the step number i is already included in the value of z_i. The same can be said about the apparent dependence of the state z_{i+1} on the states z_j and on the input signals $x_{j'}$ belonging to the previous steps $j, j' < i$. Analogously, the output signal y_i of $\mathfrak{S}$ in step i only depends on the state z_i and the input signal x_i (i.e., the *situation* $[z_i, x_i]$) in step i.

Let us collect all the input signals x which $\mathfrak{S}$ could receive in one of the steps in a set X of all input signals of $\mathfrak{S}$, and analogously let Y and Z be the set of all output signals and all states of $\mathfrak{S}$ respectively. Now the way in which $\mathfrak{S}$ functions in an arbitrary step can be described by means of a single-valued mapping γ which assigns to each pair $[z, x]$ where z is a state and x is an input signal of $\mathfrak{S}$, a pair $[y, z']$ of an output signal and a state, so that y is the output signal of $\mathfrak{S}$ in step i and z' is that state of $\mathfrak{S}$ in step $i+1$, provided that in the ith step $\mathfrak{S}$ is in the situation $[z, x]$. The quadruple $[X, Y, Z, \gamma]$ which we shall call a *deterministic abstract automaton* gives an abstract description of our system $\mathfrak{S}$.

If we drop the requirement of strong determinacy for the system $\mathfrak{S}$ then in general it will not be uniquely determined which pair $[y, z']$ of an output signal and of a next state is induced by the situation $[z, x]$. In many cases there is only a certain probability that this pair would appear in the situation $[z, x]$ as a pair of an output signal and a next state. According to the above, however, this probability only depends on $[z, x]$. When describing our system $\mathfrak{S}$ we can now choose that of the following two possibilities which best serves our purpose: either we take these probabilities into account, or we only investigate what is "possible" for the system $\mathfrak{S}$ in a sense which will be specified later.

If we choose the first possibility, then $\mathfrak{S}$ is described by a quadruple $[X, Y, Z, H]$, where H is a single-valued mapping assigning to each pair $[z, x]$ a *discrete probability measure* $H[z, x]$ on $Y \times Z$, i.e., a function whose value for the pair $[y, z']$ is exactly the probability that $\mathfrak{S}$ in the situation $[z, x]$ has the output y and in the next step the state z'. The quadruple $[X, Y, Z, H]$ is called a *stochastic* or *probabilistic automaton*. A stochastic automaton is nothing else but what is known in information theory as a transmission channel.

In order to explain the second possibility, we must first specify what we mean when we say that the pair $[y, z']$ is "possible" for the system $\mathfrak{S}$ in the situation $[z, x]$. This will depend on our reason for investigating $\mathfrak{S}$. A close connection with stochastic automata is obtained if we define as "possible" in the situation $[z, x]$ those pairs $[y, z']$ which appear in this situation with positive probability as a pair of an output signal and a next state. The functioning of $\mathfrak{S}$ can be described by means of a single-valued map h which assigns to each situation $[z, x]$ the set $h(z, x)$ of all pairs $[y, z']$ which are possible in this situation. The quadruple $[X, Y, Z, h]$ describes the possibilities of $\mathfrak{S}$ and is called a *non-deterministic automaton.*

Thus we have described the three types of automata which will be investigated in the three parts of this book. The three corresponding theories will run on parallel tracks in order to facilitate the comparison of their results. Below we shall sketch briefly the most important problems which will come under consideration in the order of their presentation.

Once a type of automata has been defined, the first problem is to derive formulas which enable use to compute what an automaton of this type does, if in a certain step i it is in one of its states z, and receives in the course of the steps $t, t+1, \ldots, t+n$ a finite sequence $x_0, x_1, \ldots, x_n$ of input signals (in each step exactly one signal). Thus we ask which states (and perhaps, with what probability) the automaton can go through, and which sequences of output signals (with what probability) can be generated in its output.

By means of these formulas the efficiency of different automata of a given type can be compared and their *equivalence* defined. The latter means that two automata can do exactly the same job. In this connection the problem immediately arises of finding equivalence criteria, and perhaps also a process for deciding the equivalence of automata. Further we have the problem of simplifying an automaton to an equivalent one and also of constructing an automaton which is optimal in a certain sense and can still do the same job as the automaton we are considering.

If this type of automata is defined in a set theoretical manner, like the three types of automata we defined above, and thus is close in its nature to algebraic structures such as groups, rings, etc. then it is natural to define *homomorphisms* and *isomorphisms* of automata in a suitable way and to investigate which properties of automata are preserved by homomorphic images.

One of the most important problems of automata theory is to characterize in an "automata-free" manner those *input-output-relations* which can be realized by the automata of the type under consideration. In other words we seek a criterion which would decide whether a relation between finite sequences of input signals and finite sequences of output signals can be realized by an automaton of a given type in the following sense: if the automaton is beginning to work in a certain state and receives a certain finite sequence of input signals, then its reaction will be as prescribed by the corresponding relations. Here the question of how to construct such an automaton is especially interesting.

In this connection we can raise the problem of the *classifying behaviour* of automata of a given type. This implies the following questions: which sequences of input signals result in a given reaction for a given automaton; when does an automaton of a given type exist such that its reaction distinguishes two such disjoint classes if the input sequence belongs to one of them; how can such an automaton be constructed, etc.

Further questions concern *experiments* on automata. By experiment we mean applying to the automata a finite sequence of input signals. If we assume that the description of the automaton is known, we can inquire as to the existence of an experiment by means of which we can decide in which state the automaton was at the beginning or at the end of the experiment. If only the set of input signals and a certain class of automata to which the automaton belongs are known, we may try to find an experiment whose result would decide which automaton of the corresponding class of automata we are dealing with.

Finally there is the *problem of stability*. Here, for example, we might ask under which conditions an automaton can "forget" a mistake in its input (i.e., in the ith step instead of the expected signal x_i another one was fed in) after a certain finite number of steps. By this of course we mean that eventually the automaton reacts as if the "correct" input signal had been put in.

All these problems can be raised in particular for *finite* automata which work with finitely many different input signals, output signals and states. The solutions of these problems, of course, has greater practical significance than the corresponding results for infinite automata, since the digital systems existing in practice can only have finitely many different states and can only work with discrete signals.

The questions not touched upon in this book include all the problems of *structural automata theory*, also known as the *theory of logical networks*. This theory deals with questions arising in the construction of automata from simpler subautomata or from the simplest elementary automata. Here, optimality problems play a special role. The theory of logical networks has so far only been worked out completely for deterministic automata. However, this single branch of automata theory is already so complex that its inclusion here would be impossible (cf. Miller [1]). A first introduction to this discipline can be found in the book by Kobrinski and Trachtenbrot [1].

Nor shall we go into the details of *algebraic automata theory*, which considers (so far only deterministic) automata as algebraic structures. Analogously to the theory of groups or rings, it deals both with relationships between algebraic structures and those between semi-groups, groups and rings on one hand, and classes of (deterministic) automata on the other. Important results of this theory can be found in the works of Deussen [2] and Glushkov [6].

A new direction in the theory of deterministic automata deals with systems in which the sets of input signals, output signals and states are structured; they can be e.g., linear spaces (*linear automata*) or topological spaces (*topological automata*) (cf. Arbib [5], Gill [12] to [14], Hartmanis and Davis [1], Pohl [1]).

Since none of those questions can be touched upon here we refer the reader to the literature. Thus the bibliography also contains works on problems we could not deal with.

The notion of an abstract automaton which is defined here as the mathematical model of digital cybernetical systems is of a high generality. In accordance with this, the field of application of this notion and therefore of automata theory is very wide. Besides applications in biology (Rosen [1]) automata theory is applied to the theory of finite sequences of symbols and thus to mathematical linguistics (Bar-Hillel, Perles and Shamir [1]) and to mathematical logic (Büchi [1], [4], Church [3]). The chief domain of application of automata theory is of course system theory, namely the analysis and synthesis of cybernetical systems. The generality and simplicity of the models (and of the related automata theoretical problems) implies that abstract automata theory can only deal with fundamental questions concerning the efficiency of digital cybernetical systems. Nonetheless the answers to these questions have great practical significance even if they only show which problems can be solved by means of finite deterministic automata, etc.

Naturally, abstract automata theory provides no answer to merely structural questions such as e.g., how a concrete switching circuit should be built in order to solve a certain problem. Abstract automata theory however can be of use in the logical design of cybernetical systems. For example, it can be applied to the global description of separate blocks which can be considered as abstract automata. The minimal number of states needed for an abstract automaton to realize a certain information processor, measures the complexity of that information processor and thus of the concrete switching circuits by which it is realized. Automata theory and especially the theory of stochastic automata however, can also be useful in the modelling of optimization situations (Pohl [1], Poljak [1], Schrejder [1]) and learning processes (Feichtinger [6], [8], Fu [1], Fu and McLaren [1], Wolf and Schmitt [1]) in particular to clarify the notion of "intelligent behaviour" (Fechner [1], Zetlin [4]).

PRELIMINARIES

In this chapter we shall explain the notations used in what follows and recal some fundamental definitions and theorems.

In order to abbreviate proofs and definitions and especially definitions of sets, it will be very convenient to apply the notation used in predicate calculus. Thus we shall use the symbols $\wedge$, $\vee$, $\rightarrow$, $\leftrightarrow$, $\exists$, $\forall$ as abbreviations for the logical connectives "and", "or", "if ... then" (or "implies") "if and only if" and the quantifiers "there exists" and "for all" respectively.

The symbol $\in$ denotes the *membership relation* (between sets and elements). Thus for instance $\{y \mid \exists z \, \exists x (z \in Z \wedge x \in X \wedge y = \lambda(z, x))\}$ denotes the set of all those y for which a z in Z and an x in X exist such that $y = \lambda(z, x)$. The following sequence of symbols

$$\exists K^{i+2}(z, z' \in K^{i+2} \in \mathfrak{z}_{i+2}) \leftrightarrow \exists K^{i+1}(z, z' \in K^{i+1} \in \mathfrak{z}_{i+1}) \\ \wedge \forall x \big(x \in X \rightarrow \exists K^{i+1}(\delta(z, x), \delta(z', x) \in K^{i+1} \in \mathfrak{z}_{i+1})\big)$$

should be read as follows: There exists a K^{i+2} in $\mathfrak{z}_{i+2}$ such that $z, z' \in K^{i+2}$ if and only if there is a K^{i+1} in $\mathfrak{z}_{i+1}$ with $z, z' \in K^{i+1}$ and for all x in X there exists a K^{i+1} in $\mathfrak{z}_{i+1}$ such that $\delta(z, x), \delta(z', x) \in K^{i+1}$. Furthermore instead of

$$\forall i (1 \leqq i \leqq n \rightarrow x_i \in X_i)$$

we shall write shortly

$$\bigwedge_{i=1}^{n} x_i \in X_i .$$

The *empty set* will be denoted by $\emptyset$. $M \cap N$ denotes the *intersection* of the sets M and N, $M \cup N$ is their *union*, $M \setminus N$ denotes their *difference*, and $M \times N$ denotes their *Cartesian product* (the set of all ordered pairs $[m, n]$ such that $m \in M$ and $n \in N$). The fact that M is a *subset* of N is denoted by $M \subseteq N$ and if $N \setminus M \neq \emptyset$ also holds (i.e., M is a *proper* subset of N) then we write $M \subset N$. The collection of all subsets of M is denoted by $\mathfrak{P}(M)$. For a system of sets $\mathfrak{N}$ the intersection (resp. the union) of all sets $N \in \mathfrak{N}$ is denoted by $\bigcap \mathfrak{N}$ (resp. $\bigcup \mathfrak{N}$).

PART I
DETERMINISTIC AUTOMATA

In the first part of this book we shall develop the fundaments of the theory of deterministic abstract automata. Here, our aim is to introduce the reader who has not yet studied automata theory, to its most important notions and methods. He will thus be able to compare the results obtained for non-deterministic and stochastic automata with the corresponding results for deterministic automata, and also to follow the rapidly increasing literature in this field. Therefore, in general, we shall not take up problems whose analogons in the theories of non-deterministic and stochastic automata have not yet been considered, such as those concerning relationships between automata and algebraic structures, for example, semi-groups or groups, which have been investigated for deterministic automata in a large number of works (see, e.g., ARBIB [10], BÜCHI [5], DEUSSEN [2], GLUSHKOV [6]).

§ 1. Basic Notions

As we have seen in the Introduction, a deterministic abstract automaton is a system working on a given discrete time scale, in a countably infinite number of steps. These steps are enumerated by the positive natural numbers 1, 2, 3, ... In each step t the automaton receives exactly one input signal value x_t in its input and in each step t it sends out exactly one output signal value y_t. In every step the system has exactly one state z, which can only be altered by changing the step. These properties of the systems we intend to investigate are contained in the following definition and its interpretation.

Definition 1.1. $\mathfrak{A} = [X, Y, Z, \gamma]$ is called a *deterministic* (abstract) *automaton* if

a) X, Y, Z are arbitrary non-empty sets and

b) γ is a function defined on $Z \times X$, whose values are taken from $Y \times Z$.

Interpretation: The set X is called the input alphabet of $\mathfrak{A}$ and its elements x are the *input signals* of $\mathfrak{A}$; Y is the output alphabet and its elements y are the *output signals* of $\mathfrak{A}$, and finally, the elements $z \in Z$ are the states of $\mathfrak{A}$. The automaton $\mathfrak{A}$ works on a discrete time scale in a countably infinite number of steps $t = 1, 2, 3, \ldots,$ according to the following rule: if z_t is the state of $\mathfrak{A}$ in step t and x_t is the input signal received by $\mathfrak{A}$ in step t, furthermore $\gamma(z_t, x_t) = [y, z']$, then the output signal of $\mathfrak{A}$ in step t is y, and in step $t+1$ it enters the state z'.

To express that in a certain step t an automaton $\mathfrak{A}$ has the state z and receives the input signal x, we shall also say that the automaton $\mathfrak{A}$ is in the *situation* $[z, x]$ in step t. Thus $Z \times X$ is also the set of all situations in which $\mathfrak{A}$ can be.

Let $\mathfrak{A} = [X, Y, Z, \gamma]$ be an arbitrary deterministic automaton. The *transition function* (or next-state function) of $\mathfrak{A}$ is defined as the single-valued mapping δ of $Z \times X$ into Z, for which for all $z \in Z$ and $x \in X$, $\delta(z, x)$ is the second component of the ordered pair $\gamma(z, x)$. The function λ defined on $Z \times X$ in such a way that for arbitrary $z \in Z$, $x \in X$ its value is the first component of the ordered pair $\gamma(z, x)$, is called the *output function* of $\mathfrak{A}$. If the deterministic automaton $\mathfrak{A}$ is in the situation $[z, x]$ in step t, then in this step, $\mathfrak{A}$ sends out the signal $y = \lambda(z, x)$ and in the next step it has the state $\delta(z, x)$.

Since for all $z \in Z$, $x \in X$

$$\gamma(z, x) = [\lambda(z, x), \delta(z, x)]$$

holds, the automaton $\mathfrak{A}$ can also be described by means of the functions λ and δ instead of the function γ. The definition of an abstract automaton for finite X, Y, Z was given in this form by MEALY. Therefore, automata given in this form are also called *Mealy automata*.

Definition 1.2. A deterministic automaton $\mathfrak{A} = [X, Y, Z, \gamma]$ is called a *deterministic Mealy automaton* if for all $z \in Z$, $x \in X$, we have

$$\gamma(z, x) = [\lambda(z, x), \delta(z, x)],$$

where λ and δ are the input and transition functions respectively of $\mathfrak{A}$.

Corollary 1.1. Every deterministic automaton is a deterministic Mealy automaton.

Thus the difference between deterministic automata and deterministic Mealy automata is only formal. The reason why we have mentioned it is because of the comparison with the theories of non-deterministic and stochastic automata. We shall see later that there exist such non-deterministic and stochastic automata which are not non-deterministic and stochastic Mealy automata, respectively, and are not even equivalent to such an automaton (although the non-deterministic and stochastic Mealy automata are defined in a completely analogous manner as in definition 1.2.).

In virtue of Corollary 1.1., in what follows, deterministic automata will always be described as deterministic Mealy automata.

The definition and interpretation of deterministic automata implies not only what happens if we apply into a deterministic automaton $\mathfrak{A} = [X, Y, Z, \delta, \lambda]$ in state z a signal $x \in X$, but also what happens if in n consecutive steps the signals $x_1, \ldots, x_n$ are fed into $\mathfrak{A}$ (for which we shall say that the word $p = x_1 \ldots x_n \in W(X)$ is fed into $\mathfrak{A}$). This definition and its interpretation lead us to extend the domains of the functions δ and λ as follows: for an arbitrary state $z \in Z$ and for every input word $p \in W(X)$, if in step t, $\mathfrak{A}$ is in state z and in the course of the steps $t, t+1, \ldots, t+l(p)-1$, the word p is fed into $\mathfrak{A}$, then the value $\delta(z, p)$ of our function δ is exactly the state $z' \in Z$ into which $\mathfrak{A}$ enters in step $t+l(p)$, and under the same conditions the value $\lambda(z, p)$ of the function λ will be the word $q \in W(Y)$ put out by $\mathfrak{A}$ in the course of the steps $t, t+1, \ldots, t+l(p)-1$ (signal by signal). The reader can readily convince himself that the following inductive definition yields us what we need, if he takes into consideration the fact that the input and output of the empty word e need no time (no step).

Let $z \in Z$ be arbitrary:

$$\delta(z, e) \underset{\text{Df}}{=} z,$$

$$\delta(z, px) \underset{\text{Df}}{=} \delta(\delta(z, p), x) \quad \text{for} \quad p \in W(X), \ x \in X,$$

$$\lambda(z, e) \underset{\text{Df}}{=} e,$$

$$\lambda(z, px) \underset{\text{Df}}{=} \lambda(z, p)\lambda(\delta(z, p), x) \quad \text{for} \quad p \in W(X), \ x \in X.$$

Since the extended functions coincide with the original functions δ and λ on $Z \times X$, they will also be denoted by δ and λ.

Theorem 1.2. *Let $\mathfrak{A} = [X, Y, Z, \delta, \lambda]$ be an arbitrary deterministic automaton. Then for all $x \in X$, $p, r \in W(X)$, $z \in Z$ we have*

1. $\delta(z, xp) = \delta(\delta(z, x), p)$,
2. $\delta(z, rp) = \delta(\delta(z, r), p)$,
3. $\lambda(z, xp) = \lambda(z, x)\lambda(\delta(z, x), p)$,
4. $\lambda(z, rp) = \lambda(z, r)\lambda(\delta(z, r), p)$.

The proofs of all these equalities will be carried out by induction on p. The initial step $p = e$ is always trivial. The steps of induction are taken from p to px', for arbitrary $x' \in X$.

Ad 1.
$$\begin{aligned} \delta(z, xpx') &= \delta(\delta(z, xp), x') && \text{(by the definition of } \delta) \\ &= \delta(\delta(\delta(z, x), p), x') && \text{(by the induction hypothesis)} \\ &= \delta(\delta(z, x), px') && \text{(by the definition of } \delta). \end{aligned}$$

Ad 2.
$$\begin{aligned} \delta(z, rpx') &= \delta(\delta(z, rp), x') = \delta(\delta(\delta(z, r), p), x') \\ &= \delta(\delta(z, r), px'). \end{aligned}$$

Ad 3. $$\begin{aligned}\lambda(z, xpx') &= \lambda(z, xp)\lambda\big(\delta(z, xp), x'\big)\\ &= \lambda(z, x)\lambda\big(\delta(z, x), p\big)\lambda\big(\delta(z, xp), x'\big)\\ &= \lambda(z, x)\lambda\big(\delta(z, x), px'\big) \qquad \text{(by 1.2.1)}.\end{aligned}$$

Ad 4. $$\begin{aligned}\lambda(z, rpx') &= \lambda(z, rp)\lambda\big(\delta(z, rp), x'\big)\\ &= \lambda(z, r)\lambda\big(\delta(z, r), p\big)\lambda\big(\delta(z, rp), x'\big)\\ &= \lambda(z, r)\lambda\big(\delta(z, r), px'\big) \qquad \text{(by 1.2.2)}.\end{aligned}$$

This proves Theorem 1.2.

In particular cases it might happen that for a certain automaton $\mathfrak{A} = [X, Y, Z, \delta, \lambda]$ the output signal $y = \lambda(z, x)$ given out by $\mathfrak{A}$ in an arbitrary situation $[z, x] \in Z \times X$ does not depend explicitely on $[z, x]$, but only on $\delta(z, x)$, i.e. the next state into which $\mathfrak{A}$ enters after this situation. Automata of this type will be called deterministic *Moore automata.*

Definition 1.3. A deterministic automaton $\mathfrak{A} = [X, Y, Z, \delta, \lambda]$ is called a *deterministic Moore automaton* if there is a function μ defined on Z (taking its value in Y) such that for all $z \in Z$, $x \in X$

$$\lambda(z, x) = \mu\big(\delta(z, x)\big).$$

If $\mathfrak{A} = [X, Y, Z, \delta, \lambda]$ then in general there might exist several functions μ satisfying the conditions of Definition 1.3. Obviously this is the case if and only if *Card* $(Y) \geqq 2$ and if there is a $z' \in Z$ which does not occur as a value of δ, since for such states the value of μ can be chosen arbitrarily. In what follows we shall assume that in one way or another, one of the possible functions has been fixed (for instance by choosing a $y^* \in Y$ and stipulating $\mu(z') = y^*$ for every $z' \in Z$ which does not lie in the range of δ). The function μ thus chosen is called the *marking function* of $\mathfrak{A}$, and we shall denote $\mathfrak{A}$ by $[X, Y, Z, \delta, \mu]$.

Since for every deterministic Moore automaton $\mathfrak{A} = [X, Y, Z, \delta, \mu]$ the function λ can be obtained by composing δ and μ, for every such automaton and every $z \in Z$ and $p \in W(X)$, $\lambda(z, p)$ is also uniquely determined by the above inductive definition.

Corollary 1.3. If $\mathfrak{A} = [X, Y, Z, \delta, \mu]$ is a Moore automaton, then for all $z \in Z$, $p \in W(X)$ we have

$$\lambda(z, px) = \lambda(z,p)\,\mu\big(\delta(z, px)\big).$$

Now we shall define some fundamental properties of deterministic automata.

Definition 1.4. Let $\mathfrak{A} = [X, Y, Z, \delta, \lambda]$ be an arbitrary deterministic automaton.

(1.4.1.) $\mathfrak{A}$ is called *X-finite, Y-finite, Z-finite,* $[X, Y]$*-finite* etc. if the corresponding sets are finite. $[X, Y, Z]$-finite automata are simply called *finite.*

(1.4.2.) $\mathfrak{A}$ is called *autonomous* if X is a singleton.

(1.4.3.) $\mathfrak{A}$ is called *weakly initial* if a non-empty subset $Z_1 \subseteq Z$ is fixed as the set of possible states in step 1 (*initial states*), i.e., in step 1, $\mathfrak{A}$ will be in one of the states $z \in Z_1$. If $Z_1 = Z$, then $\mathfrak{A}$ is called *non-initial*, and if $Z_1 = \{z_1\}$ is a singleton, then $\mathfrak{A}$ is an *initial* automaton with the *initial state* z_1. Weakly initial automata will be denoted by $[X, Y, Z, \delta, \lambda, Z_1]$ and initial automata by $[X, Y, Z, \delta, \lambda, z_1]$.

(1.4.4.) $\mathfrak{A}' = [X', Y', Z', \delta', \lambda']$ is called a *subautomaton* of $\mathfrak{A}$, if $\mathfrak{A}'$ is an automaton and furthermore we have $X' \subseteq X$, $Y' \subseteq Y$, $Z' \subset Z$, and the functions δ', λ' of $\mathfrak{A}'$ are the restrictions of the functions δ, λ (defined on $Z \times X$) of $\mathfrak{A}$ to their domains of definition $Z' \times X' \subseteq Z \times X$.

Let us add to this that for every subautomaton $\mathfrak{A}'$ of $\mathfrak{A}$, $z' \in Z'$, $x' \in X'$ implies $\delta(z', x') \in Z'$ and $\lambda(z', x') \in Y'$, since $\delta(z', x') = \delta'(z', x')$ and $\lambda(z', x') = \lambda'(z', x')$ hold and $\mathfrak{A}'$ is an automaton.

Corollary 1.4. If $\mathfrak{A}' = [X', Y', Z', \delta', \lambda']$ is a subautomaton of the deterministic automaton $\mathfrak{A} = [X, Y, Z, \delta, \lambda]$, then for all $z' \in Z'$, $p' \in W(X')$ we have

$$\delta'(z', p') = \delta(z', p') \text{ and } \lambda'(z', p') = \lambda(z', p').$$

To every deterministic automaton we can assign a directed graph in a bi-uniquely determined way. For a finite automaton not having too many input signals, output signals, and states, the way of functioning of the automaton can be easily visualized by representing its graph. It is often more convenient to represent the graph geometrically than to determine the functions δ and λ by means of formulas or tables.

Definition 1.5. Let $\mathfrak{A} = [X, Y, Z, \delta, \lambda]$ be an arbitrary deterministic automaton. Then the *graph of* $\mathfrak{A}$ is defined as

$$\mathfrak{G}_{\mathfrak{A}} = [Z, K, \alpha_{\mathfrak{A}}],$$

where

$$K = \{[z, x, y] \mid z \in Z \wedge x \in X \wedge y = \lambda(z, x)\}$$

and for all edges $[z, x, y] \in K$

$$\alpha_{\mathfrak{A}}([z, x, y]) = [z, \delta(z, x)].$$

Thus the vertices of $\mathfrak{G}_{\mathfrak{A}}$ are the states of $\mathfrak{A}$ and the edge $[z, x, y]$ of $\mathfrak{G}_{\mathfrak{A}}$ runs from the vertice z to the vertice $\delta(z, x)$. The geometrical representation of the graph $\mathfrak{G}_{\mathfrak{A}}$ of a finite automaton $\mathfrak{A}$ will be illuminated by the following example:

Let $\mathfrak{A}_1 = [\{0, 1\}, \{0, 1\}, \{a, b\}, \delta^1, \lambda^1]$, where for $z \in \{a, b\}$, $x \in \{0, 1\}$ we stipulate

$$\delta^1(z, x) = \begin{cases} a, & \text{if } x = 0, \\ b, & \text{if } x = 1; \end{cases} \qquad \lambda^1(z, x) = \begin{cases} 0, & \text{if } z = a, \\ 1, & \text{if } z = b. \end{cases}$$

In the geometrical representation of $\mathfrak{G}_{\mathfrak{A}_1}$ we only write x, y next to the edge $[x, z, y]$, since this representation clearly shows from which vertice z the edge $[z, x, y]$ originates. Such a representation of $\mathfrak{G}_{\mathfrak{A}_1}$ is shown in Figure 1. From this representation one can immediately see that $\mathfrak{A}_1$ is not a Moore automaton, since by entering into the state a under the influence of the input signal 0, the output of $\mathfrak{A}_1$ can be 0 just as well as 1, depending on whether the transition originated from the state a or from the state b.

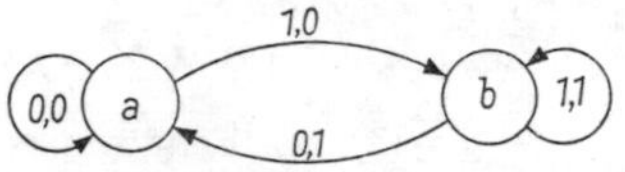

Fig. 1

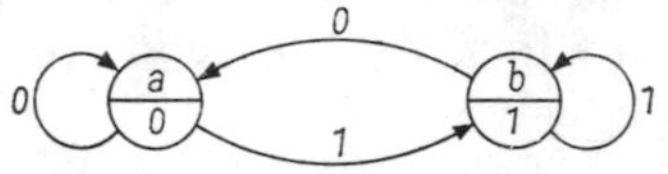

Fig. 2

Obviously an automaton $\mathfrak{A} = [X, Y, Z, \delta, \lambda]$ is a Moore automaton if and only if in $\mathfrak{G}_{\mathfrak{A}}$ at every vertice $z \in Z$, all the edges $[z', x, y]$ running to the vertice z (i.e., for which $z = \delta(z', x)$ holds), have the same third component. In accordance with this, for a Moore automaton $\mathfrak{A} = [X, Y, Z, \delta, \mu]$ the geometric representation of $\mathfrak{G}_{\mathfrak{A}}$ can be further simplified so far as the edges $[z, x, y]$ must only be labelled by the value of x, and for all $z \in Z$, at the vertice z the value $\mu(z)$ is to be indicated. The next example is the automaton $\mathfrak{A}_2 = [\{0, 1\}, \{0, 1\}, \{a, b\}, \delta^2, \mu^2]$, where for $z \in \{a, b\}$, $x \in \{0, 1\}$

$$\delta^2(z, x) = \begin{cases} a, & \text{if } x = 0, \\ b, & \text{if } x = 1; \end{cases} \qquad \mu^2(z) = \begin{cases} 0, & \text{if } z = a, \\ 1, & \text{if } z = b. \end{cases}$$

A representation of $\mathfrak{G}_{\mathfrak{A}_2}$ is shown in Figure 2.

§ 2. Equivalence and Reduction

Two arbitrary systems are considered equivalent if each of them can substitute the other in every respect. For abstract automata this should mean that both automata can do the same information processing job. Therefore, both automata must have the same input alphabet, since otherwise there would be a signal which could be processed in one of the automata but not in the other. The relation between input and output words realized by a deterministic automaton (the structure of which will be investigated in § 4) depends essentially on the initial state, i.e., the state in which the automaton is at the beginning of its work. Therefore it is natural that we should first define what we mean when we say that a state z of an automaton $\mathfrak{A}$ is *equivalent to the state* z' of an automaton $\mathfrak{A}'$. This will hold if and only if both states, as initial states of the corresponding automata, generate the same relation between input and output words (the same *input-output relation*). The automata themselves will be called *equivalent* if they can realize the same set of input-output relations.

When speaking of the equivalence of systems, the problem immediately arises whether a certain system could be equivalently simplified, i.e., whether a system equivalent to another could be constructed such that it is simpler or in a certain sense even optimal. To measure the complexity of abstract automata we can only use the number of states. Thus the *reduction* of an abstract automaton aims at finding an automaton which is equivalent to the one under consideration and has a minimal number of states.[1])

Definition 2.1. Let $\mathfrak{A} = [X, Y, Z, \delta, \lambda]$, $\mathfrak{A}' = [X, Y', Z', \delta, \lambda]$ be deterministic automata having the same input alphabet X.

(2.1.1.) The states $z \in Z$, $z' \in Z'$ are called *equivalent* (notation $z \sim z'$), if for all $p \in W(X)$ the relation $\lambda(z, p) = \lambda'(z', p)$ holds.

(2.1.2.) The automaton $\mathfrak{A}$ is called *equivalently embedded into the automaton* $\mathfrak{A}'$ (notation $\mathfrak{A} \lesssim \mathfrak{A}'$), if for every state $z \in Z$ of $\mathfrak{A}$ there is an equivalent state $z' \in Z'$ of $\mathfrak{A}'$.

(2.1.3.) The automata $\mathfrak{A}$ and $\mathfrak{A}'$ are called equivalent (notation $\mathfrak{A} \sim \mathfrak{A}'$), if both $\mathfrak{A} \lesssim \mathfrak{A}'$ and $\mathfrak{A}' \lesssim \mathfrak{A}$ hold.

Corollary 2.1.

1. The relation $\sim$ is an equivalence relation between arbitrary automata $\mathfrak{A}$, $\mathfrak{A}'$ with the same input alphabet, and between states of such automata.

2. The relation $\lesssim$ is reflexive and transitive. Instead of anti-symmetry we have

$$\mathfrak{A} \lesssim \mathfrak{A}' \wedge \mathfrak{A}' \lesssim \mathfrak{A} \rightarrow \mathfrak{A} \sim \mathfrak{A}'.$$

3. If $\mathfrak{A} \sim \mathfrak{A}'$, then

$$\{y \mid \exists z\, \exists x (z \in Z \wedge x \in X \wedge y = \lambda(z, x))\}$$
$$= \{y \mid \exists z'\, \exists x (z' \in Z' \wedge x \in X \wedge y = \lambda'(z', x))\}.$$

2.1.3. implies that equivalent automata also have the same output alphabets if they can only contain such output signals y, which the corresponding automata can in fact produce. (This means that they have to belong to the ranges of λ and λ' respectively.) In what follows we shall always assume that $\mathfrak{A} \sim \mathfrak{A}'$ implies $Y = Y'$ and this evidently does not result in any loss of generality.

Theorem 2.2. *For every deterministic automaton* $\mathfrak{A} = [X, X, Z, \delta, \lambda]$ *there is an equivalent deterministic Moore automaton* $\mathfrak{A}^*$. *If* $\mathfrak{A}$ *is* $[X, Z]$*-finite or* $[Y, Z]$*-finite, then* $\mathfrak{A}^*$ *can be chosen to be Z-finite.*

---

[1]) Pohl [2] calls input signals of $\mathfrak{A}$ to be equivalent if they cause the same internal and external reaction of $\mathfrak{A}$, and investigates the corresponding minimization problem.

Proof: $\mathfrak{A}^*$ can be constructed in two ways. In BLOCH [2] or GLUSHKOV [6], a construction is given which leads from an $[X, Z]$-finite automaton to an equivalent Z-finite Moore automaton $\big($with $Card(X) \cdot Card(Z) + 1\big)$ states. Here we shall give a construction which leads from a $[Y, Z]$-finite automaton to a Z-finite Moore automaton with $Card(Z) \cdot Card(Y)$ states. Since $[X, Z]$-finiteness implies $[Y, Z]$-finiteness, provided that Y only contains output signals which $\mathfrak{A}$ can indeed produce, this construction can be applied to a larger class of automata than the above one, in order to obtain equivalent Z-finite Moore automata.

Let $Z^* = Y \times Z$ and for $[y, z] \in Z^*$, $x \in X$ let

$$\delta^*([y, z], x) = [\lambda(z, x), \delta(z, x)],$$
$$\mu^*([y, z]) = y.$$

$\mathfrak{A}^* = [X, Y, Z^*, \delta^*, \mu^*]$ is a deterministic Moore automaton. We claim that for all $z \in Z$, $y \in Y$, the state $[y, z]$ of $\mathfrak{A}^*$ is equivalent to the state z of $\mathfrak{A}$, i.e., for all $p \in W(X)$

$$\lambda^*([y, z], p) = \lambda(z, p)$$

holds.

This will be proven by induction on p. The initial step $p = e$ is trivial, by the definition of the extension of λ. The induction hypothesis says that $\lambda^*([\gamma, z], p) = \lambda(z, p)$, and we have to show that for all $x \in X$ the relation $\lambda^*([y, z], px) = \lambda(z, px)$ holds.

So we have

$$\begin{aligned}\lambda^*([y, z], px) &= \lambda^*([y, z], p)\,\mu^*\big(\delta^*([y, z], px)\big)\\ &= \lambda(z, p)\,\mu^*\big(\delta^*([y, z], px)\big).\end{aligned}$$

Next we claim $\delta^*([y, z], px) = [\lambda\big(\delta(z, p), x\big), \delta(z, px)]$. This will be proved below by induction on p. So finally we have

$$\begin{aligned}\lambda^*([y, z], px) &= \lambda(z, p)\,\mu^*\big([\lambda(\delta(z, p), x), \delta(z, px)]\big)\\ &= \lambda(z, p)\,\lambda\big(\delta(z, p), x\big) = \lambda(z, px).\end{aligned}$$

In the inductive proof of $\delta^*([y, z], px) = [\lambda\big(\delta(z, p), x\big), \delta(z, px)]$, the initial step $p = e$ is trivial from the definition of δ^*. The induction step is carried out from p to $x_1 p$. Then we have

$$\begin{aligned}\delta^*([y, z], x_1 px) &= \delta^*\big(\delta^*([y, z], x_1), px\big) && \text{(by 1.2.1)}\\ &= \delta^*\big([\lambda(z, x_1), \delta(z, x_1)], px\big)\\ &= \big[\lambda\big(\delta(\delta(z, x_1), p), x\big), \delta\big(\delta(z, x_1), px\big)\big] && \text{(by the induction hypothesis)}\\ &= \big[\lambda\big(\delta(z, x_1 p), x\big), \delta(z, x_1 px)\big] && \text{(by 1.2.1),}\end{aligned}$$

which was to be shown. Thus theorem 2.2 is proved.

Theorem 2.3. *Let* $\mathfrak{A} = [X, Y, Z, \delta, \lambda]$, $\mathfrak{A}' = [X, Y', Z', \delta', \lambda']$ *be arbitrary automata, furthermore* $z \in Z$ *and* $z' \in Z'$.

1. *If* $z \sim z'$ *then* $\delta(z, p) \sim \delta'(z', p)$ *holds for all* $p \in W(X)$.

2. *If* $n \geqq 0$ *is an arbitrary natural number and* $\lambda(z, p) = \lambda'(z', p)$ *as well as* $\delta(z, p) \sim \delta'(z', p)$ *holds for all* $p \in W(X)$ *with* $l(p) = n$, *then* $z \sim z'$.

Proof: We shall first prove proposition 2.3.1. Let $z \sim z'$ and $p \in W(X)$. Then for all $r \in W(X)$ we have

$$\lambda(z, pr) = \lambda'(z', pr),$$

$$\lambda(z, p)\lambda(\delta(z, p), r) = \lambda'(z', p)\lambda'(\delta'(z', p), r) \qquad \text{(by 1.2.4)}.$$

So in particular

$$\lambda(\delta(z, p), r) = \lambda'(\delta'(z', p), r)$$

holds for all $r \in W(X)$, i.e., the states $\delta(z, p)$, $\delta'(z', p)$ are equivalent.

We shall now prove 2.3.2 showing that for all $q \in W(X)$ we have

$$\lambda(z, q) = \lambda'(z', q).$$

If $l(q) \geqq n$, then let q' be the *initial section of q of length n*, i.e., $q = q'q''$, where $l(q') = n$, $l(q'') = l(q) - n$. Then we have

$$\lambda(z, q) = \lambda(z, q')\lambda(\delta(z, q'), q'').$$

Since $l(q') = n$, $\lambda(z, q') = \lambda'(z', q')$ and $\delta(z, q') \sim \delta'(z', q')$ holds, and we have

$$\lambda(z, q) = \lambda'(z', q')\lambda'(\delta'(z', q'), q'') = \lambda'(z', q).$$

Assume now $n > 0$ and $l(q) = k < n$. Let us consider an arbitrary word $r \in W(X)$ such that $l(r) = n - k$. Since $l(qr) = n$, we have

$$\lambda(z, qr) = \lambda'(z', qr),$$

hence by 1.2.4,

$$\lambda(z, q)\lambda(\delta(z, q), r) = \lambda'(z', q)\lambda'(\delta'(z', q), r),$$

and in particular $\lambda(z, q) = \lambda'(z', q)$, which completes the proof.

Theorem 2.3 implies

Corollary 2.4. The states $z \in Z$, $z' \in Z'$ of the automata $\mathfrak{A} = [X, Y, Z, \delta, \lambda]$, $\mathfrak{A}' = [X, Y', Z', \delta', \lambda']$ are equivalent if and only if $\lambda(x, z) = \lambda'(z', x)$ and $\delta(z, x) \sim \delta'(z', x)$ hold for all $x \in X$.

Theorem 2.5. *If the automaton* $\mathfrak{A}' = [X, Y', Z', \delta', \lambda']$ *is equivalently embedded into the automaton* $\mathfrak{A} = [X, Y, Z, \delta, \lambda]$, *then there exists a subautomaton* $\mathfrak{A}^*$ *of* $\mathfrak{A}$ *which is equivalent to* $\mathfrak{A}'$.

Proof: Let $Z^* = \{z \mid z \in Z \wedge \exists z' (z' \in Z' \wedge z' \sim z)\}$. Z^* is a subset of Z. For $z^* \in Z^*$, $x \in X$ we have $\delta(z^*, x) \in Z^*$, since there exists a state z' of $\mathfrak{A}'$, which is equivalent to z^*, thus the states $\delta(z^*, x)$, $\delta'(z', x)$ are equivalent too, and consequently the state $\delta(z^*, x)$ belongs to Z^*. If we denote the restrictions of δ and

λ to the set $Z^* \times X$ by δ^* and λ^* respectively, then $\mathfrak{A}^* = [X, Y^*, Z^*, \delta^*, \lambda^*]$, where we put $Y^* = \{\lambda(z^*, x) \mid z^* \in Z^* \wedge x \in X\}$, is a subautomaton of $\mathfrak{A}$ equivalent to $\mathfrak{A}'$.

Theorem 2.6. *Let* $\mathfrak{A} = [X, Y, Z, \delta, \lambda]$ *be an arbitrary Z-finite deterministic automaton with* $n > 0$ *states. Two states* $z, z' \in Z$ *of* $\mathfrak{A}$ *are equivalent if and only if* $\lambda(z, p) = \lambda(z', p)$ *holds for all* $p \in W(X)$ *such that* $l(p) = n - 1$.

Proof: We shall define by induction a sequence $\mathfrak{Z}(\mathfrak{A}) = (\mathfrak{z}_i)$ of partitions of the set Z. Here we shall not make use of the fact that $\mathfrak{A}$ is Z-finite, so $\mathfrak{Z}(\mathfrak{A})$ will be defined for an arbitrary deterministic automaton $\mathfrak{A}$. The initial step is for $i = 1$. Let $\mathfrak{z}_1$ be a partition of Z such that for arbitrary $z, z' \in Z$,

(A1) there is a class $K^1 \in \mathfrak{z}_1$ for which $z \in K^1$;

(A2) there is a class $K^1 \in \mathfrak{z}_1$ containing both z and z' if and only if $\lambda(z, x) = \lambda(z', x)$ holds for all $x \in X$.

For $i \geqq 1$ let $\mathfrak{z}_{i+1}$ be a partition of Z (into non-empty classes) such that for all $z, z' \in Z$,

(I1) there is a class $K^{i+1} \in \mathfrak{z}_{i+1}$ containing z;

(I2) there is a class $K^{i+1} \in \mathfrak{z}_{i+1}$ containing both z and z' if and only if there is a class $K^i \in \mathfrak{z}_i$ such that $z, z' \in K^i$ and for every $x \in X$ there is a class $K^i \in \mathfrak{z}_i$ for which $\delta(z, x)$, $\delta(z', x) \in K^i$ holds.

Lemma 2.6a. *There exists a* $K^i \in \mathfrak{z}_i$ *containing both* z *and* z' *if and only if for all* $p \in W(X)$ *with* $l(p) = i$ *the equation* $\lambda(z, p) = \lambda(z', p)$ *is satisfied.*

Whe shall prove the lemma by induction on i. The initial step $i = 1$ is trivial from the definition of $\mathfrak{z}_1$. The induction steps are taken from i to $i + 1$. In the proof of theorem 2.3 we have shown that

$$\begin{aligned} &\forall p\big(p \in W(X) \wedge l(p) = i + 1 \to \lambda(z, p) = \lambda(z', p)\big) \\ &\leftrightarrow \forall p\big(p \in W(X) \wedge l(p) \leqq i + 1 \to \lambda(z, p) = \lambda(z', p)\big) \end{aligned}$$

holds for arbitrary $z, z' \in Z$. Using this fact and the induction hypothesis, we obtain

$$\begin{aligned} &\forall p\big(p \in W(X) \wedge l(p) = i + 1 \to \lambda(z, p) = \lambda(z', p)\big) \\ &\leftrightarrow \forall p\big(p \in W(X) \wedge l(p) \leqq i \to \lambda(z, p) = \lambda(z', p)\big) \\ &\qquad \wedge \forall x \forall p\big(x \in X \wedge p \in W(X) \wedge l(p) \leqq i \to \lambda(z, xp) = \lambda(z', xp)\big) \\ &\leftrightarrow \exists K^i(K^i \in \mathfrak{z}_i \wedge z, z' \in K^i) \wedge \forall x\big(x \in X \to \lambda(z, x) = \lambda(z', x)\big) \\ &\qquad \wedge \forall x\big(x \in X \to \forall p(p \in W(X) \wedge l(p) \leqq i \\ &\qquad\quad \to \lambda(\delta(z, x), p) = \lambda(\delta(z', x), p)\big) \\ &\leftrightarrow \exists K^i(K^i \in \mathfrak{z}_i \wedge z, z' \in K^i) \wedge \exists K^1(K^1 \in \mathfrak{z}_1 \wedge z, z' \in K^1) \\ &\qquad \wedge \forall x\big(x \in X \to \exists K^i(K^i \in \mathfrak{z}_i \wedge \delta(z, x), \delta(z', x) \in K^i)\big) \\ &\leftrightarrow \exists K^{i+1}(K^{i+1} \in \mathfrak{z}_{i+1} \wedge z, z' \in K^{i+1}), \end{aligned}$$

since the existence of a K^i with $z, z' \in K^i$ implies that there exists a class $K^1 \in \mathfrak{z}_1$ containing both z and z'.

From Lemma 2.6a it follows that every $\mathfrak{z}_i$ is a partition of Z and we can see from the construction that for each i the partition $\mathfrak{z}_{i+1}$ is a refinement of the partition $\mathfrak{z}_i$.

Lemma 2.6b. *If* $\mathfrak{z}_i = \mathfrak{z}_{i+1}$ *then* $\mathfrak{z}_i = \mathfrak{z}_{i+j}$ *holds for all* $(j = 1, 2, \ldots)$.

Obviously it suffices to show that $\mathfrak{z}_{i+2} = \mathfrak{z}_{i+1}$ holds if $\mathfrak{z}_i = \mathfrak{z}_{i+1}$. For arbitrary $z, z' \in Z$ we have

$$\begin{aligned} &\exists K^{i+2}(z, z' \in K^{i+2} \in \mathfrak{z}_{i+2}) \\ &\leftrightarrow \exists K^{i+1}(z, z' \in K^{i+1} \in \mathfrak{z}_{i+1}) \\ &\qquad \wedge \forall x\big(x \in X \rightarrow \exists K^{i+1}(\delta(z, x), \delta(z', x) \in K^{i+1} \in \mathfrak{z}_{i+1})\big) \\ &\leftrightarrow \exists K^i(z, z' \in K^i \in \mathfrak{z}_i) \wedge \forall x\big(x \in X \rightarrow \exists K^i(\delta(z, x), \delta(z', x) \in K^i \in \mathfrak{z}_i)\big), \end{aligned}$$

since $\mathfrak{z}_i = \mathfrak{z}_{i+1}$. Consequently,

$$\exists K^{i+2}(z, z' \in K^{i+2} \in \mathfrak{z}_{i+2}) \leftrightarrow \exists K^{i+1}(z, z' \in K^{i+1} \in \mathfrak{z}_{i+1}),$$

i.e., $\mathfrak{z}_{i+1} = \mathfrak{z}_{i+2}$.

Lemma 2.6c. *If* $\mathfrak{z}_i \neq \mathfrak{z}_{i+1}$ *then* $Card(\mathfrak{z}_i) \geqq i + 1$.

In order to prove lemma 2.6c it is enough to show that $\mathfrak{z}_1 = \mathfrak{z}_2$, provided that $\mathfrak{z}_1$ contains one class only. In this case, however, for all $z, z' \in Z$ and $x \in X$ we have $\lambda(z, x) = \lambda(z', x)$, i.e., all the states of $\mathfrak{A}$ are pairwise equivalent, which implies $\mathfrak{z}_1 = \mathfrak{z}_2$.

Lemma 2.6c, together with Lemma 2.6b, implies that $\mathfrak{z}_{n-1} = \mathfrak{z}_n = \mathfrak{z}_{n+j}$ holds for all $j \geqq 0$, since Z cannot be divided into more than n non-empty classes. Lemma 2.6a implies that the states z, z' are equivalent if and only if, for all $j = 1, 2, \ldots$, z and z' belong to the same class of $\mathfrak{z}_j$, which is exactly the case when these states lie in the same class of $\mathfrak{z}_{n-1}$, i.e., when for all $p \in W(X)$ with $l(p) = n - 1$ we always have $\lambda(z, p) = \lambda(z', p)$.

Corollary 2.7. If $\mathfrak{A}$ is an $[X, Z]$-finite deterministic automaton, then

1. The equivalence between states of $\mathfrak{A}$ is a decidable relation.
2. The partition $Z = \{[z] \mid z \in Z\}$, where $[z] = \{z' \mid z' \in Z \wedge z' \sim z\}$ can be constructed by means of an algorithmic process.

Definition 2.2. Let $\mathfrak{A} = [X, Y, Z, \delta, \lambda]$, $\mathfrak{A}' = [X, Y', Z', \delta, \lambda]$ be deterministic automata with the same input alphabet and (without loss of generality) disjoint state sets. Then the automaton $\mathfrak{A} + \mathfrak{A}' \underset{\text{Df}}{=} [X, Y \cup Y', Z \cup Z', \delta + \delta', \lambda + \lambda']$ where, for all $z'' \in z \cup Z'$ and $x \in X$

$$\delta + \delta'(z'', x) \underset{\text{Df}}{=} \begin{cases} \delta(z'', x), & \text{if} \quad z'' \in Z, \\ \delta'(z'', x), & \text{if} \quad z'' \in Z', \end{cases}$$

$$\lambda + \lambda'(z'', x) \underset{\text{Df}}{=} \begin{cases} \lambda(z'', x), & \text{if} \quad z'' \in Z, \\ \lambda'(z'', x), & \text{if} \quad z'' \in Z', \end{cases}$$

is called the *direct sum of* $\mathfrak{A}$ *and* $\mathfrak{A}'$.

Corollary 2.8. Let $\mathfrak{A} = [X, Y, Z, \delta, \lambda]$, $\mathfrak{A}' = [X, Y', Z', \delta', \lambda']$ be deterministic automata as in definition 2.2. Then we have

1. $\mathfrak{A}$ and $\mathfrak{A}'$ are subautomata of the direct sum $\mathfrak{A} + \mathfrak{A}'$.

2. For every $z \in Z$ (resp. $z' \in Z'$) z, as a state of $\mathfrak{A}$ (resp. z' as a state of $\mathfrak{A}'$) is equivalent to z (resp. z') as a state of $\mathfrak{A} + \mathfrak{A}'$.

3. If $z \in Z$, $z' \in Z'$ and the automata $\mathfrak{A}$ and $\mathfrak{A}'$ are Z-finite with $Card(Z) = n$, $Card(Z') = n'$, then $z \sim z'$ holds if and only if for all $p \in W(X)$ with $l(p) = n + n' - 1$ the equality $\lambda(z, p) = \lambda'(z'p)$ is satisfied.

4. If $\mathfrak{K} = \{[X, Y^i, Z^i, \delta^i, \lambda^i] \mid i \in I\}$ is a finite class of $[X, Z]$-finite automata having (without loss of generality) pairwise disjoint state sets, then the equivalence between the states of the finite set $\bigcup_{i \in I} Z^i$ is a decidable relation.

5. The equivalence of automata is a decidable relation for $[X, Z]$-finite automata.

Now we shall turn to the equivalent simplification of automata. If two states of the same automaton $\mathfrak{A} = [X, Y, Z, \delta, \lambda]$ are equivalent, then the external examination of the efficiency of $\mathfrak{A}$ suggests that one of them is superfluous. Thus the question arises whether we could internally eliminate one of these states, i.e., whether we could construct an equivalent automaton which has less states than $\mathfrak{A}$ and for which different states are perhaps no longer equivalent. We shall see that there always exists such a reduced automaton and the number of its states is uniquely determined. Thus this number can be considered as a measure of the complexity of $\mathfrak{A}$. Furthermore in the next section we shall show that up to isomorphisms there exists exactly one reduced automaton which is equivalent to the automaton $\mathfrak{A}$ under consideration.

Definition 2.3. Let $\mathfrak{A} = [X, Y, Z, \delta, \lambda]$ be a deterministic automaton.

(2.3.1.) $\mathfrak{A}$ is called *reduced* if for all $z, z' \in Z$ we have

$$z \sim z' \rightarrow z = z'.$$

(2.3.2.) A deterministic automaton $\mathfrak{A}'$ is called a *reduct of* $\mathfrak{A}$, if $\mathfrak{A}'$ is reduced and equivalent to $\mathfrak{A}$.

Corollary 2.9.

1. A Z-finite deterministic automaton $\mathfrak{A}$ is reduced if and only if the finest partition $\mathfrak{z}^* = \{\{z\} \mid z \in Z\}$ of Z appears in $\mathfrak{Z}(\mathfrak{A})$.

2. Whether or not an $[X, Z]$-finite deterministic automaton is reduced is a decidable property.

Let us consider as an example the autonomous automaton $\mathfrak{A}_3 = [\{x\}, \{0, 1\}, \boldsymbol{nz}, \delta^3, \lambda^3]$, where $\boldsymbol{nz} = \{0, 1, 2, \ldots\}$ is the set of natural numbers and for $k \in \boldsymbol{nz}$ we have

$$\delta^3(k, x) = \begin{cases} 0, & \text{if} \quad k = 0, \\ k - 1 & \text{otherwise}, \end{cases} \qquad \lambda^3(k, x) = \begin{cases} 1, & \text{if} \quad k = 0, \\ 0 & \text{otherwise}. \end{cases}$$

This automaton is obviously reduced, since for the states $k, m \in \boldsymbol{nz}$ with $k < m$

$$\lambda^3(k, x^m) = 0^k 1^{m-k} \neq 0^m = \lambda^3(m, x^m),$$

holds where x^m denotes the word consisting of m consecutive signals x ($x^0 = e$). In the sequence of partitions $\mathfrak{Z}(\mathfrak{A}_3)$ all members are different. For $i = 1, 2, \ldots$ we have

$$\mathfrak{z}_i = \{\{0\}, \{1\}, \ldots, \{i-1\}, \{i, i+1, \ldots\}\}.$$

The partition $\mathfrak{z}^* = \{\{0\}, \{1\}, \ldots\}$ does not appear in $\mathfrak{Z}(\mathfrak{A}_3)$, which shows that for Z-infinite automata, 2.9.1 holds only in that the appearance of $\mathfrak{z}^*$ in $\mathfrak{Z}(\mathfrak{A})$ implies that $\mathfrak{A}$ is reduced. For arbitrary $k \in \boldsymbol{nz}$, $k > 0$ the subautomaton $\mathfrak{A}_3^k$ of $\mathfrak{A}_3$ with the state set $\{0, 1, \ldots, k\}$, shows that there are indeed automata with $n = k + 1$ states for which the partitions $\mathfrak{Z}_1, \ldots, \mathfrak{Z}_{n-1}$ are all different. Thus the upper bound $n - 1$ appearing in Theorem 2.6 can not be improved.

Theorem 2.10. *Every automaton* $\mathfrak{A} = [X, Y, Z, \delta, \lambda]$ *possesses a reduct. If* $\mathfrak{A}$ *is* $[X, Y]$*-finite, then the reduct of* $\mathfrak{A}$ *can be constructed algorithmically.*

Proof: Let $\bar{Z} \underset{\mathrm{Df}}{=} \{[z] \mid z \in Z\}$, where for $z \in Z$ we put

$$[z] \underset{\mathrm{Df}}{=} \{z' \mid z' \sim z \wedge z' \in Z\}.$$

If $\mathfrak{A}$ is $[X, Z]$-finite, then $\bar{Z}$ has an algorithmic construction, since it is exactly the partition $\mathfrak{z}_{n-1}$, where $n = Card(Z)$. For $\bar{z} \in \bar{Z}$, $x \in X$ we define

$$\left.\begin{aligned}\bar{\delta}(\bar{z}, x) &\underset{\mathrm{Df}}{=} [\delta(z', x)],\\ \bar{\lambda}(\bar{z}, x) &\underset{\mathrm{Df}}{=} \lambda(z', x),\end{aligned}\right\} \quad \text{if} \quad \bar{z} = [z'].$$

The fact that these definitions are independent of the representative z' of the equivalence class $\bar{z}$ is implied by the following relations

$$\begin{aligned}&z \sim z' \to \forall x\big(x \in X \to \delta(z, x) \sim \delta(z', x) \wedge \lambda(z, x) = \lambda(z', x)\big),\\ &z \sim z' \leftrightarrow [z] = [z'],\end{aligned}$$

which hold for all $z, z' \in Z$. Thus $\bar{\mathfrak{A}} = [X, Y, \bar{Z}, \bar{\delta}, \bar{\lambda}]$ is in fact an automaton. We claim that for every $z \in Z$ and $p \in W(X)$

$$\lambda(z, p) = \bar{\lambda}([z], p)$$

holds, which implied that $\mathfrak{A} \sim \bar{\mathfrak{A}}$. The proof is carried out by induction on p. The initial step $p = e$ is again trivial. The step from p to xp for an $x \in X$ is as follows:

$$\begin{aligned}\lambda(z, xp) &= \lambda(z, x)\lambda\big(\delta(z, x), p\big)\\ &= \bar{\lambda}([z], x)\lambda\big(\delta(z, x), p\big)\\ &= \bar{\lambda}([z], x)\bar{\lambda}\big([\delta(z, x)], p\big)\\ &= \bar{\lambda}([z], x)\bar{\lambda}\big(\bar{\delta}([z], x), p\big) = \bar{\lambda}([z], xp).\end{aligned}$$

$\bar{\mathfrak{A}}$ is indeed reduced, since $[z] \sim [z']$ implies $z \sim z'$, i.e. $[z] = [z']$. This proves Theorem 2.10.

Theorem 2.11. *Reduced and equivalent automata have the same number of states.*

Proof: Let $\mathfrak{A} = [X, Y, Z, \delta, \lambda] \sim \mathfrak{A}' = [X, Y', Z', \delta', \lambda']$, and suppose that the automata $\mathfrak{A}$ and $\mathfrak{A}'$ are reduced. $\mathfrak{A} \sim \mathfrak{A}'$ implies that for each $z \in Z$ there exists a $z' \in Z'$ for which $z' \sim z$. Since $\mathfrak{A}'$ is reduced, for every $z \in Z$ at most one $z' \in Z'$ can exist such that $z' \sim z$, since $z' \sim z$ and $z'' \sim z$ imply $z' \sim z''$, hence $z' = z''$. The same reasoning shows that for each $z' \in Z'$ there is exactly one $z \in Z$ for which $z \sim z'$. Consequently, the mapping ζ assigning to each $z \in Z$ that $z' \in Z'$ for which $z' \sim z$ holds, is a one-to-one mapping of Z onto Z'. This however is equivalent to $Card(Z) = Card(Z')$.

Thus, by Theorem 2.11, all the reducts of a fixed automaton have the same number of states. A reduct of a Moore automaton need not be a Moore automaton, as can be shown by a simple example (cf. $\mathfrak{A}_2$).

In the theory of Moore automata, where other kinds of automata are not considered, the equivalence of the states z, z' is thus defined in a special way, namely we have the additional requirement that $\mu(z) = \mu'(z')$ holds. Thus, one can define on the corresponding partition $\bar{Z}$ a function $\bar{\mu}$ such that

$$\bar{\mu}(\bar{z}) = \mu(z'), \quad \text{if} \quad \bar{z} = [z'],$$

which implies that the reduct (in the sense of *Moore equivalence*) is again a Moore automaton. It is obvious that the *Moore reduct* constructed in this manner is in general not reduced (in the strong sense).

Definition 2.4. Let $\mathfrak{A} = [X, Y, Z, \delta, \lambda]$ be a deterministic automaton.

(2.4.1) $\mathfrak{A}$ is called *connected from the state* $z' \in Z$ if for every $z \in Z$ there exists a $p \in W(X)$ for which $z = \delta(z', p)$.

(2.4.2) $\mathfrak{A}$ is called *connected* if there is a $z' \in Z$ such that $\mathfrak{A}$ is connected from the state z'.

(2.4.3) $\mathfrak{A}$ is called *strongly connected* if it is connected from each of its states.

Corollary 2.12. $\mathfrak{A}$ is strongly connected if and only if the only subautomaton of $\mathfrak{A}$ with the input alphabet X and the output alphabet Y is $\mathfrak{A}$ itself.

Theorem 2.13. *Let* $\mathfrak{A} = [X, Y, Z, \delta, \lambda]$, $\mathfrak{A}' = [X, Y', Z', \delta', \lambda']$ *be strongly connected reduced automata with the same input alphabet and (without loss of generality) disjoint state sets. Then we have*

1. $\mathfrak{A} \sim \mathfrak{A}'$ *if and only if there are* $z \in Z$ *and* $z' \in Z'$ *such that* $z \sim z'$.

2. $\mathfrak{A} + \mathfrak{A}'$ *is reduced if and only if* $\mathfrak{A}$ *and* $\mathfrak{A}'$ *are not equivalent.*

Proof: Obviously, it is sufficient to show that the existence of states $z \in Z$, $z' \in Z'$ with $z \sim z'$ implies $\mathfrak{A} \lesssim \mathfrak{A}'$. Since $\mathfrak{A}$ is strongly connected, $Z = \{\delta(z, p) \mid p \in W(X)\}$ holds for arbitrary $z \in Z$. Because of $z \sim z'$ however, to each state $z^* = \delta(z, p) \in Z$ the state $z'' = \delta'(z' p)$ is an equivalent state of $\mathfrak{A}'$.

Corollary 2.14. If $\mathfrak{A}$ and $\mathfrak{A}'$ are connected from the states z and z' respectively, then $z \sim z'$ implies $\mathfrak{A} \sim \mathfrak{A}'$.

§ 3. Homomorphisms

The set theoretical definition of the notion of an automaton by means of a quintuple $[X, Y, Z, \delta, \lambda]$ consisting of three sets and two functions enables us to compare automata with the usual algebraic structures, such as groups, semi-groups or rings, although in the definition of these structures only one set is involved. That is why much work has been devoted to the investigation of the relationship between deterministic automata on one hand and semi-groups and groups, mainly, on the other.

Here, we shall restrict ourselves to the investigation of the "coarse" structure of deterministic automata by means of homomorphisms. By coarse structure we mean the properties of the transition and output functions, in contrast to the fine structure of an automaton given by its construction from the simplest elementary automata (i.e., its representation as a logical network of elementary automata).

Definition 3.1. Let $\mathfrak{A} = [X, Y, Z, \delta, \lambda]$, $\mathfrak{A}' = [X', Y', Z', \delta', \lambda']$ be arbitrary deterministic automata. A triple $\chi = [\xi, \eta, \zeta]$ of mappings is called a *homomorphism of* $\mathfrak{A}$ *onto* $\mathfrak{A}'$ if the following conditions hold:

a) ξ, η, and ζ respectively are single-valued mappings of X, Y, and Z respectively onto X', Y', and Z' respectively.

b) For all $z \in Z$, $x \in X$ we have

$$\zeta(\delta(z, x)) = \delta'(\zeta(z), \xi(x)), \qquad \eta(\lambda(z, x)) = \lambda'(\zeta(z), \xi(x)).$$

If in addition the mappings ξ, η, ζ are one-to-one, then χ is called an *isomorphism of* $\mathfrak{A}$ *onto* $\mathfrak{A}'$.

If $X = X'$, $Y = Y'$ and ξ, η coincide with the identity mappings I_X, I_Y of X and Y respectively, then $\chi = [I_X, I_Y, \zeta]$ is called a *Z-homomorphism* of $\mathfrak{A}$ onto $\mathfrak{A}'$. Similarly we can define $[X, Z]$-*homomorphisms*, $[X, Y]$-*homomorphisms*, etc.

Let $\chi = [\xi, \eta, \zeta]$ be a homomorphism of $\mathfrak{A} = [X, Y, Z, \delta, \lambda]$ onto $\mathfrak{A}' = [X', Y', Z', \delta', \lambda']$. We can extend the definitions of ξ and η for all $p \in W(X)$, $x \in X$, $q \in W(Y)$, $y \in Y$ by means of the following inductive stipulations:

$$\xi(e) = e, \qquad \eta(e) = e,$$

$$\xi(xp) = \xi(x)\,\xi(p), \qquad \eta(yq) = \eta(y)\,\eta(q).$$

Theorem 3.1. *If* $\chi = [\xi, \eta, \zeta]$ *is a homomorphism of* $\mathfrak{A} = [X, Y, Z, \delta, \lambda]$ *onto* $\mathfrak{A}' = [X', Y', Z', \delta', \lambda']$, *then for all* $z \in Z$, $p \in W(X)$ *we have:*

1. $\zeta(\delta(z, p)) = \delta'(\zeta(z), \xi(p))$,
2. $\eta(\lambda(z, p)) = \lambda'(\zeta(z), \xi(p))$.

The proof is carried out by induction on p. The initial step $p = e$ is trivial for both equalities. The induction step is taken from p to xp for all $x \in X$. Thus we have

$$\begin{aligned}\zeta\big(\delta(z, xp)\big) &= \zeta\big(\delta(\delta(z, x), p)\big) = \delta'\big(\zeta(\delta(z, x)), \xi(p)\big)\\ &= \delta'\big(\delta'(\zeta(z), \xi(x)), \xi(p)\big) = \delta'\big(\zeta(z), \xi(x)\,\xi(p)\big)\\ &= \delta'\big(\zeta(z), \xi(xp)\big).\end{aligned}$$

$$\begin{aligned}\eta\big(\lambda(z, xp)\big) &= \eta\big(\lambda(z, x)\,\lambda(\delta(z, x), p)\big) = \eta\big(\lambda(z, x)\big)\,\eta\big(\lambda(\delta(z, x), p)\big)\\ &= \lambda'\big(\zeta(z), \xi(x)\big)\,\lambda'\big(\zeta(\delta(z, x)), \xi(p)\big)\\ &= \lambda'\big(\zeta(z), \xi(x)\big)\,\lambda'\big(\delta'(\zeta(z), \xi(x)), \xi(p)\big) = \lambda'\big(\zeta(z), \xi(xp)\big).\end{aligned}$$

Corollary 3.2. Assume $\chi = [I_X, I_Y, \zeta]$ is a Z-homomorphism of $\mathfrak{A}$ onto $\mathfrak{A}'$. Then the following two propositions hold:

1. For all $z \in Z$ we have $z \sim \zeta(z)$.
2. The automata $\mathfrak{A}$ and $\mathfrak{A}'$ are equivalent.

Theorem 3.3. *Let $\mathfrak{A} = [X, Y, Z, \delta, \lambda]$ be an arbitrary deterministic automaton. In the class $Eq(\mathfrak{A})$ of all deterministic automata equivalent to $\mathfrak{A}$ there is an up to Z-isomorphisms uniquely determined deterministic automaton, onto which every automaton belonging to the class $Eq(\mathfrak{A})$ can be mapped Z-homomorphically. This automaton is reduced and its set of states has the minimal possible cardinality among the automata of the class $Eq(\mathfrak{A})$.*

Proof: Let $\overline{\mathfrak{A}} = [X, Y, \overline{Z}, \overline{\delta}, \overline{\lambda}]$ be the reduct of $\mathfrak{A}$ constructed in the proof of Theorem 2.10. If $\mathfrak{A}^* = [X, Y^*, Z^*, \delta^*, \lambda^*] \in Eq(\mathfrak{A})$ then $\mathfrak{A}^* \sim \mathfrak{A} \sim \overline{\mathfrak{A}}$, hence $\overline{\mathfrak{A}}$ is a reduct of $\mathfrak{A}^*$. Thus for every $z^* \in Z^*$ there is exactly one state $\bar{z} \in \overline{Z}$ for which $\bar{z} \sim z^*$. The mapping ζ assigning to each $z^* \in Z^*$ this state $\bar{z} \in \overline{Z}$ is a single valued mapping of Z^* onto $\overline{Z}$. $\mathfrak{A}^* \sim \overline{\mathfrak{A}}$ and our assumption that the output alphabets of the automata under consideration do not contain superfluous output signals imply $Y^* = Y$. We claim that $\chi = [I_X, I_Y, \zeta]$ is a Z-homomorphism of $\mathfrak{A}^* = [X, Y, Z^*, \delta^*, \lambda^*]$ onto $\overline{\mathfrak{A}}$.

By definition $\zeta\big(\delta^*(z^*, x)\big)$ is the state of $\overline{\mathfrak{A}}$ equivalent to $\delta^*(z^*, x)$. Since by 2.4, $z^* \sim \zeta(z^*)$, for all $x \in X$ we also have $\delta^*(z^*, x) \sim \overline{\delta}\big(\zeta(z^*), x\big)$, and because there is exactly one state of $\overline{\mathfrak{A}}$ which is equivalent to $\delta^*(z^*, x)$, we see that

$$\zeta\big(\delta^*(z^*, x)\big) = \overline{\delta}\big(\zeta(z^*), x\big)$$

holds for arbitrary $z^* \in Z^*$ and $x \in X$. Furthermore $z^* \sim \zeta(z^*)$ implies that for each $x \in X$

$$\lambda^*(z^*, x) = \overline{\lambda}\big(\zeta(z^*), x\big).$$

This shows that every automaton of the class $Eq(\mathfrak{A})$ admits a Z-homomorphism onto the reduced automaton $\overline{\mathfrak{A}}$.

If the automaton $\overline{\overline{\mathfrak{A}}} = [X, Y, \overline{\overline{Z}}, \overline{\overline{\delta}}, \overline{\overline{\lambda}}]$ belongs to the class $Eq(\mathfrak{A})$ and every automaton of $Eq(\mathfrak{A})$ admits a Z-homomorphism onto $\overline{\overline{\mathfrak{A}}}$ then in particular, there s a Z-homomorphism $\bar{\chi} = [I_X, I_Y, \bar{\zeta}]$ of $\overline{\mathfrak{A}}$ onto $\overline{\overline{\mathfrak{A}}}$. Because $\overline{\mathfrak{A}}$ is reduced, we can easily see that ζ is one-to-one, since $\bar{z}_1, \bar{z}_2 \in \bar{Z}$ and $\bar{\zeta}(\bar{z}_1) = \bar{\zeta}(\bar{z}_2)$ imply

$$\bar{z}_1 \sim \bar{\zeta}(\bar{z}_1) = \bar{\zeta}(\bar{z}_2) \sim \bar{z}_2,$$

hence $\bar{z}_1 \sim \bar{z}_2$ and thus $\bar{z}_1 = \bar{z}_2$. This shows that $\bar{\chi}$ is actually a Z-isomorphism of $\bar{\mathfrak{A}}$ onto $\bar{\bar{\mathfrak{A}}}$. The fact that every state set of an automaton from $Eq(\mathfrak{A})$ can be mapped onto $\bar{Z}$ immediately implies that the state set of $\bar{\mathfrak{A}}$ is of minimal cardinality among the automata from $Eq(\mathfrak{A})$.

Corollary 3.4.

1. Up to Z-isomorphisms, every deterministic automaton has exactly one reduct.
2. The number of states of an arbitrary reduct of $\mathfrak{A}$ is the minimal number of states among the automata equivalent to $\mathfrak{A}$.

Since the reduct of a Moore automaton is in general no longer a Moore automaton, we see that the property of being a Moore automaton is not invariant under homomorphisms. Furthermore we have

Theorem 3.5. *Let* $\chi = [\xi, \eta, I_Z]$ *be an arbitrary* $[X, Y]$*-homomorphism of* $\mathfrak{A} = [X, Y, Z, \delta, \lambda]$ *onto* $\mathfrak{A}' = [X', Y', Z, \delta', \lambda']$. *Then the following two propositions hold:*

1. *If* $\mathfrak{A}$ *is a Moore automaton, so is* $\mathfrak{A}'$.
2. *If* $Y = Y'$ *and* $\eta = I_Y$ *then* $\mathfrak{A}$ *is a Moore automaton if an only if* $\mathfrak{A}'$ *is.*

Proof: Let $\mathfrak{A} = [X, Y, Z, \delta, \mu]$ and put

$$\mu'(z) \underset{\mathrm{Df}}{=} \eta(\mu(z))$$

for $z \in Z$. Thus for every $z \in Z$, $x' \in X'$ and for all $x \in X$ such that $\xi(x) = x'$

$$\lambda'(z, x') = \eta(\lambda(z, x)) = \eta(\mu(\delta(z, x))) = \mu'(\delta(z, x)).$$

Now we have $\delta(z, x) = I_Z(\delta(z, x)) = \delta'(I_Z(z), \xi(x)) = \delta'(z, x')$, and also $\lambda'(z, x') = \mu'(\delta'(z, x'))$ for all $z \in Z$, $x' \in X'$, that is $\mathfrak{A}'$ is a Moore automaton.

If $\mathfrak{A}' = [X', Y, Z, \delta', \mu']$ and $\eta = I_Y$ then for all $z \in Z$, $x \in X$ we have

$$\lambda(z, x) = \lambda'(z, \xi(x)) = \mu'(\delta'(z, \xi(x))) = \mu'(\delta(z, x)),$$

which shows that $\mathfrak{A}$ is a Moore automaton if and only if $\mathfrak{A}'$ is.

In the same way it is clear that under isomorphisms Moore automata are transferred into Moore automata. Namely we can show that μ' defined by $\mu(z') = \eta(\mu(\zeta^{-1}(z')))$ (for $z' \in Z'$) satisfies our requirements. Furthermore the following theorem can easily be verified:

Theorem 3.6. *Suppose* $\chi = [\xi, \eta, \zeta]$ *is a homomorphism of* $\mathfrak{A} = [X, Y, Z, \delta, \lambda]$ *onto* $\mathfrak{A}' = [X', Y', Z', \delta', \lambda']$, *then we have:*

1. *If* $\mathfrak{A}$ *is connected from the state* z *then* $\mathfrak{A}'$ *is connected from the state* $\zeta(z)$.
2. *If* $\mathfrak{A}$ *is strongly connected, so is* $\mathfrak{A}'$.

The converse of Theorem 3.6 is obviously false.

§ 4. Word Functions

Next we turn to the investigation of the input-output relations realized by deterministic automata. If we consider a fixed state z of the deterministic automaton $\mathfrak{A} = [X, Y, Z, \delta, \lambda]$ and feed into the automaton $\mathfrak{A}$ which is in the state z an arbitrary word $p \in W(X)$, then the automaton puts out a completely determined word, namely the word $q = \lambda(z, p)$. Thus the input-output relation generated by z in $\mathfrak{A}$ yields us a single valued function which maps the set $W(X)$ into the set $W(Y)$.

Definition 4.1. If $\mathfrak{A} = [X, Y, Z, \delta, \lambda]$ is a deterministic automaton and $z \in Z$ then the word function φ which is defined for every $p \in W(X)$ by

$$\varphi(p) = \lambda(z, p)$$

is called the *word function over* $[X, Y]$ *generated by the state* z *in the automaton* $\mathfrak{A}$. A word function φ over $[X, Y]$, i.e., a function which assigns to each $p \in W(X)$ a word $\varphi(p) \in W(Y)$, is called *feasible* if there is an automaton $\mathfrak{A} = [X', Y', Z, \delta, \lambda]$ and $z \in Z$ such that $X \subseteq X'$, $Y \subseteq Y'$, and $\lambda(z, p) = \varphi(p)$ holds for every $p \in W(X)$.

Let φ be a word function over $[X, Y]$ and

$$Y_\varphi = \{y \mid y \in Y \wedge \exists p \exists q \exists s (p \in W(X) \wedge q, s \in W(Y) \wedge qys = \varphi(p))\}.$$

Then φ is also a word function over $[X, Y_\varphi]$ and $[X, Y']$, provided that $Y_\varphi \subseteq Y'$.

Theorem 4.1. *If φ is a feasible word function over $[X, Y]$, then there is a deterministic automaton $\mathfrak{A}$ with the input alphabet X and the output alphabet Y_φ, and a state z of $\mathfrak{A}$ such that φ is generated by z in $\mathfrak{A}$.*

Proof: Suppose φ is generated by z' in $\mathfrak{A}' = [X', Y', Z', \delta', \lambda']$. Then we have

$$X \subseteq X', \quad Y_\varphi \subseteq Y' \quad \text{and} \quad Z = \{z \mid \exists p (p \in W(X) \wedge z = \delta'(z', p))\} \subseteq Z'.$$

If δ and λ denote the restrictions of δ' and λ', respectively, onto $Z \times X$, then $\mathfrak{A} = [X, Y_\varphi, Z, \delta, \lambda]$ is a subautomaton of $\mathfrak{A}'$, hence for all $p \in W(X)$ we have

$$\varphi(p) = \lambda'(z', p) = \lambda(z', p),$$

which shows that φ is generated by z' in $\mathfrak{A}$. Indeed, if we had $z \in Z$ and $x \in X$ with $\lambda'(z, x) \notin Y_\varphi$, i.e., a $p \in W(X)$, $x \in X$ with $\lambda'(\delta'(z', p), x) \notin Y_\varphi$, then $\varphi(px) = \lambda'(z', px) = \lambda'(z' p)\, \lambda'(\delta'(z', p), x) \notin W(Y_\varphi)$ would hold, and thus φ would not be a word function over $[X, Y_\varphi]$.

Theorem 4.2. *Let φ be the word function over $[X, Y]$ generated by $z \in Z$ in $\mathfrak{A} = [X, Y, Z, \delta, \lambda]$. Then we have:*

1. *For all $p \in W(X)$ the equality $l(\varphi(p)) = l(p)$ holds.*
2. *If $p, r \in W(X)$ then there is an $s \in W(Y)$ such that*

$$\varphi(pr) = \varphi(p)s$$

is satisfied.

Proposition 4.2.1 is immediately obvious; we can also see that $s = \lambda(\delta(z, p), r)$ satisfies the requirements of 4.2.2. Conditions 4.2.1 and 4.2.2 are called the *automata conditions*. We shall show that these conditions are not only necessary but also sufficient for the generability of the word function φ over $[X, Y]$.

Definition 4.2. A word function φ over $[X, Y]$ is called *sequential* if it satisfies conditions 4.2.1 and 4.2.2 (the automata conditions).

In order to show that all sequential functions are generable we introduce the notion of the "state" of a word function satisfying condition 4.2.2. If φ is a word function over $[X, Y]$ satisfying 4.2.2 and furthermore $p, r \in W(X)$, then the words $\varphi(pr)$, $\varphi(p)$ are uniquely determined, and consequently the word s, whose existence is assured by 4.2.2, is also uniquely determined.

Definition 4.3. Let φ be a word function over $[X, Y]$ satisfying 4.2.2. The function assigning to each $r \in W(X)$ the word $s \in W(Y)$ for which $\varphi(pr) = \varphi(p)s$ holds, is called *the state of φ belonging to the word p* and is denoted by φ_p.

Theorem 4.3. *Let φ be a word function over $[X, Y]$.*

1. *If φ satisfies condition 4.2.2, so does each of its states φ_p.*
2. *If φ is sequential, all the states φ_p of φ are also sequential.*

Proof: Let us choose an arbitrary $p \in W(X)$. Then for all $r, u \in W(X)$

$$\varphi(p)\,\varphi_p(r)\,\varphi_{pr}(u) = \varphi(pr)\,\varphi_{pr}(u) = \varphi(pru) = \varphi(p)\,\varphi_p(ru),$$

holds, hence $\varphi_p(r)\,\varphi_{pr}(u) = \varphi_p(ru)$, which shows that φ_p satisfies condition 4.2.2. If moreover φ is sequential, then $\varphi(pr) = \varphi(p)\,\varphi_p(r)$ holds too, hence

$$l(\varphi_p(r)) = l(\varphi(pr)) - l(\varphi(p)) = l(pr) - l(p) = l(r),$$

i.e., φ_p also satisfies 4.2.1 and thus is sequential.

Corollary 4.4. Let φ be a word function over $[X, Y]$ satisfying 4.2.2. Then we have:

1. If $p, r \in W(X)$ and $(\varphi_p)_r$ is the state of φ_p belonging to the word r then $(\varphi_p)_r = \varphi_{pr}$.
2. Every state of a state of φ is again a state of φ.

Theorem 4.5. *Every sequential function φ over $[X, Y]$ can be generated in a deterministic automaton which has at most as many states as φ itself.*

Proof: Let us put $Z^\varphi \underset{\mathrm{Df}}{=} \{\varphi_p \mid p \in W(X)\}$, and for $\varphi_p \in Z^\varphi$, $x \in X$

$$\delta^\varphi(\varphi_p, x) \underset{\mathrm{Df}}{=} \varphi_{px}, \qquad \lambda^\varphi(\varphi_p, x) \underset{\mathrm{Df}}{=} \varphi_p(x).$$

We shall show by induction on r that for all $\varphi_p \in Z^\varphi$, $r \in W(X)$

$$\delta^\varphi(\varphi_p, r) = \varphi_{pr}, \qquad \lambda^\varphi(\varphi_p, r) = \varphi_p(r).$$

The initial step $r = e$ is trivial, since $\varphi_p(e) = e$ holds because of the fact that e is the only word of $W(Y)$ which has the same length as e itself. The induction step is taken from r to rx:

$$\delta^\varphi(\varphi_p, rx) = \delta^\varphi(\delta^\varphi(\varphi_p, r), x) = \delta^\varphi(\varphi_{pr}, x) = \varphi_{prx};$$

$$\lambda^\varphi(\varphi_p, rx) = \lambda^\varphi(\varphi_p, r)\, \lambda^\varphi(\delta^\varphi(\varphi_p, r), x) = \varphi_p(r)\, \lambda^\varphi(\varphi_{pr}, x)$$
$$= \varphi_p(r)\, \varphi_{pr}(x) = \varphi_p(rx).$$

In the automaton $\mathfrak{A}^\varphi = [X, Y, Z^\varphi, \delta^\varphi, \lambda^\varphi]$ the sequential function φ is generated by the state φ_e $(= \varphi)$. Also, all the states φ_p of φ can be generated in $\mathfrak{A}^\varphi$. In fact we can show that this holds for every automaton in which φ can be generated.

Theorem 4.6. *If φ is generated by z in $\mathfrak{A} = [X, Y, Z, \delta, \lambda]$, then for arbitrary $p \in W(X)$ the state $\delta(z, p)$ of $\mathfrak{A}$ generates the state φ_p of φ.*

Proof: For all $p, r \in W(X)$ we have

$$\varphi(p)\, \varphi_p(r) = \varphi(pr) = \lambda(z, pr) = \lambda(z, p)\, \lambda(\delta(z, p), r)$$
$$= \varphi(p)\, \lambda(\delta(z, p), r),$$

hence

$$\varphi_p(r) = \lambda(\delta(z, p), r).$$

As for the number of states, the automaton $\mathfrak{A}^\varphi$ is optimal. φ cannot be generated in an automaton whose state set is of smaller cardinality than Z^φ. In particular, we have

Corollary 4.7. A sequential word function φ can be generated in a Z-finite automaton if and only if it has a finite number of states.

If X and Z^φ are finite, then obviously Y_φ is also. Thus a word function φ can be generated in a finite automaton if and only if the sets X and Z^φ are finite. In the following section, word functions which can be generated in Z-finite and finite automata respectively, will be further characterized. These characterizations are based on a connection between word functions over $[X, Y]$ and partitions of the set $W(X) \setminus \{e\}$.

Now we shall show by means of an example that there are such sequential word functions over finite alphabets which possess infinitely many states and thus cannot be generated in any finite automaton.

Let us put $X = \{x\}$, $Y = \{0, 1\}$ and let φ^1 be defined for all $n = 0, 1, \ldots$ as follows:

$$\varphi^1(x^n) = y_1 y_2 \cdots y_n, \quad \text{where } y_i = \begin{cases} 1, & \text{if } i \text{ is a square number,} \\ 0 & \text{otherwise.} \end{cases}$$

We can easily verify that φ^1 is sequential. For each $x^n \in W(\{x\})$ we denote by φ^1_n the state of φ^1 belonging to x^n and show that

$$\varphi^1_n = \varphi^1_m \to n = m.$$

holds for every $n, m \in \boldsymbol{nz}$.

If $\varphi_n^1 = \varphi_m^1$ then for all $k \in \boldsymbol{nz}$ we have $\varphi_n^1(x^k) = \varphi_m^1(x^k)$. Let $i, j \geqq 1$ be chosen in such a way that $\varphi_n^1(x^i) = 0^{i-1}1$ and $\varphi_n^1(x^{i+j}) = 0^{i-1}10^{j-1}1$. Obviously for each n there exist such numbers i, j. Since $\varphi_n^1 = \varphi_m^1$, the words $\varphi^1(x^{n+i})$, $\varphi^1(x^{n+i+j})$, $\varphi^1(x^{m+i})$, $\varphi^1(x^{m+i+j})$ all end with the same letter 1. It follows from our construction that $n + i$, $n + i + j$ and $m + i$, $m + i + j$ are consecutive square numbers. Thus there are natural numbers k, l such that

$$n + i = k^2, \qquad n + i + j = (k + 1)^2,$$

$$m + i = l^2, \qquad m + i + j = (l + 1)^2.$$

Since $(m + j + i) - (m + i) = (n + j + i) - (n + i)$, we also have the equality $(l + 1)^2 - l^2 = (k + 1)^2 - k^2$. From this however we obtain $k = l$ and $m = n$. This shows that our sequential word function φ^1 has a countably infinitely number of states.

The restrictions on the generability of word functions in deterministic abstract automata which are given by the automata conditions are not essential. They follow from the fact that in the definition of automata the output of exactly one signal is required in every step. Condition 4.2.1 can immediately be dispensed with if we admit automata whose output alphabets can be certain subsets W of $W(Y)$. The sequence of words from this subset W put out by such an automaton is then "read together", i.e., all the words are concatenated in the order in which they appear to form one word. This approach is closer to reality, for example in computers, than that in which exactly one signal is put out in each step. (If a concrete automaton puts out nothing, then the corresponding abstract automaton puts out the empty word e.)

Definition 4.4. A word function φ over $[X, Y]$ is said to be *realized from the state z of the automaton* $\mathfrak{A} = [X, W, Z, \delta, \lambda]$ if $\varphi(p) = |\lambda(z, p)|$ holds for each $p \in W(X)$ (where $|\lambda(z, p)|$ denotes the word obtained by concatenating the words $\lambda(z, x_1)$, $\lambda(\delta(z, x_1), x_2), \ldots$, $\lambda(\delta(z, x_1 \ldots x_{n-1}), x_n)$, provided that $p = x_1 x_2 \ldots x_n$).

Theorem 4.8. *A word function φ over $[X, Y]$ can be realized if and only if condition 4.2.2 is satisfied and $\varphi(e) = e$ holds.*

Proof sketch: That these conditions are necessary, is obvious. In order to show that they are sufficient, we consider the automaton $\mathfrak{A}^\varphi$ defined above and replace its output alphabet Y by the set of words

$$W^\varphi = \{\varphi_p(x) \mid \varphi_p \in Z^\varphi \wedge x \in X\}.$$

Then we reason in the same way as in the proof of Theorem 4.5. We also obtain that every automaton in which the word function φ can be realized has at least as many states as φ.

In order that arbitrary word functions, including those which do not satisfy 4.2.2, and for which $\varphi(e) \neq e$, could be realized in an abstract automaton, we shall have to investigate one more characteristic of the way computers work.

A computer is informed by means of a signal (the starting signal) in its input, when all the data necessary for its work has been collected. Therefore we add a new symbol ε (the end mark) to the input alphabet X of the automaton. We say that the state z of the automaton ε-realizes the word function φ if in response to the input of $p\varepsilon$ in the state z such a sequence of words is put out whose concatenation is the word $\varphi(p)$.

Definition 4.5. Let φ be a word function over $[X, Y]$ and $\varepsilon \notin X$. We say that the state z of the automaton $\mathfrak{A} = [X \cup \{\varepsilon\}, W, Z, \delta, \lambda]$ *ε-realizes* φ if for all $p \in W(X)$

$$\varphi(p) = |\lambda(z, p\varepsilon)|.$$

In order to show that every word function can be ε-realized and to characterize those word functions which can be ε-realized in finite automata, we shall introduce (following Modrow [1]), the notion of the state system for an arbitrary word function.

Definition 4.6. Let φ be an arbitrary word function over $[X, Y]$. Then each set $\mathfrak{Z}^\varphi = \{[\sigma_p, \tau_p] \mid p \in W(X)\}$ where

(Z1) For all $p \in W(X)$ σ_p, τ_p are word functions over $[X, Y]$;

(Z2) $\forall p \forall r(p, r \in W(X) \to \varphi(pr) = \sigma_e(p)\, \tau_p(r))$;

(Z3) $\forall p \forall r(p, r \in W(X) \to \sigma_e(pr) = \sigma_e(p)\, \sigma_p(r))$

is called a *state system of* φ.

Every word function φ possesses a state system, e.g., the one in which

$$\sigma_p(r) = e, \qquad \tau_p(r) = \varphi(pr)$$

hold for all $p, r \in W(X)$. In general one word function has several state systems. We are especially interested in those $\mathfrak{Z}^\varphi$ whose cardinality is minimal.

Theorem 4.9. *Let* $\mathfrak{Z}^\varphi = \{[\sigma_p, \tau_p] \mid p \in W(X)\}$ *be a state system of* φ. *Then for all* $p, r, u \in W(X)$ *we have*

1. $\sigma_p(e) = e,$
2. $\varphi(p) = \tau_e(p),$
3. $\sigma_p(ru) = \sigma_p(r)\, \sigma_{pr}(u),$
4. $\tau_p(ru) = \sigma_p(r)\, \tau_{pr}(u),$
5. $[\sigma_p, \tau_p] = [\sigma_r, \tau_r] \to \forall u(u \in W(X) \to [\sigma_{pu}, \tau_{pu}] = [\sigma_{ru}, \tau_{ru}]).$

Proof: If in (Z3) we replace r by the word e then we obtain

$$\sigma_e(p) = \sigma_e(p)\, \sigma_p(e),$$

which yields us $\sigma_p(e) = e$, and thus proves 4.9.1. From (Z2) for $p = e$ and $e = \sigma_e(e)$ we immediately obtain 4.9.2. From (Z3) we get

$$\sigma_e(p)\,\sigma_p(r)\,\sigma_{pr}(u) = \sigma_e(pr)\,\sigma_{pr}(u) = \sigma_e(pru) = \sigma_e(p)\,\sigma_p(ru);$$

hence $\sigma_p(r)\sigma_{pr}(u) = \sigma_p(ru)$, which proves 4.9.3. Because of (Z2) and (Z3) we have

$$\sigma_e(p)\,\sigma_p(r)\,\tau_{pr}(u) = \sigma_e(pr)\,\tau_{pr}(u) = \varphi(pru) = \sigma_e(p)\,\tau_p(ru),$$

hence $\sigma_p(r)\tau_{pr}(u) = \tau_p(ru)$. This proves 4.9.4.

From $\sigma_p = \sigma_r$ it follows for all $u, w \in W(X)$ that

$$\sigma_r(u)\,\sigma_{ru}(w) = \sigma_r(uw) = \sigma_p(uw) = \sigma_p(u)\,\sigma_{pu}(w)$$

holds. Because of $\sigma_r(u) = \sigma_p(u)$, this implies $\sigma_{ru}(w) = \sigma_{pu}(w)$ for all $u, w \in W(X)$, hence $\sigma_{ru} = \sigma_{pu}$ for all $u \in W(X)$.

If moreover we have $\tau_p = \tau_r$, then for all $u, w \in W(X)$ we have

$$\sigma_r(u)\,\tau_{ru}(w) = \tau_r(uw) = \tau_p(uw) = \sigma_p(u)\,\tau_{pu}(w).$$

Since $\sigma_r = \sigma_p$, for all $u \in W(X)$ we have $\tau_{ru} = \tau_{pu}$. Thus Theorem 4.9 is proved.

Let us consider an arbitrary word function φ over $[X, Y]$ and put for $p, r \in W(X)$

$$\sigma_e^0(e) \underset{\mathrm{Df}}{=} e,$$

and for $p \neq e$

$$\sigma_e^0(p) \underset{\mathrm{Df}}{=} \text{the longest word } q \text{ with}$$

a) $\qquad \exists s\big(s \in W(Y) \wedge qs = \varphi(p)\big),$

b) $\qquad \forall r\big(r \in W(X) \to \exists s(s \in W(Y) \wedge qs = \varphi(pr))\big);$

$$\sigma_p^0(r) \underset{\mathrm{Df}}{=} \text{the word } s \text{ with } \sigma_e^0(pr) = \sigma_e^0(p)s, \text{ if } p \neq e;$$

$$\tau_p^0(r) \underset{\mathrm{Df}}{=} \text{the word } q \text{ with } \varphi(pr) = \sigma_e^0(p)q.$$

Obviously, $\mathfrak{Z}_0^\varphi = \{[\sigma_p^0, \tau_p^0] \mid p \in W(X)\}$ is a state system of φ which we shall call the *canonical* state system of φ.

Theorem 4.10. *Let* $\mathfrak{Z}^\varphi = \{[\sigma_p, \tau_p] \mid p \in W(X)\}$ *be an arbitrary state system of* φ.

1. *For each* $p \in W(X)$ *there is an* $s \in W(Y)$ *such that* $\sigma_e^0(p) = \sigma_e(p)s$.

2. *For all* $p, r \in W(X) \setminus \{e\}$ *we have: if* $[\sigma_p, \tau_p] = [\sigma_r, \tau_r]$, *then* $[\sigma_p^0, \tau_p^0] = [\sigma_r^0, \tau_r^0]$.

Proof: Proposition 4.10.1 follows from the fact that for arbitrary $p \in W(X) \setminus \{e\}$ the word $\sigma_e(p)$ satisfies conditions a) and b) of the definition of $\sigma_e^0(p)$ and that $\sigma_e(e) = e = \sigma_0^e(e)$ holds. The word s, whose existence is assured by 4.10.1, is obviously uniquely determined by p, and this justifies the following definition:

For $p \in W(X)$ we put

$$\sigma^*(p) \underset{\mathrm{Df}}{=} \text{that } s, \text{ for which } \sigma_e^0(p) = \sigma_e(p)s.$$

Thus we have $\sigma^*(e) = e$. Since for $p \in W(X)$ we have

$$\sigma_e^0(p)\,\tau_p^0(e) = \varphi(p) = \sigma_e(p)\,\tau_p(e),$$
$$\sigma_e^0(p)\,\tau_p^0(e) = \sigma_e(p)\,\sigma^*(p)\,\tau_p^0(e) = \sigma_e(p)\,\tau_p(e);$$

for all $p \in W(X)$

$$\sigma^*(p)\,\tau_p^0(e) = \tau_p(e). \tag{1}$$

Furthermore for all $p, r \in W(X)$

$$\sigma_e(p)\,\sigma_p(r)\,\tau_{pr}(e) = \sigma_e(pr)\,\tau_{pr}(e) = \varphi(pr) = \sigma_e^0(p)\,\sigma_p^0(r)\,\tau_{pr}^0(e),$$
$$\sigma_e(p)\,\sigma_p(r)\,\tau_{pr}(e) = \sigma_e(p)\,\sigma^*(p)\,\sigma_p^0(r)\,\tau_{pr}^0(e),$$

are satisfied, hence because of (1)

$$\sigma_p(r)\,\sigma^*(pr)\,\tau_{pr}^0(e) = \sigma^*(p)\,\sigma_p^0(r)\,\tau_{pr}^0(e)$$

holds, i.e., for all $p, r \in W(X)$ we have

$$\sigma_p(r)\,\sigma^*(pr) = \sigma^*(p)\,\sigma_p^0(r). \tag{2}$$

For arbitrary $p \in W(X) \setminus \{e\}$, $\sigma_e^0(p)\ \big(= \sigma_e(p)\sigma^*(p)\big)$ is the longest word q for which

a) $\exists s\big(s \in W(Y) \wedge qs = \varphi(p) = \sigma_e(p)\,\tau_p(e)\big),$

b) $\forall r\big(r \in W(X) \to \exists s\,(s \in W(Y) \wedge qs = \varphi(pr) = \sigma_e(p)\,\sigma_p(r)\,\tau_{pr}(e))\big)$

are both satisfied.

Thus for $p \in W(X) \setminus \{e\}$, $\sigma^*(p)$ is the longest word q' such that

a′) $\exists s\big(s \in W(Y) \wedge q's = \tau_p(e)\big),$

b′) $\forall r\big(r \in W(X) \to \exists s\,(s \in W(Y) \wedge q's = \sigma_p(r)\,\tau_{pr}(e) = \tau_p(r))\big).$ (3)

Let us consider now $p, r \neq e$, $[\sigma_p, \tau_p] = [\sigma_r, \tau_r]$. Because of (3) we have $\sigma^*(p) = \sigma^*(r)$ and because of 4.9.5 and (3) we also have $\sigma^*(pu) = \sigma^*(ru)$ for every $u \in W(X)$. Therefore by (2)

$$\sigma^*(p)\,\sigma_p^0(u) = \sigma_p(u)\,\sigma^*(pu) = \sigma_r(u)\,\sigma^*(ru) = \sigma^*(r)\,\sigma_r^0(u)$$
$$= \sigma^*(p)\,\sigma_r^0(u),$$

hence $\sigma_p^0 = \sigma_r^0$. As in the proof of 4.9.5, from this it follows that $\sigma_{pu}^0 = \sigma_{ru}^0$ holds for every $u \in W(X)$.

Finally we have for $u \in W(X)$

$$\begin{aligned}
\sigma^*(r)\,\tau_r^0(u) &= \sigma^*(r)\,\sigma_r^0(u)\,\tau_{ru}^0(e) && \text{(by 4.9.4)}\\
&= \sigma_r(u)\,\sigma^*(ru)\,\tau_{ru}^0(e) && \big(\text{by (2)}\big)\\
&= \sigma_r(u)\,\tau_{ru}(e) && \big(\text{by (1)}\big)\\
&= \sigma_p(u)\,\tau_{pu}(e) && (\text{by } \sigma_p = \sigma_r,\ \tau_p = \tau, \text{ and } 4.9.5)\\
&= \sigma_p(u)\,\sigma^*(pu)\,\tau_{pu}^0(e) && \big(\text{by (1), (2) and 4.9.4}\big)\\
&= \sigma^*(r)\,\tau_p^0(u) && \big(\text{by } \sigma^*(p) = \sigma^*(r)\big);
\end{aligned}$$

hence $\tau_p^0 = \tau_r^0$. Thus Theorem 4.10 is proved.

From 4.10.2 we obtain that the canonical state system $\mathfrak{Z}_0^\varphi$ of φ is "almost" minimal. If $\mathfrak{Z}_{min}^\varphi = \{[\sigma_p', \tau_p'] \mid p \in W(X)\}$ is a state system of φ with a minimal number of elements, then by 4.10.2 we have $Card\,(\mathfrak{Z}_0^\varphi) \leqq Card\,(\mathfrak{Z}_{min}^\varphi) + 1$ (which is trivial if $Card\,(\mathfrak{Z}_{min}^\varphi) \geqq \aleph_0$). If $\mathfrak{Z}_{min}^\varphi$ is finite then it might have one element less than $\mathfrak{Z}_0^\varphi$, since there might exist a $p \in W(X)$ such that $[\sigma_e', \tau_e'] = [\sigma_p', \tau_p']$ but $[\sigma_e^0, \tau_e^0] \neq [\sigma_p^0, \tau_p^0]$.

Theorem 4.11 (Modrow [1]). *Every word function φ over $[X, Y]$ can be ε-realized in a deterministic automaton with at most as many states as the cardinality of the canonical state system $\mathfrak{Z}_0^\varphi$ of φ, and it cannot be ε-realized in an automaton with fewer states than the number of elements in $\mathfrak{Z}_{min}^\varphi$.*

Proof: Let $\mathfrak{Z}^\varphi = \{[\sigma_p, \tau_p] \mid p \in W(X)\}$ be an arbitrary state system of φ and $\varepsilon \notin X$, furthermore

$$W \underset{\text{Df}}{=} \big\{q \mid \exists x\, \exists p \big(x \in X \wedge [\sigma_p, \tau_p] \in \mathfrak{Z}^\varphi \wedge (q = \sigma_p(x) \vee q = \tau_p(e))\big)\big\}.$$

For $[\sigma_p, \tau_p] \in Z^\varphi$, $x \in X$ let us put

$$\begin{aligned}
\delta([\sigma_p, \tau_p], x) &\underset{\text{Df}}{=} [\sigma_{px}, \tau_{px}], & \delta([\sigma_p, \tau_p], \varepsilon) &\underset{\text{Df}}{=} [\sigma_e, \tau_e],\\
\lambda([\sigma_p, \tau_p], x) &\underset{\text{Df}}{=} \sigma_p(x), & \lambda([\sigma_p, \tau_p], \varepsilon) &\underset{\text{Df}}{=} \tau_p(e).
\end{aligned}$$

Now we shall consider the automaton $\mathfrak{A} = [X \cup \{\varepsilon\}, W, Z^\varphi, \delta, \lambda]$. We can easily verify by induction on r, that for all $[\sigma_p, \tau_p] \in Z^\varphi$, $r \in W(X)$

$$\begin{aligned}
\delta([\sigma_p, \tau_p], r) &= [\sigma_{pr}, \tau_{pr}],\\
|\lambda([\sigma_p, \tau_p], r)| &= \sigma_p(r).
\end{aligned}$$

Thus for all $r, p \in W(X)$

$$\begin{aligned}
|\lambda([\sigma_r, \tau_r], p\varepsilon)| &= |\lambda([\sigma_r, \tau_r], p)\,\lambda\big(\delta([\sigma_r, \tau_r], p), \varepsilon\big)|\\
&= \sigma_r(p)\,\lambda([\sigma_{rp}, \tau_{rp}], \varepsilon)\\
&= \sigma_r(p)\,\tau_{rp}(e) = \tau_r(p)
\end{aligned}$$

is satisfied. This shows that the word function τ_r is ε-realized in $\mathfrak{A}$ by the state $[\sigma_r, \tau_r]$. Since $\tau_e = \varphi$, we also see that φ is ε-realized in $\mathfrak{A}$ by the state $[\sigma_e, \tau_e]$.

Thus we have shown that φ can be ε-realized in an automaton which has at most as many states as the cardinality of $\mathfrak{Z}_0^\varphi$. Finally we shall show that if φ can be realized in an automaton $\mathfrak{A}' = [X \cup \{\varepsilon\}, W', Z, \delta', \lambda']$ by a state $z^* \in Z$, then every minimal state system $\mathfrak{Z}_{min}^\varphi$ has at most *Card* (Z) elements. Without any loss of generality we can assume that $\mathfrak{A}'$ is connected from the state z^* since otherwise we could consider the corresponding subautomaton.

Let us define for $p, r \in W(X)$

$$\sigma_p(r) \underset{\mathrm{Df}}{=} |\lambda'(\delta'(z^*, p), r)|,$$

$$\tau_p(r) \underset{\mathrm{Df}}{=} |\lambda'(\delta'(z^*, p), r\varepsilon)|.$$

Thus σ_p is the word function over $[X, Y]$ realized by the state $\delta'(z^*, p)$ and τ_p is the word function over $[X, Y]$ which is ε-realized by $\delta'(z^*, p)$. We claim that $\{[\sigma_p, \tau_p] \mid p \in W(X)\}$ is a state system for φ, i.e., we want to show that

$$\forall p\, \forall r \big(p, r \in W(X) \rightarrow \varphi(pr) = \sigma_e(p)\, \tau_p(r)\big)$$

and

$$\forall p\, \forall r \big(p, r \in W(X) \rightarrow \sigma_e(pr) = \sigma_e(p)\, \sigma_p(r)\big)$$

hold.

Now for $p, r \in W(X)$ we have

$$\varphi(pr) = |\lambda'(z^*, pr\varepsilon)| = |\lambda'(z^*, p)\, \lambda'(\delta'(z^*, p), r\varepsilon)| = \sigma_e(p)\, \tau_p(r)$$

and

$$\sigma_e(pr) = |\lambda'(\delta'(z^*, e), pr)| = |\lambda'(z^*, p)\, \lambda'(\delta'(z^*, p), r)| = \sigma_e(p)\, \sigma_p(r).$$

Obviously, the state system $\mathfrak{Z}^{\mathfrak{A}, z^*} = \{[\sigma_p, \tau_p] \mid p \in W(X)\}$ contains at most *Card* (Z) elements. Now if $\mathfrak{A}'$ is an automaton in which φ can be ε-realized by the state z' then

$$\mathit{Card}\,(\mathfrak{Z}_{min}^\varphi) \leqq \mathit{Card}\,(\mathfrak{Z}^{\mathfrak{A}', z'}) \leqq \mathit{Card}\,(Z')$$

holds, and this proves Theorem 4.11.

If $\mathfrak{Z}_0^\varphi$ and X are finite, then the set

$$W = \big\{q \mid \exists x\, \exists p \big(x \in X \wedge [\sigma_p^0, \tau_p^0] \in \mathfrak{Z}_0^\varphi \wedge (q = \sigma_p^0(x) \vee q = \tau_p^0(e))\big)\big\}$$

is also finite.

Corollary 4.12. The word function φ over $[X, Y]$ can be ε-realized in a finite automaton if and only if X and $\mathfrak{Z}_0^\varphi$ are finite.

Theorem 4.13. *A word function φ over $[X, Y]$ is realizable (i.e., $\varphi(e) = e$ and 4.2.2 hold) if and only if for all $[\sigma_p^0, \tau_p^0] \in \mathfrak{Z}_0^\varphi$ we have $\sigma_p^0 = \tau_p^0$.*

Proof: If $\varphi(e) = e$ and 4.2.2 hold, then for $p \in W(X)$ we obviously have

$$\sigma_e^0(p) = \varphi(p).$$

Thus $\varphi(pr) = \sigma_e^0(p)\tau_p^0(r) = \varphi(p)\tau_p^0(r)$. Because of $\varphi(pr) = \varphi(p)\varphi_p(r)$ we also have

$$\varphi_p(r) = \tau_p^0(r)$$

for all $p, r \in W(X)$. $\varphi(e) = e$ and 4.2.2 imply that for all $p \in W(X)$

$$\varphi(p)\,\varphi_p(e) = \varphi(pe) = \varphi(p)$$

holds and thus $\varphi_p(e) = e$ and $\tau_p^0(e) = e$ are also true. Furthermore,

$$\varphi(p)\,\varphi_p(r) = \varphi(pr) = \sigma_e^0(pr)\,\tau_{pr}^0(e) = \sigma_e^0(p)\,\sigma_p^0(r) = \varphi(p)\,\sigma_p^0(r).$$

Thus for every $p, r \in W(X)$

$$\tau_p^0(r) = \varphi_p(r) = \sigma_p^0(r)$$

holds, which was to be shown.

To prove the converse, assume that $\sigma_p^0 = \tau_p^0$ holds for all $[\sigma_p^0, \tau_p^0] \in \mathfrak{Z}_0^\varphi$. Then by 4.9.1, $\tau_p^0(e) = \sigma_p^0(e) = e$ is satisfied for every $p \in W(X)$. Therefore

$$\varphi(e) = \sigma_e^0(e)\,\tau_e^0(e) = e.$$

Furthermore $\varphi(p) = \sigma_e^0(p)$ holds, and for all $p, r \in W(X)$ we have

$$\varphi(pr) = \sigma_e^0(pr) = \sigma_e^0(p)\,\sigma_p^0(r) = \varphi(p)\,\sigma_p^0(r),$$

This shows that for every $p, r \in W(X)$ there is an $s = \sigma_p^0(r)$ such that

$$\varphi(pr) = \varphi(p)s$$

is satisfied, i.e., condition 4.2.2 holds for φ. This completes the proof of Theorem 4.13.

In addition to the information about how many states an automaton in which φ can be ε-realized must have, the canonical state system $\mathfrak{Z}_0^\varphi$ of the function φ also tells us whether φ is already realizable. These two pieces of information constitute the principal advantage of the above described method over the standard sequentialization method described exhaustively in Glushkov [6].

§ 5. Events

If we apply to the input of a concrete (natural or artificial) information processing system certain signals or sequences of signals, then we observe that under suitable circumstances the system reacts in the same way to different impulses. Thus the system classifies the input impulses in such a way that all impulses from the same class generate the same reaction. This paragraph and the one that follows are devoted to the investigation of this behavior of automata. We shall discuss the following questions: which classes of impulses can be distinguished by deterministic automata or even by finite deterministic automata? Are these classes in any way structured?

An impulse for a deterministic abstract automaton consists, in the simplest case, of the input of an input signal, and in the general case, of the input of an input word. Therefore, a class of impulses for the automaton is given by a set of input words; such a set is called an event.

Definition 5.1. E is called an *event over* X if X is a non-empty set and $E \subseteq W(X)$. If $E = \emptyset$, then we call E the *impossible event* over X and the set $W(X)$ itself is also referred to as the *certain event* over X.

Corollary 5.1. If E is an event over X then E is an event over every X' such that $X' \supseteq X$.

From now on we shall consider as the reaction of the automaton $\mathfrak{A} = [X, Y, Z, \delta, \lambda]$ to a (non-empty) impulse $p \in W(X) \setminus \{e\}$ the last letter $y \in Y$ of the output word $q \in W(Y)$ put out by $\mathfrak{A}$ in response to the input of p. (The rest of the letters in q can be taken as partial results obtained by the computation of the reaction y.) Thus by saying that $\mathfrak{A}$ identifies the impulses of a certain class E we mean that in step t it puts out a definite signal y if and only if in the course of the steps $1, \ldots, t$ a word $p \in E$ is fed into its input. (We also say that in step t the event E occurs.) First we shall only consider events not containing the empty word and investigate the classifying behaviour of initial deterministic automata.

Definition 5.2. Let $\mathfrak{A} = [X, Y, Z, \delta, \lambda, z_1]$ be an initial deterministic automaton, $y \in Y$, $X' \subseteq X$ and $E \subseteq W(X') \setminus \{e\}$. The event E over X' is said to be *represented by the output signal* y *in* $\mathfrak{A}$ if for all $p \in W(X')$

$$p \in E \leftrightarrow \exists q \big(q \in W(Y) \wedge \lambda(z_1, p) = qy\big).$$

The following algorithm theoretical point of view concerning the representability of events in finite initial automata is somewhat more abstract. In the theory of computability or decidability[1]) a set of words E is called decidable if, for every word $p \in W(X)$ we can decide by means of a uniform process in finitely many steps whether or not p belongs to E. Such a process can always be carried out by means of a Turing machine.

When applying the notion of decidability one often encounters difficulties originating from the fact that in general there is no a priori (i.e., known before the application of the process to the word p) upper bound for the number of steps needed to carry the procedure to the end. If we use finite automata as instruments to decide upon sets of words, then such an upper bound, namely the length of p, can be given, provided by steps we mean the finding of a value of δ or λ in tables or in the graph of the corresponding automaton. This implies that not all decidable

[1]) Cf. Footnote on page 16.

sets of words can be decided upon by means of finite automata, since otherwise such an upper bound would exist a priori.

From Definition 5.2 (together with Definition 1.4.4 and propositions 1.3, 2.2, 4.1) we obtain

Corollary 5.2.

1. If $E \subseteq W(X') \setminus \{e\}$ and E can be represented in a (finite) automaton $\mathfrak{A}$ by means of an output signal y, then there is a (finite) automaton $\mathfrak{A}'$ with the input alphabet X' in which E can be represented by an output signal.

2. An event E can be represented in a (finite) automaton by an output signal if and only if E can be represented in a (finite) Moore automaton by an output signal.

Theorem 5.3. *Every event* $E \subseteq W(X) \setminus \{e\}$ *is representable.*

Proof: We shall give an initial (infinite) Moore automaton $\mathfrak{A}^*$ with the input alphabet X and the output alphabet $\{0, 1\}$ in which every event $E \subseteq W(X) \setminus \{e\}$ is represented by the signal 1 for a suitable choice of a marking function μ^E:

$$\mathfrak{A}^* \underset{\text{Df}}{=} [X, \{0, 1\}, W(X), \delta^*, \mu^E, e], \quad \text{where for } p \in W(X), \ x \in X$$

$$\delta^*(p, x) \underset{\text{Df}}{=} px$$

and

$$\mu^E(p) \underset{\text{Df}}{=} \begin{cases} 1, & \text{if } p \in E, \\ 0 & \text{otherwise.} \end{cases}$$

In particular we have $\mu^E(e) = 0$. Obviously $\delta^*(e, p) = p$ for all $p \in W(X)$ and for $p = x_1 x_2 \ldots x_n \in W(X) \setminus \{e\}$

$$\begin{aligned} \lambda^*(e, x_1 \ldots x_n) &= \mu^E\big(\delta^*(e, x_1)\big) \ldots \mu^E\big(\delta^*(e, x_1 \ldots x_n)\big) \\ &= \mu^E(x_1) \ldots \mu^E(x_1 \ldots x_n). \end{aligned}$$

Therefore, for $p \in W(X) \setminus \{e\}$ $\lambda^*(e, p)$ ends with 1 if and only if $\mu^E(p) = 1$ holds, i.e., if and only if $p \in E$. Moreover, $e \notin E$ and $\lambda^*(e, e)$ does not end with 1. Thus Theorem 5.4 is proved.

Remark. The automaton $\mathfrak{A}^*$ is known as a *free automaton*, i.e., its transition function is free of relations of the type $\delta(z, p) = \delta(z, r)$ over $W(X)$, where $p \neq r$ are words over the input alphabet X. More details concerning the concept of free automata can be found in Glushkov [6] (Definition 9).

Similarly to the investigation of sequential functions, the question arises whether, if not all, then which events can be represented in finite automata. Next we shall point out a connection between systems of events, or, more precisely, partitions of $W(X) \setminus \{e\}$ on one hand, and sequential functions on the other. This will enable us to reduce to each other the representability of events in finite automata and the generability of sequential functions in finite automata.

Let φ be an arbitrary sequential function over $[X, Y]$ and suppose that $Y = Y_\varphi$ holds, i.e., for each $y \in Y$ there is a $p \in W(X)$ such that y appears in $\varphi(p)$. Obviously then we also have for each $y \in Y$ a $p \in W(X)$ such that $\varphi(p)$ ends with y.

Let us define for each $y \in Y$

$$E_y = \{p \mid p \in W(X) \wedge \exists q(q \in W(Y) \wedge \varphi(p) = qy)\}.$$

It is obvious that all the sets E_y are non-empty, and each $p \in W(X) \setminus \{e\}$ belongs to exactly one of these sets, i.e. the sequential function φ uniquely determines in this way a partition $\mathfrak{E}^\varphi = \{E_y \mid y \in Y\}$ of $W(X) \setminus \{e\}$.

Conversely, let $\mathfrak{R} = \{E_i \mid i \in I\}$ be a partition of $W(X) \setminus \{e\}$. We shall define a mapping $\varphi^{\mathfrak{R}}$ of $W(X)$ into $W(I)$ as follows:

$$\varphi^{\mathfrak{R}}(p) \underset{\mathrm{Df}}{=} \begin{cases} e, & \text{if} \quad p = e; \\ i_1 i_2 \ldots i_n, & \text{if} \quad p = x_1 x_2 \ldots x_n,\ n \geqq 1 \text{ and } x_1 x_2 \ldots x_j \in E_{i_j} \\ & \text{for} \quad j = 1, 2, \ldots, n. \end{cases}$$

We can easily verify that $\varphi^{\mathfrak{R}}$ is a sequential function over $[X, I]$ and that the following theorems are true:

Theorem 5.4. *The correspondence between the sequential functions φ defined on $W(X)$ and the partitions $\mathfrak{R}$ of $W(X) \setminus \{e\}$ is one-to-one provided that we identify all the sequential functions φ which coincide up to the designation of the output signals (i.e., which are Y-isomorphic).*

Theorem 5.5. *If φ is a sequential function over $[X, Y]$ where $Y = Y_\varphi$ holds and φ is generated by the state z_1 in the automaton $\mathfrak{A} = [X, Y, Z, \delta, \lambda]$, then for every $y \in Y$ the event $E_y \in \mathfrak{E}^\varphi$ is represented by the output signal y in the initial automaton $\mathfrak{A} = [X, Y, Z, \delta, \lambda, z_1]$.*

On the basis of Theorem 5.5 we can also say that $\mathfrak{E}^\varphi$ is *represented in* $\mathfrak{A}'$.

Theorem 5.6. *If $\mathfrak{R} = \{E_i \mid i \in I\}$ is an arbitrary partition of $W(X) \setminus \{e\}$ and $\mathfrak{A} = [X, I, Z, \delta, \lambda, z_1]$ is an initial automaton in which $\mathfrak{R}$ is represented, then the state z_1 generates the sequential function $\varphi^{\mathfrak{R}}$ in the automaton $\mathfrak{A}$.*

Corollary 5.7. A sequential function φ can be generated in a finite automaton if and only if $\mathfrak{E}^\varphi$ is representable in a finite automaton.

Theorem 5.8. *There exists an event E over the one-element alphabet $X = \{x\}$ (hence by* 5.1 *over every X) which is not representable in any finite automaton.*

To show this, let us consider the sequential function φ^1 over $[\{x\}, \{0, 1\}]$. We have shown in § 4 that φ^1 cannot be generated in any finite automaton:

$$\varphi^1(x^n) = y_1 y_2 \ldots y_n \text{ where } y_i = \begin{cases} 0, & \text{if } i \text{ is not a square number,} \\ 1 & \text{otherwise.} \end{cases}$$

Here, $\mathfrak{E}^{\varphi^1} = \{E_0, E_1\}$, where $E_0 = \{x^m \mid m > 0, m$ is not a square number$\}$ and $E_1 = \{x^m \mid m$ is a square number$\}$. Now if E_0 were represented in a finite automaton $[\{x\}, Y, Z, \delta, \lambda, z_1]$ by means of a certain output signal $y_0 \in Y$ then:

$$\mathfrak{A}^* \underset{\mathrm{Df}}{=} [\{x\}, \{0, 1\}, Z, \delta, \lambda^*] \text{ where } \lambda^*(z, x) = \begin{cases} 0, & \text{if } \lambda(z, x) = y_0, \\ 1 & \text{otherwise}, \end{cases}$$

would be a finite automaton in which the state z_1 generates the function φ^1. This shows that E_0 and E_1 are events not representable in any finite automaton.

The definition of representability of events which we have used so far has the disadvantage of having to exclude the empty word e. The following definition does away with this disadvantage:

Definition 5.3. Let $\mathfrak{A} = [X, Y, Z, \delta, \lambda, z_1]$ be an initial automaton, and $M \subseteq Z$, $E \subseteq W(X)$. We say that the event E is *represented by the state set* M *in the automaton* $\mathfrak{A}$, if for all $p \in W(X)$

$$p \in E \quad \text{if and only if} \quad \delta(z_1, p) \in M.$$

The connection between Definitions 5.2 and 5.3 (in virtue of Corollary 5.2) yields us the following theorem.

Theorem 5.9. *If an event* $E \subseteq W(X) \setminus \{e\}$ *is represented in an initial Moore automaton* $\mathfrak{A} = [X, Y, Z, \delta, \mu, z_1]$ *by means of an output signal* $y^* \in Y$, *then the set* $M = \{z \mid \mu(z) = y^*\}$ *of the states of* $\mathfrak{A}$ *marked by* y^* *represents the event* $E \cup \{e\}$ *or the event* E, *depending on whether* $\mu(z_1) = y^*$ *holds or not. If the event* $E \subseteq W(X)$ *is represented in an initial Moore automaton* $\mathfrak{A} = [X, Y, Z, \delta, \mu, z_1]$ *by a set* $M \subseteq Z$ *of states, then in the initial Moore automaton* $\mathfrak{A}^* = [X, \{0, 1\}, Z, \delta, \mu^*, z_1]$, *defined by*

$$\mu^*(z) = \begin{cases} 1, & \text{if } z \in M, \\ 0 & \text{otherwise}, \end{cases}$$

the signal 1 *represents the event* $E \setminus \{e\}$ *or the event* E *according to whether* $e \in E$ $(z_1 \in M)$ *or* $e \notin E$ $(z_1 \notin M)$ *holds.*

The proof is very simple if we observe that in a Moore automaton the last letter of the word $\lambda(z_1, p)$ is always $\mu(\delta(z_1, p))$.

Definition 5.3 has the additional advantage of not claiming anything concerning the output of the automaton in which an event is represented. Therefore in what follows we shall always start from Definition 5.3 when speaking about representability and use "outputless" automata as defined below for the representation of events.

Definition 5.4. An automaton $\mathfrak{A} = [X, Y, Z, \delta, \lambda]$ is called *outputless* (or a *Medvedjev automaton*) if $Y = Z$ and $\delta = \lambda$. An outputless automaton $\mathfrak{A}$ is denoted by $[X, Z, \delta]$ or $[X, Z, \delta, z_1]$, provided that $\mathfrak{A}$ is initial.

§ 6. Representability of Events in Finite Automata

Throughout this section X will denote a *finite* (non-empty) alphabet. Our aim is to characterize those events which can be represented in a finite Medvedjev automaton with the input alphabet X. Let us denote by $\mathfrak{R}(X)$ the set of all such events. We will approach this problem from two different directions; one, algebraic, by means of equivalence relations over the set $W(X)$, and the other, syntactical, by using regular terms to describe the representable events.

Definition 6.1. An equivalence relation R over $W(X)$ is called

1. *Right invariant*, if for all $p, q, r \in W(X)$, pRq implies $prRqr$.

2. *Left invariant*, if for all $p, q, r \in W(X)$, pRq implies $rpRrq$.

3. A *congruence*, if it is both right and left invariant.

Corollary 6.1. Suppose R is a congruence over $W(X)$. Then for all $p, q, r, s \in W(X)$ we have: pRq and rRs imply $prRqs$ and $rpRsq$.

Definition 6.2. An equivalence relation R over $W(X)$ is said to be *of finite rank* if it divides the set $W(X)$ into finitely many equivalence classes only.

Theorem 6.1. (Myhill [1][1])) *Let* $E \subseteq W(X)$. *Then the following three propositions are equivalent:*

(1) $E \in \mathfrak{R}(X)$.

(2) *E is the union of certain equivalence classes of a congruence of finite rank over* $W(X)$.

(3) *The congruence* $\underset{E}{\equiv}$ *defined below is of finite rank;*

$$p \underset{E}{\equiv} q \underset{\mathrm{Df}}{\leftrightarrow} \forall r\, \forall s\big(r, s \in W(X) \to (rps \in E \leftrightarrow rqs \in E)\big).$$

Proof: I. (1) implies (2).

Suppose we have $E \in \mathfrak{R}(X)$ and let $\mathfrak{A} = [X, Z, \delta, z_1]$ be a finite initial Medvedjev automaton, furthermore $M \subseteq Z$ such that for all $p \in W(X)$

$$p \in E \leftrightarrow \delta(z_1, p) \in M.$$

We shall define a relation R over $W(X)$ by putting

$$pRq \underset{\mathrm{Df}}{\leftrightarrow} \forall z\big(z \in Z \to \delta(z, p) = \delta(z, q)\big)$$

for all $p, q \in W(X)$. It is clear that R is an equivalence relation over $W(X)$. We claim that R is even a congruence.

Let $p, q, r \in W(X)$ and pRq. We have to show that $prRqr$ and $rpRrq$ hold. By the definition of R, pRq implies $\forall z\big(z \in Z \to \delta(z, p) = \delta(z, q)\big)$, and because $\delta(z, p) = \delta(z, q) \to \delta(z, pr) = \delta(z, qr)$ we obtain $prRqr$. Furthermore,

[1]) Quoted in Rabin; Scott [2].

$\forall z(z \in Z \to \delta(z, p) = \delta(z, q))$ implies the proposition $\forall z'(z' \in Z \to \forall z(z = \delta(z'r) \to \delta(z, p) = \delta(z, q)))$, i.e., it implies the following equivalent proposition $\forall z'(z' \in Z \to \delta(z', rp) = \delta(z', rq))$, hence $rpRrq$.

Next we shall show that R is of finite rank and E a union of R-equivalence classes.

To achieve this, let us enumerate the elements of the finite set Z: $Z = \{z^1, z^2, \ldots, z^k\}$ and define for all sequences $i_1, i_2, \ldots, i_k$ with $1 \leq i_1, \ldots, i_k \leq k$ the set

$$W(i_1, i_2, \ldots, i_k) \underset{\text{Df}}{=} \left\{p \mid \bigwedge_{\varkappa=1}^{k} \delta(z^\varkappa, p) = z^{i_\varkappa}\right\}.$$

We claim that pRq holds if and only if there is a sequence of integers $i_1, i_2, \ldots, i_k$ such that $p, q \in W(i_1, i_2, \ldots, i_k)$.

If pRq holds, then we have $\delta(z^\varkappa, p) = \delta(z^\varkappa, q)$ for all $\varkappa = 1, \ldots, k$, hence there are integers $i_1, \ldots, i_k$ with the required properties, namely i_1 is the index of the state $\delta(z^1, p), \ldots, i_k$ is the index of $\delta(z^k, p)$ respectively.

Conversely, if $p, q \in W(i_1, i_2, \ldots, i_k)$, then we have

$$\delta(z^\varkappa, p) = z^{i_\varkappa} = \delta^\varkappa(z, q) \text{ for all } \varkappa = 1, \ldots, k,$$

hence pRq.

Those sets $W(i_1, \ldots, i_k)$ which are not empty, are equivalence classes of R. And since there are at most k^k sets of the form $W(i_1, \ldots, i_k)$, R is of finite rank.

Let $p \in E$ (i.e., $\delta(z_1, p) \in M$) and $q \in W(X)$ such that pRq holds. Then $\delta(z_1, p) = \delta(z_1, q)$, hence $\delta(z_1, q) \in M$ and $q \in E$. Thus pRq and $p \in E$ imply $q \in E$, which shows that E is a union of R-equivalence classes. This proves the implication $(1) \to (2)$.

II. (2) implies (3).

Let R be a congruence of finite rank over $W(X)$ and E a union of R-equivalence classes. Furthermore, let us have $p, q, r, s \in W(X)$ and pRq. Since R is a congruence, we also have $rpsRrqs$. Since R is the union of certain R-equivalence classes,

$$rpsRrqs \to (rps \in E \leftrightarrow rqs \in E).$$

Therefore we have

$$pRq \to p \underset{E}{\equiv} q,$$

i.e., the congruence $\underset{E}{\equiv}$ has at most as many equivalence classes as the congruence R and thus is of finite rank.

III. (3) implies (1).

Let Z be the set of equivalence classes of the congruence $\underset{E}{\equiv}$. Let us denote by $[p]$ the equivalence class containing the word p. For $[p] \in Z$, $x \in X$ we put $\delta([p], x) \underset{\text{Df}}{=} [px]$.

First we show that this definition is independent of the choice of representatives:

$$[p] = [q] \to [px] = [qx].$$

If $[p] = [q]$, then pRq. Because R is right invariant this implies $pxRqx$, i.e., $[px] = [qx]$ for all $x \in X$.

Let us put $M \underset{\mathrm{Df}}{=} \{[p] \mid p \in E\}$. We can easily verify by induction on p that for all $p \in W(X)$

$$\delta([e], p) = [p].$$

Therefore we have

$$p \in E \leftrightarrow [p] \in M \leftrightarrow \delta([e], p) \in M,$$

i.e., E is represented by the set M in the finite initial Medvedjev automaton $[X, Z, \delta, [e]]$.

Analogously, we can prove the following theorem:

Theorem 6.2 (Nerode [1]). *Let* $E \subseteq W(X)$. *Then the following propositions are equivalent*:

(1) $E \in \mathfrak{R}(X)$.

(2) *E is the union of equivalence classes of a certain right invariant equivalence relation of finite rank over $W(X)$.*

(3) *The right invariant equivalence relation $\underset{E}{\sim}$ defined below is of finite rank:*

$$p \underset{E}{\sim} q \underset{\mathrm{Df}}{\leftrightarrow} \forall r\big(r \in W(X) \to (pr \in E \leftrightarrow qr \in E)\big).$$

The proof runs on similiar lines to that of Theorem 6.1, but in step I the relation R is defined by

$$pRq \underset{\mathrm{Df}}{\leftrightarrow} \delta(z_1, p) = \delta(z_1, q).$$

Observe that in step III we only use the fact that R is a right invariant equivalence relation and not that it is a congruence.

Theorem 6.3. *If $E \in \mathfrak{R}(X)$, then the number of equivalence classes of the relation $\underset{E}{\sim}$ coincides with the smallest number of states of an automaton in which E can be represented.*

Proof: Suppose that E can be represented in the automaton $\mathfrak{A}^* = [X, Z, \delta^*, z_1]$ and $\mathfrak{A}^*$ has fewer states than the number of equivalence classes of $\underset{E}{\sim}$. Then the relation R^* defined by

$$pR^*q \underset{\mathrm{Df}}{\leftrightarrow} \delta^*(z_1, p) = \delta^*(z_1, q)$$

has a smaller number of classes than $\underset{E}{\sim}$. E can be obtained as a union of certain equivalence classes of R^*, and this, as in step II of the above proof, implies

$$pR^*q \to p \underset{E}{\sim} q.$$

It is, however, in contradiction to our assumption.

Theorem 6.4. *If* $E \in \mathfrak{R}(X)$, *then we can construct in a finite number of steps a finite automaton in which E is representable, provided that we have*

a) *a decision procedure for the set E,*

b) *an upper bound N for the number of the equivalence classes of* $\underset{E}{\sim}$.

Proof: In constructing the required automaton the essential step is to find the equivalence classes of the relation $\underset{E}{\sim}$. Once we have the set Z of these equivalence classes, the automaton can be constructed immediately, as in step III of the above proof. The fact that the equivalence classes of $\underset{E}{\sim}$ can be obtained in finitely many steps, follows from the next two lemmas.

Lemma 6.4a. *In each class the length of the shortest words is smaller than N.*

Lemma 6.4b. $p \underset{E}{\sim} q \leftrightarrow \forall r(r \in W(X) \wedge l(r) < N \rightarrow (pr \in E \leftrightarrow qr \in E))$.

Lemma 6.4a implies that for each equivalence class we can find a representative among the finitely many words with length smaller than N. From lemma 6.4b it follows that we can decide in a finite number of steps for any two words p, q whether $p \underset{E}{\sim} q$ holds or not, since by a) there exists a procedure by means of which we can decide in a finite number of steps whether a word belongs to E or not.

Lemma 6.4a is implied by

Theorem 6.5. *Suppose that E is represented by* $M \subseteq Z$ *in the finite initial automaton* $\mathfrak{A} = [X, Z, \delta, z_1]$. *Then E is non-empty if and only if there exists a* $p \in W(X)$ *such that* $l(p) < Card(Z)$ *and* $\delta(z_1, p) \in M$ *hold.*[1])

Proof: Assume $E \neq \emptyset$ and that p is one of the shortest words in E, $l(p) = n$, furthermore that $n \geqq Card(Z) = k$ holds. Putting $p = x_1 x_2 \ldots x_n$ we consider the states $z_{\nu+1} = \delta(z_1, x_1 \ldots x_\nu)$ for each $\nu = 0, \ldots, n$. Since there are only k different states, these $n+1$ states cannot all be different, because $n + 1 > k$. Therefore, we have integers i, j with $0 \leqq i < j \leqq n$ such that

$$\delta(z_1, x_1 \ldots x_i) = z_{i+1} = z_{j+1} = \delta(z_1, x_1 \ldots x_i \ldots x_j).$$

Therefore we have

$$\delta(z_1, x_1 x_2 \ldots x_i x_{j+1} \ldots x_n) = \delta(z_1, x_1 \ldots x_n) \in M,$$

and thus $x_1 x_2 \ldots x_i x_{j+1} \ldots x_n \in E$.

This last word, however, is shorter than p, in contradiction to the choice of p as one of the shortest words in E.

The converse is trivial.

---

[1]) A corresponding result on the infiniteness of the event E representable by M in $\mathfrak{A} = [X, Z, \delta, z_1]$ can be found in Rabin; Scott [2] and says: E is infinite if and only if there exists a $p \in E$ for which $Card(Z) \leqq l(p) < 2 \cdot Card(Z)$ holds. Consequently, it is decidable whether E is finite or infinite.

Now we shall show that Lemma 6.4a follows from Theorem 6.5. Since $E \in \mathfrak{R}(X)$, the set Z of the equivalence classes $[p]$ determined by the relation $\underset{E}{\sim}$ is finite, and in the finite initial automaton $[X, Z, \delta, [e]]$ where $\delta([p], x) = [px]$, the equivalence class $[p]$ is represented by the set $M = \{[p]\} \subseteq Z$. Thus every equivalence class of $\underset{E}{\sim}$ can be represented in an automaton with at most N states and this, together with Theorem 6.5, immediately gives us Lemma 6.4a.

Corollary 6.6. If $E \in \mathfrak{R}(X)$, then it is decidable whether $E = \emptyset$ holds.

Proof of Lemma 6.4b. The implication from the left to the right is trivial. If $E = W(X)$ or $E = \emptyset$, then again the proposition is trivial. Assume $E \neq \emptyset$ and $E \neq W(X)$. For each $i = 1, 2, \ldots$ we consider the relation $\overset{i}{\underset{E}{\sim}}$ defined as follows:

$$p \overset{i}{\underset{E}{\sim}} q \underset{\mathrm{Df}}{\leftrightarrow} \forall r \big(r \in W(X) \wedge l(r) < i \rightarrow (pr \in E \leftrightarrow qr \in E)\big).$$

Thus our proposition can be formulated as follows: $\overset{N}{\underset{E}{\sim}} = \underset{E}{\sim}$.

Obviously, the relation $\overset{1}{\underset{E}{\sim}}$ divides the set $W(X)$ into two classes, namely E and $W(X) \setminus E$, and for all i and $p, q \in W(X)$

$$p \overset{i+1}{\underset{E}{\sim}} q \rightarrow p \overset{i}{\underset{E}{\sim}} q$$

holds, i.e., the relation $\overset{i+1}{\underset{E}{\sim}}$ is finer than the relation $\overset{i}{\underset{E}{\sim}}$. We claim that

$$\text{if } \overset{k}{\underset{E}{\sim}} = \overset{k+1}{\underset{E}{\sim}} \text{ then } \overset{k}{\underset{E}{\sim}} = \overset{k+\nu}{\underset{E}{\sim}} \text{ for all } \nu = 1, 2, \ldots$$

To show this, it is enough to prove that $\overset{k+\nu-1}{\underset{E}{\sim}} = \overset{k+\nu}{\underset{E}{\sim}}$ implies that the relations $\overset{k+\nu}{\underset{E}{\sim}}$, $\overset{k+\nu+1}{\underset{E}{\sim}}$ coincide, and this readily follows from

$$p \overset{k+\nu}{\underset{E}{\sim}} q \rightarrow p \overset{k+\nu+1}{\underset{E}{\sim}} q.$$

$p \overset{k+\nu}{\underset{E}{\sim}} q$ implies the proposition

$$\forall r \forall x \big(r \in W(X) \wedge x \in X \wedge l(r) < k + \nu - 1 \rightarrow (pxr \in E \leftrightarrow qxr \in E)\big),$$

i.e., $\forall x (x \in X \rightarrow px \overset{k+\nu-1}{\underset{E}{\sim}} qx)$.

Since the relations $\overset{k+\nu-1}{\underset{E}{\sim}}$, $\overset{k+\nu}{\underset{E}{\sim}}$ are identical by our assumption, we also have

$$\forall x (x \in X \rightarrow px \overset{k+\nu}{\underset{E}{\sim}} qx)$$

and thus $p \overset{k+\nu+1}{\underset{E}{\sim}} q$, which was to be shown.

By our assumption, there are at most N classes in the partition $W(X)/\overset{i}{\underset{E}{\sim}}$. Now the relation $\overset{1}{\underset{E}{\sim}}$ divides $W(X)$ into two classes, and for $i > 1$ the partition $W(X)/\overset{i}{\underset{E}{\sim}}$ consists of at least $i+1$ classes or else the relations $\overset{i}{\underset{E}{\sim}}$, $\overset{i-1}{\underset{E}{\sim}}$ coincide. Therefore, $\overset{N}{\underset{E}{\sim}} = \overset{N+\nu}{\underset{E}{\sim}}$ must hold for each ν, i.e., $\overset{N}{\underset{E}{\sim}} = \underset{E}{\sim}$, and this completes the proof.

The syntactical description of events representable in finite automata will use certain expressions which reflect the fact that they are constructed from elementary events, which are obviously finitely representable. To prepare this description let us define operations which transform finitely representable events into such events again.

Definition 6.3. For each word $p \in W(X)$ and for each event $E \subseteq W(X)$ we define the *inverse* (or *mirror image*) p^* *and* E^* *of* p *and* E respectively by means of the following inductive definition:

$$e^* = e, \qquad (px)^* = xp^*,$$
$$E^* = \{p^* \mid p \in E\}.$$

Corollary 6.7. $(pq)^* = q^*p^*$ for all $p, q \in W(X)$; $(E^*)^* = E$ for all $E \subseteq W(X)$.

Theorem 6.8. *An event E is representable in a finite automaton if and only if E^* is.*

Proof: By Theorem 6.1 it suffices to show that $\underset{E}{\equiv}$ is of finite rank if and only if $\underset{E^*}{\equiv}$ is. Now for $p, q \in W(X)$ we have:

$$p \underset{E}{\equiv} q \leftrightarrow \forall r\, \forall s\big(r, s \in W(X) \rightarrow (rps \in E \leftrightarrow rqs \in E)\big).$$

Since $rps \in E \leftrightarrow s^*p^*r^* \in E^*$,

$$p \underset{E}{\equiv} q \leftrightarrow \forall r\, \forall s\big(r, s \in W(X) \rightarrow (rp^*s \in E^* \leftrightarrow rq^*s \in E^*)\big),$$

i.e.,

$$p \underset{E}{\equiv} q \leftrightarrow p^* \underset{E^*}{\equiv} q^*.$$

This immediately implies our proposition.

We shall denote by $\bar{E}$ the (relative) *complement* $W(X) \setminus E$ of the event E.

Theorem 6.9. $[\mathfrak{R}(X), \cap, \cup, ^-]$ *is a Boolean algebra of sets.*

Proof: It suffices to show that $\mathfrak{R}(X)$ is closed under intersection and complementation.

a) Assume $E \subseteq W(X)$ is represented in the finite initial automaton $\mathfrak{A} = [X, Z, \delta, z_1]$ by the set M, and $F \subseteq W(X)$ is represented in the finite initial automaton $\mathfrak{A}' = [X, Z', \delta', z_1']$ by M'. As the direct product $\mathfrak{A} \times \mathfrak{A}'$ of the automata $\mathfrak{A}, \mathfrak{A}'$ we define the automaton $\big[X, Z \times Z', \delta \times \delta', [z_1, z_1']\big]$, where $\delta \times \delta'([z, z'], x) = [\delta(z, x), \delta'(z', x)]$ holds for all $z \in Z, z' \in Z', x \in X$. We claim that $E \cap F$ is represented by the set $M \times M'$ in the finite initial automaton $\mathfrak{A} \times \mathfrak{A}'$. Indeed, for each $p \in W(X)$ we have

$$\begin{aligned} \delta \times \delta'([z_1, z_1'], p) \in M \times M' &\leftrightarrow [\delta(z_1, p), \delta'(z_1', p)] \in M \times M' \\ &\leftrightarrow \delta(z_1, p) \in M \wedge \delta'(z_1', p) \in M' \\ &\leftrightarrow p \in E \wedge p \in F \\ &\leftrightarrow p \in E \cap F. \end{aligned}$$

b) Assume that E is represented by M in $\mathfrak{A}$ as above. It is obvious then that $\bar{E}$ is represented in $\mathfrak{A}$ by the set $Z \setminus M$.

Definition 6.4. An event $E \subseteq W(X)$ is called *complete* if it contains the empty word and for each word $p \in E$ it contains every initial segment of p. We define as the *completion Com* (E) of E the smallest complete event containing E, i.e.,

$$Com\,(E) \underset{\mathrm{Df}}{=} \{q \mid \exists r(r \in W(X) \wedge qr \in E)\} \cup \{e\}.$$

Theorem 6.10. *If E is representable in a finite automaton, so is Com (E).*

Proof: Suppose E is represented by M in the finite automaton $\mathfrak{A} = [X, Z, \delta, z_1]$. Without loss of generality we can assume that $\delta(z_1, p) \neq z_1$ for all $p \in W(X) \setminus \{e\}$ (cf. the proof of Theorem 6.17). Furthermore let us put

$$M^* = \{z \mid \exists p \exists r(p, r \in W(X) \wedge z = \delta(z_1, p) \wedge \delta(z_1, pr) \in M)\} \cup \{z_1\}.$$

We can easily verify that M^* represents $Com\,(E)$ in $\mathfrak{A}$.

Definition 6.5. Let E, F be events over X. We define their *product* $E \cdot F$ (in this order) by

$$E \cdot F \underset{\mathrm{Df}}{=} \{pq \mid p \in E \wedge q \in F\}.$$

By the *closure* $\langle E \rangle$ *of an event* E we mean the smallest set of words containing all the powers E^ν ($\nu = 0, 1, \ldots$). Here, $E^0 \underset{\mathrm{Df}}{=} \{e\}$, $E^{n+1} \underset{\mathrm{Df}}{=} E^n \cdot E$.

Corollary 6.11. The operation $\langle\ \rangle$ possesses the closure properties, i.e., for arbitary events E, F we have:

(1) $E \subseteq \langle E \rangle$ (embedding property).

(2) If $E \subseteq F$, then $\langle E \rangle \subseteq \langle F \rangle$ (monotone property).

(3) $\langle E \rangle = \langle\langle E \rangle\rangle$ (closedness property).

Below we shall show that the set $\mathfrak{R}(X)$ is also closed under products and the closure operation. First we shall show that the finite sets and their complements belong to $\mathfrak{R}(X)$.

Theorem 6.12. *If $p \in W(X)$ then $\{p\} \in \mathfrak{R}(X)$.*

Proof: If $p = e$, then e is represented in an arbitrary finite initial automaton $[X, Z, \delta, z_1]$ by $\{z_1\}$, provided that $\delta(z, x) \neq z_1$ holds for every $z \in Z$, $x \in X$. If $p = x_1 x_2 \ldots x_n$ then we put

$Z = \{e, x_1, x_1 x_2, \ldots, x_1 x_2 \ldots x_n, z^*\}$, and for $i = 0, \ldots, n-1$, $x \in X$

$$\delta(x_1 \ldots x_i, x) = \begin{cases} x_1 \ldots x_{i+1}, & \text{if} \quad x = x_{i+1}, \\ z^* & \text{otherwise} \end{cases}$$

and $\delta(z^*, x) = \delta(x_1 \ldots x_n, x) = z^*$.

Clearly, $\{p\}$ is represented in $[X, Z, \delta, e]$ by $\{x_1 \ldots x_n\}$.

Corollary 6.13. If $E \subseteq W(X)$ is finite, or the complement of a finite set of words, then $E \in \mathfrak{R}(X)$.

Next we shall deal with a language in which the construction of events from simple events is described, namely the language of regular terms. In the literature, these terms are usually called "expressions". Here, however, we shall not do so, in order to be consistent with the terminology of mathematical logic.

Definition 6.6. The impossible event $\emptyset$ and the events $\{x\}$ for each $x \in X$ are called *elementary events over* X.

In order to construct the required language we need symbols to denote the elementary events and certain operations on the events. We introduce the following symbols:

$\mathbf{0}$ to denote the impossible event,
$\boldsymbol{x}$ to denote the event $\{x\}$ (for each $x \in X$),
$\vee$ to denote the union,
$\circ$ to denote the product,
$\langle\ \rangle$ to denote the closure,

and also the technical symbols (,).

Among the finite sequences built up from these symbols we distinguish certain special sequences of symbols which we call regular terms. This is done by means of the following inductive definition:

Definition 6.7.

(1) $\mathbf{0}$ and $\boldsymbol{x}$ (for $x \in X$) are *regular terms over* X.

(2) If Z_1, Z_2 are regular terms over X then the sequences $(Z_1 \vee Z_2)$, $(Z_1 \circ Z_2)$, $\langle Z_1 \rangle$ are regular terms over X.

(3) A sequence of symbols Z is a regular term over X only if it can be obtained by means of (1) or (2).

Finally we come to the interpretation of this language, i.e., we assign to each regular term over X that event over X whose construction from elementary events is described by this term. This event is called the *value of the term*. We shall write $Z_1 \equiv Z_2$ if the sequences of symbols Z_1, Z_2 are *identical*, i.e., if they coincide symbol to symbol.

Definition 6.8. Let T be a regular term.

(1) If $T \equiv \mathbf{0}$, then $Val\,(T) = \emptyset$.

If $T \equiv \boldsymbol{x}$, then $Val\,(T) = \{x\}$ (for each $x \in X$).

$$(2)\ Val\,(T) = \begin{cases} Val\,(T_1) \cup Val\,(T_2), & \text{if } T \equiv (T_1 \vee T_2), \\ Val\,(T_1) \cdot Val\,(T_2), & \text{if } T \equiv (T_1 \circ T_2), \\ \langle Val\,(T_1)\rangle, & \text{if } T \equiv \langle T_1 \rangle. \end{cases}$$

Definition 6.9. An event E over a finite alphabet X is called *regular* if and only if there is a regular term T over X such that $E = Val(T)$.

Corollary 6.14. The set of regular events (over a finite alphabet X) is the smallest set of events which contains all elementary events and is closed under union, product, and the closure operation.

In writing regular terms let us agree to use the following *rules in order to save parentheses:* The outermost parentheses of a term will be omitted as well as the parentheses in multiple products and unions (since these operations are associative) and finally, we agree that the symbol $\vee$ separates more strongly than $\circ$.

Theorem 6.15. (*Analysis theorem*) *Every event E representable in a finite automaton $\mathfrak{A} = [X, Z, \delta, z_1]$ by means of a set M of states is regular over X. A regular term T over X with $Val(T) = E$ can be obtained from $\mathfrak{A}$ and M in a finite number of steps.*

Proof: It suffices to prove the theorem for the case in which M is a singleton $\{z\}$. Indeed, if we denote by $E(z)$ the event represented by the set $\{z\}$ in $\mathfrak{A}$, and $T(z)$ is a regular term with $Val\big(T(z)\big) = E(z)$, then for $M = \{z^1, z^2, \ldots, z^m\}$ we have

$$E = E(z^1) \cup E(z^2) \cup \cdots \cup E(z^m),$$

and for

$$T \equiv T(z^1) \vee T(z^2) \vee \cdots \vee T(z^m), \quad Val(T) = E.$$

Suppose that E is represented in the automaton $\mathfrak{A} = [X, Z, \delta, z_1]$ by $\{z^*\}$, where Z is enumerated as $Z = \{z^1, z^2, \ldots, z^k\}$ $(k \geqq 1)$. For all $i, j, \varkappa$ with $1 \leqq i, j \leqq k$, $0 \leqq \varkappa \leqq k$ we define $E^{\varkappa}_{i,j}$ as the set of all non-empty words $p = x_1 x_2 \ldots x_r$ $(r \geqq 1)$, for which $\delta(z^i, p) = z^j$ holds, and for each $\varrho = 1, 2, \ldots, r-1$ the intermediate state $z_\varrho = \delta(z^i, x_1 \ldots x_\varrho)$ has an upper index $\nu_\varrho \leqq \varkappa$.

Thus a non-empty word belongs to $E^{\varkappa}_{i,j}$ if and only if it moves $\mathfrak{A}$ from the state z^i to the state z^j without entering any of the states $z^{\varkappa+1}, \ldots, z^k$.

We shall prove by induction on $\varkappa$ that every event $E^{\varkappa}_{i,j}$ is regular.

Initial step: $\varkappa = 0$.

$E^0_{i,j}$ is the set of all $p \neq e$, which take $\mathfrak{A}$ from the state z^i to z^j without going through any intermediate states. Hence, $E^0_{i,j}$ is either empty, or a finite set of letters $x \in X$ (and thus a finite union of elementary events). Therefore, we can find a term $T^0_{i,j}$ with the property $Val(T^0_{i,j}) = E^0_{i,j}$ in a finite number of steps.

The **induction step** is taken from $\varkappa - 1$ to $\varkappa$ $(1 \leqq \varkappa \leqq k)$:

Induction hypothesis: For all i, j with $1 \leqq i, j \leqq k$, $E^{\varkappa-1}_{i,j}$ is regular and $T^{\varkappa-1}_{i,j}$ is a regular term such that $Val(T^{\varkappa-1}_{i,j}) = E^{\varkappa-1}_{i,j}$.

Induction statement: For each i, j with $1 \leqq i, j \leqq k$ we can construct a regular term $T^{\varkappa}_{i,j}$ for which $Val(T^{\varkappa}_{i,j}) = E^{\varkappa}_{i,j}$.

We claim that the following regular term satisfies our requirements:

$$T^{\varkappa}_{i,j} \equiv T^{\varkappa-1}_{i,j} \vee T^{\varkappa-1}_{i,\varkappa} \circ \langle T^{\varkappa-1}_{\varkappa,\varkappa} \rangle \circ T^{\varkappa-1}_{\varkappa,j}.$$

For this we have to show that for every $i, j, \varkappa$ with $1 \leqq i, j, \varkappa \leqq k$

$$E^{\varkappa}_{i,j} = E^{\varkappa-1}_{i,j} \cup E^{\varkappa-1}_{i,\varkappa} \cdot \langle E^{\varkappa-1}_{\varkappa,\varkappa} \rangle \cdot E^{\varkappa-1}_{\varkappa,j}.$$

Let $p = x_1 x_2 \ldots x_n \in E^{\varkappa}_{i,j}$, and for $\varrho = 1, 2, \ldots, n-1$ let $z_\varrho = \delta(z^i, x_1 \ldots x_\varrho)$.

Case a). There is no ϱ for which $z_\varrho = z^\varkappa$. Then $p \in E^{\varkappa-1}_{i,j}$.

Case b). Let $\varrho_1, \varrho_2, \ldots, \varrho_r$ $(r \geqq 1)$ be all indices ϱ such that $z_\varrho = z^\varkappa$, where $1 \leqq \varrho_1 < \varrho_2 < \cdots < \varrho_r < n-1$. Then we have

$$x_1 x_2 \ldots x_{\varrho_1} \in E^{\varkappa-1}_{i,\varkappa},$$
$$x_{\varrho_1+1} \ldots x_{\varrho_2} \in E^{\varkappa-1}_{\varkappa,\varkappa}, \quad \ldots, \quad x_{\varrho_{r-1}+1} \ldots x_{\varrho_r} \in E^{\varkappa-1}_{\varkappa,\varkappa}, \quad x_{\varrho_r+1} \ldots x_n \in E^{\varkappa-1}_{\varkappa,j}.$$

Therefore p belongs to the set $E^{\varkappa-1}_{i,\varkappa} \cdot \langle E^{\varkappa-1}_{\varkappa,\varkappa} \rangle \cdot E^{\varkappa-1}_{\varkappa,j}$. This shows that the left hand side of our equality is contained in the right hand side. However it is obvious that the converse also holds.

Now there are such indices i_0, j_0 for which $z_1 = z^{i_0}$, $z^* = z^{j_0}$. Therefore

$$E = \begin{cases} E^k_{i_0,j_0}, & \text{if } i_0 \neq j_0, \\ E^k_{i_0,i_0} \cup \{e\}, & \text{if } i_0 = j_0, \end{cases}$$

hence

$$T \equiv \begin{cases} T^k_{i_0,j_0}, & \text{if } i_0 \neq j_0, \\ T^k_{i_0,i_0} \vee \langle 0 \rangle, & \text{if } i_0 = j_0, \end{cases}$$

is the required term. This proves the analysis theorem.

For an arbitrary regular term T we put

$$A(T) \underset{\text{Df}}{=} \{x \mid \exists p (p \in W(X) \wedge xp \in Val(T))\},$$
$$E(T) \underset{\text{Df}}{=} \{x \mid \exists p (p \in W(X) \wedge px \in Val(T))\},$$
$$f^T(x) \underset{\text{Df}}{=} \{x' \mid \exists p \exists r (p, r \in W(X) \wedge pxx'r \in Val(T))\}$$

for all $x \in X$.

The following lemma will play an important role in the construction by means of which we shall prove the synthesis theorem.

Lemma 6.16. *Let T be a regular term over X in which every symbol $\mathbf{x}$ (for $x \in X$) appears at most once. Then for all $n \geqq 1$, $x_1 \ldots x_n \in W(X)$ we have*

$$x_1 \ldots x_n \in Val(T) \leftrightarrow x_1 \in A(T) \wedge \bigwedge_{i=1}^{n-1} x_{i+1} \in f^T(x_i) \wedge x_n \in E(T).^{1)}$$

Proof: The implication "from the left to the right" immediately follows from the above definitions. We shall prove the converse by induction on T. If T is one

---

[1]) The empty conjunction $\bigwedge_{i=1}^{0} x_{i+1} \in f^T(x_i)$ is always true.

of the terms $\mathbf{0}$, $\boldsymbol{x}$ (for $x \in X$) then our statement is trivial. The induction step is taken from T_1, T_2 to $T_1 \vee T_2$, $T_1 \circ T_2$ and $\langle T_1 \rangle$.

I. $T \equiv T_1 \vee T_2$.

We have an $x_1 \in A(T) = A(T_1) \cup A(T_2)$. Since $\boldsymbol{x}_1$ appears in the term T exactly once, there is a uniquely determined $j \in \{1, 2\}$ for which $x_1 \in A(T_j)$. Clearly, $x_1 \in A(T_j)$ and $x_2 \in f^T(x_1)$ imply $x_1 \in f^{T_j}(x_1)$ and then again $x_3 \in f^{T_j}(x_2)$ etc. Thus we have

$$x_1 \in A(T_j) \wedge \bigwedge_{i=1}^{n-1} x_{i+1} \in f^{T_j}(x_i).$$

Finally $x_n \in E(T) = E(T_1) \cup E(T_2)$ and $x_n \in f^{T_j}(x_{n-1})$. Therefore $x_n \in E(T_j)$, and from the induction hypothesis we obtain

$$x_1 \dots x_n \in Val(T_j) \subseteq Val(T_1 \vee T_2) = Val(T).$$

II. $T \equiv T_1 \circ T_2$.

Suppose that j is chosen as above and thus $x_1 \in A(T_j)$ (and consequently, $x_1 \notin A(T_{2-j+1})$) holds. If $j = 2$, then obviously $e \in Val(T_1)$. Now $x_{i+1} \in f^T(x_i)$ and

$$\exists p \exists r \big(p, r \in W(X) \wedge p x_i r \in Val(T_2)\big)$$

imply that there is a word in $Val(T_2)$, in which x_{i+1} appears. Thus if $x_1 \in A(T_2)$ we have

$$x_1 \in A(T_2) \wedge \bigwedge_{i=1}^{n-1} x_{i+1} \in f^{T_2}(x_i) \wedge x_n \in E(T_2).$$

Consequently, $x_1 \dots x_n \in Val(T_2)$ and because $e \in Val(T_1)$ we also have $x_1 \dots x_n \in Val(T_1 \circ T_2)$.

Suppose $x_1 \in A(T_1)$. If furthermore

$$\bigwedge_{i=1}^{n-1} x_{i+1} \in f^{T_1}(x_i) \wedge x_n \in E(T_1),$$

then $x_1 \dots x_n \in Val(T_1)$. Since $x_n \in E(T_1) \cap E(T_1 \circ T_2)$, $e \in Val(T_2)$ hence $x_1 \dots x_n \in Val(T_1 \circ T_2)$. Otherwise, there is a k with $1 \leqq k < n$ such that

$$x_1 \in A(T_1) \wedge \bigwedge_{i=1}^{k-1} x_{i+1} \in f^{T_1}(x_i) \wedge x_{k+1} \notin f^{T_1}(x_k) \wedge x_{k+1} \in f^{T_1 \circ T_2}(x_k)$$

Here, $x_k \in E(T_1)$ and $x_{k+1} \in A(T_2)$, and as above we obtain

$$\bigwedge_{i=k+1}^{n-1} x_{i+1} \in f^{T_2}(x_i) \wedge x_n \in E(T_2).$$

By the induction hypothesis we have $x_1 \dots x_k \in Val(T_1)$, $x_{k+1} \dots x_n \in Val(T_2)$ hence $x_1 \dots x_n \in Val(T_1 \circ T_2)$.

III. $T = \langle T_1 \rangle$.

In this case, $A(T) = A(T_1)$, $E(T) = E(T_1)$, and there is an m with $0 \leqq m \leqq n$ and furthermore numbers $1 \leqq l_1 < l_2 < \cdots < l_m < n$ such that

$$x_1 \in A(T_1) \wedge \bigwedge_{i=1}^{l_1-1} x_{i+1} \in f^{T_1}(x_i) \wedge x_{l_1+1} \notin f^{T_1}(x_{l_1}) \wedge x_{l_1+1} \in f^T(x_{l_1})$$
$$\wedge \bigwedge_{i=l_1+1}^{l_2-1} x_{i+1} \in f^{T_1}(x_i) \wedge x_{l_2+1} \notin f^{T_1}(x_{l_2}) \wedge x_{l_2+1} \in f^T(x_{l_2}) \wedge \cdots$$
$$\wedge \bigwedge_{i=l_{m-1}+1}^{l_m-1} x_{i+1} \in f^{T_1}(x_i) \wedge x_{l_m+1} \notin f^{T_1}(x_{l_m}) \wedge x_{l_m+1} \in f^T(x_{l_m})$$
$$\wedge \bigwedge_{i=l_m+1}^{n-1} x_{i+1} \in f^{T_1}(x_i) \wedge x_n \in E(T_1).$$

From this, as in II, we obtain that for $\mu = 1, \ldots m$

$$x_{l_\mu} \in E(T_1), \qquad x_{l_\mu+1} \in A(T_1)$$

and

$$x_1 \ldots x_{l_1}, \quad x_{l_1+1} \ldots x_{l_2}, \quad \ldots, \quad x_{l_{m-1}+1} \ldots x_{l_m}, \quad x_{l_m+1} \ldots x_n \in Val(T_1)$$

and therefore $x_1 \ldots x_n \in Val(\langle T_1 \rangle)$. Thus Lemma 6.16 is proved.

Theorem 6.17 (*Synthesis theorem*). *There is a procedure which, when applied to an arbitrary finite system* $\mathfrak{E} = \{E_1, \ldots, E_s\}$ $(s \geqq 1)$ *of regular events over a finite alphabet* X *given by the regular terms* $T_1, T_2, \ldots, T_s$, *yields us in a finite number of steps a finite initial automaton* $\mathfrak{A} = [X, Z, \delta, z_1]$ *and sets of states* $M_1, M_2, \ldots, M_s \subseteq Z$ *such that for any* $\sigma = 1, \ldots, s$ *the event* E_σ *is represented by* M_σ *in* $\mathfrak{A}$. *If we denote by* $d(x)$ *the number of all occurences of the symbol* $\boldsymbol{x}$ *in the terms* T_σ *(for* $x \in X$*), then*

$$Card\,(Z) \leqq 1 + \sum_{x \in X} 2^{d(x)}.$$

Proof: Having constructed $\mathfrak{A}$ we see that in this automaton, for all $z \in Z$, $x \in X$ we have $\delta(z, x) \neq z_1$. Since the impossible event $\emptyset$ and the event $\{e\}$ can be represented in every such automaton (by $M = \emptyset$ and $M = \{z_1\}$ respectively), we can assume without loss of generality that these events do not occur among the E_σ.

1st Construction Step. We write the terms T_σ in an arbitrary order, and index the places at which the symbol $\boldsymbol{x}$, which stands for a non-empty elementary event $\{x\}$ in one of the terms T_σ, appears. This index i will be indicated as a lower index of the symbol $\boldsymbol{x}$ appearing at the ith place. Let $1, 2, \ldots, n$ be the indices needed for this proceedure.

The indexed terms are denoted by T'_σ, and E'_σ denotes the "value" of T'_σ in the computation of which the indices are taken into consideration. Thus a word $p' \in E'_\sigma$ differs from a word in E_σ in that every letter x in p' has the index i of that place of the symbol $\boldsymbol{x}$ in T_σ on account of which x appears in it.

We shall illustrate this by means of the following example: Let

$$X = \{x^{(1)}, x^{(2)}\},\ T_1 \equiv x^{(1)} \circ (x^{(2)} \vee x^{(2)}).$$

Then $E_1 = \{x^{(1)}x^{(2)}\}$, $T_1' \equiv x_1^{(1)} \circ (x_2^{(2)} \vee x_3^{(2)})$ and $E_1' = \{x_1^{(1)}x_2^{(2)},\ x_1^{(1)}x_3^{(2)}\}$.

Let us denote by I_σ the set of all indices appearing in the term T_σ', and by I_x the set of all the indices with which x appears in one of the terms T_σ'. By this indexing procedure we achieve that the terms T_σ' satisfy the conditions of Lemma 6.16.

2nd Construction Step. Let $z_1 \notin \mathfrak{P}(\{1, 2, \ldots, n\})$. We choose z_1 as the initial state of our automaton $\mathfrak{A}$ and construct successively further states (namely subsets of the sets I_x), by defining first $\delta(z_1, x)$ for all $x \in X$, then $\delta(z, x)$ for the states z of the form $\delta(z_1, x)$ etc. Since all the sets I_x are finite, this procedure must end in a finite number of steps. Let us put for $x \in X$

$$\delta(z_1, x) \underset{\mathrm{Df}}{=} \{i \mid \exists \sigma(1 \leqq \sigma \leqq s \wedge x_i \in A(T_\sigma'))\}.$$

If z is a state already constructed (a subset of $\{1, 2, \ldots, n\}$) and $x \in X$, then we put

$$\delta(z, x) \underset{\mathrm{Df}}{=} \{i \mid \exists j \exists \sigma \exists x' (j \in z \wedge 1 \leqq \sigma \leqq s \wedge x_i \in f^{T_\sigma'}(x_j'))\}.$$

Let Z be the set containing z_1 and all the subsets of $\{1, 2, \ldots, n\}$ constructed in this way. We see that for $z \in Z$, $x \in X$ we have $\delta(z, x) \subseteq I_x$.

3rd Construction Step. Let us put for $1 \leqq \sigma \leqq s$

$$M_\sigma \underset{\mathrm{Df}}{=} \{z \mid \exists i \exists x(x \in X \wedge i \in z \wedge x_i \in E(T_\sigma'))\} \cup \begin{cases} \{z_1\}, & \text{if } e \in E_\sigma, \\ \emptyset & \text{otherwise.} \end{cases}$$

We shall show that for all σ with $1 \leqq \sigma \leqq s$ and $p \in W(X)$

$$p \in E_\sigma \leftrightarrow \delta(z_1, p) \in M_\sigma.$$

For the empty word e this equivalence is trivial. Let $p = x^{(1)}x^{(2)} \ldots x^{(n)}$ be an arbitrary non-empty word over X, and for $\nu = 1, \ldots, n$ let us put

$$z_{\nu+1} = \delta(z_1, x^{(1)} \ldots x^{(\nu)}).$$

The word p belongs to E_σ, if and only if there are integers $i_1, \ldots, i_n \in I_\sigma$ such that $x_{i_1}^{(1)} x_{i_2}^{(2)} \ldots x_{i_n}^{(n)} \in E_\sigma'$. By Lemma 6.16 we see that $p \in E_\sigma$ if and only if there are integers $i_1, \ldots, i_n \in I_\sigma$ for which

$$x_{i_1}^{(1)} \in A(T_\sigma') \wedge \bigwedge_{\nu=1}^{n-1} x_{i_{\nu+1}}^{(\nu+1)} \in f^{T_\sigma'}(x_{i_\nu}^{(\nu)}) \wedge x_{i_n}^{n} \in E(T_\sigma')$$

hold, i.e., if and only if integers $i_1 \ldots, i_n \in I_\sigma$ satisfying

$$i_1 \in \delta(z_1, x^{(1)}) \wedge \bigwedge_{\nu=1}^{n-1} i_{\nu+1} \in z_{\nu+2} \wedge z_{n+1} \in M_\sigma,$$

exist, and this is the case if and only if $z_{n+1} = \delta(z_1, p) \in M_\sigma$.

The inequality $Card(Z) \leqq 1 + \sum_{x \in X} 2^{d(x)}$ follows from the definition of δ and $d(x) = Card(I_x)$.

This proves the synthesis theorem.

We shall now carry out the above construction on an example. Let $X = \{a, b\}$, $\mathfrak{E} = \{E_1, E_2, E_3\}$, $T_1 \equiv \langle \boldsymbol{a} \rangle$, $T_2 \equiv \langle \boldsymbol{b} \vee \boldsymbol{a} \rangle \circ \boldsymbol{b}$ and $T_3 \equiv \langle \boldsymbol{b} \circ \boldsymbol{a} \rangle \vee \langle \boldsymbol{a} \circ \boldsymbol{b} \rangle \vee \boldsymbol{0} \circ \boldsymbol{a}$. Then $T_1' \equiv \langle \boldsymbol{a}_1 \rangle$, $T_2' \equiv \langle \boldsymbol{b}_2 \vee \boldsymbol{a}_3 \rangle \circ \boldsymbol{b}_4$, $T_3' \equiv \langle \boldsymbol{b}_5 \circ \boldsymbol{a}_6 \rangle \vee \langle \boldsymbol{a}_7 \circ \boldsymbol{b}_8 \rangle \vee \boldsymbol{0} \circ \boldsymbol{a}_9$;

$$I_a = \{1, 3, 6, 7, 9\}, \quad I_b = \{2, 4, 5, 8\},$$
$$I_1 = \{1\}, \quad I_2 = \{2, 3, 4\}, \quad I_3 = \{5, 6, 7, 8, 9\}.$$

For δ^4 we have the following table:

δ^4	z_1	{1, 3, 7}	{2, 4, 5}	{1, 3}	{2, 4, 8}	{3, 6}	{2, 4}	{3, 7}	{3}
a	{1, 3, 7}	{1, 3}	{3, 6}	{1, 3}	{3, 7}	{3}	{3}	{3}	{3}
b	{2, 4, 5}	{2, 4, 8}	{2, 4}	{2, 4}	{2, 4}	{2, 4, 5}	{2, 4}	{2, 4, 8}	{2, 4}

and for M_1, M_2, M_3 we have

$$M_1 = \{z_1, \{1, 3, 7\}, \{1, 3\}\},$$
$$M_2 = \{\{2, 4, 5\}, \{2, 4\}, \{2, 4, 8\}\},$$
$$M_3 = \{z_1, \{3, 6\}, \{2, 4, 8\}\}.$$

The graph of the automaton $\mathfrak{A}_4 = [X, Z, \delta^4, z_1]$ is shown on Figure 3.

Corollary 6.18 (Kleene [1]). An event E over a finite alphabet X is regular if and only if it is representable in a finite initial Medvedjev automaton by a set of states.

Corollary 6.19. A sequential function φ over $[X, Y]$ can be generated in a finite automaton if and only if the system $E^\varphi = \{E_y \mid y \in Y\}$ is a finite system of regular events.

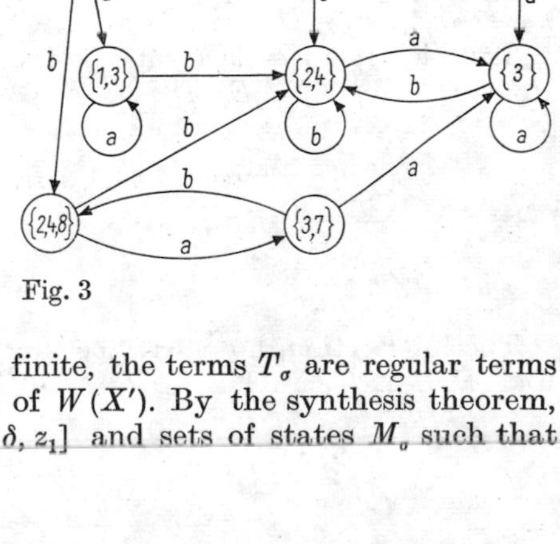

Fig. 3

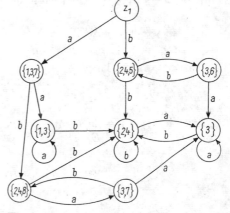

Remark. The synthesis theorem can easily be generalized for regular events over an inifinite alphabet X. Let X be infinite and T_σ for $\sigma = 1, 2, \ldots, s$, be regular terms over X with $E_\sigma = Val(T_\sigma) \subseteq W(X)$. Then in the words $p \in E_\sigma$ only those finitely many letters $x \in X$ appear for which the corresponding symbol $\boldsymbol{x}$ appears in T_σ. Let X' be the set of all these letters. Then X' is finite, the terms T_σ are regular terms over X', and the events E_σ are subsets of $W(X')$. By the synthesis theorem, there are a finite automaton $\mathfrak{A} = [X', Z, \delta, z_1]$ and sets of states M_σ such that for all $\sigma = 1, 2, \ldots, s$, $p \in W(X')$ we have $p \in E_\sigma$ if and only if $\delta(z_1, p) \in M_\sigma$. Let $z^* \notin Z$. We define δ^* on the set $(Z \cup \{z^*\}) \times X$ as follows:

$$\delta^*(z, x) = \begin{cases} \delta(z, x), & \text{if } z \in Z,\ x \in X', \\ z^*, & \text{if } z \in Z,\ x \in X \setminus X' \text{ or } z = z^*,\ x \in X. \end{cases}$$

It is clear that for each $\sigma = 1, 2, \ldots, s$, the event E_σ is represented in the X-infinite but Z-finite automaton $\mathfrak{A}^* = [X, Z \cup \{z^*\}, \delta^*, z_1]$ by the set M_σ. A characterization of events over an arbitrary X which are representable in Z-finite automata can be found in Pohl [3].

We have already noted the existence of intersection, complementation, completion and inversion operations, which lead from regular events to regular events. Therefore, if E, E' are regular events and T, T' regular terms such that $E = Val(T)$, $E' = Val(T')$, then we can construct in a finite number of steps regular terms T_1, T_2, T_3, T_4, for which $Val(T_1) = E \cap E'$, $Val(T_2) = \bar{E}$, $Val(T_3) = Com(E)$ and $Val(T_4) = E^*$. The question arises whether the intersection, complementation, completion and inversion operations can already be defined with the help of union, product and the closure operations, i.e., whether these operations can be obtained by combining the union, product and closure operations.

Theorem 6.20. *The intersection, complementation and completion operations cannot be explicitely defined with the help of the union, product and closure operations, however the inversion can, provided that X contains only one letter.*

Proof: If the complementation is definable, so is the intersection. Therefore we first show that the intersection is not definable. Let E, E' be arbitrary, non-empty events over X. Then we have

$$\begin{aligned} &\{x \mid \exists p \exists r (pxr \in E \cup E')\} \\ &= \{x \mid \exists p \exists r (pxr \in E)\} \cup \{x \mid \exists p \exists r (pxr \in E')\} \\ &= \{x \mid \exists p \exists r (pxr \in E \cdot E')\}, \end{aligned}$$

$$\{x \mid \exists p \exists r (pxr \in \langle E \rangle)\} = \{x \mid \exists p \exists r (pxr \in E)\}.$$

Thus if f is an n-place superposition of the union, product and closure operations, then for $\emptyset \neq E_1, E_2, \ldots, E_n \subseteq W(X)$

$$\begin{aligned} \{x \mid \exists p \exists r (pxr \in f(E_1, \ldots, E_n))\} &= \bigcup_{\nu=1}^{n} \{x \mid \exists p \exists r (pxr \in E_\nu)\} \\ &= \left\{x \mid \exists p \exists r \left(pxr \in \bigcup_{\nu=1}^{n} E_\nu\right)\right\}. \end{aligned}$$

The intersection, however, does not have this property, since if $E \cap E' = \{e\}$ and $E, E' \supset \{e\}$ we have

$$\{x \mid \exists p \exists r (pxr \in E \cap E')\} = \emptyset \neq \{x \mid \exists p \exists r (pxr \in E \cup E')\}.$$

This implies that the intersection and complementation cannot be explicitely defined with the help of the union, product and closure.

Let $a \in X$, $\emptyset \neq E$, $E' \subseteq W(X)$ and $p = x_1 x_2 \ldots x_n \in W(X)$. Then we define

$$p^{E'} = \begin{cases} \{e\}, & \text{if} \quad p = e, \\ X_1 \cdot X_2 \cdot \ldots \cdot X_n, & \text{where} \quad X_i = \begin{cases} E', & \text{if} \quad x_i = a, \\ \{x_i\} & \text{otherwise,} \end{cases} \end{cases}$$

and

$$E^{E'} = \bigcup_{p \in E} p^{E'}.$$

We can easily see that, for arbitrary non-empty events E_1, E_2, E'

$$(E_1 \cup E_2)^{E'} = E_1^{E'} \cup E_2^{E'}, \quad (E_1 \cdot E_2)^{E'} = E_1^{E'} \cdot E_2^{E'}, \quad (\langle E_1 \rangle)^{E'} = \langle E_1^{E'} \rangle.$$

Thus for every (one-place) superposition f of the union, product and closure

$$\big(f(E)\big)^{E'} = f(E^{E'}).$$

The operation *Com* does not have this property, since for example

$$Com(\{a\}) = \{e, a\},$$

$$\big(Com(\{a\})\big)^{\{aa\}} = \{e, aa\} \neq \{e, a, aa\} = Com(\{aa\}) = Com(\{a\}^{\{aa\}}),$$

and this shows that *Com* cannot be explicitely defined by means of the union, product and closure operations.

Whether the inversion is explicitely definable or not depends on the alphabet being used. If $X = \{a\}$ is a singleton, then $E^* = E$ holds for every $E \subseteq W(X)$, i.e., the inversion is trivially definable. However, if X contains at least two different letters, say a and b, then

$$(\{ab\}^{\{ab\}})^* = \{abb\}^* \neq \{bab\} = \{ba\}^{\{ab\}} = (\{ab\}^*)^{\{ab\}},$$

and consequently the inversion is not a one-place superposition of the union, product and closure operations. This completes the proof of Theorem 6.20.

§ 7. Term Equalities

When we say that an event E is regular over a finite alphabet X we mean that an initial finite automaton $\mathfrak{A}$ and a set M are given in such a way that E is represented by M in $\mathfrak{A}$, or equivalently, that a regular term T over X is given such that $Val(T) = E$. It is clear that the same event E can be described by means of a multitude of different terms, e.g.,

$$Val\,(\langle \mathbf{0} \rangle \circ T \vee \mathbf{0} \circ T') = Val\,(T) = E,$$

where T' can be chosen as a completely arbitrary term. Here we may ask whether a procedure exists by means of which we can decide in a finite number of steps for any two regular terms T_1, T_2 whether $Val(T_1) = Val(T_2)$ holds or not. To express this relation conveniently, we shall say that the equality $T_1 = T_2$ is valid. In other words, we add the symbol "=" to the fundamental symbols of our language and introduce the following definition:

Definition 7.1. A sequence of symbols Z is called an *equality over* X if there are regular terms T_1, T_2 over X such that $Z \equiv T_1 = T_2$. We shall say that the equality $T_1 = T_2$ *is valid* if $Val(T_1) = Val(T_2)$ holds.

Theorem 7.1. *There exists a procedure by means of which we can decide about every equality over an arbitrary non-empty alphabet X in a finite number of steps whether it is valid or not. In other words, the set of all valid equalities over an arbitrary non-empty alphabet X is decidable.*

Proof: Let $T_1 = T_2$ be an arbitrary equality over X. According to the proof of the synthesis theorem, there is a procedure by means of which we can construct an initial Medvedjev automaton $\mathfrak{A}$ with a finite set of states Z and sets $M_1, M_2 \subseteq Z$ such that $Val(T_1)$ and $Val(T_2)$ are represented in $\mathfrak{A}$ by M_1 and M_2 respectively. Now $T_1 = T_2$ is valid if and only if $M_1 = M_2$ holds, and the latter can be decided in a finite number of steps, since M_1 and M_2 are finite.

Remark. This decision procedure is "semantic" in the sense that it makes essential use of the interpretation of terms (by means of their values). A procedure is called syntactic if only purely structural rules can be used in working with the terms.

Theorem 7.1 implies that the *axiomatization problem* for term equalities is also solvable. By this we mean the following question:

Does there exist a decidable set A (of valid equalities) and a decidable set $\mathfrak{R}$ of transformation rules for equalities such that every valid equality and only these can be obtained from the equalities belonging to the set A by applying in a finite number of steps the rules of $\mathfrak{R}$?

This problem has a trivial solution, namely, we can choose as A the set of all valid equalities (which is decidable by Theorem 7.1) and as $\mathfrak{R}$ the empty set. Of course this solution is not satisfactory, since the set of all valid equalities is much too complicated. In general, we cannot see immediately whether a given equality is valid or not. However, we can readily see that an equality G is of the form

$$T \vee T = T,$$

for which we also say that it satisfies the schema $T \vee T = T$ (where T denotes an arbitrary regular term). Obviously, a set of equalities which can be described by at most finitely many such schemas is much more satisfactory as a set A of fundamental equalities. Similarly, the set $\mathfrak{R}$ which we choose is not only decidable, but of a simple nature, and in general it is even finite.

In what follows we shall present a set A of equalities which is simple (in the above sense) and a finite set $\mathfrak{R}$ of transformation rules such that the system $[A, \mathfrak{R}]$ yields a solution of the axiomatization problem.

Let A be the set of all term equalities over an arbitrary non-empty alphabet X which satisfy one of the following 11 schemas S_1 to S_{11}:[1])

$$\begin{array}{lll}
(S_1) & T_1 \vee (T_2 \vee T_3) & = (T_1 \vee T_2) \vee T_3 \\
(S_2) & T_1 \circ (T_2 \circ T_3) & = (T_1 \circ T_2) \circ T_3 \\
(S_3) & T_1 \vee T_2 & = T_2 \vee T_1 \\
(S_4) & T_1 \circ (T_2 \vee T_3) & = T_1 \circ T_2 \vee T_1 \circ T_3 \\
(S_5) & (T_1 \vee T_2) \circ T_3 & = T_1 \circ T_3 \vee T_2 \circ T_3 \\
(S_6) & T \vee T & = T \\
(S_7) & \langle 0 \rangle \circ T & = T \\
(S_8) & 0 \circ T & = 0 \\
(S_9) & T \vee 0 & = T \\
(S_{10}) & \langle T \rangle & = \langle 0 \rangle \vee \langle T \rangle \circ T \\
(S_{11}) & \langle T \rangle & = \langle \langle 0 \rangle \vee T \rangle
\end{array}$$

It is easy to verify the following theorem:

Theorem 7.2. *If G is a term equality over X which is obtained from one of the schemas $S_1, S_2, \ldots, S_{11}$ by substituting definite regular terms over X for the term variables T, T_1, T_2, T_3 occuring in it, (i.e., $G \in A$), then G is valid.*

The transformation rules of the set $\mathfrak{R}$ are formulated together with the inductive definition of the relation "G is deducible from A", which will be briefly denoted by $\vdash G$. Before this, however, we shall define one more syntactic property, namely the e-property of regular terms and a syntactic relation *Rep* between regular terms.

Definition 7.2. Let T, T_1, T_2, T' be regular terms.

(7.2.1) We shall say that T *has the e-property* if one of the following conditions holds:

a) there is a term T'' such that $T \equiv \langle T'' \rangle$;

b) there are terms $T^1, \ldots, T^n$, such that $T \equiv T^1 \vee \ldots \vee T^n$ and at least one of the terms T^i has the e-property;

c) there are terms $T^1, \ldots, T^n$ such that $T \equiv T^1 \circ T^2 \circ \ldots \circ T^n$ and all the terms T^i have the e-property.

---

[1]) Topi Urponen has shown, that the schemas S_6 and S_9 are superfluous but the remaining schemas are all independent (under our choice of transformation rules). Publ. in Ann. Univ. Turku, Ser. A, I, No. 145 (1971).

(7.2.2) We shall write $Rep(T, T_1, T_2, T')$ to abbreviate the following assertion: the term T' is obtained from the term T in such a way the term T_1 is replaced by the term T_2 wherever it occurs in T.

Corollary 7.3. A regular term T has the e-property if and only if $e \in Val(T)$ holds.

Definition 7.3.

Initial step: If $G \in A$ then $\vdash G$.

Induction step:

(R_1) If $\vdash T_1 = T_2$ and $\vdash T_1 = T_3$, then $\vdash T_2 = T_3$.

(R_2) If $Rep(T, T_1, T_2, T')$, $\vdash T_1 = T_2$ and $\vdash T = T_3$, then $\vdash T = T'$ and $\vdash T' = T_3$.

(R_3) If T_2 does not have the e-property and $\vdash T_1 = T_1 \circ T_2 \vee T_3$, then $\vdash T_1 = T_3 \circ \langle T_2 \rangle$.

Thus an equality is deducible from A if and only if it belongs to A or can be obtained from equalities belonging to A by applying the rules of the set $\mathfrak{R} = \{R_1, R_2, R_3\}$ in a finite number of steps. Now we claim:

Theorem 7.4. *If $\vdash G$, then G is valid (i.e., the system $[A, \mathfrak{R}]$ is consistent).*

Proof: Since by Theorem 7.2 the equalities $G \in A$ are valid, it suffices to show that the application of R_1, R_2, R_3 to valid equalities results in a valid equality again. (We can also say that R_1, R_2, R_3 *preserve validity*.) The cases of R_1 and R_2 are trivial.

Now let T_2 be a term which does not have the e-property, $T_1 = T_1 \circ T_2 \vee T_3$ a valid equality and $E_i = Val(T_i)$ for $i = 1, 2, 3$. Then we have

$$E_1 = E_1 \cdot E_2 \cup E_3.$$

By successive substitutions of E_1 into the right hand side of this identity, and using the distributivity of the product and union (which are, by the way, described in S_4 and S_5) we obtain:

$$E_1 = E_1 \cdot E_2^2 \cup E_3 \cdot E_2 \cup E_3,$$

$$E_1 = E_1 \cdot E_2^3 \cup E_3 \cdot E_2^2 \cup E_3 \cdot E_2 \cup E_3.$$

By induction on n we obtain that for all $n \geqq 1$

$$E_1 = E_1 \cdot E_2^n \cup E_3 \cdot (E_2^{n-1} \cup \cdots \cup E_2 \cup E_2^0). \qquad (*)$$

T_2 does not have the e-property, hence $e \notin Val(T_2) = E_2$, and for all words $p \in E_2^n$ and thus for all words $p \in E_1 \cdot E_2^n$ we have $l(p) \geqq n$.

We assert that, for each $p \in W(X)$, $p \in E_1$ holds, if and only if there is an integer $m \geqq 0$ such that $p \in E_3 \cdot E_2^m$.

It follows immediately from (*) that $p \in E_1$ holds, if there exists an m such that $p \in E_3 \cdot E_2^m$. Conversely, assume $p \in E_1$, $l(p) = k \geqq 0$. Then, because of

(*) we have $p \in E_1 \cdot E_2^{k+1} \cup E_3 \cdot (E_2^k \cup \ldots \cup E_2 \cup E_2^0)$. The words $q \in E_1 \cdot E_2^{k+1}$ are of length greater than k, consequently $p \in E_3 \cdot (E_2^k \cup \ldots \cup E_2 \cup E_2^0)$. Thus there is an m with $0 \leqq m \leqq k = l(p)$ such that $p \in E_3 \cdot E_2^m$ holds.

We also obtain from this proof that $E_1 = \bigcup_{n \geqq 0} E_3 \cdot E_2^n = E_3 \cdot \langle E_2 \rangle$, and this implies that the equality $T_1 = T_3 \circ \langle T_2 \rangle$ is valid, completing the proof.

It is much more difficult to prove the *completeness* of the system $[A, \mathfrak{R}]$, i.e., to show that every valid equality can be deduced from A. In order to do this, we shall first establish several propositions concerning deducibility (including derived rules of inference) and show that every term can be characterized by means of equalities.

(S_{12}) $\vdash T = T$.

Proof: By S_6 we have $\vdash T \vee T = T$. Therefore if we put $T_1 \equiv T \vee T$, $T_2 \equiv T_3 \equiv T$, then $\vdash T_1 = T_2$, $\vdash T_1 = T_3$ hence by R_1 $\vdash T_2 = T_3$, i.e., $\vdash T = T$.

(R_4) If $\vdash T_1 = T_2$, then $\vdash T_2 = T_1$.

Proof: We put $T_3 \equiv T_1$ and because of S_{12} we have $\vdash T_1 = T_2$ and $\vdash T_1 = T_3$, thus by R_1 $\vdash T_2 = T_3$ i.e., $\vdash T_2 = T_1$.

(R_5) If $\vdash T_1 = T_2$ and $\vdash T_2 = T_3$, then $\vdash T_1 = T_3$.

The proof follows from R_1 and R_4.

(R_6) If $\vdash T_1 = T_2$ and $\vdash T_3 = T_4$, then $\vdash T_1 \vee T_3 = T_2 \vee T_4$, $\vdash T_1 \circ T_3 = T_2 \circ T_4$ and $\vdash \langle T_1 \rangle = \langle T_2 \rangle$.

Proof: First we show that $\vdash T_1 \vee T_3 = T_2 \vee T_4$. By S_{12} we have $\vdash T_1 \vee T_3 = T_1 \vee T_3$, further $Rep(T_1 \vee T_3, T_1, T_2, T_2 \vee T_3)$ and $\vdash T_1 = T_2$, hence by R_2 $\vdash T_1 \vee T_3 = T_2 \vee T_3$. Now $Rep(T_2 \vee T_3, T_3, T_4, T_2 \vee T_4)$ and $\vdash T_3 = T_4$ hence by R_2 $\vdash T_2 \vee T_3 = T_2 \vee T_4$, and by R_5 we have $\vdash T_1 \vee T_3 = T_2 \vee T_4$. The proposition $\vdash T_1 \circ T_3 = T_2 \circ T_4$ can be proved analogously and $\vdash \langle T_1 \rangle = \langle T_2 \rangle$ follows immediately from $Rep(\langle T_1 \rangle, T_1, T_2, \langle T_2 \rangle)$ and $\vdash T_1 = T_2$, by R_2.

(S_{13}) $\vdash T \circ \mathbf{0} = \mathbf{0}$.

Proof: From S_8 we have $\vdash \mathbf{0} \circ \mathbf{0} = \mathbf{0}$, and from S_{12}, $\vdash T = T$, hence by R_6 we also have $\vdash T \circ (\mathbf{0} \circ \mathbf{0}) = T \circ \mathbf{0}$. By S_9, $\vdash T \circ \mathbf{0} \vee \mathbf{0} = T \circ \mathbf{0}$, hence by R_4 $\vdash T \circ \mathbf{0} = T \circ \mathbf{0} \vee \mathbf{0}$. Furthermore we have $Rep\big(T \circ \mathbf{0} \vee \mathbf{0}, T \circ \mathbf{0}, T \circ (\mathbf{0} \circ \mathbf{0}), T \circ (\mathbf{0} \circ \mathbf{0}) \vee \mathbf{0}\big)$, and by R_4 $\vdash T \circ \mathbf{0} = T \circ (\mathbf{0} \circ \mathbf{0})$, hence using R_2 we obtain $\vdash T \circ \mathbf{0} = T \circ (\mathbf{0} \circ \mathbf{0}) \vee \mathbf{0}$. Because of S_2 we have $\vdash T \circ (\mathbf{0} \circ \mathbf{0}) = (T \circ \mathbf{0}) \circ \mathbf{0}$, $Rep\big(T \circ (\mathbf{0} \circ \mathbf{0}) \vee \mathbf{0}, T \circ (\mathbf{0} \circ \mathbf{0}), (T \circ \mathbf{0}) \circ \mathbf{0}, (T \circ \mathbf{0}) \circ \mathbf{0} \vee \mathbf{0}\big)$, hence $\vdash T \circ (\mathbf{0} \circ \mathbf{0}) \vee \mathbf{0} = (T \circ \mathbf{0}) \circ \mathbf{0} \vee \mathbf{0}$, and by R_5, $\vdash T \circ \mathbf{0} = (T \circ \mathbf{0}) \circ \mathbf{0} \vee \mathbf{0}$. Now, $\mathbf{0}$ does not have the e-property, and thus by R_3 we get $\vdash T \circ \mathbf{0} = \mathbf{0} \circ \langle \mathbf{0} \rangle$. Because of S_8 $\vdash \mathbf{0} \circ \langle \mathbf{0} \rangle = \mathbf{0}$ holds, and using R_5, S_{13} follows.

(S_{14}) $\vdash T = T \circ \langle \mathbf{0} \rangle$.

Proof: By S_9 $\vdash T \vee \mathbf{0} = \mathbf{0}$ holds, hence using R_4 we get $\vdash T = T \vee \mathbf{0}$. S_8 and R_4 imply $\vdash \mathbf{0} = T \circ \mathbf{0}$. Furthermore we have $Rep(T \vee \mathbf{0}, \mathbf{0}, T \circ \mathbf{0}, T \vee T \circ \mathbf{0})$ and using R_2 and R_5 we obtain $\vdash T = T \vee T \circ \mathbf{0}$. Because of S_3 $\vdash T \vee T \circ \mathbf{0} = T \circ \mathbf{0} \vee T$, hence, by R_5, $\vdash T = T \circ \mathbf{0} \vee T$, and since $\mathbf{0}$ does not have the e-property, using R_3 we obtain $\vdash T = T \circ \langle \mathbf{0} \rangle$, which was to be shown.

In what follows we shall not give all the details of the proofs and leave it to the reader to convince himself that in each step only equalities and rules of inference which have already been derived are used.

(R_7) Let $n \geqq 1$ and for $i = 1, 2, \ldots, n$ we put

$$\vdash T_i = T_1 \circ T_{i1} \vee T_2 \circ T_{i2} \vee \ldots \vee T_n \circ T_{in} \vee T_i^*$$

and

$$\vdash T_i' = T_1' \circ T_{i1} \vee T_2' \circ T_{i2} \vee \ldots \vee T_n' \circ T_{in} \vee T_i^*,$$

where no term T_{ij} $(1 \leqq i, j \leqq n)$ has the e-property.

Then for $i = 1, 2, \ldots, n$ we have

$$\vdash T_i = T_i'.$$

The proof goes by induction on n. The initial step is $n = 1$. Thus we have

$$\vdash T_1 = T_1 \circ T_{11} \vee T_1^* \quad \text{and} \quad \vdash T_1' = T_1' \circ T_{11} \vee T_1^*.$$

Since T_{11} does not have the e-property, using R_3 we get

$$\vdash T_1 = T_1^* \circ \langle T_{11} \rangle \quad \text{and} \quad \vdash T_1' = T_1^* \circ \langle T_{11} \rangle,$$

and this together with R_2 implies that $\vdash T_1 = T_1'$.

The induction step is taken from $n - 1$ to n, for $n \geqq 2$.

According to the hypothesis, we have

$$\vdash T_n = (T_1 \circ T_{n1} \vee \ldots \vee T_{n-1} \circ T_{nn-1}) \vee T_n \circ T_{nn} \vee T_n^*,$$
$$\vdash T_n' = (T_1' \circ T_{n1} \vee \ldots \vee T_{n-1}' \circ T_{nn-1}) \vee T_n' \circ T_{nn} \vee T_n^*,$$

$$\vdash T_n = T_n \circ T_{nn} \vee (T_1 \circ T_{n1} \vee \ldots \vee T_{n-1} \circ T_{nn-1} \vee T_n^*),$$
$$\vdash T_n' = T_n' \circ T_{nn} \vee (T_1' \circ T_{n1} \vee \ldots \vee T_{n-1}' \circ T_{nn-1} \vee T_n^*).$$

Since T_{nn} does not have the e-property, using R_3 we get

$$\left.\begin{aligned} &\vdash T_n = (T_1 \circ T_{n1} \vee \ldots \vee T_{n-1} \circ T_{nn-1} \vee T_n^*) \circ \langle T_{nn} \rangle, \\ &\vdash T_n' = (T_1' \circ T_{n1} \vee \ldots \vee T_{n-1}' \circ T_{nn-1} \vee T_n^*) \circ \langle T_{nn} \rangle. \end{aligned}\right\} \quad (*)$$

For $i = 1, 2, \ldots, n - 1$ we have

$$\vdash T_i = T_1 \circ T_{i1} \vee \ldots \vee T_{n-1} \circ T_{in-1} \vee T_n \circ T_{in} \vee T_i^*,$$

hence

$$\vdash T_i = T_1 \circ T_{i1} \vee \ldots \vee T_{n-1} \circ T_{in-1}$$
$$\vee (T_1 \circ T_{n1} \vee \ldots \vee T_{n-1} \circ T_{nn-1} \vee T_n^*) \circ \langle T_{nn} \rangle \circ T_{in} \vee T_i^*,$$

$$\vdash T_i = T_1 \circ (T_{i1} \vee T_{n1} \circ \langle T_{nn} \rangle \circ T_{in}) \vee \ldots$$
$$\vee T_{n-1} \circ (T_{in-1} \vee T_{nn-1} \circ \langle T_{nn} \rangle \circ T_{in}) \vee (T_n^* \circ \langle T_{nn} \rangle \circ T_{in} \vee T_i^*).$$

Similarly, we show that for all $i = 1, \ldots, n-1$

$$\vdash T_i' = T_1' \circ (T_{i1} \vee T_{n1} \circ \langle T_{nn} \rangle \circ T_{in}) \vee \ldots$$
$$\vee T_{n-1}' \circ (T_{in-1} \vee T_{nn-1} \circ \langle T_{nn} \rangle \circ T_{in}) \vee (T_n^* \circ \langle T_{nn} \rangle \circ T_{in} \vee T_i^*).$$

For arbitrary $i, j = 1, \ldots, n-1$ the terms $T_{ij} \vee T_{nj} \circ \langle T_{nn} \rangle \circ T_{in}$ do not have the e-property, since T_{ij}, T_{nj} do not have this property. By the induction hypothesis we have for $i = 1, 2, \ldots, n-1$

$$\vdash T_i = T_i'.$$

This, together with (*) implies that $\vdash T_n = T_n'$, and proves R_7.

Definition 7.4 (Salomaa [1], [5]). Let T be a regular term over X and $X' = \{x^{(1)}, x^{(2)}, \ldots, x^{(r)}\}$ a finite subset of X. We say that T is *X'-characterizable*, if there are a natural number n and terms $T_1, T_2, \ldots, T_n$ over X' such that $T \equiv T_1$ and for all $i = 1, 2, \ldots, n$

$$\vdash T_i = T_{i1} \circ \boldsymbol{x}^{(1)} \vee T_{i2} \circ \boldsymbol{x}^{(2)} \vee \ldots \vee T_{ir} \circ \boldsymbol{x}^{(r)} \vee \delta(T_i)$$

where for each pair i, j with $1 \leqq i \leqq n$, $1 \leqq j \leqq r$ there is a k with $1 \leqq k \leqq n$, for which $T_{ij} \equiv T_k$, and where $\delta(T_i)$ is either the term $\mathbf{0}$ or the term $\langle \mathbf{0} \rangle$.

It is clear that $\delta(T_i) \equiv \langle \mathbf{0} \rangle$ holds, if and only if T_i has the e-property, furthermore that T can only be X'-characterizable if all the letters x for which the symbol $\boldsymbol{x}$ appears in T belong to X' (i.e., if T is a term over X').

Examples of the characterization of regular terms can be found at the end of this section.

Lemma 7.5. *If T is X'-characterizable, $X' \subseteq X'' \subseteq X$ and X'' is finite, then T is also X''-characterizable.*

Proof: Suppose $X' = \{x^{(1)}, x^{(2)}, \ldots, x^{(r)}\}$, $X'' = \{x^{(1)}, \ldots, x^{(r)}, x^{(r+1)}, \ldots, x^{(r+k)}\}$, and $T_1, T_2, \ldots, T_n$ are terms over X' such that $T \equiv T_1$ and for $i = 1, 2, \ldots, n$

$$\vdash T_i = T_{i1} \circ \boldsymbol{x}^{(1)} \vee T_{i2} \circ \boldsymbol{x}^{(2)} \vee \ldots \vee T_{ir} \circ \boldsymbol{x}^{(r)} \vee \delta(T_i)$$

with the properties given in Definition 7.4. For $T^* \equiv \mathbf{0}$ we obviously have

$$\vdash T_i = T_{i1} \circ \boldsymbol{x}^{(1)} \vee \ldots \vee T_{ir} \circ \boldsymbol{x}^{(r)} \vee T^* \circ \boldsymbol{x}^{(r+1)} \vee \ldots$$
$$\vee T^* \circ \boldsymbol{x}^{(r+k)} \vee \delta(T_i) \qquad (1 \leqq i \leqq n),$$

$$\vdash T^* = T^* \circ \boldsymbol{x}^{(1)} \vee \ldots \vee T^* \circ \boldsymbol{x}^{(r)} \vee T^* \circ \boldsymbol{x}^{(r+1)} \vee \ldots \vee T^* \circ \boldsymbol{x}^{(r+k)} \vee \mathbf{0}.$$

If T^* does not appear among the terms $T_1, \ldots, T_n$, then we add it as T_{n+1}. Since all the terms $T_1, \ldots, T_n, T^*$ are also terms over X'' (because $X' \subseteq X''$), this proves Lemma 7.5.

If T is a regular term over X we denote by X_T the *smallest* (finite) *subset* X' *of* X *such that* T *is a term over* X'. Evidently, X_T is the set of all those $x \in X$ for which the symbol $\boldsymbol{x}$ appears in T.

Lemma 7.6. *Every regular term* T *over* X *is* X_T*-characterizable.*

The proof goes by induction. First we show that $\mathbf{0}$ is $\emptyset$-characterizable and that for every $x \in X$ the term $\boldsymbol{x}$ is $\{x\}$-characterizable.

It is clear that for $T \equiv \mathbf{0}$, $\delta(T) \equiv \mathbf{0}$ and $n = 1$, $T_1 \equiv \mathbf{0}$ satisfy our requirements, since

$$\vdash T_1 = \delta(T_1), \text{ i.e. } \vdash \mathbf{0} = \mathbf{0}.$$

If $T \equiv \boldsymbol{x}$ then for $n = 3$, $T_1 \equiv \boldsymbol{x}$, $T_2 \equiv \langle \mathbf{0} \rangle$, $T_3 \equiv \mathbf{0}$ we have:

$$\begin{aligned}
&\vdash T_1 = T_2 \circ \boldsymbol{x} \vee \mathbf{0},\\
&\vdash T_2 = T_3 \circ \boldsymbol{x} \vee \langle \mathbf{0} \rangle,\\
&\vdash T_3 = T_3 \circ \boldsymbol{x} \vee \mathbf{0}.
\end{aligned}$$

In the induction step we assume that the terms T and T' are X_T and $X_{T'}$-characterizable, respectively, and we show that under these conditions the terms $T \vee T'$, $T \circ T'$ and $\langle T \rangle$ are $X_{T \vee T'}$, $X_{T \circ T'}$, X_T-characterizable.

It is easy to see that $X_{T \vee T'} = X_{T \circ T'} = X_T \cup X_{T'}$. Now let $X_T \cup X_{T'} = \{x^{(1)}, x^{(2)}, \ldots, x^{(r)}\}$.

By Lemma 7.5 T and T' are $(X_T \cup X_{T'})$-characterizable.

Let $T_1, T_2, \ldots, T_n$ be terms such that $T \equiv T'$ and for $i = 1, 2, \ldots, n$

$$\vdash T_i = T_{i1} \circ \boldsymbol{x}^{(1)} \vee \ldots \vee T_{ir} \circ \boldsymbol{x}^{(r)} \vee \delta(T_i)$$

where $T_{i\varrho} \in \{T_1, \ldots, T_n\}$ for $\varrho = 1, \ldots, r$; $i = 1, \ldots, n$. Furthermore, let $T'_1, T'_2, \ldots, T'_m$ be terms with $T' \equiv T'_1$ and for $j = 1, \ldots, m$:

$$\vdash T'_j = T'_{j1} \circ \boldsymbol{x}^{(1)} \vee \ldots \vee T'_{jr} \circ \boldsymbol{x}^{(r)} \vee \delta(T'_j),$$

where $T'_{j\varrho} \in \{T'_1, \ldots, T'_m\}$ for $\varrho = 1, \ldots, r$; $j = 1, \ldots, m$. Finally let be $T(i, j) \equiv T_i \vee T'_j$ for $1 \leq i \leq n$, $1 \leq j \leq m$; let us denote by $\mathfrak{t}$ the set of all these terms. Then using R_6, S_1, S_3, S_4 and S_5 we have for all i, j

$$\vdash T(i, j) = (T_{i1} \vee T'_{j1}) \circ \boldsymbol{x}^{(1)} \vee \ldots \vee (T_{ir} \vee T'_{jr}) \circ \boldsymbol{x}^{(r)} \vee \delta(T_i) \vee \delta(T'_j).$$

Here the terms $T_{i\varrho} \vee T'_{j\varrho}$ belong to $\mathfrak{t}$. Furthermore

$$\begin{aligned}
&\vdash \mathbf{0} \vee \mathbf{0} = \mathbf{0}, \ \vdash \mathbf{0} \vee \langle \mathbf{0} \rangle = \langle \mathbf{0} \rangle, \ \vdash \langle \mathbf{0} \rangle \vee \langle \mathbf{0} \rangle = \langle \mathbf{0} \rangle,\\
&\vdash \delta\big(T(i, j)\big) = \delta(T_i) \vee \delta(T'_j),
\end{aligned}$$

where $\delta(T(i, j)) \equiv \mathbf{0}$ or $\delta(T(i, j)) \equiv \langle \mathbf{0} \rangle$. This shows that all the terms belonging to $\mathfrak{t}$ are $X_{T \vee T'}$-characterizable, hence in particular $T(1, 1) \equiv T \vee T'$ is also.

Let us consider for $1 \leqq j \leqq m$, $1 \leqq i_1 < i_2 < \cdots < i_k \leqq h$, $k \geqq 0$ the following regular terms (over $X_{T \circ T'}$): $T'(j, i_1, \ldots, i_k) \equiv T \circ T'_j \vee T_{i_1} \vee \ldots \vee T_{i_k}$. The set of these terms which we denote by $\mathfrak{t}'$ is finite. Obviously we have

$$\begin{aligned} \vdash T'(j, i_1, \ldots, i_k) = T \circ \big(T'_{j1} \circ \boldsymbol{x}^{(1)} \vee \ldots \vee T'_{jr} \circ \boldsymbol{x}^{(r)} \vee \delta(T'_j)\big) \\ \vee \big(T_{i_1 1} \circ \boldsymbol{x}^{(1)} \vee \ldots \vee T_{i_1 r} \circ \boldsymbol{x}^{(r)} \vee \delta(T_{i_1})\big) \vee \ldots \\ \vee \big(T_{i_k 1} \circ \boldsymbol{x}^{(1)} \vee \ldots \vee T_{i_k r} \circ \boldsymbol{x}^{(r)} \vee \delta(T_{i_k})\big) \end{aligned}$$

and thus

$$\begin{aligned} \vdash T'(j, i_1, \ldots, i_k) = (T \circ T'_{j1} \vee T_{i_1 1} \vee \ldots \vee T_{i_k 1}) \circ \boldsymbol{x}^{(1)} \vee \ldots \\ \vee (T \circ T'_{jr} \vee T_{i_1 r} \vee \ldots \vee T_{i_k r}) \circ \boldsymbol{x}^{(r)} \\ \vee \big(T \circ \delta(T'_j) \vee \delta(T_{i_1}) \vee \ldots \vee \delta(T_{i_k})\big). \end{aligned}$$

Case 1. $\delta(T'_j) \equiv \mathbf{0}$. Then the term $T \circ \delta(T'_j)$ can be deleted from the right hand side of the last equality giving us an equality for $T'(j, i_1, \ldots, i_n)$ in which only terms belonging to $\mathfrak{t}'$ appear as coefficients of $\boldsymbol{x}^{(\varrho)}$, and the last summand is either $\equiv \mathbf{0}$ or $\equiv \langle \mathbf{0} \rangle$.

Case 2. $\delta(T'_j) \equiv \langle \mathbf{0} \rangle$.

Because of $\vdash T = T_{11} \circ \boldsymbol{x}^{(1)} \vee \ldots \vee T_{1r} \circ \boldsymbol{x}^{(r)} \vee \delta(T)$ we have

$$\begin{aligned} \vdash T'(j, i_1, \ldots, i_k) = (T \circ T'_{j1} \vee T_{11} \vee T_{i_1 1} \vee \ldots \vee T_{i_k 1}) \circ \boldsymbol{x}^{(1)} \vee \ldots \\ \vee (T \circ T'_{jr} \vee T_{1r} \vee T_{i_1 r} \vee \ldots \vee T_{i_k r}) \circ \boldsymbol{x}^{(r)} \\ \vee \big(\delta(T) \vee \delta(T_{i_1}) \vee \ldots \vee \delta(T_{i_k})\big). \end{aligned}$$

Now for all $\varrho = 1, 2, \ldots, r$ the coefficient $T \circ T'_{j\varrho} \vee T_{1\varrho} \vee T_{i_1\varrho} \vee \ldots \vee T_{i_k\varrho}$ lies in $\mathfrak{t}'$, or otherwise there is a term $T'(j', i'_1, \ldots, i'_{k'}) \in \mathfrak{t}'$ such that $\vdash (T \circ T'_{j\varrho} \vee T_{1\varrho} \vee T_{i_1\varrho} \vee \ldots \vee T_{i_k\varrho}) = T'(j', i'_1, \ldots, i'_{k'})$. Thus also in this case we have an equality for $T'(j, i_1, \ldots, i_k)$, in which only terms belonging to $\mathfrak{t}'$ appear as coefficients of $\boldsymbol{x}^{(\varrho)}$ and the last summand is either $\mathbf{0}$ or $\langle \mathbf{0} \rangle$. This shows that all the terms in the set $\mathfrak{t}'$ are $X_{T \circ T'}$-characterizable, thus in particular the term $T'(1) \equiv T \circ T_1 \equiv T \circ T'$ is also.

Let us put now $X_T = \{x^{(1)}, x^{(2)}, \ldots, x^{(r)}\}$, and then consider the term $T''(0) = \langle T \rangle$ and for $k \geqq 1$, $1 \leqq i_1 < \cdots < i_k \leqq n$ the terms $T''(i_1, \ldots, i_k) \equiv \langle T \rangle \circ (T_{i_1} \vee \ldots \vee T_{i_k})$. The set $\mathfrak{t}''$ of these terms over X_T is finite. We have

$$\vdash T = T_{11} \circ \boldsymbol{x}^{(1)} \vee \ldots \vee T_{1r} \circ \boldsymbol{x}^{(r)} \vee \delta(T),$$

hence by R_6, S_9, S_{11}

$$\vdash \langle T \rangle = \langle T_{11} \circ \boldsymbol{x}^{(1)} \vee \ldots \vee T_{1r} \circ \boldsymbol{x}^{(r)} \rangle.$$

Thus by S_{10}

$$\vdash \langle T_{11} \circ x^{(1)} \vee \ldots \vee T_{1r} \circ x^{(r)} \rangle$$
$$= \langle T_{11} \circ x^{(1)} \rangle \vee \ldots \vee T_{1r} \circ x^{(r)} \rangle \circ (T_{11} \circ x^{(1)} \vee \ldots \vee T_{1r} \circ x^{(r)}) \vee \langle \mathbf{0} \rangle$$

and thus

$$\vdash \langle T \rangle = \langle T \rangle \circ (T_{11} \circ x^{(1)} \vee \ldots \vee T_{1r} \circ x^{(r)}) \vee \langle \mathbf{0} \rangle,$$
$$\vdash T''(0) = \langle T \rangle \circ T_{11} \circ x^{(1)} \vee \ldots \vee \langle T \rangle \circ T_{1r} \circ x^{(r)} \vee \delta\big(T''(0)\big)$$

where $\delta\big(T''(0)\big) \equiv \langle \mathbf{0} \rangle$. Thus we have derived an equality for $T''(0)$ in which only terms from t″ appear as coefficients and the last summand is $\langle \mathbf{0} \rangle$. Assume $k \geqq 1,\ 1 \leqq i_1 < \cdots < i_k \leqq n$.

Case 1. The term $T_{i_1} \vee \ldots \vee T_{i_k}$ does not have the e-property. Then for $\varkappa = 1, \ldots, k$ $\delta(T_{i_\varkappa}) \equiv \mathbf{0}$ and $\vdash T_{i_\varkappa} = T_{i_\varkappa 1} \circ x^{(1)} \vee \ldots \vee T_{i_\varkappa r} \circ x^{(r)}$ and thus

$$T''(i_1, \ldots, i_k) = \langle T \rangle \circ (T_{i_1 1} \vee \ldots \vee T_{i_k 1}) \circ x^{(1)} \vee \ldots$$
$$\vee \langle T \rangle \circ (T_{i_1 r} \vee \ldots \vee T_{i_k r}) \circ x^{(r)} \vee \mathbf{0},$$

i.e., we have an equality for $T''(i_1, \ldots, i_k)$ in which every coefficient is from t″ and the last summand is $\mathbf{0}$.

Case 2. The term $T_{i_1} \vee \ldots \vee T_{i_k}$ has the e-property.
Then

$$\vdash T''(i_1, \ldots, i_k) = \langle T \rangle \circ (T_{i_1 1} \vee \ldots \vee T_{i_k 1}) \circ x^{(1)} \vee \ldots$$
$$\vee \langle T \rangle \circ (T_{i_1 r} \vee \ldots \vee T_{i_k r}) \circ x^{(r)} \vee \langle T \rangle$$

hence

$$\vdash T''(i_1, \ldots, i_k) = \langle T \rangle \circ (T_{11} \vee T_{i_1 1} \vee \ldots \vee T_{i_k 1}) \circ x^{(1)} \vee \ldots$$
$$\vee \langle T \rangle \circ (T_{1r} \vee T_{i_1 r} \vee \ldots \vee T_{i_k r}) \circ x^{(r)} \vee \langle \mathbf{0} \rangle.$$

Here for all $\varrho = 1, 2, \ldots, r$ we have: the coefficient $\langle T \rangle \circ (T_{1\varrho} \vee T_{i_1 \varrho} \vee \ldots \vee T_{i_k \varrho})$ belongs to t″, or there is a term $T_\varrho^{**} \in$ t″ such that

$$\vdash T_\varrho^{**} = \langle T \rangle \circ (T_{1\varrho} \vee T_{i_1 \varrho} \vee \ldots \vee T_{i_k \varrho}).$$

Thus in this case too we have obtained an equality for the term $T''(i_1, \ldots, i_k)$ with all the coefficients in t″, and in which the last summand is $\langle \mathbf{0} \rangle$. We have shown that every term from t″ is X_T-characterizable, including $T''(0) = \langle T \rangle$. This proves Lemma 7.6.

Lemma 7.7. *If the equality* $T = T'$ *is valid, and* $\vdash T = T_1 \circ x^{(1)} \vee \ldots \vee T_r \circ x^{(r)} \vee \delta(T)$, $\vdash T' = T'_1 \circ x^{(1)} \vee \ldots \vee T'_r \circ x^{(r)} \vee \delta(T')$, *where* $\delta(T)$ *and* $\delta(T')$ *denote one of the terms* $\mathbf{0}, \langle \mathbf{0} \rangle$, *then* $\delta(T) \equiv \delta(T')$ *and the equalities* $T_i = T'_i$ *are valid (for* $i = 1, 2, \ldots, r$*).*

Proof: Since $T = T'$ is valid, T has the e-property if and only if T' has (Corollary 7.3), and this implies $\delta(T) \equiv \delta(T')$. For $1 \leqq i, j \leqq r$ and $i \neq j$ we have

$$Val(T_i \circ \boldsymbol{x}^{(i)}) \cap Val(T_j \circ \boldsymbol{x}^{(j)}) = \emptyset,$$
$$Val(T) \cap W(X) \cdot \{x^{(i)}\} = Val(T_i \circ \boldsymbol{x}^{(i)}),$$
$$Val(T') \cap W(X) \cdot \{x^{(i)}\} = Val(T'_i \circ \boldsymbol{x}^{(i)}).$$

Thus $Val(T) = Val(T')$ implies $Val(T_i \circ \boldsymbol{x}^{(i)}) = Val(T'_i \circ \boldsymbol{x}^{(i)})$ hence $Val(T_i) = Val(T'_i)$, and the equality $T_i = T'_i$ is indeed valid for all $i = 1, 2, \ldots, r$.

Theorem 7.8 (Salomaa's *completeness theorem*). *If* $T_1 = T'_1$ *is a valid equality over* $X_{T_1} \cup X_{T'_1} = X' = \{x^{(1)}, \ldots, x^{(r)}\} \subseteq X$, *then*

$$\vdash T_1 = T'_1.$$

Proof: By Lemmas 7.6 and 7.5, there exist finite sets $\mathfrak{t} = \{T_1, T_2, \ldots, T_n\}$ and $\mathfrak{t}' = \{T'_1, T'_2, \ldots, T'_m\}$ of terms over X' such that for $\nu = 1, 2, \ldots, n$ and $\mu = 1, 2, \ldots, m$

$$\vdash T_\nu = T_{\nu 1} \circ \boldsymbol{x}^{(1)} \vee \ldots \vee T_{\nu r} \circ \boldsymbol{x}^{(r)} \vee \delta(T_\nu), \qquad (*)$$
$$\vdash T'_\mu = T'_{\mu 1} \circ \boldsymbol{x}^{(1)} \vee \ldots \vee T'_{\mu r} \circ \boldsymbol{x}^{(r)} \vee \delta(T'_\mu) \qquad (**)$$

where for $\varrho = 1, 2, \ldots, r$; $\nu = 1, 2, \ldots, n$; $\mu = 1, 2, \ldots, m$

$$T_{\nu\varrho} \in \mathfrak{t},\ T'_{\mu\varrho} \in \mathfrak{t}',\ \delta(T'_\mu),\ \delta(T_\nu) \in \{0, \langle 0 \rangle\}$$

are satisfied.

$(*)$ for $\nu = 1$, $(**)$ for $\mu = 1$, and the validity of $T_1 = T'_1$ imply by Lemma 7.7,

$$\delta(T_1) \equiv \delta(T'_1)$$

and for $\varrho = 1, 2, \ldots, r$ the validity of the equality

$$T_{1\varrho} = T'_{1\varrho}.$$

Since $T_{1\varrho} \in \mathfrak{t}$, and $T'_{1\varrho} \in \mathfrak{t}'$, there are such expressions in $(*)$ and $(**)$ in which these terms appear on the left hand side:

$$\vdash T_{1\varrho} = T_{1\varrho 1} \circ \boldsymbol{x}^{(1)} \vee \ldots \vee T_{1\varrho r} \circ \boldsymbol{x}^{(r)} \vee \delta(T_{1\varrho}),$$
$$\vdash T'_{1\varrho} = T'_{1\varrho 1} \circ \boldsymbol{x}^{(1)} \vee \ldots \vee T'_{1\varrho r} \circ \boldsymbol{x}^{(r)} \vee \delta(T'_{1\varrho}).$$

Since $T_{1\varrho} = T'_{1\varrho}$ is valid, by Lemma 7.7 we obtain that $\delta(T_{1\varrho}) \equiv \delta(T'_{1\varrho})$ and for all $\varrho' = 1, 2, \ldots, r$ the equality

$$T_{1\varrho\varrho'} = T'_{1\varrho\varrho'}$$

is valid. Here $T_{1\varrho\varrho'}$, $T'_{1\varrho\varrho'}$ are terms belonging to $\mathfrak{t}$ and $\mathfrak{t}'$ respectively. We continue this procedure until no new equalities with the left hand side from $\mathfrak{t}$ and the right hand side from $\mathfrak{t}'$ can be obtained. The process will end in a finite number of steps and result in a finite sequence $\mathfrak{G} = [T_1^* = T_1^{**}, \ldots, T_k^* = T_k^{**}]$ of such equalities since their number $k \leqq n \cdot m$. Among these equalities, the initial equality $T_1 = T_1'$ can be found, say as $T_1^* = T_1^{**}$. For each $\varkappa = 1, 2, \ldots, k$ we have $T_\varkappa^* \in \mathfrak{t}$, $T_\varkappa^{**} \in \mathfrak{t}'$. Because of (*) and (**) we obtain

$$\vdash T_\varkappa^* = T_{\varkappa 1}^* \circ \boldsymbol{x}^{(1)} \vee \ldots \vee T_{\varkappa r}^* \circ \boldsymbol{x}^{(r)} \vee \delta(T_\varkappa^*),$$
$$\vdash T_\varkappa^{**} = T_{\varkappa 1}^{**} \circ \boldsymbol{x}^{(1)} \vee \ldots \vee T_{\varkappa r}^{**} \circ \boldsymbol{x}^{(r)} \vee \delta(T_\varkappa^{**}).$$

By our construction

$$\delta(T_\varkappa^*) \equiv \delta(T_\varkappa^{**}),$$

and for each $\varrho = 1, 2, \ldots, r$ the equality $T_{\varkappa\varrho}^* = T_{\varkappa\varrho}^{**}$ belongs to $\mathfrak{G}$. Thus the terms $T_{\varkappa\varrho}^*$ appear in the sequence $T_1^*, \ldots, T_k^*$ and the terms $T_{\varkappa\varrho}^{**}$ appear in the sequence $T_1^{**}, \ldots, T_k^{**}$. Using S_3 to S_5, S_9 and S_{13}, the right hand sides of the above equalities can be augmented in such a way that all the terms $T_1^*, \ldots, T_k^*$ and $T_1^{**}, \ldots, T_k^{**}$, respectively appear there in this order. Then we have

$$\vdash T_\varkappa^* = T_1^* \circ T_{\varkappa 1}^0 \vee T_2^* \circ T_{\varkappa 2}^0 \vee \ldots \vee T_k^* \circ T_{\varkappa k}^0 \vee \delta(T_\varkappa^*),$$
$$\vdash T_\varkappa^{**} = T_1^{**} \circ T_{\varkappa 1}^0 \vee T_2^{**} \circ T_{\varkappa 2}^0 \vee \ldots \vee T_k^{**} \circ T_{\varkappa k}^0 \vee \delta(T_\varkappa^{**}),$$

where, for $i = 1, \ldots, k$, either $T_{\varkappa i}^0 \equiv \mathbf{0}$ or

$$T_{\varkappa i}^0 \equiv \boldsymbol{x}^{(\nu_1)} \vee \ldots \vee \boldsymbol{x}^{(\nu_j)} \qquad (\text{for } 1 \leqq j \leqq r,\ 1 \leqq \nu_1 < \cdots < \nu_j \leqq r).$$

Therefore, these terms do not have the e-property and applying R_7 we obtain that for $\varkappa = 1, \ldots, k$

$$\vdash T_\varkappa^* = T_\varkappa^{**}.$$

Because of $T_1 \equiv T_1^*$ and $T_1' = T_1^{**}$ we have $\vdash T = T'$, which was to be shown.

R e m a r k. The proof of the completeness theorem also yields us a *syntactic* decision procedure for the set of valid equalities. Namely if we start from an equality $T = T'$ which is not valid, then the steps which in the case of a valid equality lead to the construction of a proof of this equality, can be carried out in the same way. However $T = T'$ is not valid and by Theorem 7.4 it is not deducible, hence there must exist a $\varkappa$ such that $\delta(T_\varkappa^*) \not\equiv \delta(T_\varkappa^{**})$, which can be determined in a single step. Now the syntactic decision procedure consists of constructing the terms $\delta(T_1^*), \ldots, \delta(T_k^*), \delta(T_1^{**}), \ldots, \delta(T_k^{**})$. If $\delta(T_\varkappa^*) \equiv \delta(T_\varkappa^{**})$ holds for each $\varkappa = 1, \ldots, k$, then the equality $T = T'$ is valid, otherwise it is not.

As an example we construct a proof of the valid equality

$$T_1 \equiv \langle \boldsymbol{a} \vee \boldsymbol{a} \circ \boldsymbol{b} \vee \boldsymbol{b} \circ \boldsymbol{a} \rangle = \big\langle \boldsymbol{b} \circ \boldsymbol{a} \vee \langle \boldsymbol{a} \rangle \circ \boldsymbol{a} \circ \boldsymbol{b} \big\rangle \circ \langle \boldsymbol{a} \rangle \equiv T_1'.$$

using the above procedure.

We have $X' = \{a, b\}$ and

$$\vdash T_1 = \langle \boldsymbol{a} \vee \boldsymbol{a} \circ \boldsymbol{b} \vee \boldsymbol{b} \circ \boldsymbol{a} \rangle \circ (\boldsymbol{a} \vee \boldsymbol{a} \circ \boldsymbol{b} \vee \boldsymbol{b} \circ \boldsymbol{a}) \vee \langle \boldsymbol{0} \rangle,$$

$$\vdash T_1 = (\langle \boldsymbol{a} \vee \boldsymbol{a} \circ \boldsymbol{b} \vee \boldsymbol{b} \circ \boldsymbol{a} \rangle \vee \langle \boldsymbol{a} \vee \boldsymbol{a} \circ \boldsymbol{b} \vee \boldsymbol{b} \circ \boldsymbol{a} \rangle \circ \boldsymbol{b}) \circ \boldsymbol{a} \vee ((\langle \boldsymbol{a} \vee \boldsymbol{a} \circ \boldsymbol{b} \vee \boldsymbol{b} \circ \boldsymbol{a} \rangle \circ \boldsymbol{a}) \circ \boldsymbol{b} \vee \langle \boldsymbol{0} \rangle,$$

$$\vdash T_1 = (T_1 \vee T_1 \circ \boldsymbol{b}) \circ \boldsymbol{a} \vee (T_1 \circ \boldsymbol{a}) \circ \boldsymbol{b} \vee \langle \boldsymbol{0} \rangle.$$

We put

$$T_2 \underset{\mathrm{Df}}{\equiv} T_1 \vee T_1 \circ \boldsymbol{b} \qquad \text{and} \qquad T_3 \underset{\mathrm{Df}}{\equiv} T_1 \circ \boldsymbol{a}$$

and obtain

$$\vdash T_1 = T_2 \circ \boldsymbol{a} \vee T_3 \circ \boldsymbol{b} \vee \langle \boldsymbol{0} \rangle. \tag{1}$$

Because $T_2 \equiv T_1 \vee T_1 \circ \boldsymbol{b}$,

$$\vdash T_2 = T_2 \circ \boldsymbol{a} \vee T_3 \circ \boldsymbol{b} \vee \langle \boldsymbol{0} \rangle \vee T_1 \circ \boldsymbol{b},$$

$$\vdash T_2 = T_2 \circ \boldsymbol{a} \vee (T_3 \vee T_1) \circ \boldsymbol{b} \vee \langle \boldsymbol{0} \rangle.$$

Thus

$$\vdash T_3 \vee T_1 = T_1 \circ \boldsymbol{a} \vee T_2 \circ \boldsymbol{a} \vee T_3 \circ \boldsymbol{b} \vee \langle \boldsymbol{0} \rangle,$$

$$\vdash T_3 \vee T_1 = (T_1 \vee T_2) \circ \boldsymbol{a} \vee T_3 \circ \boldsymbol{b} \vee \langle \boldsymbol{0} \rangle.$$

However,

$$\vdash T_1 \vee T_2 = T_2,$$

thus

$$\vdash T_3 \vee T_1 = T_2 \circ \boldsymbol{a} \vee T_3 \circ \boldsymbol{b} \vee \langle \boldsymbol{0} \rangle;$$

hence

$$\vdash T_3 \vee T_1 = T_1$$

and

$$\vdash T_2 = T_2 \circ \boldsymbol{a} \vee T_1 \circ \boldsymbol{b} \vee \langle \boldsymbol{0} \rangle. \tag{2}$$

Furthermore,

$$\vdash T_3 = T_1 \circ \boldsymbol{a} \vee \boldsymbol{0} \circ \boldsymbol{b} \vee \boldsymbol{0}.$$

We put $T_4 \equiv \boldsymbol{0}$ and obtain

$$\vdash T_3 = T_1 \circ \boldsymbol{a} \vee T_4 \circ \boldsymbol{b} \vee \boldsymbol{0}, \tag{3}$$

$$\vdash T_4 = T_4 \circ \boldsymbol{a} \vee T_4 \circ \boldsymbol{b} \vee \boldsymbol{0}. \tag{4}$$

Thus T_1 is characterized in the equalities (1) to (4) by means of the terms $T_1, \ldots, T_4$.

We have $\vdash \langle \boldsymbol{a} \rangle = \langle \boldsymbol{a} \rangle \circ \boldsymbol{a} \vee \langle \boldsymbol{0} \rangle$, thus

$$\vdash T_1' = \langle \boldsymbol{b} \circ \boldsymbol{a} \vee \langle \boldsymbol{a} \rangle \circ \boldsymbol{a} \circ \boldsymbol{b} \rangle \circ (\langle \boldsymbol{a} \rangle \circ \boldsymbol{a} \vee \langle \boldsymbol{0} \rangle),$$
$$\vdash T_1' = (T_1' \vee \langle \boldsymbol{b} \circ \boldsymbol{a} \vee \langle \boldsymbol{a} \rangle \circ \boldsymbol{a} \circ \boldsymbol{b} \rangle \circ \boldsymbol{b}) \circ \boldsymbol{a} \vee (T_1' \circ \boldsymbol{a}) \circ \boldsymbol{b} \vee \langle \boldsymbol{0} \rangle.$$

We put $T_2' \underset{\mathrm{Df}}{\equiv} T_1' \vee \langle \boldsymbol{b} \circ \boldsymbol{a} \vee \langle \boldsymbol{a} \rangle \circ \boldsymbol{a} \circ \boldsymbol{b} \rangle \circ \boldsymbol{b}$; $T_3' \equiv T_1' \circ \boldsymbol{a}$ and obtain

$$\vdash T_1' = T_2' \circ \boldsymbol{a} \vee T_3' \circ \boldsymbol{b} \vee \langle \boldsymbol{0} \rangle. \tag{5}$$

Furthermore,

$$\vdash T_2' = T_2' \circ \boldsymbol{a} \vee T_3' \circ \boldsymbol{b} \vee \langle \boldsymbol{0} \rangle \vee \langle \boldsymbol{b} \circ \boldsymbol{a} \vee \langle \boldsymbol{a} \rangle \circ \boldsymbol{a} \circ \boldsymbol{b} \rangle \circ \boldsymbol{b},$$
$$\vdash T_2' = T_2' \circ \boldsymbol{a} \vee (T_3' \vee \langle \boldsymbol{b} \circ \boldsymbol{a} \vee \langle \boldsymbol{a} \rangle \circ \boldsymbol{a} \circ \boldsymbol{b} \rangle) \circ \boldsymbol{b} \vee \langle \boldsymbol{0} \rangle.$$

By $T_4' \underset{\mathrm{Df}}{\equiv} T_3' \vee \langle \boldsymbol{b} \circ \boldsymbol{a} \vee \langle \boldsymbol{a} \rangle \circ \boldsymbol{a} \circ \boldsymbol{b} \rangle$, we have

$$\vdash T_2' = T_2' \circ \boldsymbol{a} \vee T_4' \circ \boldsymbol{b} \vee \langle \boldsymbol{0} \rangle. \tag{6}$$

Furthermore, by $T_5' \underset{\mathrm{Df}}{\equiv} \boldsymbol{0}$

$$\vdash T_3' = T_1' \circ \boldsymbol{a} \vee T_5' \circ \boldsymbol{b} \vee \boldsymbol{0}. \tag{7}$$

Finally we see that

$$\vdash T_4' = T_2' \circ \boldsymbol{a} \vee T_3' \circ \boldsymbol{b} \vee \langle \boldsymbol{0} \rangle, \tag{8}$$
$$\vdash T_5' = T_3' \circ \boldsymbol{a} \vee T_5' \circ \boldsymbol{b} \vee \boldsymbol{0}. \tag{9}$$

From (5) and (8) it follows that $\vdash T_1' = T_4'$ holds. Therefore, the term T_4' is superfluous. Now we obtain successively the following (valid) equalities:

$$T_1^* \equiv T_1 = T_1' \equiv T_1^{**},$$
$$T_2^* \equiv T_2 = T_2' \equiv T_2^{**},$$
$$T_3^* \equiv T_3 = T_3' \equiv T_3^{**},$$
$$T_4^* \equiv T_1 = T_4' \equiv T_4^{**},$$
$$T_5^* \equiv T_4 = T_5' \equiv T_5^{**}$$

and thus by (1) and (5)

$$\vdash T_1^* = T_1^* \circ \boldsymbol{0} \vee T_2^* \circ \boldsymbol{a} \vee T_3^* \circ \boldsymbol{b} \vee T_4^* \circ \boldsymbol{0} \vee T_5^* \circ \boldsymbol{0} \vee \langle \boldsymbol{0} \rangle,$$
$$\vdash T_1^{**} = T_1^{**} \circ \boldsymbol{0} \vee T_2^{**} \circ \boldsymbol{a} \vee T_3^{**} \circ \boldsymbol{b} \vee T_4^{**} \circ \boldsymbol{0} \vee T_5^{**} \circ \boldsymbol{0} \vee \langle \boldsymbol{0} \rangle,$$

by (2) and (6) (and $T_1^* \equiv T_4^*$)

$$\vdash T_2^* = T_1^* \circ \boldsymbol{0} \vee T_2^* \circ \boldsymbol{a} \vee T_3^* \circ \boldsymbol{0} \vee T_4^* \circ \boldsymbol{b} \vee T_5^* \circ \boldsymbol{0} \vee \langle \boldsymbol{0} \rangle,$$
$$\vdash T_2^{**} = T_1^{**} \circ \boldsymbol{0} \vee T_2^{**} \circ \boldsymbol{a} \vee T_3^{**} \circ \boldsymbol{0} \vee T_4^{**} \circ \boldsymbol{b} \vee T_5^{**} \circ \boldsymbol{0} \vee \langle \boldsymbol{0} \rangle,$$

by (3) and (7)

$$\vdash T_3^* \;= T_1^* \circ \boldsymbol{a} \vee T_2^* \circ \mathbf{0} \vee T_3^* \circ \mathbf{0} \vee T_4^* \circ \mathbf{0} \vee T_5^* \circ \boldsymbol{b} \vee \mathbf{0},$$
$$\vdash T_3^{**} = T_1^{**} \circ \boldsymbol{a} \vee T_2^{**} \circ \mathbf{0} \vee T_3^{**} \circ \mathbf{0} \vee T_4^{**} \circ \mathbf{0} \vee T_5^{**} \circ \boldsymbol{b} \vee \mathbf{0},$$

by (1) and (8)

$$\vdash T_4^* \;= T_1^* \circ \mathbf{0} \vee T_2^* \circ \boldsymbol{a} \vee T_3^* \circ \boldsymbol{b} \vee T_4^* \circ \mathbf{0} \vee T_5^* \circ \mathbf{0} \vee \langle \mathbf{0} \rangle,$$
$$\vdash T_4^{**} = T_1^{**} \circ \mathbf{0} \vee T_2^{**} \circ \boldsymbol{a} \vee T_3^{**} \circ \boldsymbol{b} \vee T_4^{**} \circ \mathbf{0} \vee T_5^{**} \circ \mathbf{0} \vee \langle \mathbf{0} \rangle,$$

by (5) and (9)

$$\vdash T_5^* \;= T_1^* \circ \mathbf{0} \vee T_2^* \circ \mathbf{0} \vee T_3^* \circ \mathbf{0} \vee T_4^* \circ \mathbf{0} \vee T_5^* \circ (\boldsymbol{a} \vee \boldsymbol{b}) \vee \mathbf{0},$$
$$\vdash T_5^{**} = T_1^{**} \circ \mathbf{0} \vee T_2^{**} \circ \mathbf{0} \vee T_3^{**} \circ \mathbf{0} \vee T_4^{**} \circ \mathbf{0} \vee T_5^{**} \circ (\boldsymbol{a} \vee \boldsymbol{b}) \vee \mathbf{0}.$$

Now we apply R_7 and obtain in particular

$$\vdash T_1 \;= T_1'.$$

The set A, our axiom system, is, of course, infinite. The answer to the question of whether there are also finite axiom systems for the set of valid equalities, depends largely on the set $\mathfrak{R}$ of admissible rules of inference. If X contains at least three different letters $a, b, c,$ we can immediately construct a complete finite system $[A^*, \mathfrak{R}^*]$. A^* consists of the 11 equalities which we obtain by substituting the term $\boldsymbol{a}$ for T and T_1, the term $\boldsymbol{b}$ for T_2 and finally $\boldsymbol{c}$ for T_3 in $S_1, S_2, \ldots, S_{11}$; $\mathfrak{R}^* \underset{\mathrm{Df}}{=} \{R_1, R_2, R_3, R_4^*\}$, where R_4^* denotes the following *substitution rule*:

(R_4^*) If $\vdash T_1 = T_2$, $x^0 \in X$ and T^* is a regular term over X then $\vdash T_1^* = T_2^*$ holds, where T_1^* and T_2^* are obtained from T_1 and T_2 respectively, by replacing *every* appearance of the symbol x^0 by the term T^*.

We can easily see that this rule of inference preserves validity and applying it, every equality belonging to A can be deduced from A^*. From Theorem 7.8 it follows then that every valid equality is deducible in $[A^*, \mathfrak{R}^*]$.

§ 8. Stable and Definite Automata

In this section we shall deal with automata whose efficiency is restricted in a special way. In general, the storing capacity and thus the efficiency of an abstract deterministic automaton depend only on its number of states. (See e.g., MARTYNJUK [1]). Here we shall consider automata whose storing capacity is also restricted in time. These machines automatically forget about the input signal x_t

received in step t after a certain time interval of length k, and therefore the signal put out in step $t+k$ does not depend on the input signal received in step t. If $t \geqq k$, then the signal put out in step t depends only on one part of the "past" namely on the signals received in steps $t-k+1, \ldots, t$.

This clearly represents a certain kind of stability property of automata. Indeed, if for example in step t the automaton's input is incorrect, i.e., the input signal described by the program is not fed in, but another signal, or the automaton makes a mistake in this step in calculating the next state, entering a state into which it would have entered had some other signal been fed in, then these mistakes automatically cease to have any effect after k steps. In other words, the automaton functions as though the mistake had never occured, provided no further mistakes have been made.

Automata of this kind are referred to as self correcting or self adjusting automata, and in practice are mainly used in coding and decoding messages. (See e.g. LÖWENSTEIN [1], [3]—[6], WINOGRAD [2].)

It is obvious that the transition functions of the automata which are stable in this sense, have special properties. Outputless automata with such transition functions were used in PERLES and others [1] to represent events. We shall characterize these events and show that they are exactly those which can in a certain sense be represented in non-initial automata.

Definition 8.1. Let $\mathfrak{A} = [X, Y, Z, \delta, \lambda]$ be a deterministic automaton $z \in Z$, and k a positive natural number.

(8.1.1) $\mathfrak{A}$ is called *weakly k-stable over z* if for all $p, r \in W(X)$ and $x \in X$ with $l(r) = k-1$

$$\lambda(\delta(z, pr), x) = \lambda(\delta(z, r), x).$$

(8.1.2) $\mathfrak{A}$ is called *weakly k-stable* if $\mathfrak{A}$ is weakly k-stable over each $z \in Z$.

(8.1.3) We say that $\mathfrak{A}$ is *k-stable* (*over z*) if $\mathfrak{A}$ is weakly k-stable (over z) and either $k = 1$ or $\mathfrak{A}$ is not weakly $(k-1)$-stable (over z).

(8.1.4) $\mathfrak{A}$ is called *stable* (*over z*) if there is a positive natural number k such that $\mathfrak{A}$ is k-stable (over z).

Theorem 8.1. *Let $\mathfrak{A} = [X, Y, Z, \delta, \lambda]$, $\mathfrak{A}' = [X, Y, Z', \delta', \lambda']$ be deterministic automata, furthermore let $z' \in Z'$, $z \in Z$.*

1. *If $z \sim z'$, then $\mathfrak{A}$ is (weakly) k-stable over z if and only if $\mathfrak{A}'$ is (weakly) k-stable over z'.*

2. *If $\mathfrak{A} \sim \mathfrak{A}'$, then $\mathfrak{A}$ is stable if and only if $\mathfrak{A}'$ is.*

3. *Stability is preserved under homomorphisms.*

4. *If $\mathfrak{A}$ is weakly k-stable over z, then $\mathfrak{A}$ is also weakly $(k+n)$-stable over z, for each $n \in \boldsymbol{nz}$.*

5. *$\mathfrak{A}$ is weakly k-stable over z if and only if for all $p, r \in W(X)$ and $x \in X$ with $l(r) \geqq k-1$ the equality $\lambda(\delta(z, pr), x) = \lambda(\delta(z, r), x)$ holds.*

6. *$\mathfrak{A}$ is weakly k-stable over z if and only if $\mathfrak{A}$ is weakly k-stable over each state $\delta(z, p)$ for $p \in W(X)$.*

7. *If* $\mathfrak{A}$ *is connected from the state* z *then* $\mathfrak{A}$ *is weakly* k*-stable over* z *if and only if* $\mathfrak{A}$ *is weakly* k*-stable.*

8. *If* $\mathfrak{A}$ *is strongly connected, and there is a* z *such that* $\mathfrak{A}$ *is weakly* k*-stable over* z*, then* $\mathfrak{A}$ *is weakly* k*-stable.*

Proof: Propositions 8.1.1 and 8.1.2 can be seen immediately if we remember that $z \sim z'$ always implies $\delta(z, pr) \sim \delta'(z', pr)$ and $\delta(z, r) \sim \delta'(z', r)$.

Suppose $\mathfrak{A}$ is weakly k-stable over z and $\chi = [\xi, \eta, \zeta]$ is a homomorphism of $\mathfrak{A}$ onto $\mathfrak{A}'' = [X'', Y'', Z'', \delta'', \lambda'']$. Then for $p, r \in W(X)$ and $x \in X$ with $l(r) = k - 1$

$$\lambda(\delta(z, pr), x) = \lambda(\delta(z, r), x),$$

hence

$$\eta(\lambda(\delta(z, pr), x)) = \eta(\lambda(\delta(z, r), x)),$$

i.e., by Theorem 3.1

$$\lambda''(\delta''(\zeta(z), \xi(pr)), \xi(x)) = \lambda''(\delta''(\zeta(z), \xi(r)), \xi(x));$$

and because ξ is a length invariant mapping of $W(X)$ onto $W(X'')$, for all $p'', r'' \in W(X'')$ and $x'' \in X''$ with $l(r'') = k - 1$ we have

$$\lambda''(\delta''(\zeta(z), p''r''), x'') = \lambda''(\delta''(\zeta(z), r''), x''),$$

hence $\mathfrak{A}''$ is weakly k-stable over $\zeta(z)$. This immediately implies Proposition 8.1.3.

If $\mathfrak{A}$ is weakly k-stable over z, then for all $p, r, u \in W(X)$ and $x \in X$ with $l(r) = k - 1$ and $l(u) = n$

$$\lambda(\delta(z, pur), x) = \lambda(\delta(z, r), x) = \lambda(\delta(z, ur), x),$$

and therefore $\mathfrak{A}$ is weakly $(k+n)$-stable over z. Propositions 8.1.4 and 8.1.5 follow immediately from this.

Suppose now $p \in W(X)$. Then for all $u, r \in W(X)$ and $x \in X$ with $l(r) \geqq k - 1$

$$\begin{aligned}\lambda(\delta(\delta(z, p), ur), x) &= \lambda(\delta(z, pur), x) = \lambda(\delta(z, r), x)\\ &= \lambda(\delta(z, pr), x) = \lambda(\delta(\delta(z, p), r), x),\end{aligned}$$

and thus $\mathfrak{A}$ is also weakly k-stable over $\delta(z, p)$. This proves 8.1.6. 8.1.7 and 8.1.8 follow from 8.1.6. Thus Theorem 8.1 is proved.

If $\mathfrak{A} = [X, Y, Z, \delta, \lambda]$ is an automaton and $M \subseteq Z$, then we denote by $\langle M\rangle$ the set of all states of the form $\delta(z, p)$, for $z \in M$ and $p \in W(X)$. By means of the same methods used in the proof of Theorem 6.5 (page 55) we can easily verify that $\langle M\rangle = \{\delta(z,p) \mid z \in M \wedge p \in W(X) \wedge l(p) \leqq Card(Z) - 1\}$, which is trivial, unless the set Z is finite.

Theorem 8.2. *Assume* $\mathfrak{A} = [X, Y, Z, \delta, \lambda]$ *is an automaton and* $z \in Z$.

1. $\mathfrak{A}$ *is weakly k-stable over z if and only if for all* $r \in W(X)$ *and* $x \in X$ *with* $l(r) = k - 1$ *(and consequently for all* $r \in W(X)$ *with* $l(r) \geqq k - 1$) *and for each* $z' \in \langle\{z\}\rangle$

$$\lambda(\delta(z', r), x) = \lambda(\delta(z, r), x).$$

2. $\mathfrak{A}$ *is weakly k-stable over z if and only if for all* $r \in W(X)$ *and* $x \in X$ *with* $l(r) \geqq k - 1$ *and each* $z' \in \langle\{z\}\rangle$

$$\delta(z, r) \sim \delta(z', r).$$

Proof: Proposition 8.2.1 is trivial. To prove 8.2.2, it suffices to show that $\delta(z, r) \sim \delta(z', r')$ if $\mathfrak{A}$ is weakly k-stable over z, $r \in W(X)$, $l(r) \geqq k - 1$ and $z' \in \langle\{z\}\rangle$ holds.

For such z, z' and r we shall prove by induction on p that

$$\lambda(\delta(z, r), p) = \lambda(\delta(z', r), p)$$

for all $p \in W(X)$. The initial step is trivial.

The induction step is taken from p to px for all $x \in X$: We have

$$\lambda(\delta(z', r), px) = \lambda(\delta(z', r), p)\, \lambda(\delta(z', rp), x).$$

By the induction hypothesis $\lambda(\delta(z', r), p) = \lambda(\delta(z, r), p)$, and because of $l(rp) \geqq l(r) \geqq k - 1$, we have $\lambda(\delta(z', rp), x) = \lambda(\delta(z, rp), x)$ and therefore $\lambda(\delta(z', r), px) = \lambda(\delta(z, r), px)$.

Definition 8.2. Let $\mathfrak{A} = [X, Y, Z, \delta, \lambda]$ be an automaton, $z \in Z$, and k a positive natural number.

(8.2.1) $\mathfrak{A}$ is called *weakly k-definite over z* if for all $p, r \in W(X)$ with $l(r) = k - 1$

$$\delta(z, pr) = \delta(z, r).$$

(8.2.2) $\mathfrak{A}$ is called *weakly k-definite* if $\mathfrak{A}$ is weakly k-definite over each $z \in Z$.

(8.2.3) We say that $\mathfrak{A}$ is *k-definite (over z)*, provided that $\mathfrak{A}$ is weakly k-definite over z and either $k = 1$ or $\mathfrak{A}$ is not weakly $(k-1)$-definite (over z).

(8.2.4) $\mathfrak{A}$ is called *definite (over z)* if there is a positive natural number k such that $\mathfrak{A}$ is k-definite (over z).

Corollary 8.3.

1. If $\mathfrak{A}$ is weakly k-definite (over z) then $\mathfrak{A}$ is weakly k-stable (over z).
2. Every definite automaton is stable.
3. If $\mathfrak{A}$ is reduced, then $\mathfrak{A}$ is stable if and only if it is definite.
4. $\mathfrak{A}$ is weakly k-definite over z if and only if $\mathfrak{A}$ is weakly k-definite over each state $z' \in \langle\{z\}\rangle$.
5. $\mathfrak{A}$ is weakly k-definite over z if and only if $\forall p \forall z' \forall z'' (p \in W(X) \wedge l(p) = k - 1 \wedge z', z'' \in \langle\{z\}\rangle \rightarrow \delta(z', p) = \delta(z'', p))$.

6. If $\mathfrak{A}$ is connected from the state z, then $\mathfrak{A}$ is weakly k-definite if and only if $\mathfrak{A}$ is weakly k-definite over z.

Theorem 8.4. (PERLES, RABIN, SHAMIR [1].)

1. *If* $\mathfrak{A} = [X, Y, Z, \delta, \lambda]$ *is k-definite over* $z \in Z$ *or k-stable over z, then* $Card\,(Z) \geqq Card\,(\langle\{z\}\rangle) \geqq k$.

2. *If* $Card\,(\langle\{z\}\rangle) = n$ *and* $\mathfrak{A}$ *is definite over z (or stable over z) then* $\mathfrak{A}$ *is weakly n-definite over z (or weakly n-stable over z).*

Proof: First we show that $Card\,(\langle\{z\}\rangle) \geqq k$ holds, if $\mathfrak{A}$ is k-definite over z. For $k = 1$ this is trivial because of $z \in \langle\{z\}\rangle$. Assume now $k \geqq 2$. We construct by induction a sequence of partitions $\mathfrak{R}_1, \mathfrak{R}_2, \ldots$ of the set $\langle\{z\}\rangle$:

$$\mathfrak{R}_1 \underset{\mathrm{Df}}{=} \{\{z'\} \mid z' \in \langle\{z\}\rangle\}.$$

If the partition $\mathfrak{R}_i$ $(i \geqq 1)$ has already been defined, then we put as $\mathfrak{R}_{i+1}$ the partition of $\langle\{z\}\rangle$ for which

a) $$\forall z'\big(z' \in \langle\{z\}\rangle \to \exists M^{i+1}(M^{i+1} \in \mathfrak{R}_{i+1} \wedge z' \in M^{i+1})\big),$$

b) $$\forall z'\,\forall z''\big(z', z'' \in \langle\{z\}\rangle \to \big[\exists M^{i+1}(z', z'' \in M^{i+1} \in \mathfrak{R}_{i+1}) \leftrightarrow \forall x\big(x \in X \to \exists M^i(\delta(z', x), \delta(z'', x) \in M^i \in \mathfrak{R}_i)\big)\big]\big).$$

Lemma 8.4a. *For all* $z', z'' \in \langle\{z\}\rangle$, $i = 1, 2, \ldots,$

$$\exists M^i(z', z'' \in M^i \in \mathfrak{R}_i) \leftrightarrow \forall p\big(p \in W(X) \wedge l(p) \geqq i - 1 \to \delta(z', p) = \delta(z'', p)\big).$$

We shall prove this by induction on i. The initial step $i = 1$ is trivial, since $\forall p\big(p \in W(X) \wedge l(p) \geqq 0 \to \delta(z', p) = \delta(z'', p)\big)$ holds obviously if and only if $z' = z''$. The induction step is taken from i to $i + 1$. We have

$$\begin{aligned}
&\forall p\big(p \in W(X) \wedge l(p) \geqq i \to \delta(z', p) = \delta(z'', p)\big)\\
&\leftrightarrow \forall x\,\forall p\big(x \in X \wedge p \in W(X) \wedge l(p) \geqq i - 1\\
&\qquad\qquad \to \delta(\delta(z', x), p) = \delta(\delta(z'', x), p)\big)\\
&\leftrightarrow \forall x\big(x \in X \to \exists M^i(\delta(z', x), \delta(z'', x) \in M^i \in \mathfrak{R}_i)\big)\\
&\leftrightarrow \exists M^{i+1}(z', z'' \in M^{i+1} \in \mathfrak{R}_{i+1}).
\end{aligned}$$

Thus, for all $i = 1, 2, \ldots,$ $\mathfrak{R}_i$ is a partition of $\langle\{z\}\rangle$. Clearly, the partition $\mathfrak{R}_i$ is always a refinement of the partition $\mathfrak{R}_{i+1}$ (or $\mathfrak{R}_{i+1}$ is a "coarsening" of $\mathfrak{R}_i$). We can easily verify that $\mathfrak{R}_i = \mathfrak{R}_{i+1}$ implies $\mathfrak{R}_{i+1} = \mathfrak{R}_{i+2}$, hence $\mathfrak{R}_i = \mathfrak{R}_{i+j}$ for all $j \in \boldsymbol{nz}$. Thus if $\mathfrak{R}_{i+1} \neq \mathfrak{R}_i$, then $\mathfrak{R}_1 \neq \mathfrak{R}_2 \neq \ldots \neq \mathfrak{R}_{i-1} \neq \mathfrak{R}_i \neq \mathfrak{R}_{i+1}$.

Lemma 8.4b. $\mathfrak{A}$ *is weakly i-definite over z if and only if* $\mathfrak{R}_i = \{\langle\{z\}\rangle\}$ *holds.*

This follows immediately from the fact that $\mathfrak{A}$ is weakly i-definite over z if and only if one of the following assertions holds:

$$\forall z' \forall z'' \forall p \big(p \in W(X) \wedge l(p) \geqq i - 1 \wedge z', z'' \in \langle\{z\}\rangle \rightarrow \delta(z', p) = \delta(z'', p)\big),$$

$$\forall z' \forall z'' \big(z', z'' \in \langle\{z\}\rangle \rightarrow \exists M^i (z', z'' \in M^i \in \mathfrak{K}_i)\big),$$

$$\mathfrak{K}_i = \big\{\langle\{z\}\rangle\big\}.$$

Now we have $k \geqq 2$; $\mathfrak{A}$ is weakly k-definite over z and not weakly $(k-1)$-definite over z. Consequently $\mathfrak{K}_{k-1} \neq \mathfrak{K}_k$, and therefore $\mathfrak{K}_1 \neq \mathfrak{K}_2 \neq \cdots \neq \mathfrak{K}_{k-1} \neq \mathfrak{K}_k = \mathfrak{K}_{k+1}$.

The partition $\mathfrak{K}_k$ contains exactly one class and is a proper coarsening of $\mathfrak{K}_{k-1}$. Therefore $\mathfrak{K}_{k-1}$ contains at least two classes, and $\mathfrak{K}_1$ contains at least k classes, i.e., we have $Card\ (\langle\{z\}\rangle) \geqq k$ and, consequently also $Card\ (Z) \geqq k$.

If $\mathfrak{A}$ is k-stable over z then the reduct $\overline{\mathfrak{A}} = [X, Y, \overline{Z}, \overline{\delta}, \overline{\lambda}]$ of $\mathfrak{A}$ is k-definite over $[z]$. Therefore, by $Card\ (\langle\{z\}\rangle) \geqq Card\ (\langle\{[z]\}\rangle) \geqq k$, the second part of Proposition 8.4.1 is also verified. Proposition 8.4.2 follows immediately from 8.4.1.

From 8.2.1, 8.3.5, and 8.4.2 we obtain

Corollary 8.5. Definiteness and stability are decidable properties of finite automata.

Let us consider the automaton $\mathfrak{A}_3^n = [\{x\}, \{0, 1\}, \{0, 1, \ldots, n\}, \delta^3, \lambda^3]$ (cf. § 2), whose graph is represented in Fig. 4 for the case $n = 3$. We can easily see that $\mathfrak{A}_3^n$ is both stable and definite over the state n. Furthermore we have $\langle\{n\}\rangle = \{0, 1, 2, \ldots, n\}$. $\mathfrak{A}_3^n$ is weakly $(n+1)$-definite over n, since for all x^m with $m \geqq n$, and k, l with $0 \leqq k, l \leqq n$, $\delta^3(k, x^m) = 0 = \delta^3(l, x^m)$; however, it is not weakly n-definite, since $\delta^3(n, x^{n-1}) = 1 \neq 0 = \delta^3(0, x^{n-1})$. Consequently $\mathfrak{A}_3^n$ is $(n+1)$-definite over the state n. Moreover $\mathfrak{A}_3^n$ is also $(n+1)$-stable over n. Since $\mathfrak{A}_3^n$ has exactly $n+1$ states, the upper bound $Card\ (\langle\{z\}\rangle)$ given in Theorem 8.4 cannot be improved.

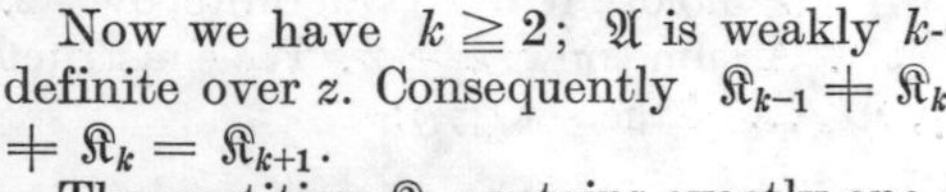

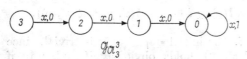

Fig. 4

Definition 8.3. A sequential function φ over $[X, Y]$ is said to be (*weakly*) *k-stable*, if φ can be generated in an automaton $\mathfrak{A}$ by z, where A is (weakly) k-stable over z.

Theorem 8.6. *Let φ be a sequential function over $[X, Y]$.*

1. *φ is weakly k-stable if and only if for all $p, r \in W(X)$ with $l(r) = k - 1$ the equality $\varphi_{pr} = \varphi_r$ holds.*
2. *φ is (weakly) k-stable if and only if $\mathfrak{A}^\varphi$ is (weakly) k-definite.*
3. *If φ is k-stable, then $k \leqq Card\ \big(\{\varphi_p \mid p \in W(X)\}\big)$.*

4. *If X is finite, and φ is k-stable, then φ only possesses a finite number of states, namely at least k and at most $(Card\,(X))^k$.*

Proof: Suppose that φ is generated by z in $\mathfrak{A} = [X, Y, Z, \delta, \lambda]$. Consequently, φ is weakly k-stable if and only if $\mathfrak{A}$ is weakly k-stable over z, i.e., if and only if for all $p, r \in W(X)$ with $l(r) = k - 1$

$$\delta(z, pr) \sim \delta(z, r).$$

By 4.6, this holds if and only if for all $p, r \in W(X)$ with $l(r) = k - 1$ the equality $\varphi_{pr} = \varphi_r$ is satisfied.

Since φ is generated by φ_e in $\mathfrak{A}^\varphi$ (cf. 4.5) and $\mathfrak{A}^\varphi$ is connected from the state φ_e, φ is (weakly) k-stable if and only if $\mathfrak{A}^\varphi$ is (weakly) k-stable. Since $\mathfrak{A}^\varphi$ is reduced, this holds if and only if $\mathfrak{A}^\varphi$ is (weakly) k-definite. Since the number of states of $\mathfrak{A}^\varphi$ is equal to $Card\,(\{\varphi_p \mid p \in W(X)\})$, Theorem 8.4 implies that $k \leq Card\,(\{\varphi_p \mid p \in W(X)\})$, provided that φ is k-stable. (For sequential functions with infinitely many states this is trivial.)

Proposition 8.6.4 follows immediately from 8.6.1, 8.6.2, and 8.4.1.

Definition 8.4. An event E over X is called *(weakly) k-definite* if there is an initial outputless automaton $\mathfrak{A} = [X, Z, \delta, z_1]$ which is (weakly) $(k+1)$-definite over z_1 and a set $M \subseteq Z$ such that E is represented in $\mathfrak{A}$ by M.

Corollary 8.7. The impossible event $\emptyset$ and the certain event $W(X)$ are weakly k-definite for each $k = 0, 1, 2, \ldots,$ and thus 0-definite. All the other events can only be k-definite for $k > 0$.

Theorem 8.8. *Let E be an event over X, and k a natural number.*

1. *E is weakly k-definite if and only if $E = E' \cup W(X) \cdot E''$, where $E' = \{p \mid p \in E \wedge l(p) < k\}$ and $E'' = \{p \mid p \in E \wedge l(p) = k\}$.*

2. *If E is (weakly) k-definite, and X is finite, then E is regular.*

Proof: Suppose E is weakly k-definite and $\mathfrak{A} = [X, Z, \delta, z_1]$, $M \subseteq Z$ are such that $\mathfrak{A}$ is weakly $(k+1)$-*definite* over z_1, and for all $p \in W(X)$

$$p \in E \leftrightarrow \delta(z_1, p) \in M.$$

For $pr \in W(X)$ with $l(r) = k$ we have $\delta(z_1, pr) = \delta(z_1, r)$, hence for all $pr \in W(X)$ with $l(r) = k$

$$pr \in E \leftrightarrow \delta(z_1, pr) \in M \leftrightarrow r \in E.$$

Consequently, $E = E' \cup W(X) \cdot E''$.

Conversely, if this equality is satisfied, then we consider the automaton $\mathfrak{A}^* = [X, Z^*, \delta^*, e]$, where $Z^* = \{p \mid p \in W(X) \wedge l(p) \leqq k\}$ and for $p \in Z^*$, $x \in X$ we have

$$\delta^*(p, x) = \begin{cases} px, & \text{if } l(p) < k, \\ e, & \text{if } p = e \text{ and } k = 0, \\ x_2 \ldots x_k x, & \text{if } p = x_1 \ldots x_k,\ l(p) = k \geqq 1. \end{cases}$$

(Thus for $k = 0$ we put $Z^* = \{e\}$.) $M^* = E' \cup E'' \subseteq Z^*$, and obviously E is represented by M^* in $\mathfrak{A}^* = [X, Z^*, \delta^*, e]$. $\mathfrak{A}^*$ is weakly $(k+1)$-definite over e, since for all $p, r \in W(X)$ with $l(r) = k$ $\delta^*(e, pr) = r = \delta^*(e, r)$ holds. If X is finite, so is $\mathfrak{A}^*$, and therefore E is regular. Thus Theorem 8.8 is proved.

Corollary 8.9. Every finite event E is weakly k-definite if we put

$$k = \max_{p \in E} l(p) + 1.$$

Theorem 8.10. *The automaton* $\mathfrak{A} = [X, Y, Z, \delta, \lambda]$ *is weakly k-stable over* $z \in Z$, *if and only if every event* E_y^z, *which is representable in the initial automaton* $\mathfrak{A}_z = [X, Y, Z, \delta, \lambda, z]$ *by means of an output signal* $y \in Y$, *is weakly k-definite.*

Proof: The automaton $\mathfrak{A}$ is weakly k-stable over z if and only if

$$\forall p \forall r \forall x (p, r \in W(X) \wedge x \in X \wedge l(r) = k - 1 \\ \rightarrow \lambda(\delta(z, pr), x) = \lambda(\delta(z, r), x))$$

i.e., if

$$\forall p \forall r \forall x \Big(p, r \in W(X) \wedge x \in X \wedge l(r) = k - 1 \\ \rightarrow \forall y \big(y \in Y \rightarrow \big(\lambda(\delta(z, pr), x) = y \leftrightarrow \lambda(\delta(z, r), x) = y\big)\big)\Big)$$

is satisfied, or if

$$\forall p \forall r \forall x (p, r \in W(X) \wedge x \in X \wedge l(r) = k - 1 \\ \rightarrow \forall y (y \in Y \rightarrow (prx \in E_y^z \leftrightarrow rx \in E_y^z))).$$

This is true if and only if

$$\forall y \big(y \in Y \rightarrow \forall p \forall r (p, r \in W(X) \wedge l(r) = k \rightarrow (pr \in E_y^z \leftrightarrow r \in E_y^z))\big).$$

is satisfied.

The last proposition is equivalent to saying that, for all $y \in Y$, the event E_y^z represented by the output signal y in $\mathfrak{A}_z$ is weakly k-definite.

We can prove analogously the following

Theorem 8.11. *An outputless automaton* $\mathfrak{A} = [X, Z, \delta]$ *is weakly k-definite over* $z \in Z$ *if and only if every event* $E_{z'}^z$, *which is representable in the initial (outputless) automaton* $\mathfrak{A}_z = [X, Z, \delta, z]$ *by means of a singleton* $\{z'\} \subseteq Z$, *is weakly* $(k-1)$*-definite.*

Next we shall deal with the representability of events in *non-initial* automata. We have no information about the initial state of such an automaton. Therefore, whether the state of the automaton, after application of a word p, belongs to the representing set M or not, must not depend on the initial state, if, from the property of this state (namely that it belongs to M) we wish to infer a property of the input word p (namely that it belongs to E). For reasons which will become clear later, we define the representability of events in non-initial automata in such a way that it depends on a parameter k.

Definition 8.5. We say that the event E over X is *k-represented* in the non-initial automaton $\mathfrak{A} = [X, Z, \delta]$ *by the set* M if

$$\forall z \forall p\big(z \in Z \wedge p \in W(X) \wedge l(p) \geqq k \to (p \in E \leftrightarrow \delta(z, p) \in M)\big).$$

Thus for k-representability it is only for the words $p \in W(X)$ with $l(p) \geqq k$ that we require that the automaton should function "correctly", in that we can decide after the application of p whether or not $p \in E$ holds. It is clear that there are automata in which only the trivial events $W(X)$ and $\emptyset$ (by the sets Z and $\emptyset$ respectively) can be k-represented and in which no set M with $\emptyset \neq M \subset Z$ k-represents any event. Let us consider as an example the automaton $\mathfrak{A}_5 = [\{0, 1\}, \{a, b\}, \delta^5]$ where

$$\delta^5(z, x) = \begin{cases} a, & \text{if} \quad z = a,\ x = 0 \quad \text{or} \quad z = b,\ x = 1, \\ b & \text{otherwise}. \end{cases}$$

$M = \{a\}$ does not k-represent any event, since

$$\delta^5(a, 0^k) = a \in M, \qquad \delta^5(b, 0^k) = b \notin M.$$

From $a \in Z$, $0^k \in W(X)$, $l(0) = k$ and $\delta^5(a, 0^k) \in M$

$$0^k \in E$$

would follow if $\{a\}$ represented an event E in $\mathfrak{A}_5$, in contradiction to $\delta^5(b, 0^k) = b \notin M$. Similarly we can show that no event is k-represented by $\{b\}$.

Theorem 8.12. *Suppose* $E \subseteq W(X)$ *is k-represented by* $M \subseteq Z$ *in* $\mathfrak{A} = [X, Z, \delta]$. *Then we have*

1. $\forall p\big(p \in W(X) \wedge l(p) \geqq k \to \big(\exists z(z \in Z \wedge \delta(z, p) \in M) \leftrightarrow \forall z(z \in Z \to \delta(z, p) \in M)\big)\big).$
2. $\forall p \forall r\big(p \in W(X) \wedge r \in E \to pr \in E\big).$
3. $\forall p \forall r\big(p \in W(X) \wedge pr \in E \wedge l(r) \geqq k \to r \in E\big).$
4. *The event E is weakly k-definite.*

Proof: Suppose $p \in W(X)$ and $l(p) \geqq k$. If $p \in E$ then by Definition 8.5, $\forall z\big(z \in Z \to \delta(z, p) \in M\big)$ holds. If $p \notin E$, then for *all* $z \in Z$ we have $\delta(z,p) \notin M$, hence the hypothesis $\exists z\big(z \in Z \wedge \delta(z, p) \in M\big)$ is not satisfied. This shows that Proposition 8.12.1 is true.

Next we show that $r \in E$ implies $pr \in E$. Since (by $r \in E$) $\delta(z, r) \in M$ holds for each $z \in Z$, a fortiori we have $\delta\big(\delta(z, p), r\big) = \delta(z, pr) \in M$ for each $z \in Z$, hence $pr \in E$.

If $pr \in E$ then $\delta(z, pr) \in M$ holds for each $z \in Z$. Therefore, there exists at least one state z^* for which $\delta(z^*, r) \in M$ (namely $z^* \in \{\delta(z, p) \mid z \in Z\}$).

Consequently, we have by 8.12.1, and because of $l(r) \geqq k$, $\delta(z, r) \in M$ for each $z \in Z$, i.e., $r \in E$. Putting $E' = \{p \mid p \in E \wedge l(p) < k\}$, and $E'' = \{p \mid p \in E \wedge l(p) = k\}$ we have, by 8.12.2 and 8.12.3,

$$E = E' \cup W(X) \cdot E'',$$

i.e., E is weakly k-definite.

Corollary 8.13.

1. An event is k-representable (in a non-initial automaton) if and only if it is weakly k-definite.

2. An event E over X is k-representable in a finite non-initial automaton if and only if X is finite and E is weakly k-definite.

Thus an event E is 0-representable (and this corresponds to the usual definition of representability) if and only if E is weakly 0-definite and hence 0-definite. Therefore, only the trivial events $\emptyset$ and $W(X)$ are 0-representable (cf. 8.7). This is the reason why the parameter k appears in Definition 8.5.

Theorem 8.14. *Every k-definite event can be k-represented in a $(k+1)$-definite non-initial automaton.*

Proof: For $\emptyset$ and $W(X)$ this is trivial. Assume $k \neq 0$, $E = E' \cup W(X) \cdot E''$ where E' and E'' are as above.

If $E'' = \emptyset$, then the assertion is again trivial, because every automaton of the required type yields what we need by putting $M = \emptyset$. Let us put

$$Z = \{p \mid p \in W(X) \wedge l(p) = k\},$$
$$\delta(x_1 \ldots x_k, x) = x_2 \ldots x_k x \quad \text{for all} \quad x_1 \ldots x_k \in Z,\ x \in X.$$

Here for every $p, r \in W(X)$, $z \in Z$ with $l(r) = k$

$$\delta(z, pr) = \delta(z, r) = r,$$

Thus, $\mathfrak{A} = [X, Z, \delta]$ is $(k+1)$-definite and E is k-represented in $\mathfrak{A}$ by $E'' \subseteq Z$.

§ 9. Experiments

In this section we shall investigate some of the problems which arise when abstract deterministic automata are considered as "black boxes". This means we shall try to obtain information about the inside of the black box from certain external behaviour which develops if we feed into it certain signals. A psychiatrist is in a similar situation when he uses tests to find out what is wrong with his patient's nervous system; or a pyrotechnist who has to find out how the fuse of an unexploded infernal machine works.

It is clear that in general such a problem cannot be solved unless we already have some information about the black box, or, in this case, about the automaton under consideration.

An experiment on an abstract automaton means the application of a certain sequence of input signals $x_1 x_2 \dots x_n$. Thus, an experiment can only be carried out if the input alphabet of the automaton is at least partially known. Whenever we assume, as the experiment dictates, certain information about the black box, we obtain what we call a *black-box-situation.*

Suppose that we are given a concrete system described by a weakly initial automaton $\mathfrak{A} = [X, Y, Z, \delta, \lambda, Z_1]$. In step 1, $\mathfrak{A}$ is in one of the states belonging to the set Z_1; however if $Card\,(Z_1) \geqq 2$ then we cannot say in exactly which state. Thereby a black-box-situation is given: the problem to find out in which state $\mathfrak{A}$ is in step 1. If we can solve this problem, then we can immediately answer the second question arising in this black-box-situation, namely the question: in which state is $\mathfrak{A}$ at the end of the experiment? Obviously, this is the state $\delta(z, x_1 \dots x_n)$, provided that, by applying the word $x_1 \dots x_n$, we have decided that the state of $\mathfrak{A}$ in step 1 was z.

First we shall deal with the problem of identifying the state of $\mathfrak{A}$ in step 1. This situation can be described as a game between the black box (i.e. the automaton $\mathfrak{A}$) and the experimenter, in which the automaton tries to keep its initial state hidden. A move of the experimenter consists in applying an input signal, and the counter move of the automaton consists in putting out an output signal. The experimenter wins the game if we can find out in a finite number of moves in which state $\mathfrak{A}$ was in step 1. Therefore, this problem is solvable if and only if there is a winning strategy for the experimenter. We shall call such a winning strategy an *identification strategy of the first kind* (in abbreviation: IS 1).

The experimenter's work, described by a winning strategy, actually consists of pulse-wise information processing; therefore it can always be carried out (cf. § 4) by an automaton.

We can assume without any loss of generality that in the automaton $\mathfrak{A} = [X, Y, Z, \delta, \lambda, Z_1]$ under consideration, the intersection $Z_1 \cap X$ is empty. Suppose $\hat{\mathfrak{A}} = [Y, Z_1 \cup X, \hat{Z}, \hat{\delta}, \hat{\lambda}, x_1]$ is an initial automaton with the initial state x_1, where $x_1 \in X$. For the sake of brevity we shall put for $z \in Z_1$

$$x_1^z = x_1, \quad y_1^z = \lambda(z, x_1), \quad x_2^z = \hat{\lambda}(x_1, y_1^z),$$

and for $i \geqq 2,\ z \in Z_1$

$$y_i^z \underset{\mathrm{Df}}{=} \begin{cases} \lambda\big(\delta(z, x_1^z \dots x_{i-1}^z), x_i^z\big), & \text{if } x_1^z, \dots, x_i^z \in X, \\ \text{not defined} & \text{otherwise;} \end{cases}$$

$$x_{i+1}^z \underset{\mathrm{Df}}{=} \begin{cases} \hat{\lambda}\big(\hat{\delta}(x_1, y_1^z \dots y_{i-1}^z), y_i^z\big), & \text{if } y_1^z, \dots, y_i^z \text{ are defined} \\ \text{not defined} & \text{otherwise.} \end{cases}$$

We can readily see that $\hat{\mathfrak{A}}$ (or more precisely the initial state of $\hat{\mathfrak{A}}$) realizes an identification strategy of the first kind for $\hat{\mathfrak{A}}$, if and only if the following two conditions hold:

a) There exists a natural number n such that y_n^z is not defined for each $z \in Z_1$.

b) For every $z \in Z_1$ there exists an i with $1 \leqq i \leqq n$ such that $x_i^z = z$.

We shall illustrate this with the following example: Let us put $\mathfrak{A}_6 = [X, Y, Z, \delta^6, \lambda^6, Z_1]$, where

$$Z = \{a, b, c, d, e\},\ Z_1 = \{a, b, c, d\},\ X = \{0, 1, 2\},\ Y = \{0, 1\}$$

and δ^6, λ^6 are given by the following table:

δ^6	a	b	c	d	e	λ^6	a	b	c	d	e
0	a	b	c	d	e	0	0	0	1	1	1
1	a	b	e	d	e	1	1	0	0	0	0
2	e	d	c	d	e	2	0	0	1	0	0

Then $\hat{\mathfrak{A}}_6 = [Y, Z_1 \cup X, \{0, A, B\}\ \hat{\delta}^6, \hat{\lambda}^6, 0]$, realizes an IS 1 for $\mathfrak{A}_6$, provided that δ^6, λ^6 are given by the following table:

$\hat{\delta}^6$	0	A	B	$\hat{\lambda}^6$	0	A	B
0	A	A	B	0	1	b	d
1	B	A	B	1	2	a	c

since

$$x_1^z = 0,$$
$$y_1^a = y_1^b = 0; \quad y_1^c = y_1^d = 1,$$
$$x_2^a = x_2^b = 1; \quad x_2^c = x_2^d = 2,$$
$$y_2^a = 1, \quad y_2^b = 0; \quad y_2^c = 1, \quad y_2^d = 0,$$
$$x_3^a = a, \quad x_3^b = b; \quad x_3^c = c, \quad x_3^d = d.$$

If $\hat{\mathfrak{A}}$ realizes an IS 1 for A, then we call the smallest n, for which x_{n+1}^z belongs to Z_1 or is not defined for each $z \in Z_1$, the *length* of this strategy. Thus the automaton $\mathfrak{A}_6$ has an IS 1 of length 2.

If the game with the weakly initial automaton $\mathfrak{A} = [X, Y, Z, \delta, \lambda, Z_1]$ (with *Card* $(Z_1) \geqq 2$) is aimed at finding out in which state the automaton is at the end of the experiment, then we call a winning strategy for the experimenter an *identification strategy of the second kind* (abbreviated: IS 2). As we have already mentioned, each IS 1 yields us an IS 2 since, if by applying the word p to $\mathfrak{A}$ we can decide that in step 1, $\mathfrak{A}$ was in the state $z_1 \in Z_1$, then at the end of the application of p, $\mathfrak{A}$ is in the state $\delta(z_1, p)$.

The following problems arise in the investigation of the above mentioned types of strategies.

1. *The existence problem*

Here, we seek a criterion (a necessary and sufficient condition) for the possession by a given weakly initial automaton $\mathfrak{A}$ of an identification strategy of the first or second kind.

It is obviously necessary, for the existence of an IS 1 for $\mathfrak{A}$, that the states from Z_1 be pairwise inequivalent. However, this condition is only sufficient for the existence of an IS 2 and not for the possession by $\mathfrak{A}$ of an IS 1, as has already been shown by Moore [1].

By the length of an identification strategy of first or second kind on a weakly initial automaton, we mean the number of steps the experimenter needs in the worst case, in order to find the answer to the given question. For the natural numbers $n \geqq k \geqq 2$ let $\alpha(n, k)$ (resp. $\beta(n, k)$) be the maximum of the lengths of the shortest identification strategies of the first (resp. second) kind, on automata $[X, Y, Z, \delta, \lambda, Z_1]$ with $Card\,(Z) = n$ and $Card\,(Z_1) = k$.

2. *The length problem*

Here we seek a formula for $\alpha(n, k)$ and $\beta(n, k)$, respectively.

Both problems are unsolved in the general case. Therefore, we shall consider here a special type of identification strategy which we shall call *identification experiments*. By this we mean an identification strategy without ramifications, where the input word applied is not constructed step by step in the course of the experiment, in dependence of the output signals of the automaton, but is already known before the experiment.

We shall first consider identification experiments of the first kind.

Let $\mathfrak{A} = [X, Y, Z, \delta, \lambda, Z_1]$ be an arbitrary weakly initial automaton with $Card\,(Z_1) \geqq 2$. Without any loss of generality we can assume that for each $z \in Z$ there are a $z_1 \in Z_1$, and $p \in W(X)$ such that $z = \delta(z_1, p)$, since otherwise we can consider the corresponding subautomaton. Let us put for $p \in W(X)$

$$\mathfrak{A}(p) \underset{\mathrm{Df}}{=} \{q \mid \exists z_1 (z_1 \in Z_1 \wedge \lambda(z_1, p) = q)\}.$$

Definition 9.1. A word $p \in W(X)$ is called *identification experiment of the first kind* (IE 1) for $\mathfrak{A} = [X, Y, Z, \delta, \lambda, Z_1]$, if the function

$$\lambda_p(z) \underset{\mathrm{Df}}{=} \lambda(z, p) \quad \text{für} \quad z \in Z_1$$

establishes a one-to-one mapping of Z_1 onto $\mathfrak{A}(p)$.

Thus if an IE 1 p is known for $\mathfrak{A}$ then we only have to apply p to $\mathfrak{A}$ and the resulting output word $q \in \mathfrak{A}(p)$ will show us in which state $\mathfrak{A}$ was in step 1.

Corollary 9.1.

1. A word p is an IE 1 for $\mathfrak{A}$ if and only if, for all $z, z' \in Z_1$, $z \neq z'$ implies $\lambda(z, p) \neq \lambda(z', p)$.
2. If Z_1 is finite, then p is an IE 1 for $\mathfrak{A}$ if and only if $Card(Z_1) = Card(\mathfrak{A}(p))$.
3. If p is an IE 1 for $\mathfrak{A}$ and $r \in W(X)$, then pr is also an IE 1 for $\mathfrak{A}$.
4. If $\mathfrak{A}$ has an IE 1, then the states belonging to Z_1 are pairwise inequivalent.
5. If $\mathfrak{A}$ has an IE 1 p, and Y is finite, then $\mathfrak{A}(p)$ ($\subseteq Y^{l(p)}$) is finite, and consequently Z_1 is finite.
6. There are automata which have an IS 1 but no IE 1.

As an example which illustrates Proposition 9.1.6, we can take the automaton $\mathfrak{A}_6$ mentioned above (cf. page 95 below).

Now we shall solve the *existence problem* for identification experiments of the first kind. Let $\mathfrak{A} = [X, Y, Z, \delta, \lambda, Z_1]$ be an arbitrary weakly initial automaton with $Card\,(Z_1) \geqq 2$ and (according to our above convention)

$$Z = \{\delta(z_1, p) \mid z_1 \in Z_1 \wedge p \in W(X)\}.$$

By induction we shall define a function $\mathfrak{Z}_{\mathfrak{A}}$ on $W(X)$, whose values will be partitions of Z.

Initial step: $\mathfrak{Z}_{\mathfrak{A}}(e) = \{Z\}$.

Induction step: Suppose that $\mathfrak{Z}_{\mathfrak{A}}(p)$ has already been defined and $x \in X$. Then we define as $\mathfrak{Z}_{\mathfrak{A}}(px)$ that partition of Z for which

$$\forall z\, \forall z' \big(z, z' \in Z \to \big[\exists M\, (z, z' \in M \in \mathfrak{Z}_{\mathfrak{A}}(px)) \leftrightarrow \lambda(z, x) = \lambda(z', x) \wedge \exists N\, (\delta(z, x), \delta(z', x) \in N \in \mathfrak{Z}_{\mathfrak{A}}(p))\big]\big).$$

Let $\mathfrak{Z}^*$ be the set of all partitions $\mathfrak{z}$ of Z such that for arbitrary $z, z' \in Z_1$

$$\exists M\, (z, z' \in M \in \mathfrak{z}) \to z = z'.$$

We shall denote by p^* the inverse of the word p (cf. § 6).

Theorem 9.2. *Let* $\mathfrak{A} = [X, Y, Z, \delta, \lambda, Z_1]$ *be a weakly initial automaton.*

1. *For all* $z, z' \in Z$, $p \in W(X)$ *we have*

$$\exists M \big(z, z' \in M \in \mathfrak{Z}_{\mathfrak{A}}(p)\big) \leftrightarrow \lambda(z, p^*) = \lambda(z', p^*).$$

2. *A word* $p \in W(X)$ *is an IE* 1 *for* $\mathfrak{A}$ *if and only if* $\mathfrak{Z}_{\mathfrak{A}}(p^*) \in \mathfrak{Z}^*$.
3. *For all* $p, r, u \in W(X)$ *we have*

$$\mathfrak{Z}_{\mathfrak{A}}(p) = \mathfrak{Z}_{\mathfrak{A}}(r) \to \mathfrak{Z}_{\mathfrak{A}}(pu) = \mathfrak{Z}_{\mathfrak{A}}(ru).$$

4. *If X and Z are finite sets, then the question whether $\mathfrak{A}$ has an IE 1 is decidable and the set of all IE 1's for $\mathfrak{A}$ is regular.*

Proof: We shall prove 9.2.1 by induction on p. The initial step $p = e$ is trivial. The step from p to px is as follows:

For $z, z' \in Z$ we have

$$\begin{aligned}
&\exists M\big(z, z' \in M \in \mathfrak{Z}_{\mathfrak{A}}(px)\big)\\
&\leftrightarrow \lambda(z, x) = \lambda(z', x) \wedge \exists N\big(\delta(z, x), \delta(z', x) \in N \in \mathfrak{Z}_{\mathfrak{A}}(p)\big)\\
&\leftrightarrow \lambda(z, x) = \lambda(z', x) \wedge \lambda\big(\delta(z, x), p^*\big) = \lambda\big(\delta(z', x), p^*\big)\\
&\leftrightarrow \lambda(z, xp^*) = \lambda(z', xp^*)\\
&\leftrightarrow \lambda\big(z, (px)^*\big) = \lambda\big(z', (px)^*\big).
\end{aligned}$$

Proposition 9.2.2 follows immediately from 9.2.1, the definition of $\mathfrak{Z}^*$, and 9.1.1, while 9.2.3 can easily be shown by induction on u.

If Z is finite, then $\tilde{\mathfrak{Z}} \underset{\mathrm{Df}}{=} \{\mathfrak{Z}_{\mathfrak{A}}(p) \mid p \in W(X)\}$ and $\mathfrak{Z}^*$ are finite sets.

If moreover X is finite, then $\tilde{\mathfrak{Z}}$ can be constructed algorithmically. For $\tilde{\mathfrak{z}} \in \tilde{\mathfrak{Z}}$ and $x \in X$ we put

$$\tilde{\delta}(\tilde{\mathfrak{z}}, x) = \mathfrak{Z}_{\mathfrak{A}}(px), \quad \text{if} \quad \tilde{\mathfrak{z}} = \mathfrak{Z}_{\mathfrak{A}}(p).$$

This definition is justified by 9.2.3. $\tilde{\mathfrak{A}} = [X, \tilde{\mathfrak{Z}}, \tilde{\delta}, \mathfrak{Z}_{\mathfrak{A}}(e)]$ is a finite initial outputless automaton such that

$$\tilde{\delta}\big(\mathfrak{Z}_{\mathfrak{A}}(e), p\big) = \mathfrak{Z}_{\mathfrak{A}}(p),$$

for all $p \in W(X)$. Suppose E is the event represented in $\tilde{\mathfrak{A}}$ by the set $\tilde{\mathfrak{Z}} \cap \mathfrak{Z}^*$. Clearly then, E^* is the set of all identification experiments of the first kind for $\mathfrak{A}$ and this set (the inverse of E) is regular. By Theorem 6.6 it is decidable whether E^* (or E) is empty.

Now we show that the automaton $\mathfrak{A}_6$ given above has no IE1. We have

$$\begin{aligned}
\mathfrak{Z}_{\mathfrak{A}_6}(e) &= \big\{\{a, b, c, d, e\}\big\},\\
\mathfrak{Z}_{\mathfrak{A}_6}(0) &= \big\{\{a, b\}, \{c, d, e\}\big\},\\
\mathfrak{Z}_{\mathfrak{A}_6}(1) &= \big\{\{a\}, \{b, c, d, e\}\big\},\\
\mathfrak{Z}_{\mathfrak{A}_6}(2) &= \big\{\{a, b, d, e\}, \{c\}\big\},
\end{aligned}$$

$$\begin{aligned}
\mathfrak{Z}_{\mathfrak{A}_6}(00) &= \big\{\{a, b\}, \{c, d, e\}\big\} = \mathfrak{Z}_{\mathfrak{A}_6}(0),\\
\mathfrak{Z}_{\mathfrak{A}_6}(01) &= \big\{\{a\}, \{b\}, \{c, d, e\}\big\},\\
\mathfrak{Z}_{\mathfrak{A}_6}(02) &= \big\{\{a, b, d, e\}, \{c\}\big\} = \mathfrak{Z}_{\mathfrak{A}_6}(2),
\end{aligned}$$

$$\begin{aligned}
\mathfrak{Z}_{\mathfrak{A}_6}(10) &= \big\{\{a\}, \{b\}, \{c, d, e\}\big\} = \mathfrak{Z}_{\mathfrak{A}_6}(01),\\
\mathfrak{Z}_{\mathfrak{A}_6}(11) &= \big\{\{a\}, \{b, c, d, e\}\big\} = \mathfrak{Z}_{\mathfrak{A}_6}(1),\\
\mathfrak{Z}_{\mathfrak{A}_6}(12) &= \big\{\{a, b, d, e\}, \{c\}\big\} = \mathfrak{Z}_{\mathfrak{A}_6}(2),
\end{aligned}$$

$$
\begin{aligned}
\mathfrak{Z}_{\mathfrak{A}_6}(20) &= \{\{a, b\}, \{c\}, \{d, e\}\}, \\
\mathfrak{Z}_{\mathfrak{A}_6}(21) &= \{\{a\}, \{b, c, d, e\}\} &&= \mathfrak{Z}_{\mathfrak{A}_6}(1), \\
\mathfrak{Z}_{\mathfrak{A}_6}(22) &= \{\{a, b, d, e\}, \{c\}\} &&= \mathfrak{Z}_{\mathfrak{A}_6}(2), \\
\\
\mathfrak{Z}_{\mathfrak{A}_6}(010) &= \{\{a\}, \{b\}, \{c, d, e\}\} &&= \mathfrak{Z}_{\mathfrak{A}_6}(01), \\
\mathfrak{Z}_{\mathfrak{A}_6}(011) &= \{\{a\}, \{b\}, \{c, d, e\}\} &&= \mathfrak{Z}_{\mathfrak{A}_6}(01), \\
\mathfrak{Z}_{\mathfrak{A}_6}(012) &= \{\{a, b, d, e\}, \{c\}\} &&= \mathfrak{Z}_{\mathfrak{A}_6}(2), \\
\\
\mathfrak{Z}_{\mathfrak{A}_6}(200) &= \{\{a, b\}, \{c\}, \{d, e\}\} &&= \mathfrak{Z}_{\mathfrak{A}_6}(20), \\
\mathfrak{Z}_{\mathfrak{A}_6}(201) &= \{\{a\}, \{b\}, \{c, d, e\}\} &&= \mathfrak{Z}_{\mathfrak{A}_6}(01), \\
\mathfrak{Z}_{\mathfrak{A}_6}(202) &= \{\{a, b, d, e\}, \{c\}\} &&= \mathfrak{Z}_{\mathfrak{A}_6}(2).
\end{aligned}
$$

hence $\tilde{\mathfrak{Z}}_6 = \{\mathfrak{Z}_{\mathfrak{A}_6}(e), \mathfrak{Z}_{\mathfrak{A}_6}(0), \mathfrak{Z}_{\mathfrak{A}_6}(1), \mathfrak{Z}_{\mathfrak{A}_6}(2), \mathfrak{Z}_{\mathfrak{A}_6}(01), \mathfrak{Z}_{\mathfrak{A}_6}(20)\}$ and $\tilde{\mathfrak{Z}}_6 \cap \mathfrak{Z}_6^* = \emptyset$.

Consequently $\mathfrak{A}_6$ has no IE1.

Remark on the *length problem* for identification experiments of the first kind: Suppose that $a(n, k)$ for $n \geqq k \geqq 2$ is the maximum of the lengths of the shortest identification experiments of the first kind for automata $\mathfrak{A} = [X, Y, Z, \delta, \lambda, Z_1]$ with $Card\,(Z) = n$, $Card\,(Z_1) = k$. For all n, k $(n \geqq k \geqq 2)$ we have

$$1 \leqq \alpha(n, k) \leqq a(n, k) < n!.$$

Indeed, there are at most $n!$ partitions of the n-element set Z, since the mapping assigning to each permutation π of Z that partition $\mathfrak{z}$ of Z in which the states z, z' belong to the same class if and only if they belong to the same cycle of π, is a single-valued mapping of the set of all permutations of Z onto the set of all partitions of Z. Therefore, the automaton $\tilde{\mathfrak{A}}$ has at most $n!$ states, and thus for each shortest p with $\tilde{\delta}(\mathfrak{Z}_{\mathfrak{A}}(e), p) \in \tilde{\mathfrak{Z}} \cap \mathfrak{Z}^*$ we have $l(p) < n!$.

Moreover, Theorem 2.6 and the example $\mathfrak{A}_3^k$ imply

$$a(n, 2) = n - 1.$$

We shall show below, following the solution of the length problem for identification experiments of the second kind (or shortly IE 2) that

$$a(n, k) \geqq \frac{k-1}{2}(2n - k).$$

The length problem for identification experiments of the first kind (on finite automata) is unsolved. Using methods developed in the solution of the length problem for identification experiments of the second kind on reduced automata, we can easily show that

$$\alpha(n, k) \leqq a(n, k) < 2^n.$$

For automata $\mathfrak{A} = [X, Y, Z, \delta, \lambda, Z_1]$ with

$$\forall z \forall z' \forall x \big(z, z' \in Z \wedge z \neq z' \wedge x \in X \to \delta(z, x) \neq \delta(z', x)\big)$$

every IS 2 is obviously an IS 1 and every IE 2 is an IE 1. Therefore, the length problem for IE 1 on such automata is solvable, as we shall see below.

Definition 9.2. A word $p \in W(X)$ is called an *identification experiment of the second kind* (IE 2) on the weakly initial automaton $\mathfrak{A} = [X, Y, Z, \delta, \lambda, Z_1]$, if there is a function ψ from $\mathfrak{A}(p)$ into Z such that for each $z \in Z_1$

$$\psi\big(\lambda(z, p)\big) = \delta(z, p).$$

Corollary 9.3.

1. Every IE1 for $\mathfrak{A}$ is an IE2 for $\mathfrak{A}$.
2. A word $p \in W(X)$ is an IE2 for $\mathfrak{A}$ if and only if for all $z, z' \in Z_1$ we have

$$\lambda(z, p) = \lambda(z', p) \to \delta(z, p) = \delta(z', p).$$

3. If $\mathfrak{A}$ has an IE2, then there is an IS2 for $\mathfrak{A}$.
4. There are automata which have an IS2 but no IE2.

An example which illustrates Proposition 9.3.4 is the automaton $\mathfrak{A}_6$ defined above, which has an IS 1 and hence an IS 2.

To solve the *existence problem* for IE 2's on finite weakly initial automata $\mathfrak{A} = [X, Y, Z, \delta, \lambda, Z_1]$, we define by induction a function $\mathfrak{M}_{\mathfrak{A}}$ on $W(X)$ whose values are subsets of $\mathfrak{P}(Z)$.

Initial step: $\mathfrak{M}_{\mathfrak{A}}(e) \underset{\mathrm{Df}}{=} \{Z_1\}$.

Induction step: $p \to px$:

$$\mathfrak{M}_{\mathfrak{A}}(px) \underset{\mathrm{Df}}{=} \big\{M \mid \mathit{Card}\,(M) \geqq 2$$
$$\wedge \exists N \exists y\big(N \in \mathfrak{M}_{\mathfrak{A}}(p) \wedge M = \{\delta(z, x) \mid z \in N \wedge y = \lambda(z, x)\}\big)\big\}.$$

Theorem 9.4. *Let* $\mathfrak{A} = [X, Y, Z, \delta, \lambda, Z_1]$ *be a weakly initial automaton.*

1. *For all* $z, z' \in Z$ *with* $z \neq z'$, $p \in W(X)$,

$$\exists M\big(M \in \mathfrak{M}_{\mathfrak{A}}(p) \wedge z, z' \in M\big)$$
$$\leftrightarrow \exists z_1 \exists z_1'\big(z_1, z_1' \in Z_1 \wedge \lambda(z_1, p) = \lambda(z_1', p)$$
$$\wedge z = \delta(z_1, p) \wedge z' = \delta(z_1', p)\big).$$

2. *For all* $p, r, u \in W(X)$, $\mathfrak{M}_{\mathfrak{A}}(p) = \mathfrak{M}_{\mathfrak{A}}(r) \to \mathfrak{M}_{\mathfrak{A}}(pu) = \mathfrak{M}_{\mathfrak{A}}(ru)$.
3. *A word* $p \in W(X)$ *is an IE 2 for* $\mathfrak{A}$ *if and only if* $\mathfrak{M}_{\mathfrak{A}}(p) = \emptyset$.

Proof: We shall prove 9.4.1 by induction on p. The initial step $p = e$ is trivial. Suppose $z, z' \in Z$ and $z \neq z'$. Then we have

$$\begin{aligned}
&\exists M\big(z, z' \in M \in \mathfrak{M}_{\mathfrak{A}}(px)\big)\\
&\leftrightarrow \exists M \exists N \exists y\big(N \in \mathfrak{M}_{\mathfrak{A}}(p) \wedge Card(M) \geqq 2\\
&\qquad\qquad \wedge z, z' \in M = \{\delta(z'', x) \mid z'' \in N \wedge \lambda(z'', x) = y\}\big)\\
&\leftrightarrow \exists N\big(N \in \mathfrak{M}_{\mathfrak{A}}(p) \wedge \exists z^* \exists z^{**}(z^*, z^{**} \in N \wedge \lambda(z^*, x) = \lambda(z^{**}, x)\\
&\qquad\qquad \wedge \delta(z^*, x) = z \wedge \delta(z^{**}, x) = z')\big)\\
&\leftrightarrow \exists z_1 \exists z_1' \exists z^* \exists z^{**}\big(z_1, z_1' \in Z_1 \wedge \lambda(z_1, p) = \lambda(z_1', p) \wedge z^* = \delta(z_1, p)\\
&\qquad\qquad \wedge z^{**} = \delta(z_1', p) \wedge z = \delta(z^*, x) \wedge z' = \delta(z^{**}, x)\\
&\qquad\qquad \wedge \lambda(z^*, x) = \lambda(z^{**}, x)\big)\\
&\leftrightarrow \exists z_1 \exists z_1'\big(z_1, z_1' \in Z_1 \wedge z = \delta(z_1, px) \wedge z' = \delta(z_1', px)\\
&\qquad\qquad \wedge \lambda(z_1, px) = \lambda(z_1', px)\big).
\end{aligned}$$

Proposition 9.4.2 can be easily verified by induction on u. A word $p \in W(X)$ is an IE 2 for $\mathfrak{A}$ if and only if for $z_1, z_1' \in Z_1$ with $z_1 \neq z_1'$

$$\lambda(z_1, p) = \lambda(z_1', p) \rightarrow \delta(z_1, p) = \delta(z_1', p),$$

that is if and only if $\mathfrak{M}_{\mathfrak{A}}(p)$ is empty.

This proves Theorem 9.4.

Let us put

$$\tilde{\mathfrak{M}}_{\mathfrak{A}} \underset{\mathrm{Df}}{=} \{\mathfrak{M}_{\mathfrak{A}}(p) \mid p \in W(X)\} \cup \{\emptyset\}.$$

If Z is finite, so is $\tilde{\mathfrak{M}}_{\mathfrak{A}}$. If moreover X is finite, then $\tilde{\mathfrak{M}}_{\mathfrak{A}}$ can be constructed in finitely many steps. For $m \in \tilde{\mathfrak{M}}_{\mathfrak{A}}$ and $x \in X$ we put

$$\tilde{\delta}(m, x) = \begin{cases} \mathfrak{M}_{\mathfrak{A}}(px), & \text{if} \quad m = \mathfrak{M}_{\mathfrak{A}}(p);\\ \emptyset & \text{otherwise}. \end{cases}$$

By 9.4.2 this definition is justified. Now the set of all IE 2's for $\mathfrak{A}$ is represented in the initial automaton $\tilde{\mathfrak{A}} = [X, \tilde{\mathfrak{M}}_{\mathfrak{A}}, \tilde{\delta}, \{Z_1\}]$ by the set $\{\emptyset\}$.

Corollary 9.5. If X and Z_1 are finite sets, then the question whether $\mathfrak{A}$ has an IE2 is decidable, and the set of all IE2's for $\mathfrak{A}$ is regular.

Let us consider as an example the (reduced) automaton

$$\mathfrak{A}_7 = [\{0, 1\}, \{0, 1\}, \{1, 2, 3, 4\}, \delta^7, \lambda^7, \{1, 2, 3, 4\}],$$

where δ^7, λ^7 are given in the following table:

δ^7	1	2	3	4	λ^7	1	2	3	4
0	2	3	4	1	0	0	0	0	0
1	3	2	1	4	1	0	0	0	1

The graph of the corresponding automaton $\tilde{\tilde{\mathfrak{A}}}_7$ is shown on Fig. 5. The lexicographically first (shortest) IE 2 for $\mathfrak{A}_7$ is the word 100101.

Using the same method we can easily show that the automaton $\mathfrak{A}_6$ has no IE 2. Namely we have:

$\mathfrak{M}_{\mathfrak{A}_6}(e) \;\; = \{\{a, b, c, d\}\}$;

$\mathfrak{M}_{\mathfrak{A}_6}(0) \;\; = \{\{a, b\}, \{c, d\}\}$;

$\mathfrak{M}_{\mathfrak{A}_6}(1) \;\; = \{\{b, d, e\}\}$;

$\mathfrak{M}_{\mathfrak{A}_6}(2) \;\; = \{\{d, e\}\}$;

furthermore

$\mathfrak{M}_{\mathfrak{A}_6}(00) = \mathfrak{M}_{\mathfrak{A}_6}(0)$,

$\mathfrak{M}_{\mathfrak{A}_6}(01) = \mathfrak{M}_{\mathfrak{A}_6}(2) = \mathfrak{M}_{\mathfrak{A}_6}(02)$;

$\mathfrak{M}_{\mathfrak{A}_6}(10) = \mathfrak{M}_{\mathfrak{A}_6}(2)$,

$\mathfrak{M}_{\mathfrak{A}_6}(11) = \mathfrak{M}_{\mathfrak{A}_6}(1)$,

$\mathfrak{M}_{\mathfrak{A}_6}(12) = \mathfrak{M}_{\mathfrak{A}_6}(2)$;

$\mathfrak{M}_{\mathfrak{A}_6}(20) = \mathfrak{M}_{\mathfrak{A}_6}(21) = \mathfrak{M}_{\mathfrak{A}_6}(22) = \mathfrak{M}_{\mathfrak{A}_6}(2)$;

consequently there is no p with $\mathfrak{M}_{\mathfrak{A}_6}(p) = \emptyset$.

The length problem for IE 2's is unsolved.

Now we turn to the solution of the length problem for IE 2's on *reduced* (Z-finite) automata. In this we shall follow GINSBURG's work [10]. Theorem 9.7 below is due to HIBBARD [1].

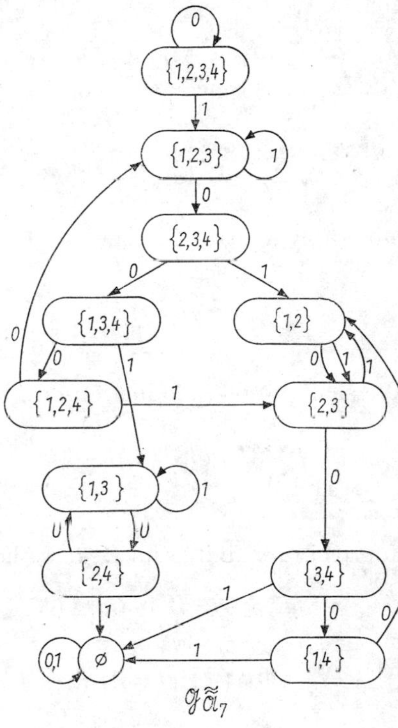

Fig. 5

Lemma 9.6. *Let* $\mathfrak{M} = \{M(\alpha) \mid \alpha \in A\}$ *be a finite system of finite non-empty sets. For* $M, N \in \mathfrak{M}$ *let* $M * N$ *abbreviate the following statement: There are sets* $M_1, M_2, \ldots, M_i \in \mathfrak{M}$ *such that* $M = M_1$, $N = M_i$ *and* $M_j \cap M_{j+1} \neq \emptyset$ *for each* $j = 1, \ldots, i-1$. *Furthermore we put*

$$[M] = \bigcup_{M * N,\, N \in \mathfrak{M}} N$$

for $M \in \mathfrak{M}$, *and finally let* $\overline{\mathfrak{M}} = \{[M] \mid M \in \mathfrak{M}\}$. *Then we have*

1. $\overline{\mathfrak{M}}$ *is a partition of* $\bigcup \mathfrak{M}$.
2. $\sum_{\alpha \in A} \mathit{Card}\,(M(\alpha)) - \mathit{Card}\,(\bigcup \mathfrak{M}) \geqq \mathit{Card}\,(A) - \mathit{Card}\,(\overline{\mathfrak{M}})$.

Proof: Ad 9.6.1. Since $M \in \mathfrak{M}$ implies $M * M$, $M \subseteq [M]$, hence $\bigcup \overline{\mathfrak{M}} = \bigcup \mathfrak{M}$. Now we show that $[M] \cap [N] \neq \emptyset$ implies $[M] = [N]$. Let

$$\bigcup_{M * M^*} M^* \cap \bigcup_{N * N^*} N^* \neq \emptyset .$$

Then there are $M^*, N^* \in \mathfrak{M}$ with $M^* \cap N^* \neq \emptyset$, $M * M^*$ and $N * N^*$. Consequently $M * N$ is satisfied and because the relation $*$ is transitive, we have $[M] = [N]$.

Ad 9.6.2. Let $[M] \in \overline{\mathfrak{M}}$ be arbitrary and $D = \{\alpha \mid \in A \wedge M(\alpha) \subseteq [M]\}$, $\mathit{Card}\,(D) = d$. Since the elements of $\overline{\mathfrak{M}}$ are pairwise disjoint, proposition 9.6.2 is implied by

$$\sum_{\alpha \in D} \mathit{Card}\,(M(\alpha)) - \mathit{Card}\,([M]) \geqq \mathit{Card}\,(D) - 1 = d - 1 .$$

Obviously we can re-enumerate the set D in such a way that $D = \{\alpha_1, \alpha_2, \ldots, \alpha_d\}$, and for $1 \leqq i < d$

$$\bigcup_{j=1}^{i} M(\alpha_j) \cap M(\alpha_{i+1}) \neq \emptyset .$$

We shall prove by induction on i that for $1 \leqq i \leqq d$ we have

$$\sum_{j=1}^{i} \mathit{Card}\,(M(\alpha_j)) - \mathit{Card}\left(\bigcup_{j=1}^{i} M(\alpha_j)\right) \geqq i - 1 .$$

For $i = 1$ this is trivial. The step from i to $i + 1$:
For arbitrary finite sets K, L we have

$$K \cap L \neq \emptyset \rightarrow \mathit{Card}\,(K) + \mathit{Card}\,(L) - \mathit{Card}\,(K \cup L) \geqq 1,$$

$$\mathit{Card}\left(\bigcup_{j=1}^{i} M(\alpha_j)\right) + \mathit{Card}\,(M(\alpha_{i+1})) - \mathit{Card}\left(\bigcup_{j=1}^{i+1} M(\alpha_j)\right) \geqq 1,$$

$$\begin{aligned} &\sum_{j=1}^{i+1} \mathit{Card}\,(M(\alpha_j)) - \mathit{Card}\left(\bigcup_{j=1}^{i+1} M(\alpha_j)\right) \\ &= \sum_{j=1}^{i} \mathit{Card}\,(M(\alpha_j)) + \mathit{Card}\,(M(\alpha_{i+1})) - \mathit{Card}\left(\bigcup_{j=1}^{i+1} M(\alpha_j)\right) \\ &\geqq \sum_{j=1}^{i} \mathit{Card}\,(M(\alpha_j)) + \mathit{Card}\,(M(\alpha_{i+1})) + 1 - \mathit{Card}\left(\bigcup_{j=1}^{i} M(\alpha_j)\right) \\ &\quad - \mathit{Card}\,(M(\alpha_{i+1})) \geqq i - 1 + 1 = i . \end{aligned}$$

Thus Lemma 9.6 is proved.

Theorem 9.7 (Hibbard [1]). *Let* $\mathfrak{A} = [X, Y, Z, \delta, \lambda]$ *be a reduced Z-finite automaton,* $\mathfrak{M} = \{Z_i \mid 1 \leqq i \leqq d\}$ *a non-empty system of pairwise disjoint non-empty subsets of* Z, $Card\,(Z) = n \geqq 2$ *and* $Card\,(\bigcup \mathfrak{M}) = m > d$. *Then there is a* $p \in W(X)$ *such that* p *is an IE 2 for all the weakly initial automata* $\mathfrak{A}^i = [X, Y, Z, \delta, \lambda, Z_i]$ *and*

$$l(p) \leqq \sum_{\nu=n-m+d}^{n-1} \nu.$$

Proof: The proof will be carried out by induction on $m-d$. (The assumption $m > d$ assures us that there is a set Z_i which contains at least two elements.) If $m - d = 1$, then we have exactly one set $Z_{i*} \in \mathfrak{M}$, which is not a singleton, and this set Z_{i*} contains exactly two states z_1, z_2. Since $\mathfrak{A}$ is reduced, there is a $p \in W(X)$ for which

$$l(p) \leqq n - 1 = \sum_{\nu=n-(m-d)}^{n-1} \nu.$$

Obviously, p is an IE 2 for each $\mathfrak{A}^i$ $(1 \leqq i \leqq d)$.

The induction step is taken from $m' - d' < m - d$ to $m - d$, where $m - d > 1$. We shall first show that there is a $p \in W(X)$ with $l(p) \leqq n - m + d$ such that at least one $Z_i \in \mathfrak{M}$ contains two different states z, z' for which $\lambda(z, p) \neq \lambda(z', p)$.

$m > d$ implies $n - m + d \leqq n - 1$, and because $\mathfrak{A}$ is reduced, the partition $\mathfrak{z}_{n-m+d}$ has at least $n - m + d + 1$ classes (cf. § 2). Suppose that for each $i = 1, \ldots, d$ there exists a class $K_i \in \mathfrak{z}_{n-m+d}$ for which $Z_i \subseteq K_i$. Now we have $Card\,(\bigcup \mathfrak{M}) = m$, hence $Card\,(Z \setminus \bigcup \mathfrak{M}) = n - m$. Consequently, there are at most $n-m$ classes K in $\mathfrak{z}_{n-m+d}$ such that no i exists with $Z_i \subseteq K$, moreover there are at most d classes K for which such an i exists. Thus we obtain that $\mathfrak{z}_{n-m+d}$ has at most $n - m + d$ classes, which is in contradiction to our above result. This shows that there is a set $Z_i \in \mathfrak{M}$ which contains two different states z, z' lying in different classes of the partition $\mathfrak{z}_{n-m+d}$, and therefore we also have a $p \in W(X)$ with $l(p) \leqq n - m + d$ and $\lambda(z, p) \neq \lambda(z', p)$.

We choose such a word $p \in W(X)$ and define

$$A = \{[i, q] \mid 1 \leqq i \leqq d \wedge \exists z(z \in Z_i \wedge \lambda(z, p) = q)\}.$$

We have $Card(A) \geqq d + 1$, since for each i with $1 \leqq i \leqq d$ there is at least one $q \in W(Y)$ with $[i, q] \in A$, and thus, by the choice of p, for at least one i there are words q, q' $(q = \lambda(z, p), q' = \lambda(z', p))$ with $[i, q] \in A$, $[i, q'] \in A$ and $q \neq q'$.

For $[i, q] \in A$ we put

$$Z_{i,q} = \{\delta(z, p) \mid z \in Z_i \wedge \lambda(z, p) = q\}.$$

We shall distinguish two cases.

I. For all $[i, q] \in A$ we have $Card(Z_{i,q}) \leqq 1$.

In this case p satisfies our requirements. Indeed we have

$$l(p) = n - m + d \leqq \sum_{\nu=n-m+d}^{n-1} \nu,$$

and p is an IE2 for each $\mathfrak{A}^i$, since $z, z' \in Z_i$ and $\lambda(z, p) = \lambda(z', p)$ imply $[i, \lambda(z, p)] \in A$ and $\delta(z, p)$, $\delta(z', p) \in Z_{i,\lambda(z,p)}$; because $Card(Z_{i,\lambda(z,p)}) \leqq 1$ we have $\delta(z, p) = \delta(z', p)$. By 9.3.2 it follows that p is an IE2 for $\mathfrak{A}^i$.

II. There is an $[i, q] \in A$ with $Card(Z_{i,q}) \geqq 2$.

Let us put $\mathfrak{N} = \{Z_{i,q} \mid [i, q] \in A\}$. $\mathfrak{N}$ satisfies the assumptions of Lemma 9.6, since

$$A = \bigcup_{i=1}^{d} \Big(\{i\} \times \bigcup_{z \in Z_i} \{\lambda(z, p)\}\Big)$$

is finite, because for each i the set $\bigcup_{z \in Z_i} \{\lambda(z, p)\}$ has at most as many elements as Z_i. The sets $Z_{i,q}$ are also non-empty and finite $\big(Card(Z_{i,q}) \leqq Card(Z_i) \leqq n\big)$. Therefore the partition $\overline{\mathfrak{N}}$ exists (cf. Lemma 9.6). Let us put

$$d' \underset{\mathrm{Df}}{=} Card\,(\overline{\mathfrak{N}}), \qquad m' \underset{\mathrm{Df}}{=} Card\,(\bigcup \overline{\mathfrak{N}}).$$

Then

$$\bigcup \overline{\mathfrak{N}} = \bigcup_{[i,q] \in A} Z_{i,q}, \qquad \text{hence} \qquad m' = Card\Big(\bigcup_{[i,q] \in A} Z_{i,q}\Big).$$

$\overline{\mathfrak{N}}$ is a non-empty finite system of non-empty pairwise disjoint subsets of Z. Since at least one of the sets $Z_{i,q}$ is not a singleton, we have $m' > d'$. Now we show that

$$m' - d' < m - d.$$

By Lemma 9.6.2 we have

$$\sum_{[i,q] \in A} Card\,(Z_{i,q}) - Card\,(\bigcup \mathfrak{N}) \geqq Card\,(A) - Card\,(\overline{\mathfrak{N}}).$$

On the other hand, we have $A = \{[i, q] \mid 1 \leqq i \leqq d \wedge q \in \mathfrak{A}^i(p)\}$, and for all i

$$\sum_{q \in \mathfrak{A}^i(p)} Card\,(Z_{i,q}) \leqq Card\,(Z_i).$$

because the sets Z_i are pairwise disjoint,

$$\sum_{[i,q] \in A} Card\,(Z_{i,q}) = \sum_{i=1}^{d} \sum_{q \in \mathfrak{A}^i(p)} Card\,(Z_{i,q}) \leqq \sum_{i=1}^{d} Card\,(Z_i) = m.$$

Hence,

$$m - m' \geqq \sum_{[i,q] \in A} Card\,(Z_{i,q}) - m' \geqq Card\,(A) - d'$$

$$\geqq d + 1 - d' > d - d',$$

which implies $m' - d' < m - d$. By the induction hypothesis, there exists a word r with

$$l(r) \leqq \sum_{\nu=n-m'+d'}^{n-1} \nu$$

such that r is an IE2 for every automaton $\mathfrak{A}^N = [X, Y, Z, \delta, \lambda, N]$ for $N \in \overline{\mathfrak{N}}$. We claim that pr is an IE2 for each $\mathfrak{A}^i$. Let $1 \leqq i \leqq d$ and $z, z' \in Z_i$ with $\lambda(z, pr) = \lambda(z', pr)$. Then we have $\lambda(z, p) = \lambda(z' p)$ and $\delta(z, p), \delta(z', p) \in Z_{i,\lambda(z,p)}$. There is an $N \in \overline{\mathfrak{N}}$ such that $Z_{i,\lambda(z,p)} \subseteq N$. Now $\lambda(\delta(z, p), r) = \lambda(\delta(z', p), r)$ implies $\delta(z, pr) = \delta(\delta(z, p), r) = \delta(\delta(z', p), r) = \delta(z', pr)$, because r is an IE2 for $\mathfrak{A}^N$. Thus the word pr is an IE2 for $\mathfrak{A}^i$.

Moreover we have

$$l(pr) \leqq n - m + d + \sum_{\nu=n-m'+d'}^{n-1} \nu \leqq \sum_{\nu=n-m+d}^{n-1} \nu,$$

because $m' - d' < m - d$ implies $n - m + d < n - m' + d'$. This completes the proof of Hibbard's theorem.

Corollary 9.8. If $\mathfrak{A} = [X, Y, Z, \delta, \lambda]$ is a reduced Z-finite automaton, then for each weakly initial automaton

$$\mathfrak{A}^{Z_1} = [X, Y, Z, \delta, \lambda, Z_1] \text{ with } Z_1 \subseteq Z,\ Card(Z) = n \geqq 2,\ Card(Z_1) = k \geqq 2$$

there is an IE2 p for which

$$l(p) \leqq \sum_{\nu=n-k+1}^{n-1} \nu = \frac{k-1}{2}(2n-k).$$

Next we show (cf. GINSBURG [10]) that this upper bound cannot be improved. We consider for $n \geqq 2$, $2 \leqq k \leqq n$ the automata $\mathfrak{A}_n^k = [X, Y, Z, \delta, \lambda, Z^k]$, where $Z = \{1, 2, \ldots, n\}$, $Z^k = \{1, 2, \ldots, k\}$, $X = \{1, 2, \ldots, n-1\}$, $Y = \{0, 1\}$ and for $1 \leqq i \leqq n$, $1 \leqq j \leqq n-1$

$$\delta(i, j) = \begin{cases} i, & \text{if } i \leqq j \vee j = n-1, \\ i+1, & \text{if } i = j+1,\ j \leqq n-2, \\ i-1, & \text{if } i = j+2,\ j \leqq n-2, \\ i, & \text{if } i > j+2,\ j \leqq n-2, \end{cases}$$

$$\lambda(i, j) = \begin{cases} 1, & \text{if } i = n,\ j = n-1, \\ 0 & \text{otherwise.} \end{cases}$$

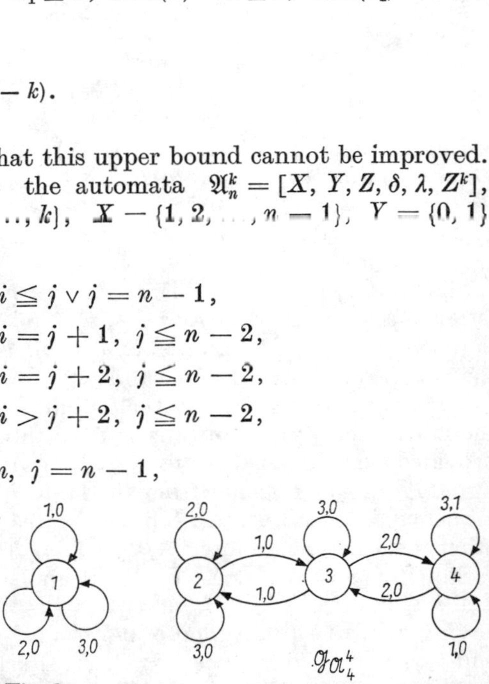

Fig. 6

(Figure 6 shows the graph of $\mathfrak{A}_4^4$). By the definition of δ we have, for all i, j with $1 \leqq i, j \leqq n$, and $p \in W(X)$

$$i = j \leftrightarrow \delta(i, p) = \delta(j, p).$$

A word p is an IE2 for $\mathfrak{A}_n^k$ if and only if for all i, j with $1 \leqq i, j \leqq k$

$$\lambda(i, p) = \lambda(j, p) \rightarrow \delta(i, p) = \delta(j, p),$$

i.e. if and only if for all i, j with $1 \leqq i, j \leqq k$ and $i \neq j$ we have

$$\delta(i, p) \neq \delta(j, p) \rightarrow \lambda(i, p) \neq \lambda(j, p),$$

and this is the case if and only if $Card(\mathfrak{A}_n^k(p)) = k$. Therefore, a word p is an IE2 for $\mathfrak{A}^k$ if and only if it is an IE1 for $\mathfrak{A}_n^k$.

Suppose $2 \leqq i \leqq n$ and p is the word consisting of the input signals $i-1, i, i+1, \ldots, n-1$, in this order. An easy computation shows that $\delta(j, p) = j$ for each $j < i$, since $j < i$ implies $j \leqq i - 1 + l$ and thus (for $0 \leqq l \leqq n - i$)

$$\delta(j, i-1 \ldots i-1+l) = j,$$

and therefore we have $\lambda(j, p) = 0^{n-i+1}$. On the other hand we have

$$\delta(i, i-1) = i+1, \quad \delta(i+1, i) = i+2, \ldots, \delta(n-1, n-2) = n,$$
$$\delta(n, n-1) = n$$

and consequently $\lambda(i, p) = 0^{n-1}1$. Therefore the automaton $\mathfrak{A}_n = [X, Y, Z, \delta, \lambda]$ is reduced and $\mathfrak{A}_n^k$ has an IE2, say p, for which

$$l(p) \leqq \frac{k-1}{2}(2n-k).$$

Lemma. *If* $p = x_1 \ldots x_m \in W(X)$, $2 \leqq i \leqq n$ *and* $\lambda(1, p) \neq \lambda(i, p)$, *then for every* j *with* $i \leqq j \leqq n$ *there is an integer* $m_{i,j}$ *such that*

$$1 \leqq m_{i,j} \leqq m \wedge \delta(i, x_1 \ldots x_{m_{i,j}-1}) = j \wedge x_{m_{i,j}} = j - 1. \tag{*}$$

Since $\delta(1, x) = 1$, for all $x \in X$ we have $\lambda(1, p) = 0^m$. Consequently, the letter 1 appears in the word $\lambda(i, p)$, and thus the state n must appear in the sequence $i, \delta(i, x_1), \delta(i, x_1x_2), \ldots, \delta(i, p)$. Therefore, there is an integer $m_{i,n}$ such that $\delta(i, x_1 \ldots x_{m_{i,n}-1}) = n$ and $x_{m_{i,n}} = n - 1$, which proves the lemma for $j = n$. Suppose $j < n$. By the definition of δ, $\mathfrak{A}_n$ can move from the state i to the state n only if meanwhile it runs through all the states j with $i \leqq j < n$, provided that $\mathfrak{A}_n$ is in a state $i \leqq j$. Furthermore, only by applying the input signal $j - 1$ can $\mathfrak{A}_n$ get from the state j to the state $j + 1$. Therefore in the sequence $i, \delta(i, x_1), \ldots, \delta(i, p)$ the states $j, j+1$ appear one right after the other, i.e., there is an integer $m_{i,j}$ ($\leqq m_{i,n}$) with the required property (*).

Suppose $p = x_1 \ldots x_m \in W(X)$ is an IE2 for $\mathfrak{A}_n^k$. Then $\lambda(1, p) \neq \lambda(i, p)$ for $2 \leqq i \leqq k$. If $2 \leqq i \leqq k$ and $1 \leqq j \leqq n$, let $m_{i,j}^*$ be the smallest integer $m_{i,j}$ having property (*). Suppose $m_{i',j'}^* = m_{i,j}^* = l$. Then we have both $x_l = j - 1$ and $x_l = j' - 1$, hence $j = j'$. Furthermore $\delta(i, x_1 \ldots x_{l-1}) = j = j' = \delta(i', x_1 \ldots x_l)$, hence $i = i'$. Therefore, $[i, j] \neq [i', j']$ implies $m_{i,j}^* \neq m_{i',j'}^*$. The number of all such pairs $[i, j]$ is

$$\sum_{i=2}^{k} \sum_{j=i}^{n} 1 = \sum_{i=2}^{k} (n - i + 1) = \frac{k-1}{2} (2n - k);$$

hence

$$m \geqq \frac{k-1}{2} (2n - k).$$

Thus every shortest IE2 for $\mathfrak{A}_n^k$ has the length $\frac{k-1}{2} (2n - k)$, and every shortest IE1 for $\mathfrak{A}_n^k$ has the same length. This implies

$$a(n, k) \geqq \frac{k-1}{2} (2n - k), \quad b(n, k) \geqq \frac{k-1}{2} (2n - k),$$

where $b(n, k)$ is the maximum of the lengths of the shortest IE2's on automata with n states and $Card(Z_1) = k$. We also see that the upper bound given in Theorem 9.7 cannot be improved. Clearly, every IS2 for $\mathfrak{A}_n^k$ yields us an IS1 of the same length. We can easily verify that the length of every IS2 for $\mathfrak{A}_n^k$ is at least

$$\frac{k-1}{2} (2n - k),$$

hence

$$\alpha(n, k) \geqq \beta(n, k) \geqq \frac{k-1}{2} (2n - k).$$

It is possible that the experimenter identifying the terminal state by means of an experiment p does not have to know the word $q \in \mathfrak{A}(p)$ put out by the automaton in order to find out the state of $\mathfrak{A}$. This is obviously the case if and only if $\{\delta(z, p) \mid z \in Z_1\}$ is a singleton. Such an IE2 is called a homogeneous experiment.

Definition 9.3. A word $p \in W(X)$ is called a *homogeneous experiment* (HE) for the weakly initial automaton $\mathfrak{A} = [X, Y, Z, \delta, \lambda, Z_1]$, if there exists a state $z^* \in Z$ such that $\delta(z_1, p) = z^*$ for each $z_1 \in Z_1$.

Let $\mathfrak{A} = [X, Y, Z, \delta, \lambda, Z_1]$ be a weakly initial automaton. For $M \subseteq Z$, $M \neq \emptyset$, $x \in X$ we put

$$\delta'(M, x) = \{\delta(z, x) \mid z \in M\}.$$

Then for $p \in W(X)$, $M \in \mathfrak{P}(Z) \setminus \{\emptyset\}$

$$\delta'(M, p) = \{\delta(z, p) \mid z \in M\}.$$

If $\mathfrak{M}' = \{M \mid \exists p(p \in W(X) \wedge M = \delta'(Z_1, p))\}$, $\mathfrak{M}'' = \{\{\delta(z, p)\} \mid z \in Z_1 \wedge p \in W(X)\}$, then the set of homogeneous experiments for $\mathfrak{A}$ is represented in the initial automaton $[X, \mathfrak{M}', \delta', Z_1]$ by the set $\mathfrak{M}' \cap \mathfrak{M}''$. Thus we have

Theorem 9.9.

1. *There is an HE for* $\mathfrak{A}$ *if and only if* $\mathfrak{M}' \cap \mathfrak{M}'' \neq \emptyset$.

2. *If* p *is an HE for* $\mathfrak{A}$ *and* $r \in W(X)$, *then* pr *also is an HE for* $\mathfrak{A}$.

3. *If* X *and* Z *are finite, then the question whether there is a homogeneous experiment for* $\mathfrak{A}$ *is decidable, and the set of all HE's for* $\mathfrak{A}$ *is regular.*

This solves the existence problem for homogeneous experiments. Next we turn to their length problem. From the construction of the automaton $[X, \mathfrak{M}', \delta', Z_1]$ it follows that if Z is finite, and $\mathfrak{A}$ has an HE, then there is also an HE p for $\mathfrak{A}$ with

$$l(p) \leqq \sum_{\varkappa=2}^{k} \binom{n}{\varkappa},$$

since this is the greatest possible number of states in this automaton which are not singletons.

Theorem 9.10. *Let* $\mathfrak{A} = [X, Y, Z, \delta, \lambda, Z_1]$ *be a Z-finite weakly initial automaton* $\left(\textit{with } Z = \langle Z_1\rangle,\ \textit{Card}(Z) = n,\ \textit{Card}(Z_1) = k\right)$.

1. *For arbitrary* $z, z' \in Z$, *if there is a* $p \mathrel{\dot\in} W(X)$ *with* $\delta(z, p) = \delta(z', p)$, *then there is a* $p' \in W(X)$ *such that* $\delta(z', p') = \delta(z, p')$ *and* $l(p') \leqq \binom{n}{2}$.

2. *If* $\mathfrak{A}$ *has an HE then it also has an HE* p *with*

$$l(p) \leqq (k-1)\binom{n}{2}.$$

If $n = k$ *then there is an HE* p' *for* $\mathfrak{A}$ *with*

$$l(p') \leqq 1 + (n-2)\binom{n}{2},$$

and for $n = k \geqq 3$ *with*

$$l(p') \leqq 1 + n + (n-3)\binom{n}{2}.$$

Proof: 9.10.1 can be proved as follows: If $z \neq z'$ and $p = x_1 \ldots x_m$ is the shortest word with $\delta(z, p) = \delta(z', p)$ then for $\mu = 0, 1, \ldots, m-1$ the sets $\{\delta(z, x_1 \ldots x_\mu), \delta(z', x_1 \ldots x_\mu)\}$ are pairwise different two element sets, and since there are exactly $\binom{n}{2}$ such sets we have $m \leqq \binom{n}{2}$. If $p = x_1 \ldots x_m$ is one of the shortest HE's for $\mathfrak{A}$ and μ the smallest integer such that $\delta'(Z_1, x_1 \ldots x_\mu)$ contains at most $k-1$ states, then as can be readily seen,

$$\mu \leqq \min\left(\binom{n}{2}, \binom{n}{k}\right),$$

and $x_{\mu+1} \dots x_m$ is a shortest HE for $\mathfrak{A}_\mu = [X, Y, Z, \delta, \lambda, \delta'(Z_1, x_1 \dots x_\mu)]$. By induction we obtain

$$m \leqq (k-1)\binom{n}{2}.$$

If $n = k$, then there are $z, z' \in Z_1$, $z \neq z'$ and $x \in X$ with

$$\delta(z, x) = \delta(z', x).$$

Hence

$$m \leqq 1 + (n-2)\binom{n}{2},$$

and for $n = k \geqq 3$

$$m \leqq 1 + n + (n-3)\binom{n}{2}.$$

Thus Theorem 9.10 is proved.

Černy [1] has shown that for each n there is an automaton $[X, Y, Z, \delta, \lambda, Z]$ with $Card(Z) = n$, for which every shortest HE has the length $(n-1)^2$. Let us consider as an example the automaton $\mathfrak{A}_8$ which was given by him for the case $n = 4$. The transition function of this automaton is summarized by the following table $(X = \{0, 1\}, Z = \{1, 2, 3, 4\})$:

δ_8	1	2	3	4
0	2	3	4	1
1	1	2	3	1

The graph of the corresponding automaton $[X, \mathfrak{M}', \{1, 2, 3, 4\}]$ is represented in Fig. 7. This shows that the shortest HE for the automaton under consideration is the word 100010001 whose length is $9 = (4-1)^2$.

Finally we shall deal with a very general black box situation in which only the input alphabet of our automaton and a certain class $\mathfrak{K}_X$ of automata with the same input alphabet to which this automaton belongs, are known. The problem is to identify the given automaton, i.e., the experimenter has to find out which automaton of the class $\mathfrak{K}_X$ is represented by the black box.

It is clear that the solvability of this problem depends heavily on the choice of the class $\mathfrak{K}_X$ namely whether the automata $\mathfrak{A} \in \mathfrak{K}_X$ are pairwise distinguishable by their external reactions. For simplicity's sake, here we shall restrict ourselves to non-initial automata. There is no difficulty in transferring these results to weakly initial automata. Let us first clarify the concept of distinguishability.

Definition 9.4. Suppose $\mathfrak{A}, \mathfrak{A}'$ are automata with the same input alphabet X.

(9.4.1.) $\mathfrak{A}, \mathfrak{A}'$ are said to be *distinguishable* if there is a word $p \in W(X)$ with $\mathfrak{A}(p) \neq \mathfrak{A}'(p)$.

(9.4.2.) $\mathfrak{A}$, $\mathfrak{A}'$ are said to be *strongly distinguishable* if there is a word $p \in W(X)$ for which $\mathfrak{A}(p) \cap \mathfrak{A}'(p) = \emptyset$.

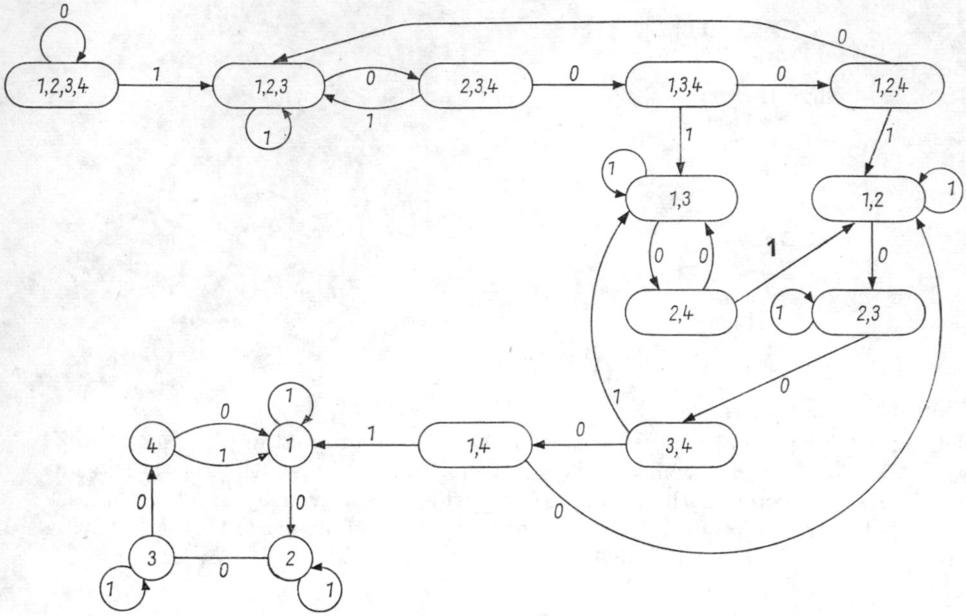

Fig. 7

Clearly, equivalent automata can not be either distinguishable or strongly distinguishable. The automata $\mathfrak{A}_9$, $\mathfrak{A}_{10}$ constructed by Moore [1], and whose graphs are represented in Fig. 8, show, on the other hand, that indistinguishable automata are not necessarily equivalent. Indeed, $1 \sim 1'$, $2 \sim 2'$, $3 \sim 3'$ are obviously satisfied, but no state in the automaton $\mathfrak{A}_{10}$ is equivalent to state 4 of $\mathfrak{A}_9$. For each $p \in W(\{0, 1\})$, however, we have

$$\lambda^9(4, p) = \begin{cases} \lambda^{10}(1', p), & \text{if} \quad p = 0r, \\ \lambda^{10}(3', p), & \text{if} \quad p = 1r; \end{cases}$$

whence $\mathfrak{A}_9$, $\mathfrak{A}_{10}$ are indistinguishable.

Theorem 9.11 (Moore [1]). *If* $\mathfrak{A} = [X, Y, Z, \delta, \lambda]$, $\mathfrak{A}' = [X, Y', Z', \delta', \lambda']$ *are indistinguishable strongly connected Z-finite automata, then* $\mathfrak{A} \sim \mathfrak{A}'$.

Proof: It suffices to show that for each $z \in Z$ there is a $z' \in Z'$ with $z \sim z'$. For $z \in Z$, $p \in W(X)$ let

$$M(z, p) = \{\delta'(z', p) \mid z' \in Z' \wedge \lambda'(z', p) = \lambda(z, p)\}.$$

Since $\mathfrak{A}(p) = \mathfrak{A}'(p)$ for every $p \in W(X)$, $M(z, p)$ is non-empty and finite, since Z' is finite. Furthermore, for each $r \in W(X)$ we have

$$Card\big(M(z, p)\big) \geqq Card\big(M(z, pr)\big).$$

Since $\mathfrak{A}'$ is Z-finite, for every $z \in Z$ there is a word $p \in W(X)$ such that for all $r \in W(X)$ $Card\big(M(z, pr)\big) = Card\big(M(z, p)\big)$. Since $\mathfrak{A}$ is strongly connected, there is a $w \in W(X)$ with $\delta(z, pw) = z$. We claim that every state $z' \in M(z, pw)$ is equivalent to z. Indeed, $z' \in M(z, pw)$ implies that there exists a $z'' \in Z'$ with $z' = \delta(z'', pw)$ and $\lambda'(z'', pw) = \lambda(z, pw)$. If $\lambda'(z', u) \neq \lambda(z, u)$ hold for some $u \in W(X)$ then we would have

$$\lambda'\big(\delta'(z'', pw), u\big) \neq \lambda(z, u) = \lambda\big(\delta(z, pw), u\big),$$

$$\lambda'(z'', pw) = \lambda(z, pw);$$

thus $\delta'(z', u) \notin M(z, pwu)$ would hold, hence

$$Card\big(M(z, pwu)\big) < Card\big(M(z, pw)\big),$$

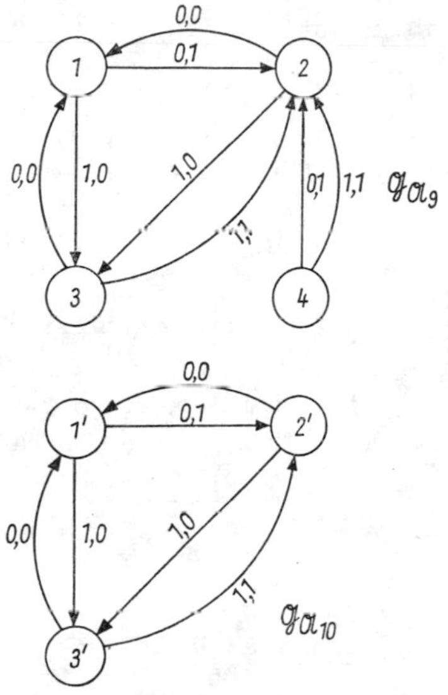

Fig. 8

which is in contradiction to the choice of p. Thus Theorem 9.11 is proved.

Let $\mathfrak{K}_X = \{\mathfrak{A}^i \mid i \in I\}$ be a class of automata $\mathfrak{A}^i = [X, Y^i, Z^i, \delta^i, \lambda^i]$ with the input alphabet X. We can assume without loss of generality that the sets Z^i are pairwise disjoint. Moreover let

$$\Sigma \mathfrak{K}_X = \Big[X, \bigcup_{i \in I} Y^i, \bigcup_{i \in I} Z^i, \delta^\Sigma, \lambda^\Sigma\Big]$$

be the direct sum of the automata $\mathfrak{A}^i$. Thus for $z \in \bigcup_{i \in I} Z^i$, $x \in X$ we have

$$\delta^\Sigma(z, x) = \delta^i(z, x), \quad \text{if} \quad z \in Z^i,$$
$$\lambda^\Sigma(z, x) = \lambda^i(z, x), \quad \text{if} \quad z \in Z^i.$$

A procedure is called a *distinguishing strategy* for the class $\mathfrak{K}_X$ if for arbitrary $\mathfrak{A} \in \mathfrak{K}_X$ it enables us to determine in finitely many steps for which index $i \in I$ we have $\mathfrak{A} = \mathfrak{A}^i$. Obviously, a distinguishing strategy for $\mathfrak{K}_X$ exists if and only if there is a strategy which allows us to decide in a finite number of steps to which set Z^i an arbitrary state of $\Sigma \mathfrak{K}_X$ belongs. If $\Sigma \mathfrak{K}_X$ is Z-finite and reduced, then there is a distinguishing strategy for $\mathfrak{K}_X$, since, as we know, there is an identification strategy of the second kind for $\Sigma \mathfrak{K}_X$.

Suppose now that the class $\mathfrak{K}_X$ contains exactly two distinguishable automata $\mathfrak{A}, \mathfrak{A}'$. We can assume without loss of generality that there is a state z of $\mathfrak{A}$ and a word $p \in W(X)$ with $\lambda(z, p) \notin \mathfrak{A}'(p)$. If z is the only such state of $\mathfrak{A}$, and $\mathfrak{A}'(p) \subseteq \mathfrak{A}(p)$, then the experimenter can distinguish between $\mathfrak{A}$ and $\mathfrak{A}'$ only if $\mathfrak{A}$ is the given black box and happens to be in the state z. Thus the distinguishability of the automata $\mathfrak{A}, \mathfrak{A}'$ is too weak a condition to imply the existence of a winning strategy over the class $\mathfrak{K}_X = \{\mathfrak{A}, \mathfrak{A}'\}$. This notion of distinguishability is of use only in such a black box situation where several copies of the black box are given and we know that they are all in different states (multiple experiments, cf. e.g., MOORE [1], DUSHSKI [1]).

Let $\mathfrak{K}_X = \{\mathfrak{A}^i \mid i \in I\}$ be an arbitrary non-empty class of automata $\mathfrak{A}^i = [X, Y^i, Z^i, \delta^i, \lambda^i]$, (where for $i, j \in I$ we have: $i = j \leftrightarrow \mathfrak{A}^i = \mathfrak{A}^j$). Let us put for $p \in W(X)$

$$\mathfrak{K}_X(p) = \bigcup_{i \in I} \mathfrak{A}^i(p).$$

Definition 9.5. A word $p \in W(X)$ is called a *distinguishing experiment* (DE) for $\mathfrak{K}_X$ if there is a single valued mapping α of $\mathfrak{K}_X(p)$ onto I such that for all $i \in I$, $q \in \mathfrak{A}^i(p)$

$$\alpha(q) = i.$$

Corollary 9.12.

1. A word $p \in W(X)$ is a DE for $\mathfrak{K}_X$ if and only if for all $i, j \in I$ we have

$$i = j \leftrightarrow \mathfrak{A}^i(p) \cap \mathfrak{A}^j(p) \neq \emptyset.$$

2. If there is a DE for $\mathfrak{K}_X$ then the automata in $\mathfrak{K}_X$ are pairwise strongly distinguishable.

3. If $\mathfrak{K}_X$ is finite, then the automata in $\mathfrak{K}_X$ are pairwise strongly distinguishable if and only if there is a DE for $\mathfrak{K}_X$.

4. If $\bigcup_{i \in I} Y^i$ is finite and there exists a DE for $\mathfrak{K}_X$ then $\mathfrak{K}_X$ is finite.

The proof of 9.12.3 can be found in STARKE [9], and is so simple that we omit it here.

Now we solve the *existence problem* for distinguishing experiments.

Theorem 9.13. *Suppose* $\mathfrak{K}_X = \{\mathfrak{A}^i \mid i \in I\}$.

1. *A word* $p \in W(X)$ *is a DE for* $\mathfrak{K}_X$ *if and only if for every* $i \in I$, $M \in \mathfrak{Z}_{\Sigma\mathfrak{K}_X}(p^*)$ *we have*

$$Z^i \cap M \neq \emptyset \rightarrow M \subseteq Z^i.$$

2. *A word* $p \in W(X)$ *is a DE for* $\mathfrak{K}_X$ *if and only if for all* $i \in I$, $M \in \mathfrak{M}_{\Sigma\mathfrak{K}_X}(p)$ *we have*

$$\{\delta^i(z, p) \mid z \in Z^i\} \cap M \neq \emptyset \rightarrow M \subseteq \{\delta^i(z, p) \mid z \in Z^i\}.$$

Proof: p is a DE for $\mathfrak{K}_X$ if and only if for all $i, j \in I$ with $i \neq j$ $\mathfrak{A}^i(p) \cap \mathfrak{A}^j(p) = \emptyset$ holds, hence if and only if $i, j \in I$, $i \neq j$, $z^i \in Z^i$, and $z^j \in Z^j$ imply $\lambda^i(z^i, p) \neq \lambda^j(z^j, p)$. In other words, p is a DE for $\mathfrak{K}_X$ if and only if for all $i \in I$, $z^i \in Z^i$ we have:

$$\forall j \forall z^j \big(j \in I \setminus \{i\} \wedge z^j \in Z^j \rightarrow \lambda^\Sigma(z_i, p) \neq \lambda^\Sigma(z_j, p)\big).$$

Now $\lambda^\Sigma(z^i, p) \neq \lambda^\Sigma(z^j, p)$ holds if and only if for each $M \in \mathfrak{Z}_{\Sigma\mathfrak{K}_X}(p^*)$

$$z^i \in M \rightarrow z^j \notin M$$

is true.

Therefore p is a DE for $\mathfrak{K}_X$ if and only if for all $i \in I$, $M \in \mathfrak{Z}_{\Sigma\mathfrak{K}_X}(p^*)$ we have: If $M \cap Z^i \neq \emptyset$, then for every $j \in I \setminus \{i\}$ $M \cap Z^j = \emptyset$, hence $M \subseteq Z^i$ is satisfied.

On the other hand for $z^i \in Z^i$, $z^j \in Z^j$, $i \neq j$ we have $z^i \neq z^j$ and $\delta^\Sigma(z^i, p) \neq \delta^\Sigma(z^j, p)$. Here

$$\begin{aligned} &\exists M\big(M \in \mathfrak{M}_{\Sigma\mathfrak{K}_X}(p) \wedge \delta^\Sigma(z^i, p), \delta^\Sigma(z^j, p) \in M\big) \\ &\leftrightarrow \exists z_1^i \exists z_1^j \big(z_1^i \in Z^i \wedge z_1^j \in Z^j \wedge \lambda^\Sigma(z_1^i, p) = \lambda^\Sigma(z_1^j, p) \\ &\qquad \wedge \delta^\Sigma(z_1^i, p) = \delta^\Sigma(z^i, p) \wedge \delta^\Sigma(z_1^j, p) = \delta^\Sigma(z^j, p)\big). \end{aligned}$$

Consequently, p is a DE for $\mathfrak{K}_X$ if and only if for all $i, j \in I$ with $i \neq j$ and every $M \in \mathfrak{M}_{\Sigma\mathfrak{K}_X}(p)$ we have

$$M \cap \{\delta^i(z, p) \mid z \in Z^i\} \neq \emptyset \rightarrow M \cap \{\delta^j(z, p) \mid z \in Z^j\},$$

which immediately implies Proposition 9.13.2.

Corollary 9.14.

1. If the sets X, I and Z^i (for $i \in I$) are finite, i.e., $\Sigma\mathfrak{K}_X$ is $[X, Z]$-finite, then the question whether $\mathfrak{K}_X$ has a DE is decidable and the set of all distinguishing experiments for $\mathfrak{K}_X$ is regular.

2. If $\Sigma\mathfrak{K}_X$ is Z-finite and reduced, then $\mathfrak{K}_X$ has a DE.

Lastly we consider a simple example. Let $X = \{0, 1\}$, $\mathfrak{K}_X = \{\mathfrak{A}^1, \mathfrak{A}^2, \mathfrak{A}^3, \mathfrak{A}^4\}$, $Y^i = \{0, 1\}$, $Z^1 = \{1\}$, $Z^2 = \{2\}$, $Z^3 = \{3, 4\}$, $Z^4 = \{5, 6, 7, 8\}$ and the functions δ^Σ, λ^Σ belonging to the direct sum Σ of $\mathfrak{A}^1, \ldots, \mathfrak{A}^4$ be given by the following table:

δ^Σ	1	2	3	4	5	6	7	8	λ^Σ	1	2	3	4	5	6	7	8
0	1	2	4	3	7	8	5	7	0	0	1	1	0	1	0	1	1
1	1	2	3	3	6	5	6	8	1	1	1	1	0	0	1	0	1

The lexicographically first DE for $\{\mathfrak{A}^1, \ldots, \mathfrak{A}^4\}$ is the word 0001, as can be easily seen. We have $\mathfrak{K}_X(0001) = \{0001, 1111, 1010, 0101, 1110, 0110\}$ and the corresponding mapping α is summarized in the following table:

q	0001	1111	1010	0101	1110	0110
$\alpha(q)$	1	2	3	3	4	4

§ 10. Partial Automata

If an automaton is a subsystem of an encompassing information processing system, it can happen that the behaviour of the whole system remains unchanged if the automaton $\mathfrak{A}$ under consideration is replaced by another automaton $\mathfrak{A}'$, which is not equivalent to $\mathfrak{A}$, i.e., which, in certain situations, behaves completely differently from $\mathfrak{A}$. For instance, suppose the input alphabet of $\mathfrak{A}$ is $\{0, 1\}$ and the whole system is constructed in such a way that the sequence 111 never occurs among the input sequences entering into $\mathfrak{A}$. Then we can obviously not deduce, from the prescribed behaviour of the whole system and from its structure, how $\mathfrak{A}$ should behave if the sequence 111 is fed into it (in a certain fixed or arbitrary state). In other words, the prescribed behaviour of the whole system only allows us to obtain *partial* data on the necessary behaviour of $\mathfrak{A}$.

Assume that from the behaviour prescribed for the whole system, we can deduce that the automaton $\mathfrak{A}$ has to solve the following decoding problem. The input word of $\mathfrak{A}$ is composed of the subwords $p_1 = 001$, $p_2 = 010$, and $p_3 = 011$. In step $t + 3$, $\mathfrak{A}$ has to put out the signal i provided that in the course of the steps $t + 1$, $t + 2$, $t + 3$ the word p_i is fed into $\mathfrak{A}$. Here it is obviously not specified what $\mathfrak{A}$ does if for instance the word 111 is fed into it, nor what it should put out in step 1. From the viewpoint of the behaviour of the whole system, this is completely irrelevant. An automaton which solves the above problem is therefore only partially specified, hence we refer to it as a *partial automaton*. Such is for example the initial automaton

$$\mathfrak{A}_{11} = [\{0, 1\}, \{1, 2, 3\}, \{a, b, c, d, e\}, \delta^{11}, \lambda^{11}, a]$$

with

δ^{11}	a	b	c	d	e	λ^{11}	a	b	c	d	e
0	b	c	—	a	—	0	—	—	—	2	—
1	e	d	a	a	—	1	—	—	1	3	—

whose graph is represented in Fig. 9. For this automaton, the transition function is not defined in the situation $[c, 0]$ (a dash is represented in the corresponding square of the table defining δ^{11}, and in the graph of $\mathfrak{A}_{11}$ no edge designated by $0, y$ originates from the vertice c). This does not mean that the automaton $\mathfrak{A}_{11}$ "does nothing" in the situation $[c, 0]$ (i.e., it remains in the same state c) but only that it is not specified into which state $\mathfrak{A}_{11}$ enters from this situation. Since λ^{11} is also not defined for $[c, 0]$, the output signal put out by $\mathfrak{A}_{11}$ in this situation is not specified either.

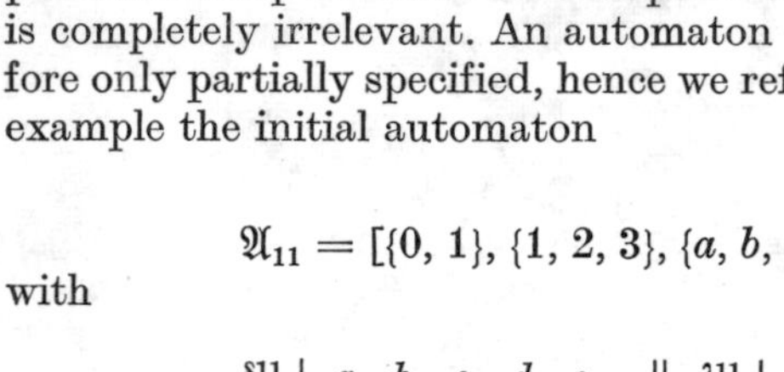

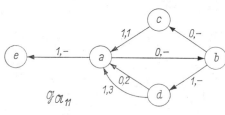

Fig. 9

Definition 10.1. $\mathfrak{A} = [X, Y, Z, \delta, \lambda]$ is called a *partial automaton* if X, Y, Z are non-empty sets and δ, λ are functions mapping certain subsets of $Z \times X$ into Z and Y respectively.

In order to describe the *behaviour* of partial automata, we introduce the notion of a partial word. A *partial word* q of length n over Y is a single-valued mapping from a subset of the set $\{0, 1, \ldots, n-1\}$ into the set Y. We denote partial words as usual, i.e., $q = y_1 y_2 \ldots y_n$ where $y_i = q(i-1)$, however y_i is replaced by a dash ("—") if q is not defined for $i-1$. Thus e.g., 00– and ––– are partial words of length 3 over $\{0, 1\}$. The set of all partial words over the set Y is denoted by $P(Y)$. Obviously, $W(Y) \subseteq P(Y)$. A function which maps the set $W(X)$ into the set $P(Y)$ is referred to as an *incomplete word function over* $[X, Y]$.

Thus in a partial automaton, a fixed initial state generates an incomplete word function. Here we have for $\mathfrak{A} = [X, Y, Z, \delta, \lambda]$, $z \in Z$, $x \in X$, $p \in W(X)$:

$$\delta(z, e) \underset{\mathrm{Df}}{=} z,$$

$$\delta(z, px) \underset{\mathrm{Df}}{=} \begin{cases} \delta\big(\delta(z, p), x\big), & \text{if } \delta(z, p),\ \delta\big(\delta(z, p), x\big) \text{ are defined,} \\ \text{not defined otherwise;} \end{cases}$$

$$\lambda(z, e) \underset{\mathrm{Df}}{=} e$$

and for $p = x_1 x_2 \ldots x_n$, $0 \leqq i < n \geqq 1$

$$\lambda(z, p)(i) \underset{\mathrm{Df}}{=} \begin{cases} \lambda\big(\delta(z, x_1 \ldots x_i), x_{i+1}\big), \text{ if } \delta(z, x_1 \ldots x_i) \text{ and} \\ \qquad\qquad \lambda\big(\delta(z, x_1 \ldots x_i), x_{i+1}\big) \text{ are defined,} \\ \text{not defined otherwise.} \end{cases}$$

In the above example, $\lambda^{11}(a, 0111x) =$ ––3–– for arbitrary $x \in \{0, 1\}$, and for all $p \in W(\{0, 1\})$, $\lambda^{11}(a, 1p)$ is the nowhere defined word of length $l(p) + 1$.

The most important problem arising in the investigation of partial automata is their "equivalent" simplification. This means that for a given partial automaton $\mathfrak{A}$ we seek an automaton $\mathfrak{A}'$ with a minimum number of states which can replace $\mathfrak{A}$ in every encompassing system. The required automaton is, in general, not equivalent to $\mathfrak{A}$ (if, as usual, equivalence is understood to mean that in both automata the same incomplete word functions are generable. However, $\mathfrak{A}'$ "covers" $\mathfrak{A}$ in a sense which we shall now clarify.

Definition 10.2. Let $q, q' \in P(Y)$ and φ, φ' be incomplete word functions over $[X, Y]$.

(10.2.1) The partial word q is said to *be covered by* q' (notation: $q \doteq q'$), if $l(q) = l(q')$, $Dom(q) \subseteq Dom(q')$ and $q(i) = q'(i)$ for all $i \in Dom(q)$.

(10.2.2) We say that φ *is covered by* φ' if $\varphi(p) \doteq \varphi'(p)$ for all $p \in W(X)$.

Thus for $Y = \{0, 1\}$ we have ––– ≐ –1– ≐ 01– ≐ 011, however *not* 0– ≐ –0. The incomplete word function generated by the state e in $\mathfrak{A}_{11}$ is covered by the word function generated by the state a in $\mathfrak{A}_{11}$.

Definition 10.3. Let $\mathfrak{A} = [X, Y, Z, \delta, \lambda]$, $\mathfrak{A}' = [X, Y, Z', \delta', \lambda']$ be arbitrary partial automata.

(10.3.1) A state z of $\mathfrak{A}$ is said to *be covered by the state* z' of $\mathfrak{A}'$ (notation: $z \preceq z'$) if the word function generated by z in $\mathfrak{A}$ is covered by the word function generated by z' in $\mathfrak{A}'$.

(10.3.2) We say that $\mathfrak{A}$ *is covered by* $\mathfrak{A}'$ (notation: $\mathfrak{A} \preceq \mathfrak{A}'$) if

$$\forall z\big(z \in Z \to \exists z' (z' \in Z' \wedge z \preceq z')\big).$$

Corollary 10.1.

1. The relation $\preceq$ is reflexive and transitive (a quasi ordering) over $P(Y)$, over the set of incomplete word functions over $[X, Y]$, and over the set of all partial automata with the given alphabets X, Y.

2. If $z \preceq z'$ and for all $p \in W(X)$ $\lambda(z, p) \in W(Y)$, then $\lambda'(z', p) \in W(Y)$ for all $p \in W(X)$ and $z \sim z'$.

3. If $\mathfrak{A}$ is a completely specified automaton and $\mathfrak{A} \preceq \mathfrak{A}'$, then $\mathfrak{A}$ can be equivalently embedded into $\mathfrak{A}'$ and there exists a completely specified subautomaton of $\mathfrak{A}'$ which is equivalent to $\mathfrak{A}$.

Definition 10.4. Let $\mathfrak{A} = [X, Y, Z, \delta, \lambda]$ be a partial automaton. An automaton $\mathfrak{A}' = [X, Y, Z', \delta', \lambda']$ is called a *minimum of* $\mathfrak{A}$ if $\mathfrak{A} \preceq \mathfrak{A}'$ and every automaton $\mathfrak{A}''$ satisfying $\mathfrak{A} \preceq \mathfrak{A}''$ has at least as many states as $\mathfrak{A}'$. If every minimum of $\mathfrak{A}$ has the same number of states as $\mathfrak{A}$, then $\mathfrak{A}$ is called *minimal.*

Corollary 10.2. If $\mathfrak{A}$ is a completely specified automaton and $\mathfrak{A}'$ is a minimum of $\mathfrak{A}$, then $\mathfrak{A}'$ is completely specified and is a reduct of $\mathfrak{A}$.

Clearly, every minimum $\mathfrak{A}'$ of $\mathfrak{A}$ has the above formulated properties, that is, $\mathfrak{A}'$ is a "simplest" automaton which can substitute $\mathfrak{A}$ in every encompassing system. We shall show that in general, partial automata have *several minima.*

In the automaton $\mathfrak{A}_{11}$ the state e generates the word function which assigns to each $p \in W(X) \setminus \{e\}$ the nowhere defined word of the same length. Such a state is called *degenerate*. Obviously, a degenerate state z is covered by any other state, hence all the degenerate states can be eliminated from each partial automaton in the following way, without affecting its behaviour.

Let $\mathfrak{A} = [X, Y, Z, \delta, \lambda]$ be a partial automaton which has at least one non-degenerate state, and Z_d the set of all degenerate states of $\mathfrak{A}$. Then we consider $\mathfrak{A}' = [X, Y, Z', \delta', \lambda']$ where $Z' \underset{\mathrm{Df}}{=} Z \setminus Z_d$ and, for $z \in Z'$, $x \in X$,

$$\delta'(z, x) = \begin{cases} \delta(z, x), & \text{if } [z, x] \in Dom(\delta) \text{ and } \delta(z, x) \notin Z_d, \\ \text{not defined otherwise,} \end{cases}$$

and λ' is the restriction of λ to the set $Z' \times X$. Obviously then, $\mathfrak{A} \preceq \mathfrak{A}'$.

In what follows we assume that the partial automata under consideration have no degenerate states.

Let $\mathfrak{A} = [X, Y, Z, \delta, \lambda]$ be a partial automaton. For $z \in Z$ let

$$D(z) \underset{\mathrm{Df}}{=} \{px \mid p \in W(X) \wedge x \in X \wedge \lambda(\delta(z, p), x) \in Y\}.$$[1]

Theorem 10.3. *Let* $\mathfrak{A} = [X, Y, Z, \delta, \lambda]$, $\mathfrak{A}' = [X, Y, Z', \delta', \lambda']$ *be partial automata*, $z \in Z$ *and* $z' \in Z'$. *Then*

$$z \mathrel{\dot{\leq}} z' \leftrightarrow \forall p\, \forall x \big(x \in X \wedge px \in D(z) \rightarrow px \in D'(z') \wedge \lambda(\delta(z, p), x)) \\ = \lambda'(\delta'(z', p), x\big).$$

Proof: We have

$$\begin{aligned} z \mathrel{\dot{\leq}} z' &\leftrightarrow \forall p \big(p \in W(X) \rightarrow \lambda(z, p) \mathrel{\dot{\leq}} \lambda'(z', p)\big) \\ &\leftrightarrow \forall p\, \forall x \big(p \in W(X) \wedge x \in X \rightarrow \lambda(z, px) \mathrel{\dot{\leq}} \lambda'(z', px)\big) \text{ (by } e \mathrel{\dot{\leq}} e) \\ &\leftrightarrow \forall p\, \forall i \big(p \in W(X) \setminus \{e\} \wedge 0 \leqq i < l(p) \wedge i \in Dom\big(\lambda(z, p)\big) \rightarrow \\ &\qquad \rightarrow i \in Dom\big(\lambda'(z', p)\big) \wedge \lambda(z, p)(i) = \big(\lambda'(z', p)(i)\big). \end{aligned}$$

Now, for $p = x_1 \dots x_n$ $(n \geqq 1)$, $0 \leqq i < n$

$$\begin{aligned} i \in Dom\big(\lambda(z, x_1 \dots x_n)\big) &\leftrightarrow \lambda\big(\delta(z, x_1 \dots x_i), x_{i+1}\big) \in Y \\ &\leftrightarrow x_1 \dots x_i x_{i+1} \in D(z), \end{aligned}$$

and analogously,

$$i \in Dom\big(\lambda'(z', x_1 \dots x_n)\big) \leftrightarrow x_1 \dots x_i x_{i+1} \in D'(z'),$$

because

$$\lambda(z, x_1 \dots x_n)(i) = \begin{cases} \lambda\big(\delta(z, x_1 \dots x_i), x_{i+1}\big), & \text{if it is defined} \\ \text{not defined otherwise.} \end{cases}$$

Consequently,

$$\begin{aligned} z \mathrel{\dot{\leq}} z' &\leftrightarrow \forall i\, \forall x_1 \dots x_i\, \forall x \big(\lambda(\delta(z, x_1 \dots x_i), x) \in Y \rightarrow \\ &\qquad \rightarrow \lambda'(\delta'(z', x_1 \dots x_i), x) \in Y \wedge \\ &\qquad \wedge \lambda(\delta(z, x_1 \dots x_i), x) = \lambda'(\delta'(z', x_1 \dots x_i), x)\big) \\ &\leftrightarrow \forall p\, \forall x \big(px \in D(z) \rightarrow px \in D'(z') \wedge \lambda(\delta(z, p), x) \\ &\qquad = \lambda'(\delta'(z', p), x)\big), \end{aligned}$$

which was to be shown.

By using the relation $\dot{\leq}$ alone, we can achieve a more efficient simplification of automata than by eliminating degenerate states, but in general this will not yield us a minimum. Therefore in what follows we shall consider the compatibility of partial words and states.

---

[1] $\lambda(\delta(z, p), x) \in Y$ obviously means that $\delta(z, p)$ and $\lambda(\delta(z, p), x)$ are defined

Definition 10.5.

(10.5.1) The partial *words* $q, q' \in P(Y)$ are called *compatible* (notation: $q V q'$) if

$$\forall i\big(i \in Dom(q) \cap Dom(q') \rightarrow q(i) = q'(i)\big).$$

(10.5.2) The *states* $z \in Z$, $z' \in Z'$ of the partial automata $\mathfrak{A} = [X, Y, Z, \delta, \lambda]$, $\mathfrak{A}' = [X, Y, Z', \delta', \lambda']$ are called *compatible* (notation: $z V z'$) if for all $p \in W(X)$ the partial words $\lambda(z, p)$ and $\lambda'(z', p)$ are compatible.

(10.5.3) Every non-empty set consisting of pairwise compatible states of $\mathfrak{A}$ is called a *compatibility class of* $\mathfrak{A}$.

(10.5.4) A compatibility class K of $\mathfrak{A}$ is called *maximal* if for each state z of $\mathfrak{A}$

$$\forall z'(z' \in K \rightarrow z V z') \rightarrow z \in K.$$

Corollary 10.4. Let $\mathfrak{A} = [X, Y, Z, \delta, \lambda]$ be a partial automaton and $z, z^* \in Z$.

1. $z V z \leftrightarrow \forall p \forall x\big(px \in D(z) \cap D(z^*) \rightarrow \lambda(\delta(z, p), x) = \lambda(\delta(z^*, p), x)\big)$.

2. The system $\mathfrak{K}_{max}$ of all maximal compatibility classes of $\mathfrak{A}$ is a covering of Z, i.e., $\bigcup \mathfrak{K}^{\mathfrak{A}}_{max} = Z$, moreover for $K, K' \in \mathfrak{K}^{\mathfrak{A}}_{max}$, we have $K \not\subset K'$.

We are especially interested in coverings of Z which are invariant under the transition function. For $N \subseteq Z$, $x \in X$ let

$$\delta(N, x) \underset{\mathrm{Df}}{=} \{\delta(z, x) \mid z \in N \wedge [z, x] \in Dom(\delta)\}.$$

Definition 10.6. A covering $\mathfrak{N}$ of Z is called an *automaton covering for* $\mathfrak{A} = [X, Y, Z, \delta, \lambda]$ if

$$\forall N \forall x\big(N \in \mathfrak{N} \wedge x \in X \rightarrow \exists N'(N' \in \mathfrak{N} \wedge \delta(N, x) \subseteq N')\big).$$

Our interest in automaton coverings consisting of compatibility classes is motivated by the following two theorems.

Theorem 10.5. *Let* $\mathfrak{A} = [X, Y, Z, \delta, \lambda]$, $\mathfrak{A}' = [X, Y, Z', \delta', \lambda']$ *be partial automata and* $\mathfrak{A} \doteq \mathfrak{A}'$. *Then there exists an automaton covering* $\mathfrak{N}$ *of* $\mathfrak{A}$ *whose elements are compatibility classes of* $\mathfrak{A}$ *such that* $Card(\mathfrak{N}) \leqq Card(Z')$.

Proof: For $z' \in Z'$ let $N_{z'} \underset{\mathrm{Df}}{=} \{z \mid z \in Z \wedge z \doteq z'\}$, furthermore

$$\mathfrak{M} \underset{\mathrm{Df}}{=} \{N_{z'} \mid z' \in Z'\} \quad \text{and} \quad \mathfrak{N} \underset{\mathrm{Df}}{=} max\, \mathfrak{M}$$

(i.e., $\mathfrak{N}$ consists of all elements of $\mathfrak{M}$ which are maximal with respect to $\subseteq$). We claim that $\mathfrak{N}$ satisfies our requirements. Clearly, $Card(\mathfrak{N}) \leqq Card(Z')$.

Lemma 10.5a. *Every* $N \in \mathfrak{N}$ *is a compatibility class of* $\mathfrak{A}$.

Let $N = N_{z'} \in \mathfrak{N}$, $z, z^* \in N_{z'}$. Then $z \doteq z'$ and $z^* \doteq z'$, consequently for all $p \in W(X)$

$$\lambda(z, p) \doteq \lambda'(z', p) \wedge \lambda(z^*, p) \doteq \lambda'(z', p).$$

Suppose $i \in Dom(\lambda(z, p)) \cap Dom(\lambda(z^*, p))$. Then $i \in Dom(\lambda'(z', p))$ and

$$\lambda(z, p)(i) = \lambda'(z', p)(i) = \lambda(z^*, p)(i).$$

Consequently

$$\forall p\big(p \in W(X) \to \forall i\big(i \in Dom(\lambda(z, p)) \cap Dom(\lambda(z^*, p)) \to \\ \to \lambda(z, p)(i) = \lambda(z^*, p)(i)\big)\big),$$

i.e., $z\, V z^*$, which was to be shown.

Lemma 10.5b. *$\mathfrak{N}$ is an automaton covering of $\mathfrak{A}$.*

Let $z \in Z$ be arbitrary. Since $\mathfrak{A} \doteq \mathfrak{A}'$, there is a $z' \in Z'$ with $z \doteq z'$, i.e., $z \in N_{z'}$. Hence $Z = \bigcup \mathfrak{M} = \bigcup \mathfrak{N}$. Since the elements of $\mathfrak{N}$ are maximal with respect to $\subseteq$, we have

$$\forall N\, \forall N' (N, N' \in \mathfrak{N} \to N \not\subset N').$$

Let $N = N_{z'} \in \mathfrak{N}$, $x \in X$. We claim that

$$\delta(N, x) \neq \emptyset \to \delta(N, x) = \delta(N_{z'}, x) \subseteq N_{\delta'(z', x)},$$

which immediately implies the existence of a class $N' \in \mathfrak{N}$ with $\delta(N, x) \subseteq N'$.

Let $z^* \in \delta(N_{z'}, x)$. Then there is a $z \in N_{z'}$ with $[z, x] \in Dom(\delta)$ and $z^* = \delta(z, x)$ and with $z \doteq z'$. Next we have to show that $[z', x] \in Dom(\delta')$. $z \doteq z'$ implies $D(z) \subseteq D'(z')$. If $[z', x] \notin Dom(\delta')$, then for arbitrary $p \in W(X)$, $xp \notin D'(z')$, hence $xp \notin D(z)$ and $p \notin D(\delta(z, x)) = D(z^*)$. Thus $[z', x] \notin Dom(\delta')$ implies that z^* is degenerate, which is in contradiction to our assumption that $\mathfrak{A}$ has no degenerate states. Consequently, $[z', x] \in Dom(\delta')$ and the set $N_{\delta'(z', x)}$ exists. $z \doteq z'$, $[z, x] \in Dom(\delta)$ and $[z', x] \in Dom(\delta')$ obviously imply $z^* = \delta(z, x) \doteq \delta'(z', x)$, hence $z^* \in N_{\delta'(z', x)}$, i.e., $\delta(N, x) \subseteq N_{\delta'(z', x)}$. Thus Theorem 10.5 is proved.

Theorem 10.6. *For each automaton covering $\mathfrak{N}$ of $\mathfrak{A}$ consisting of compatibility classes of $\mathfrak{A} = [X, Y, Z, \delta, \lambda]$, there exists an automaton $\mathfrak{A}_{\mathfrak{N}}$ with the set of states $\mathfrak{N}$ and $\mathfrak{A} \doteq \mathfrak{A}_{\mathfrak{N}}$.*

Proof: Let

$$\delta_{\mathfrak{N}}(N, x) \underset{\mathrm{Df}}{=} \begin{cases} \text{a fixed } N' \in \mathfrak{N} \text{ with } \delta(N, x) \subseteq N', & \text{if } \delta(N, x) \neq \emptyset, \\ \text{not defined otherwise,} \end{cases}$$

$$\lambda_{\mathfrak{N}}(N, x) \underset{\mathrm{Df}}{=} \begin{cases} \lambda(z, x), & \text{if } [z, x] \in Dom(\lambda) \text{ for some } z \in N, \\ \text{not defined otherwise,} \end{cases}$$

for arbitrary $N \in \mathfrak{N}$, $x \in X$. Since every $N \in \mathfrak{N}$ is a compatibility class of $\mathfrak{A}$, the definition of $\lambda_{\mathfrak{N}}$ is justified (indeed $z\, V z'$, $[z, x] \in Dom(\lambda)$ and $[z', x] \in Dom(\lambda)$ imply $\lambda(z, x) = \lambda(z', x)$), and the definition of $\delta_{\mathfrak{N}}$ is justified because $\mathfrak{N}$ is an automaton covering.

To show that $\mathfrak{A} \doteq \mathfrak{A}_{\mathfrak{N}}$, i.e., that for each $z \in Z$ there is an $N \in \mathfrak{N}$ with $z \doteq N$, we prove

$$\forall N \forall z (z \in N \in \mathfrak{N} \rightarrow z \doteq N).$$

Let $N \in \mathfrak{N}$, $z \in N$, furthermore $px \in D(z)$ with $p = x_1 \dots x_n$. Then $z_j = \delta(z, x_1 \dots x_j)$ is defined for $j = 1, \dots, n$, since $\delta(z, p)$ is. Consequently, $\delta(N, x_1 \dots x_j)$ is non-empty and therefore $N_j \underset{\mathrm{Df}}{=} \delta_{\mathfrak{N}}(N, x_1 \dots x_j)$ is defined. Since $\mathfrak{N}$ is an automaton covering of $\mathfrak{A}$ and $z \in N$, we have $z_j \in N_j$ for $j = 1, \dots, n$. In particular, $\delta(z, p) \in \delta_{\mathfrak{N}}(N, p)$, hence

$$\lambda_{\mathfrak{N}}\big(\delta_{\mathfrak{N}}(N, p), x\big) = \lambda\big(\delta(z, p), x\big) \in Y,$$

i.e., $px \in D_{\mathfrak{N}}(N)$ and $\lambda\big(\delta(z, p), x\big) = \lambda_{\mathfrak{N}}\big(\delta_{\mathfrak{N}}(N, p), x\big)$ for all $px \in D(x)$. Thus, by 10.3, $z \doteq N$. This proves Theorem 10.6.

Corollary 10.7.

1. By finding one (or all) of the automaton coverings $\mathfrak{N}$ of $\mathfrak{A}$ which consist of compatibility classes of $\mathfrak{A}$ and have minimal cardinality, and by constructing $\mathfrak{A}_{\mathfrak{N}}$, we obtain a minimum (or all minima) of a given partial automaton $\mathfrak{A}$.

2. $\mathfrak{A}$ is minimal if and only if every automaton covering of $\mathfrak{A}$ consisting of compatibility classes has at least *Card* (Z) elements.

Thus it is necessary to have a view of the possible automaton coverings of $\mathfrak{A}$ consisting of compatibility classes, and in particular of the systems of compatibility classes of $\mathfrak{A}$. $\mathfrak{K}^{\mathfrak{A}}_{\max}$, the system of maximal compatibility classes of $\mathfrak{A}$, enables us to obtain such a view. First we prove

Theorem 10.8. $\mathfrak{K}^{\mathfrak{A}}_{\max}$ *is an automaton covering of* $\mathfrak{A}$.

Proof: We have already shown that $\mathfrak{K}^{\mathfrak{A}}_{\max}$ is a covering of Z. Suppose $K \in \mathfrak{K}^{\mathfrak{A}}_{\max}$, $x \in X$. To show that there is a $K' \in \mathfrak{K}^{\mathfrak{A}}_{\max}$ with $\delta(K, x) \subseteq K'$, it suffices to show that $\delta(K, x)$ is either a compatibility class, or empty. Let $z_1, z_2 \in \delta(K, x) \neq \emptyset$. Then there are states $z_1', z_2' \in K$ with

$$[z_1', x], [z_2', x] \in Dom(\delta), \quad z_1 = \delta(z_1', x), \quad z_2 = \delta(z_2', x).$$

Since $K \in \mathfrak{K}^{\mathfrak{A}}_{\max}$, we have $z_1' V z_2'$,

$$\forall p \forall x \big(p \in W(X) \wedge x \in X \rightarrow \lambda(z_1', xp) V \lambda(z_2', xp)\big),$$

consequently, by $\lambda(z_i', xp) = \lambda(z_i', x)\lambda\big(\delta(z_i', x), p\big)$ we have for $i \in \{1, 2\}$

$$\forall p \big(p \in W(X) \rightarrow \lambda(\delta(z_1', x), p) V \lambda(\delta(z_2, x), p)\big),$$

hence $z_1 V z_2$.

Obviously, two states of a completely specified automaton are compatible if and only if they are equivalent. Consequently, for a completely specified automaton $\mathfrak{A}$, $\mathfrak{K}^{\mathfrak{A}}_{\max}$ is a partition of Z, namely $\bar{Z} = Z/\sim$, and $Card(\mathfrak{K}^{\mathfrak{A}}_{\max})$ is the minimal number of states among the automata equivalent to $\mathfrak{A}$. For partial automata this is not the case, since there is such a partial automaton $\mathfrak{A}$, for which $\mathfrak{K}^{\mathfrak{A}}_{\max}$ has more classes than the number of states of $\mathfrak{A}$.

The system $\mathfrak{K}^{\mathfrak{A}}_{\max}$ of maximal compatibility classes is not constructed directly, but we construct the system $\mathfrak{K}^{\mathfrak{A}}_{2}$ of all two element sets $\{z, z'\}$ with $z V z'$, and thus we obtain a view of the structure of the relation V. It is obvious how the system $\mathfrak{K}^{\mathfrak{A}}_{\max}$ can be obtain from $\mathfrak{K}^{\mathfrak{A}}_{2}$.

Let $\mathfrak{A} = [X, Y, Z, \delta, \lambda]$ be a finite partial automaton. We define by induction a sequence whose terms are systems of two-element sets as follows:

$$\mathfrak{M}_1 \underset{\mathrm{Df}}{=} \{\{z, z'\} \mid z, z' \in Z \wedge z \neq z' \wedge \wedge \forall x (x \in D(z) \cap D(z') \rightarrow \lambda(z, x) = \lambda(z', x))\}.$$

$$\mathfrak{M}_{i+1} \underset{\mathrm{Df}}{=} \{\{z, z'\} \mid \{z, z'\} \in \mathfrak{M}_i \wedge \forall x ([z, x], [z', x] \in Dom(\delta) \wedge \wedge \delta(z, x) \neq \delta(z', x) \rightarrow \{\delta(z, x), \delta(z', x)\} \in \mathfrak{M}_i)\}.$$

Obviously,

$$\mathfrak{M}_1 \supseteq \mathfrak{M}_2 \supseteq \cdots \supseteq \mathfrak{M}_i \supseteq \mathfrak{M}_{i+1} \supseteq \cdots$$

Lemma 10.9. *For* $z, z' \in Z$ *with* $z \neq z'$, $i = 1, 2, \ldots$

$$\{z, z'\} \in \mathfrak{M}_i \leftrightarrow \forall p \forall x (px \in D(z) \cap D(z') \wedge l(px) \leqq i \rightarrow \rightarrow \lambda(\delta(z, p), x) = \lambda(\delta(z', p), x)).$$

The proof is carried out by induction on i, where the initial step $i = 1$ is trivial by the definition of $\mathfrak{M}_1$. The step from i to $i+1$:

$$\begin{aligned}\{z, z'\} \in \mathfrak{M}_{i+1} \leftrightarrow & \{z, z'\} \in \mathfrak{M}_i \wedge \forall x' ([z, x'], [z', x'] \in Dom(\delta) \wedge \\ & \wedge \delta(z, x') \neq \delta(z', x') \rightarrow \{\delta(z, x'), \delta(z', x')\} \in \mathfrak{M}_i) \\ \leftrightarrow & \forall p \forall x (px \in D(z) \cap D(z') \wedge l(px) \leqq i \rightarrow \\ & \rightarrow \lambda(\delta(z, p), x) = \lambda(\delta(z', p), x)) \wedge \\ & \wedge \forall x' \forall p \forall x ([z,x'], [z',x'] \in Dom(\delta) \wedge \delta(z, x') \neq \delta(z',x') \wedge \\ & \wedge px \in D(\delta(z, x')) \cap D(\delta(z', x')) \wedge l(px) \leqq i \rightarrow \\ & \rightarrow \lambda(\delta(\delta(z', x'), p), x) = \lambda(\delta(\delta(z, x'), p), x)),\end{aligned}$$

applying the definition of $\mathfrak{M}_{i+1}$ and the induction hypothesis. The assumption $\delta(z, x') \neq \delta(z', x')$ can be omitted, since for $\delta(z, x') = \delta(z', x')$ the stated equality is trivially true. We can easily verify that

$$[z, x'], [z', x'] \in Dom(\delta) \wedge px \in D(\delta(z, x')) \cap D(\delta(z', x')) \leftrightarrow \leftrightarrow x'px \in D(z) \cap D(z').$$

Thus we obtain

$$\{z, z'\} \in \mathfrak{M}_{i+1} \leftrightarrow \forall p \, \forall x \big(px \in D(z) \cap D(z') \wedge l(px) \leqq i \rightarrow$$
$$\rightarrow \lambda(\delta(z, p), x) = \lambda(\delta(z', p), x)\big) \wedge$$
$$\wedge \forall p \, \forall x \big(px \in D(z) \cap D(z') \wedge 1 \leqq l(px) \leqq i + 1 \rightarrow$$
$$\rightarrow \lambda(\delta(z, p), x) = \lambda(\delta(z', p), x)\big)$$
$$\leftrightarrow \forall p \, \forall x \big(px \in D(z) \cap D(z') \wedge l(px) \leqq i + 1 \rightarrow$$
$$\rightarrow \lambda(\delta(z, p), x) = \lambda(\delta(z', p), x)\big),$$

which was to be shown.

Lemma 10.10. *There exists an* $i^* \leqq \binom{n}{2}$ *(with* $n = Card\,(Z)$*) such that* $\mathfrak{M}_{i^*} = \mathfrak{K}_2^{\mathfrak{A}})$.

Proof: We can readily see that $\mathfrak{M}_i = \mathfrak{M}_{i+1}$ always implies $\mathfrak{M}_{i+1} = \mathfrak{M}_{i+2}$. If $\mathfrak{M}_1 = \big\{\{z, z'\} \mid z, z' \in Z \wedge z \neq z'\big\}$, then $M_2 = M_1$, hence all the $\mathfrak{M}_i$'s coincide with $\mathfrak{M}_1$. Therefore the system $\mathfrak{M}_1$ cannot contain more than $\binom{n}{2} - 1$ elements if $\mathfrak{M}_2 \neq \mathfrak{M}_1$. If $\mathfrak{M}_i \neq \mathfrak{M}_{i+1}$, then the latter has fewer elements than $\mathfrak{M}_i$. Hence if $\mathfrak{M}_i \neq \mathfrak{M}_{i+1}$, then $\mathfrak{M}_{i+1}$ contains at most $\binom{n}{2} - (i+1)$ elements. Thus, for $i^* \underset{\mathrm{Df}}{=} min\,\{i \mid \mathfrak{M}_i = \mathfrak{M}_{i+1}\}$,

$$i^* \leqq \binom{n}{2}.$$

Hence for $z, z' \in Z$ with $z \neq z'$

$$\{z, z'\} \in \mathfrak{K}_2^{\mathfrak{A}} \leftrightarrow \forall p \, \forall x \big(px \in D(z) \cap D(z') \rightarrow \lambda(\delta(z, p), x)$$
$$= \lambda(\delta(z', p), x)\big)$$
$$\leftrightarrow \forall i (i \in nz \setminus \{0\} \rightarrow \{z, z'\} \in \mathfrak{M}_i)$$
$$\leftrightarrow \{z, z'\} \in \mathfrak{M}_{i^*}.$$

Thus Lemma 10.10 is proved.

From the definition of the sequence $\mathfrak{M}_1, \mathfrak{M}_2, \ldots$ we can easily derive an algorithm by means of which we can construct the system $\mathfrak{K}_2^{\mathfrak{A}}$ for every finite partial automaton.

Now we clarify this construction by an example: Let

$$\mathfrak{A}_{12} = [\{0, 1\}, \{a, b\}, \{1, 2, 3, 4, 5, 6\}, \delta^{12}, \lambda^{12}],$$

where δ^{12} and λ^{12} are specified in the following tables:

δ^{12}	1	2	3	4	5	6
0	3	6	5	2	1	4
1	6	—	—	—	4	1

λ^{12}	1	2	3	4	5	6
0	—	—	—	a	—	b
1	b	—	—	—	b	—

First we determine $\mathfrak{K}_2^{\mathfrak{A}}$ and $\mathfrak{K}_{\max}^{\mathfrak{A}}$. Then we have for $\mathfrak{M}^* = \{\{i, j\} \mid 1 \leqq i < j \leqq 6\}$,

$$\mathfrak{M}_1 = \mathfrak{M}^* \setminus \{\{4, 6\}\},$$
$$\mathfrak{M}_2 = \mathfrak{M}^* \setminus \{\{1, 5\}, \{2, 6\}, \{4, 6\}\},$$
$$\mathfrak{M}_3 = \mathfrak{M}^* \setminus \{\{1, 5\}, \{2, 4\}, \{2, 6\}, \{3, 5\}, \{4, 6\}\},$$
$$\mathfrak{M}_4 = \mathfrak{M}^* \setminus \{\{1, 3\}, \{1, 5\}, \{2, 4\}, \{2, 6\}, \{3, 5\}, \{4, 6\}\} = \mathfrak{M}_{4+i}.$$

Hence,

$$\mathfrak{K}_2^{\mathfrak{A}_{12}} = \{\{1, 2\}, \{1, 4\}, \{1, 6\}, \{2, 3\}, \{2, 5\}, \{3, 4\}, \{3, 6\}, \{4, 5\}, \{5, 6\}\}$$
$$= \mathfrak{K}_{\max}^{\mathfrak{A}_{12}}.$$

A covering of $\{1, \ldots, 6\}$ by compatibility classes of $\mathfrak{A}_{12}$ has to contain at least three classes. All coverings (in fact partitions) of this kind are listed below.

$$\mathfrak{N}_1 = \{\{1, 2\}, \{3, 4\}, \{5, 6\}\}, \qquad \mathfrak{N}_2 = \{\{1, 2\}, \{3, 6\}, \{4, 5\}\},$$
$$\mathfrak{N}_3 = \{\{1, 4\}, \{2, 3\}, \{5, 6\}\}, \qquad \mathfrak{N}_4 = \{\{1, 4\}, \{2, 5\}, \{3, 6\}\},$$
$$\mathfrak{N}_5 = \{\{1, 6\}, \{2, 3\}, \{4, 5\}\}, \qquad \mathfrak{N}_6 = \{\{1, 6\}, \{2, 5\}, \{3, 4\}\}.$$

One can easily verify that $\mathfrak{N}_2$, $\mathfrak{N}_3$ and $\mathfrak{N}_6$ are automaton coverings of $\mathfrak{A}_{12}$. Consequently, the automaton $\mathfrak{A}_{12}$ has three minima, $\mathfrak{A}_{\mathfrak{N}_2}$, $\mathfrak{A}_{\mathfrak{N}_3}$, and $\mathfrak{A}_{\mathfrak{N}_6}$, whose graphs are represented in Fig. 10. These three minima are essentially different in that no two of these automata can be completed in such a way that the resulting completely specified automata are Z-isomorphic.

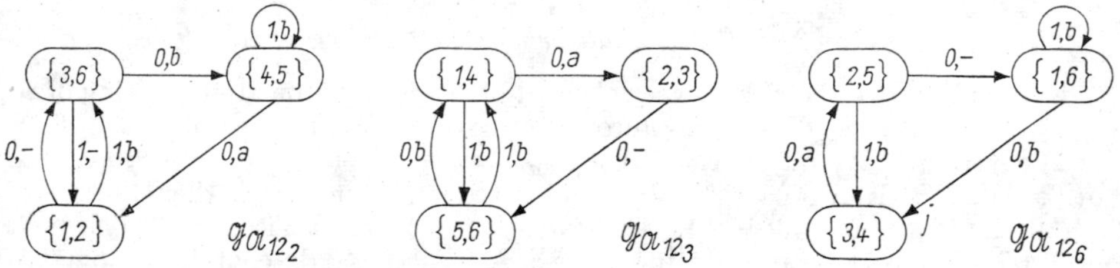

Fig. 10

In our example, the minimal automaton coverings were constructed by first finding all the coverings of minimal cardinality and consisting of compatibility classes, and then selecting from among these the automaton coverings $\mathfrak{N}_2$, $\mathfrak{N}_3$, and $\mathfrak{N}_6$. This procedure is in general not feasible, because it may happen that among the coverings of minimal cardinality consisting of compatibility classes, no automaton covering occurs. Then, the cardinalities of the coverings must be successively increased until we find an automaton covering. The surest way to avoid these difficulties is to construct all automaton coverings containing compatibility classes only for the given finite automaton, and select from among these all the coverings of minimal cardinality. In what follows we give an algorithm for the construction of *all* automaton coverings of a given finite partial automaton. If in the first step we apply this algorithm to compatibility classes only and contain $\{Z\}$ into $\mathfrak{M}$ only if Z is a compatibility class the set of all automaton coverings consisting of compatibility classes is constructed.

Let $\mathfrak{A} = [X, Y, Z, \delta, \lambda]$ be a partial automaton with $k = Card(Z) \geqq 2$.

1st Step: Let $M_1, M_2, \ldots, M_{2^k-(k+2)}$ be an enumeration of the elements of the set $\mathfrak{P}(Z) \setminus \left(\{\{z\} \mid z \in Z\} \cup \{\emptyset, Z\}\right)$.

2nd Step: For $i = 1, 2, \ldots, 2^k - (k+2)$ let

$$\langle \mathfrak{M}_i \rangle \underset{\mathrm{Df}}{=} \left\{M' \mid \exists p\left(p \in W(X) \wedge M' = \delta(M_i, p)\right)\right\},$$

$$\mathfrak{N}_{\langle M_i \rangle} \underset{\mathrm{Df}}{=} max\left(\langle M_i \rangle \cup \{\{z\} \mid z \in Z\}\right);$$

and put

$$\mathfrak{M} \underset{\mathrm{Df}}{=} \{\mathfrak{N}_{\langle M_i \rangle} \mid i = 1, \ldots, 2^k - (k+2)\} \cup \left\{\{Z\}, \{\{z\} \mid z \in Z\}\right\}.$$

3rd Step: Let $\mathfrak{M}_{\mathfrak{A}} = \{\bigsqcup \mathfrak{M}' \mid \mathfrak{M}' \subseteq \mathfrak{M} \wedge \mathfrak{M}' \neq \emptyset\}$, where for $\mathfrak{M}' = \{\mathfrak{N}_1, \ldots, \mathfrak{N}_m\}$ we set

$$\bigsqcup \mathfrak{M}' \underset{\mathrm{Df}}{=} \mathfrak{N}_1 \sqcup \ldots \sqcup \mathfrak{N}_m,$$

and for the coverings $\mathfrak{N}, \mathfrak{N}'$ of Z,

$$\mathfrak{N} \sqcup \mathfrak{N}' \underset{\mathrm{Df}}{=} \max(\mathfrak{N} \cup \mathfrak{N}').$$

Theorem 10.11. *$\mathfrak{M}_{\mathfrak{A}}$ is the set of all automaton coverings of $\mathfrak{A}$.*

Proof: First we show that every element of $\mathfrak{M}_{\mathfrak{A}}$ is an automaton covering of $\mathfrak{A}$.

If $M \subseteq Z$, then $\mathfrak{N}_{\langle M \rangle}$ is an automaton covering of $\mathfrak{A}$, since obviously $\mathfrak{N}_{\langle M \rangle}$ is a covering of Z and for each $N \in \mathfrak{N}_{\langle M \rangle}$, $x \in X$ there is an $N' \in \mathfrak{N}_{\langle M \rangle}$ with $\delta(N, x) \subseteq N'$. If N is a singleton, this is trivial. If it is not, then there is a $p \in W(X)$ with $N = \delta(M, p)$. Then $\delta(N, x) = \delta(M, px)$ is either an element of $\mathfrak{N}_{\langle M \rangle}$ or a subset of an element N' of $\mathfrak{N}_{\langle M \rangle}$. Hence $\mathfrak{M}$ only contains automaton coverings of $\mathfrak{A}$. To prove the rest it suffices to show that $\mathfrak{N}_1 \sqcup \mathfrak{N}_2$ is an automaton covering of $\mathfrak{A}$ if $\mathfrak{N}_1$ and $\mathfrak{N}_2$ are.

Let $N \in \mathfrak{N}_1 \sqcup \mathfrak{N}_2$ and $x \in X$. Then there is an $i \in \{1, 2\}$ with $N \in \mathfrak{N}_i$ anp consequently an $N' \in \mathfrak{N}_i$ with $\delta(N, x) \subseteq N'$. By $\mathfrak{N}_1 \sqcup \mathfrak{N}_2 = max(\mathfrak{N}_1 \cup \mathfrak{N}_2)$, there exists an $N'' \in \mathfrak{N}_1 \sqcup \mathfrak{N}_2$ with $N' \subseteq N''$, i.e., with $\delta(N, x) \subseteq N''$.

Now we show that every automaton covering of $\mathfrak{A}$ belongs to $\mathfrak{M}_{\mathfrak{A}}$. Let $\mathfrak{N}$ be an arbitrary automaton covering of $\mathfrak{A}$ and $N_1, N_2, \ldots, N_n$ all the elements N of $\mathfrak{N}$ with $Card(N) \geqq 2$. If $n = 0$, then $\mathfrak{N} = \{\{z\} \mid z \in Z\}$ hence $\mathfrak{N} \in \mathfrak{M}_{\mathfrak{A}}$. Let us consider the case $n \geqq 1$. We claim

$$\mathfrak{N} = \bigsqcup_{i=1}^{n} \mathfrak{N}_{\langle N_i \rangle}.$$

We have $\mathfrak{N} = \{N_i \mid i = 1, \ldots, n\} \cup \left\{\{z\} \mid z \in Z \setminus \bigcup_{i=1}^{n} N_i\right\}$ and, since $\mathfrak{N}$ is an automaton covering,

$$\max\left(\bigcup_{i=1}^{n} \langle N_i \rangle\right) \subseteq \mathfrak{N}.$$

Thus, $\{N_1, \ldots, N_n\} \subseteq \max\left(\bigcup_{i=1}^{n} \langle N_i \rangle\right) \subseteq \mathfrak{N}$, because all the sets $N_1, \ldots, N_n$ have at least two elements. Therefore the system of sets $\max\left(\bigcup_{i=1}^{n} \langle N_i \rangle\right) \setminus \{N_1, \ldots, N_n\}$ can only contain singletons. Consequently

$$\begin{aligned}
\mathfrak{N} &= \max\left(\{N_1, \ldots, N_n\} \cup \left\{\{z\} \mid z \in Z\right\}\right) \\
&= \max\left(\bigcup_{i=1}^{n} \langle N_i \rangle \cup \left\{\{z\} \mid z \in Z\right\}\right) \\
&= \max\left(\bigcup_{i=1}^{n} \left(\max\left(\langle N_i \rangle \cup \{\{z\} \mid z \in Z\}\right)\right)\right) \\
&= \max\left(\bigcup_{i=1}^{n} \mathfrak{N}_{\langle N_i \rangle}\right) \\
&= \bigsqcup_{i=1}^{n} \mathfrak{N}_{\langle N_i \rangle}.
\end{aligned}$$

Thus Theorem 10.11. is proved.

A comparison between the minimization procedures for partial automata on one hand and completely specified automata on the other will obviously not be in favor of the former as developped here. This suggests that we should try to apply the reduction procedure developped for completely specified automata for partial automata, by first obtaining all possible completions of the partial automaton under consideration. In other words, we should try the following algorithm:

1st Step: Completion of the given automaton in all possible ways.

2nd Step: Reduction of the automata thus obtained.

3rd Step: Search among the resulting reducts for one or all automata with the minimal number of states.

Unfortunately, this procedure does not necessarily take us to our goal, i.e., to a minimum of the given partial automaton. This is shown by the example (due to Booth [5]), of the non-minimal automaton

$$\mathfrak{A}_{13} = [\{0, 1\}, \{a, b\}, \{1, 2, 3\}, \delta^{13}, \lambda^{13}]$$

with

δ^{13}	1	2	3	λ^{13}	1	2	3
0	1	3	2	0	$-$	a	b
1	2	1	1	1	a	a	a

as can be easily verified.

§ 11. Decomposition of Automata

In the theory of abstract automata we can deal with problems concerning the structure of automata, i.e., the connections within them. Here, in the notion of connection we abstract from the technical data. The elements of the connection we consider are not technical, such as transistors, resistances, etc.) but automata themselves, whose technical realization is irrelevant. Our next problem can be described shortly as follows: how can we "realize" a finite automaton, by composing simpler automata (i.e., automata with fewer states), connecting some of their outputs with certain inputs to a connection (perhaps with given structural properties)? This should be done in such a way that the resulting switching circuit can do the same job as the original. In this section we shall touch upon some of the most important results concerning this problem. They were considered for instance by BOOTH [5], BRZOZOWSKI [5], [7], GERACE and GESTRI [2], [3], GINZBURG [3], HARTMANIS [2], [5], [7], [9], HARTMANIS and STEARNS [5], KROHN and RHODES [1], [3], [5], SUNAGA [1], YOELI [1], [3], and ZEIGER [1], [2]. In our considerations we always include partial automata too, although we shall not call attention to the fact each time.

parallel connection $P(\alpha_1, \alpha_2, \eta)$

series or cascade connection $S(\alpha_1, \alpha_2)$

feedback connection $R(\alpha_1, \alpha_2, \zeta)$

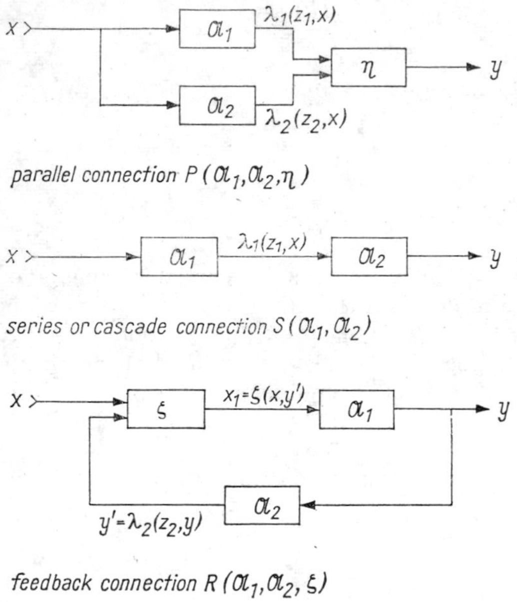

Fig. 11

We shall distinguish three basic connections by means of which two automata $\mathfrak{A}_1 = [X_1, Y_1, Z_1, \delta_1, \lambda_1]$, $\mathfrak{A}_2 = [X_2, Y_2, Z_2, \delta_2, \lambda_2]$ can be composed, namely the *parallel connection*, the *series* or *cascade connection*, and the *feedback connection* (cf. Fig. 11). A *parallel connection* of $\mathfrak{A}_1, \mathfrak{A}_2$ is only possible if $X_1 = X_2$. On the output side, we connect a combinatorial switch (an automaton with exactly one state), which realizes a function η from $Y_1 \times Y_2$ into the output alphabet Y of the parallel connection. In the simplest case we have $Y = Y_1 \times Y_2$ and $\eta = I_{Y_1 \times Y_2}$. The *parallel connection* $P(\mathfrak{A}_1, \mathfrak{A}_2, \eta)$ is the automaton $[X_1, Y, Z_1 \times Z_2, \delta_P, \lambda_P]$, where

$$\delta_P([z_1, z_2], x) = \begin{cases} [\delta_1(z_1, x), \delta_2(z_2, x)], & \text{if } [z_i, x] \in Dom(\delta_i),\ i \in \{1, 2\} \\ \text{not defined otherwise;} \end{cases}$$

$$\lambda_P([z_1, z_2], x) = \begin{cases} \eta\big(\lambda_1(z_1, x), \lambda_2(z_2, x)\big), & \text{if } [z_i, x] \in Dom(\lambda_i),\ i \in \{1, 2\} \\ \text{not defined otherwise,} \end{cases}$$

for all $z_1 \in Z_1$, $z_2 \in Z_2$, $x \in X_1 = X_2$.

In order to obtain a *series connection* of $\mathfrak{A}_1, \mathfrak{A}_2$, $Y_1 \subseteq X_2$ must be satisfied. In this case, the series connection is the automaton

$$S(\mathfrak{A}_1, \mathfrak{A}_2) \underset{\mathrm{Df}}{=} [X_1, Y_2, Z_1 \times Z_2, \delta_S, \lambda_S],$$

where

$$\delta_S([z_1, z_2], x) = \begin{cases} \big[\delta_1(z_1, x), \delta_2\big(z_2, \lambda_1(z_1, x)\big)\big], & \text{if all functions are defined,} \\ \text{not defined otherwise;} \end{cases}$$

$$\lambda_S([z_1, z_2], x) = \begin{cases} \lambda_2\big(z_2, \lambda_1(z_1, x)\big), & \text{if } \lambda_1, \lambda_2 \text{ are defined,} \\ \text{not defined otherwise,} \end{cases}$$

for all $z_1 \in Z_1$, $z_2 \in Z_2$, $x \in X_1$.

In a *feedback connection*, certain difficulties might arise which can only be avoided by imposing restrictions on the corresponding automata. If we consider the feedback connection represented in Fig. 11, we see that for the output signal y of this connection,

$$\begin{aligned} y = \lambda_R([z_1, z_2], x) &= \lambda_1(z_1, x_1) \\ &= \lambda_1\big(z_1, \zeta(x, \lambda_2(z_2, y))\big) \end{aligned}$$

is satisfied. We can easily construct examples where this equality has no solution for y, hence the result of the connection of $\mathfrak{A}_1, \mathfrak{A}_2$ according to Fig. 11, is not an automaton. This can be avoided by assuming that λ_2 does not depend on its second argument. If this assumption holds, and $X_2 \subseteq Y_1$, then the *feedback connection* $R(A_1, A_2, \zeta)$ of A_1 over A_2 by means of the function ζ which maps

$X \times Y_2$ into X_1 is the automaton $[X, Y_1, Z_1 \times Z_2, \delta_R, \lambda_R]$ with

$$\delta_R([z_1, z_2], x) = \begin{cases} \left[\delta_1\big(z_1, \zeta(x, \lambda_2(z_2))\big), \ \delta_2\big(z_2, \lambda_1(z_1, \zeta(x, \lambda_2(z_2)))\big)\right], \\ \qquad\qquad \text{if all these functions are defined,} \\ \text{not defined otherwise;} \end{cases}$$

$$\lambda_R([z_1, z_2], x) = \begin{cases} \lambda_1\big(z_1, \zeta(x, \lambda_2(z_2))\big), & \text{if } \lambda_2, \lambda_1 \text{ are defined,} \\ \text{not defined otherwise,} \end{cases}$$

for all $z_1 \in Z_1$, $z_2 \in Z_2$, $x \in X$.

Thus automata in which the output function does not depend on its second argument can be used in arbitrary connections. Consider an automaton $\mathfrak{A}$ obtained by composing the automata $\mathfrak{A}_i = [X_i, Y_i, Z_i, \delta_i, \lambda_i]$. The set Z of all states of $\mathfrak{A}$ is obviously a Cartesian product of the sets Z_i, and the output function λ of $\mathfrak{A}$ only depends on the input signal x of $\mathfrak{A}$ and the states $z^i \in Z_i$ of the automata $\mathfrak{A}_i$. Consequently, the output function of $\mathfrak{A}$ can be realized by a combinatorial automaton having the input alphabet $X \times \bigtimes_{i=1}^{n} Z_i$, and the rest of the connection can be constructed from automata of special types which we call *components*.

Definition 11.1. The automaton $\mathfrak{A} = [X, Y, Z, \delta, \lambda]$ is called a *component* if $Y = Z$, $\mathit{Card}(Z) \geqq 2$, $\mathit{Dom}(\lambda) = Z \times X$ and for all $z \in Z$, $x \in X$ we have $\lambda(z, x) = z$. We denote the component $\mathfrak{A}$ by $[X, Z, \delta]$.

It is obvious that only using components in a connection can be more costly than using ordinary automata, if the necessary channel capacity of the connections between the components is bigger (e.g., if the automaton to be replaced by a component has fewer output signals than states). However here we shall only consider some fundamental problems of the decomposition of automata, and therefore we restrict ourselves to connections consisting of components. In this way, problems of existence can obviously be avoided. Now we clarify the notions of a connection and a decomposition.

Definition 11.2. $\mathfrak{S} = [X, Y, Z_{\mathfrak{S}}, \delta_{\mathfrak{S}}, \lambda_{\mathfrak{S}}]$ is a *connection of the components* $\mathfrak{A}_1 = [X_1, Z_1, \delta_1], \ldots, \mathfrak{A}_k = [X_k, Z_k, \delta_k]$ $(k \geqq 2)$, if $\mathfrak{S}$ is a partial automaton with $Z_{\mathfrak{S}} = Z_1 \times \cdots \times Z_k$, and for every $\varkappa = 1, \ldots, k$ there is a non-empty subset $\{i(\varkappa, 1), \ldots, i(\varkappa, n_\varkappa)\}$ of the set $\{0, 1, \ldots, k\} \setminus \{\varkappa\}$ $\big($with $i(\varkappa, 1) < \cdots < i(\varkappa, n_\varkappa)\big)$ such that (putting $Z_0 = X$)

$$X_\varkappa = \bigtimes_{\nu=1}^{n_\varkappa} Z_{i(\varkappa,\nu)}$$

and for all $[z^1, \ldots, z^k] \in Z_\gamma$, $z^0 \in X$

$$\delta([z^1, \ldots, z^k], z^0) = \begin{cases} \left[\delta_1(z^1, [z^{i(1,1)}, \ldots, z^{i(1,n_1)}]), \ldots, \delta_k(z^k, [z^{i(k,1)} \ldots, z^{i(k,n_k)}])\right], \\ \qquad\qquad \text{if all } \delta_\varkappa \text{ are defined,} \\ \text{not defined otherwise.} \end{cases}$$

Definition 11.3. The connection $\mathfrak{S}$ of the components $\mathfrak{A}_1, \ldots, \mathfrak{A}_k$ is called *loop-free* if there is an enumeration of the components such that for all $\varkappa = 1, \ldots, k$ we have $i(\varkappa, n_\varkappa) < \varkappa$.

Thus in a loop-free connection, the components can be enumerated in such a way that every component can only receive information in its input from components with a smaller index. Consequently, any loop-free connection can be divided into levels, where the components of the ith level can only receive the output signals of the components belonging to the levels $1, \ldots, i-1$, as input signals. Hence the components of the first level only receive the input signals of the connection itself.

Definition 11.4. The connection $\mathfrak{S} = [X', Y', Z_{\mathfrak{S}}, \delta_{\mathfrak{S}}, \lambda_{\mathfrak{S}}]$ of the components $\mathfrak{A}_1 = [X_1, Z_1, \delta_1], \ldots, \mathfrak{A}_k = [X_k, Z_k, \delta_k]$ $(k \geqq 2)$ is called a *decomposition of the automaton* $\mathfrak{A} = [X, Y, Z, \delta, \lambda]$ if

a) $X = X'$, $Y = Y'$;

b) $Card(Z_\varkappa) < Card(Z)$ for $\varkappa = 1, \ldots, k$ and

c) $\mathfrak{A} \trianglelefteq \mathfrak{S}$.

If moreover $\mathfrak{S}$ is loop-free, then it is referred to as a *loop-free decomposition*. If all components of the decomposition $\mathfrak{S}$ of $\mathfrak{A}$ have the input alphabet $X_\varkappa = X$, then $\mathfrak{S}$ is called a *parallel decomposition* of $\mathfrak{A}$. If for each $\varkappa$, $X_\varkappa = X \times Z_{\varkappa-1}$ or $X_\varkappa = X$ or $X_\varkappa = Z_{\varkappa-1}$, then $\mathfrak{S}$ is called a *series decomposition* of $\mathfrak{A}$.

Obviously, every loop-free decomposition consisting of exactly two components is a series decomposition.

In what follows we shall need certain notions and notations. Let Z be an arbitrary non-empty set and $\mathfrak{N}, \mathfrak{N}'$ coverings of Z. Then we define

$$\mathfrak{N} \leq \mathfrak{N}' \underset{\mathrm{Df}}{\leftrightarrow} \forall K\big(K \in \mathfrak{N} \to \exists K'(K' \in \mathfrak{N}' \wedge K \subseteq K')\big),$$

$$\mathfrak{N} < \mathfrak{N}' \underset{\mathrm{Df}}{\leftrightarrow} \mathfrak{N} \neq \mathfrak{N}' \wedge \mathfrak{N} \leq \mathfrak{N}',$$

i.e., $\leq$ (or $<$) denotes the relation "finer or equal" (or "properly finer") between coverings of Z. Furthermore we set

$$\mathfrak{N} \sqcap \mathfrak{N}' = max\,\{K \cap K' \mid K \in \mathfrak{N} \wedge K' \in \mathfrak{N}'\}.$$

We can readily see that $\mathfrak{N} \sqcap \mathfrak{N}'$ is the coarsest covering $\mathfrak{N}^*$ of Z such that $\mathfrak{N}^* \leq \mathfrak{N}$ and $\mathfrak{N}^* \leq \mathfrak{N}'$. It is just as clear that $\mathfrak{N} \sqcap \mathfrak{N}'$ is a partition of Z, provided $\mathfrak{N}, \mathfrak{N}'$ are partitions of Z and that $\mathfrak{N} \sqcap \mathfrak{N}'$ is an automaton covering (or an automaton partition) if $\mathfrak{N}$ and $\mathfrak{N}'$ are.

The finest partition $\big\{\{z\} \mid z \in Z\big\}$ of Z is denoted by $\mathfrak{z}^0$ and the coarsest partition $\{Z\}$ by $\mathfrak{z}^1$. If $\mathfrak{N}, \mathfrak{N}'$ are coverings (or partitions) of the set Z of all states of an automaton $\mathfrak{A} = [X, Y, Z, \delta, \lambda]$, and for every $N \in \mathfrak{N}$, $x \in X$, there is a class $N' \in \mathfrak{N}'$ with $\delta(N, x) \subseteq N'$, then $[\mathfrak{N}, \mathfrak{N}']$ is called a *covering pair* (or a *partition pair*) *of* $\mathfrak{A}$.

In the above references, several algorithms were developped by means of which the sets of all automaton coverings, all covering pairs and all partition pairs can be constructed for an arbitrary finite automaton. The set of all automaton coverings can be obviously obtained by means of the algorithm given in the preceeding section. Since covering and partition pairs are only of interest in the case of series decompositions, and this type of decomposition is not dealt with here in detail, the corresponding construction algorithms are also omitted.

Theorem 11.1. *Every Z-finite automaton* $\mathfrak{A} = [X, Y, Z, \delta, \lambda]$ *with* $Card\,(Z) \geqq 3$ *has a decomposition.*

Proof: Since $Card\,(Z) \geqq 3$, there is an $n \geqq 2$ and pairwise distinct partitions $\mathfrak{z}_1, \ldots, \mathfrak{z}_n$ of Z such that $\mathfrak{z}^0 < \mathfrak{z}_i < \mathfrak{z}^1$ for $i = 1, \ldots, n$ and $\mathfrak{z}_1 \sqcap \cdots \sqcap \mathfrak{z}_n = \mathfrak{z}^0$. We fix this set of partitions and put for $i = 1, \ldots, n$

$$Z_i = \mathfrak{z}_i,$$
$$X_i = X \times \mathfrak{z}_1 \times \cdots \times \mathfrak{z}_{i-1} \times \mathfrak{z}_{i+1} \times \cdots \times \mathfrak{z}_n,$$

and for $N_i \in \mathfrak{z}_i$ $(1 \leqq i \leqq n)$, $x \in X$

$$\delta_i(N_i, x, N_1, \ldots, N_{i-1}, N_{i+1}, \ldots, N_n) \underset{\mathrm{Df}}{=} \begin{cases} \text{that } N' \in \mathfrak{z}_i \text{ for which } \delta\left(\bigcap_{i=1}^{n} N_i, x\right) \subseteq N', \text{ if } \delta\left(\bigcap_{i=1}^{n} N_i, x\right) \neq \emptyset, \\ \text{not defined otherwise.} \end{cases}$$

If $\delta\left(\bigcap_{i=1}^{n} N_i, x\right) \neq \emptyset$, then $\bigcap_{i=1}^{n} N_i \neq \emptyset$. Because of $\prod_{i=1}^{n} \mathfrak{z}_i = \mathfrak{z}^0$, $\bigcap_{i=1}^{n} N_i$ hence $\delta\left(\bigcap_{i=1}^{n} N_i, x\right)$ too is a singleton. If $M \subseteq Z$ is a singleton, we denote its single element by $\zeta(M)$.

Let $\mathfrak{S} = [X, Y, \mathfrak{z}_1 \times \cdots \times \mathfrak{z}_n, \delta_\mathfrak{S}, \lambda_\mathfrak{S}]$ be the connection consisting of the components $\mathfrak{A}_1 = [X_1, z_1, \delta_1], \ldots, \mathfrak{A}_n = [X_n, z_n, \delta_n]$, whose output function $\lambda_\mathfrak{S}$ is defined as follows:

$$\lambda_\mathfrak{S}([N_1, \ldots, N_n], x) = \begin{cases} \lambda\left(\zeta\left(\bigcap_{i=1}^{n} N_i\right), x\right), & \text{if } \bigcap_{i=1}^{n} N_i \neq \emptyset \\ & \text{and } \lambda \text{ is defined.} \end{cases}$$

Since $\mathfrak{z}^0 < \mathfrak{z}_i < \mathfrak{z}^1$, we have $2 \leqq Card\,(\mathfrak{z}_i) < Card\,(\mathfrak{z}^0) = Card\,(Z)$. We still have to show that $\mathfrak{A} \preceq \mathfrak{S}$. For this we prove that for each $z \in Z$ the state $[N_1, \ldots, N_n]$ of $\mathfrak{S}$ with $\zeta\left(\bigcap_{i=1}^{n} N_i\right) = z$ covers the state z of Z. For each $z \in Z$ there exists an n-tuple $[N_1, \ldots, N_n] \in \mathfrak{z}_1 \times \cdots \times \mathfrak{z}_n$ with $\bigcap_{i=1}^{n} N_i = \{z\}$, since $\prod_{i=1}^{n} \mathfrak{z}_i = \mathfrak{z}^0$. By 10.3 we have to prove

$$\forall p\, \forall x \big(px \in D_\mathfrak{S}(z) \to px \in D_\mathfrak{S}([N_1, \ldots, N_n]) \wedge$$
$$\wedge\, \lambda(\delta(z, p), x) = \lambda_\mathfrak{S}(\delta_\mathfrak{S}([N_1, \ldots, N_n], p), x)\big).$$

The proof is carried out by induction on p. The initial step is $p = e$. $x \in D(z)$ implies $[z, x] \in Dom(\lambda)$, i.e., $\left[\zeta\left(\bigcap_{i=1}^{n} N_i\right), x\right] \in Dom(\lambda_{\mathfrak{S}})$, i.e., $[[N_1, \ldots, N_n], x] \in Dom(\lambda_{\mathfrak{S}})$, $x \in D_{\mathfrak{S}}([N_1, \ldots, N_n])$ and $\lambda(z, x) = \lambda_{\mathfrak{S}}([N_1, \ldots, N_n], x)$.

The induction step is taken from p to $x_1 p$. $x_1 p x \in D(z)$ implies $[z, x_1] \in Dom(\delta)$ and $px \in D(\delta(z, x_1))$. Since $[z, x_1] \in Dom(\delta)$ and $\bigcap_{i=1}^{n} N_i = \{z\}$, $\delta\left(\bigcap_{i=1}^{n} N_i, x_1\right) \neq \emptyset$, consequently, $[[N_1, \ldots, N_n], x_1] \in Dom(\delta_{\mathfrak{S}})$. Let $\delta_{\mathfrak{S}}([N_1, \ldots, N_n], x_1) = [N_1', \ldots, N_n']$. Then $\emptyset \neq \delta\left(\bigcap_{i=1}^{n} N_i, x_1\right) \subseteq \bigcap_{i=1}^{n} N_i'$, hence $\bigcap_{i=1}^{n} N_i' = \{\delta(z, x_1)\}$. This and $px \in D(\delta(z, x_1))$ imply by the induction hypothesis

$$px \in D_{\mathfrak{S}}(\delta_{\mathfrak{S}}[N_1, \ldots, N_n], x_1)) \quad \text{i.e.,} \quad x_1 px \in D_{\mathfrak{S}}([N_1, \ldots, N_n]).$$

Furthermore,

$$\begin{aligned} \lambda(\delta(z, x_1 p), x) &= \lambda(\delta(\delta(z, x_1), p), x) \\ &= \lambda_{\mathfrak{S}}(\delta_{\mathfrak{S}}([N_1', \ldots, N_n'], p), x) \\ &= \lambda_{\mathfrak{S}}(\delta_{\mathfrak{S}}([N_1, \ldots, N_n], x_1 p), x), \end{aligned}$$

which was to be shown.

Remark. If $\mathfrak{A}$ is a completely specified automaton, then the mapping χ which assigns to every state $[N_1, \ldots, N_n]$ of $\mathfrak{S}$ with $\bigcap_{i=1}^{n} N_i \neq \emptyset$ the state $\zeta\left(\bigcap_{i=1}^{n} N_i\right)$ of $\mathfrak{A}$, is a Z-homomorphism of the subautomaton $\mathfrak{S}^*$ of $\mathfrak{S}$ with the set of states $Z^* = \left\{[N_1, \ldots, N_n] \mid \bigcap_{i=1}^{n} N_i \neq \emptyset \wedge \bigwedge_{i=1}^{n} N_i \in \mathfrak{Z}_i\right\}$ onto the automaton $\mathfrak{A}$.

Theorem 11.2. *If a automaton* $\mathfrak{A} = [X, Y, Z, \delta, \lambda]$ *has a loop-free decomposition, then there are a* $k \geq 2$ *and automaton coverings* $\mathfrak{N}_1^*, \ldots, \mathfrak{N}_k^*$ *of* $\mathfrak{A}$ *with* $\mathfrak{z}^1 > \mathfrak{N}_1^* > \cdots > \mathfrak{N}_k^* \geq \mathfrak{z}^0$, $\prod_{\varkappa=1}^{k} \mathfrak{N}_\varkappa^* = \mathfrak{z}^0$ *and* $Card(\mathfrak{N}_1) < Card(Z)$.

Proof: Let $\mathfrak{S} = [X, Y, Z_{\mathfrak{S}}, \delta_{\mathfrak{S}}, \lambda_{\mathfrak{S}}]$ be a loop-free decomposition of $\mathfrak{A}$ consisting of the components $\mathfrak{A}_i = [X_i, Z_i, \delta_i]$ in this enumeration $(1 \leq i \leq n)$. For $i = 1, \ldots, n$ we put

$$\mathfrak{z}_i = \left\{\{z^1\} \times \cdots \times \{z^i\} \times Z_{i+1} \times \cdots \times Z_n \mid \bigwedge_{j=1}^{i} z^j \in Z_j\right\},$$

$$\mathfrak{N}_i = max\left(\{\{z \mid z \in Z \wedge \exists z^* (z^* \in K^i \wedge z \doteq z^*) \mid K^i \in \mathfrak{z}_i\}\right).$$

Lemma 11.2a. *For each* $j = 1, \ldots, n$, $\mathfrak{N}_j$ *is an automaton covering of* $\mathfrak{A}$.

Let $N_j \in \mathfrak{N}_j$ and $x \in X$. Then there is a $[z_0^1, \ldots, z_0^j] \in Z_1 \times \cdots \times Z_j$ such that

$$N_j = \{z \mid z \in Z \wedge \exists z^* (z^* \in \{z_0^1\} \times \cdots \times \{z_0^j\} \times Z_{j+1} \times \cdots \times Z_n \wedge z \doteq z^*)\}.$$

If $\delta(N_j, x) = \emptyset$, then $\delta(N_j, x) \subseteq N'_j$ for every $N'_j \in \mathfrak{N}_j$. Suppose $z' \in \delta(N_j, x)$, then $z' = \delta(z, x)$ for a certain $z \in N_j$. There is a $[z_0^{j+1}, \ldots, z_0^n] \in Z_{j+1} \times \cdots \times Z_n$ with $z \doteq [z_0^1, \ldots, z_0^j, z_0^{j+1}, \ldots, z_0^n]$. We have $[z, x] \in Dom(\delta)$ and since $\mathfrak{A}$ has no degenerate states, $\big[[z_0^1, \ldots, z_0^n], x\big] \in Dom(\delta_{\mathfrak{S}})$, because $z \doteq [z_0^1, \ldots, z_0^n]$. Consequently, for $z_0^0 = x$ we obtain

$$\begin{aligned} z' = \delta(z, x) &\doteq \delta_{\mathfrak{S}}([z_0^1, \ldots, z_0^n], z_0^0) = \\ &= \big[\delta_1(z_0^1, x), \ldots, \delta_j(z_0^j, [z_0^{i(j,1)}, \ldots, z_0^{i(j,n_j)}]), \ldots \\ &\qquad \ldots, \delta_n(z_0^n, [z_0^{i(n,1)}, \ldots, z_0^{i(n,n_n)}])\big] \in \\ &\in \{\delta_1(z_0^1, x)\} \times \cdots \times \{\delta_j(z_0^j, [z_0^{i(j,1)}, \ldots, z_0^{i(j,n_j)}])\} \times Z_{j+1} \times \cdots \times Z_n. \end{aligned}$$

Thus for each $z' \in \delta(N_j, x)$ there is a z^* in a class $K \in \mathfrak{z}_j$ with $z' \doteq z^*$, hence there is an $N'_j \in \mathfrak{N}_j$ with $\delta(N_j, x) \subseteq N'_j$. Thus Lemma 11.2a is proved.

Obviously,

$$\begin{aligned} \mathfrak{N}_n &= max\left(\left\{\{z \mid z \in Z \wedge z \doteq [z^1, \ldots, z^n]\} \mid \bigwedge_{i=1}^{n} z^i \in Z_i\right\}\right) \\ &\geq \big\{\{z\} \mid z \in Z\big\} = \mathfrak{z}^0. \end{aligned}$$

Furthermore $\mathfrak{N}_i \geq \mathfrak{N}_{i+1}$, since for every $z^{i+1} \in Z_{i+1}$

$$\left.\begin{aligned} &\big\{z \mid z \in Z \wedge \exists z^* (z \doteq z^* \in \{z_0^1\} \times \cdots \times \{z_0^i\} \times \{z^{i+1}\} \times Z_{i+2} \times \cdots \times Z_n)\big\} \\ &\subseteq \big\{z \mid z \in Z \wedge \exists z^* (z \doteq z^* \in \{z_0^1\} \times \cdots \times \{z_0^i\} \times Z_{i+1} \times \cdots \times Z_n)\big\}. \end{aligned}\right\} \qquad (*)$$

Let j be the smallest i with $\mathfrak{z}^1 > \mathfrak{N}_i$, hence

$$\mathfrak{z}^1 = \mathfrak{N}_1 = \cdots = \mathfrak{N}_{j-1} > \mathfrak{N}_j.$$

Then, as can be easily seen using (*),

$$Card(\mathfrak{N}_j) \leqq Card(Z_j) < Card(Z),$$

and $\mathfrak{z}^1 > \mathfrak{N}_j > \mathfrak{z}^0 \underset{\mathrm{Df}}{=} \mathfrak{N}_{n+1}$. If l is the smallest i with $\mathfrak{N}_i = \mathfrak{z}^0$, then $j < l \leq n + 1$ and

$$\mathfrak{z}^1 > \mathfrak{N}_j \geq \cdots \geq \mathfrak{N}_l = \mathfrak{z}^0.$$

Thus there is a k with $l - j + 1 \geqq k \geqq 2$, and automaton coverings $\mathfrak{N}_j = \mathfrak{N}_1^*$, $\ldots$, $\mathfrak{N}_k^* = \mathfrak{N}_l$ of $\mathfrak{A}$ such that $\mathfrak{z}^1 > \mathfrak{N}_1^* > \cdots > \mathfrak{N}_k^* = \mathfrak{z}^0$, $\prod_{i=1}^{k} \mathfrak{N}_i^* = \mathfrak{z}^0$ and $Card(\mathfrak{N}_1^*) < Card(Z)$, which was to be shown.

Corollary 11.3. If the automaton $\mathfrak{A}$ has a loop-free decomposition, then there is an automaton covering $\mathfrak{N}$ of $\mathfrak{A}$ with $\mathfrak{z}^1 > \mathfrak{N} > \mathfrak{z}^0$ and $Card(\mathfrak{N}) < Card(Z)$.

As an example, consider the automaton $\mathfrak{A}_{14} = [\{0, 1\}, \{0, 1\}, \{1, 2, 3, 4\}, \delta^{14}, \lambda^{14}]$ with

δ^{14}	1	2	3	4	λ^{14}	1	2	3	4
0	1	3	4	2	0	1	0	—	—
1	2	—	1	3	1	0	1	—	—

and the loop-free connection $\mathfrak{S} = [\{0, 1\}, \{0, 1\}, Z_1 \times Z_2, \delta_{\mathfrak{S}}, \lambda_{\mathfrak{S}}]$ of the components $\mathfrak{A}_1 = [\{0, 1\}, Z_1, \delta_1]$, $\mathfrak{A}_2 = [\{0, 1\} \times Z_1, Z_2, \delta_2]$, where $Z_1 = \{a, b, c\}$, $Z_2 = \{d, e, f\}$ and the functions δ_1, δ_2 and $\lambda_{\mathfrak{S}}$ are given in the following tables:

δ_1	a	b	c
0	c	a	b
1	b	a	a

δ_2	d	e	f
$[0, a]$	d	e	f
$[0, b]$	d	f	e
$[0, c]$	d	f	e
$[1, a]$	e	d	d
$[1, b]$	e	e	f
$[1, c]$	e	e	f

$\lambda_{\mathfrak{S}}$	$[a, d]$	$[a, e]$	$[a, f]$	$[b, d]$	$[b, e]$	$[b, f]$	$[c, d]$	$[c, e]$	$[c, f]$
0	1	0	—	1	0	—	1	—	—
1	0	1	—	0	1	—	0	—	—

We can easily see that

$$1 \triangleq [a, d], [b, d], [c, d],$$
$$2 \triangleq [a, e], [b, e],$$
$$3 \triangleq [a, f], [c, e],$$
$$4 \triangleq [b, f], [c, f],$$

hence $\mathfrak{S}$ is a loop-free decomposition (a series decomposition) of $\mathfrak{A}$. We have

$$\mathfrak{z}_1 = \{\{a\} \times Z_2, \{b\} \times Z_2, \{c\} \times Z_2\},$$

hence

$$\mathfrak{R}_1 = \{\{1, 2, 3\}, \{1, 2, 4\}, \{1, 3, 4\}\}$$

is an automaton covering of $\mathfrak{A}_{14}$ with the properties required in 11.3. We remark that the automaton $\mathfrak{A}_{14}$ has no non-trivial automaton partitions. Hence the condition given in the following theorem is not necessary for the existence of a loop-free decomposition.

Theorem 11.4. *If* $k \geqq 2$ *and* $\mathfrak{z}_1, \ldots, \mathfrak{z}_k$ *are pairwise different automaton partitions of the Z-finite automaton* $\mathfrak{A} = [X, Y, Z, \delta, \lambda]$ *with* $\prod_{\varkappa=1}^{k} \mathfrak{z}_\varkappa = \mathfrak{z}^0$ *and* $\bigwedge_{\varkappa=1}^{k} \mathfrak{z}_\varkappa \neq \mathfrak{z}^1$, *then* $\mathfrak{A}$ *has a loop-free decomposition.*

Proof: If $\mathfrak{Z}$ is a set of partitions of Z, then we denote by $max(\mathfrak{Z})$ the set of those elements of $\mathfrak{Z}$ which are maximal (i.e., the coarsest) with respect to the relation $\leq$.

Let $\mathfrak{Z} = \{\mathfrak{z}_1, \ldots, \mathfrak{z}_k\}$ be a set of partitions of Z having the above properties and

$$\mathfrak{Z}^1 \underset{\text{Df}}{=} max(\mathfrak{Z}) = \{\mathfrak{z}_1, \ldots, \mathfrak{z}_{r_1}\}.$$

Here, $1 \leqq r_1 \leqq k$ and $\mathfrak{z}^0 \notin \mathfrak{Z}^1$ (since otherwise $\mathfrak{Z}^1 = \{\mathfrak{z}^0\} = \mathfrak{Z}$ hence $k = 1$ would hold). Consequently $Card(\mathfrak{z}_i) < Card(Z)$ for $i = 1, \ldots, r_1$. For each $i = 1, \ldots, r_1$ we define the component $\mathfrak{A}_i \underset{\text{Df}}{=} [X, \mathfrak{z}_i, \delta_i]$ as follows:

$$\delta_i(N_i, x) \underset{\text{Df}}{=} \begin{cases} \text{a fixed } N_i' \in \mathfrak{z}_i \text{ with } \delta(N_i, x) \subseteq N_i', \text{ if } \delta(N_i, x) \neq \emptyset, \\ \text{not defined otherwise,} \end{cases}$$

for all $N_i \in \mathfrak{z}_i$, $x \in X$.

We compose these components into a parallel connection, which is the first level $\mathfrak{S}_1 = [X, \mathfrak{z}_1 \times \cdots \times \mathfrak{z}_{r_1}, \delta^1]$ (a new component) of the connection we want to construct. Thus we have

$$\delta^1([N_1, \ldots, N_{r_1}], x) = [\delta_1(N_1, x), \ldots, \delta_{r_1}(N_{r_1}, x)].$$

Case 1: $r_1 = k$.

In this case the desired decomposition (which is even a parallel decomposition) is given by $\mathfrak{S}_1$ by defining its output function $\lambda_\mathfrak{S}$ as follows:

$$\lambda_\mathfrak{S}([N_1, \ldots, N_k], x) \underset{\text{Df}}{=} \begin{cases} \text{the unique } y \in \lambda\left(\bigcap_{\varkappa=1}^{k} N_\varkappa, x\right), \text{ if} \\ \qquad\qquad \lambda\left(\bigcap_{\varkappa=1}^{n} N_\varkappa, x\right) \neq \emptyset, \\ \text{not defined otherwise.} \end{cases}$$

Hence the connection $\mathfrak{S} = [X, Y, \mathfrak{z}_1 \times \cdots \times \mathfrak{z}_k, \delta^1, \lambda_\mathfrak{S}]$ has only one level. Since $\prod_{\varkappa=1}^{k} \mathfrak{z}_\varkappa = \mathfrak{z}^0$ for each $z \in Z$, there is exactly one $[N_1, \ldots, N_k] \in \mathfrak{z}_1 \times \cdots \times \mathfrak{z}_k$ with $\bigcap_{\varkappa=1}^{n} N_\varkappa = \{z\}$. Now we show that for $z \in \bigcap_{\varkappa=1}^{n} N_\varkappa$, $[N_1, \ldots, N_k] \in \mathfrak{z}_1 \times \cdots \times \mathfrak{z}_k$ we have $z \doteq [N_1, \ldots, N_k]$, hence

$$\forall p \, \forall x \big(px \in D(z) \to px \in D_\mathfrak{S}([N_1, \ldots, N_k]) \wedge$$
$$\wedge \, \lambda(\delta(z, p), x) = \lambda_\mathfrak{S}(\delta^1([N_1, \ldots, N_k], p), x)\big).$$

The proof is carried out by induction on p. The initial step is $p = e$. If $x \in D(z)$, then $[z, x] \in Dom(\lambda)$, hence by $\bigcap_{\varkappa=1}^{n} N_\varkappa = \{z\}$, we have $\big[[N_1, \ldots, N_k], x\big] \in Dom(\lambda_\mathfrak{S})$, i.e., $x \in D_\mathfrak{S}([N_1, \ldots, N_k])$ and $\lambda(z, x) = \lambda_\mathfrak{S}([N_1, \ldots, N_k], x)$.

The induction step is taken from p to $x_1 p$. $x_1 p x \in D(z)$ implies $[z, x_1] \in Dom(\delta)$ and $px \in D\big(\delta(z, x_1)\big)$. By $[z, x_1] \in Dom(\delta)$ and $\bigcap_{\varkappa=1}^{n} N_\varkappa = \{z\}$ we have $\delta(N_\varkappa, x_1) \neq \emptyset$ for all $\varkappa = 1, \ldots, k$, hence $\big[[N_1, \ldots, N_k], x_1\big] \in Dom(\delta^1)$. Let $\delta^1([N_1, \ldots, N_k], x_1) = [N_1', \ldots, N_k']$. Then $\bigcap_{\varkappa=1}^{k} N_\varkappa' = \{\delta(z, x_1)\}$. Thus $px \in D\big(\delta(z, x_1)\big)$ implies $px \in D_\mathfrak{S}([N_1', \ldots, N_k'])$, which together with $[N_1', \ldots, N_k'] = \delta^1([N_1, \ldots, N_k], x_1)$ implies the proposition $x_1 p x \in D_\mathfrak{S}([N_1, \ldots, N_k])$. We have

$$\begin{aligned} \lambda\big(\delta(z, x_1 p), x\big) &= \lambda\big(\delta(\delta(z, x_1), p), x\big) \\ &= \lambda_\mathfrak{S}\big(\delta^1([N_1', \ldots, N_k'], p), x\big) \quad \text{(by the induction hypothesis)} \\ &= \lambda_\mathfrak{S}\big(\delta^1([N_1, \ldots, N_k], x_1 p), x\big), \end{aligned}$$

which was to be shown.

Case 2: $r_1 < k$.

Let $\mathfrak{Z}^2 = max(\mathfrak{Z} \setminus \mathfrak{Z}^1) = \{\mathfrak{z}_{r_1+1}, \ldots, \mathfrak{z}_{r_2}\}$. Then $r_1 < r_2 \leqq k$. Moreover, for $\varrho = r_1 + 1, \ldots, r_2$ let

$$\mathfrak{Z}_\varrho^1 = \{\mathfrak{z} \mid \mathfrak{z} \in \mathfrak{Z}^1 \wedge \mathfrak{z} > \mathfrak{z}_\varrho\}.$$

We have $\emptyset \neq \mathfrak{Z}_\varrho^1 \subseteq \mathfrak{Z}^1$, since for each $\mathfrak{z} \in \mathfrak{Z}^2$ there is a $\mathfrak{z}' \in \mathfrak{Z}^1$ with $\mathfrak{z}' > \mathfrak{z}$ (since otherwise $\mathfrak{z} \in \mathfrak{Z}^1$ would hold). For $\varrho = r_1 + 1, \ldots, r_2$ we put

$$\mathfrak{z}_\varrho^* \underset{\mathrm{Df}}{=} \bigsqcap_{\mathfrak{z} \in \mathfrak{Z}_\varrho^1} \mathfrak{z}$$

and specify a partition $\bar{\mathfrak{z}}_\varrho$ as follows:

$$\bar{\mathfrak{z}}_\varrho \sqcap \mathfrak{z}_\varrho^* = \mathfrak{z}_\varrho, \quad 2 \leqq Card(\bar{\mathfrak{z}}_\varrho) < Card(Z).$$

Since every $\mathfrak{z} \in \mathfrak{Z}_\varrho^1$ is properly coarser than $\mathfrak{z}_\varrho$, we have $\mathfrak{z}_\varrho^* \geq \mathfrak{z}_\varrho$, consequently there exists a partition $\mathfrak{z}$ with $\mathfrak{z} \sqcap \mathfrak{z}_\varrho^* = \mathfrak{z}_\varrho$. $Card(\mathfrak{z}_\varrho^*) \geqq 2$ (since for every $\mathfrak{z} \in \mathfrak{Z}_\varrho^1$ we have $\mathfrak{z}_\varrho^* \leq \mathfrak{z} < \mathfrak{z}^1$), hence $\bar{\mathfrak{z}}_\varrho$ has at most $Card(Z)$-1 classes. On the other hand, $\bar{\mathfrak{z}}_\varrho$ has at least m_ϱ classes, where m_ϱ is the maximal number of classes of the partition $\mathfrak{z}_\varrho$ which are contained in one fixed class of $\mathfrak{z}_\varrho^*$. For $\varrho = r_1 + 1, \ldots, r_2$ we set

$$\begin{aligned} &\mathfrak{Z}_\varrho^1 = \{\mathfrak{z}_{\varrho,1}, \ldots, \mathfrak{z}_{\varrho,n_\varrho}\}, \\ &\mathfrak{A}_\varrho = [X_\varrho, \bar{\mathfrak{z}}_\varrho, \delta_\varrho], \quad \text{where} \\ &X_\varrho = X \times \mathfrak{z}_{\varrho,1} \times \cdots \times \mathfrak{z}_{\varrho,n_\varrho} \end{aligned}$$

which means that the output of the component $\mathfrak{A}_\sigma = \mathfrak{A}_{\varrho,\tau}$ $(1 \leq \sigma \leq r_1,$ $r_1 + 1 \leq \varrho \leq r_2,$ $1 \leq \tau \leq n_\varrho)$ of the first level $\mathfrak{S}_1$ of the required connection is linked to the input of the component $\mathfrak{A}_\varrho$ of the second level just constructed. For $\overline{N}_\varrho \in \bar{\mathfrak{z}}_\varrho$, $x \in X$, $N_{\varrho,\tau} \in \mathfrak{z}_{\varrho,\tau}$ we put

$$\delta_\varrho(\overline{N}_\varrho, [x, N_{\varrho,1}, \ldots, N_{\varrho,n_\varrho}]) \underset{\mathrm{Df}}{=}$$

$$\underset{\mathrm{Df}}{=} \begin{cases} \text{a fixed } \overline{N}'_\varrho \in \bar{\mathfrak{z}}_\varrho \text{ with } \delta\left(\bigcap\limits_{\tau=1}^{n_\varrho} N_{\varrho,\tau} \cap \overline{N}_\varrho, x\right) \subseteq \overline{N}'_\varrho, \\ \qquad\qquad\qquad\qquad \text{if } \delta\left(\bigcap\limits_{\tau=1}^{n_\varrho} N_{\varrho,\tau} \cap \overline{N}_\varrho, x\right) \neq \emptyset, \\ \text{not defined otherwise.} \end{cases}$$

This definition is justified because $\bigcap\limits_{\tau=1}^{n_\varrho} N_{\varrho,\tau} \cap \overline{N}_\varrho$ is either empty or a class of $\mathfrak{z}_\varrho = \mathfrak{z}_\varrho^* \sqcap \bar{\mathfrak{z}}_\varrho$, and because $\mathfrak{z}_\varrho \leq \bar{\mathfrak{z}}_\varrho$ is an automaton partition of $\mathfrak{A}$.

Case 3: $r_2 = k$.

In this case $\mathfrak{S} = [X, Y, \mathfrak{z}_1 \times \cdots \times \mathfrak{z}_{r_1} \times \bar{\mathfrak{z}}_{r_1+1} \times \cdots \times \bar{\mathfrak{z}}_k, \delta_\mathfrak{S}, \lambda_\mathfrak{S}]$ is the desired connection, if we define $\lambda_\mathfrak{S}$ as follows:

$$\lambda_\mathfrak{S}([N_1, \ldots, N_{r_1}, \overline{N}_{r_1+1}, \ldots, \overline{N}_k], x) \underset{\mathrm{Df}}{=}$$

$$\underset{\mathrm{Df}}{=} \begin{cases} \text{the unique } y \in \lambda\left(\bigcap\limits_{\varrho=1}^{r_1} N_\varrho \cap \bigcap\limits_{\varrho=r_1+1}^{k} \overline{N}_\varrho, x\right), \text{ if this set is non-empty,} \\ \text{not defined otherwise.} \end{cases}$$

To justify this definition, we show that:

$$\mathfrak{z}^* \underset{\mathrm{Df}}{=} \prod_{\varrho=1}^{r_1} \mathfrak{z}_\varrho \sqcap \prod_{\varrho=r_1+1}^{k} \bar{\mathfrak{z}}_\varrho = \mathfrak{z}^0. \tag{**}$$

Let $K \in \mathfrak{z}^*$, $K = N_1 \cap N_2 \cap \cdots \cap N_{r_1} \cap \overline{N}_{r_1+1} \cap \cdots \cap \overline{N}_k \neq \emptyset$. Then

$$K = N_1 \cap \cdots \cap N_{r_1} \cap \left(\overline{N}_{r_1+1} \cap \bigcap_{\tau=1}^{n_{r_1+1}} N_{r_1+1,\tau}\right) \cap \cdots \cap \left(\overline{N}_k \cap \bigcap_{\tau=1}^{n_k} N_{k,\tau}\right) \neq \emptyset,$$

where $N_{\varrho,\tau} \in \{N_1, \ldots, N_{r_1}\} \cap \mathfrak{z}_{\varrho,\tau}$. Now $\bigcap\limits_{\tau=1}^{n_\sigma} N_{\sigma,\tau} \neq \emptyset$, hence it is a class of the partition $\mathfrak{z}^*_{\sigma}$, i.e., $\overline{N}_\sigma \cap \bigcap\limits_{\tau=1}^{n_\sigma} N_{\sigma,\tau}$ is a class N_σ of $\mathfrak{z}_\sigma$. Thus we obtain

$$K = N_1 \cap \cdots \cap N_{r_1} \cap N_{r_1+1} \cdots \cap \cdots \cap N_k \neq \emptyset,$$

i.e., K is a class of the partition $\mathfrak{z}^0 = \prod\limits_{\varkappa=1}^{k} \mathfrak{z}_\varkappa$, which was to be shown.

Next we prove that for $z^* = [N_1, \ldots, N_{r_1}, \overline{N}_{r_1+1}, \ldots, \overline{N}_k]$ with $\bigcap_{\varrho=1}^{r_1} N_\varrho \cap \bigcap_{\varrho=r_1+1}^{k} \overline{N}_\varrho = \{z\}$ we have $z \trianglelefteq z^*$, i.e.,

$$\forall p \, \forall x \big(px \in D(z) \to px \in D_{\mathfrak{S}}(z^*) \wedge \lambda(\delta(z, p), x) = \lambda_{\mathfrak{S}}(\delta_{\mathfrak{S}}(z^*, p), x)\big).$$

The proof is given by induction on p. The initial step $p = e$ is trivial. The induction step is taken from p to $x_1 p$.

$$x_1 px \in D(z) \text{ implies } [z, x_1] \subset Dom(\delta) \text{ and } px \in D\big(\delta(z, x_1)\big).$$

Since $\{z\} = \bigcap_{\varrho=1}^{r_1} N_\varrho \cap \bigcap_{\varrho=r_1+1}^{k} \overline{N}_\varrho$ and $[z, x_1] \in Dom(\delta)$, we have

$$\delta\left(\bigcap_{\varrho=1}^{r_1} N_\varrho \cap \bigcap_{\varrho=r_1+1}^{k} \overline{N}_\varrho, x_1\right) \neq \emptyset, \quad \delta\left(\bigcap_{\varrho=1}^{r_1} N_\varrho, x_1\right) \neq \emptyset.$$

Consequently, $[z^*, x_1] \in Dom(\delta_{\mathfrak{S}})$ and (**) implies for $\delta_{\mathfrak{S}}(z^*, x_1) = [N'_1, \ldots, N'_{r_1}, \overline{N}'_{r_1+1}, \ldots, \overline{N}'_k]$

$$\{\delta(z, x_1)\} = \bigcap_{\varrho=1}^{r_1} N'_\varrho \cap \bigcap_{\varrho=r_1+1}^{k} \overline{N}'_\varrho.$$

The rest of the proof is similar to that of Case 1.

Case 4. $r_2 < k$.

In this case the construction is continued in the same way, i.e., we put

$$\mathfrak{Z}^3 \underset{\text{Df}}{=} max\big(\mathfrak{Z} \setminus (\mathfrak{Z}^1 \cup \mathfrak{Z}^2)\big) = \{\mathfrak{z}_{r_2+1}, \ldots, \mathfrak{z}_{r_3}\}$$

and for $\varrho = r_2 + 1, \ldots, r_3$

$$\mathfrak{Z}^2_\varrho \underset{\text{Df}}{=} \{\mathfrak{z} \mid \mathfrak{z} \in \mathfrak{Z}^1 \cup \mathfrak{Z}^2 \wedge \mathfrak{z} > \mathfrak{z}_\varrho\} = \{\mathfrak{z}_{\varrho,1}, \ldots, \mathfrak{z}_{\varrho,n_\varrho}\},$$

furthermore

$$\mathfrak{z}^*_\varrho \underset{\text{Df}}{=} \prod_{\tau=1}^{n} \mathfrak{z}_{\varrho,\tau}$$

and determine a partition $\bar{\mathfrak{z}}_\varrho$ with $2 \leq Card(\mathfrak{z}_\varrho) < Card(Z)$ and $\mathfrak{z}^*_\varrho \sqcap \bar{\mathfrak{z}}_\varrho = \mathfrak{z}_\varrho$.

Finally the components $\mathfrak{A}_\varrho$ are defined as above. Obviously this procedure must stop in at most k steps and thus yields a loop-free decomposition of $\mathfrak{A}$ (with at most k levels).

Corollary 11.5. If the Z-finite automaton $\mathfrak{A}$ has a non-trivial automaton partition, then it also has a loop-free decomposition.

Let us consider for example the automaton $\mathfrak{A}_{15} = [\{0, 1\}, \{0, 1\}, \{1, 2, 3, 4, 5\}, \delta^{15}, \lambda^{15}]$, where

δ^{15}	1	2	3	4	5	λ^{15}	1	2	3	4	5
0	—	3	5	5	3	0	0	—	0	1	—
1	2	4	4	—	1	1	1	—	1	1	—

and the automaton partitions of $\mathfrak{A}_{15}$:

$$\mathfrak{z}_1 = \{\{1, 2, 4\}, \{3, 5\}\}, \qquad \mathfrak{z}_2 = \{\{1, 4\}, \{2, 3, 5\}\},$$
$$\mathfrak{z}_3 = \{\{1, 4\}, \{2\}, \{3\}, \{5\}\}, \qquad \mathfrak{z}_4 = \{\{1\}, \{2\}, \{3\}, \{4\}, \{5\}\} = \mathfrak{z}^0.$$

Here $k = 4$, $\mathfrak{Z}^1 = \{\mathfrak{z}_1, \mathfrak{z}_2\}$, $r_1 = 2$ and we obtain the components

$\mathfrak{A}_1 = [\{0, 1\}, \mathfrak{z}_1, \delta_1]$, $\mathfrak{A}_2 = [\{0, 1\}, \mathfrak{z}_2, \delta_2]$, where

δ_1	{1, 2, 4}	{3, 5}	δ_2	{1, 4}	{2, 3, 5}
0	{3, 5}	{3, 5}	0	{2, 3, 5}	{2, 3, 5}
1	{1, 2, 4}	{1, 2, 4}	1	{2, 3, 5}	{1, 4}

In the second step we obtain

$$\mathfrak{Z}^2 = \{\mathfrak{z}_3\}, \; r_2 = 3, \; \mathfrak{Z}_3^1 = \{\mathfrak{z}_1, \mathfrak{z}_2\} \text{ and}$$
$$\mathfrak{z}_3^* = \{\{1, 4\}, \{2\}, \{3, 5\}\}.$$

Now we choose

$$\bar{\mathfrak{z}}_3 = \{\{2, 5\}, \{1, 3, 4\}\}$$

and obtain the component $\mathfrak{A}_3 = [\{0, 1\} \times \mathfrak{z}_1 \times \mathfrak{z}_2, \bar{\mathfrak{z}}_3, \delta_3]$ with

δ_3	{2, 5}	{1, 3, 4}
[0, {1, 2, 4}, {1, 4}]	—	{2, 5}
[0, {1, 2, 4}, {2, 3, 5}]	{1, 3, 4}	—
[0, {3, 5}, {1, 4}]	—	—
[0, {3, 5}, {2, 3, 5}]	{1, 3, 4}	{2, 5}
[1, {1, 2, 4}, {1, 4}]	—	{2, 5}
[1, {1, 2, 4}, {2, 3, 5}]	{1, 3, 4)	—
[1, {3, 5}, {1, 4}]	—	—
[1, {3, 5}, {2, 3, 5}]	{1, 3, 4}	{1, 3, 4}

Here we see that by computing the next state of $\mathfrak{A}_3$ the information concerning the state either of $\mathfrak{A}_1$ or of $\mathfrak{A}_2$ can be omitted. This is reflected by the fact that both $[\mathfrak{z}_1 \sqcap \bar{\mathfrak{z}}_3, \bar{\mathfrak{z}}_3]$ and $[\mathfrak{z}_2 \sqcap \bar{\mathfrak{z}}_3, \bar{\mathfrak{z}}_3]$ are partition pairs of $\mathfrak{A}_{15}$. The corresponding simplified components are $\mathfrak{A}_3' = [\{0, 1\} \times \mathfrak{z}_1, \bar{\mathfrak{z}}_3, \delta_3']$, $\mathfrak{A}_3'' = [\{0, 1\} \times \mathfrak{z}_2, \mathfrak{z}_3, \delta_3'']$, where

δ_3'	{2, 5}	{1, 3, 4}
[0, {1, 2, 4}]	{1, 3, 4}	{2, 5}
[0, {3, 5}]	{1, 3, 4}	{2, 5}
[1, {1, 2, 4}]	{1, 3, 4}	{2, 5}
[1, {3, 5}]	{1, 3, 4}	{1, 3, 4}

δ_3''	{2, 5}	{1, 3, 4}
[0, {1, 4}]	—	{2, 5}
[0, {2, 3, 5}]	{1, 3, 4}	{2, 5}
[1, {1, 4}]	—	{2, 5}
[1, {2, 3, 5}]	{1, 3, 4}	{1, 3, 4}

In the third step we obtain

$$\mathfrak{Z}^3 = \{\mathfrak{z}_4\}, \qquad \mathfrak{Z}_4^2 = \{\mathfrak{z}_1, \mathfrak{z}_2, \mathfrak{z}_3\}, \qquad \mathfrak{z}_4^* = \mathfrak{z}_3 .$$

Now we seek a partition $\bar{\mathfrak{z}}_4$ with

$$\bar{\mathfrak{z}}_4 \sqcap \mathfrak{z}_3 = \bar{\mathfrak{z}}_4 \sqcap \mathfrak{z}_4^* = \mathfrak{z}_4 = \mathfrak{z}^0$$

and possibly with a small number of classes. Here all partitions with exactly two classes, and such that the states 1 and 4 belong to different classes, come into consideration. We choose

$$\bar{\mathfrak{z}}_4 = \{\{2, 4\}, \{1, 3, 5\}\}$$

and we see that

$$\bar{\mathfrak{z}}_3 \sqcap \bar{\mathfrak{z}}_4 = \{\{2\}, \{4\}, \{5\}, \{1, 3\}\},$$

consequently $[\mathfrak{z}_3 \sqcap \bar{\mathfrak{z}}_4, \bar{\mathfrak{z}}_4]$ is a partition pair of $\mathfrak{A}_{15}$. Therefore, in computing the next state of the component $\mathfrak{A}_4$ by applying the input signal of $\mathfrak{A}_{15}$, it suffices to know the state of $\mathfrak{A}_3$. We obtain $\mathfrak{A}_4 = [\{0, 1\} \times \bar{\mathfrak{z}}_3, \bar{\mathfrak{z}}_4, \delta_4]$ with

δ_4	{2, 4}	{1, 3, 5}
[0, {2, 5}]	{1, 3, 5}	{1, 3, 5}
[0, {1, 3, 4}]	{1, 3, 5}	{1, 3, 5}
[1, {2, 5}]	{2, 4}	{1, 3, 5}
[1, {1, 3, 4}]	—	{2, 4}

Thus we have

$$\mathfrak{z}_1 \sqcap \bar{\mathfrak{z}}_3 \sqcap \bar{\mathfrak{z}}_4 = \mathfrak{z}^0 \quad \text{and} \quad \mathfrak{z}_2 \sqcap \bar{\mathfrak{z}}_3 \sqcap \bar{\mathfrak{z}}_4 = \mathfrak{z}^0,$$

hence the combinatorial automaton which computes the output function $\lambda_{\mathfrak{S}}$ of the whole connection only has to know either the state of $\mathfrak{A}_1$ or of $\mathfrak{A}_2$ in addition to the states of $\mathfrak{A}_3$ and $\mathfrak{A}_4$. According to whether we choose the first or the second alternative, $\lambda^1_{\mathfrak{S}}$ or $\lambda^2_{\mathfrak{S}}$ can be obtained as follows (where only those triples of states are indicated for which the corresponding function is defined):

$\lambda^1_{\mathfrak{S}}$	[{1, 2, 4}, {1, 3, 4}, {1, 3, 5}]	[{3, 5}, {1, 3, 4}, {1, 3, 5}]
0	0	0
1	1	1

$\lambda^1_{\mathfrak{S}}$	[{1, 2, 4}, {1, 3, 4}, {2, 4}]
0	1
1	1

$\lambda^2_{\mathfrak{S}}$	[{1, 4}, {1, 3, 4}, {1, 3, 5}]	[{2, 3, 5}, {1, 3, 4}, {1, 3, 5}]
0	0	0
1	1	1

$\lambda^2_{\mathfrak{S}}$	[{1, 4}, {1, 3, 4}, {2, 4}
0	1
1	1

Thus one of the components $\mathfrak{A}_1$ or $\mathfrak{A}_2$ can be omitted from the connection provided $\mathfrak{A}_3$ is replaced by $\mathfrak{A}_3''$ or $\mathfrak{A}_3'$. Thus we obtain two loop-free decompositions $\mathfrak{S}_1$, $\mathfrak{S}_2$ of $\mathfrak{A}_{15}$ (cf. Fig. 12), namely series decompositions.

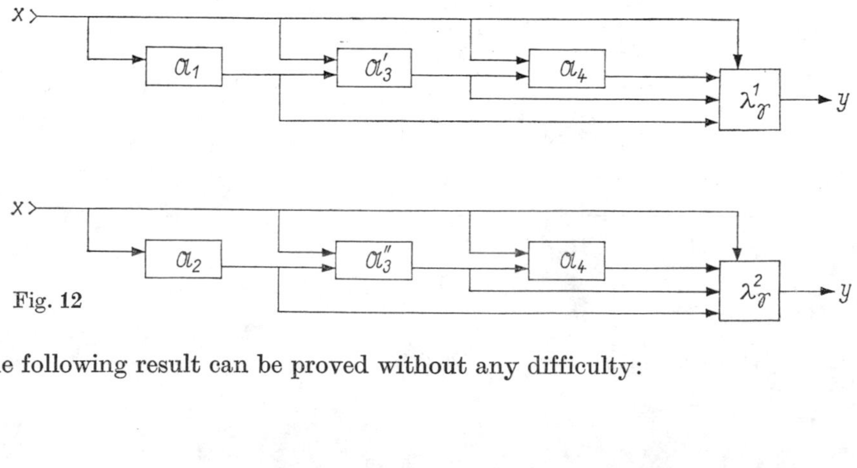

Fig. 12

The following result can be proved without any difficulty:

Theorem 11.6. *Let* $\mathfrak{A} = [X, Y, Z, \delta, \lambda]$ *be a Z-finite automaton.*

1. *If there exists a set* $\mathfrak{Z} = \{\mathfrak{z}_1, \ldots, \mathfrak{z}_k\}$ *of* $k \geqq 2$ *automaton partitions of* $\mathfrak{A}$ *with* $\mathfrak{Z} = max(\mathfrak{Z})$ *and* $\prod_{\varkappa=1}^{k} \mathfrak{z}_\varkappa = \mathfrak{z}^0$, *then* $\mathfrak{A}$ *has a parallel decomposition.*

2. *If there are* $k \geqq 2$ *automaton coverings,* $\mathfrak{z}_1, \ldots, \mathfrak{z}_k$ *of* $\mathfrak{A}$ *with* $\mathfrak{z}^1 > \mathfrak{z}_1 > \mathfrak{z}_2 > > \cdots > \mathfrak{z}_k \geqq \mathfrak{z}^0$ *and* $\prod_{\varkappa=1}^{k} \mathfrak{z}_\varkappa = \mathfrak{z}^0$, *moreover partitions* $\bar{\mathfrak{z}}_2, \ldots, \bar{\mathfrak{z}}_k$ *of* Z *such that for* $\varkappa = 1, \ldots, k-1$, $\mathfrak{z}_\varkappa \sqcap \bar{\mathfrak{z}}_{\varkappa+1} = \mathfrak{z}_{\varkappa+1}$ *and (if we put* $\bar{\mathfrak{z}}_1 = \mathfrak{z}_1$) $[\bar{\mathfrak{z}}_\varkappa \sqcap \bar{\mathfrak{z}}_{\varkappa+1}, \bar{\mathfrak{z}}_{\varkappa+1}]$ *is a partition pair of* $\mathfrak{A}$, *then* $\mathfrak{A}$ *has a series decomposition of k levels.*

Theorem 11.7. *A Z-finite automaton* $\mathfrak{A} = [X, Y, Z, \delta, \lambda]$ *has a loop-free decomposition if and only if it has an automaton covering* $\mathfrak{N}$ *with*

$$2 \leqq Card(\mathfrak{N}) < Card(Z).$$

Proof: By 11.3, it suffices to show that $\mathfrak{A}$ has a loop-free decomposition, provided there is an automaton covering $\mathfrak{N}$ with the above properties. Let $\mathfrak{N} = \{N_1, N_2, \ldots, N_n\}$ $\big(2 \leqq n < Card(Z)\big)$ be an automaton covering of $\mathfrak{A}$.

Lemma 11.7a. *There is an automaton* $\mathfrak{A}' = [X, Y, Z', \delta', \lambda']$ *and an automaton partition* $\mathfrak{z}'$ *of* $\mathfrak{A}'$ *with*

$$\mathfrak{A} \triangleq \mathfrak{A}' \quad \text{and} \quad 2 \leqq Card(\mathfrak{z}') < Card(Z).$$

Proof: We set for $i = 1, \ldots, n$

$$K_i = N_i \times \{i\},$$

furthermore let

$$Z' = \bigcup_{i=1}^{n} K_i, \qquad \mathfrak{z}' = \{K_i \mid 1 \leqq i \leqq n\}$$

and for $[z, j] \in Z'$, $x \in X$

$$\delta'([z, j], x) = \begin{cases} [\delta(z, x), i], \text{ if } [z, x] \in Dom(\delta), \text{ where } i \text{ is the} \\ \qquad\qquad \text{smallest } l \text{ with } \delta(N_j, x) \subseteq N_l, \\ \text{not defined otherwise;} \end{cases}$$

$$\lambda'([z, j], x) = \begin{cases} \lambda(z, x), \text{ if } [z, x] \in Dom(\lambda), \\ \text{not defined otherwise.} \end{cases}$$

If $[z, j] \in Z'$, then $z \in N_j$. Hence for $[z, x] \in Dom(\delta)$ $\delta(N_j, x) \neq \emptyset$. Since $\mathfrak{N}$ is an automaton covering, there exists an $N' \in \mathfrak{N}$ with $\delta(N_j, x) \subseteq N'$, i.e., $\delta(z, x) \in N'$. Consequently, $\delta([z, j], x) = [\delta(z, x), i] \in Z'$. Thus $\mathfrak{A}'$ is an automaton and $\mathfrak{z}'$ is a partition of Z'. Furthermore, for $K_j \in z'$, $x \in X$ we have

$$\delta'(K_j, x) = \delta'(N_j \times \{j\}, x) = \delta(N_j, x) \times \{i\} \subseteq N_i \times \{i\} = K_i \in \mathfrak{z}'$$

if i denotes the smallest l with $\delta(N_j, x) \subseteq N_l$. Thus $\mathfrak{z}'$ is an automaton partition of $\mathfrak{A}'$. $Card(\mathfrak{N}) = Card(\mathfrak{z}')$ implies $2 \leqq Card(\mathfrak{z}') < Card(Z)$. It remains to show that $\mathfrak{A} \preceq \mathfrak{A}'$. For this we prove by induction on p that for all $z \in Z$, $[z, i] \in Z'$.

$$\forall p \forall x (px \in D(z) \to px \in D'([z, i]) \wedge \\ \wedge \lambda(\delta(z, p), x) = \lambda'(\delta'([z, i], p), x)),$$

i.e., $z \preceq [z, i]$.

The initial step $p = e$ is trivial. The step from p to $x_1 p$: $x_1 px \in D(z)$ implies $[z, x_1] \in Dom(\delta)$ and $px \in D(z, x_1)$. This and $z \in N_i$ imply $\delta(N_i, x_1) \neq \emptyset$. Let j be the smallest l with $\delta(N_i, x_1) \subseteq N_l$. Then we have $\delta(z, x_1) \in N_j$ and $\delta'([z, i], x_1) = [\delta(z, x_1), j]$, $[[z, i], x_1] \in Dom(\delta')$. By the induction hypothesis, $px \in D(\delta(z, x_1))$ and $[\delta(z, x_1), j] \in Z'$ imply $px \in D'(\delta[(z, x_1), j])$, hence $x_1 px \in D'([z, i])$. Finally we obtain

$$\begin{aligned} \lambda(\delta(z, x_1 p), x) &= \lambda(\delta(\delta(z, x_1), p), x) \\ &= \lambda'(\delta'([\delta(z, x_1), j], p), x) \text{ (by the induction hypothesis)} \\ &= \lambda'(\delta'([z, i], x_1 p), x). \end{aligned}$$

Thus Lemma 11.7a is proved.

Remark. If $\mathfrak{A}$ is a completely specified automaton, then the mapping ζ' with $\zeta'([z, i]) = z$ is a Z-homomorphism of $\mathfrak{A}'$ onto $\mathfrak{A}$.

Now by Theorem 11.4 and putting $\mathfrak{z}_1 = \mathfrak{z}'$, $\mathfrak{z}_2 = \mathfrak{z}^0$, the automaton $\mathfrak{A}'$ has a loop-free decomposition. The resulting connection $\mathfrak{S}$ covers $\mathfrak{A}'$ hence $\mathfrak{A} \preceq \mathfrak{S}$. We still have to show that the second component $\mathfrak{A}_2$ of $\mathfrak{S}$ has less states than $\mathfrak{A}$, i.e., that there is a partition $\bar{\mathfrak{z}}_2$ of Z' with $\mathfrak{z}' \sqcap \bar{\mathfrak{z}}_2 = \mathfrak{z}^0$ and $Card(\bar{\mathfrak{z}}_2) < Card(Z)$. Obviously, $\bar{\mathfrak{z}}_2$ might have at most k classes, where $k = max\{Card(K_i) \mid 1 \leq i \leq n\}$. We have, for $i = 1, \ldots, n$,

$$Card(K_i) = Card(N_i) < Card(Z),$$

because Z is not an element of $\mathfrak{N}$ (otherwise $\mathfrak{N} = \mathfrak{z}^1$ would hold). Thus theorem 11.7 is proved.

Let us again consider the automaton $\mathfrak{A}_{14}$ (see page 131) and the automaton covering $\mathfrak{N} = \{N_1, N_2, N_3\}$ of $\mathfrak{A}_{14}$ where $N_1 = \{1, 2, 3\}$, $N_2 = \{1, 2, 4\}$, $N_3 = \{1, 3, 4\}$. By the construction of Lemma 11.7a, we obtain the automaton $\mathfrak{A}'_{14} = [\{0, 1\}, \{0, 1\}, Z', \delta'_{14}, \lambda'_{14}]$ with

δ'_{14}	[1, 1]	[2, 1]	[3, 1]	[1, 2]	[2, 2]	[4, 2]	[1, 3]	[3, 3]	[4, 3]
0	[1, 3]	[3, 3]	[4, 3]	[1, 1]	[3, 1]	[2, 1]	[1, 2]	[4, 2]	[2, 2]
1	[2, 1]	—	[1, 1]	[2, 1]	—	[3, 1]	[2, 1]	[1, 1]	[3, 1]

λ'_{14}	[1, 1]	[2, 1]	[3, 1]	[1, 2]	[2, 2]	[4, 2]	[1, 3]	[3, 3]	[4, 3]
0	1	0	—	1	0	—	1	—	—
1	0	1	—	0	1	—	0	—	—

Proposition 11.6.1 can be generalized as follows:

Theorem 11.8. *Let* $\mathfrak{M} = \{\mathfrak{N}_1, \ldots, \mathfrak{N}_k\}$ *be a set of automaton coverings of the automaton* $\mathfrak{A} = [X, Y, Z, \delta, \lambda]$ *with* $\prod_{\varkappa=1}^{k} \mathfrak{N}_\varkappa = \mathfrak{z}^0$, *and* $\bigwedge_{\varkappa=1}^{k} Card(\mathfrak{N}_\varkappa) < Card(Z)$. *Then* $\mathfrak{A}$ *has a parallel decomposition.*

The proof is analogous to the first step in the proof of Theorem 11.4; the details are omitted. The converse of 11.8 is not true, as is shown by the following example.

Consider the automaton $\mathfrak{A}_{16} = [\{0, 1\}, \{a, b\}, \{1, 2, 3\}, \delta^{16}, \lambda^{16}]$

δ^{16}	1	2	3	λ^{16}	1	2	3
0	1	—	2	0	a	b	a
1	—	1	3	1	b	a	a

on one hand, and the parallel connection $\mathfrak{S}$ of the components $\mathfrak{A}_1 = [\{0,1\}, \{A, B\}, \delta^1]$, $\mathfrak{A}_2 = [\{0, 1\}, \{C, D\}, \delta^2]$ with the output function $\lambda_{\mathfrak{S}}$, where

δ^1	A	B
0	B	A
1	A	B

δ^2	C	D
0	D	C
1	D	D

λ_γ	$[A, C]$	$[A, D]$	$[B, C]$	$[B, D]$
0	b	a	a	a
1	a	b	b	a

We can easily verify that $1 \trianglelefteq [A, D]$, $1 \trianglelefteq [B, C]$, $2 \trianglelefteq [A, C]$ and $3 \trianglelefteq [B, D]$, hence $\mathfrak{A}_{16} \trianglelefteq \mathfrak{S}$. Using the algorithm given in § 10 we construct the set of all automaton coverings of $\mathfrak{A}_{16}$ and obtain

$$\mathfrak{M}_{\mathfrak{A}_{16}} = \{\{\{1\}, \{2\}, \{3\}\}, \{\{1, 2\}, \{3\}\}, \{\{1, 3\}, \{1, 2\}\}, \{\{2, 3\}, \{1, 3\}, \{1, 2\}\}, \{\{1, 2, 3\}\}\}.$$

Thus the automaton $\mathfrak{A}_{16}$ has exactly two non-trivial automaton coverings with fewer classes than states, namely $\mathfrak{N}_1 = \{\{1, 2\}, \{3\}\}$ and $\mathfrak{N}_2 = \{\{1, 2\}, \{1, 3\}\}$, moreover $\mathfrak{N}_1 \sqcap \mathfrak{N}_2 = \mathfrak{N}_1 \neq \mathfrak{z}^0$, although $\mathfrak{A}_{16}$ does have a parallel decomposition.

PART II

NON-DETERMINISTIC AUTOMATA

In the second part of this book we consider systems which work pulse-wise, with input signals, output signals and states, such as the deterministic automata investigated so far. These however function with a certain degree of freedom. For a deterministic automaton, the output signal and the next state are uniquely determined in a given situation $[z, x]$. In general, this is not the case for the systems we now consider, called non-deterministic automata. Often, the situation $[z, x]$ only determines a non-empty set of ordered pairs, $h(z, x)$, independent of the step in which the situation occurs, and in which the ordered pair $[y^*, z^*]$ of the corresponding output signal y^* and next state z^* must be contained. If $h(z, x)$ contains several elements, then the system has several possibilities for carrying on its work. We do not distinguish these possibilities from each other, as is done for instance in a stochastic automaton by assigning them probabilities (cf. Part III, § 1).

We can apply non-deterministic automata to describe the "possibilities" of a given stochastic automaton in that we call "possible" those things which have a positive probability of being turned out. Thus we can assign to each stochastic automaton $\mathfrak{C}$ with the set of input signals X, the set of output signals Y and the set of states Z, a non-deterministic automaton $\mathfrak{B} = [X, Y, Z, h]$, by defining for every situation $[z, x]$ the set $h(z, x)$ consisting of those pairs $[y, z']$ for which the output signal y and the next state z' appear with a positive probability in the situation $[z, x]$. Then the non-deterministic automaton $\mathfrak{B}$ describes the "possibilities" of the stochastic automaton $\mathfrak{C}$ in the above sense. For stochastic automata, however, we also assume that for each pair consisting of an output signal and a next state, the probability with which it occurs in a situation $[z, x]$ is independent of the number of the step in which the situation appears. If we only want to study the possibilities of a stochastic system which works pulse-wise with input signals, output signals and states, then this restriction is unnecessary. It is obviously enough to assume that the possibility of $[y, z']$ in the situation $[z, x]$ is independent of the number t of the step in which this situation appears. Using our concept of possibility this means that the probability that the pair $[y, z']$ occurs in the situation $[z, x]$ in step t is either positive for each t or zero for each t.

These conditions can also be applied in cases where the term "possible" is specified in another way, for instance when an event is called possible if and only if the probability of its occurence exceeds a given bound ε $(0 \leqq \varepsilon < 1)$. It can very well happen in this case that for a certain situation $[z, x]$ no pair $[y, z']$ is "possible", because for each such pair the probability of its occurence is less than ε. In this case, $h(z, x)$ is the empty set which is excluded in Definition 1.1. Similarly to partial deterministic automata, a system $[X, Y, Z, h]$ in which, for certain pairs $[z, x] \in Z \times X$, the subset $h(z, x)$ of $Y \times Z$ is empty, is called a partial non-deterministic automaton (cf. SCHMITT [1]). From the point of view of the functioning of these system it is obviously immaterial whether h is not-defined in the situation $[z, x]$ or whether it is defined, but empty, since in either case, the system can not function in a well-defined way.

If we consider a concrete stochastic information processing system, then in general it is difficult to describe it as a stochastic automaton. If however the exact probability with which a certain operation is carried out in the system is indifferent, and we only want to know whether this probability is positive or not, then we can try to describe the system as a non-deterministic automaton. Obviously this is easier than to describe it as a stochastic automaton.

In addition to stochastic automata, to be investigated in Part III, the class of all digital systems to which we can assign a fixed non-deterministic automaton as above, also contains other systems. Also, there are non-deterministic automata which can not be assigned to any stochastic automaton. Indeed, the definition of a stochastic automaton implies that the set of possibilities $[y, z']$ is always at most countable, and this for instance is not satisfied in a non-deterministic automaton with an uncountable set of states.

Non-deterministic automata were first considered, in the particular case of finite outputless automata, by RABIN and SCOTT [2], where they were used in the proof of KLEENE's theorem (Part I, 6.18). Special cases of this concept can also be found implicitely in works on problems of structural grammatics, as finite-state-grammars (cf. e.g. BAR-HILLEL et al. [1], CHOMSKY [1], CHOMSKY, MILLER [1], CULIK I [1]). The systematic development of the theory of non-deterministic automata was begun in STARKE [4].

§ 1. Fundamental Concepts

For any set M we denote by $\mathfrak{P}^*(M)$ the set of all *non-empty* subsets of M.

Definition 1.1. $\mathfrak{B} = [X, Y, Z, h]$ is called a *non-deterministic automaton* (shortly, *ND-automaton*) if

a) X, Y, Z are non-empty sets;

b) h is a single valued mapping of $Z \times X$ into $\mathfrak{P}^*(Y \times Z)$.

Interpretation: The elements $x \in X$ are called *input signals*, the y's of Y *output signals* and the elements z of the set Z *states* of the ND-automaton $\mathfrak{B}$.

The ND-automaton $\mathfrak{B}$ works on a discrete time-scale in a countable number of steps $t = 1, 2, \ldots$ In every step t, $\mathfrak{B}$ has exactly one of the states $z \in Z$, receives exactly one input signal $x \in X$, and sends out an output signal $y \in Y$. If in step t, z_t is the state of $\mathfrak{B}$, and x_t is the input signal received in this step, then for the output signal y_t in step t and the state z_{t+1} in step $t+1$ we have

$$[y_t, z_{t+1}] \in h(z_t, x_t).$$

In what follows we shall define fundamental functions and properties of non-deterministic automata. For the sake of brevity we shall make extensive use of the notation of predicate calculus.

Definition 1.2. Let $\mathfrak{B} = [X, Y, Z, h]$ be an ND-automaton.
(1.2.1) The *transition function* f of $\mathfrak{B}$ is the single-valued mapping of the set $Z \times X$ into $\mathfrak{P}^*(Z)$ defined as follows:

$$f(z, x) \underset{\mathrm{Df}}{=} \{z' \mid \exists y([y, z'] \in h(z, x))\}.$$

(1.2.2) Accordingly, the *output function* g of $\mathfrak{B}$ is defined by

$$g(z, x) \underset{\mathrm{Df}}{=} \{y \mid \exists z'([y, z'] \in h(z, x))\}.$$

(1.2.3) The *conditional transition function* h_y and the *conditional output function* $h_{z'}$ of $\mathfrak{B}$ are defined for $z, z' \in Z$, $x \in X$, $y \in Y$ as follows:

$$h_y(z, x) \underset{\mathrm{Df}}{=} \{z' \mid [y, z'] \in h(z, x)\},$$

$$h_{z'}(z, x) \underset{\mathrm{Df}}{=} \{y \mid [y, z'] \in h(z, x)\}.$$

Interpretation: If $[z, x]$ is an arbitrary situation of the ND-automaton $\mathfrak{B}$, then the value $f(z, x)$ of the transition function f of $\mathfrak{B}$ in this situation is obviously the set of all states z' into which $\mathfrak{B}$ can enter from this situation, and $g(z, x)$ is the set of all output signals which $\mathfrak{B}$ can send out in this situation. $h_y(z, x)$ is the set of all states into which $\mathfrak{B}$ can enter from the situation $[z, x]$, while simultaneously emitting the output signal y. $h_{z'}(z, x)$ is the set of all output signals y which $\mathfrak{B}$ can put out while simultaneously entering the state z' from the situation $[z, x]$.

As for the connections between the above functions we immediately obtain

Corollary 1.1. If $\mathfrak{B} = [X, Y, Z, h]$ is an ND-automaton, f its transition function, g its output function, h_y and $h_{z'}$ its conditional transition and output functions respectively, then for every $z, z' \in Z$, $x \in X$, $y \in Y$, the following relations are satisfied:

1. $h_{z'}(z, x) \neq \emptyset$ if and only if $z' \in f(z, x)$,
2. $h_y(z, x) \neq \emptyset$ if and only if $y \in g(z, x)$,
3. $h(z, x) = \bigcup_{z' \in Z} h_{z'}(z, x) \times \{z'\} = \bigcup_{z' \in f(z,x)} h_{z'}(z, x) \times \{z'\}$,

4. $h(z, x) = \bigcup_{y \in Y} \{y\} \times h_y(z, x) = \bigcup_{y \in g(z,x)} \{y\} \times h_y(z, x)$,

5. $f(z, x) = \bigcup_{y \in Y} h_y(z, x) = \bigcup_{y \in g(z,x)} h_y(z, x)$,

6. $g(z, x) = \bigcup_{z' \in Z} h_{z'}(z, x) = \bigcup_{z' \in f(z,x)} h_{z'}(z, x)$.

Definition 1.3. Let $\mathfrak{B} = [X, Y, Z, h]$ be an ND-automaton.

(1.3.1) $\mathfrak{B}$ is said to be *obversable* if for all $z \in Z$, $x \in X$ and $y \in Y$ we have $Card(h_y(z, x)) \leqq 1$.[1])

(1.3.2) $\mathfrak{B}$ is called *Z-deterministic* (*Y-deterministic*) if for all $[z, x] \in Z \times X$, $y', y'' \in Y$, $z', z'' \in Z$, $[y', z'] \in h(z, x)$ and $[y'', z''] \in h(z, x)$ imply that $z' = z''$ ($y' = y''$).

(1.3.3) $\mathfrak{B}$ is called *deterministic* if it is both Z-deterministic and Y-deterministic.

(1.3.4) We say that $\mathfrak{B}$ is *X-finite, Y-finite, Z-finite, [X, Y]-finite,* etc. if the indicated sets are finite. $[X, Y, Z]$-finite automata are simply called *finite.*

(1.3.5) $\mathfrak{B}$ is called *autonomous* if X is a singleton.

(1.3.6) We call $\mathfrak{B}$ *weakly-inital* (*inital*), if a non-empty set $M_1 \subseteq Z$ of states (a state $z_1 \in Z$) is prescribed as the set of all possible initial states (the initial state) of $\mathfrak{B}$. Thus the state z of $\mathfrak{B}$ in step 1 always belongs to the set M_1 (is equal to z_1). Weakly initial (initial) ND-automata are denoted by $[X, Y, Z, h, M_1]$ ($[X, Y, Z, h, z_1]$). If $M_1 = Z$, then we refer to $\mathfrak{B}$ as a *non-initial* ND-automaton.

(1.3.7) A function α which maps a non-empty set A into the set of all non-empty subsets of a non-empty set $\mathfrak{B}$, is called *deterministic* if for each $a \in A$, $\alpha(a)$ is a singleton.

For a Z-deterministic (or Y-deterministic) ND-automaton, in every situation $[z, x]$, the state z' in the next step (or the output signal y of the same step) is uniquely determined by $[z, x]$. If an obversable ND-automaton in step t has the state z_t, and receives the input signal x_t, furthermore the output signal y_t is observed, then $\{z_{t+1}\} = h_{y_t}(z_t, x_t)$.

Corollary 1.2.

1. Every Z-deterministic ND-automaton is observable.

2. An ND-automaton is Z-deterministic, Y-deterministic, or deterministic, if and only if its transition function, its output function or its function h respectively, are deterministic.

Definition 1.1 decides in which way an ND-automaton $\mathfrak{B} = [X, Y, Z, h]$ behaves if, in a certain state $z_1 \in Z$, it receives an input signal $x_1 \in X$, i.e., it decides which pairs of an output signal and a next state can occur. Now we describe the possible (external) global behaviour of ND-automata in that we decide which words $q \in W(Y)$ the ND-automaton $\mathfrak{B}$ can emit if it receives a certain finite sequence p of input signals in the state $z_1 \in Z$. From the interpretation of Definition 1.1 it follows that the function $v_{\mathfrak{B}}$ defined below and which

---

[1]) This is analogous to "observer-state-calculability" defined for stochastic automata by CARLYLE [4], [5]; SCHMITT [1] calls such automata "einspurig".

we call the *behaviour function* of the ND-automaton $\mathfrak{B}$, satisfies these requirements. For all $z_1 \in Z$, $p \in W(X)$ let $v_{\mathfrak{B}}(z_1, p)$ be the set of those words which $\mathfrak{B}$ can emit, if in state z_1 it receives the word p:

$$v_{\mathfrak{B}}(z_1, p) \underset{\text{Df}}{=} \begin{cases} \{e\}, & \text{if } p = e; \\ \left\{y_1 \ldots y_n \mid \exists z_2 \ldots \exists z_{n+1} \left(\bigwedge_{i=1}^{n} [y_i, z_{i+1}] \in h(z_i, x_i) \right) \right\}, & \text{if } p = x_1 \ldots x_n,\ n \geqq 1. \end{cases}$$

Obviously, for all $z \in Z$, $x \in X$

$$v_{\mathfrak{B}}(z, x) = g(z, x).$$

One can see easily

Theorem 1.3. *If* $\mathfrak{B} = [X, Y, Z, h]$ *is an ND-automaton, then for* $z \in Z$, $x \in X$, $p \in W(X)$

$$v_{\mathfrak{B}}(z, xp) = \bigcup_{z' \in Z} h_{z'}(z, x) \cdot v_{\mathfrak{B}}(z', p) = \bigcup_{z' \in f(z,x)} h_{z'}(z, x) \cdot v_{\mathfrak{B}}(z', p).$$

For an arbitrary ND-automaton $\mathfrak{B} = [X, Y, Z, h]$ we extend the domains of definition of the functions $v_{\mathfrak{B}}$, $f, g, h_{z'}, h_y$, and for every $q \in W(Y)$ and certain sets $Q \subseteq W(Y)$ we define the functions h_q, h_Q, as follows.

Definition 1.4. Let $\mathfrak{B} = [X, Y, Z, h]$ be an ND-automaton.
(1.4.1) For $z_1 \in Z$, $p \in W(X)$ let

$$f(z_1, p) \underset{\text{Df}}{=} \begin{cases} \{z_1\}, & \text{if } p = e, \\ \left\{z_{n+1} \mid \exists y_1 \ldots \exists y_n \exists z_2 \ldots \exists z_n \left(\bigwedge_{i=1}^{n} [y_i, z_{i+1}] \in h(z_i, x_i) \right) \right\}, & \text{if } p = x_1 \ldots x_n,\ n \geqq 1; \end{cases}$$

and for $M \subseteq Z$, $p \in W(X)$ let

$$f(M, p) \underset{\text{Df}}{=} \bigcup_{z \in M} f(z, p).$$

(1.4.2) For $M \subseteq Z$, $p \subseteq W(X)$ let

$$v_{\mathfrak{B}}(M, p) \underset{\text{Df}}{=} \bigcup_{z \in M} v_{\mathfrak{B}}(z, p).$$

(1.4.3) For $z_1, z_{n+1} \in Z$, $p \in W(X)$ let

$$h_{z_{n+1}}(z_1, p) \underset{\text{Df}}{=} \begin{cases} \{e\}, & \text{if } p = e \text{ and } z_1 = z_{n+1}, \\ \left\{y_1 \ldots y_n \mid \exists z_2 \ldots \exists z_n \left(\bigwedge_{i=1}^{n} [y_i, z_{i+1}] \in h(z_i, x_i) \right) \right\}, & \text{if } p = x_1 \ldots x_n,\ n \geqq 1, \\ \emptyset & \text{otherwise}; \end{cases}$$

and for $M \subseteq Z,\ z^* \in Z,\ p \in W(X)$ let

$$h_{z^*}(M, p) \underset{\mathrm{Df}}{=} \bigcup_{z \in M} h_{z^*}(z, p).$$

(1.4.4) For each $q \in W(Y)$ we define for $M \subseteq Z,\ p \in W(X)$

$$h_q(M, p) \underset{\mathrm{Df}}{=} \begin{cases} \emptyset, & \text{if } l(p) \neq l(q), \\ \left\{z_{n+1} \mid \exists z_1 \exists z_2 \ldots \exists z_n \left(z_1 \in M \wedge \bigwedge_{i=1}^{n} [y_i, z_{i+1}] \in h(z_i, x_i)\right)\right\}, & \\ & \text{if } p = x_1 \ldots x_n,\ q = y_1 \ldots y_n,\ n = l(p) \geqq 1, \\ M, & \text{if } p = q = e; \end{cases}$$

and for $M \subseteq Z,\ p \in W(X),\ \emptyset \neq Q \subseteq Y^{l(p)}$ let

$$h_Q(M, p) = \bigcup_{q \in Q} h_q(M, p).$$

(1.4.5) For $M \subseteq Z,\ x \in X$ let

$$g(M, x) = \bigcup_{z \in M} g(z, x) \ \left(= v_{\mathfrak{B}}(M, x)\right).$$

The above definitions can be interpreted as follows: $f(M, p)$ is the set of all those states which are possible for $\mathfrak{B}$ in step $t + l(p)$, provided that in step t exactly the states of M are possible for $\mathfrak{B}$ and the word p is fed into $\mathfrak{B}$ in the course of the steps $t, \ldots, t + l(p) - 1$. (For the input of the empty word e no time, hence no step is needed.) $v_{\mathfrak{B}}(M, p)$ is the set of words which can be emitted by $\mathfrak{B}$ in the course of the steps $t, \ldots, t + l(p) - 1$, under the same conditions. $h_{z^*}(M, p)$ is the set of words which $\mathfrak{B}$ can put out in the course of the same steps under the additional condition that in step $t + l(p)$ the state of $\mathfrak{B}$ is z^*; $h_Q(M, p)$ is the set of states of $\mathfrak{B}$ which can appear in step $t + l(p)$, provided that in step t exactly the states of M had been possible for $\mathfrak{B}$, and in the course of the steps $t, \ldots, t + l(p) - 1$ the word p has been fed into $\mathfrak{B}$ and a word $q \in Q$ put out by $\mathfrak{B}$.

Corollary 1.4. Let $\mathfrak{B} = [X, Y, Z, h]$ be an ND-automaton. Then for $M \subseteq Z,\ p \in W(X),\ z' \in Z,\ q \in W(Y)$ we have

1. $$f(M, p) = \begin{cases} M, & \text{if } p = e, \\ \left\{z_{n+1} \mid \exists z_1 \exists z_2 \ldots \exists z_n \left(z_1 \in M \wedge \bigwedge_{i=1}^{n} z_{i+1} \in f(z_i, x_i)\right)\right\}, & \\ & \text{if } p = x_1 \ldots x_n,\ n \geqq 1. \end{cases}$$

2. $h_{z'}(M, p) \neq \emptyset$ if and only if $z' \in f(M, p)$.

3. $$h_{z'}(M, e) = \begin{cases} \{e\}, & \text{if } z' \in M, \\ \emptyset & \text{otherwise.} \end{cases}$$

4. $h_q(M, p) \neq \emptyset$ if and only if $q \in v_{\mathfrak{B}}(M, p)$.

5. $f(M, p) = \bigcup_{q \in W(Y)} h_q(M, p) = \bigcup_{q \in Y^{l(p)}} h_q(M, p) = \bigcup_{q \in v_{\mathfrak{B}}(M,p)} h_q(M, p)$.

6. $v_{\mathfrak{B}}(M, p) = \bigcup_{z' \in Z} h_{z'}(M, p) = \bigcup_{z' \in f(M,p)} h_{z'}(M, p)$.

7. If $\mathfrak{B}$ is observable, then $Card(h_q(z, p)) \leqq 1$ and $Card(h_q(M, p)) \leqq Card(M)$.

Theorem 1.5. *Let* $\mathfrak{B} = [X, Y, Z, h]$ *be an ND-automaton* $M \subseteq Z$, $z' \in Z$, $p, r \in W(X)$, $q, s \in W(Y)$, $Q \subseteq Y^{l(p)}$, $S \subseteq Y^{l(r)}$, $x \in X$, $y \in Y$. *Then*

1. $f(M, pr) = f(f(M, p), r)$.

2. $h_{z'}(M, xp) = \bigcup_{z^* \in Z} h_{z^*}(M, x) h_{z'}(z^*, p) = \bigcup_{z^* \in f(M,x)} h_{z^*}(M, x) h_{z'}(z^*, p)$.

3. $h_{z'}(M, pr) = \bigcup_{z^* \in Z} h_{z^*}(M, p) h_{z'}(z^*, r) = \bigcup_{z^* \in f(M,p)} h_{z^*}(M, p) h_{z'}(z^*, r)$.

4. $h_{yq}(M, xp) = h_q(h_y(M, x), p)$.

5. $h_{qs}(M, pr) = h_s(h_q(M, p), r)$, *if* $l(q) = l(p)$ *or* $l(r) = l(s)$.

6. $v_{\mathfrak{B}}(M, pr) = \bigcup_{z' \in Z} h_{z'}(M, p) v_{\mathfrak{B}}(z', r) = \bigcup_{z' \in f(M,p)} h_{z'}(M, p) v_{\mathfrak{B}}(z', r)$.

7. $v_{\mathfrak{B}}(M, xp) = \bigcup_{y \in Y} \{y\} \cdot v_{\mathfrak{B}}(h_y(M, x), p) = \bigcup_{y \in g(M,x)} \{y\} \cdot v_{\mathfrak{B}}(h_y(M, x), p)$.

8. $v_{\mathfrak{B}}(M, pr) = \bigcup_{q \in W(Y)} \{q\} \cdot v_{\mathfrak{B}}(h_q(M, p), r) = \bigcup_{q \in v_{\mathfrak{B}}(M,p)} \{q\} \cdot v_{\mathfrak{B}}(h_q(M, p), r)$.

9. $v_{\mathfrak{B}}(M, p) = \{q \mid \exists x \exists y (x \in X \wedge y \in Y \wedge qy \in v_{\mathfrak{B}}(M, px))\}$.

10. $h_{QS}(M, pr) = h_S(h_Q(M, p), r)$.

Proof: Proposition 1.5.1 is obviously true. Suppose $M \subseteq Z$, $z_{n+1} \in Z$, $x_1 \in X$, $p = x_2 \ldots x_n \in W(X)$ $(n \geqq 1)$. Thus for $n = 1$ we have $p = e$. $q \in h_{z_{n+1}}(M, x_1 p)$ can only be satisfied if $l(q) = n$. Furthermore for $y_1 \ldots y_n \in W(Y)$

$$\begin{aligned} y_1 \ldots y_n \in h_{z_{n+1}}(M, x_1 p) &\leftrightarrow \exists z_1 \exists z_2 \ldots \exists z_n \Big(z_1 \in M \\ &\qquad \wedge \bigwedge_{i=1}^{n} [y_i, z_{i+1}] \in h(z_i, x_i)\Big) \\ &\leftrightarrow \exists z_2 \Big[\exists z_1 (z_1 \in M \wedge [y_1, z_2] \in h(z_1, x_1)) \\ &\qquad \wedge \exists z_3 \ldots \exists z_n \Big(\bigwedge_{i=2}^{n} [y_i, z_{i+1}] \in h(z_i, x_i)\Big)\Big] \\ &\leftrightarrow \exists z_2 [y_1 \in h_{z_2}(M, x_1) \\ &\qquad \wedge y_2 \ldots y_n \in h_{z_{n+1}}(z_2, x_2 \ldots x_n)] \\ &\leftrightarrow \exists z_2 (y_1 \ldots y_n \in h_{z_2}(M, x_1) h_{z_{n+1}}(z_2, x_2 \ldots x_n)) \end{aligned}$$

is satisfied. Therefore,

$$h_{z_{n+1}}(M, x_1 p) = \bigcup_{z_2 \in Z} h_{z_2}(M, x_1) h_{z_{n+1}}(z_2, p).$$

Since $h_{z_2}(M, x_1) = \emptyset$ holds for $z_2 \notin f(M, x_1)$, this proves Proposition 1.5.2. Proposition 1.5.3 can be easily shown by induction on p, using 1.5.2 and 1.4.3.

Let $M \subseteq Z$, $x \in X$, $y \in Y$, $p \in W(X)$, $q \in W(Y)$. $l(p) \neq l(q)$ implies $h_q(N, p) = \emptyset$ for arbitrary $N \subseteq Z$. Thus in this case 1.5.4 is trivial. Suppose $p = x_1 \ldots x_n$, $q = y_1 \ldots y_n$. If $n = 0$, then $p = q = e$, hence

$$h_q\big(h_y(M, x), p\big) = h_y(M, x),$$

by Definition 1.4.4.

For $n \geqq 1$ and arbitrary $z_{n+1} \in Z$ we have

$$\begin{aligned} z_{n+1} \in h_{yq}(M, xp) &\leftrightarrow \exists z' \exists z_1 \ldots \exists z_n \Big(z' \in M \wedge [y, z_1] \in h(z', x) \\ &\qquad \wedge \bigwedge_{i=1}^{n} [y_i, z_{i+1}] \in h(z_i, x_i)\Big) \\ &\leftrightarrow \exists z_1 \Big[\exists z' \big(z' \in M \wedge [y, z_1] \in h(z', x)\big) \\ &\qquad \wedge \exists z_2 \ldots \exists z_n \Big(\bigwedge_{i=1}^{n} [y_i, z_{i+1}] \in h(z_i, x_i)\Big)\Big] \\ &\leftrightarrow \exists z_1 \big(z_1 \in h_y(M, x) \wedge z_{n+1} \in h_q(z_1, p)\big) \\ &\leftrightarrow z_{n+1} \in h_q\big(h_y(M, x), p\big). \end{aligned}$$

This proves 1.5.4. Proposition 1.5.5 can be proved by induction on p, using 1.5.4.

Next we prove Proposition 1.5.6 by induction on p. If $p = e$, then for any $M \subseteq Z$, $r \in W(X)$

$$\begin{aligned} \bigcup_{z' \in Z} h_{z'}(M, e)\, v_{\mathfrak{B}}(z', r) &= \bigcup_{z' \in Z} \bigcup_{z \in M} h_{z'}(z, e)\, v_{\mathfrak{B}}(z', r) \\ &= \bigcup_{z \in M} v_{\mathfrak{B}}(z, r) = v_{\mathfrak{B}}(M, r) \end{aligned}$$

is satisfied.

The induction step is taken from p to xp:

$$\begin{aligned} v_{\mathfrak{B}}(M, xpr) &= \bigcup_{z \in M} v_{\mathfrak{B}}(z, xpr) \\ &= \bigcup_{z \in M} \bigcup_{z' \in Z} h_{z'}(z, x) \Big[\bigcup_{z^* \in Z} h_{z^*}(z', p)\, v_{\mathfrak{B}}(z^*, r)\Big] \end{aligned}$$

by Theorem 1.3 and the induction hypothesis. Thus we have

$$\begin{aligned} v_{\mathfrak{B}}(M, xpr) &= \bigcup_{z \in M} \bigcup_{z^* \in Z} \Big[\bigcup_{z' \in Z} h_{z'}(z, x)\, h_{z^*}(z', p)\Big] v_{\mathfrak{B}}(z^*, r) \\ &= \bigcup_{z^* \in Z} \Big[\bigcup_{z \in M} h_{z^*}(z, xp)\Big] v_{\mathfrak{B}}(z^*, r) = \bigcup_{z^* \in Z} h_{z^*}(M, xp)\, v_{\mathfrak{B}}(z^*, r). \end{aligned}$$

Because of 1.4.2, this proves Proposition 1.5.6.

Let $M \subseteq Z$, $x \in X$, $p \in W(X)$. Then for all $y \in Y$, $q \in W(Y)$

$$\begin{aligned} yq \in v_{\mathfrak{B}}(M, xp) &\leftrightarrow \exists z\, \exists z^* \big(z \in M \wedge [y, z^*] \in h(z, x) \wedge q \in v_{\mathfrak{B}}(z^*, p)\big) \\ &\leftrightarrow \exists z^* \big(z^* \in h_y(M, x) \wedge q \in v_{\mathfrak{B}}(z^*, p)\big) \\ &\leftrightarrow q \in v_{\mathfrak{B}}\big(h_y(M, x), p\big). \end{aligned}$$

From this, using 1.4.4, we obtain Proposition 1.5.7. Proposition 1.5.8 can be verified by induction on p using 1.5.7 and 1.5.4.

By 1.4.4 and 1.5.8 we have for $M \subseteq Z$, $p \in W(X)$, $q \in W(Y)$

$$\begin{aligned} q \in v_{\mathfrak{B}}(M, p) &\leftrightarrow h_q(M, p) \neq \emptyset \\ &\leftrightarrow \exists x \big(x \in X \wedge v_{\mathfrak{B}}(h_q(M, p), x) \neq \emptyset\big) \\ &\leftrightarrow \exists x\, \exists y \big(x \in X \wedge y \in Y \wedge qy \in \{q\} \cdot v_{\mathfrak{B}}(h_q(M, p), x)\big) \\ &\leftrightarrow \exists x\, \exists y \big(x \in X \wedge y \in Y \wedge qy \in v_{\mathfrak{B}}(M, px)\big). \end{aligned}$$

Thus 1.5.9 is proved.

Finally let $M \subseteq Z$, $p, r \in W(X)$, $\emptyset \neq Q \subseteq Y^{l(p)}$, $\emptyset \neq S \subseteq Y^{l(r)}$.

If $p = e$ or $r = e$, then Proposition 1.5.10 is trivial. So assume $p, r \neq e$. Then for arbitrary $z^* \in Z$ by 1.5.5

$$\begin{aligned} z^* \in h_{QS}(M, pr) &\leftrightarrow \exists q\, \exists s \big(q \in Q \wedge s \in S \wedge z^* \in h_{qs}(M, pr)\big) \\ &\leftrightarrow \exists q\, \exists s\, \exists z^{**} \big(q \in Q \wedge s \in S \wedge z^{**} \in h_q(M, p) \\ &\qquad \wedge z^* \in h_s(z^{**}, r)\big) \\ &\leftrightarrow \exists z^{**} \big(z^{**} \in h_Q(M, p) \wedge z^* \in h_S(z^{**}, r)\big) \\ &\leftrightarrow z^* \in h_S\big(h_Q(M, p), r\big) \end{aligned}$$

is satisfied. Thus Theorem 1.5 is proved.

In analogy to deterministic Mealy and Moore automata, we define non-deterministic Mealy and non-deterministic Moore automata.

Definition 1.5. Let $\mathfrak{B} = [X, Y, Z, h]$ be an ND-automaton.

(1.5.1) $\mathfrak{B}$ is called a *non-deterministic Mealy automaton* if for all $[z, x] \in Z \times X$

$$h(z, x) = g(z, x) \times f(z, x)$$

(1.5.2) $\mathfrak{B}$ is called a *non-deterministic Moore automaton*, if there is a function m mapping the set Z into $\mathfrak{P}^*(Y)$ in such a way that for $z, z' \in Z$, $x \in X$ and $y \in Y$

$$[y, z'] \in h(z, x) \leftrightarrow z' \in f(z, x) \wedge y \in m(z').$$

The function m is called a *marking function* of $\mathfrak{B}$.

Non-deterministic Mealy (Moore) automata are denoted by $[X, Y, Z, f, g]$ ($[X, Y, Z, f, m]$). Obviously, the marking function m of an ND-Moore automaton need not be defined for those $z' \in Z$ which are not contained in any set $f(z, x)$, in order to satisfy the equivalence (1.5.2). However we require that m be defined on the whole Z, so that when investigating an ND-Moore automaton, we do not have to worry whether, for a given $z \in Z$, m is defined or not. This can be achieved for instance by choosing a $y^* \in Y$ and setting $m(z) = \{y^*\}$ for each $z \in Z \setminus \bigcup_{x \in X} f(Z, x)$. For convenience we refer to this m as *the* marking function of the ND-Moore automaton $\mathfrak{B}$.

Corollary 1.6. Let $\mathfrak{B} = [X, Y, Z, f, g]$ be an ND-Mealy automaton, and for all $z \in Z$, $x \in X$ let $h(z, x) \underset{\mathrm{Df}}{=} g(z, x) \times f(z, x)$.

1. For all $z_1 \in Z$, $p \in W(X)$,

$$v_{\mathfrak{B}}(z_1, p) = \begin{cases} \{e\}, & \text{if } p = e, \\ \Big\{y_1 \dots y_n \,|\, y_1 \in g(z_1, x_1) \\ \quad \wedge \exists z_2 \dots \exists z_n \Big[\bigwedge_{i=1}^{n-1} [z_{i+1} \in f(z_i, x_i) \wedge y_{i+1} \in g(z_{i+1}, x_{i+1})]\Big]\Big\}, & \\ & \text{if } p = x_1 \dots x_n,\ n > 0. \end{cases}$$

2. For all $z, z' \in Z$, $x \in X$, $y \in Y$,

$$h_{z'}(z, x) = \begin{cases} g(z, x), & \text{if } z' \in f(z, x), \\ \emptyset & \text{otherwise.} \end{cases}$$

$$h_y(z, x) = \begin{cases} f(z, x), & \text{if } y \in g(z, x), \\ \emptyset & \text{otherwise.} \end{cases}$$

3. For all $z \in Z$, $x \in X$, $p \in W(X)$,

$$v_{\mathfrak{B}}(z, xp) = g(z, x) \bigcup_{z' \in f(z, x)} v_{\mathfrak{B}}(z', p) = g(z, x)\, v_{\mathfrak{B}}(f(z, x), p).$$

4. An ND-automaton $\mathfrak{B} = [X, Y, Z, h]$ is an ND-Mealy automaton if and only if for any $z \in Z$, $x \in X$ the set $h_{z'}(z, x)$ does not depend on z', provided that $z' \in f(z, x)$.

5. Every Z-deterministic (Y-deterministic) ND-automaton is a Z-deterministic (Y-deterministic) ND-Mealy automaton.

6. An ND-Mealy automaton is observable if and only if it is Z-deterministic.

Corollary 1.7. Let $\mathfrak{B} = [Y, Y, Z, f, m]$ be an ND-Moore automaton and h the function which belongs to f and m by (1.5.2).

1. For all $z_1 \in Z$, $p \in W(X)$,

$$v_{\mathfrak{B}}(z_1, p) = \begin{cases} \{e\}, & \text{if } p = e, \\ \Big\{y_1 \dots y_n \mid \exists z_2 \dots \exists z_{n+1} \Big(\bigwedge_{i=1}^{n} [z_{i+1} \in f(z_i, x_i) \wedge y_i \in m(z_{i+1})]\Big)\Big\}, & \\ & \text{if } p = x_1 \dots x_n,\ n > 0. \end{cases}$$

2. For all $z\,z' \in Z,\; x \in X$,

$$h_{z'}(z, x) \;=\; \begin{cases} m(z'), & \text{if } z' \in f(z, x), \\ \emptyset & \text{otherwise}. \end{cases}$$

3. For all $z \in Z,\; x \in X,\; p \in W(X)$,

$$v_{\mathfrak{B}}(z, xp) = \bigcup_{z' \in f(z,x)} m(z')\, v_{\mathfrak{B}}(z', p).$$

4. An ND-automaton $\mathfrak{B} = [X, Y, Z, h]$ is an ND-Moore automaton if and only if the set $h_{z'}(x, z)$ does not depend on $[z, x]$, provided that $z' \in f(z, x)$.

It is clear that every deterministic ND-automaton (i.e. every deterministic ND-Mealy automaton) in practice works like an ordinary deterministic (abstract) automaton. Therefore, we canonically assign to each such ND-automaton an abstract deterministic automaton.

Definition 1.6.

(1.6.1) Let $\mathfrak{B} = [X, Y, Z, h]$ be a deterministic ND-automaton. Then $Det(\mathfrak{B}) = [X, Y, Z, \delta, \lambda]$ denotes the deterministic automaton for which

$$h(z, x) = \{[\lambda(z, x), \delta(z, x)]\}$$

is satisfied for any $z \in Z,\; x \in X$.

(1.6.2) If α is a function mapping the set A into the set of all singletons of the set $\mathfrak{B}$, then $Det(\alpha)$ denotes the function on A into B such that $\alpha(a) = \{Det(\alpha)(a)\}$ for each $a \in A$.

Clearly, *Det* is a one-to-one mapping which possesses the properties usually required from an isomorphism. Thus in this sense, the class (or the theory) of deterministic automata can be isomorphically embedded into the class (or the theory) of ND-automata.

Now we assign to each non-deterministic automaton $\mathfrak{B} = [X, Y, Z, h]$ a directed graph $\mathfrak{G}_{\mathfrak{B}}$. The graphs of finite automata with a small number of input signals, output signals and states enable them to be easily described and visualized. We shall use them in our examples.

Definition 1.7. Let $\mathfrak{B} = [X, Y, Z, h]$ be an ND-automaton. The *graph* $\mathfrak{G}_{\mathfrak{B}}$ *of* $\mathfrak{B}$ is the triple $[P, K, \alpha]$, where

$$P \underset{\text{Df}}{=} Z,$$

$$K \underset{\text{Df}}{=} \{[z, x, y, z'] \mid [y, z'] \in h(z, x)\}$$

and for all $k = [z, x, y, z'] \in K$

$$\alpha(k) \underset{\text{Df}}{=} [z, z'] \in P \times P.$$

The graphical representation of the graph of a finite ND-automaton is illustrated by the example of the following automaton $\mathfrak{B}_1 = [\{x\}, \{0, 1\}, \{1, 2, 3, 4\}, h^1]$, where h^1 is given by the table below:

h^1	1	2	3	4
x	$\{[0, 2], [1, 3]\}$	$\{[0, 3], [1, 4]\}$	$\{[0, 4]\}$	$\{[0, 1], [1, 3]\}$

The graph $\mathfrak{G}_{\mathfrak{B}_1}$ is represented in Fig. 13.

We conclude this section by defining the concept of a "subautomaton" in the usual way.

Definition 1.8. The ND-automaton $\mathfrak{B}' = [X', Y', Z', h']$ is called a *subautomaton of the ND-automaton* $\mathfrak{B} = [X, Y, Z, h]$, if $X' \subseteq X$, $Z' \subseteq Z$ and h' is the restriction of h onto $Z' \times X' \subseteq Z \times X$.

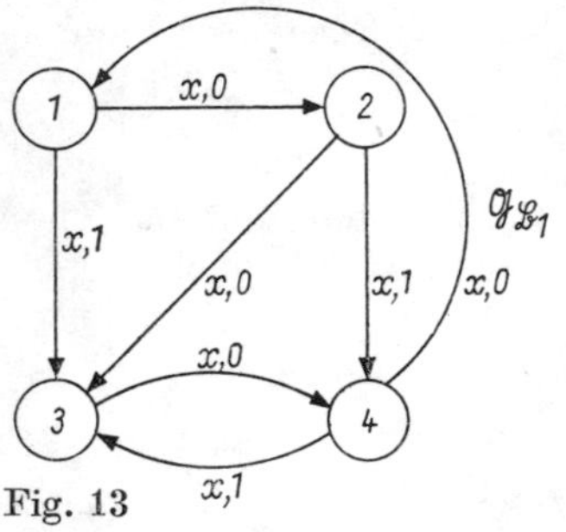

Fig. 13

In particular, if $\mathfrak{B}'$ is a subautomaton of $\mathfrak{B}$, then for all $z' \in Z'$, $x' \in X'$

$$\big(h(z', x') =\big) \quad h'(z', x') \subseteq Y' \times Z'.$$

If $\mathfrak{B}'$ has no "superfluous" output signals, i.e., output signals which do not occur in any of the sets $g'(z', x')$, then we also have $Y' \subseteq Y$.

§ 2. Equivalence, Distinguishability and Reduction

If we feed an input word p into an ND-automaton $\mathfrak{B}$ having a certain state z, then it is in general not uniquely determined which word q will be put out in response. What we know is only that the word q must belong to the set $v_{\mathfrak{B}}(z, p)$ of all "possible" output words. By choosing an initial state z or a set M of possible initial states, we specify a certain "behaviour" of our automaton, i.e., a single valued mapping which assigns to every input word p the set $v_{\mathfrak{B}}(z, p)$ or $v_{\mathfrak{B}}(M, p)$ respectively. However, before we investigate more closely the various behaviours of ND-automata, which we shall call non-deterministic operators (cf. § 4), it would be expedient to take up identity problems in the behaviour of various non-deterministic automata. Systems which, when looked at from outside are indistinguishable, are usually called equivalent. Since the behaviour of an automaton is only specified after we have chosen an initial state, the equivalence between states must be distinguished from that between automata, unless we confine ourselves to considering only initial automata, where the initial states are specified once and for all. Thus it is not sufficient for two automata to have only one realizable behaviour in common in order to be called equivalent: every realizable behaviour of one must be realizable in the other. In particular it is necessary that both automata should be able to receive the same input signals, i.e., that their input alphabets coincide.

Definition 2.1. Let $\mathfrak{B}$ and $\mathfrak{B}'$ be (not necessarily different) ND-automata with the same input alphabet X.

(2.1.1] A state z of $\mathfrak{B}$ is said to be *equivalent* to a state z' of $\mathfrak{B}'$ (written: $z \sim z'$), if for all $p \in W(X)$

$$v_{\mathfrak{B}}(z, p) = v_{\mathfrak{B}'}(z', p).$$

(2.1.2) A set M of states of $\mathfrak{B}$ is *equivalent* to a set M' of states of $\mathfrak{B}'$ (written: $M \sim M'$), if for all $p \in W(X)$

$$v_{\mathfrak{B}}(M, p) = v_{\mathfrak{B}'}(M', p).$$

(2.1.3) The ND-automaton $\mathfrak{B}$ is called *equivalently embedded* into the ND-automaton $\mathfrak{B}'$ (written: $\mathfrak{B} \subseteq \mathfrak{B}'$), if for each state z of $\mathfrak{B}$ there is an equivalent state z' of $\mathfrak{B}'$.

(2.1.4) The ND-automaton $\mathfrak{B}$ is called equivalent to $\mathfrak{B}'$ (written: $\mathfrak{B} \sim \mathfrak{B}'$) if both $\mathfrak{B} \subseteq \mathfrak{B}'$ and $\mathfrak{B}' \subseteq \mathfrak{B}$.

(2.1.5) We say that the ND-automaton $\mathfrak{B}$ is *weakly equivalently embedded* into the ND-automaton $\mathfrak{B}'$ (written: $\mathfrak{B} \lessapprox \mathfrak{B}'$) if for each set M of states of $\mathfrak{B}$ there is an equivalent set M' of states of $\mathfrak{B}'$.

(2.1.6) The ND-automata $\mathfrak{B}$ and $\mathfrak{B}'$ are called *weakly equivalent* (written: $\mathfrak{B} \approx \mathfrak{B}'$) if either is weakly equivalently embedded into the other.

Corollary 2.1.

1. The relations $\sim$, $\approx$ are equivalence relations.
2. The relations $\subseteq$, $\lessapprox$ are reflexive and transitive. Instead of anti-symmetry we have

$$\mathfrak{B} \subseteq \mathfrak{B}' \wedge \mathfrak{B}' \subseteq \mathfrak{B} \rightarrow \mathfrak{B} \sim \mathfrak{B}'; \qquad \mathfrak{B} \lessapprox \mathfrak{B}' \wedge \mathfrak{B}' \lessapprox \mathfrak{B} \rightarrow \mathfrak{B} \approx \mathfrak{B}'.$$

3. If $\mathfrak{B} \subseteq \mathfrak{B}'$, then $\mathfrak{B} \lessapprox \mathfrak{B}'$.
4. If $\mathfrak{B} \sim \mathfrak{B}'$, then $\mathfrak{B} \approx \mathfrak{B}'$.
5. An ND-automaton $\mathfrak{B}$ is weakly equivalently embedded into the ND-automaton $\mathfrak{B}'$ if and only if for every singleton $\{z\}$ containing a state of $\mathfrak{B}$ there is an equivalent set M' of states of $\mathfrak{B}'$.
6. Deterministic ND-automata are equivalent if and only if they are weakly equivalent.

The following example readily convinces us that the converses of 2.1.2 and 2.1.4 are not valid. We consider the (autonomous) ND-automata $\mathfrak{B}_2$ and $\mathfrak{B}_3$ with the input alphabet $X = \{x\}$ and the output alphabet $Y = \{0, 1\}$, whose graphs $\mathfrak{G}_{\mathfrak{B}_2}$, $\mathfrak{G}_{\mathfrak{B}_3}$ are shown in Fig. 14.

The ND-Moore automata $\mathfrak{B}_2$, $\mathfrak{B}_3$ are weakly equivalent, since $\{a\} \sim \{d, e\}$, $\{b\} \sim \{d\}$, $\{c\} \sim \{e\}$. However, there is no state in $\mathfrak{B}_3$ which is equivalent to a. Therefore $\mathfrak{B}_2$ and $\mathfrak{B}_3$ are not equivalent.

In the definition of equivalence and weak equivalence, we have made no assumptions on the output alphabets of the corresponding automata. Now we show that the output alphabets must coincide if they contain no superfluous elements.

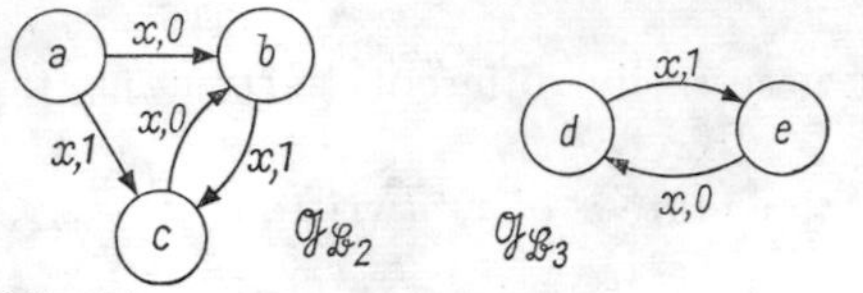

Fig. 14

Theorem 2.2. *If the ND-automata* $\mathfrak{B} = [X, Y, Z, h]$, $\mathfrak{B}' = [X, Y', Z', h']$ *are weakly equivalent, and the sets* Y, Y' *are minimal in the sense that for every* $y \in Y$ *(or* $y' \in Y'$*) there exist an* $x \in X$ *and a* $z \in Z$ *(or* $z' \in Z'$*) such that* $y \in g(z, x)$ *(or* $y' \in g'(z', x)$*), then we have* $Y = Y'$.

Proof: Let $y \in Y$. Then there is a $z \in Z$ and an $x \in X$ with $y \in g(z, x)$. $\mathfrak{B} \approx \mathfrak{B}'$ implies that there exists a set $M' \subseteq Z'$ such that $\{z\} \sim M'$, hence $g(z, x) = g'(M', x)$. Therefore, $y \in g'(M', z)$ i.e., there is a $z' \in M' \subseteq Z'$ with $y \in g'(z', x)$ which implies $y \in Y'$. The converse can be shown analogously.

In what follows we always assume that the output alphabets of the ND-automata under consideration contain no superfluous elements (signals).

Theorem 2.3. *Let* $\mathfrak{B} = [X, Y, Z, h]$ *be an arbitrary ND-automaton.*

1. *There is an ND-Moore automaton* $\mathfrak{B}'$ *which is equivalent to* $\mathfrak{B}$. $\mathfrak{B}'$ *can be chosen in such a way that it is Z-deterministic, finite,* $[X, Z]$*-finite, if* $\mathfrak{B}$ *is Z-deterministic, finite, or* $[X, Z]$*-finite respectively.*

2. *There is an ND-Moore automaton* $\mathfrak{B}''$ *with a deterministic marking function such that* $\mathfrak{B}''$ *is equivalent to* $\mathfrak{B}$. *This can be chosen in such a way that* $\mathfrak{B}''$ *is finite or* $[Y, Z]$*-finite if* $\mathfrak{B}$ *is finite or* $[Y, Z]$*-finite respectively.*

Remark: We shall show later that a corresponding theorem for ND-Mealy automata is not valid.

Proof: To verify 2.3.1, let us consider the system $\mathfrak{B}' = [X, Y, Z \times X \times Z, f', m']$ with

$$f'([z_0, x_0, z_1], x_1) \underset{\mathrm{Df}}{=} \{[z_1, x_1, z_2] \mid z_2 \in f(z_1, x_1)\},$$

$$m'([z_0, x_0, z_1]) = \begin{cases} h_{z_1}(z_0, x_0), & \text{if this set is non-empty,} \\ \{y^*\} & \text{otherwise,} \end{cases}$$

where $y^* \in Y$ is arbitrary, but fixed. $\mathfrak{B}'$ is an ND-Moore automaton and for all $z, z' \in Z$, $x \in X$ we have

$$z' \sim [z, x, z']$$

i.e., for every $p \in W(X)$ we have $v_{\mathfrak{B}}(z', p) = v_{\mathfrak{B}'}([z, x, z'], p)$. We prove this assertion by induction on p. The initial step $p = e$ is trivial and the induction step is taken from p to xp for every $x \in X$. We have

$$v_{\mathfrak{B}}(z, xp) = \bigcup_{z' \in f(z,x)} h_{z'}(z, x)\, v_{\mathfrak{B}}(z', p)$$
$$= \bigcup_{z' \in f(z,x)} m'([z, x, z'])\, v_{\mathfrak{B}'}([z, x, z'], p)$$

and for arbitrary $z_0 \in Z$, $x_0 \in X$

$$z' \in f(z, x) \leftrightarrow [z, x, z'] \in f'([z_0, x_0, z], x).$$

Thus for arbitrary $z_0 \in Z$, $x_0 \in X$

$$v_{\mathfrak{B}}(z, xp) = \bigcup_{[z,x,z'] \in f'([z_0,x_0,z],x)} m'([z, x, z'])\, v_{\mathfrak{B}'}([z, x, z'], p) = v_{\mathfrak{B}'}([z_0, x_0, z], xp),$$

which was to be shown. To prove Proposition 2.3.2, consider the system $\mathfrak{B}'' = [X, Y, Y \times Z, f'', m'']$, where

$$f''([y, z], x) = h(z, x) \quad \text{for all } [y, z] \in Y \times Z,\ x \in X,$$
$$m''([y, z]) = \{y\} \quad \text{for all } [y, z] \in Y \times Z.$$

We shall show by induction on p that $[y_0, z] \sim z$ for all $y_0 \in Y$, $z \in Z$, or in other words that for all $z \in Z$, $y_0 \in Y$, $p \in W(X)$

$$v_{\mathfrak{B}}(z, p) = v_{\mathfrak{B}''}([y_0, z], p).$$

The initial step $p = e$ is again trivial, and the induction step is taken from p to xp for any $x \in X$. We can easily see that

$$v_{\mathfrak{B}}(z, xp) = \bigcup_{[y,z'] \in h(z,x)} \{y\} \cdot v_{\mathfrak{B}}(z', p).$$

Thus by the induction hypothesis, for arbitrary $y_0 \in Y$

$$v_{\mathfrak{B}}(z, xp) = \bigcup_{[y,z'] \in f''([y_0,z],x)} m''([y, z'])\, v_{\mathfrak{B}''}([y, z'], p) = v_{\mathfrak{B}''}([y_0, z], xp).$$

This proves Theorem 2.3.

Theorem 2.4. *For every ND-automaton* $\mathfrak{B} = [X, Y, Z, h]$ *there is an observable ND-automaton* $\mathfrak{B}^* = [X, Y, Z^*, h^*]$, *which is weakly equivalent to* $\mathfrak{B}$ *and into which* $\mathfrak{B}$ *is equivalently embedded. If* $\mathfrak{B}$ *is finite (Z-finite), then* $\mathfrak{B}^*$ *can be chosen finite (Z-finite).*

Proof: Let $Z^* = \{h_q(z, p) \mid z \in Z \wedge p \in W(X) \wedge q \in v_{\mathfrak{B}}(z, p)\}$, and for $z^* \in Z^*$, $x \in X$

$$h^*(z^*, x) = \{[y, h_y(z^*, x)] \mid y \in g(z^*, x)\}.$$

Thus the elements of Z are non-empty subsets of Z. If $z^* = h_q(z, p)$, $y \in g(h_q(z, p), x)$, then $h_y(h_q(z, p), x) = h_{qy}(z, px) \neq \emptyset$; since $z^* = h_q(z, p) \neq \emptyset$ implies $q \in v_{\mathfrak{B}}(z, p)$, and by $y \in g(h_q(z, p), x)$ we have

$$qy \in \bigcup_{q \in W(Y)} \{q\} \cdot v_{\mathfrak{B}}(h_q(z, p), x) = v_{\mathfrak{B}}(z, px).$$

Thus, $\mathfrak{B}^* = [X, Y, Z^*, h^*]$ is an observable ND-automaton, since either $h_y^*(z^*, x) = \{h_y(z^*, x)\}$ or it is empty. Now we show by induction on r that for $z \in Z$, $p, r \in W(X)$, $q \in v_{\mathfrak{B}}(z, p)$

$$v_{\mathfrak{B}}(h_q(z, p), r) = v_{\mathfrak{B}^*}(h_q(z, p), r).$$

The initial step $r = e$ is trivial. The step from r to xr:

$$v_{\mathfrak{B}}(h_q(z, p), xr) = \bigcup_{y \in g(h_q(z, p), x)} \{y\} \cdot v_{\mathfrak{B}}(h_y(h_q(z, p), x), r).$$

We have $h_y(h_q(z, p), x) = h_{qy}(z, px)$ and by the induction hypothesis $v_{\mathfrak{B}}(h_{qy}(z, px), r) = v_{\mathfrak{B}^*}(h_{qy}(z, px), r)$. Hence,

$$\begin{aligned} v_{\mathfrak{B}}(h_q(z, p), xr) &= \bigcup_{y \in g(h_q(z, p), x)} \{y\} \cdot v_{\mathfrak{B}^*}(h_{qy}(z, px), r) \\ &= \bigcup_{y \in g^*(h_q(z, p), x)} \{y\} \cdot v_{\mathfrak{B}^*}(h_y^*(h_q(z, p), x), r) \\ &= v_{\mathfrak{B}^*}(h_q(z, p), xr). \end{aligned}$$

Because of $h_e(z, e) = \{z\}$, the state $\{z\} \in Z^*$ is equivalent to the state z of $\mathfrak{B}$, hence $\mathfrak{B} \subsetsim \mathfrak{B}^*$. On the other hand, for every state $z^* = h_q(z, p) \in Z^*$ of $\mathfrak{B}^*$, the set z^* as a set of states of $\mathfrak{B}$ is equivalent to z^* as a state of $\mathfrak{B}^*$, and therefore $\mathfrak{B}^* \subsetsim \mathfrak{B}$, and consequently $\mathfrak{B} \approx \mathfrak{B}^*$.

Theorem 2.5. *Let* $\mathfrak{B} = [X, Y, Z, h]$, $\mathfrak{B}' = [X, Y, Z', h']$ *be ND-automata, and let* $M \subseteq Z$, $M' \subseteq Z'$, $p \in W(X)$.

1. *If* $Q \subseteq v_{\mathfrak{B}}(M, p)$ *and* $M \sim M'$, *then* $h_Q(M, p) \sim h'_Q(M', p)$.

2. $M \sim M'$ *holds if and only if there is an* $n \geqq 0$ *such that for all* $p \in W(X)$, $q \in W(Y)$ *with* $l(p) = l(q) = n$ *the sets* $h_q(M, p)$, $h'_q(M', p)$ *are equivalent.*

Proof: Suppose $M \sim M'$ and $Q \subseteq v_{\mathfrak{B}}(M, p)$. If $Q = \emptyset$, then $h_Q(M, p) = h'_Q(M', p) = \emptyset$. Suppose now that the sets M, M', Q are non-empty and $q' \in Q$ is arbitrary. By $q' \in v_{\mathfrak{B}}(M, p) = v_{\mathfrak{B}'}(M', p)$, the sets $h_{q'}(M, p)$, $h'_{q'}(M, p)$, are non-empty, and therefore for all $r \in W(X)$ we have

$$\begin{aligned} v_{\mathfrak{B}}(M, pr) &= \bigcup_{q \in W(Y)} \{q\} \cdot v_{\mathfrak{B}}(h_q(M, p), r) \\ &= \bigcup_{q \in W(Y)} \{q\} \cdot v_{\mathfrak{B}'}(h'_q(M', p), r) \\ &= v_{\mathfrak{B}'}(M', pr), \end{aligned}$$

from which

$$v_{\mathfrak{B}}\big(h_{q'}(M, p), r\big) = v_{\mathfrak{B}'}\big(h'_{q'}(M', p), r\big).$$

For $q' \in Q$ we have $h_{q'}(M, p) \sim h'_{q'}(M', p)$; consequently,

$$h_Q(M, p) = \bigcup_{q \in Q} h_q(M, p) \sim \bigcup_{q \in Q} h'_q(M', p) = h'_Q(M, p),$$

which proves 2.5.1. Thus to verify 2.5.2 we only have to show that the existence of an $n \geq 0$ such that $h_q(M, p) \sim h'_q(M', p)$ for all $p \in X^n$, $q \in Y^n$, implies the equivalence of M and M'. For $n = 0$ this is trivial. Suppose $n \geqq 1$. For $r' \in W(X)$ with $l(r') \geqq n$, we obtain $v_{\mathfrak{B}}(M, r') = v_{\mathfrak{B}'}(M', r')$ by putting $r' = pr$ with $l(p) = n$ into the above chain of equations. Suppose $r' \in W(X)$ with $0 < l(r') < n$. Then

$$\begin{aligned} s' \in v_{\mathfrak{B}}(M, r') &\leftrightarrow h_{s'}(M, r') \neq \emptyset \\ &\leftrightarrow \exists p\big(p \in W(X) \wedge l(p) = n - l(r') \wedge v_{\mathfrak{B}}(h_{s'}(M, r'), p) \neq \emptyset\big) \\ &\leftrightarrow \exists p\, \exists q\big(p \in X^{n-l(r')} \wedge q \in W(Y) \wedge h_{s'q}(M, r'p) \neq \emptyset\big). \end{aligned}$$

We have $l(r'p) = n$, hence $h_{s'q}(M, r'p) \sim h'_{s'q}(M', r'p)$, from which in particular

$$h_{s'q}(M, r'p) \neq \emptyset \leftrightarrow h'_{s'q}(M', r'p) \neq \emptyset$$

and we get

$$\begin{aligned} s' \in v_{\mathfrak{B}}(M, r') &\leftrightarrow \exists p\, \exists q\big(p \in X^{n-l(r')} \wedge q \in W(Y) \wedge h'_{s'q}(M', r'p) \neq \emptyset\big) \\ &\leftrightarrow s' \in v_{\mathfrak{B}'}(M', r'), \end{aligned}$$

which was to be shown. This proves Theorem 2.5.

From 1.4.5 and the above considerations we obtain

Corollary 2.6.

1. If $M \sim M'$, then $f(M, p) \sim f'(M', p)$ for every $p \in W(X)$.

2. If the equation $v_{\mathfrak{B}}(M, p') = v_{\mathfrak{B}'}(M', p')$ is satisfied for each $p' \in X^n$, then we have $v_{\mathfrak{B}}(M, p) = v_{\mathfrak{B}'}(M', p)$ for each $p \in W(X)$ with $l(p) \leqq n$.

Next we define the distinguishability of ND-automata and their states.

Definition 2.2. Let $\mathfrak{B} = [X, Y, Z, h]$, $\mathfrak{B}' = [X, Y', Z', h']$ be ND-automata with the same input alphabet.

(2.2.1) The states $z \in Z$, $z' \in Z'$ (or the sets of states $M \subseteq Z$, $M' \subseteq Z'$) are called *distinguishable* if there is a $p \in W(X)$ with $v_{\mathfrak{B}}(z, p) \neq v_{\mathfrak{B}'}(z', p)$ (or $v_{\mathfrak{B}}(M, p) \neq v_{\mathfrak{B}'}(M', p)$).

(2.2.2) The states $z \in Z$, $z' \in Z'$ (or the sets of states $M \subseteq Z$, $M' \subseteq Z'$) are called *separable* if there is a $p \in W(X)$ with $v_{\mathfrak{B}}(z, p) \cap v_{\mathfrak{B}}(z', p) = \emptyset$ (or $v_{\mathfrak{B}}(M, p) \cap v_{\mathfrak{B}'}(M', p) = \emptyset$).

(2.2.3) The ND-automata $\mathfrak{B}$, $\mathfrak{B}'$ are called *distinguishable* (or *separable*) if the sets Z, Z' are distinguishable (or separable).

Corollary 2.7.

1. Separable states, sets of states and automata respectively, are distinguishable.
2. States or sets of states are distinguishable if and only if they are not equivalent.
3. Equivalent ND-automata are neither distinguishable nor separable.
4. There exist indistinguishable ND-automata which are not equivalent.
5. The ND-automata $\mathfrak{B}, \mathfrak{B}'$ are separable if and only if every set M of states of $\mathfrak{B}$ is separable from every set M' of states of $\mathfrak{B}'$.

The ND-automata $\mathfrak{B}_2, \mathfrak{B}_3$ whose graphs are represented in Fig. 14 (page 158) illustrate Proposition 2.7.4.

Theorem 2.8. *Weakly equivalent ND-automata are indistinguishable.*

Proof: Let $\mathfrak{B} = [X, Y, Z, h] \approx \mathfrak{B}' = [X, Y', Z', h']$. Then there is a set $M' \subseteq Z'$ with $M' \sim Z$. If $M' = Z'$, the assertion is trivial. If $M' \subset Z'$, then there is a set $M \subseteq Z$ with $M \sim Z' \setminus M'$. Thus, for each $p \in W(X)$ we have

$$v_{\mathfrak{B}'}(Z' \setminus M', p) = v_{\mathfrak{B}}(M, p) \subseteq v_{\mathfrak{B}}(Z, p) = v_{\mathfrak{B}'}(M', p),$$

$$v_{\mathfrak{B}}(Z, p) = v_{\mathfrak{B}'}(M', p) = v_{\mathfrak{B}'}(M', p) \cup v_{\mathfrak{B}'}(Z' \setminus M', p) = v_{\mathfrak{B}'}(Z', p),$$

which was to be shown.

There exist indistinguishable but not weakly equivalent ND-automata. To illustrate this we consider the ND-automata $\mathfrak{B}_4 = [\{x\}, \{0,1\}, \{a, b\}, h^4]$ and $\mathfrak{B}_5 = [\{x\}, \{0, 1\}, \{c\}, h^5]$, whose graphs are shown in Fig. 15. We have $v_{\mathfrak{B}_4}(\{a, b\}, p) = \{0, 1\}^{l(p)} = v_{\mathfrak{B}_5}(\{c\}, p)$, hence $\mathfrak{B}_4$ and $\mathfrak{B}_5$ are indistinguishable. However since the state c of $\mathfrak{B}_5$ is not equivalent to the state a of $\mathfrak{B}_4$, $\mathfrak{B}_4$ and $\mathfrak{B}_5$ are not weakly equivalent.

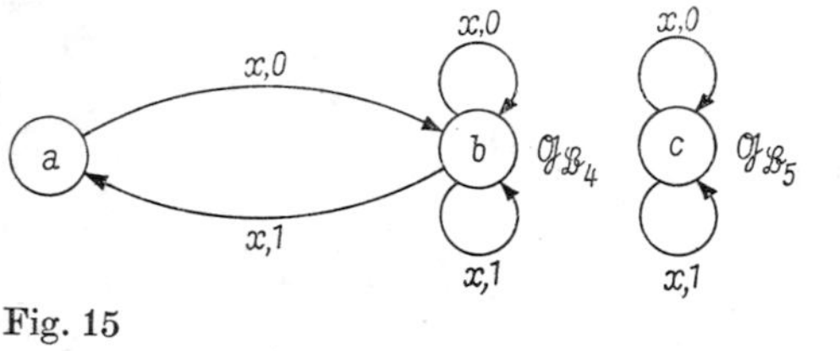

Fig. 15

We can also see from this example that for ND-automata, $\mathfrak{B}' \lesssim \mathfrak{B}$ does not necessarily imply the existence of a subautomaton of $\mathfrak{B}$ equivalent to $\mathfrak{B}'$, as is the case for deterministic automata. Indeed, $\mathfrak{B}_5 \lesssim \mathfrak{B}_4$ is satisfied because $c \sim b$.

Theorem 2.9. *Let* $\mathfrak{B} = [X, Y, Z, h]$ *be a Z-finite ND-automaton with* $k > 0$ *states,* $M, N \subseteq Z$. *If M and N are distinguishable, then there is a word* $p \in W(X)$ *with* $l(p) = 2^k - 2$ *such that* $v_{\mathfrak{B}}(M, p) \neq v_{\mathfrak{B}}(N, p)$.

Proof: If M or N is empty, then the assertion is trivial. Suppose $M, N \in \mathfrak{P}^*(Z)$. We define by induction a sequence $\mathfrak{Z}(\mathfrak{B}) = (\mathfrak{z}_i)$ of partitions of the set $\mathfrak{P}^*(\mathfrak{Z})$, and here we make no use of the fact that $\mathfrak{B}$ is Z-finite. Thus, $\mathfrak{Z}(\mathfrak{B})$ is defined for an arbitrary ND-automaton $\mathfrak{B}$.

Initial step: $i = 1$. Let $\mathfrak{z}_1$ be that partition of $\mathfrak{P}^*(Z)$ where for all $M, N \in \mathfrak{P}^*(Z)$ we have the following assertions:

(A1) There is a class $K^1 \in \mathfrak{z}_1$ with $M \in K^1$.

(A2) There is a class $K^1 \in \mathfrak{z}_1$ with $M, N \in K^1$ if and only if $v_{\mathfrak{B}}(M,x) = v_{\mathfrak{B}}(N,x)$ for all $x \in X$.

Induction step: $i \to i+1$. Let $\mathfrak{z}_{i+1}$ be the partition of $\mathfrak{P}^*(Z)$ where, for all $M, N \in \mathfrak{P}^*(Z)$ we have:

(I1) There is a class $K^{i+1} \in \mathfrak{z}_{i+1}$ with $M \in K^{i+1}$.

(I2) There is a class $K^{i+1} \in \mathfrak{z}_{i+1}$ with $M, N \in K^{i+1}$, if and only if

a) there is a class $K^i \in \mathfrak{z}_i$ with $M, N \in K^i$ and

b) for every $x \in X$, $y \in v_{\mathfrak{B}}(M, x)$ $\big(= v_{\mathfrak{B}}(N, x)\big)$ there is a class $K^i \in \mathfrak{z}_i$ with $h_y(M, x), h_y(N, x) \in K^i$.

Now we prove a series of lemmas on the sequence $\mathfrak{Z}(\mathfrak{B})$, which will immediately imply Theorem 2.9.

Lemma 2.9a. *For all $M, N \in \mathfrak{P}^*(Z)$ and every $i = 1, 2, \ldots$ we have: There is a class $K^i \in \mathfrak{z}_i$ with $M, N \in K^i$, if and only if $v_{\mathfrak{B}}(M, p) = v_{\mathfrak{B}}(N, p)$ for each $p \in W(X)$ with $l(p) \leqq i$.*

We prove this by induction on i. The initial step $i = 1$ is trivial because of (A2). Using (I2) we have, for all $M, N \in \mathfrak{P}^*(Z)$: the assertion

$$\exists K^{i+1}(M, N \in K^{i+1} \in \mathfrak{z}_{i+1}) \tag{1}$$

holds if and only if

$$\exists K^i(K^i \in \mathfrak{z}_i \wedge M, N \in K^i), \tag{2}$$

$$\forall x \forall y\big(x \in X \wedge y \in g(M, x) \to \exists K^i(h_y(M, x), h_y(N, x) \in K^i \in \mathfrak{z}_i)\big) \tag{3}$$

are satisfied. By (I2a), (1) or (2) implies

$$\exists K^1(K^1 \in \mathfrak{z}_1 \wedge M, N \in K^1),$$

i.e., by (A2),

$$\forall x\big(x \in X \to g(M, x) = g(N, x)\big). \tag{4}$$

By the induction hypothesis, (3) is equivalent to the following

$$\begin{aligned}&\forall x \forall y\,\big(x \in X \wedge y \in g(M, x)\\ &\to \forall p\big(p \in W(X) \wedge l(p) \leqq i \to v_{\mathfrak{B}}(h_y(M, x), p) = v_{\mathfrak{B}}(h_y(N, x), p)\big)\big),\end{aligned} \tag{5}$$

hence to

$$\begin{aligned}&\forall x \forall y \forall p\big(x \in X \wedge y \in g(M, x) \wedge p \in W(X) \wedge l(p) \leqq i\\ &\qquad \to \{y\} \cdot v_{\mathfrak{B}}(h_y(M, x), p) = \{y\} \cdot v_{\mathfrak{B}}(h_y(N, x), p)\big).\end{aligned} \tag{6}$$

By (4), (6) is equivalent to the assertion

$$\forall x \forall p \big(xp \in W(X) \wedge l(xp) \leqq i + 1 \\ \rightarrow \bigcup_{y \in g(M,x)} \{y\} \cdot v_{\mathfrak{B}}(h_y(M, x), p) = \bigcup_{y \in g(N,x)} \{y\} \cdot v_{\mathfrak{B}}(h_y(N, x), p)\big). \quad (7)$$

By Theorem 1.5.7, (7) is equivalent to

$$\forall p \big(p \in W(X) \wedge l(p) \leqq i + 1 \rightarrow v_{\mathfrak{B}}(M, p) = v_{\mathfrak{B}}(N, p)\big). \quad (8)$$

Thus (1) implies (8). On the other hand, we immediately obtain from (8) the statement (4) and

$$\forall p \big(p \in W(X) \wedge l(p) \leqq i \rightarrow v_{\mathfrak{B}}(M, p) = v_{\mathfrak{B}}(N, p)\big),$$

i.e., by the induction hypothesis, the statement (2). Because of (4) however, (8) is equivalent to (3). Hence (8) holds if and only if (1) does.

We can easily prove the following

Lemma 2.9b. *If* $\mathfrak{z}_i = \mathfrak{z}_{i+1}$, *then* $\mathfrak{z}_i = \mathfrak{z}_{i+1}$ *for every* $j \in \boldsymbol{nz}$.

Next we show

Lemma 2.9c. *If* $\mathfrak{z}_i \neq \mathfrak{z}_{i+1}$, *then* $\mathfrak{z}_i$ *contains at least* $i + 1$ *classes.*

If $\mathfrak{z}_i \neq \mathfrak{z}_{i+1}$ and $i \geqq 1$, then $\mathfrak{z}_{i+1}$ is a proper refinement of $\mathfrak{z}_i$, hence $\mathfrak{z}_{i+1}$ contains at least one class more than $\mathfrak{z}_i$. Thus by 2.9b, it suffices to show that $\mathfrak{z}_1 = \mathfrak{z}_2$, if $\mathfrak{z}_1$ contains only one class, i.e., $\mathfrak{z}_1 = \{\mathfrak{P}^*(Z)\}$. Indeed, for all $M, N \in \mathfrak{P}^*(Z)$, $x \in X$, we have $g(M, x) = g(N, x)$, and for arbitrary $x_1, x_2 \in X$, $y \in g(M, x_1) = g(N, x_1)$ the sets $h_y(M, x_1), h_y(N, x_1)$ are non-empty, and therefore

$$v_{\mathfrak{B}}(h_y(M, x_1), x_2) = v_{\mathfrak{B}}(h_y(N, x_1), x_2).$$

This, together with 1.5.7, implies that $v_{\mathfrak{B}}(M, x_1x_2) = v_{\mathfrak{B}}(N, x_1x_2)$, hence by Lemma 2.9a, we have $\mathfrak{z}_2 = \{\mathfrak{P}^*(Z)\} = \mathfrak{z}_1$.

Our above results can be summarized as follows:

Corollary 2.10. Let $\mathfrak{B} = [X, Y, Z, h]$ be an ND-automaton.

1. $\mathfrak{Z}(\mathfrak{B}) = (\mathfrak{z}_i)$ is a sequence of partitions of the set $\mathfrak{P}^*(Z)$ such that $\mathfrak{z}_{i+1}$ is a refinement of $\mathfrak{z}_i$.

2. If $\mathfrak{z}_{i+1}$ is a proper refinement of $\mathfrak{z}_i$, then $\mathfrak{z}_{j+1}$ is also a proper refinement of $\mathfrak{z}_j$ for all $j = 1, \ldots, i$, and $\mathfrak{z}_i$ contains at least $i + 1$ classes.

3. If $\mathfrak{B}$ is Z-finite, with $Card(Z) = k$, then there is an i with $1 \leqq i \leqq 2^k - 2$ such that $\mathfrak{z}_i = \mathfrak{z}_{i+1}$.

4. If $\mathfrak{B}$ is Z-finite, and i^* is the smallest number i with $\mathfrak{z}_i = \mathfrak{z}_{i+1}$, then two non-empty sets of states M, N are equivalent if and only if they belong to the same class of $\mathfrak{z}_{i^*}$ i.e., if and only if $v_{\mathfrak{B}}(M, p) = v_{\mathfrak{B}}(N, p)$ is satisfied for each $p \in W(X)$ with $l(p) \leqq i^*$.

Since $i^* \leqq 2^k - 2$, the non-empty sets of states M, N are equivalent (or indistinguishable) if and only if $v_{\mathfrak{B}}(M, p) = v_{\mathfrak{B}}(N, p)$ for each $p \in W(X)$ with

$l(p) \leqq 2^k - 2$. It follows from 2.6.2 that this holds if and only if the equality $v_{\mathfrak{B}}(M, p) = v_{\mathfrak{B}}(N, p)$ is satisfied for every $p \in X^{2^k-2}$. Thus Theorem 2.9 is proved.

We compute the sequence $\mathfrak{Z}(\mathfrak{B})$ for the example of the ND-Mealy automaton $\mathfrak{B}_6 = [\{0, 1, 2, 3\}, \{a, b\}, \{1, 2, 3, 4\}, f^6, g^6]$, where the functions f^6, g^6 are given in the following table:

f^6	1	2	3	4	g^6	1	2	3	4
0	{1}	{1}	{1}	{1}	0	{a}	{a, b}	{a, b}	{a}
1	{2}	{2}	{3}	{2}	1	{a}	{a}	{a}	{a}
2	{2}	{3}	{1}	{2}	2	{a}	{a}	{a}	{a}
3	{2, 3}	{2}	{3}	{1, 2, 3}	3	{a}	{a}	{a}	{a}

Here,

$$\mathfrak{z}_1 = \{\{\{1\}, \{4\}, \{1, 4\}\}, \{\{2\}, \{3\}, \{1, 2\}, \{1, 3\}, \{2, 3\}, \{2, 4\}, \{3, 4\}, \{2, 3, 4\}, \{1, 3, 4\}, \{1, 2, 4\}, \{1, 2, 3\}, \{1, 2, 3, 4\}\}\};$$

$$\mathfrak{z}_2 = \{\{\{1\}, \{4\}, \{1, 4\}\}, \{\{3\}\}, \{\{2\}, \{1, 2\}, \{1, 3\}, \{2, 3\}, \{2, 4\}, \{3, 4\}, \{2, 3, 4\}, \{1, 3, 4\}, \{1, 2, 4\}, \{1, 2, 3\}, \{1, 2, 3, 4\}\}\};$$

$$\mathfrak{z}_3 = \{\{\{1\}, \{4\}, \{1, 4\}\}, \{\{2\}\}, \{\{3\}\}, \{\{1, 2\}, \{1, 3\}, \{2, 3\}, \{2, 4\}, \{3, 4\}, \{2, 3, 4\}, \{1, 3, 4\}, \{1, 2, 4\}, \{1, 2, 3\}, \{1, 2, 3, 4\}\}\};$$

$$\mathfrak{z}_4 = \{\{\{1\}, \{4\}, \{1, 4\}\}, \{\{2\}\}, \{\{3\}\}, \{\{1, 2\}, \{2, 4\}, \{1, 2, 4\}\}, \{\{1, 3\}, \{2, 3\}, \{3, 4\}, \{2, 3, 4\}, \{1, 3, 4\}, \{1, 2, 3\}, \{1, 2, 3, 4\}\}\};$$

$$\mathfrak{z}_5 = \{\{\{1\}, \{4\}, \{1, 4\}\}, \{\{2\}\}, \{\{3\}\}, \{\{1, 2\}, \{2, 4\}, \{1, 2, 4\}\}, \{\{1, 3\}, \{3, 4\}, \{1, 3, 4\}\}, \{\{2, 3\}, \{2, 3, 4\}, \{1, 2, 3\}, \{1, 2, 3, 4\}\}\};$$

$$\mathfrak{z}_6 = \{\{\{1\}, \{4\}, \{1, 4\}\}, \{\{2\}\}, \{\{3\}\}, \{\{1, 2\}, \{2, 4\}, \{1, 2, 4\}\}, \{\{1, 3\}, \{3, 4\}, \{1, 3, 4\}\}, \{\{2, 3\}\}, \{\{1, 2, 3\}, \{1, 2, 3, 4\}, \{2, 3, 4\}\}\};$$

$$\mathfrak{z}_7 = \mathfrak{z}_{7+j} = \{\{\{1\}\}, \{\{4\}, \{1, 4\}\}, \{\{2\}\}, \{\{3\}\}, \{\{1, 2\}\}, \{\{2, 4\}, \{1, 2, 4\}\}, \{\{1, 3\}\}, \{\{3, 4\}, \{1, 3, 4\}\}, \{\{2, 3\}\}, \{\{1, 2, 3\}\}, \{\{2, 3, 4\}, \{1, 2, 3, 4\}\}\}.$$

For the ND-automaton $\mathfrak{B}_6$ the states 1 and 4 are distinguishable, and the shortest word p with $v_{\mathfrak{B}_6}(1, p) \neq v_{\mathfrak{B}_6}(4, p)$ has the length 7 (e.g. the word 3221220 satisfies our requirements). Thus, for non-deterministic automata, distinguishable states cannot, in general, be distinguished by means of a word p of length $Card(Z) - 1$ as is the case for deterministic automata (cf. Part I, 2.6) and stochastic automata (cf. Part III, 2.11).

Theorem 2.11 (Schmitt [1]). *The states z, z' of a Z-finite observable ND-automaton $\mathfrak{B} = [X, Y, Z, h]$ are distinguishable if and only if there is a word $p \in W(X)$ with $l(p) \leqq Card(Z) - 1$ and $v_{\mathfrak{B}}(z, p) \neq v_{\mathfrak{B}}(z', p)$.*

Proof: First we define a function δ on a subset of $Z \times X \times Y$ as follows: If $h_y(z, x) = \emptyset$, then δ is not defined for $[z, x, y]$, while if $h_y(z, x) = \{z'\}$, we set $\delta(z, x, y) = z'$. Then we define a sequence $(\mathfrak{z}_i')$ of partitions of Z by induction:

Initial step: Let $\mathfrak{z}_1'$ be the partition of Z where the states $z, z' \in Z$ belong to a class $N^1 \in \mathfrak{z}_i'$ if and only if for all $x \in X$ we have $g(z, x) = g(z', x)$.

Induction step: If $\mathfrak{z}_i'$ has already been defined, let $\mathfrak{z}_{i+1}$ be the partition of Z where two states $z, z' \in Z$ belong to a class $N^{i+1} \in \mathfrak{z}_{i+1}'$ if and only if

$$\exists N^i(z, z' \in N^i \in \mathfrak{z}_i') \wedge \forall x \forall y \big(x \in X \wedge y \in g(z, x) \\ \rightarrow \exists N^i(\delta(z, x, y), \delta(z', x, y) \in N^i \in \mathfrak{z}_i')\big).$$

From $\exists N^i(z, z' \in N^i \in \mathfrak{z}_i')$ it follows that for $x \in X$ we have $g(z, x) = g(z', x)$, and $y \in g(z, x) = g(z', x)$ implies that the sets $h_y(z, x)$, $h_y(z', x)$ are non-empty, hence δ is defined for $[z, x, y]$, and $[z', x, y]$.

We can easily show that for the states $z, z' \in Z$

$$\exists N^i(z, z' \in N^i \in \mathfrak{z}_i') \leftrightarrow \forall p\big(p \in W(X) \wedge l(p) \leqq i \rightarrow v_{\mathfrak{B}}(z, p) = v_{\mathfrak{B}'}(z', p)\big).$$

For every $i = 1, 2, \ldots$ the partition $\mathfrak{z}_{i+1}'$ is a refinement of the partition $\mathfrak{z}_i'$, and $\mathfrak{z}_i' = \mathfrak{z}_{i+1}'$ implies $\mathfrak{z}_i' = \mathfrak{z}_{i+k}'$ for every $k = 0, 1, 2, \ldots$ If the partition $\mathfrak{z}_1'$ contains only one class, then obviously all states of $\mathfrak{B}$ are equivalent. Consequently, we have $\mathfrak{z}_1' = \mathfrak{z}_2'$. Therefore, if $\mathfrak{z}_i' \neq \mathfrak{z}_{i+1}'$, then $\mathfrak{z}_i'$ contains at least $i + 1$ classes. Since every partition of Z has at most $Card(Z)$ classes, there exists a minimal i^* with $1 \leqq i^* \leqq Card(Z) - 1$ and $\mathfrak{z}_{i^*}' = \mathfrak{z}_{i^*+1}'$. Clearly, the states $z, z' \in Z$ are distinguishable, (non-equivalent) if and only if they belong to different classes of $\mathfrak{z}_{i^*}'$, that is, they can be distinguished by means of a word p with $l(p) \leqq Card(Z) - 1$. Thus Theorem 2.11 is proved.

It is easy to see that the upper bound $Card(Z) - 1$, given in Theorem 2.11 for the length of a word distinguishing the states z, z' of an observable ND-automaton, cannot be improved. Burkhard [1] has shown that the upper bound $2^{Card(Z)} - 2$ given in Theorem 2.9 for the lengths of words distinguishing the (distinguishable) sets of states of an arbitrary Z-finite ND-automaton, cannot be improved either.

Definition 2.3. Let $\mathfrak{B} = [X, Y, Z, h]$, $\mathfrak{B}' = [X, Y', Z', h']$ be ND-automata with the same input alphabet and (without any loss of generality) disjoint sets of states. The *direct sum* $\mathfrak{B} + \mathfrak{B}'$ of the ND-automata $\mathfrak{B}$, $\mathfrak{B}'$ is defined as the ND-automaton $[X, Y \cup Y', Z \cup Z', h + h']$, where for $z \in Z \cup Z'$, $x \in X$ we have

$$h + h'(z, x) = \begin{cases} h(z, x), & \text{if} \quad z \in Z, \\ h'(z', x), & \text{if} \quad z \in Z'. \end{cases}$$

Corollary 2.12. Let $\mathfrak{B}$, $\mathfrak{B}'$ be ND-automata as in Definition 2.3.

1. If $\mathfrak{B}$ and $\mathfrak{B}'$ both are ND-Mealy automata, or ND-Moore automata, or observable or Z-deterministic or Y-deterministic or deterministic, then $\mathfrak{B} + \mathfrak{B}'$ has the same properties.

2. If $\mathfrak{B}$ and $\mathfrak{B}'$ are Z-finite with $Card\,(Z) = n$, $Card\,(Z') = n'$, then two sets of states M, M' of $\mathfrak{B}$ and $\mathfrak{B}'$ respectively are distinguishable, if and only if there is a word $p \in W(X)$ with $l(p) \leqq 2^{n+n'} - 2$ and $v_{\mathfrak{B}}(M, p) \neq v_{\mathfrak{B}'}(M', p)$. If moreover $\mathfrak{B}, \mathfrak{B}'$ are observable, then two states z, z' of $\mathfrak{B}$ and $\mathfrak{B}'$ respectively, are distinguishable if and only if there is a $p \in W(X)$ with $l(p) \leqq n + n' - 1$ and $v_{\mathfrak{B}}(z, p) \neq v_{\mathfrak{B}'}(z', p)$.

3. If $\mathfrak{B}, \mathfrak{B}'$ are Z-finite, then they are distinguishable if and only if there is a $p \in W(X)$ with $l(p) \leqq 2^{n+n'} - 2$ and $v_{\mathfrak{B}'}(Z, p) \neq v_{\mathfrak{B}'}(Z', p)$.

4. The relations $\sim$, $\approx$, $\subsetsim$, $\subsetapprox$ are decidable for finite ND-automata.

Proposition 2.12 follows directly from the fact that for $M \subseteq Z$ and $p \in W(X)$ we have

$$v_{\mathfrak{B}}(M, p) = v_{\mathfrak{B}+\mathfrak{B}'}(M, p).$$

If in an ND-automaton $\mathfrak{B}$ there are two equivalent states, then seen from the outside, one of them is superfluous. The question arises whether one can omit this state internally as well, i.e., whether it is possible to construct an automaton $\mathfrak{B}'$ which is equivalent to $\mathfrak{B}$ (hence does the same job as $\mathfrak{B}$), and has one state less than $\mathfrak{B}$. If this is possible, and $\mathfrak{B}$ is Z-finite, then by successive elimination of "superfluous" states, we obtain, in a finite number of steps, an automaton $\overline{\mathfrak{B}}$, which is equivalent to $\mathfrak{B}$ and has no more superfluous states. Thus, any two different states of $\overline{\mathfrak{B}}$ are inequivalent, for which we say that $\overline{\mathfrak{B}}$ is reduced, and $\overline{\mathfrak{B}}$ is called a reduct of $\mathfrak{B}$. Next we show that the reduction problem has a relatively simple solution. The number of states of a reduct $\overline{\mathfrak{B}}$ of $\mathfrak{B}$ is the minimal number of states among the automata equivalent to $\mathfrak{B}$. However, the number of states of $\overline{\mathfrak{B}}$ cannot (as for deterministic automata) be considered as a measure of the complexity of $\mathfrak{B}$, since there may exist an ND-automaton $\mathfrak{B}'$ which is weakly equivalent to $\mathfrak{B}$ and has fewer states than $\overline{\mathfrak{B}}$.

Definition 2.4. Let $\mathfrak{B} = [X, Y, Z, h]$ be an arbitrary ND-automaton.

(2.4.1) $\mathfrak{B}$ is called *reduced* if, for arbitrary $z, z' \in Z$, $z \sim z'$ implies $z = z'$.

(2.4.2) An ND-automaton $\mathfrak{B}'$ is called a *reduct of* $\mathfrak{B}$ if it is reduced and equivalent to $\mathfrak{B}$.

(2.4.3) $\mathfrak{B}$ is called *minimal*, if for every $z \in Z$, $M \subseteq Z$, $\{z\} \sim M$ implies $\{z\} = M$.

(2.4.4) The ND-automaton $\mathfrak{B}'$ is said to be a *minim of* $\mathfrak{B}$ if $\mathfrak{B}'$ is minimal and weakly equivalent to $\mathfrak{B}$.

(2.4.5) $\mathfrak{B}$ is called *strongly reduced*, if for arbitrary subsets $M, N \subseteq Z$, $M \sim N$ implies $M = N$.

(2.4.6) $\mathfrak{B}'$ is called a *strong reduct of* $\mathfrak{B}$ if it is strongly reduced and weakly equivalent to $\mathfrak{B}$.

Corollary 2.13.

1. Every strongly reduced ND-automaton is minimal and every minimal ND-automaton is reduced.

2. Every strong reduct of $\mathfrak{B}$ is a minim of $\mathfrak{B}$.

3. A Z-finite ND-automaton $\mathfrak{B}$ is reduced if and only if the sequence $\mathfrak{Z}(\mathfrak{B})$ leads to such a partition $\mathfrak{z}_{i^*}$, where every class K^{i^*} contains at most one singleton $\{z\}$. Whether or not a finite ND-automaton is reduced, is a decidable property.

4. A Z-finite ND-automaton $\mathfrak{B}$ is minimal if and only if the sequence $\mathfrak{Z}(\mathfrak{B})$ leads to a partition $\mathfrak{z}_{i^*}$ where, for every class K^{i^*} and every singleton $\{z\}$ consisting of an element of Z we have: If $\{z\} \in K^{i^*}$, then $K^{i^*} = \{\{z\}\}$. Minimality is a decidable property of finite ND-automata.

5. A Z-finite ND-automaton $\mathfrak{B}$ is strongly reduced if and only if the sequence $\mathfrak{Z}(\mathfrak{B})$ leads to the finest partition of $\mathfrak{P}^*(Z)$ as $\mathfrak{z}_{i^*}$, i.e. if every class K^{i^*} consists of exactly one element of $\mathfrak{P}^*(Z)$. Whether or not a given finite ND-automaton is strongly reduced, is a decidable property.

The converses of 2.13.1 and 2.13.2 are not valid. The ND-automaton $\mathfrak{B}_4$ described above (see Fig. 15), is reduced but not minimal because $\{b\}$ is equivalent to $\{a, b\}$. $\mathfrak{B}_7$ is an example of a minimal ND-automaton which is not strongly reduced, where $\mathfrak{B}_7 = [\{0, 1\}, \{A, B, C\}, \{1, 2, 3, 4, 5\}, h^7]$. Its graph $\mathfrak{G}_{\mathfrak{B}_7}$ is represented in Fig. 16. We can easily verify that $\mathfrak{B}_7$ is minimal but

$$M = \{1, 3\} \sim \{1, 2, 3, 4\} = N,$$

The latter can be shown by using 2.5.2, since for all $x \in \{0, 1\}$, $y \in \{A, B, C\}$ we have $h_y^7(M, x) = h_y^7(N, x)$. Thus $\mathfrak{B}_7$ is not strongly reduced. The ND-automaton $\mathfrak{B}_1$ given in § 1 is an example of a strongly reduced ND-automaton.

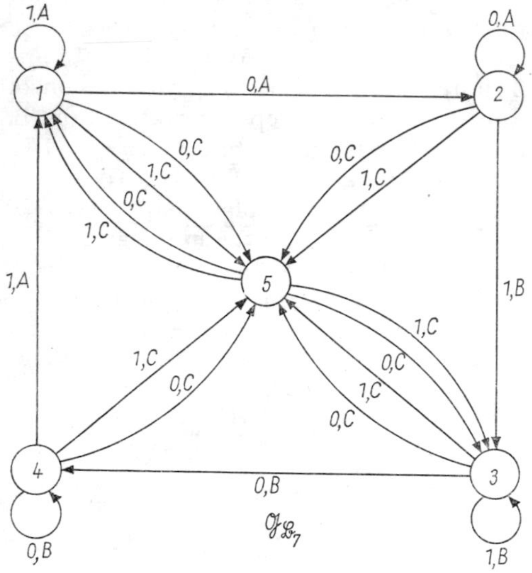

Fig. 16

Theorem 2.14. *Let* $\mathfrak{B} = [X, Y, Z, h]$ *be an ND-automaton.*

1. *All the reducts* $\mathfrak{B}'$ *of* $\mathfrak{B}$ *have the same number of states.*

2. *If* $\mathfrak{B}$ *is reduced and equivalent to a minimal ND-automaton* $\mathfrak{B}^*$, *then* $\mathfrak{B}$ *is minimal.*

3. *If* $\mathfrak{B}$ *is reduced and equivalent to a strongly reduced ND-automaton* $\mathfrak{B}^{**}$, *then* $\mathfrak{B}$ *is strongly reduced.*

Proof: Proposition 2.14.1 can be proved in exactly the same way as Theorem 2.11 in Part I.

Suppose $\mathfrak{B}^* = [X, Y, Z^*, h^*]$ is minimal and $\mathfrak{B}^* \sim \mathfrak{B}$, where $\mathfrak{B}$ is reduced. Since $\mathfrak{B}^*$ is also reduced, there is a one-to-one mapping ζ of Z onto Z^*, which assigns to each $z \in Z$ that state $z^* \in Z^*$ which is equivalent to z. For $z \in Z$, $M \subseteq Z$ with $\{z\} \sim M$ we obviously have

$$\{\zeta(z)\} \sim \{z\} \sim M \sim \{\zeta(z) \mid z \in M\}.$$

Because $\mathfrak{B}^*$ is minimal, $\{\zeta(z)\} = \{\zeta(z) \mid z \in M\}$ must be satisfied, and because ζ is one-to-one, this implies $\{z\} = M$, hence $\mathfrak{B}$ is minimal. This proves Proposition 2.14.2. The proof of Proposition 2.14.3. is completely analogous.

For an arbitrary ND-automaton $\mathfrak{B}$, the number of states of any reduct of $\mathfrak{B}$ is the minimal number of states of ND-automata equivalent to $\mathfrak{B}$. However, the reducts of $\mathfrak{B}$ are not pairwise Z-isomorphic, which is the case for deterministic automata, as we shall see in the next section. If we consider the class $\mathfrak{M}(\mathfrak{B})$ of all ND-automata weakly equivalent to $\mathfrak{B}$, then in certain cases we may find an ND-automaton $\mathfrak{B}^*$ in $\mathfrak{M}(\mathfrak{B})$ which has fewer states than any reduct of $\mathfrak{B}$. Such a $\mathfrak{B}^*$ is of course not equivalent to $\mathfrak{B}$, but only weakly equivalent, and can be obtained for example from a reduct $\overline{\mathfrak{B}}$ of $\mathfrak{B}$ by eliminating a certain state of $\overline{\mathfrak{B}}$ for which there is an equivalent set of states in $\overline{\mathfrak{B}}$ not containing this state. Sometimes this elimination procedure can be carried out in such a way that we obtain a minimal ND-automaton (i.e., a minim of $\mathfrak{B}$). The example of the ND-automaton $\mathfrak{B}_7$ shows that this minim need not be strongly reduced. We see, however, that for a minim of $\mathfrak{B}$, a further elimination of states is impossible if we want to keep the resulting automaton weakly equivalent to $\mathfrak{B}$. But not all ND-automata have a minim. Therefore we introduce the weak minims (cf. Def. 2.5) and shall show that the weak minims of $\mathfrak{B}$, independently of whether they are minimal or not, have the smallest number of states among the ND-automata weakly equivalent to $\mathfrak{B}$.

Theorem 2.15.

1. *Every ND-automaton has a reduct.*

2. *Every reduct of a finite ND-automaton is finite, and can be constructed in a finite number of steps.*

3. *Every observable ND-automaton has an observable reduct.*

4. *Every Z-deterministic ND-automaton has a Z-deterministic reduct.*

5. *Every ND-Mealy automaton has a reduct which is an ND-Mealy automaton.*

Proof: Let $\mathfrak{B} = [X, Y, Z, h]$ be an arbitrary ND-automaton. For $z \in Z$, the $\sim$-equivalence class of z is denoted by $[z]$, i.e., $[z] = \{z' \mid z' \in Z \wedge z' \sim z\}$; furthermore let $\bar{Z} = \{[z] \mid z \in Z\}$.

If $\mathfrak{B}$ is finite, then $\bar{Z}$ can be constructed in finitely many steps (Theorem 2.9). For $\bar{z}, \bar{\bar{z}} \in \bar{Z}$, $x \in X$ let

$$\bar{h}_{\bar{\bar{z}}}(\bar{z}, x) \underset{\mathrm{Df}}{=} \bigcup_{z' \in \bar{\bar{z}},\, z \in \bar{z}} h_{z'}(z, x) = \bigcup_{z' \in \bar{\bar{z}}} h_{z'}(\bar{z}, x)$$

and thus for $\bar{z} \in \bar{Z}$, $x \in X$

$$\bar{h}(\bar{z}, x) = \bigcup_{\bar{\bar{z}} \in \bar{Z}} \bar{h}_{\bar{\bar{z}}}(\bar{z}, x) \times \{\bar{\bar{z}}\}.$$

$\overline{\mathfrak{B}} = [X, Y, \bar{Z}, \bar{h}]$ is an ND-automaton. We claim that $\overline{\mathfrak{B}}$ is a reduct of $\mathfrak{B}$. For this purpose we first show by induction on p that for all $z \in Z$, $p \in W(X)$

$$v_{\mathfrak{B}}(z, p) = v_{\overline{\mathfrak{B}}}([z], p).$$

The initial step $p = e$ is trivial. The step from p to xp for $x \in X$: By the definition of $[z]$ we have

$$v_{\mathfrak{B}}(z, xp) = \bigcup_{z' \in [z]} v_{\mathfrak{B}}(z', xp) = \bigcup_{z' \in [z],\, z'' \in Z} h_{z''}(z', x) \cdot v_{\mathfrak{B}}(z'', p)$$
$$= \bigcup_{z' \in [z]} \bigcup_{\bar{z} \in \bar{Z},\, z'' \in \bar{z}} h_{z''}(z', x) \cdot v_{\mathfrak{B}}(z'', p).$$

By the induction hypothesis, for $z'' \in \bar{z}$ (i.e., $\bar{z} = [z'']$)

$$v_{\mathfrak{B}}(z'', p) = v_{\bar{\mathfrak{B}}}(\bar{z}, p).$$

We obtain thus,

$$v_{\mathfrak{B}}(z, xp) = \bigcup_{\bar{z} \in \bar{Z}} \left[\bigcup_{z' \in [z],\, z'' \in \bar{z}} h_{z''}(z', x) \right] \cdot v_{\bar{\mathfrak{B}}}(\bar{z}, p)$$
$$= \bigcup_{\bar{z} \in \bar{Z}} \bar{h}_{\bar{z}}([z], x) v_{\bar{\mathfrak{B}}}(\bar{z}, p) = v_{\bar{\mathfrak{B}}}([z], xp).$$

Hence, $\mathfrak{B} \sim \bar{\mathfrak{B}}$. The ND-automaton $\bar{\mathfrak{B}}$ is reduced, since $[z]$, $[z'] \in Z$ and $[z] \sim [z']$ imply $z \sim [z] \sim [z'] \sim z'$, thus $z \sim z'$ i.e., $[z] = [z']$. Therefore the automaton $\bar{\mathfrak{B}}$ is a reduct of $\mathfrak{B}$. Because $Card(\bar{Z}) \leq Card(Z)$, it follows from 2.14.1 that every reduct of a finite ND-automaton is finite. Thus Propositions 2.15.1 and 2.15.2 are proved.

Let ϱ be a choice function on $\bar{Z}$. Hence the function ϱ assigns to each $\bar{z} \in \bar{Z}$ one of its members $\varrho(\bar{z}) \in \bar{z}$. For $\bar{z}, \bar{\bar{z}} \in \bar{Z}$, $x \in X$ we set

$$\bar{h}^{\varrho}_{\bar{\bar{z}}}(\bar{z}, x) = \bigcup_{z' \in \bar{\bar{z}}} h_{z'}\bigl(\varrho(\bar{z}), x\bigr).$$

We can show as above that $\bar{\mathfrak{B}}_{\varrho} = [X, Y, \bar{Z}, \bar{h}^{\varrho}]$ is a reduct of $\mathfrak{B}$. In the induction step we use the fact that

$$v_{\mathfrak{B}}(z, xp) = v_{\mathfrak{B}}\bigl(\varrho([z]), xp\bigr),$$

because $\varrho([z]) \sim z$. Now for $\bar{z} \in \bar{Z}$, $x \in X$, $y \in Y$

$$\bar{h}^{\varrho}_{y}(\bar{z}, x) = \bigl\{\bar{\bar{z}} \mid \exists z' \bigl(z' \in h_y(\varrho(\bar{z}), x) \wedge \bar{\bar{z}} = [z']\bigr)\bigr\}$$
$$= \bigl\{[z'] \mid z' \in h_y\bigl(\varrho(\bar{z}), x\bigr)\bigr\};$$

consequently $Card\bigl(\bar{h}^{\varrho}_{y}(\bar{z}, x)\bigr) \leq Card\,\bigl(h_y(\varrho(\bar{z}), x)\bigr)$. This shows that $\bar{\mathfrak{B}}_{\varrho}$ is observable, provided that $\mathfrak{B}$ is. Hence 2.15.3 is proved. One can easily verify that $\bar{\mathfrak{B}}_{\varrho}$ is a (Z-deterministic) ND-Mealy automaton, if $\mathfrak{B}$ is a (Z-deterministic) ND-Mealy automaton.

Theorem 2.16. *Let* $\mathfrak{B} = [X, Y, Z, h]$ *be an arbitrary ND-automaton.*

1. *Every minim* $\mathfrak{B}' = [X, Y, Z', h']$ *of* $\mathfrak{B}$ *is equivalently embedded into* $\mathfrak{B}$.
2. *Weakly equivalent minimal ND-automata are equivalent.*

Proof: Clearly, it suffices to prove Proposition 2.16.1. For this we have to show that for each $z' \in Z'$ there is a $z \in Z$ with $z \sim z'$. Suppose z' is an arbitrary state of $\mathfrak{B}'$. Since $\mathfrak{B}' \approx \mathfrak{B}$, there is a non-empty set of states $M_{z'} \subseteq Z$ with $\{z'\} \sim M_{z'}$, and for each $z \in Z$ there is a non-empty set $N'_z \subseteq Z'$ with $\{z\} \sim N'_z$. Thus we have

$$\{z'\} \sim M_{z'} = \bigcup_{z \in M_{z'}} \{z\} \sim \bigcup_{z \in M_{z'}} N'_z \underset{\mathrm{Df}}{=} N_{z'}.$$

Since $\mathfrak{B}'$ is minimal, $\{z'\} \sim N_{z'}$ implies $N_{z'} = \{z'\}$. Hence for all $z \in M_{z'}$ we have $N'_z = \{z'\}$. Therefore, the states belonging to the set $M_{z'}$ are all equivalent to z' and thus any $z \in M_{z'}$ satisfies our requirements.

Theorem 2.17. *Let* $\mathfrak{B} = [X, Y, Z, h]$ *be an arbitrary ND-automaton.*

1. *All the minims and strong reducts of* $\mathfrak{B}$ *are pairwise equivalent and have the same number of states.*

2. *Every strong reduct of* $\mathfrak{B}$ *is equivalently embedded into* $\mathfrak{B}$.

3. *If* $\mathfrak{B}$ *has a minim which is not strongly reduced, then* $\mathfrak{B}$ *has no strong reduct.*

4. $\mathfrak{B}$ *has a strong reduct if and only if* $\mathfrak{B}$ *has a minim and every minim of* $\mathfrak{B}$ *is strongly reduced.*

Proposition 2.17.2 is implied by 2.16.1 and the fact that every strong reduct of $\mathfrak{B}$ is a minim of $\mathfrak{B}$. Since all the minims of $\mathfrak{B}$ are pairwise weakly equivalent, Proposition 2.17.1 follows from 2.16.2 and 2.14.1. By 2.14.3, a strongly reduced automaton cannot be equivalent to a minimal automaton unless it is also strongly reduced. Therefore, Propositions 2.17.3 and 2.17.4 are implied by 2.17.1.

Let us again consider the ND-automata $\mathfrak{B}_2$, $\mathfrak{B}_3$ (see Fig. 14, page 158). We have already shown that $\mathfrak{B}_2 \approx \mathfrak{B}_3$. Just as easily we can see that $\mathfrak{B}_2$ is reduced but not minimal (since $\{a\} \sim \{b, c\}$), while $\mathfrak{B}_3$ is minimal and even strongly reduced. Therefore, $\mathfrak{B}_3$ is a minim and a strong reduct of $\mathfrak{B}_2$.

2.17.1 and 2.17.4 explain why we do not investigate the reduction of an ND-automaton $\mathfrak{B}$ to a strongly reduced automaton which is weakly equivalent to $\mathfrak{B}$. If $\mathfrak{B}$ has a strong reduct at all, then every minim of $\mathfrak{B}$ is already a strong reduct of $\mathfrak{B}$.

It is not always possible to reduce an automaton to a minim, as is shown by the above ND-automaton $\mathfrak{B}_4$ (Fig. 15, page 162). The states a and b of $\mathfrak{B}_4$ are not equivalent (they are distinguishable), however we have $\{a, b\} \sim b$, and for every $p \in W(\{x\}) \setminus \{e\}$, $v_{\mathfrak{B}_4}(a, p) \subset v_{\mathfrak{B}_4}(b, p)$. Suppose $\mathfrak{B} = [\{x\}, \{0, 1\}, Z, h]$ is a minim of $\mathfrak{B}_4$. Then by 2.16.1, $\mathfrak{B}$ can be equivalently embedded into $\mathfrak{B}_4$, i.e., every $z \in Z$ is equivalent to a or b. Since $\mathfrak{B}$ is reduced, it contains at most two states. If $\mathfrak{B}$ had only one state, it certainly could not be weakly equivalent to $\mathfrak{B}_4$. Hence, $\mathfrak{B}$ has exactly two states, z^*, z^{**}, where e.g., $z^* \sim a$ and $z^{**} \sim b$. Consequently, we have $\{z^*, z^{**}\} \sim \{a, b\} \sim \{b\} \sim \{z^{**}\}$, which means that $\mathfrak{B}$ is not minimal, in contradiction to our assumption. Thus $\mathfrak{B}_4$ has no minims and consequently no strong reducts.

The next natural problem is to find a criterion for the existence of a minim of an ND-automaton. It is enough to solve this problem for reduced ND-automata, since clearly an ND-automaton has a minim if and only if there exists a minim for a (certain) reduct of $\mathfrak{B}$ (and hence for all the reducts of $\mathfrak{B}$).

Theorem 2.18. *Let* $\mathfrak{B} = [X, Y, Z, h]$ *be a reduced ND-automaton and* $Z^* = \{z \mid \exists M (M \subseteq Z \wedge M \sim \{z\} \wedge M \neq \{z\})\}$. $\mathfrak{B}$ *has a minim if and only if for each* $z \in Z^*$ *there is a set* $M_z \subseteq Z$ *with* $M_z \sim \{z\}$ *and* $M_z \cap Z^* = \emptyset$.

Proof: First we show that the above condition is necessary. Let $\mathfrak{B}' = [X, Y, Z', h']$ be a minim of $\mathfrak{B}$.

Lemma 2.18a. *There are no* $z^* \in Z^*$ *and* $z' \in Z'$ *with* $z^* \sim z'$.

Suppose that the state $z^* \in Z^*$ is equivalent to the state $z' \in Z'$. Let M^* be a subset of Z such that $M^* \sim \{z^*\}$ and $M^* \neq \{z^*\}$. Since $\mathfrak{B} \approx \mathfrak{B}'$, for each $z \in M^* \subseteq Z$ there is a set $N'_z \subseteq Z'$ with $\{z\} \sim N'_z$. Then we have $M^* \sim N' \underset{\mathrm{Df}}{=} \bigcup_{z \in M^*} N'_z$, hence $N' \sim M^* \sim \{z^*\} \sim \{z'\}$ implies $N' = \{z'\}$, because $\mathfrak{B}'$ is minimal. Thus for each $z \in M^*$ we have $N'_z = \{z'\} \sim \{z\}$, i.e., $\{z\} \sim \{z'\} \sim \{z^*\}$, consequently $z = z^*$, because $\mathfrak{B}$ is reduced. This implies $M^* = \{z^*\}$, which is in contradiction to $M^* \neq \{z^*\}$.

Let us consider an arbitrary $z^* \in Z^*$. Then there is a set $N'_{z^*} \subseteq Z'$ with $N'_{z^*} \sim \{z^*\}$. We set $M_{z^*} = \{z \mid z \in Z \wedge \exists z' (z' \in N'_{z^*} \wedge z \sim z')\}$. Since $\mathfrak{B}' \subsetneq \mathfrak{B}$, for each $z' \in N'_{z^*}$ there is a $z \in Z$ with $z' \sim z$, hence M_{z^*} and N'_{z^*} are equivalent. Thus we have $M_{z^*} \subset Z$ and $M_{z^*} \sim \{z^*\}$. If there were a $z^{**} \in Z^* \cap M_{z^*}$, then by the definition of M_{z^*} there would exist a $z' \in N'_{z^*} \subseteq Z'$ with $z^{**} \sim z'$, which is in contradiction to Lemma 2.18a.

Suppose $\mathfrak{B}$ is a reduced ND-automaton, and for each $z \in Z^*$ we choose a set $M_z \subseteq Z \setminus Z^*$ such that $M_z \sim \{z\}$. Furthermore, let $\mathfrak{B}' = [X, Y, Z \setminus Z^*, h']$, where for $z' \in Z \setminus Z^*$, $x \in X$ we set:

$$h'(z', x) = \{[y, z''] \mid ([y, z''] \in h(z', x) \wedge z'' \in Z \setminus Z^*) \vee \exists z^* (z^* \in Z^* \wedge [y, z^*] \in h(z', x) \wedge z'' \in M_{z^*})\}.$$

Lemma 2.18b. *For all* $N' \subseteq Z \setminus Z^*$, $p \in W(X)$

$$v_{\mathfrak{B}}(N', p) = v_{\mathfrak{B}'}(N', p).$$

We prove this by induction on p. The initial step is trivial and the induction step is taken from p to xp for each $x \in X$. By the induction hypothesis we have

$$v_{\mathfrak{B}'}(N', xp) = \bigcup_{z' \in N'} \bigcup_{y \in Y} \{y\} \cdot v_{\mathfrak{B}'}(h'_y(z', x), p)$$

$$= \bigcup_{z' \in N'} \bigcup_{y \in Y} \{y\} \cdot v_{\mathfrak{B}}(h'_y(z', x), p).$$

Now,

$$h'_y(z', x) = (h_y(z', x) \setminus Z^*) \cup \bigcup_{z^* \in Z^* \cap h_y(z', x)} M_{z^*},$$

and according to the choice of the sets M_{z^*}, the last above mentioned set, as a set of states of $\mathfrak{B}$, is equivalent to the set $h_y(z', x)$ of states of $\mathfrak{B}$. This implies

$$v_{\mathfrak{B}'}(N', xp) = \bigcup_{z' \in N'} \bigcup_{y \in Y} \{y\} \cdot v_{\mathfrak{B}}\big(h_y(z', x), p\big) = v_{\mathfrak{B}}(N', xp),$$

which was to be shown.

Lemma 2.18b implies $\mathfrak{B}' \subseteq \mathfrak{B}$ and also that $\mathfrak{B}'$ is reduced.

We can immediately see that $\mathfrak{B}'$ is weakly equivalent to $\mathfrak{B}$, because if $z \in Z \setminus Z^*$, then z as a state of $\mathfrak{B}'$ is equivalent to z as a state of $\mathfrak{B}$, and if $z \in Z^*$, then the set $M_z \subseteq Z \setminus Z^*$ of states of $\mathfrak{B}'$ is equivalent to $\{z\}$. Next we show that $\mathfrak{B}'$ is minimal. Suppose $z' \in Z \setminus Z^*$, $N' \subseteq Z \setminus Z^*$ are such that $\{z'\}, N'$ as sets of states of $\mathfrak{B}'$ are equivalent. By Lemma 2.18b, they are also equivalent as sets of states of $\mathfrak{B}$. Now if we had $N' \neq \{z'\}$, then z' would belong to Z^*. However $z' \in Z \setminus Z^*$, hence $N' = \{z'\}$, i.e., $\mathfrak{B}'$ is a minim of $\mathfrak{B}$. This proves Theorem 2.18.

Since the criterion for the existence of minims, given by Theorem 2.18, is difficult to visualize, in what follows we formulate another sufficient condition ($\overline{\mathrm{M}}$) for the non-existence of minims of an ND-automaton. Then we show that a reduced ND-automaton which does not satisfy this condition, has a minim, provided it satisfies a certain finiteness condition, which holds for all Z-finite ND-automata.

Theorem 2.19. *If the ND-automaton* $\mathfrak{B} = [X, Y, Z, h]$ *satisfies the condition*

$$\exists z\big(z \in Z \wedge \exists N(N \subseteq Z \wedge N \sim \{z\} \wedge N \setminus \{z\} \neq \emptyset) \\ \wedge \forall M(M \subseteq Z \wedge M \sim \{z\} \rightarrow z \in M)\big) \qquad (\overline{\mathrm{M}})$$

then $\mathfrak{B}$ *has no minim.*

Our proof is indirect. Suppose that $\mathfrak{B}' = [X, Y, Z', h']$ is a minim of $\mathfrak{B}$. Let z^* be a state of $\mathfrak{B}$, whose existence is assured by ($\overline{\mathrm{M}}$), and $N^* \subseteq Z$ with $N^* \sim \{z^*\}$ and $N^* \setminus \{z^*\} \neq \emptyset$. Because of $\mathfrak{B} \approx \mathfrak{B}'$, there is an $M' \subseteq Z'$ with $M' \neq \emptyset$ and $M' \sim \{z^*\}$. Let us put

$$M^* = \{z \mid z \in Z \wedge \exists z'(z' \in M' \wedge z \sim z')\}.$$

Since $\mathfrak{B}' \subseteq \mathfrak{B}$, for each $z' \in Z'$ there is a $z \in Z$ with $z \sim z'$. We therefore have $M^* \sim M' \sim \{z^*\}$. According to the choise of z^* and by ($\overline{\mathrm{M}}$), we have $z^* \in M^*$, i.e., there is a $z'' \in M'$ with $z'' \sim z^*$.

Since $N^* \setminus \{z^*\} \neq \emptyset$, there is a set $N' \subseteq Z'$ with $N' \neq \emptyset$ and $N' \sim N^* \setminus \{z^*\}$.

We claim $z'' \notin N'$; otherwise, for all $p \in W(X)$, we could replace $\subseteq$ by $=$ everywhere in the following formula:

$$v_{\mathfrak{B}'}(N', p) = v_{\mathfrak{B}}(N^* \setminus \{z^*\}, p) \subseteq v_{\mathfrak{B}}(N^*, p) \\ = v_{\mathfrak{B}}(z^*, p) = v_{\mathfrak{B}'}(z'', p) \subseteq v_{\mathfrak{B}'}(N', p)$$

hence we would have $N^* \setminus \{z^*\} \sim \{z^*\}$, which contradicts the fact that $M \subseteq Z$ with $M \sim \{z^*\}$ implies $z^* \in M$.

On the other hand, for every $p \in W(X)$,

$$v_{\mathfrak{B}'}(N', p) \subseteq v_{\mathfrak{B}'}(z'', p),$$

which implies that $N' \cup \{z''\} \sim \{z''\}$. Since $\emptyset \neq N' \neq \{z''\}$, this is a contradiction, because $\mathfrak{B}'$ is minimal. Thus Theorem 2.19 is proved.

Using the example of the ND-automaton $\mathfrak{B}_8$ that the condition $(\overline{\mathrm{M}})$ is not necessary for the non-existence of minims of an ND-automaton. We denote by $(0, 1)$ the open interval of the rationals r such that $0 < r < 1$. We put $\mathfrak{B}_8 = [\{x\}, Y, Z, h^8]$, where $Y = Z = (0, 1)$ and for $z \in (0, 1)$

$$h^8(z, x) \underset{\mathrm{Df}}{=} \{[y, z] \mid 0 < y < z \wedge y \in (0, 1)\}.$$

Thus $\mathfrak{B}_8$ is a Z-deterministic autonomous ND-automaton with a countably infinite set of states. For all $n \geqq 1$, $z \in Z$

$$v_{\mathfrak{B}_8}(z, x^n) = \{y_1 \ldots y_n \mid \bigwedge_{\nu=1}^{n} y_\nu \in Y \wedge 0 < y_\nu < z\}.$$

Obviously $\mathfrak{B}_8$ is reduced. Moreover, for each $z \in Z$, the set $M_z = \{z' \mid z' \in Z \wedge \wedge z' < z\}$ is equivalent to $\{z\}$ and does not contain z. Thus $\mathfrak{B}_8$ does not satisfy condition $(\overline{\mathrm{M}})$, but it does satisfy its negation (M):

$$\forall z\big(z \in Z \to \forall N(N \subseteq Z \wedge N \sim \{z\} \to N = \{z\}) \\ \vee \exists M(M \subseteq Z \wedge M \sim \{z\} \wedge z \notin M)\big). \qquad \text{(M)}$$

Still, $\mathfrak{B}_8$ has no minims. Indeed, suppose $\mathfrak{B}' = [\{x\}, Y, Z', h']$ is a minim of $\mathfrak{B}_8$. Then $\mathfrak{B}'$ has at least two states, z^*, z^{**}, and by 2.16.1, we can find states $z', z'' \in Z$ which are equivalent to z^*, z^{**} respectively. Without any loss of generality, we can assume $z' < z''$. Then we have $\{z', z''\} \sim \{z''\}$, hence $\{z^*, z^{**}\} \sim \{z^{**}\}$, which is a contradiction, since $\mathfrak{B}'$ is minimal.

Theorem 2.20. *Let* $\mathfrak{B} = [X, Y, Z, h]$ *be a reduced ND-automaton satisfying condition* (M) *and such that the set*

$$Z^{**} \underset{\mathrm{Df}}{=} \big\{z \mid \exists M(M \subseteq Z \wedge M \sim \{z\} \wedge z \notin M)\big\}$$

is finite. Then $\mathfrak{B}$ *has a minim.*

Proof: Suppose $Z^{**} = \{z_1, z_2, \ldots, z_k\}$. If $k = 0$, i.e., $Z^{**} = \emptyset$, then the assertion is trivial, since $\mathfrak{B}$ itself is minimal. Let $k > 0$. We shall prove by induction on $\varkappa$ that for each $\varkappa = 1, \ldots, k$ and every $j = 1, \ldots, k$ there is a set $M_j^\varkappa \subseteq Z$ with $\{z_j\} \sim M_j^\varkappa$ and $(\{z_1, \ldots, z_\varkappa\} \cup \{z_j\}) \cap M_j^\varkappa = \emptyset$.

The initial step is $\varkappa = 1$. If $j = 1$, then by our conditions, there is a set $M_1^1 \subseteq Z$ with $\{z_1\} \sim M_1^1$ and $z_1 \notin M_1^1$, i.e., $\{z_1\} \cap M_1^1 = \emptyset$. Suppose $j \in \{2, \ldots, k\}$. Then there is a set M_j with $M_j \subseteq Z$, $\{z_j\} \sim M_j$ and $z_j \notin M_j$. We put

$$M_j^1 = \begin{cases} M_j, & \text{if} \quad z_1 \notin M_j, \\ (M_j \setminus \{z_1\}) \cup M_1^1, & \text{if} \quad z_1 \in M_j. \end{cases}$$

Obviously, $M_j^1 \subseteq Z$, $M_j^1 \sim \{z_j\}$ and $z_1 \notin M_j^1$. Assume that $z_j \in M_j^1$. Then $z_1 \in M_j$ and $z_j \in M_1^1$, and for each $p \in W(X)$ we have

$$v_{\mathfrak{B}}(z_1, p) \subseteq v_{\mathfrak{B}}(M_j, p) = v_{\mathfrak{B}}(z_j, p) \subseteq v_{\mathfrak{B}}(M_1^1, p) = v_{\mathfrak{B}}(z_1, p),$$

i.e., $z_1 \sim z_j$. Since $\mathfrak{B}$ is reduced, this shows that z_j cannot belong to M_j^1, and therefore M_j^1 satisfies our requirements.

In the induction step we construct the sets $M_j^{\varkappa+1}$ for fixed $1 \leqq \varkappa < k$. If $j = 1, \ldots, k$, we set

$$M_j^{\varkappa+1} = \begin{cases} M_j^\varkappa, & \text{if} \quad z_{\varkappa+1} \notin M_j^\varkappa, \\ (M_j^\varkappa \setminus \{z_{\varkappa+1}\}) \cup M_{\varkappa+1}^\varkappa, & \text{if} \quad z_{\varkappa+1} \in M_j^\varkappa. \end{cases}$$

Clearly, $M_j^{\varkappa+1} \subseteq Z$, $\{z_j\} \sim M_j^{\varkappa+1}$ and $\{z_1, \ldots, z_{\varkappa+1}\} \cap M_j^{\varkappa+1} = \emptyset$. Assume that $z_j \in M_j^{\varkappa+1}$. Then by $z_j \notin M_j^\varkappa$ we have $z_{\varkappa+1} \in M_j^\varkappa$ and $z_j \in M_{\varkappa+1}^\varkappa$, hence for all $p \in W(X)$

$$v_{\mathfrak{B}}(z_{\varkappa+1}, p) \subseteq v_{\mathfrak{B}}(M_j^\varkappa, p) = v_{\mathfrak{B}}(z_j, p) \subseteq v_{\mathfrak{B}}(M_{\varkappa+1}^\varkappa, p) = v_{\mathfrak{B}}(z_{\varkappa+1}, p),$$

i.e., $z_{\varkappa+1} \sim z_j$. Since $\mathfrak{B}$ is reduced, this implies $j = \varkappa + 1$, which is in contradiction to $z_{\varkappa+1} \notin M_j^{\varkappa+1}$ and $z_j \in M_j^{\varkappa+1}$. Hence $z_j \notin M_j^{\varkappa+1}$.

For $\varkappa = k$ we obtain that for each $z \in Z^{**}$ there is a set $M_z \subseteq Z \setminus Z^{**}$ with $\{z\} \sim M_z$.

To show that $\mathfrak{B}$ has a minim, it suffices to prove by Theorem 2.18 that condition (M) implies $Z^{**} = Z^*$. $Z^{**} \subseteq Z^*$ holds trivially. Suppose $z^* \in Z^*$. Then there is a set $M^* \subseteq Z$ with $M^* \sim \{z^*\}$, $M^* \neq \{z^*\}$. Thus the condition

$$\forall N (N \subseteq Z \wedge N \sim \{z\} \rightarrow N = \{z\})$$

is not satisfied for $z = z^*$. Applying (M), we see that there exists a set M with $M \subseteq Z$, $M \sim \{z^*\}$ and $z^* \notin M$, hence $z^* \in Z^{**}$. This proves Theorem 2.20.

From the last two theorems we obtain

Corollary 2.21. A Z-finite reduced ND-automaton $\mathfrak{B} = [X, Y, Z, h]$ has a minim if and only if it satisfies condition (M).

We have seen that there are ND-automata $\mathfrak{B}$ such that no ND-automaton $\mathfrak{B}$, which is weakly equivalent with $\mathfrak{B}$, is minimal. Let us finally look for such ND-automata which are weakly equivalent with $\mathfrak{B}$ and have the smallest number of states among all these ND-automata.

Definition 2.5. Let $\mathfrak{B} = [X, Y, Z, h]$ be an arbitrary ND-automaton.

(2.5.1) $\mathfrak{B}$ is said to be *weakly minimal*, if $z \in Z$, $N \subseteq Z$ and $\{z\} \sim N$ implies $z \in N$.

(2.5.2) The ND-automaton $\mathfrak{B}'$ is said to be a *weak minim of* $\mathfrak{B}$, if $\mathfrak{B}'$ is weakly minimal and weakly equivalent to $\mathfrak{B}$.

Corollary 2.22.

1. Every minimal ND-automaton is weakly minimal and every weakly minimal ND-automaton is reduced.

2. Every minim of $\mathfrak{B}$ is a weak minim of $\mathfrak{B}$.

Theorem 2.23. *Let* $\mathfrak{B} = [X, Y, Z, h]$ *be an arbitrary ND-automaton.*

1. *Every weak minim of* $\mathfrak{B}$ *is equivalently embedded into* $\mathfrak{B}$.

2. *All the weak minims of* $\mathfrak{B}$ *are pairwise equivalent and therefore have the same number of states.*

3. *Every Z-finite ND-automaton possesses a weak minim and if* $\mathfrak{B}$ *is finite, a weak minim of* $\mathfrak{B}$ *can be constructed algorithmically.*

4. *The weak minims of* $\mathfrak{B}$ *have the smallest number of states among the ND-automata weakly equivalent with* $\mathfrak{B}$.

5. *If* $\mathfrak{B}$ *has a minim, all the weak minims of* $\mathfrak{B}$ *are minimal.*

Proof. Let $\mathfrak{B}' = [X, Y, Z', h']$ be a weak minim of $\mathfrak{B}$ and $z' \in Z'$ a state of $\mathfrak{B}'$. Since $\mathfrak{B}' \approx \mathfrak{B}$ there is a set $N \subseteq Z$ with $\{z'\} \sim N$ and to every $z \in N$ there corresponds a set $N'_z \subseteq Z'$ with $\{z\} \sim N'_z$. Thus we have $\{z'\} \sim N \sim \bigcup_{z \in N} N'_z$. Because $\mathfrak{B}'$ is weakly minimal this implies $z' \in \bigcup_{z \in N} N'_z$, i.e. there exists a $z_0 \in N$ such that $z' \in N'_{z_0}$. Hence for all $p \in W(X)$ we have

$$v_{\mathfrak{B}}(z', p) = v_{\mathfrak{B}}(N, p) \supseteq v_{\mathfrak{B}}(z_0, p) = v_{\mathfrak{B}'}(N'_{z_0}, p) \supseteq v_{\mathfrak{B}'}(z', p)$$

from which follows $z' \sim z_0$ and, consequently, $\mathfrak{B}' \subsetneq \mathfrak{B}$. Thus Proposition 2.23.1 is proved.

The assertion 2.23.2 is implied by 2.23.1 since for two weak minims $\mathfrak{B}'$, $\mathfrak{B}''$ of $\mathfrak{B}$ we have $\mathfrak{B}' \approx \mathfrak{B} \approx \mathfrak{B}''$, i.e. $\mathfrak{B}'$ is a weak minim of $\mathfrak{B}''$ (thus $\mathfrak{B}' \subsetneq \mathfrak{B}''$ by 2.23.1) and $\mathfrak{B}''$ is a weak minim of $\mathfrak{B}'$ (thus $\mathfrak{B}'' \subsetneq \mathfrak{B}'$).

If $\mathfrak{B}$ is not weakly minimal there are $z_0 \in Z$, $N_0 \subseteq Z$ with $\{z_0\} \sim N_0$ and $z_0 \notin N_0$. Now let $Z' = Z \setminus \{z_0\}$ and for $z' \in Z'$, $x \in X$, $y \in Y$

$$h'_y(z', x) = \big(h_y(z', x) \setminus \{z_0\}\big) \cup \begin{cases} N_0, & \text{if} \quad z_0 \in h_y(z', x), \\ \emptyset, & \text{otherwise}, \end{cases}$$

and

$$h'(z', x) = \bigcup_{y \in Y} \{y\} \times h'_y(z', x).$$

Obviously $\mathfrak{B}' = [X, Y, Z', h']$ is an ND-automaton having one state less than $\mathfrak{B}$. We can show without difficulties that for $N \subseteq Z'$, $p \in W(X)$ the equation $v_{\mathfrak{B}}(N, p) = v_{\mathfrak{B}'}(N, p)$ holds, which by $\{z_0\} \sim N_0$ implies $\mathfrak{B}' \approx \mathfrak{B}$. If $\mathfrak{B}'$ is weakly minimal, $\mathfrak{B}'$ is a weak minim of $\mathfrak{B}$; if not, the whole procedure will be repeated with $\mathfrak{B}'$ instead of $\mathfrak{B}$. Since Z is finite the construction will come to an end after finitely many steps.

For proof of 2.23.4 let be $\mathfrak{B}'$ a weak minim of $\mathfrak{B}$ and $\mathfrak{B}'' \approx \mathfrak{B}$. Then $\mathfrak{B}' \approx \mathfrak{B}''$, i.e. $\mathfrak{B}'$ is a weak minim of $\mathfrak{B}''$ and therefore equivalently embedded into $\mathfrak{B}''$. This implies the existence of a single-valued mapping from a certain subset of the state set Z'' of $\mathfrak{B}''$ onto the state set Z' of $\mathfrak{B}'$, i.e. $Card(Z'') \geq Card(Z')$.

Concerning 2.23.5, by 2.23.2 and 2.22.2 it suffices to show that a weakly minimal (consequently, reduced) ND-automaton, which is equivalent with a minimal ND-automaton, is minimal. This follows from 2.14.2.

Finally, we prove the following theorem:

Theorem 2.24. *Deterministic ND-automata are reduced if and only if they are minimal.*

Proof: Let $\mathfrak{B} = [X, Y, Z, h]$ be a reduced deterministic ND-automaton, $z \in Z$, $N \subseteq Z$ and $N \sim \{z\}$. Then for each $p \in W(X)$ we have

$$v_{\mathfrak{B}}(N, p) = v_{\mathfrak{B}}(z, p).$$

Since $\mathfrak{B}$ is deterministic, the set $v_{\mathfrak{B}}(z, p)$ contains exactly one word. For every $z' \in N$

$$\emptyset \neq v_{\mathfrak{B}}(z', p) \subseteq v_{\mathfrak{B}}(N, p) = v_{\mathfrak{B}}(z, p).$$

Since $v_{\mathfrak{B}}(N, p)$ also contains only one word, for all $p \in W(X)$, $z' \in N$ we have

$$v_{\mathfrak{B}}(z', p) = v_{\mathfrak{B}}(N, p) = v_{\mathfrak{B}}(z, p),$$

i.e., $\{z'\} \sim N \sim \{z\}$. Hence every $z' \in N$ is equivalent to z. Since $\mathfrak{B}$ is reduced, this implies $N = \{z\}$, hence $\mathfrak{B}$ is minimal.

The example of the ND-automaton $\mathfrak{B}_8$ shows that 2.24 is no longer valid for Z-deterministic automata. Also, there are deterministic reduced ND-automata which are not strongly reduced. As an example, we can consider the ND-automaton $\mathfrak{B}_9^* = [\{0, 1\}, \{0, 1\}, \{1, 2, 3, 4\}, h_9]$ with $Det(\mathfrak{B}_9^*) = \mathfrak{A}_9$ (cf. Part I, § 9). The graph of $\mathfrak{A}_9$ is represented in Fig. 8 (page 109). As we showed earlier, for $p \in W(\{0, 1\})$

$$\lambda^9(4, p) = \begin{cases} \lambda^9(1, p), & \text{if} \quad p = 0r, \\ \lambda^9(3, p), & \text{if} \quad p = 1r, \end{cases}$$

consequently, the sets of states $\{1, 2, 3\}$, $\{1, 2, 3, 4\}$ of $\mathfrak{B}_9^*$ are equivalent. Hence $\mathfrak{B}_9^*$ is not strongly reduced, although it is reduced.

§ 3. Homomorphisms

By the fine structure of an automaton we mean the construction of the system from simple, elementary automata; by the coarse structure of an ND-automaton $\mathfrak{B} = [X, Y, Z, h]$ we mean the properties of its function h. Thus for instance, the properties of being a Moore automaton or of being Z-deterministic are considered as belonging to the coarse structure of the ND-automaton. In investigating abstract automata, where the construction of the systems under consideration is completely ignored, only their coarse structures can be compared. The algebraic concepts of a homomorphism and an isomorphism lend themselves well for this purpose.

In this section we consider two possible definitions of a homomorphism and an isomorphism between ND-automata. One of these turns out to be an adequate counterpart of the concept of homomorphisms of deterministic automata in that the deterministic ND-automata $\mathfrak{B}$, $\mathfrak{B}'$ are homomorphic by this definition if and only if $Det(\mathfrak{B})$, $Det(\mathfrak{B}')$ are homomorphic under the same triple of mappings (in the sense of the theory of deterministic automata).

Definition 3.1. Let $\mathfrak{B} = [X, Y, Z, h]$, $\mathfrak{B}' = [X', Y', Z', h']$ be arbitrary ND-automata and ξ, η, ζ single-valued mappings of X onto X', Y onto Y', and Z onto Z' respectively.

(3.1.1) $\chi = [\xi, \eta, \zeta]$ is called a *strong homomorphism of* $\mathfrak{B}$ *onto* $\mathfrak{B}'$ if for all $z, z^* \in Z$, $x \in X$, $y \in Y$ we have

$$[y, z^*] \in h(z, x) \leftrightarrow [\eta(y), \zeta(z^*)] \in h'(\zeta(z), \xi(x)).$$

(3.1.2) $\chi = [\xi, \eta, \zeta]$ is called a *homomorphism of* $\mathfrak{B}$ *onto* $\mathfrak{B}'$ if for all $z \in Z$, $x \in X$ we have

$$h'(\zeta(z), \xi(x)) = \{[y', z''] \mid \exists y \exists z^* ([y, z^*] \in h(z, x) \wedge \eta(y) = y' \wedge \zeta(z^*) = z'')\}.$$

Moreover, if the mappings ξ, η, ζ are one-to-one, then χ is called a *strong isomorphism of* $\mathfrak{B}$ *onto* $\mathfrak{B}'$ if (3.1.1) is satisfied, and an *isomorphism of* $\mathfrak{B}$ *onto* $\mathfrak{B}'$ if (3.1.2) holds. If $X = X'$, $Y = Y'$ and ξ, η are the corresponding identity mappings I_X, I_Y respectively, then $[I_X, I_Y, \zeta]$ is called a *strong Z-homomorphism* or a *Z-homomorphism*, depending on whether (3.1.1) or (3.1.2) is satisfied. Similarly, we can define strong *[X, Z]-homomorphisms*, *Z-isomorphisms*, etc.

Suppose ξ, η, ζ are single-valued mappings of X onto X', Y onto Y', and Z onto Z' respectively. Then we set

a) for $p \in W(X)$, $x \in X$

$$\xi(e) = e, \quad \xi(xp) = \xi(x)\,\xi(p);$$

b) for $q \in W(Y)$, $y \in Y$, $Q \subseteq W(Y)$

$$\eta(e) = e, \quad \eta(yq) = \eta(y)\,\eta(q), \quad \eta(Q) = \{\eta(q) \mid q \in Q\};$$

c) for $M \subseteq Z$

$$\zeta(M) = \{\zeta(z) \mid z \in M\},$$

d) for $z \in Z$, $y \in Y$, $M \subseteq Y \times Z$

$$\eta\zeta(y, z) = [\eta(y), \zeta(z)], \quad \eta\zeta(M) = \{[\eta(y), \zeta(z)] \mid [y, z] \in M\}.$$

A triple $[\xi, \eta, \zeta]$ is therefore a homomorphism of $\mathfrak{B}$ onto $\mathfrak{B}'$ if and only if for all $z \in Z$, $x \in X$

$$h'(\zeta(z), \xi(x)) = \eta\zeta(h(z, x)).$$

Corollary 3.1.

1. Every strong homomorphism of $\mathfrak{B}$ onto $\mathfrak{B}'$ is a homomorphism of $\mathfrak{B}$ onto $\mathfrak{B}'$.

2. $[\xi, \eta, \zeta]$ is a strong isomorphism of $\mathfrak{B}$ onto $\mathfrak{B}'$ if and only if $[\xi, \eta, \zeta]$ is an isomorphism of $\mathfrak{B}$ onto $\mathfrak{B}'$.

Corollary 3.2. Let $[\xi, \eta, \zeta]$ be a strong homomorphism of $\mathfrak{B}$ onto $\mathfrak{B}'$. Then for all $z, z^* \in Z$, $x \in X$, $y \in Y$ we have

1. $z^* \in f(z, x) \leftrightarrow \zeta(z^*) \in f'(\zeta(z), \xi(x))$.
2. $y \in g(z, x) \leftrightarrow \eta(y) \in g'(\zeta(z), \xi(x))$.
3. $y \in h_{z^*}(z, x) \leftrightarrow \eta(y) \in h'_{\zeta(z^*)}(\zeta(z), \xi(x))$.
4. $z^* \in h_y(z, x) \leftrightarrow \zeta(z^*) \in h'_{\eta(y)}(\zeta(z), \xi(x))$.
5. If $\mathfrak{B}$ is observable, so is $\mathfrak{B}'$.
6. $\mathfrak{B}$ is an ND-Mealy automaton if and only if $\mathfrak{B}'$ is.

Corollary 3.3. Let $[\xi, \eta, \zeta]$ be a homomorphism of $\mathfrak{B}$ onto $\mathfrak{B}'$. Then for $z \in Z$, $x \in X$, $z' \in Z'$, $y' \in Y'$ we have

1. $\zeta(f(z, x)) = f'(\zeta(z), \xi(x))$.
2. $\eta(g(z, x)) = g'(\zeta(z), \xi(x))$.
3. $h'_{y'}(\zeta(z), \xi(x)) = \bigcup_{\eta(y)=y'} \zeta(h_y(z, x))$.
4. $h'_{z'}(\zeta(z), \xi(x)) = \bigcup_{\zeta(z^*)=z'} \eta(h_{z^*}(z, x))$.
5. If $\mathfrak{B}$ is an ND-Mealy automaton, so is $\mathfrak{B}'$.
6. If $\mathfrak{B}$ is Z-deterministic or Y-deterministic, then $\mathfrak{B}'$ is Z-deterministic or Y-deterministic.
7. If $Y = Y'$ and $[\xi, \eta, \zeta]$ is an $[X, Z]$-homomorphism of $\mathfrak{B}$ onto $\mathfrak{B}'$ (hence $\eta = I_Y$), then $\mathfrak{B}$ is Y-deterministic if and only if $\mathfrak{B}'$ is, and $\mathfrak{B}'$ is observable provided $\mathfrak{B}$ is.
8. If $Z = Z'$ and $[\xi, \eta, I_Z]$ is an $[X, Y]$-homomorphism of $\mathfrak{B}$ onto $\mathfrak{B}'$, then $\mathfrak{B}$ is Z-deterministic if and only if $\mathfrak{B}'$ is.

The converse of 3.3.5 is false. This is shown by the example of the ND-automaton $\mathfrak{B}_9 = [\{x\}, \{0, 1\}, \{a, b\}, h^9]$, $\mathfrak{B}_9' = [\{x\}, \{0\}, \{a, b\}, h^{9\prime}]$ where

$$h^9(a, x) = \{[0, a], [0, b], [1, a]\}, \quad h^9(b, x) = \{[0, b], [1, b]\}$$

and

$$h^{9\prime}(a, x) = \{[0, a], [0, b]\}, \quad h^{9\prime}(b, x) = \{[0, b]\}.$$

The triple $[I_{\{x\}}, \eta, I_{\{a,b\}}]$, where $\eta(0) = \eta(1) = 0$ is a homomorphism of $\mathfrak{B}_9$ onto $\mathfrak{B}_9'$. $\mathfrak{B}_9'$ is Y-deterministic, hence is an ND-Mealy automaton. However, $\mathfrak{B}_9$ is not an ND-Mealy automaton, since

$$h^9(a, x) \neq \{0, 1\} \times \{a, b\} = g^9(a, x) \times f^9(a, x).$$

Furthermore, $\mathfrak{B}_9'$ is an ND-Moore automaton, while $\mathfrak{B}_9$ is not, hence the homomorphic image of an ND automaton $\mathfrak{B}$ can be an ND-Moore automaton without

$\mathfrak{B}$ being an ND-Moore automaton. The triple $[I_{\{x\}}, \eta, I_{\{a,b\}}]$ is not a strong homomorphism of $\mathfrak{B}_9$ onto $\mathfrak{B}_9'$, since

$$[0, b] = [\eta(1), b] \in h^{9'}(a, x), \text{ but } [1, b] \notin h^9(a, x).$$

Also, the homomorphic image of an ND-Moore automaton need not be an ND-Moore automaton, as is shown by the following example. Let

$$\mathfrak{B}_{10} = [\{x, x'\}, \{0, 1\}, \{a, b\}, h^{10}], \qquad \mathfrak{B}_{11} = [\{x, x'\}, \{0, 1\}, \{c\}, h^{11}],$$

where

$$h^{10}(a, x) = \{[0, a]\} = h^{10}(b, x), \qquad h^{11}(c, x) = \{[0, c]\},$$

$$h^{10}(a, x') = \{[1, b]\} = h^{10}(b, x'), \qquad h^{11}(c, x') = \{[1, c]\}.$$

The triple $[I_{\{x,x'\}}, I_{\{0,1\}}, \zeta]$, where $\zeta(a) = \zeta(b) = c$, is a Z-homomorphism of $\mathfrak{B}_{10}$ onto $\mathfrak{B}_{11}$. $\mathfrak{B}_{10}$ is an ND-Moore automaton (consider $m(a) = \{0\}$, $m(b) = \{1\}$), however $\mathfrak{B}_{11}$ is not. Obviously, $[I_{\{x,x'\}}, I_{\{0,1\}}, \zeta]$ is not a strong homomorphism of $\mathfrak{B}_{10}$ onto $\mathfrak{B}_{11}$, since

$$[0, \zeta(b)] = [0, c] \in h^{11}(\zeta(a), x), \text{ but } [0, b] \notin h^{10}(a, x).$$

Let us consider the ND-automata $\mathfrak{B}_{12} = [\{0, 1\}, \{0, 1\}, \{a, b, c\}, h^{12}]$, $\mathfrak{B}_{13} = [\{0, 1\}, \{0, 1\}, \{A, B\}, h^{13}]$, where h^{12}, h^{13} are given by the following tables:

h^{12}	a	b	c
0	$\{[0, b], [0, c]\}$	$\{0, 1\} \times \{b, c\}$	$\{0, 1\} \times \{b, c\}$
1	$\{[1, b], [1, c]\}$	$\{0, 1\} \times \{b, c\}$	$\{0, 1\} \times \{b, c\}$

h^{13}	A	B
0	$\{[0, B]\}$	$\{[0, B], [1, B]\}$
1	$\{[1, B]\}$	$\{[0, B], [1, B]\}$

We can easily see that $[I_{\{0,1\}}, I_{\{0,1\}}, \zeta]$, where $\zeta(a) = A$, $\zeta(a) = \zeta(b) = B$, is a strong Z-homomorphism of $\mathfrak{B}_{12}$ onto $\mathfrak{B}_{13}$. $\mathfrak{B}_{13}$ is Z-deterministic, hence observable, while $\mathfrak{B}_{12}$ is not. Thus the converse of 3.2.5 is false. One can just as easily construct ND-automata $\mathfrak{B}$, $\mathfrak{B}'$ and a strong homomorphism of $\mathfrak{B}$ onto $\mathfrak{B}'$ such that $\mathfrak{B}'$ is Y-deterministic but $\mathfrak{B}$ is not. Thus the converse of 3.3.6 is false, even for strong homomorphisms.

Contrary to homomorphisms, strong homomorphisms carry ND-Moore automata into ND-Moore automata.

Theorem 3.4. *If $\chi = [\xi, \eta, \zeta]$ is a strong homomorphism of $\mathfrak{B} = [X, Y, Z, h]$ onto $\mathfrak{B}' = [X', Y', Z', h']$, then $\mathfrak{B}$ is an ND-Moore automaton if and only if $\mathfrak{B}'$ is.*

Proof: If $\mathfrak{B}$ is an ND-Moore automaton, then for all $z, z^* \in Z$, $x \in X$, the set $h_{z^*}(z, x)$ does not depend on $[z, x]$ (according to 1.7.4), provided $z^* \in f(z, x)$.

Thus 3.2.3 implies

$$\eta\big(h_{z^*}(z, x)\big) = h'_{\zeta(z^*)}\big(\zeta(z), \xi(x)\big).$$

Therefore the set $h'_{\zeta(z^*)}\big(\zeta(z), \xi(x)\big)$ does not depend on $[\zeta(z), \xi(x)]$ if $z^* \in f(z, x)$, i.e., by **3.2.1**, if $\zeta(z^*) \in f\big(\zeta(z), \xi(x)\big)$. Since ζ and ξ are mappings onto Z' and X' respectively, the set $h'_{z''}(z', x')$ does not depend on $[z', x']$, provided $z'' \in f'(z, x')$, hence $\mathfrak{B}'$ is an ND-Moore automaton.

Conversely, if $\mathfrak{B}'$ is an ND-Moore automaton, i.e., $\mathfrak{B}' = [X', Y', Z', f', m']$ then we put for $z \in Z$

$$m(z) = \{y \mid \eta(y) \in m'\big(\zeta(z)\big)\}.$$

Here, for all $z, z^* \in Z$, $x \in X$, $y \in Y$

$$\begin{aligned}[y, z^*] \in h(z, x) &\leftrightarrow [\eta(y), \zeta(z^*)] \in h'\big(\zeta(z), \xi(x)\big)\\ &\leftrightarrow \zeta(z^*) \in f'\big(\zeta(z), \xi(x)\big) \wedge \eta(y) \in m'\big(\zeta(z^*)\big)\\ &\leftrightarrow z^* \in f(z, x) \wedge y \in m(z^*),\end{aligned}$$

thus $\mathfrak{B}$ is an ND-Moore automaton.

Next we prove that Z-homomorphic (and a fortiori strongly Z-homomorphic) ND-automata are equivalent. For this we prove the following somewhat more general result.

Theorem 3.5. *If* $[\xi, \eta, \zeta]$ *is a homomorphism of* $\mathfrak{B} = [X, Y, Z, h]$ *onto* $\mathfrak{B}' = [X', Y', Z', h']$, *then for all* $M \subseteq Z$, $p \in W(X)$

$$\eta\big(v_{\mathfrak{B}}(M, p)\big) = v_{\mathfrak{B}'}\big(\zeta(M), \xi(p)\big).$$

The proof is carried out by induction on p. The initial step $p = e$ is trivial. The step from p to xp:

$$\begin{aligned}\eta\big(v_{\mathfrak{B}}(M, xp)\big) &= \bigcup_{z \in M} \eta\big(v_{\mathfrak{B}}(z, xp)\big)\\ &= \bigcup_{z \in M} \bigcup_{z^* \in Z} \eta\big(h_{z^*}(z, x)\big)\, \eta\big(v_{\mathfrak{B}}(z^*, p)\big)\\ &= \bigcup_{z \in M} \bigcup_{z' \in Z'} \bigcup_{\zeta(z^*) = z'} \eta\big(h_{z^*}(z, x)\big)\, \eta\big(v_{\mathfrak{B}}(z^*, p)\big)\\ &= \bigcup_{z \in M} \bigcup_{z' \in Z'} \Big[\bigcup_{\zeta(z^*) = z'} \eta\big(h_{z^*}(z, x)\big)\Big]\, v_{\mathfrak{B}'}\big(z', \xi(p)\big)\\ &= \bigcup_{z \in M} \bigcup_{z' \in Z'} h'_{z'}\big(\zeta(z), \xi(x)\big)\, v_{\mathfrak{B}'}\big(z', \xi(p)\big)\\ &= \bigcup_{z \in M} v_{\mathfrak{B}'}\big(\zeta(z), \xi(xp)\big) = v_{\mathfrak{B}'}\big(\zeta(M), \xi(xp)\big).\end{aligned}$$

Corollary 3.6. If $[I_X, I_Y, \zeta]$ is a Z-homomorphism of $\mathfrak{B}$ onto $\mathfrak{B}'$, then

1. For all $M \subseteq Z$ we have $M \sim \zeta(M)$.
2. $\mathfrak{B}$ and $\mathfrak{B}'$ are equivalent.

If $\mathfrak{A}$ is a deterministic automaton, then up to Z-isomorphisms there is exactly one reduct $\overline{\mathfrak{A}}$ of $\mathfrak{A}$, and every automaton which is equivalent to $\mathfrak{A}$ can be Z-homomorphically mapped onto $\overline{\mathfrak{A}}$. For ND-automata, this is no longer valid.

Let $\mathfrak{B} = [X, Y, Z, h]$ be an arbitrary ND-automaton, and $\mathfrak{B}' = [X, Y, Z', h']$ a reduct of $\mathfrak{B}$. Since all the reducts of $\mathfrak{B}$ have the same number of states, we can assume without loss of generality, that $Z' = \overline{Z}$ and for each $z \in Z$, $[z]$ is the state of $\mathfrak{B}'$ which is equivalent to z. For any Z-homomorphism $[I_X, I_Y, \zeta]$ of $\mathfrak{B}$ onto $\mathfrak{B}'$ we have $z \sim \zeta(z)$ for each $z \in Z$. Consequently, only the mapping ζ with $\zeta(z) = [z]$ for $z \in Z$ could establish a Z-homomorphism of $\mathfrak{B}$ onto $\mathfrak{B}'$. This is the case if and only if for all $z \in Z$, $x \in X$, $y \in Y$

$$h'_y(\zeta(z), x) = \zeta(h_y(z, x)),$$

i.e., if

$$h'_y([z], x) = \{[z'] \mid z' \in h_y(z, x)\}.$$

This equality can be used to define h'_y (and thus h') if and only if the right hand side is independent of the representative z of the class $[z]$. Therefore we have:

Theorem 3.7. *There exists a reduct $\mathfrak{B}'$ of the ND-automaton $\mathfrak{B} = [X, Y, Z, h]$ such that $\mathfrak{B}$ can be Z-homomorphically mapped onto $\mathfrak{B}'$, if and only if $\mathfrak{B}$ satisfies the following condition:*

For all $z_1, z_2 \in Z$, $x \in X$, $y \in Y$, with $z_1 \sim z_2$ we have

$$\{[z'_1] \mid z'_1 \in h_y(z_1, x)\} = \{[z'_2] \mid z'_2 \in h_y(z_2, x)\}. \tag{R}$$

There are ND-automata which do not satisfy the above condition (R). As an example we consider the ND-Mealy automaton $\mathfrak{B}_{14} = [\{x\}, \{0, 1\}, \{a, b, c, d\}, h^{14}]$, whose graph is represented in Fig. 17. Here we can easily see that $[a] = \{a, b\}$, $[c] = \{c\}$, $[d] = \{d\}$. Thus $a \sim b$, but

$$\{[z'] \mid z' \in h_0(a, x)\} = \{[a], [c], [d]\} \neq$$
$$\neq \{[a], [d]\} = \{[z'] \mid z' \in h_0^{14}(b, x)\}.$$

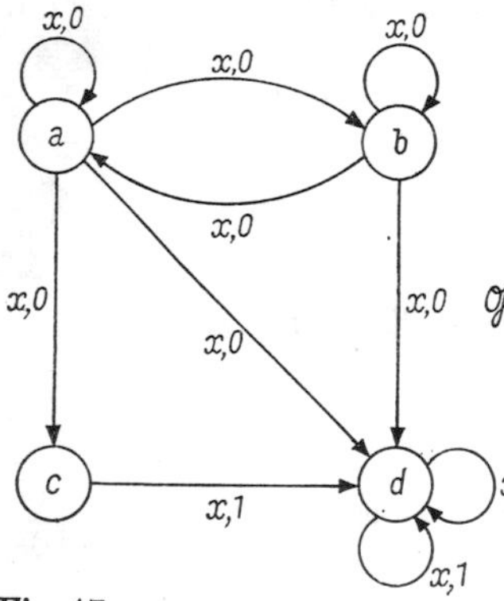

Fig. 17

Consequently, $\mathfrak{B}_{14}$ does not satisfy condition (R) and hence it cannot be Z-homomorphically mapped onto any of its reducts. An ND-automaton cannot in general be Z-homomorphically mapped onto one of its weak minims, minims or strong reducts, since a weak minim of $\mathfrak{B}$ is not even necessarily equivalent to $\mathfrak{B}$.

Furthermore, there are ND-automata with reducts and minims such that they are not pairwise Z-isomorphic. As an example we consider the minimal ND-automaton $\mathfrak{B}_7 = [\{0, 1\}, \{A, B, C\}, \{1, 2, 3, 4, 5\}]$ (cf. page 168). We have already shown that the sets of states $\{1, 3\}, \{1, 2, 3, 4\}$ are equivalent in $\mathfrak{B}_7$. We have

$\{1, 3\} = h_C^7(5, 0) = h_C^7(5, 1)$. For $z \in \{1, 2, 3, 4, 5\}$, $x \in \{0, 1\}$ we set

$$h^*(z, x) = \begin{cases} h^7(z, x), & \text{if } z \neq 5, \\ \{[C, 1], [C, 2], [C, 3], [C, 4]\}, & \text{if } z = 5, \end{cases}$$

and thus obtain the ND-automaton $\mathfrak{B}_7^* = [\{0, 1\}, \{A, B, C\}, \{1, 2, 3, 4, 5\}, h^*]$, which is also minimal and equivalent to $\mathfrak{B}_7$. Hence $\mathfrak{B}_7$ and $\mathfrak{B}_7^*$ are minims and reducts of $\mathfrak{B}_7$, and are obviously not Z-isomorphic.

Theorem 3.8. *All strong reducts of the same ND-automaton are pairwise Z-isomorphic.*

Proof: By 2.16.2, it suffices to show that equivalent strongly reduced ND-automata, say $\mathfrak{B} = [X, Y, Z, h]$, $\mathfrak{B}' = [X, Y, Z', h']$, are Z-isomorphic. The mapping ζ which assigns to each $z \in Z$ the state $z' \in Z'$ to which z is equivalent, is a one-to-one mapping of Z onto Z'. We show that for all $z, z^* \in Z$, $x \in X$, $y \in Y$

$$[y, z^*] \in h(z, x) \leftrightarrow [y, \zeta(z^*)] \in h'(\zeta(z), x),$$

which is the case if and only if for all $z \in Z$, $x \in X$, $y \in Y$

$$\zeta(h_y(z, x)) = h'_y(\zeta(z), x),$$

because ζ is one-to-one.

By 2.6.1 $z \sim \zeta(z)$ implies $h_y(z, x) \sim h'_y(\zeta(z), x)$, for $x \in X$, consequently $\zeta(h'_y(z, x)) \sim h_y(\zeta(z), x)$. Since $\mathfrak{B}'$ is strongly reduced, the latter implies $\zeta(h_y(z, x) = h'_y(\zeta(z), x)$, which was to be shown.

On the other hand, we can easily verify the following theorem:

Theorem 3.9. *Let $\mathfrak{B}$ be an ND-automaton and $\mathfrak{B}'$ a reduct (a minim) of $\mathfrak{B}$. Then there is an ND-automaton $\mathfrak{B}^*$ in the set of all ND-automata equivalent (weakly equivalent) to $\mathfrak{B}$ and having the same number of states as $\mathfrak{B}$, which can be Z-homomorphically mapped onto $\mathfrak{B}'$.*

Theorem 3.10. *If $\mathfrak{B} = [X, Y, Z, h]$ is an observable ND-automaton, then $\mathfrak{B}$ can be Z-homomorphically mapped onto each observable reduct $\bar{\mathfrak{B}} = [X, Y, \bar{Z}, \bar{h}]$ of $\mathfrak{B}$, and all the observable reducts of $\mathfrak{B}$ are pairwise Z-isomorphic.*

Proof: Let ζ be the single valued mapping of Z onto $\bar{Z}$, which assigns to each $z \in Z$ that state $\bar{z} = \zeta(z)$ of $\mathfrak{B}$ which is equivalent to z. Furthermore, we set

$$\delta(z, x, y) \underset{\text{Df}}{=} \begin{cases} \text{the unique element } z' \in h_y(z, x), & \text{if } h_y(z, x) \neq \emptyset, \\ \text{not defined otherwise;} \end{cases}$$

$$\bar{\delta}(\bar{z}, x, y) \underset{\text{Df}}{=} \begin{cases} \text{the unique element } \bar{\bar{z}} \in \bar{h}_y(\bar{z}, x), & \text{if } \bar{h}_y(\bar{z}, x) \neq \emptyset, \\ \text{not defined otherwise.} \end{cases}$$

$z \sim \zeta(z)$, implies $g(z, x) = \bar{g}(\zeta(z), x)$; hence $\delta(z, x, y)$ is defined if and only if $\bar{\delta}(\zeta(z), x, y)$ is. If $y \in g(z, x)$, then $h_y(z, x) \sim \bar{h}_y(\zeta(z), x)$, thus $\delta(z, x, y) \sim \bar{\delta}(\zeta(z), x, y)$, i.e $\zeta(\delta(z, x, y)) = \bar{\delta}(\zeta(z), x, y)$. Now for $z \in Z$, $x \in X$

$$\begin{aligned} I_Y \zeta(h(z, x)) &= \{[y, \bar{z}] \mid \exists z' (\bar{z} = \zeta(z') \wedge z' \in h_y(z, x))\} \\ &= \{[y, \bar{z}] \mid \bar{z} = \zeta(\delta(z, x, y))\} \\ &= \{[y, \bar{z}] \mid \bar{z} = \bar{\delta}(\zeta(z), x, y)\} \\ &= \bar{h}(\zeta(z), x). \end{aligned}$$

Thus $[I_X, I_Y, \zeta]$ is a Z-homomorphism of $\mathfrak{B}$ onto $\mathfrak{B}'$. If $\mathfrak{B}$ itself is reduced, then the map ζ is one-to-one, hence $[I_X, I_Y, \zeta]$ is a Z-isomorphism of $\mathfrak{B}$ onto $\mathfrak{B}'$. Thus Theorem 3.10 is proved.

Corollary 3.11.

1. In the set of all observable ND-automata equivalent to a given observable ND-automaton, up to Z-isomorphisms there is exactly one (observable) ND-automaton which is reduced, and onto which every member of this set can be mapped Z-isomorphically.

2. Every observable ND-automaton satisfies the condition (R) of Theorem 3.7.

In general, an observable ND-automaton, in addition to its observable reducts, has others which are not observable. The graphs of two equivalent reduced ND-automata of which one is observable and the other is not, are shown in Fig. 18.

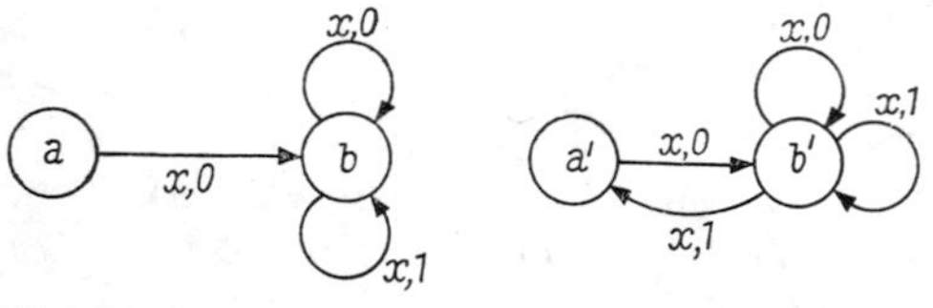

Fig. 18

One can easily see, however, that an observable, or even a Z-deterministic ND-automaton, cannot necessarily be mapped onto an observable or Z-deterministic reduct by means of a strong Z-homomorphism. This is illustrated by any two ND-automata $\mathfrak{B}$, $\mathfrak{B}'$ such that $X = X'$, $Y = Y'$, $Z \neq Z'$ and X, Y, Z, Z' are singletons, and by their direct sum $\mathfrak{B} + \mathfrak{B}'$. Then $\mathfrak{B}$ is a reduct of $\mathfrak{B} + \mathfrak{B}'$; however there is no strong Z-homomorphism of $\mathfrak{B} + \mathfrak{B}'$ onto $\mathfrak{B}$, although both ND-automata are deterministic.

Theorem 3.12. *If* $\mathfrak{B} = [X, Y, Z, h]$, $\mathfrak{B}' = [X', Y', Z', h']$ *are deterministic ND-automata, then* $[\xi, \eta, \zeta]$ *is a homomorphism of* $\mathfrak{B}$ *onto* $\mathfrak{B}'$ *if and only if* $[\xi, \eta, \zeta]$ *is a homomorphism of* $Det(\mathfrak{B})$ *onto* $Det(\mathfrak{B}')$ *in the sense of the theory of deterministic automata.*

Proof: Let $Det(\mathfrak{B}) = [X, Y, Z, \delta, \lambda]$, $Det(\mathfrak{B}') = [X', Y', Z', \delta', \lambda']$. Then $[\xi, \eta, \zeta]$ is a homomorphism of $\mathfrak{B}$ onto $\mathfrak{B}'$ if and only if the following (pairwise equivalent) assertions are satisfied.

$$\forall z\, \forall x\big(z \in Z \wedge x \in X \rightarrow h'(\zeta(z), \xi(x)) = \eta\zeta(h(z, x))\big),$$

$$\forall z\, \forall x\big(z \in Z \wedge x \in X \rightarrow \{[\lambda'(\zeta(z), \xi(x)), \delta'(\zeta(z), \xi(x))]\} = \{[\eta(\lambda(z, x)), \zeta(\delta(z, x))]\}\big),$$

$$\forall z\, \forall x\big(z \in Z \wedge x \in X \rightarrow \eta(\lambda(z, x)) = \lambda'(\zeta(z), \xi(x)) \wedge \zeta(\delta(z, x)) = \delta'(\zeta(z), \xi(x))\big),$$

hence if and only if $[\xi, \eta, \zeta]$ is a homomorphism of $Det(\mathfrak{B})$ onto $Det(\mathfrak{B}')$.

§ 4. Non-Deterministic Operators

In this section we shall deal with the possible behaviours of ND-automata, that is, with the question of the kind of relationship which exists between the input words and the ND-automaton's responses to them, as well as with the properties of this relationship. The response of the automaton is thought to be the set of all output words which can be put out by the automaton after feeding in the corresponding input word. It is clear that this set depends on which state the ND-automaton is in step 1. Every state z of an ND-automaton $\mathfrak{B} = [X, Y, Z, h]$ generates a single-valued mapping of $W(X)$ into $\mathfrak{P}^*(W(Y))$, namely the mapping $\varphi(p) = v_{\mathfrak{B}}(z, p)$.

Definition 4.1. Let X, Y be non-empty sets. A function φ which maps the set $W(X)$ into $\mathfrak{P}^*(W(Y))$ is called a *non-deterministic operator over* $[X, Y]$ (shortly: *ND-operator*).

Definition 4.2. An ND-operator φ over $[X, Y]$ is called *generable* if there are an ND-automaton $\mathfrak{B}' = [X', Y', Z', h']$ and a (non-empty) set $M \subseteq Z'$ of states of $\mathfrak{B}'$ such that

a) $X \subseteq X'$;

b) for all $p \in W(X)$ we have $\varphi(p) = v_{\mathfrak{B}'}(M, p)$.

To express the situation described by a) and b) we say that φ is *generated in* $\mathfrak{B}'$ *by the set of states* M. If $M = \{z\}$, then we refer to φ as the ND-operator generated *by the state* z in $\mathfrak{B}'$.

Theorem 4.1. *An ND-operator φ over $[X, Y]$ is generable if and only if there is an ND-automaton with the input alphabet X and the output alphabet Y and in which φ is generated by a state.*

Proof: Let $\mathfrak{B}' = [X', Y', Z', h']$ and $M \subseteq Z'$, with $X \subseteq X'$ and $\varphi(p) = v_{\mathfrak{B}'}(M, p)$ for all $p \in W(X)$. We consider the following system $\mathfrak{B} = [X, Y, Z, h]$, where

$$Z \underset{\mathrm{Df}}{=} \bigcup_{p \in W(X)} f'(M, p),$$

$$h(z, x) \underset{\mathrm{Df}}{=} h'(z, x) \text{ for all } z \in Z,\ x \in X.$$

To show that $\mathfrak{B}$ is an ND-automaton, we have to show that for every $y \in Y'$ we have

$$\exists z \exists x \big(z \in Z \wedge x \in X \wedge y \in g'(z, x)\big) \rightarrow y \in Y,$$

i.e., that Y can be chosen as the output alphabet of the system $\mathfrak{B}$. If this formula did not hold, then there would exist a situation $[z, x] \in Z \times X$ for the system $\mathfrak{B}$, in which an output signal y, not belonging to Y, could be put out, and thus $h(z, x) \subseteq Y \times X$ would not hold.

Suppose $y \in Y'$, $z \in Z$, $x \in X$ are arbitrary, and $y \in g'(z, x)$. Since $z \in Z$, there is a $p \in W(X)$ with $z \in f'(M, p)$. By 1.4.5, the latter implies the existence of a word $q \in W(Y')$ with $l(q) = l(p)$ and $z \in h'_q(M, p)$. Now by 1.5.8 we have

$$v_{\mathfrak{B}'}(M, px) = \bigcup_{q' \in W(Y')} \{q'\} \cdot g'\big(h'_{q'}(M, p), x\big).$$

Thus there is a $p \in W(X)$ and a $q \in W(Y')$ with $l(p) = l(q)$, $z \in h'_q(M, p)$ and $qy \in v_{\mathfrak{B}'}(M, px) = \varphi(px)$. Consequently, $qy \in W(Y)$, hence $y \in Y$.

If we assume that the alphabet Y is minimal for the ND-operator φ, i.e., for each $y \in Y$ there are $p \in W(X)$ and words $q, s \in W(Y)$ with $qys \in \varphi(p)$, then we can easily verify the converse of the above formula, that is, that Y is minimal for $\mathfrak{B}$.

Thus $\mathfrak{B}$ is an ND-automaton, and $M \subseteq Z$. We can easily see that φ is generated by M in $\mathfrak{B}$. We shall show later (cf. § 6), that every ND-operator generated by a non-empty set N of states in $\mathfrak{B}$, can also be generated in the ND-automaton $\tilde{\mathfrak{B}} = [X, Y, \mathfrak{P}^*(Z), \tilde{h}]$ by the state $N \in \mathfrak{P}^*(Z)$. Here, $\tilde{h}$ is defined for $N \in \mathfrak{P}^*(Z)$, $x \in X$ by the following formula:

$$\tilde{h}(N, x) \underset{\mathrm{Df}}{=} \big\{[y, \{z'\}] \mid \exists z\big(z \in N \wedge [y, z'] \in h(z, x)\big)\big\}.$$

The fact that every generable ND-operator can be generated by a single state is also obtained in the proof of Theorem 4.6.

Corollary 4.2. Every ND-operator φ over $[X, Y]$ has the following properties:

1. $\forall p \forall q \big(p \in W(X) \wedge q \in \varphi(p) \rightarrow l(q) = l(p)\big)$.
2. $\forall p \forall q \forall r \big(pr \in W(X) \wedge q \in \varphi(p) \rightarrow \exists s (qs \in \varphi(pr))\big)$.
3. $\forall p \forall q \forall r \forall s \big(pr \in W(X) \wedge l(p) = l(q) \wedge qs \in \varphi(pr) \rightarrow q \in \varphi(p)\big)$.

Definition 4.3. An ND-operator φ over $[X, Y]$ is called *sequential* if it has the properties 4.2.1, 4.2.2 and 4.2.3.

In the theory of deterministic automata, a word function α over $[X, Y]$ is called sequential if it satisfies the automata conditions:

I. $\forall p(p \in W(X) \rightarrow l(\alpha(p)) = l(p))$

II. $\forall p \forall r(pr \in W(X) \rightarrow \exists s(\alpha(pr) = \alpha(p)s))$.

We have defined a mapping *Det* which assigns to each deterministic ND-operator φ over $[X, Y]$ a word function $\alpha = Det(\varphi)$ over $[X, Y]$ in such a way that for $p \in W(X)$, $Det(\varphi)(p)$ is the unique element of the set $\varphi(p)$.[1] We can easily verify the following theorem:

Theorem 4.3. *A deterministic ND-operator φ is sequential if and only if $Det(\varphi)$ satisfies the automata conditions.*

Thus Theorem 4.3 justifies the term "sequential" for ND-operators satisfying the conditions 4.2.1, 4.2.2, and 4.2.3.

We define the states of sequential ND-operators (in analogy to the concept of states of a sequential word function).

Definition 4.4. Let φ be a sequential ND-operator over $[X, Y]$, $p \in W(X)$, $Q \subseteq \varphi(p)$, $Q \neq \emptyset$. For all $r \in W(X)$ we set

$$\varphi_{p,Q}(r) = \{s \mid \exists q(q \in Q \wedge qs \in \varphi(pr))\},$$

and call the (single-valued) mapping $\varphi_{p,Q}$ the *state of φ belonging to the pair $[p, Q]$*. If $Q = \{q\}$ is a singleton, then we write $\varphi_{p,q}$ instead of $\varphi_{p,Q}$ and refer to $\varphi_{p,q}$ as a *proper state of φ*.

Corollary 4.4. If φ is a sequential ND-operator over $[X, Y]$, $pr \in W(X)$, then we have

1. $\varphi(pr) = \bigcup_{q \in \varphi(p)} \{q\} \cdot \varphi_{p,q}(r)$.

2. $\varphi(pr) \subseteq \varphi(p) \cdot \varphi_{p,\varphi(p)}(r)$.

Theorem 4.5. *Every state of a sequential ND-operator over $[X, Y]$ is again a sequential ND-operator over $[X, Y]$.*

Proof: Let $p \in W(X)$, $\emptyset \neq Q \subseteq \varphi(p)$. By 4.2.2, for $r \in W(X)$

$$\varphi_{p,Q}(r) = \bigcup_{q \in Q} \varphi_{p,q}(r) = \bigcup_{q \in Q} \{s \mid qs \in \varphi(pr)\} \neq \emptyset.$$

Thus the function $\varphi_{p,Q}$ is an ND-operator over $[X, Y]$, which obviously satisfies condition 4.2.1. If $ru \in W(X)$, $s \in \varphi_{p,Q}(r)$, then there is a $q \in Q$ with $s \in \varphi_{p,q}(r)$, i.e., $qs \in \varphi(pr)$. Thus because of 4.2.2, there exists a $v \in W(Y)$ with $qsv \in \varphi(pru)$, i.e. $sv \in \varphi_{p,q}(ru) \subseteq \varphi_{p,Q}(ru)$, hence $\varphi_{p,Q}$ satisfies 4.2.2. If $ru \in W(X)$, $sv \in \varphi_{p,Q}(ru)$ and $l(r) = l(s)$, then there is a $q \in Q$ with $sv \in \varphi_{p,q}(ru)$ (and $l(p) = l(q)$), i.e., $qsv \in \varphi(pru)$, which, together with 4.2.3 implies that

[1] Cf. Definition (1.3.7.) and (1.6.2.).

$qs \in \varphi(pr)$, hence $s \in \varphi_{p,Q}(r)$. Therefore, $\varphi_{p,Q}$ also satisfies condition 4.2.3, and Theorem 4.5 is proved.

Theorem 4.6. *An ND-operator φ over $[X, Y]$ is generable if and only if it is sequential.*

Proof: By 4.2 it suffices to show that sequential ND-operators are generable. Let Z be the set of proper states of the sequential ND-operator φ over $[X, Y]$, i.e.,

$$Z \underset{\text{Df}}{=} \{\varphi_{p,q} \mid p \in W(X) \wedge q \in \varphi(p)\},$$

furthermore, let h be defined on $Z \times X$ as follows:

$$h(\varphi_{p,q}, x) \underset{\text{Df}}{=} \{[y, \varphi_{px,qy}] \mid y \in \varphi_{p,q}(x)\}.$$

Since $\varphi_{p,q} = \varphi_{r,s}$ implies that, for arbitrary $x \in X$, $y \in Y$, $\varphi_{px,qy}$ exists if and only if $\varphi_{rx,sy}$ exists, and $\varphi_{px,qy} = \varphi_{rx,sy}$ holds for all $y \in \varphi_{p,q}(x)$, this definition is justified.

Since $\varphi_{p,q}(x)$ is always non-empty, we also have $h(\varphi_{p,q}, x) \neq \emptyset$, thus $\mathfrak{B} = [X, Y, Z, h]$ is an observable ND-automaton. We show by induction on r that for all $\varphi_{p,q} \in Z$

$$\varphi_{p,q}(r) = v_{\mathfrak{B}}(\varphi_{p,q}, r).$$

The initial step is trivial. The step from r to xr:

$$\begin{aligned}\varphi_{p,q}(xr) &= \bigcup_{y \in \varphi_{p,q}(x)} \{y\} \cdot \varphi_{px,qy}(r)\\ &= \bigcup_{y \in g(\varphi_{p,q},x)} \{y\} \cdot v_{\mathfrak{B}}(\varphi_{px,qy}, r)\\ &= \bigcup_{y \in g(\varphi_{p,q},x)} \{y\} \cdot v_{\mathfrak{B}}\big(h_y(\varphi_{p,q}, x), r\big) = v_{\mathfrak{B}}(\varphi_{p,q}, xr).\end{aligned}$$

Therefore we see that every proper state $\varphi_{p,q}$ of φ (including $\varphi = \varphi_{e,e}$) is generated by a state in $\mathfrak{B}$.

Theorem 4.7. *If the ND-operator φ is generated by the set $M \subseteq Z$ in the ND-automaton $\mathfrak{B} = [X, Y, Z, h]$, then every state $\varphi_{p,Q}$ of φ can also be generated in $\mathfrak{B}$.*

Proof: Let $\emptyset \neq M \subseteq Z$, and φ be generated by M in $\mathfrak{B}$. Furthermore for $p \in W(X)$, $\emptyset \neq Q \subseteq \varphi(p)$

$$h_Q(M, p) = \bigcup_{q \in Q} h_q(M, p).$$

We claim that the set $h_Q(M, p)$ generates the ND-operator $\varphi_{p,Q}$ in $\mathfrak{B}$, i.e., for $p, r \in W(X)$, $\emptyset \neq Q \subseteq \varphi(p)$,

$$v_{\mathfrak{B}}\big(h_Q(M, p), r\big) = \varphi_{p,Q}(r).$$

For $s \in W(Y)$ we have

$$\begin{aligned} s \in v_{\mathfrak{B}}(h_Q(M, p), r) &\leftrightarrow \exists q(q \in Q \wedge s \in v_{\mathfrak{B}}(h_q(M, p), r)) \\ &\leftrightarrow \exists q(q \in Q \wedge qs \in v_{\mathfrak{B}}(M, pr)) \\ &\leftrightarrow \exists q(q \in Q \wedge qs \in \varphi(pr)) \\ &\leftrightarrow s \in \varphi_{p,Q}(r). \end{aligned}$$

Corollary 4.8.

1. A sequential ND-operator φ can be generated in a Z-finite ND automaton if and only if φ only has a finite number of states.

2. A sequential ND-operator φ has a finite number of states if and only if it has finitely many proper states.

3. If φ is the ND-operator generated by M in $\mathfrak{B} = [X, Y, Z, h]$, moreover $pr \in W(X)$, $\emptyset \neq Q \subseteq \varphi(p)$, $\emptyset \neq S \subseteq \varphi_{p,Q}, (r)$, then

$$h_S(h_Q(M, p), r) = h_{Q \cdot S}(M, pr) \quad \text{and} \quad (\varphi_{p,Q})_{r,S} = \varphi_{pr, Q \cdot S}.$$

By Theorems 3.2 and 4.1, every sequential ND-operator φ can be generated by a state in an ND-Moore automaton. However, the obviously sequential ND-operator φ^* over $[\{x\}, \{0, 1\}]$ with

$$\varphi^*(x^n) = \{0^n, 1^n\}$$

cannot be generated *by a state* in any ND-Mealy automaton. Indeed, for an ND-Mealy automaton $\mathfrak{B}$ we have

$$v_{\mathfrak{B}}(z, xp) = g(z, x) \cdot v_{\mathfrak{B}}(f(z, x), p);$$

but the set $\{0^n, 1^n\}$ for $n \geqq 2$ cannot be written in the form $\{0, 1\} \cdot E$ (for any $E \subseteq W(\{0, 1\})$). On the other hand, φ^* can be generated in an ND-Mealy automaton by a set of states.

Theorem 4.9. *Every sequential ND-operator φ over $[X, Y]$ can be generated in an ND-Mealy automaton by a set of states.*

Proof: Let $\Phi = \{\varphi_{p,q} \mid q \in \varphi(p) \wedge p \in W(X)\}$ be the set of proper states of φ, and η a single valued mapping of X into Y, such that for every $\varphi_{p,q} \in \Phi$, $x \in X$'

$$\eta(\varphi_{p,q}, x) \in \varphi_{p,q}(x).$$

Furthermore, let $Z \underset{\mathrm{Df}}{=} \Phi \times Y$ and for $z = [\varphi_{p,q}, y] \in Z$, $x \in X$

$$g(z, x) = g([\varphi_{p,q}, y], x) \underset{\mathrm{Df}}{=} \begin{cases} \{y\}, & \text{if } y \in \varphi_{p,q}(x), \\ \{\eta(\varphi_{p,q}, x)\}, & \text{if } y \notin \varphi_{p,q}(x); \end{cases}$$

$$f(z, x) = f([\varphi_{p,q}, y], x) \underset{\mathrm{Df}}{=} \begin{cases} \{\varphi_{px, qy}\} \times Y, & \text{if } y \in \varphi_{p,q}(x), \\ \{\varphi_{px, q\eta(\varphi_{p,q}, x)}\} \times Y, & \text{if } y \notin \varphi_{p,q}(x). \end{cases}$$

$\mathfrak{B} = [X, Y, Z, f, g]$ is an ND-Mealy automaton. We claim that for every state $\varphi_{p,q} \in \Phi$ the set $\{\varphi_{p,q}\} \times Y$ generate the ND-operator $\varphi_{p,q}$ in $\mathfrak{B}$. We prove by induction on r that for all $r \in W(X)$,

$$v_{\mathfrak{B}}(\{\varphi_{p,q}\} \times Y, r) = \varphi_{p,q}(r).$$

The initial step $r = e$ is trivial. The induction step is taken from r to xr:

$$\begin{aligned} v_{\mathfrak{B}}(\{\varphi_{p,q}\} \times Y, xr) &= \bigcup_{y \in Y} g([\varphi_{p,q}, y], x) \cdot v_{\mathfrak{B}}\big(f([\varphi_{p,q}, y], x), r\big) \\ &= \bigcup_{y \in \varphi_{p,q}(x)} \{y\} \cdot v_{\mathfrak{B}}(\{\varphi_{px,qy}\} \times Y, r) \\ &\quad \cup \{\eta(\varphi_{p,q}, x)\} \cdot v_{\mathfrak{B}}(\{\varphi_{px,q\eta(\varphi_{p,q},x)}\} \times Y, r) \\ &= \bigcup_{y \in \varphi_{p,q}(x)} \{y\} \cdot v_{\mathfrak{B}}(\{\varphi_{px,qy}\} \times Y, r) \\ &= \bigcup_{y \in \varphi_{p,q}(x)} \{y\} \cdot \varphi_{px,qy}(r) \qquad \text{(by the induction hypothesis)} \\ &= \varphi_{p,q}(xr) \qquad \text{(by 4.4.1, 4.5, 4.8.3)}, \end{aligned}$$

which was to be shown.

Theorem 4.10. *A sequential ND-operator φ over $[X, Y]$ can be generated by a state in an ND-Mealy automaton if and only if for all $x \in X$, $p \in W(X)$*

$$\varphi(xp) = \varphi(x)\, \varphi_{x,\varphi(x)}(p).$$

Proof: Let $\mathfrak{B} = [X, Y, Z, f, g]$ be an ND-Mealy automaton, $z \in Z$ and φ the ND-operator generated by z in $\mathfrak{B}$. Then $yq \in \varphi(xp)$ if and only if $y \in g(z, x)$ and $q \in v_{\mathfrak{B}}\big(f(z, x), p\big)$, i.e., if for all $y \in \varphi(x)$

$$\varphi_{x,y}(p) = v_{\mathfrak{B}}\big(f(z, x), p\big);$$

thus we have $\varphi_{x,\varphi(x)}(p) = v_{\mathfrak{B}}\big(f(z, x), p\big)$ and $\varphi(xp) = \varphi(x) \cdot \varphi_{x,\varphi(x)}(p)$. Conversely, if for all $x \in X$, $p \in W(X)$

$$\varphi(xp) = \varphi(x) \cdot \varphi_{x,\varphi(x)}(p),$$

then by Theorem 4.9, for each $x \in X$ there is an ND-Mealy automaton $\mathfrak{B}_x = [X, Y, Z_x, f_x, g_x]$ and a set $M_x \subseteq Z_x$ such that for all $p \in W(X)$

$$\varphi_{x,\varphi(x)}(p) = v_{\mathfrak{B}_x}(M_x, p).$$

Without loss of generality we can assume that the sets Z_x are pairwise disjoint. Let $z^* \notin \bigcup_{x \in X} Z_x$ and $Z \underset{\mathrm{Df}}{=} \{z^*\} \cup \bigcup_{x \in X} Z_x$, furthermore for $z \in Z$, $x \in X$,

$$f(z, x) \underset{\mathrm{Df}}{=} \begin{cases} M_x, & \text{if } z = z^*, \\ f_{x'}(z, x), & \text{if } z \in Z_{x'}; \end{cases}$$

$$g(z, x) \underset{\mathrm{Df}}{=} \begin{cases} \varphi(x), & \text{if } z = z^*, \\ g_{x'}(z, x), & \text{if } z \in Z_{x'}. \end{cases}$$

The ND-operator φ is generated by the state z^* in the MD-Mealy automaton $\mathfrak{B} = [X, Y, Z, f, g]$:

$$\begin{aligned} v_{\mathfrak{B}}(z^*, xp) &= g(z^*, x) \cdot v_{\mathfrak{B}}\big(f(z^*, x), p\big) = \varphi(x) \cdot v_{\mathfrak{B}}(M_x, p) \\ &= \varphi(x) \cdot v_{\mathfrak{B}_x}(M_x, p) = \varphi(x) \cdot \varphi_{x, \varphi(x)}(p) = \varphi(xp). \end{aligned}$$

We have already pointed out (cf. 4.8.1) that an ND-operator can be generated in a Z-finite ND-automaton if and only if it has only finitely many states. Below we shall give a characterization of these ND-operators (we call them regular) which is analogous to the theory of regular events. That is, we construct ND-operators by means of certain operations from what we call elementary operators and show that the regular ND-operators and only they can be obtained in this way. For this it will be necessary to generalize the concept of ND-operators, namely to achieve that the empty set be admissible as a value.

Definition 4.5. Let X, Y be arbitrary non-empty sets.

(4.5.1) Every single-valued mapping ψ of $W(X)$ into $\mathfrak{P}\big(W(Y)\big)$ is called a *generalized non-deterministic operator* (*GND-operator*) *over* $[X, Y]$.

(4.5.2) A generalized non-deterministic operator ψ over $[X, Y]$ is called a *non-deterministic elementary operator* (*ND-elementary operator*), if $\psi(p) \neq \emptyset$ implies $p \in X$ and $\psi(p) \subseteq Y$. The ND-elementary operator ψ with $\psi(p) \equiv \emptyset$ is denotes by Λ.

(4.5.3) The GND-operator ψ over $[X, Y]$ is said to be *represented* in the ND-automaton $\mathfrak{B} = [X, Y, Z, h]$ *by* $[z_1, M]$ (where $z_1 \in Z$, $M \subseteq Z$) if $\psi(p) = h_M(z_1, p)$ for all $p \in W(X)$.

(4.5.4) A GND-operator is called *regular* if it can be generated in a Z-finite ND-automaton.

Corollary 4.11.

1. Every (regular) ND-operator is a (regular) GND-operator.
2. Every ND-elementary operator is regular.

Let ψ be an ND-elementary operator over $[X, Y]$ and consider the ND-automaton $\mathfrak{B}^\psi = [X, Y, \{a, b, c\}, h^\psi]$, where

$$h^\psi(a, x) \underset{\mathrm{Df}}{=} \{[y, b] \mid y \in \psi(x)\} \cup Y \times \{c\},$$

$$h^\psi(b, x) \underset{\mathrm{Df}}{=} h^\psi(c, x) \underset{\mathrm{Df}}{=} Y \times \{c\}.$$

Obviously, ψ is generated in $\mathfrak{B}^{\psi}$ by $[a, \{b\}]$.

The following theorem implies that without any loos of generality we can assume that the representing ND-automaton has the same alphabets as the GND-operator to be represented, and that the representation is by an initial state z_1 instead of by an initial set M_1.

Theorem 4.12. *A GND-operator ψ over $[X, Y]$ is representable if and only if*

$$\forall p \forall q \big(p \in W(X) \wedge q \in \psi(p) \rightarrow l(p) = l(q)\big).$$

Proof: It is obvious that the given condition is necessary. To show that it is also sufficient, we consider the free ND-automaton $\mathfrak{B} = [X, Y, Z, h]$, where

$$Z \underset{\text{Df}}{=} \{[p, q] \mid p \in W(x) \wedge q \in Y^{l(p)}\}$$

and

$$h([p, q], x) \underset{\text{Df}}{=} \big\{[y, [px, qy]] \mid y \in Y\big\}$$

for all $[p, q] \in Z$, $x \in X$. As can be easily seen, ψ is represented in $\mathfrak{B}$ by $\big[[e, e], M_\psi\big]$, where

$$M_\psi \underset{\text{Df}}{=} \{[p, q] \mid p \in W(X) \wedge q \in \psi(p)\}.$$

Now we define operations on GND-operators, and show that they preserve regularity.

Definition 4.6. Let ψ, ψ' be GND-operators over $[X, Y]$, then the GND-operators $[\psi \cup \psi']$, $[\psi \cdot \psi']$, $\langle\psi\rangle$ are defined for all $p = x_1 \ldots x_n \in W(X)$ as follows:

$$[\psi \cup \psi'](p) = \psi(p) \cup \psi'(p),$$

$$[\psi \cdot \psi'](p) = \bigcup_{i=0}^{n} \psi(x_1 \ldots x_i)\, \psi'(x_{i+1} \ldots x_n),$$

$$\langle\psi\rangle(p) = \begin{cases} \{e\}, \text{ if } n = 0 \ (p = e), \\ \displaystyle\bigcup_{k=1}^{n} \bigcup_{\substack{p_1 \ldots p_k = p \\ p_1, \ldots, p_k \neq e}} \psi(p_1) \ldots \psi(p_k), \text{ if } n > 0. \end{cases}$$

Corollary 4.13.

1. The operation $\cup$ is associative, commutative, and the operation $\cdot$ is associative.
2. The operation $\langle\ \rangle$ is the analogon of a closure operation, i.e., if we define

$$\psi \subseteq \psi' \underset{\text{Df}}{\leftrightarrow} \forall p (p \in W(X) \rightarrow \psi(p) \subseteq \psi'(p))$$

we have

a) $\psi \subseteq \langle\psi\rangle$,

b) $\psi \subseteq \psi' \rightarrow \langle\psi\rangle \subseteq \langle\psi'\rangle$,

c) $\langle\langle\psi\rangle\rangle = \langle\psi\rangle$.

Theorem 4.14. *Every regular GND-operator ψ over $[X, Y]$ can be obtained in a finite number of steps from ND-elementary operators over $[X, Y]$, using the operations* $\cup, \cdot, \langle\,\rangle$.

The proof is analogous to that of the analysis theorem for regular events (Part I, Theorem 6.15). Let ψ be represented in the Z-finite ND-automaton $\mathfrak{B} = [X, Y, Z, h]$ by $[z_1, M]$, where we assume $Z = \{1, 2, \ldots, k\}$ and $z_1 = 1$. For $i, j \in Z$, $\varkappa \in Z \cup \{0\}$, $p = x_1 \ldots x_n \in W(X)$ we define

$$[\psi^{\varkappa}_{i,j}](p) = \begin{cases} \emptyset, \text{ if } n = 0 \ (p = e), \\ \Big\{\{y_1 \ldots y_n \mid \exists i_1 \ldots \exists i_{n+1} \Big(\bigwedge_{\nu=1}^{n} [y_\nu, i_{\nu+1}] \in h(i_\nu, x_\nu) \wedge i_1 = i \\ \wedge\, i_{n+1} = j \wedge \bigwedge_{\nu=2}^{n} i_\nu \leqq \varkappa\Big)\Big\}, \text{ if } n > 0. \end{cases}$$

Hence, $[\psi^{\varkappa}_{i,j}](p)$ is the set of all non-empty words which can be put out by the ND-automaton $\mathfrak{B}$ in response to the application of the word p, under the condition that meanwhile $\mathfrak{B}$ moves from the state i to the state j without entering any of the states i_ν with $i_\nu > \varkappa$. For $p \neq e$ we have

$$\psi(p) = \bigcup_{j \in M} [\psi^{k}_{1,j}](p)$$

$$\psi = \begin{cases} \bigcup_{j \in M} [\psi^{k}_{1,j}] \cup \langle \Lambda \rangle, \text{ if } 1 \in M \ \big(\text{i.e. } \psi(e) = \{e\}\big), \\ \bigcup_{j \in M} [\psi^{k}_{1,j}], \text{ if } 1 \notin M \ \big(\text{i.e. } \psi(e) = \emptyset\big). \end{cases}$$

Hence it suffices to show that every $[\psi^{\varkappa}_{i,j}]$ can be obtained from ND-elementary operators. We shall prove this by induction on $\varkappa$.

We have $[\psi^{0}_{i,j}](e) = \emptyset$ and $\bigwedge_{\nu=2}^{n} i_\nu \leqq 0$ can only be valid if $n \leqq 1$, i.e., if the conjunction is empty. Thus,

$$y_1 \ldots y_n \in [\psi^{0}_{i,j}](x_1 \ldots x_n)$$

implies $n = 1$, i.e., every $[\psi^{0}_{i,j}]$ is an ND-elementary operator. In the induction step from $\varkappa - 1$ to $\varkappa$ (for $1 \leqq \varkappa \leqq k$) it suffices to show that

$$[\psi^{\varkappa}_{i,j}] = [\psi^{\varkappa-1}_{i,j}] \cup [\psi^{\varkappa-1}_{i,\varkappa}] \cdot \langle [\psi^{\varkappa-1}_{\varkappa,\varkappa}] \rangle \cdot [\psi^{\varkappa-1}_{\varkappa,j}]$$

for all $i, j \in Z$.

The proof requires a certain amount of calculating, however it is straightforward, and therefore we omit it.

Theorem 4.15. *If ψ_1, ψ_2 are regular GND-operators, then the GND-operators* $[\psi_1 \cup \psi_2]$, $[\psi_1 \cdot \psi_2]$ *and* $\langle \psi_1 \rangle$ *are also regular.*

Proof: Suppose that for $i \in \{1, 2\}$, ψ_i is generated in the Z-finite ND-automaton $\mathfrak{B}_i = [X, Y, Z_i, h^i]$ by $[z_1^i, M_i]$, where $Z_1 \cap Z_2 = \emptyset$. Furthermore let

$$z_1^* \notin Z_1 \cup Z_2,$$
$$Z \underset{\mathrm{Df}}{=} Z_1 \cup Z_2 \cup \{z_1^*\},$$

and for $z \in Z$, $x \in X$

$$h^{\cup}(z, x) \underset{\mathrm{Df}}{=} \begin{cases} h^i(z, x), & \text{if } z \in Z_i, \\ h^1(z_1^1, x) \cup h^2(z_1^2, x), & \text{if } z = z_1^*, \end{cases}$$

furthermore,

$$M_{\cup} \underset{\mathrm{Df}}{=} M_1 \cup M_2 \cup \begin{cases} \{z_1^*\}, & \text{if } z_1^1 \in M_1 \vee z_1^2 \in M_2, \\ \emptyset & \text{otherwise.} \end{cases}$$

We can easily verify that $[\psi_1 \cup \psi_2]$ is represented in $\mathfrak{B}^0 = [X, Y, Z, h^{\cup}]$ by $[z_1^*, M_{\cup}]$.

For $z \in Z$, $x \in X$ we define

$$h^0(z, x) \underset{\mathrm{Df}}{=} \begin{cases} h^2(z, x), & \text{if } z \in Z_2, \\ h^1(z, x) \cup \bigcup\limits_{z' \in M_1} \{[y, z_1^2] \mid [y, z'] \in h^1(z, x)\}, & \text{if } z \in Z_1, \end{cases}$$

$$h^0(z_1^*, x) \underset{\mathrm{Df}}{=} h^0(z_1^1, x) \cup \begin{cases} \emptyset, & \text{if } z_1^1 \notin M_1, \\ h^2(z_1^2, x), & \text{if } z_1^1 \in M_1 \end{cases}$$

and

$$M_0 \underset{\mathrm{Df}}{=} M_2 \cup \begin{cases} \{z_1^*\}, & \text{if } z_1^1 \in M_1 \wedge z_1^2 \in M_2, \\ \emptyset & \text{otherwise.} \end{cases}$$

We shall show that $[\psi_1 \cdot \psi_2]$ is represented in the Z-finite ND-automaton $\mathfrak{B}^0 = [X, Y, Z, h^0]$ by $[z_1^*, M_0]$. We have

$$\begin{aligned} z^* \in M_0 &\leftrightarrow z_1^1 \in M_1 \wedge z_1^2 \in M_2 \\ &\leftrightarrow e \in \psi_1(e) \wedge e \in \psi_2(e) \\ &\leftrightarrow e \in [\psi_1 \cdot \psi_2](e), \end{aligned}$$

hence

$$h^0_{M_0}(z_1^*, e) = [\psi_1 \cdot \psi_2](e).$$

If $p = x_1 \ldots x_n \in W(X)$ and $n > 0$ we have

$$y_1 \ldots y_n \in h^0_{M_0}(z^*, p) \leftrightarrow$$
$$\leftrightarrow \exists z_2^* \ldots \exists z_{n+1}^* \left(\bigwedge_{i=1}^{n} [y_i, z_{i+1}^*] \in h^0(z_i^*, x_i) \wedge z_{n+1}^* \in M_0 \right).$$

Now, $z^*_{n+1} \in h^0_{y_n}(z^*_n, x_n)$ and $n > 0$, hence $z^*_{n+1} \neq z^*_1$. For all i $z^*_i \in Z_2$ implies $\{z^*_i, \ldots, z^*_{n+1}\} \subseteq Z_2$. Since $z^*_{n+1} \in M_2 \subseteq Z_2$, there is a j with $1 \leqq j \leqq n$ and $z^*_j \notin Z_2$, $z^*_{j+1} \in Z_2$. If $j \geqq 2$, then $z^*_2 \notin Z_2$, hence $[y_1, z^*_2] \in h^1(z^1_1, x_1)$ and

$$\bigwedge_{i=2}^{j-1} ([y_i, z^*_{i+1}] \in h^1(z^*_i, x_i) \wedge z^*_{i+1} \in Z_1) \wedge z^*_{j+1} = z^2_1$$
$$\wedge \exists z_{j+1}([y_j, z_{j+1}] \in h^1(z^*_j, x_j) \wedge z_{j+1} \in M_1)$$
$$\wedge \bigwedge_{i=j+1}^{n} ([y_i, z^*_{i+1}] \in h^2(z^*_i, x_i) \wedge z^*_i \in Z_2) \wedge z^*_{n+1} \in M_2,$$

hence in this case we obtain $y_1 \ldots y_j \in \psi_1(x_1 \ldots x_j)$ and $y_{j+1} \ldots y_n \in \psi_2(x_{j+1} \ldots x_n)$. If $j = 1$ i.e. $z^*_2 \in Z_2$, then

$$\big(z^1_1 \in M_1 \wedge [y_1, z^*_2] \in h^2(z^2_1, x_1)\big) \vee \big(z^*_2 = z^2_1 \wedge \exists z_2(z_2 \in M_1 \wedge [y_1, z_2] \in$$
$$\in h^1(z^1_1, x_1))\big)$$

consequently

$$\big(e \in \psi_1(e) \wedge y_1 \ldots y_n \in \psi_2(x_1 \ldots x_n)\big)$$
$$\vee \big(y_1 \in \psi_1(x_1) \wedge y_2 \ldots y_n \in \psi_2(x_2 \ldots x_n)\big).$$

Thus we have

$$y_1 \ldots y_n \in h^0_{M_0}(z^*_1, x_1 \ldots x_n)$$
$$\leftrightarrow \exists j\big(0 \leqq j \leqq n \wedge y_1 \ldots y_j \in \psi_1(x_1 \ldots x_j) \wedge y_{j+1} \ldots y_n \in \psi_2(x_{j+1} \ldots x_n)\big)$$
$$\leftrightarrow y_1 \ldots y_n \in [\psi_1 \cdot \psi_2]\,(x_1 \ldots x_n),$$

which was to be shown.

Finally, let $Z^* \underset{\mathrm{Df}}{=} Z_1 \cup \{z^*_1\}$ and for $z \in Z^*$, $x \in X$

$$h^*(z, x) \underset{\mathrm{Df}}{=} \begin{cases} h^1(z, x) \cup \bigcup_{z' \in M_1} \{[y, z^*_1] \mid [y, z'] \in h^1(z, x)\}, & \text{if } z \in Z_1, \\ h^1(z^1_1, x) \cup \bigcup_{z' \in M_1} \{[y, z^*_1] \mid [y, z'] \in h^1(z^1_1, x)\}, & \text{if } z = z^*_1. \end{cases}$$

We shall show that $\langle\psi_1\rangle$ is represented in $\mathfrak{B}^* = [X, Y, Z^*, h^*]$ by $[z^*_1, \{z^*_1\}]$. Indeed,

$$h^*_{z^*_1}(z^*_1, e) = \{e\} = \langle\psi_1\rangle(e)$$

and for $p = x_1 \ldots x_n \in W(X)$, $n \geqq 1$, $q = y_1 \ldots y_n$ we have

$$q \in \langle\psi_1\rangle(p) \leftrightarrow \exists k\, \exists p_1 \ldots \exists p_k\, \exists q_1 \ldots \exists q_k \Big(1 \leqq k \leqq n \wedge p_1 \ldots p_k = p$$
$$\wedge\, q_1 \ldots q_k = q \wedge \bigwedge_{\varkappa=1}^{k} \big(p_\varkappa \neq e \wedge q_\varkappa \in h^1_{M_1}(z^1_1, p_\varkappa)\big)\Big).$$

$q_\varkappa \in h^1_{M_1}(z^1_1, p_\varkappa)$ implies $q_\varkappa \in h^*_{z^*_1}(z^*_1, p_\varkappa)$, hence $q \in h^*_{z^*_1}(z^*_1, p)$, i.e. $\langle\psi_1\rangle(p) \subseteq h^*_{z^*_1}(z^*_1, p)$.

Conversely, let

$$q = y_1 \dots y_n \in h^*_{z_1^*}(z_1^*, x_1 \dots x_n).$$

Then there is a sequence of states $z_2^*, \dots, z_n^*, z_{n+1}^*$ with

$$z_{n+1}^* = z_1^* \text{ and } \bigwedge_{\nu=1}^{n} [y_\nu, z_{\nu+1}^*] \in h^*(z_\nu^*, x_\nu).$$

Let $0 = l_0 < l_1 < \dots < l_k = n$ be those integers j for which $z_{j+1}^* = z_1^*$. Then we have

$$y_{l_\varkappa+1} \dots y_{l_{\varkappa+1}} \in h^*_{z_1^*}(z_1^*, x_{l_\varkappa+1} \dots x_{l_{\varkappa+1}})$$

or $\varkappa = 0, \dots, k$, and

$$z_{l_\varkappa+2}^*, \dots, z_{l_{\varkappa+1}}^* \in Z_1,$$

hence

$$y_{l_\varkappa+1} \dots y_{l_{\varkappa+1}} \in h^1_{M_1}(z_1^1, x_{l_\varkappa+1} \dots x_{l_{\varkappa+1}}) = \psi_1(x_{l_\varkappa+1} \dots x_{l_{\varkappa+1}}).$$

Hence, $q \in \langle \psi_1 \rangle (p)$.

Corollary 4.16. A GND-operator is regular if and only if it can be constructed in a finite number of steps from ND-elementary operators using the operations $\cup, \cdot, \langle\,\rangle$.

Theorem 4.17. *A sequential ND-operator φ over $[X, Y]$ is regular if and only it can be constructed in a finite number of steps from ND-elementary operators over $[X, Y]$ using the operations $\cup, \cdot, \langle\,\rangle$.*

Proof: Since every regular ND-operator is a regular GND-operator, it suffices to show that every ND-operator which can be obtained in a finite number of steps from ND-elementary operators using the operations $\cup, \cdot, \langle\,\rangle$, is regular.

If φ is such an ND-operator, then by 4.11.2 and 4.15 there is a Z-finite ND-automaton $\mathfrak{B} = [X, Y, Z, h]$, a state $z_1 \in Z$ and a set $M \subseteq Z$ such that for all $p \in W(X)$

$$\varphi(p) = h_M(z_1, p).$$

We put

$$Z^* \underset{\text{Df}}{=} \{h_q(z_1, p) \mid p \in W(X) \wedge q \in \varphi(p)\}$$

and for $z^* = h_q(z_1, p) \in Z^*$, $x \in X$

$$h^*(z^*, x) \underset{\text{Df}}{=} \{[y, h_y(z^*, x)] \mid y \in h_M(z^*, x)\}.$$

Here, $Z^* \subseteq \mathfrak{P}(Z)$, consequently it is finite, and for all $z^* \in Z^*$, $z^* \cap M \neq \emptyset$. Furthermore, $h_y(z^*, x) = h_y(h_q(z_1, p), x) = h_{qy}(z_1, px)$, and

$$\begin{aligned} y \in h_M\big(h_q(z_1, p), x\big) &\leftrightarrow \exists z' \,(z' \in h_q(z_1, p) \wedge y \in h_M(z', x)) \\ &\leftrightarrow \exists z' \big(q \in h_{z'}(z_1, p) \wedge y \in h_M(z', x)\big) \\ &\leftrightarrow qy \in h_M(z_1, px). \end{aligned}$$

The relation $z^* = h_q(z_1, p) \in Z^*$ implies $q \in \varphi(p) = h_M(z_1, p)$. Since φ is sequential, for each $x \in X$ there is a $y \in Y$ with $qy \in \varphi(px) = h_M(z_1, px)$, i.e., a $y \in h_M(z^*, x)$ and a $z^{**} = h_{qy}(z_1, px)$ with $[y, z^{**}] \in h^*(z^*, x)$. Hence the system $\mathfrak{B}^* = [X, Y, Z^*, h^*]$ is a Z-finite ND-automaton. Furthermore, $\{z_1\} = h_e(z_1, e) \in Z^*$ (because $\varphi(e) = \{e\}$) and

$$\{e\} = \varphi(e) = v_{\mathfrak{B}^*}(\{z_1\}, e).$$

We show that for $p \neq e$

$$q \in \varphi(p) \leftrightarrow q \in v_{\mathfrak{B}^*}(\{z_1\}, p),$$

which is trivial if $l(p) \neq l(q)$. Let $p = x_1 \dots x_n$, $q = y_1 \dots y_n$ and $n \geqq 1$. Then

$$\begin{aligned} q \in v_{\mathfrak{B}^*}(\{z_1\}, p) \leftrightarrow\ & [y_1, h_{y_1}(\{z_1\}, x_1)] \in h^*(\{z_1\}, x_1) \\ & \wedge \bigwedge_{i=2}^{n} [y_i, h_{y_1 \dots y_i}(z_1, x_1 \dots x_i)] \\ & \qquad\qquad \in h^*\big(h_{y_1 \dots y_{i-1}}(z_1, x_1 \dots x_{i-1}), x_i\big) \\ \leftrightarrow\ & y_1 \in h_M(\{z_1\}, x_1) = h_M(z_1, x_1) \\ & \wedge \bigwedge_{i=2}^{n} y_i \in h_M\big(h_{y_1 \dots y_{i-1}}(z_1, x_1 \dots x_{i-1}), x_i\big). \end{aligned}$$

Now, for $i = 1, \dots, n$

$$\begin{aligned} & y_i \in h_M\big(h_{y_1 \dots y_{i-1}}(z_1, x_1 \dots x_{i-1}), x_i\big) \\ & \leftrightarrow \exists z_i\big(y_i \in h_M(z_i, x_i) \wedge y_1 \dots y_{i-1} \in h_{z_i}(z_1, x_1 \dots x_{i-1})\big) \\ & \leftrightarrow y_1 \dots y_i \in h_M(z_1, x_1 \dots x_i) = \varphi(x_1 \dots, x_i). \end{aligned}$$

and thus

$$\begin{aligned} q \in v_{\mathfrak{B}^*}(\{z_1\}, p) \leftrightarrow\ & \bigwedge_{i=0}^{n} y_1 \dots y_i \in \varphi(x_1 \dots x_i) \\ \leftrightarrow\ & q \in \varphi(p), \end{aligned}$$

since according to our assumption, φ is sequential. Thus Theorem 4.17 is proved.

To conclude this section, we establish a third criterion for the regularity of an ND-operator.

Theorem 4.18. *A sequential ND-operator over* $[X, Y]$ *is regular if and only if there is a finite set* $\{\varphi^1, \dots, \varphi^n\}$ *of sequential ND-operators over* $[X, Y]$ *such that*

a) *there is a subset* $M \subseteq \{1, \dots, n\}$ *with*

$$\varphi(p) = \bigcup_{j \in M} \varphi^j(p) \quad \textit{for all} \quad p \in W(X);$$

b) *for each* $i \in \{1, \dots, n\}$, $x \in X$, $y \in \varphi^i(x)$ *there is a set* $M(i, x, y) \subseteq \{1, \dots, n\}$ *with*

$$\varphi^i_{x,y}(p) = \bigcup_{j \in M(i,x,y)} \varphi^j(p) \quad \textit{for all} \quad p \in W(X).$$

Proof: I. Let φ be regular and $\mathfrak{B} = [X, Y, Z, h]$ be a Z-finite ND-automaton with $Z = \{1, \ldots, n\}$ in which φ is generated by the set $M \subseteq Z$. Then the ND-operators defined by

$$\varphi^i(p) = v_{\mathfrak{B}}(i, p) \text{ for } p \in W(X)$$

satisfy our requirements, since

$$\varphi(p) = \bigcup_{j \in M} v_{\mathfrak{B}}(j, p) = \bigcup_{j \in M} \varphi^j(p)$$

and for $i \in \{1, \ldots, n\}$, $x \in X$, $y \in \varphi_i(x)$ we have

$$\varphi^i_{x,y}(p) = \bigcup_{j \in h_y(i,x)} v_{\mathfrak{B}}(j, p) = \bigcup_{j \in h_y(i,x)} \varphi^j(p).$$

II. Conversely, if $\varphi^1, \ldots, \varphi^n$ are ND-operators with the above properties, we put

$$Z = \{1, \ldots, n\},$$

and for $i \in Z$, $x \in X$

$$h(i, x) = \{[y, j] \mid y \in \varphi^i(x) \wedge j \in M(i, x, y)\}.$$

Since φ^i is a sequential ND-operator, for each $x \in X$ there is a $y \in Y$ with $y \in \varphi^i(x)$, i.e., such that $M(i, x, y)$ is defined and non-empty. Consequently, $h(i, x) \neq \emptyset$, hence $\mathfrak{B} = [X, Y, Z, h]$ is an ND-automaton. We show by induction on p that for all $i \in Z$, $p \in W(X)$

$$\varphi^i(p) = v_{\mathfrak{B}}(i, p).$$

The initial step $p = e$ is trivial. The step from p to xp:

$$\begin{aligned} v_{\mathfrak{B}}(i, xp) &= \bigcup_{y \in Y} \{y\} \cdot v_{\mathfrak{B}}\big(h_y(i, x), p\big) \\ &= \bigcup_{y \in \varphi^i(x)} \{y\} \cdot v_{\mathfrak{B}}\big(M(i, x, y), p\big) \\ &= \bigcup_{y \in \varphi^i(x)} \{y\} \bigcup_{j \in M(i,x,y)} \varphi^j(p) \\ &= \bigcup_{y \in \varphi^i(x)} \{y\} \cdot \varphi^i_{x,y}(p) = \varphi^i(xp). \end{aligned}$$

Consequently,

$$\varphi(p) = \bigcup_{j \in M} \varphi^j(p) = v_{\mathfrak{B}}(M, p),$$

i.e., φ is generated by the set M in the Z-finite ND-automaton $\mathfrak{B}$ and thus is regular.

§ 5. Homogeneity

In this section we shall deal with a special class of ND-automata including all Z-deterministic ND-automata, as well as the class of non-deterministic operators which can be generated in the ND-automata of this class.

Definition 5.1. Let $\mathfrak{B} = [X, Y, Z, h]$ be an ND-automaton.

(5.1.1) $\mathfrak{B}$ is called *homogeneous with respect to the set of states* $M \subseteq Z$, if for all $p \in W(X)$, $x \in X$, $y \in Y$ we have: $qy \in v_{\mathfrak{B}}(M, px)$ does not depend on q, provided $q \in v_{\mathfrak{B}}(M, p)$.

If $\mathfrak{B}$ is homogeneous with respect to the singleton $\{z\}$, then we say that $\mathfrak{B}$ is *homogeneous with respect to* z.

(5.1.2) $\mathfrak{B}$ is called *homogeneous* if it is homogeneous with respect to each of its states.

(5.2.3) $\mathfrak{B}$ is called *strongly homogeneous* if it is homogeneous with respect to every (non-empty) set of states $M \subseteq Z$.

Corollary 5.1. Let $\mathfrak{B} = [X, Y, Z, h]$, $\mathfrak{B}' = [X, Y, Z', h']$ be ND-automata with the same input alphabet and the same output alphabet.

1. If $M \subseteq Z$, $M' \subseteq Z'$ and $M \sim M'$, then $\mathfrak{B}$ is homogeneous with respect to M if and only if $\mathfrak{B}'$ is homogeneous with respect to M'.
2. If $\mathfrak{B} \approx \mathfrak{B}'$, then $\mathfrak{B}$ is strongly homogeneous if and only if $\mathfrak{B}'$ is.
3. If $\mathfrak{B} \sim \mathfrak{B}'$, then $\mathfrak{B}$ is homogeneous if and only if $\mathfrak{B}'$ is.
4. Every homogeneous ND-automaton is equivalent to a homogeneous ND-Moore automaton with a deterministic marking function m.

Clearly there are ND-automata which are homogeneous but not strongly homogeneous. Such is for example the automaton $\mathfrak{B}_{15} = [\{x\}, \{0, 1\}, \{a, b\}, h^{15}]$, where we set $h^{15}(a, x) = \{[0, a]\}$ and $h^{15}(b, x) = \{[1, b]\}$. $\mathfrak{B}_{15}$ is not homogeneous with respect to $\{a, b\}$.

Let $\mathfrak{B} = [X, Y, Z, h]$ be an ND-automaton and $\emptyset \neq M \subseteq Z$. For all $p \in W(X)$, $x \in X$, $q \in W(Y)$ we put

$$Y^M_{px,q} \underset{\mathrm{Df}}{=} \{y \mid qy \in v_{\mathfrak{B}}(M, px)\}.$$

Lemma 5.2.

1. $Y^M_{px,q} \neq \emptyset \leftrightarrow q \in v_{\mathfrak{B}}(M, p)$.

2. $\mathfrak{B}$ *is homogeneous with respect to* M *if and only if for all* $p \in W(X)$, $x \in X$, $q, q' \in v_{\mathfrak{B}}(M, p)$

$$Y^M_{px,q} = Y^M_{px,q'}.$$

3. $\mathfrak{B}$ *is homogeneous with respect to* M *if and only if for all* $p \in W(X)$, $x \in X$, $q \in v_{\mathfrak{B}}(M, p)$ *we have* $Y^M_{px,q} = g(f(M, p), x)$.

Proof: Propositions 5.2.1 und 5.2.2 are obvious. To prove 5.2.3 (by 5.2.2), it suffices to show that the given equality is satisfied if $\mathfrak{B}$ is homogeneous with respect to M. It is clear that

$$Y^M_{px,q} \subseteq g\big(f(M, p), x\big)$$

independently of whether $\mathfrak{B}$ is homogeneous with respect to M or not. Let $p \in W(X)$, $x \in X$, $y \in g\big(f(M, p), x\big)$. Then there is a $z' \in f(M, p)$ with $y \in g(z', x)$.

By 5.2.2, $Y^M_{px,q}$ does not depend on q, provided $q \in v_{\mathfrak{B}}(M, p)$, hence, if $\mathfrak{B}$ is homogeneous with respect to M, for all $q \in v_{\mathfrak{B}}(M, p)$ we have

$$g\big(f(M, p), x\big) \subseteq Y^M_{px,q}.$$

Thus Lemma 5.2 is proved.

Theorem 5.3. *The ND-automaton* $\mathfrak{B} = [X, Y, Z, h]$ *is homogeneous with respect to the set of states* $M \subseteq Z$ *if and only if for all* $p \in W(X)$, $x \in X$

$$v_{\mathfrak{B}}(M, px) = v_{\mathfrak{B}}(M, p)g\big(f(M, p), x\big).$$

Proof: $\mathfrak{B}$ is homogeneous with respect to M if and only if

$$\forall p\, \forall x\, \forall q\big(p \in W(X) \wedge x \in X \wedge q \in v_{\mathfrak{B}}(M, p) \\ \rightarrow Y^M_{px,q} = g(f(M, p), x)\big),$$

i.e., if the following assertion is true:

$$\forall p\, \forall x\, \forall q\, \forall y\big(p \in W(X) \wedge x \in X \wedge q \in v_{\mathfrak{B}}(M, p) \wedge y \in Y \\ \rightarrow \big(qy \in v_{\mathfrak{B}}(M, px) \leftrightarrow y \in g(f(M, p), x)\big)\big).$$

This assertion is equivalent to

$$\forall p\, \forall x\, \forall q\, \forall y\big(p \in W(X) \wedge x \in X \wedge q \in W(Y) \wedge y \in Y \\ \rightarrow \big(qy \in v_{\mathfrak{B}}(M, px) \leftrightarrow q \in v_{\mathfrak{B}}(M, p) \wedge y \in g(f(M, p), x)\big)\big),$$

and thus to

$$\forall p\, \forall x\big(p \in W(X) \wedge x \in X \rightarrow v_{\mathfrak{B}}(M, px) = v_{\mathfrak{B}}(M, p)g(f(M, p), x)\big),$$

which was to be shown.

By an easy induction on r we can prove the following result:

Corollary 5.4. The ND-automaton $\mathfrak{B} = [X, Y, Z, h]$ is homogeneous with respect to $M \subseteq Z$, if and only if

$$v_{\mathfrak{B}}(M, pr) = v_{\mathfrak{B}}(M, p) \cdot v_{\mathfrak{B}}(f(M, p), r) \quad \text{for all} \quad p, r \in W(X).$$

Theorem 5.5. *The ND-automaton* $\mathfrak{B} = [X, Y, Z, h]$ *is homogeneous with respect to* $M \subseteq Z$ *if and only if for all* $p \in W(X)$, $\mathfrak{B}$ *is homogeneous with respect to* $f(M, p)$.

Proof: Since $f(M, e) = M$, it suffices to show that $\mathfrak{B}$ is homogeneous with respect to $f(M, p)$, provided it is homogeneous with respect to M. In this case for all $p, r \in W(X)$, $x \in X$

$$v_{\mathfrak{B}}(M, p) v_{\mathfrak{B}}\big(f(M, p), rx\big) = v_{\mathfrak{B}}(M, prx)$$
$$= v_{\mathfrak{B}}(M, p) v_{\mathfrak{B}}\big(f(M, p), r\big) g\big(f(f(M, p), r), x\big),$$

which implies the equality

$$v_{\mathfrak{B}}\big(f(M, p), rx\big) = v_{\mathfrak{B}}\big(f(M, p), r\big) g\big(f(f(M, p), r), x\big).$$

Thus, by 5.3, $\mathfrak{B}$ is homogeneous with respect to $f(M, p)$.

Theorem 5.6. *The ND-automaton* $\mathfrak{B} = [X, Y, Z, h]$ *is homogeneous with respect to* $M \subseteq Z$ $(M \neq \emptyset)$, *if and only if for all* $p \in W(X)$, $Q \subseteq v_{\mathfrak{B}}(M, p)$ *with* $Q \neq \emptyset$, $\mathfrak{B}$ *is homogeneous with respect to the set* $h_Q(M, p)$.

Proof: If $\mathfrak{B}$ is homogeneous with respect to M, for $p, r \in W(X)$

$$\bigcup_{q \in v_{\mathfrak{B}}(M, p)} \{q\} \cdot v_{\mathfrak{B}}\big(h_q(M, p), r\big) = v_{\mathfrak{B}}(M, pr) = v_{\mathfrak{B}}(M, p) v_{\mathfrak{B}}\big(f(M, p), r\big).$$

Hence for $p, r \in W(X)$, $q \in v_{\mathfrak{B}}(M, p)$, $s \in W(Y)$

$$s \in v_{\mathfrak{B}}\big(h_q(M, p), r\big) \leftrightarrow s \in v_{\mathfrak{B}}\big(f(M, p), r\big),$$

i.e., for all $p \in W(X)$, $q \in v_{\mathfrak{B}}(M, p)$ we have $h_q(M, p) \sim f(M, p)$, consequently for all Q with $\emptyset \neq Q \subseteq v_{\mathfrak{B}}(M, p)$, $h_Q(M, p) \sim f(M, p)$.

By 5.5, $\mathfrak{B}$ is homogeneous with respect to $f(M, p)$, hence $\mathfrak{B}$ is also homogeneous with respect to $h_Q(M, p)$. The converse is trivial because $h_e(M, e) = M$.

Corollary 5.7.

1. $\mathfrak{B}$ is homogeneous with respect to $M \neq \emptyset$, if and only if for all $p \in W(X)$ and Q, Q' with $\emptyset \neq Q, Q' \subseteq v_{\mathfrak{B}}(M, p)$ we have $h_Q(M, p) \sim h_{Q'}(M, p)$ $(\sim f(M, p))$.
2. If $\mathfrak{B}$ is homogeneous, and for each $M \subseteq Z$, $M \neq \emptyset$ there are $z \in Z$, $p \in W(X)$, $Q \subseteq v_{\mathfrak{B}}(M, p)$ with $M = h_Q(z, p)$, then $\mathfrak{B}$ is strongly homogeneous.
3. If $\mathfrak{B}$ is reduced, homogeneous and observable, then $\mathfrak{B}$ is Z-deterministic.

Clearly, Propositions 5.7.1 and 5.7.2 are valid. If $\mathfrak{B} = [X, Y, Z, h]$ is observable and homogeneous, then by 5.7.1, for $z \in Z$, $x \in X$, $y, y' \in g(z, x)$, the sets $h_y(z, x)$, $h_{y'}(z, x)$ are equivalent singletons. Since $\mathfrak{B}$ is reduced, this implies $h_y(z, x) = h_{y'}(z, x) = h_{g(z,x)}(z, x) = f(z, x)$. Thus for every $z \in Z$, $x \in X$, $f(z, x)$ is a singleton, hence $\mathfrak{B}$ is Z-deterministic.

Theorem 5.8. *Every Z-deterministic ND-automaton is homogeneous.*

This follows immediately from the fact that for every Z-deterministic ND-automaton $\mathfrak{B} = [X, Y, Z, h]$, and for all $z \in Z$, $x_1 \dots x_n \in W(X)$

$$v_{\mathfrak{B}}(z, x_1 \dots x_n) = g(z, x_1) g\big(f(z, x_1), x_2\big) \dots g\big(f(z, x_1 \dots x_{n-1}), x_n\big).$$

Theorem 5.9. *For each (finite) homogeneous ND-automaton $\mathfrak{B}$, there is a (finite) homogeneous Z-determistic ND-automaton $\mathfrak{B}^*$, which is weakly equivalent to $\mathfrak{B}$ and into which $\mathfrak{B}$ is equivalently embedded.*

Proof: Let $\mathfrak{B} = [X, Y, Z, h]$, $Z^* \underset{\mathrm{Df}}{=} \{M \mid \exists z \, \exists p \big(z \in Z \wedge p \in W(X) \wedge M = f(z, p)\big)\}$, and for $z^* \in Z^*$ and $x \in X$ put

$$f^*(z^*, x) \underset{\mathrm{Df}}{=} \{f(z^*, x)\}, \qquad g^*(z^*, x) \underset{\mathrm{Df}}{=} g(z^*, x).$$

$\mathfrak{B}^* = [X, Y, Z^*, f^*, g^*]$ is a Z-deterministic, hence homogeneous ND-Mealy automaton. For all $z \in Z$, $p \in W(X)$ we have

$$f^*(z^*, p) = \{f(z^*, p)\},$$

as can be easily shown (for instance by induction on p). Next we show by induction on p that for all $z^* \in Z^*$

$$v_{\mathfrak{B}}(z^*, p) = v_{\mathfrak{B}^*}(z^*, p)$$

i.e., the state z^* of $\mathfrak{B}^*$ is equivalent to z^* as a set of states of $\mathfrak{B}$.

Thus we show that, a) for each state $z \in Z$ of $\mathfrak{B}$, there is an equivalent state $z^* = \{z\}$ of $\mathfrak{B}^*$, hence $\mathfrak{B} \subsetneq \mathfrak{B}^*$, and b) for each state z^* of $\mathfrak{B}^*$ there is an equivalent set of states of $\mathfrak{B}$, namely $M = z^*$, which together with a) implies $\mathfrak{B}^* \approx \mathfrak{B}$.

The initial step of the induction is trivial; the induction step is taken from p to px:

$$v_{\mathfrak{B}}(z^*, px) = v_{\mathfrak{B}}(z^*, p) g\big(f(z^*, p), x\big),$$

since z^* is a set of the form $f(z, r)$ for $z \in Z$, $r \in W(X)$, and by 5.5 $\mathfrak{B}$ is homogeneous with respect to all such sets. By the induction hypothesis, we have

$$v_{\mathfrak{B}}(z^*, p) = v_{\mathfrak{B}^*}(z^*, p).$$

Furthermore,

$$\{f(z^*, p)\} = f^*(z^*, p),$$
$$g\big(f(z^*, p), x\big) = g^*\big(f(z^*, p), x\big) = g^*\big(\{f(z^*, p)\}, x\big),$$

thus we have

$$v_{\mathfrak{B}}(z^*, px) = v_{\mathfrak{B}^*}(z^*, p) g^*\big(f^*(z^*, p), x\big) = v_{\mathfrak{B}^*}(z^*, px),$$

because $\mathfrak{B}^*$, as a Z-deterministic automaton, is homogeneous.

Theorem 5.10. *Let* $\mathfrak{B} = [X, Y, Z, h]$ *be an ND-automaton and* $\mathfrak{B}_M = [X, Y$ $Z, f, g]$ *the ND-Mealy automaton with the transition and output functions of* $\mathfrak{B}$. *Then we have*

1. *If* $\mathfrak{B}$ *is homogeneous with respect to* $M \subseteq Z$, *then* $v_{\mathfrak{B}}(M, p) = v_{\mathfrak{B}_M}(M, p)$ *for all* $p \in W(X)$ *and* $\mathfrak{B}_M$ *is also homogeneous with respect to* M.

2. *If* $\mathfrak{B}$ *is homogeneous, or strongly homogeneous, then* $\mathfrak{B} \sim \mathfrak{B}_M$, *and* $\mathfrak{B}_M$ *is also homogeneous or strongly homogeneous.*

Proof: Obviously it suffices to prove the first part of Proposition 5.10.1. For $x \in X$, $z \in Z$, let $h^M(z, x) = g(z, x) \times f(z, x)$, hence $\mathfrak{B}_M = [X, Y, Z, h^M]$. Furthermore, let $\mathfrak{H}$ be the system of all subsets $M \subseteq Z$ with respect to which $\mathfrak{B}$ is homogeneous.

If $M \in \mathfrak{H}$, then for all $x \in X$, $y \in g(M, x)$

$$f(M, x) \sim h_y(M, x),$$

as was shown in the proof of Theorem 5.6. On the other hand, for $x \in X$, $y \in g(M, x)$ we have

$$h_y(M, x) \subseteq h_y^M(M, x) = f(M, x).$$

Thus for all $M \in \mathfrak{H}$, $x \in X$, $y \in g(M, x)$, $p \in W(X)$ we have

$$v_{\mathfrak{B}}\big(h_y(M, x), p\big) = v_{\mathfrak{B}}\big(h_y^M(M, x), p\big) = v_{\mathfrak{B}}\big(f(M, x), p\big)$$

and

$$f(M, x) \in \mathfrak{H}, \quad h_y^M(M, x) \in \mathfrak{H}, \quad h_y(M, x) \in \mathfrak{H}.$$

We show by induction on p that for all $M \in \mathfrak{H}$, $p \in W(X)$

$$v_{\mathfrak{B}}(M, p) = v_{\mathfrak{B}_M}(M, p).$$

The initial step $p = e$ is trivial. The step from p to xp:

$$\begin{aligned} v_{\mathfrak{B}}(M, xp) &= \bigcup_{y \in g(M,x)} \{y\} \cdot v_{\mathfrak{B}}\big(h_y(M, x), p\big) \\ &= \bigcup_{y \in g(M,x)} \{y\} \cdot v_{\mathfrak{B}}\big(h_y^M(M, x), p\big) \\ &= \bigcup_{y \in g(M,x)} \{y\} \cdot v_{\mathfrak{B}_M}\big(h_y^M(M, x), p\big) \quad \text{(by the induction hypothesis)} \\ &= v_{\mathfrak{B}_M}(M, xp). \end{aligned}$$

Thus Theorem 5.10 is proved.

Theorem 5.11. *Let* $\mathfrak{B} = [X, Y, Z, h]$, $\mathfrak{B}' = [X', Y', Z', h']$ *be ND-automata and* $\chi = [\xi, \eta, \zeta]$ *a homomorphism of* $\mathfrak{B}$ *onto* $\mathfrak{B}'$.

1. *If $\mathfrak{B}$ is homogeneous with respect to the set $M \subseteq Z$, then $\mathfrak{B}'$ is homogeneous with respect to $\zeta(M)$.*

2. *If $\mathfrak{B}$ is homogeneous, or strongly homogeneous, so is $\mathfrak{B}'$.*

Proof: Since ζ is a mapping of Z onto Z', or of $\mathfrak{P}(Z)$ onto $\mathfrak{P}(Z')$, 5.11.1 implies Proposition 5.11.2. Let $M \subseteq Z$; then $\mathfrak{B}$ is homogeneous with respect to M, if and only if for all $p, r \in W(X)$

$$v_{\mathfrak{B}}(M, pr) = v_{\mathfrak{B}}(M, p) \cdot v_{\mathfrak{B}}\big(f(M, p), r\big).$$

From this equality it follows that for all $p, r \in W(X)$

$$\eta\big(v_{\mathfrak{B}}(M, pr)\big) = \eta\big(v_{\mathfrak{B}}(M, p)\big) \cdot \eta\big(v_{\mathfrak{B}}(f(M, p), r)\big),$$

i.e., since χ is a homomorphism of $\mathfrak{B}$ onto $\mathfrak{B}'$, we have

$$v_{\mathfrak{B}'}\big(\zeta(M), \xi(pr)\big) = v_{\mathfrak{B}'}\big(\zeta(M), \xi(p)\big) \cdot v_{\mathfrak{B}'}\big(\zeta(f(M, p)), \xi(r)\big).$$

We can easily show that for all $M \subseteq Z$, $p \in W(X)$

$$\zeta\big(f(M, p)\big) = f'\big(\zeta(M), \xi(p)\big)$$

is satisfied.

Since ξ is a mapping of $W(X)$ onto $W(X')$, this implies for all $p', r' \in W(X')$

$$v_{\mathfrak{B}'}\big(\zeta(M), p'r'\big) = v_{\mathfrak{B}'}\big(\zeta(M), p'\big) v_{\mathfrak{B}'}\big(f'(\zeta(M), p'), r'\big),$$

hence $\mathfrak{B}'$ is homogeneous with respect to $\zeta(M)$.

From the proof it is obvious that the following assertions hold:

Corollary 5.12. If $\mathfrak{B} = [X, Y, Z, h]$, $\mathfrak{B}' = [X', Y', Z', h']$ are ND-automata and $\chi = [\xi, I_Y, \zeta]$ is an $[X, Z]$-homomorphism of $\mathfrak{B}$ onto $\mathfrak{B}'$, then for any $M \subseteq Z$, the ND-automaton $\mathfrak{B}$ is homogeneous with respect to M if and only if $\mathfrak{B}'$ is homogeneous with respect to $\zeta(M)$. Furthermore, $\mathfrak{B}$ is homogeneous or strongly homogeneous if and only if $\mathfrak{B}'$ is.

To conclude this section, we shall examine certain properties of sequential ND-operators which are generable in homogeneous ND-automata.

Definition 5.2. A sequential ND-operator φ over $[X, Y]$ is called *homogeneous* if there is an ND-automaton $\mathfrak{B} = [X, Y, Z, h]$ and a (non-empty) set $M \subseteq Z$ such that $\mathfrak{B}$ is homogeneous with respect to M and φ is generated by M in $\mathfrak{B}$.

Let φ be an arbitrary sequential ND-operator over $[X, Y]$. If φ is generated by $M \subseteq Z$ $(M \neq \emptyset)$ in $\mathfrak{B} = [X, Y, Z, h]$, then for $p \in W(X)$, $x \in X$, $q \in W(Y)$, we have

$$Y^M_{px,q} = \{y \mid qy \in v_{\mathfrak{B}}(M, px)\} = \{y \mid qy \in \varphi(px)\} = \begin{cases} \varphi_{p,q}(x), & \text{if } q \in \varphi(p), \\ \emptyset & \text{otherwise.} \end{cases}$$

This, together with Propositions 5.2 to 5.5, implies the assertions of the following theorem.

Theorem 5.13. *If φ is a sequential ND-operator over $[X, Y]$, then the following propositions are equivalent.*

(1) *φ is homogeneous.*

(2) *For all $p \in W(X)$, $x \in X$, $q, q' \in \varphi(p)$ we have $\varphi_{p,q}(x) = \varphi_{p,q'}(x)$.*

(3) *For all $p \in W(X)$, $x \in X$, $Q \subseteq \varphi(p)$ with $Q \neq \emptyset$, $q \in \varphi(p)$ we have $\varphi_{p,Q}(x) = \varphi_{p,q}(x)$.*

(4) *For all $p \in W(X)$, $x \in X$, $\varphi(px) = \varphi(p)\varphi_{p,\varphi(p)}(x)$.*

(5) *For all $p, r \in W(X)$, $\varphi(pr) = \varphi(p)\varphi_{p,\varphi(p)}(r)$.*

(6) *For all $p \in W(X)$, $\emptyset \neq Q \subseteq \varphi(p)$, $q \in \varphi(p)$, $\varphi_{p,Q} = \varphi_{p,q}$.*

(7) *All the states of φ are homogeneous.*

Clearly, every deterministic ND operator is homogeneous. Therefore in the theory of deterministic abstract automata, the concept of homogeneity has no significance.

Theorem 5.14. *A sequential ND-operator φ over $[X, Y]$ is homogeneous if and only if φ can be generated by a state in a Z-deterministic (hence homogeneous) ND-(Mealy)-automaton, which has at most as many states as φ.*

To prove this, we consider the ND-automaton $\mathfrak{B} = [X, Y, Z, f, g]$ where $Z \underset{\mathrm{Df}}{=} \{\varphi_{p,\varphi(p)} \mid p \in W(X)\}$ and f, g are defined for $\varphi_{p,\varphi(p)} \in Z$, $x \in X$ as follows:

$$f(\varphi_{p,\varphi(p)}, x) \underset{\mathrm{Df}}{=} \{\varphi_{px,\varphi(px)}\}, \qquad g(\varphi_{p,\varphi(p)}, x) \underset{\mathrm{Df}}{=} \varphi_{p,\varphi(p)}(x).$$

We can easily show that $\varphi_{p,\varphi(p)} = \varphi_{r,\varphi(r)}$ implies $\varphi_{px,\varphi(px)} = \varphi_{rx,\varphi(rx)}$ for arbitrary $x \in X$, hence the definition of f is admissible. Thus $\mathfrak{B}$ is an ND-automaton of the desired type, since Z consists of exactly the states of φ, and as can be easily seen, the state $\varphi_{e,\varphi(e)}$ generates in $\mathfrak{B}$ the ND-operator φ.

Finally, we give one more criterion of whether a homogeneous ND-operator φ over the finite alphabets X, Y can be generated in a finite ND-automaton, (i.e., whether φ has only a finite number of states).

Theorem 5.15. *Let X, Y be finite, non-empty sets, and φ a homogeneous ND-operator over $[X, Y]$. φ can be generated in a finite ND-automaton if and only if for all $y \in Y$, the set $E_y = \{px \mid y \in \varphi_{p,\varphi(p)}(x)\}$ is a regular event.*

Proof: We first assume that φ can be generated in a finite ND-automaton. Then by 4.8.1, φ only has a finite number of states und therefore by Theorem 5.14, it can be generated by a state in a finite Z-deterministic ND-automaton, and consequently by Theorem 2.3, it can be generated in a finite Z-deterministic ND-Moore automaton $\mathfrak{B} = [X, Y, Z, f, m]$ by a state $z^* \in Z$. Let us put for $y \in Y$

$$M_y \underset{\mathrm{Df}}{=} \{z \mid z \in Z \wedge y \in m(z)\}.$$

Since f is deterministic, the function $\delta = Det(f)$ exists, and for all $z \in Z$, $p \in W(X)$ we have $f(z, p) = \{\delta(z, p)\}$.

Let $z^0 \notin Z$, and for $x \in X$

$$\delta(z^0, x) \underset{\text{Df}}{=} \delta(z^*, x).$$

Thus for all $p \in W(X) \setminus \{e\}$

$$f(z^*, p) = \{\delta(z^0, p)\}.$$

The system $[X, Z \cup \{z^0\}, \delta, z^0]$ is a finite outputless initial deterministic abstract automaton. We claim that for all $p \in W(X)$

$$p \in E_y \leftrightarrow \delta(z^0, p) \in M_y.$$

For $p = e$ this is trivial. Suppose $p = rx \in W(X) \setminus \{e\}$. Then we have

$$\begin{aligned} rx \in E_y &\leftrightarrow y \in \varphi_{r, \varphi(r)}(x) \\ &\leftrightarrow \exists s\big(s \in \varphi(r) \wedge sy \in \varphi(rx)\big) \\ &\leftrightarrow \exists s\big(s \in v_{\mathfrak{B}}(z^*, r) \wedge sy \in v_{\mathfrak{B}}(z^*, rx)\big) \\ &\leftrightarrow \exists s\big(s \in v_{\mathfrak{B}}(z^*, r) \wedge y \in v_{\mathfrak{B}}(f(z^*, r), x)\big) \\ &\leftrightarrow y \in v_{\mathfrak{B}}\big(f(z^*, r), x\big) \\ &\leftrightarrow y \in m\big(\delta(z^*, rx)\big) \\ &\leftrightarrow y \in m\big(\delta(z^0, rx)\big) \\ &\leftrightarrow \delta(z^0, rx) \in M_y. \end{aligned}$$

Thus, for any $y \in Y$, the event E_y is representable in a finite outputless deterministic automaton, and consequently it is regular.

Conversely, assume that E_y is a regular event for each $y \in Y$. Therefore, since X and Y are finite, there is a finite deterministic outputless (initial) automaton $\mathfrak{A} = [X, Z, \delta, z^0]$, which is connected from the state z^0, such that for each $y \in Y$ there is a set $M_y \subseteq Z$ which represents E_y in $\mathfrak{A}$. Clearly,

$$\bigcup_{y \in Y} E_y = W(X) \setminus \{e\},$$

and $\mathfrak{A}$ can be chosen in such a way that for all $p \in W(X) \setminus \{e\}$

$$\delta(z^0, p) \neq z^0.$$

Let us put for $z \in Z$, $x \in X$

$$f(z, x) \underset{\text{Df}}{=} \{\delta(z, x)\},$$

$$m(z) \underset{\text{Df}}{=} \begin{cases} Y, & \text{if} \quad z = z^0, \\ \{y \mid z \in M_y\}, & \text{if} \quad z \in Z \setminus \{z^0\}. \end{cases}$$

$\mathfrak{B} = [X, Y, Z, f, m]$ is a finite Z-deterministic, hence homogeneous, ND-Moore automaton. Since $\mathfrak{A}$ is connected, for each $z \in Z \setminus \{z^0\}$ there is a $p \in W(X) \setminus \{e\}$ $= \bigcup_{y \in Y} E_y$ with $\delta(z^0, p) = Z$ i.e., a $y \in Y$ and a $p \in E_y$ with $\delta(z^0, p) = z$, hence

$z \in M_y$. This implies $m(z) \neq \emptyset$ for all $z \in Z$. We claim that the state $z^0 \in Z$ generates the ND-operator φ in $\mathfrak{B}$, i.e., for all $p \in W(X)$

$$\varphi(p) = v_{\mathfrak{B}}(z^0, p).$$

We prove this by induction on p. The initial step $p = e$ is trivial. The step from p to px:

$$\begin{aligned}\varphi(px) &= \varphi(p) \cdot \varphi_{p,\varphi(p)}(x) \\ &= v_{\mathfrak{B}}(z^0, p) \cdot \{y \mid px \in E_y\} \\ &= v_{\mathfrak{B}}(z^0, p) \cdot \{y \mid \delta(z^0, px) \in M_y\} \\ &= v_{\mathfrak{B}}(z^0, p) \cdot m\big(\delta(z^0, px)\big) \\ &= v_{\mathfrak{B}}(z^0, p) \cdot v_{\mathfrak{B}}\big(f(z^0, p), x\big) = v_{\mathfrak{B}}(z^0, px).\end{aligned}$$

Thus Theorem 5.15 is proved.

If φ is a sequential ND-operator over $[X, Y]$, then we define a function $\mathfrak{E}^\varphi$ on Y as follows:

$$\mathfrak{E}^\varphi(y) \underset{\mathrm{Df}}{=} \{px \mid px \in W(X) \setminus \{e\} \wedge y \in \varphi_{p,\varphi(p)}(x)\}.$$

Thus the values of $\mathfrak{E}^\varphi$ are subsets of $W(X) \setminus \{e\}$ and

$$\bigcup_{y \in Y} \mathfrak{E}^\varphi(y) = W(X) \setminus \{e\}.$$

Theorem 5.16. *For each non-empty set Y, and every function $\mathfrak{E}$ defined on Y, whose values are subsets of $W(X) \setminus \{e\}$ for a certain non-empty set X, and for which $\bigcup_{y \in Y} \mathfrak{E}(y) = W(X) \setminus \{e\}$, there is exactly one homogeneous ND-operator φ over $[X, Y]$ such that $\mathfrak{E}^\varphi = \mathfrak{E}$.*

Proof: One can easily verify by induction on p that the ND-operator φ over $[X, Y]$ defined below, is homogeneous:

$$\begin{aligned}\varphi(e) &= \{e\}, \\ \varphi(px) &= \varphi(p) \cdot \{y \mid px \in \mathfrak{E}(y)\}.\end{aligned}$$

Clearly, $\mathfrak{E}^\varphi = \mathfrak{E}$. It remains to show that for homogeneous ND-operators φ, φ' over $[X, Y]$, $\mathfrak{E}^\varphi = \mathfrak{E} = \mathfrak{E}^{\varphi'}$ implies $\varphi = \varphi'$, i.e., $\varphi(p) = \varphi'(p)$ for all $p \in W(X)$. This is shown by induction on p, where the initial step $p = e$ is trivial. The step from p to px:

$$\begin{aligned}\varphi(px) &= \varphi(p)\varphi_{p,\varphi(p)}(x) = \varphi(p) \cdot \{y \mid px \in \mathfrak{E}^\varphi(y)\} \\ &= \varphi'(p) \cdot \{y \mid px \in \mathfrak{E}^{\varphi'}(y)\} = \varphi'(p)\varphi'_{p,\varphi'(p)}(x) = \varphi'(px).\end{aligned}$$

Corollary 5.17. For homogeneous ND-operators over $[X, Y]$, the correspondence between φ and $\mathfrak{E}^\varphi$ is one-to-one. If φ is a sequential ND-operator and $\bar{\varphi}$ denotes the homogeneous ND-operator over $[X, Y]$ corresponding to $\mathfrak{E}^\varphi$, then for all $p \in W(X)$

$$\varphi(p) \subseteq \bar{\varphi}(p).$$

§ 6. Closure Operations for Non-Deterministic Automata

In § 4 we have shown that every sequential ND-operator can be generated by a state in an ND-automaton. Furthermore, every state $\varphi_{p,Q}$ of an ND-operator φ generated by a state or a set of states in an ND-automaton $\mathfrak{B}$, can be generated in the same automaton $\mathfrak{B}$ by a set of states (Theorem 4.7). Starting from an arbitrary ND-automaton $\mathfrak{B}$, we can construct an ND-automaton $\tilde{\mathfrak{B}}$, in which exactly those ND-operators can be generated by a state which can be generated in $\mathfrak{B}$ by a set of states. In this section, we shall also describe a construction which, from an arbitrary ND-automaton $\mathfrak{B}$, leads to an ND-automaton $\hat{\mathfrak{B}}$, in which exactly those ND-operators can be generated by states which are generable in $\mathfrak{B}$ by states, or are states of such ND-operators. Further, we shall investigate the relationships between $\mathfrak{B}$, $\hat{\mathfrak{B}}$ and $\tilde{\mathfrak{B}}$ and the connection between $\hat{\mathfrak{B}}$, $\tilde{\mathfrak{B}}$ on one hand, and the ND-automata $\hat{\tilde{\mathfrak{B}}}$, $\tilde{\hat{\mathfrak{B}}}$, $\hat{\hat{\mathfrak{B}}}$, etc., on the other. The latter automata are obtained by repeated applications of the above constructions. It will turn out that these constructions have properties analogous to those of the closure operations.

Definition 6.1. If $\mathfrak{B} = [X, Y, Z, h]$ is an ND-automaton, then the ND-automaton $\tilde{\mathfrak{B}} = [X, Y, \mathfrak{P}^*(Z), \tilde{h}]$, where $\tilde{h}$ is defined for $N \in \mathfrak{P}^*(Z)$, $x \in X$ by

$$\tilde{h}(N, x) \underset{\mathrm{Df}}{=} \{[y, \{z'\}] \mid \exists z(z \in N \wedge [y, z'] \in h(z, x))\},$$

is called the *closure of* $\mathfrak{B}$.

Theorem 6.1. *If M is an arbitrary non-empty set of states of $\mathfrak{B}$, then the set M generates the same ND-operator in $\mathfrak{B}$, as the state M in $\tilde{\mathfrak{B}}$.*

Proof: We have to show that for all $M \in \mathfrak{P}^*(Z)$, $p \in W(X)$

$$v_{\mathfrak{B}}(M, p) = v_{\tilde{\mathfrak{B}}}(M, p).$$

The proof is carried out by induction on p. The initial step is trivial. To step from p to xp, we first remark that for all $M, N \in \mathfrak{P}^*(Z)$, $x \in X$, the set $\tilde{h}_N(M, x)$ can only be non-empty if N is a singleton; this is immediately clear from the definition of $\tilde{h}$. Furthermore we have $h_{z'}(M, x) = \tilde{h}_{\{z'\}}(M, x)$, since

$$\begin{aligned} y \in h_{z'}(M, x) &\leftrightarrow \exists z(z \in M \wedge [y, z'] \in h(z, x)) \\ &\leftrightarrow [y, \{z'\}] \in \tilde{h}(M, x) \\ &\leftrightarrow y \in \tilde{h}_{\{z'\}}(M, x). \end{aligned}$$

Using 1.5.6 we obtain

$$\begin{aligned} v_{\mathfrak{B}}(M, xp) &= \bigcup_{z' \in Z} h_{z'}(M, x) \cdot v_{\mathfrak{B}}(z', p) \\ &= \bigcup_{z' \in Z} \tilde{h}_{\{z'\}}(M, x) \cdot v_{\tilde{\mathfrak{B}}}(\{z'\}, p) \\ &= \bigcup_{N \in \mathfrak{P}^*(Z)} \tilde{h}_N(M, x) \cdot v_{\tilde{\mathfrak{B}}}(N, p) = v_{\tilde{\mathfrak{B}}}(M, xp). \end{aligned}$$

Corollary 6.2.

1. $\mathfrak{B}$ is equivalently embedded into $\tilde{\mathfrak{B}}$.
2. The ND-automata $\mathfrak{B}$, $\mathfrak{B}'$ are weakly equivalent if and only if their closures are.
3. $\mathfrak{B}$ and $\tilde{\mathfrak{B}}$ are weakly equivalent.

In $\tilde{\mathfrak{B}}$, the closure of the ND-automaton $\mathfrak{B}$, exactly those ND-operators can be generated by states which are generable in $\mathfrak{B}$ by sets of states. On the other hand, $\tilde{\mathfrak{B}}$ is weakly equivalent to $\mathfrak{B}$ (as can be easily seen by 2.1.5). Therefore, every ND-operator which can be generated by a set of states in $\tilde{\mathfrak{B}}$, can also be generated by a set of states in $\mathfrak{B}$, and consequently by a state in $\tilde{\mathfrak{B}}$. Thus the construction of $\tilde{\mathfrak{B}}$ leads to a saturation with respect to the generability of ND-operators. Exactly the same ND-operators can be generated in $\mathfrak{B}$ as in $\tilde{\mathfrak{B}}$, except that in $\tilde{\mathfrak{B}}$, they can already be generated by states. Therefore in general in the transition from $\mathfrak{B}$ to $\tilde{\mathfrak{B}}$, the property of being reduced is lost.

Theorem 6.3. *Let $\mathfrak{B}$, $\mathfrak{B}'$ be ND-automata with the same input and output alphabets.*

1. *If* $\mathfrak{B} \underset{\sim}{\subset} \mathfrak{B}'$, *then* $\tilde{\mathfrak{B}} \underset{\sim}{\subset} \tilde{\mathfrak{B}}'$.
2. $\tilde{\mathfrak{B}} \sim \tilde{\tilde{\mathfrak{B}}}$.

Proof: Proposition 6.3.1 can be easily verified if we recall that by 2.1.3, $\mathfrak{B} \underset{\sim}{\subset} \mathfrak{B}'$ implies $\mathfrak{B} \underset{\approx}{\subset} \mathfrak{B}'$. To prove 6.3.2 by 6.2.1, it suffices to show that for each state $\mathfrak{M} \in \mathfrak{P}^*(\mathfrak{P}^*(Z))$ of $\tilde{\tilde{\mathfrak{B}}}$ there is an equivalent state $M \in \mathfrak{P}^*(Z)$ of $\tilde{\mathfrak{B}}$. We claim that the set $M = \bigcup \mathfrak{M}$ satisfies this requirement. Namely we have

$$v_{\tilde{\tilde{\mathfrak{B}}}}(\mathfrak{M}, p) = v_{\tilde{\tilde{\mathfrak{B}}}}(\mathfrak{M}, p) = \bigcup_{N \in \mathfrak{M}} v_{\tilde{\mathfrak{B}}}(N, p) = \bigcup_{N \in \mathfrak{M}} v_{\mathfrak{B}}(N, p)$$

$$= \bigcup_{N \in \mathfrak{M}} \bigcup_{z \in N} v_{\mathfrak{B}}(z, p) = \bigcup_{z \in \bigcup \mathfrak{M}} v_{\mathfrak{B}}(z, p) = v_{\tilde{\mathfrak{B}}}\left(\bigcup \mathfrak{M}, p\right).$$

Thus Theorem 6.3 is proved.

Propositions 6.2.1, 6.3.1, and 6.3.2 characterize the construction of $\tilde{\mathfrak{B}}$ as an analogon of a closure operator. 6.2.1 corresponds to the embedding property, 6.3.1 to the monotonity, and 6.3.2 to the closedness property. This justifies the designation "closure of $\mathfrak{B}$" for $\tilde{\mathfrak{B}}$.

If we are interested in ND-operators which can be generated in $\mathfrak{B}$ by states, or which are states of such ND-operators, we can construct a corresponding closure $\hat{\mathfrak{B}}$ of $\mathfrak{B}$. This differs from $\tilde{\mathfrak{B}}$ in that it only contains certain non-empty subsets of Z as states, namely the sets of states realizable in $\mathfrak{B}$.

Definition 6.2. A non-empty set M of states of an ND-automaton $\mathfrak{B} = [X, Y, Z, h]$ is called *realizable in* $\mathfrak{B}$ if there are $z \in Z$, $p \in W(X)$ and a non-empty subset $Q \subseteq v_{\mathfrak{B}}(z, p)$ such that $M = h_Q(z, p)$.

We showed earlier that the set $h_Q(z, p)$ generates in $\mathfrak{B}$ the state $\varphi_{p,Q}$ of the ND-operator φ generated in $\mathfrak{B}$ by z.

Corollary 6.4.

1. All singletons $\{z\} \subseteq Z$ are realizable in $\mathfrak{B}$.

2. If $M = h_Q(z, p)$ is realizable in $\mathfrak{B}$, φ is the ND-operator generated by M in $\mathfrak{B}$, $r \in W(X)$ and $\emptyset \neq S \subseteq \varphi(r)$, then the set $h_S(M, r)$ is realizable in $\mathfrak{B}$ and

$$h_S(M, r) = h_S(h_Q(z, p), r) = h_{QS}(z, pr).$$

Corollary 6.4.2 follows directly from 4.8.3 and 1.5.5. From Theorem 5.6 we obtain

Corollary 6.5. $\mathfrak{B}$ is homogeneous if and only if $\mathfrak{B}$ is homogeneous with respect to each realizable set of states in $\mathfrak{B}$.

Definition 6.3. The ND-automata $\mathfrak{B}$, $\mathfrak{B}'$ with the same input and output alphabets are called *realizable equivalent* ($\mathfrak{B} \underset{r}{\sim} \mathfrak{B}'$), if for each set of states realizable in $\mathfrak{B}$, there is an equivalent set of states realizable in $\mathfrak{B}'$ and conversely, for each set of states realizable in $\mathfrak{B}'$ there is an equivalent set of states realizable in $\mathfrak{B}$.

Corollary 6.6.

1. If $\mathfrak{B} \sim \mathfrak{B}'$, then $\mathfrak{B} \underset{r}{\sim} \mathfrak{B}'$.

2. If $\mathfrak{B} \underset{r}{\sim} \mathfrak{B}'$, then $\mathfrak{B} \approx \mathfrak{B}'$.

To prove 6.6.1, it suffices to show that for states $z \in Z$, $z' \in Z'$, for all $p \in W(X)$, $\emptyset \neq Q \subseteq v_{\mathfrak{B}}(z, p) = v_{\mathfrak{B}'}(z', p)$, $z \sim z'$ implies the assertion $h_Q(z, p) \sim h'_Q(z', p)$. This follows immediately from Theorem 2.5.2. Proposition 6.6.2 is implied by 2.1.5 and by the fact that all singletons are realizable.

Definition 6.4. If $\mathfrak{B} = [X, Y, Z, h]$ is an arbitrary automaton, then the ND-automaton $\hat{\mathfrak{B}} = [X, Y, \mathfrak{Z}_r, \hat{h}]$, where $\mathfrak{Z}_r$ is the set of all subsets of $\mathfrak{Z}$ realizable in $\mathfrak{B}$, and $\hat{h}$ is the restriction of $\tilde{h}$ onto $\mathfrak{Z}_r \times X$, is called the *realizable closure of* $\mathfrak{B}$.

We denote by $\mathfrak{Z}_1$ the set of all singletons consisting of elements of Z. Since the values of the function $\tilde{h}$ are subsets of $Y \times \mathfrak{Z}_1$, $\tilde{h}$ could be restricted not only to $\mathfrak{Z}_r \times X$ but also to $\mathfrak{Z}_1 \times X$. The latter restriction is denoted by h_1. Thus for each ND-automaton $\mathfrak{B} = [X, Y, Z, h]$ the automata $\mathfrak{B}^1 = [X, Y, \mathfrak{Z}_1, h_1]$, $\hat{\mathfrak{B}} = [X, Y, \mathfrak{Z}_r, \hat{h}]$ and $\tilde{\mathfrak{B}} = [X, Y, \mathfrak{P}^*(Z), \tilde{h}]$ are defined. Clearly, $\mathfrak{B}^1$ is a subautomaton of both $\hat{\mathfrak{B}}$ and $\tilde{\mathfrak{B}}$, and $\hat{\mathfrak{B}}$ is a subautomaton of $\tilde{\mathfrak{B}}$ (cf. Definition 1.8). Furthermore, $\mathfrak{B}^1$ is obviously Z-isomorphic to $\mathfrak{B}$. Therefore, $\hat{\mathfrak{B}}$ and $\tilde{\mathfrak{B}}$ contain a subautomaton which is isomorphic to $\mathfrak{B}$. To express this we say that $\mathfrak{B}$ can be *isomorphically embedded* into $\hat{\mathfrak{B}}$ and $\tilde{\mathfrak{B}}$.

In the same way as we proved Theorem 6.1, we can verify

Theorem 6.7. *If M is a set of states realizable in the ND-automaton $\mathfrak{B}$, then M generates the same ND-operator in $\mathfrak{B}$ as the state M in $\hat{\mathfrak{B}}$.*

Corollary 6.8. Let $\mathfrak{B}$, $\mathfrak{B}'$ be ND-automata with the same input and output alphabets.

1. $\mathfrak{B}$ is equivalently embedded into $\hat{\mathfrak{B}}$.

2. $\mathfrak{B} \underset{r}{\sim} \mathfrak{B}'$ if and only if $\hat{\mathfrak{B}} \sim \hat{\mathfrak{B}}'$.

3. If $\mathfrak{B} \subseteq \mathfrak{B}'$, then $\hat{\mathfrak{B}} \subseteq \hat{\mathfrak{B}}'$.

4. $\mathfrak{B} \approx \hat{\mathfrak{B}}$.

Theorem 6.9. *Let* $\mathfrak{B} = [X, Y, Z, h]$ *be an arbitrary ND-automaton.*

1. *If* $\mathfrak{M}$ *is a realizable set of states in* $\hat{\mathfrak{B}}$, *(i.e., a state of* $\hat{\hat{\mathfrak{B}}}$*) and* $Card(\mathfrak{M}) \geqq 2$, *then* $\mathfrak{M}$ *only contains singletons and the set* $M = \bigcup \mathfrak{M}$ *is a realizable set of states in* $\mathfrak{B}$.

2. *There exists a strong Z-homomorphism of* $\hat{\hat{\mathfrak{B}}}$ *onto* $\hat{\mathfrak{B}}$.

3. $\hat{\mathfrak{B}} \sim \hat{\hat{\mathfrak{B}}}$.

Proof: By Corollary 3.6.2, it suffices to prove Propositions 6.9.1 and 6.9.2.

Let $\mathfrak{M}$ be a realizable set of states in $\hat{\mathfrak{B}}$, i.e.,

$$\mathfrak{M} = \hat{h}_Q(M, p),$$

where $M \in \mathfrak{Z}_r$, $p \in W(X)$, $\emptyset \neq Q \subseteq v_{\hat{\mathfrak{B}}}(M, p)$. $Card(\mathfrak{M}) \geqq 2$ implies $l(p) > 0$, since for $p = e$ $Q = \{e\}$, and $\hat{h}_e(M, e) = \{M\}$ is a singleton. Let $p = x_1 \ldots x_n$ $(n \geqq 1)$. Then

$$\begin{aligned}\mathfrak{M} &= \hat{h}_Q(M, p) \\ &= \Big\{M_{n+1} \mid \exists M_2 \ldots \exists M_n \exists y_1 \ldots \exists y_n \Big(y_1 \ldots y_n \in Q \\ &\qquad \wedge \bigwedge_{i=1}^{n} [y_i, M_{i+1}] \in \hat{h}(M_i, x_i)\Big)\Big\},\end{aligned}$$

where $M_1 = M$. From the definition of $\hat{h}$ (i.e., of $\tilde{h}$), it follows that the sets $M_2, \ldots, M_n, M_{n+1}$ are all singletons. Thus $\mathfrak{M}$ indeed contains only singletons. Furthermore

$$\begin{aligned}\mathfrak{M} = \Big\{\{z_{n+1}\} \mid \exists z_1 \exists z_2 \ldots \exists z_n \exists y_1 \ldots \exists y_n \Big(y_1 \ldots y_n \in Q \wedge z_1 \in M \\ \wedge \bigwedge_{i=1}^{n} [y_i, \{z_{i+1}\}] \in \hat{h}(\{z_i\}, x_i)\Big)\Big\}.\end{aligned}$$

Hence by the definitions of h

$$\begin{aligned}\mathfrak{M} &= \Big\{\{z_{n+1}\} \mid \exists z_1 \exists z_2 \ldots \exists z_n \exists y_1 \ldots \exists y_n \Big(z_1 \in M \wedge y_1 \ldots y_n \in Q \\ &\qquad \wedge \bigwedge_{i=1}^{n} [y_i, z_{i+1}] \in h(z_i, x_i)\Big)\Big\} \\ &= \Big\{\{z_{n+1}\} \mid z_{n+1} \in h_Q(M, p)\Big\}.\end{aligned}$$

Consequently, $\bigcup \mathfrak{M} = h_Q(M, p)$ and this set is realizable in $\mathfrak{B}$, since M is realizable in $\mathfrak{B}$ and $Q \subseteq v_{\hat{\mathfrak{B}}}(M, p) = v_{\mathfrak{B}}(M, p)$. Thus Proposition 6.9.1 is proved.

If $\mathfrak{M}$ is a state of $\hat{\hat{\mathfrak{B}}}$, then let

$$\zeta(\mathfrak{M}) \underset{\mathrm{Df}}{=} \bigcup \mathfrak{M}.$$

ζ is a single-valued mapping from the set of states of $\hat{\hat{\mathfrak{B}}}$ onto $\mathfrak{Z}_r$, since for all $M \in \mathfrak{Z}_r$ the set $\{M\}$ is realizable in $\hat{\mathfrak{B}}$. We claim that $\chi = [I_X, I_Y, \zeta]$ is a strong Z-homomorphism of $\hat{\hat{\mathfrak{B}}}$ onto $\hat{\mathfrak{B}}$. It suffices to show that for arbitrary states $\mathfrak{M}, \mathfrak{M}'$ of $\hat{\hat{\mathfrak{B}}}$, and all $x \in X$, $y \in Y$

$$[y, \mathfrak{M}'] \in \hat{\hat{h}}(\mathfrak{M}, x) \leftrightarrow [y, \zeta(\mathfrak{M}')] \in \hat{h}\big(\zeta(\mathfrak{M}), x\big).$$

If $\mathfrak{M}'$ is not a singleton, then $\zeta(\mathfrak{M}') = \bigcup \mathfrak{M}'$ is not either. In this case, both sides of the equivalence under consideration are false. Now we turn to the case where $\zeta(\mathfrak{M}') = \bigcup \mathfrak{M}'$ is a singleton. Then

$$\begin{aligned}
[y, \{M'\}] \in \hat{\hat{h}}(\mathfrak{M}, x) &\leftrightarrow \exists M\big(M \in \mathfrak{M} \wedge [y, M'] \in \hat{h}(M, x)\big)\\
&\leftrightarrow \exists M\big(M \in \mathfrak{M} \wedge \exists z' \exists z (M' = \{z'\} \wedge z \in M\\
&\qquad\qquad \wedge [y, z'] \in h(z, x))\big)\\
&\leftrightarrow \exists z \exists z' \big(z \in \bigcup \mathfrak{M} \wedge M' = \{z'\} \wedge [y, z'] \in h(z, x)\big)\\
&\leftrightarrow \exists z' \big(M' = \{z'\} \wedge [y, \{z'\}] \in \hat{h}(\bigcup \mathfrak{M}, x)\big)\\
&\leftrightarrow [y, M'] \in \hat{h}(\bigcup \mathfrak{M}, x)\\
&\leftrightarrow [y, \zeta(\{M'\})] \in \hat{h}\big(\zeta(\mathfrak{M}), x\big).
\end{aligned}$$

Thus Theorem 6.9 is proved.

Propositions 6.8.1, 6.8.3 and 6.9.3 justify the designation "realizable closure" for $\hat{\mathfrak{B}}$.

In the same way as in 6.9.2, we can prove

Corollary 6.10. There exist strong Z-homomorphisms of $\tilde{\tilde{\mathfrak{B}}}$, $\hat{\tilde{\mathfrak{B}}}$ and $\tilde{\hat{\mathfrak{B}}}$ onto $\tilde{\mathfrak{B}}$. These automata are pairwise equivalent.

In all these cases, the single-valued mapping ζ with $\zeta(\mathfrak{M}) = \bigcup \mathfrak{M}$ satisfies the requirements, as was shown in the proof of 6.9.2. The only thing we still have to show is that the range of ζ is in every case $\mathfrak{P}^*(Z)$. For this, in the case of $\tilde{\tilde{\mathfrak{B}}}$, we have to show that every non-empty subset of Z is a union of sets realizable in $\mathfrak{B}$. This immediately follows from the realizability of all singletons.

In what follows, we shall investigate which properties of $\mathfrak{B}$ are preserved by $\hat{\mathfrak{B}}$ and $\tilde{\mathfrak{B}}$.

Theorem 6.11. *$\mathfrak{B} = [X, Y, Z, h]$ is Z-deterministic if and only if every set of states realizable in $\mathfrak{B}$ is a singleton, i.e., if and only if $\hat{\mathfrak{B}} = \mathfrak{B}^1$.*

Proof: Let $M = h_Q(z, p)$ be a set realizable in the Z-deterministic ND-automaton $\mathfrak{B}$. Then by 1.4.5

$$\emptyset \neq M = h_Q(z, p) \subseteq \bigcup_{q \in W(Y)} h_q(z, p) = f(z, p).$$

Since $\mathfrak{B}$ is Z-deterministic, $f(z, p)$, hence M also, is a singleton. Conversely, if every set realizable in $\mathfrak{B}$ is a singleton, then, in particular, the sets

$$h_{g(z,x)}(z, x) = f(z, x)$$

are singletons; hence $\mathfrak{B}$ is Z-deterministic.

Corollary 6.12. If $\mathfrak{B}$ is Z-deterministic, then $\mathfrak{B}$ and $\hat{\mathfrak{B}}$ are Z-isomorphic.

It is obvious that for Z-finite ND-automata the converse of 6.12 is also valid. Indeed, if $\mathfrak{B}$ and $\hat{\mathfrak{B}}$ are Z-isomorphic, then the sets Z, $\mathfrak{Z}_1$ and $\mathfrak{Z}_r$ have the same cardinalities. This and $\mathfrak{Z}_1 \subseteq \mathfrak{Z}_r$ imply for finite $\mathfrak{Z}_r$ that $\mathfrak{Z}_1 = \mathfrak{Z}_r$.

Theorem 6.13. *$\mathfrak{B}$ is Z-deterministic if and only if $\hat{\mathfrak{B}}$ is.*

Proof: It suffices to show by 6.12 that $\mathfrak{B}$ is Z-deterministic, provided $\hat{\mathfrak{B}}$ is. Suppose $\hat{\mathfrak{B}}$ is Z-deterministic, then $\hat{f}$, the transition function of $\hat{\mathfrak{B}}$, is deterministic. Thus

$$\begin{aligned} \{z'\} \in \hat{f}(\{z\}, x) &\leftrightarrow \exists y([y, \{z'\}] \in \hat{h}(\{z\}, x)) \\ &\leftrightarrow \exists y([y, z'] \in h(z, x)) \\ &\leftrightarrow z' \in f(z, x). \end{aligned}$$

Since $\hat{f}(\{z\}, x)$ is a singleton (containing a singleton), $f(z, x)$ is again a singleton (of a state). Therefore the transition function f of $\mathfrak{B}$ is deterministic, which was to be shown.

Theorem 6.14. *If $\mathfrak{B}$ is reduced, and Z-isomorphic to $\hat{\mathfrak{B}}$, then $\mathfrak{B}$ is Z-deterministic.*

Proof: Let $\chi = [I_X, I_Y, \zeta]$ be a Z-isomorphism of $\hat{\mathfrak{B}}$ onto $\mathfrak{B}$. Then for $M \in \mathfrak{Z}_r$, we have $\zeta(M) \in Z$ and $M \sim \zeta(M)$.

We assert that for all $z \in Z$ $\zeta(\{z\}) = z$. Indeed, $\zeta(\{z_1\}) = z_2 \neq z_1$ would imply that the state $\{z_1\}$ of $\hat{\mathfrak{B}}$ is equivalent to the state z_2 of $\mathfrak{B}$. On the other hand, the state z_1 of $\mathfrak{B}$ is also equivalent to the state $\{z_1\}$ of $\hat{\mathfrak{B}}$. Thus z_1 and z_2 would be two different but equivalent states of $\mathfrak{B}$, which is impossible because $\mathfrak{B}$ is reduced. Consequently, ζ is a one-to-one mapping of $\mathfrak{Z}_1$ onto Z, while on the other hand, by the definition of a Z-isomorphism, ζ is a one-to-one mapping of $\mathfrak{Z}_r$ onto Z. This implies $\mathfrak{Z}_r = \mathfrak{Z}_1$. Applying 6.11, the assertion follows.

It follows directly from the definitions of $\tilde{h}$ and $\hat{h}$ that the following theorem is valid.

Theorem 6.15. *Let $\mathfrak{B} = [X, Y, Z, h]$ be an ND-automaton.*

1. *$\mathfrak{B}$ is an ND-Moore automaton if and only if $\hat{\mathfrak{B}}$ and $\tilde{\mathfrak{B}}$ are.*
2. *If $\hat{\mathfrak{B}}$ or $\tilde{\mathfrak{B}}$ is an ND-Mealy automaton, so is $\mathfrak{B}$.*
3. *If $\hat{\mathfrak{B}}$ or $\tilde{\mathfrak{B}}$ is Y-deterministic, so is $\mathfrak{B}$.*

The converse of 6.15.2 fails to be true, since otherwise, every sequential ND-operator φ could be generated by a state in an ND-Mealy automaton, which however is not the case. By Theorem 4.9, every sequential ND-operator can be generated in an ND-Mealy automaton $\mathfrak{B}$ by a set of states. Every ND-automaton can be "extended" in an obvious way so that any given set of states would be realizable in the "extension" $\mathfrak{B}^*$, which can also be chosen to be an ND-Mealy automaton. Then φ is generated by a state in $\mathfrak{B}^*$, hence in general $\mathfrak{B}^*$ is not an ND-Mealy automaton.

Easy examples show that the converse of Proposition 6.15.3 is also false.

From Proposition 6.1, 5.1.1 and 5.6 we obtain

Corollary 6.16. Let $\mathfrak{B}$ be an ND-automaton.

1. $\mathfrak{B}$ is homogeneous with respect to a non-empty set of states M if and only if $\tilde{\mathfrak{B}}$ is homogeneous with respect to the state M.
2. $\mathfrak{B}$ is strongly homogeneous if and only if $\tilde{\mathfrak{B}}$ is homogeneous.
3. $\mathfrak{B}$ is homogeneous if and only if $\hat{\mathfrak{B}}$ is.

Theorem 6.17. *Let* $\chi = [\xi, \eta, \zeta]$ *be a homomorphism of* $\mathfrak{B} = [X, Y, Z, h]$ *onto* $\mathfrak{B}' = [X', Y', Z', h']$, *furthermore let* $\tilde{\zeta}(M) = \{\zeta(z) \mid z \in M\}$ *for* $M \in \mathfrak{P}^*(Z)$. *Then* $[\xi, \eta, \tilde{\zeta}]$ *is a homomorphism of* $\tilde{\mathfrak{B}}$ *onto* $\tilde{\mathfrak{B}}'$.

Proof: For arbitrary $M \in \mathfrak{P}^*(Z)$, $x \in X$, $y' \in Y'$, $N' \in \mathfrak{P}^*(Z')$ we have

$$
\begin{aligned}
&[y', N'] \in \tilde{h}'\big(\tilde{\zeta}(M), \xi(x)\big) \\
&\leftrightarrow \exists z'\big(N' = \{z'\} \wedge [y', z'] \in h'(\tilde{\zeta}(M), \xi(x))\big) \\
&\leftrightarrow \exists z' \,\exists z^{**}\big(N' = \{z'\} \wedge z^{**} \in M \wedge [y', z'] \in h'(\zeta(z^{**}), \xi(x))\big) \\
&\leftrightarrow \exists z' \,\exists z^{**} \,\exists y \,\exists z^{*}\big(N' = \{z'\} \wedge z^{**} \in M \wedge \eta(y) = y' \wedge \zeta(z^{*}) = z' \\
&\qquad\qquad \wedge [y, z^{*}] \in h(z^{**}, x)\big) \\
&\leftrightarrow \exists y \,\exists z^{*}\big(N' = \{\zeta(z^{*})\} \wedge \eta(y) = y' \wedge [y, \{z^{*}\}] \in \tilde{h}(M, x)\big) \\
&\leftrightarrow \exists y \,\exists N\big(N' = \tilde{\zeta}(N) \wedge y' = \eta(y) \wedge [y, N] \in \tilde{h}(M, x)\big).
\end{aligned}
$$

Thus, $\tilde{h}'\big(\tilde{\zeta}(M), \xi(x)\big) = \eta\tilde{\zeta}\big(\tilde{h}(M, x)\big)$, hence, $[\xi, \eta, \tilde{\zeta}]$ is a homomorphism of $\tilde{\mathfrak{B}}$ onto $\tilde{\mathfrak{B}}'$.

In general the existence of a homomorphism of $\mathfrak{B}$ onto $\mathfrak{B}'$ does not imply that of a homomorphism of $\hat{\mathfrak{B}}$ onto $\hat{\mathfrak{B}}'$. As an example consider the ND-automata $\mathfrak{B}_{16} = [\{x\}, \{0, 1\}, \{a, b, c\}, h^{16}]$, $\mathfrak{B}_{17} = [\{x\}, \{0\}, \{a, b, c\}, h^{17}]$, whose graphs are represented in Fig. 19. Obviously, $[I_{\{x\}}, \eta, I_{\{a,b,c\}}]$ with $\eta(0) = \eta(1) = 0$ is a Y-homomorphism of $\mathfrak{B}_{16}$ onto $\mathfrak{B}_{17}$. In $\mathfrak{B}_{16}$ exactly the sets $\{a\}, \{b\}, \{c\}, \{b, c\}$ $\big(= h_0^{16}(a, x)\big)$, $\{a, b, c\}$ $\big(= h_{\{0,1\}}^{16}(a, x)\big)$ are realizable, while in $\mathfrak{B}_{17}$ only the sets $\{a\}, \{b\}, \{c\}$, and $\{a, b, c\}$ are realizable. Suppose $[\xi', \eta', \zeta']$ is a homomorphism of $\hat{\mathfrak{B}}_{16}$ onto $\hat{\mathfrak{B}}_{17}$. Then $\xi' = I_{\{x\}}$, $\eta' = \eta$, furthermore $\zeta'(\{b, c\})$ is a realizable set of states in $\mathfrak{B}_{17}$, hence we have

$$
\begin{aligned}
\hat{h}^{17}\big(\zeta'(\{b, c\}), x\big) &= \eta\zeta'\big(\hat{h}^{16}(\{b, c\}, x)\big) = \eta\zeta'\big(\{[0, \{b\}], [0, \{c\}]\}\big) \\
&= \big\{[0, \zeta'(\{b\})], [0, \zeta'(\{c\})]\big\}.
\end{aligned}
$$

$$
\begin{aligned}
\hat{h}^{17}\big(\zeta'(\{a\}), x\big) &= \eta\zeta'\big(\{[0, \{b\}], [0, \{c\}], [1, \{a\}]\}\big) \\
&= \big\{[0, \zeta'(\{b\})], [0, \zeta'(\{c\})], [0, \zeta'(\{a\})]\big\}.
\end{aligned}
$$

We can easily verify that for each state $\hat{z}$ of $\hat{\mathfrak{B}}_{17}$, the set $\hat{h}^{17}(\hat{z}, x)$ is either a singleton or a three element set. Now if $\hat{h}^{17}(\zeta'(\{a\}), x)$ is a singleton, then $\zeta'(\{a\}) = \zeta'(\{b\}) = \zeta'(\{c\})$, which is in contradiction to the fact that ζ' is a single-valued mapping of the set $\{\{a\}, \{b\}, \{c\}, \{b, c\}, \{a, b, c\}\}$ onto the set $\{\{a\}, \{b\}, \{c\}, \{a, b, c\}\}$. If $h^{17}(\zeta'(\{a\}), x)$ is a three element set, then $\zeta'(\{b\})$ and $\zeta'(\{c\})$ must be different. Therefore, $\hat{h}^{17}(\zeta'(\{b, c\}), x)$ is a two element set, contradicting the fact that $\hat{h}^{17}(\hat{z}, x)$ cannot be a two element set for any state $\hat{z}$ of $\hat{\mathfrak{B}}_{17}$. Thus there is no homomorphism of $\hat{\mathfrak{B}}_{16}$ onto $\hat{\mathfrak{B}}_{17}$.

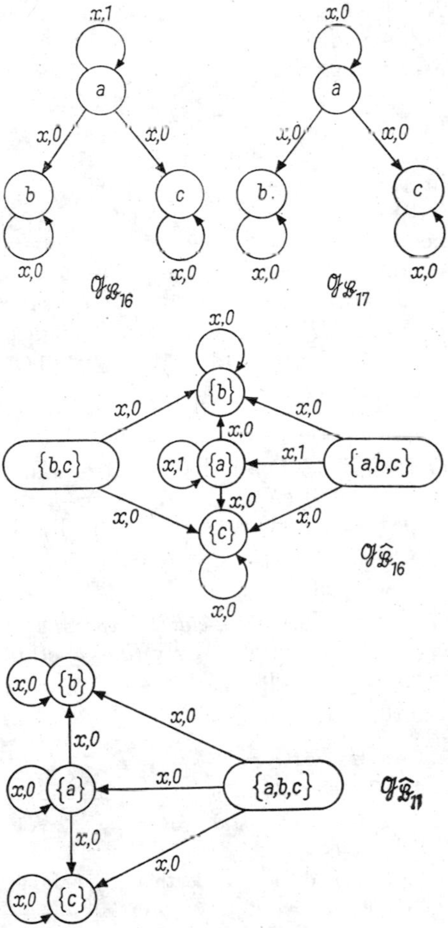

Fig. 19

Theorem 6.18. *If $[\xi, \eta, \zeta]$ is a homomorphism of $\mathfrak{B} = [X, Y, Z, h]$ onto $\mathfrak{B}' = [X', Y', Z', h']$ and η is one-to-one, then $[\xi, \eta, \hat{\zeta}]$, with $\hat{\zeta}(M) = \{\zeta(z) \mid z \in M\}$ for $M \in \mathfrak{Z}_r$, is a homomorphism of $\hat{\mathfrak{B}}$ onto $\hat{\mathfrak{B}}'$.*

Proof: As can be seen from the proof of Theorem 6.17, we only have to show that $\hat{\zeta}$ is a single-valued mapping of the set $\mathfrak{Z}_r$ onto $\mathfrak{Z}'_r$. By 3.3.3, since η is one-to-one, for $M \subseteq Z$, $x \in X$, $y \in Y$ we have

$$\begin{aligned}\hat{\zeta}(h_y(M, x)) &= \bigcup_{z \in M} \hat{\zeta}(h_y(z, x)) \\ &= \bigcup_{z \in M} h'_{\eta(y)}(\zeta(z), \xi(x)) \\ &= h'_{\eta(y)}(\hat{\zeta}(M), \xi(x)).\end{aligned}$$

From this, by induction on p we can show that

$$\hat{\zeta}(h_q(M, p)) = h'_{\eta(q)}(\hat{\zeta}(M), \xi(p))$$

for all

$$M \in \mathfrak{Z}_r, \quad p \in W(X), \quad q \in v_{\mathfrak{B}}(M, p).$$

In particular we have

$$\hat{\zeta}(h_q(z, p)) = h'_{\eta(q)}(\zeta(z), \xi(p)),$$

for $z \in Z$, $p \in W(X)$, $q \in v_{\mathfrak{B}}(z, p)$, and thus for $\emptyset \neq Q \subseteq v_{\mathfrak{B}}(z, p)$

$$\hat{\zeta}(h_Q(z, p)) = \bigcup_{q \in Q} \hat{\zeta}(h_q(z, p)) = \bigcup_{q \in Q} h'_{\eta(q)}(\zeta(z), \xi(p)) = h'_{\eta(Q)}(\zeta(z), \xi(p)).$$

Thus $\hat{\zeta}$ assigns to each set realizable in $\mathfrak{B}$ a uniquely determined set realizable in $\mathfrak{B}'$, and every set realizable in $\mathfrak{B}'$ occurs as a value of $\hat{\zeta}$. Thus Theorem 6.18 is proved.

§ 7. Stability and Terminal Equivalence

In this section we shall deal with ND-automata whose efficiency is restricted in a special way. In general, the efficiency of abstract automata only depends on the number of states (cf. Martinjuk [1]). Here we consider ND-automata, whose function h is constructed in such a way that these automata "forget" about the input signals after a certain length of time. Thus the output signal of such an automaton in a certain step t does not depend on the whole "past", i.e., on all input signals fed into it up to the moment t, or on a property of the number t (e.g. that t is even), but only on a certain "final segment" of the past of a fixed length $k > 0$, as soon as $t > k$. In other words, only the input signals applied in the steps $t-k+1, \ldots, t$ have an influence on whether in step t a certain output signal can be put out or not. It is clear that this property is closely connected to a certain stability property, as was investigated, for instance, by Perles, Rabin, Shamir [1], Winograd [2] and Lowenstein [3], [6] for deterministic automata and by Fischer, Lindner, Thiele [1] for stochastic automata. In such ND-automata, the effects of a failure in the input or in the work of the input unit of the automaton, disappear after k steps.

Definition 7.1. Let $\mathfrak{B} = [X, Y, Z, h]$ be an ND-automaton, M a non-empty subset of Z, and k a positive natural number.

(7.1.1) The ND-automaton $\mathfrak{B}$ is called *weakly k-stable over M* if for each $x \in X$, $y \in Y$, $pr \in W(X)$ with $l(r) = k-1$ there is a $q \in W(Y)$ with $qy \in v_{\mathfrak{B}}(M, prx)$ if and only if there is an $s \in W(Y)$ with $sy \in v_{\mathfrak{B}}(M, rx)$.

(7.1.2) $\mathfrak{B}$ is called *weakly k-stable if* $\mathfrak{B}$ is weakly k-stable over every non-empty subset M of Z.

(7.1.3) $\mathfrak{B}$ is called *k-stable (over M)* if $\mathfrak{B}$ is weakly k-stable (over M) and either $k = 1$ or $\mathfrak{B}$ is not weakly $(k-1)$-stable (over M).

(7.1.4) $\mathfrak{B}$ is called *stable (over M)* if there is a number $k > 0$ such that $\mathfrak{B}$ is k-stable (over M).

Corollary 7.1.

1. If $\mathfrak{B}$ is weakly k-stable over M, and $M \sim N$, then $\mathfrak{B}$ is weakly k-stable over N.

2. $\mathfrak{B}$ is weakly k-stable over the set of states M if and only if $\tilde{\mathfrak{B}}$ is weakly k-stable over the state M.

3. If $\mathfrak{B}$ is deterministic, then $\mathfrak{B}$ is stable if and only if $Det(\mathfrak{B})$ is stable, in the sense of the theory of deterministic automata.

Theorem 7.2. *Let* $\mathfrak{B} = [X, Y, Z, h]$ *be an ND-automaton,* $\emptyset \neq M \subseteq Z$, $k > 0$.

1. $\mathfrak{B}$ *is weakly k-stable over M if and only if for all* $pr \in W(X)$ *with* $l(r) = k-1$, $x \in X$.

$$g\bigl(f(M, pr), x\bigr) = g\bigl(f(M, r), x\bigr).$$

2. *If* $\mathfrak{B}$ *is k-stable over M, then* $\mathfrak{B}$ *is weakly* $(k+n)$*-stable over M for each* $n = 0, 1, \ldots$

Proof of 7.2.1. For all $y \in Y,\ p \in W(X),\ x \in X$ (cf. 1.5.8 and 1.4.5)

$$\begin{aligned}\exists q\big(qy \in v_{\mathfrak{B}}(M, px)\big) &\leftrightarrow \exists q\big(q \in v_{\mathfrak{B}}(M, p) \wedge y \in v_{\mathfrak{B}}(h_q(M, p), x)\big)\\ &\leftrightarrow y \in g\Big(\bigcup_{q \in v_{\mathfrak{B}}(M, p)} h_q(M, p), x\Big)\\ &\leftrightarrow y \in g\big(f(M, p), x\big).\end{aligned}$$

This immediately implies Proposition 7.2.1.

Proof of 7.2.2. By 7.2.1 it suffices to show that for all $pr \in W(X)$, $l(r) = n + k - 1,\ x \in X$

$$g\big(f(M, pr), x\big) = g\big(f(M, r), x\big).$$

Let $r = r'r''$ with $l(r') = n,\ l(r'') = k-1$. Then

$$\begin{aligned}g\big(f(M, r), x\big) &= g\big(f(M, r'r''), x\big) = g\big(f(M, r''), x\big),\\ g\big(f(M, pr), x\big) &= g\big(f(M, pr'r''), x\big) = g\big(f(M, r''), x\big),\end{aligned}$$

since $\mathfrak{B}$ is weakly k-stable over M.

Corollary 7.3. Let $\mathfrak{B} \approx [X, Y, Z, h]$ be an ND-automaton, $\emptyset \neq M \subseteq Z,\ k > 0$.

1. $\mathfrak{B}$ is weakly k-stable over M if and only if for all $pr \in W(X)$ with $l(r) \geqq k - 1$

$$g(f(M, pr), x) = g(f(M, r), x).$$

2. If $\mathfrak{M} \subseteq \mathfrak{P}^*(Z)$, $\mathfrak{M} \neq \emptyset$ and $\mathfrak{B}$ is weakly k-stable over each $M \in \mathfrak{M}$, then $\mathfrak{B}$ is weakly k-stable over $\bigcup \mathfrak{M}$.

3. $\mathfrak{B}$ is weakly k-stable over M if and only if $\mathfrak{B}$ is weakly k-stable over all the sets $f(M, p)$ for $p \in W(X)$.

Theorem 7.4. *If $\mathfrak{B} = [X, Y, Z, h]$ is weakly k-stable over $M \subseteq Z$ and homogeneous with respect to all the sets $f(M, q)$ for $q \in W(X)$ with $l(q) \geqq k - 1$, then for all $pr \in W(X)$ with $l(r) \geqq k - 1$ we have*

$$f(M, pr) \sim f(M, r).$$

First we prove by induction on u that for all $u \in W(X),\ p, r \in W(X)$ with $l(r) \geqq k - 1$

$$v_{\mathfrak{B}}\big(f(M, pr), u\big) = v_{\mathfrak{B}}\big(f(M, r), u\big).$$

The initial step is trivial. The step from u to xu:

$$v_{\mathfrak{B}}\big(f(M, pr), xu\big) = g\big(f(M, pr), x\big)v_{\mathfrak{B}}\big(f(M, prx), u\big),$$

since $l(pr) \geqq k - 1$, $\mathfrak{B}$ is homogeneous with respect to $f(M, pr)$ (cf. 5.5),

$$= g\big(f(M, r), x\big)v_{\mathfrak{B}}\big(f(M, rx), u\big) = v_{\mathfrak{B}}\big(f(M, r), xu\big).$$

Since $\mathfrak{B}$ is weakly k-stable over M, by the induction hypothesis

$$v_{\mathfrak{B}}\big(f(M, prx), u\big) = v_{\mathfrak{B}}\big(f(M, rx), u\big)$$

and $\mathfrak{B}$ is homogeneous with respect to $f(M, r)$.

Theorem 7.5. *Let $\mathfrak{B} = [X, Y, Z, h]$ be an ND-automaton, and M a non-empty subset of Z such that the set $\mathfrak{Z}_M = \{N \mid \exists p(p \in W(X) \wedge N = f(M, p))\}$ has only a finite number of equivalence classes by the relation $\sim$, and k_M is the number of these equivalence classes. If $\mathfrak{B}$ is stable over M, then $\mathfrak{B}$ is weakly k_M-stable over M.*

Proof: First we define a sequence of equivalence relations $\underset{i}{-}$ over $\mathfrak{Z}_M$ by induction on i. For $N, N' \in \mathfrak{Z}_M$ let

$$N \underset{1}{-} N' \underset{\mathrm{Df}}{\leftrightarrow} \forall p \forall x\big(p \in W(X) \wedge x \in X \rightarrow g(f(N, p), x) = g(f(N', p), x)\big)$$

$$N \underset{i+1}{-} N' \underset{\mathrm{Df}}{\leftrightarrow} \forall x\big(x \in X \rightarrow f(N, x) \underset{i}{-} f(N', x)\big).$$

Lemma 7.5a. *For all $N, N' \in \mathfrak{Z}_M$, $j = 1, 2, \ldots$*

$$N \underset{j}{-} N' \leftrightarrow \forall p \forall x\big(p \in W(X) \wedge l(p) \geqq j - 1 \wedge x \in X \rightarrow g(f(N, p), x) = g(f(N', p), x)\big).$$

We prove Lemma 7.5a by induction on j. The initial step $j = 1$ is trivial. The step from j to $j + 1$:

$$\begin{aligned} N \underset{j+1}{-} N' &\leftrightarrow \forall x'\Big(x' \in X \rightarrow \forall p \forall x(p \in W(X) \wedge l(p) \geqq j - 1 \wedge x \in X \\ &\qquad \rightarrow g\big(f(f(N, x'), p), x\big) = g\big(f(f(N', x'), p), x\big)\Big) \\ &\leftrightarrow \forall x' \forall p \forall x\big(p \in W(X) \wedge l(p) \geqq j - 1 \wedge x, x' \in X \\ &\qquad \rightarrow g(f(N, x' p), x) = g(f(N', x'p), x)\big) \\ &\leftrightarrow \forall p \forall x\big(p \in W(X) \wedge l(p) \geqq j \wedge x \in X \\ &\qquad \rightarrow g(f(N, p), x) = g(f(N', p), x)\big). \end{aligned}$$

It is easy to verify the following lemma.

Lemma 7.5b. *For all $j = 1, 2, \ldots$ we have: If $\underset{j}{-} = \underset{j+1}{-}$ then $\underset{j}{-} = \underset{j+i}{-}$ for all $i = 0, 1, 2, \ldots$.*

Let $\mathfrak{R}^i$ be the partition of $\mathfrak{Z}_M$ induced by the equivalence relation $\underset{i}{-}$. Lemma 7.5a implies that $\mathfrak{R}^j$ is a refinement of $\mathfrak{R}^{j+1}$ or in other words $\mathfrak{R}^{j+1}$ is coarser than $\mathfrak{R}^j$. Lemma 7.5b implies $\mathfrak{R}^j = \mathfrak{R}^{j+i}$ for all $i = 0, 1, \ldots$ provided $\mathfrak{R}^j = \mathfrak{R}^{j+1}$. If $\mathfrak{R}^j \neq \mathfrak{R}^{j+1}$, then $\mathfrak{R}^{j+1}$ is properly coarser than $\mathfrak{R}^j$, $\mathfrak{R}^j$ is properly coarser than $\mathfrak{R}^{j-1}$, etc. and finally $\mathfrak{R}^2$ is properly coarser than $\mathfrak{R}^1$.

Lemma 7.5c. *$\mathfrak{B}$ is weakly i-stable over M if and only if $\mathfrak{R}^i$ is a singleton* (i.e., if $\mathfrak{R}^i = \{\mathfrak{Z}_M\}$).

Proof: Let i be a positive natural number. $\mathfrak{B}$ is weakly i-stable over M if and only if the following assertion holds:

$$\forall p \forall r \forall x (pr \in W(X) \wedge x \in X \wedge l(r) \geqq i - 1 \rightarrow g(f(M, pr), x) = g(f(M, r), x)).$$

This is equivalent to each of the following assertions:

$$\forall N \forall r \forall x (N \in \mathfrak{Z}_M \wedge r \in W(X) \wedge l(r) \geqq i - 1 \wedge x \in X \rightarrow g(f(N, r), x) = g(f(M, r), x)),$$

$$\forall N \forall N' (N, N' \in \mathfrak{Z}_M \rightarrow \forall r \forall x (r \in W(X) \wedge l(r) \geqq i - 1 \wedge x \in X \rightarrow g(f(N, r), x) = g(f(N', r), x))),$$

$$\forall N \forall N' (N, N' \in \mathfrak{Z}_M \rightarrow N \underset{i}{-} N'),$$

$$\mathfrak{K}^i = \{\mathfrak{Z}_M\}.$$

Let $\mathfrak{B}$ be k-stable over M. Since $k_M \geqq 1$, our proposition is trivial for $k = 1$. Suppose $k \geqq 2$. Then $\mathfrak{B}$ is also weakly k-stable over M; consequently $\mathfrak{K}^k = \{\mathfrak{Z}_M\}$, and $\mathfrak{B}$ is not weakly $(k-1)$-stable over M. Therefore, $\mathfrak{K}^{k-1}$ contains at least two classes, and $\mathfrak{K}^k$ is properly coarser than $\mathfrak{K}^{k-1}$ and thus for each i with $1 < i \leq k$ the partition $\mathfrak{K}^i$ is properly coarser than $\mathfrak{K}^{i-1}$. This implies that $\mathfrak{K}^1$ contains at least k classes, hence $\mathfrak{Z}_M$ has at least k elements $N_1, \ldots, N_k$ such that for all i, j with $1 \leqq i < j \leqq k$, $N_i \underset{1}{-} N_j$ is not valid. It is easy to see that $N \sim N'$ implies $N \underset{1}{-} N'$, hence we also have $N_i \nsim N_j$. Thus the partition of $\mathfrak{Z}_M$ induced by the relation $\sim$ has at least k different equivalence classes, i.e., $k_M \geqq k$.

Corollary 7.6.

1. If $\mathfrak{B}$ is a Z-finite ND-automaton with $Card(Z) = n$, and $\mathfrak{B}$ is stable over M ($\emptyset \neq M \subseteq Z$), then $\mathfrak{B}$ is weakly $(2^n - 1)$-stable over M.

2. If $M \subseteq Z$ and $\mathfrak{B}$ is k-stable over M, then $Card(Z) \geqq ld(k+1)$. (ld denotes the logarithm with base 2.)

3. $\mathfrak{B}$ is 1-stable over M if and only if $g(N, x) = g(N', x)$ for all $N, N' \in \mathfrak{Z}_M$ and $x \in X$.

Now we show that the upper bound $k_M = Card(\mathfrak{Z}_M/\sim)$ in general cannot be improved. Let $n \geqq 2$ be a natural number,

$$Z = \{1, 2, \ldots, n\}, \quad X = \{1, 2, \ldots, 2^n - 2\} \quad \text{and} \quad Y = Z \times X.$$

Furthermore, let $N_1, N_2, \ldots, N_{2^n-1}$ be an enumeration of $\mathfrak{P}^*(Z)$ such that for $1 \leqq i, j \leqq 2^n - 1$:

If $i < j$, then $Card(N_i) \leqq Card(N_j)$.

In particular, we have $N_{2^n-1} = Z$. For $i \in Z$, $j \in X$ we put

$$f(i, j) = \begin{cases} N_{j+1}, & \text{if } i \in N_j, \\ Z & \text{otherwise.} \end{cases} \qquad g(i, j) = \{[i, j]\} \subseteq Y.$$

The system $\mathfrak{B} = [X, Y, Z, f, g]$ is an ND-Mealy automaton such that for $N, N' \subseteq Z$, $j \in X$

$$g(N, j) = g(N', j) \quad \text{if and only if} \quad N = N'.$$

Furthermore, for all $j = 1, \ldots, 2^n - 2$

$$f(N_1, 1\,2 \ldots j) = N_{j+1};$$

thus $\mathfrak{Z}_{N_1} = \mathfrak{P}^*(Z)$, $k_{N_1} = 2^n - 1$.

Lemma 7.7. *For all* $N \in \mathfrak{P}^*(Z)$, $p \in W(X)$ *with* $l(p) \geqq 2^n - 2$ *we have* $f(N, p) = Z$.

Proof: Let $p = x_1 \ldots x_m \in W(X)$ and $f(N, x_1 \ldots x_m) \neq Z$.
Then

$$f(N, x_1) = \begin{cases} N_{x_1+1}, & \text{if} \quad N \subseteq N_{x_1}, \\ Z & \text{otherwise}, \end{cases}$$

and for $\mu = 1, \ldots, m-1$

$$f(Z, x_\mu) = Z,$$

$$f(N_{x_\mu+1}, x_{\mu+1}) = \begin{cases} N_{x_{\mu+1}+1}, & \text{if} \quad N_{x_\mu+1} \subseteq N_{x_{\mu+1}}, \\ Z & \text{otherwise.} \end{cases}$$

Since $f(N, x_1 \ldots x_m) \neq Z$, $f(N, x_1 \ldots x_m) = N_{x_m+1} \neq N_{2^n-1} = Z$ must be satisfied hence

$$N \subseteq N_{x_1}, \quad N_{x_1+1} \subseteq N_{x_2}, \quad \ldots, \quad N_{x_{m-1}+1} \subseteq N_{x_m}.$$

From this, however

$$1 \leqq x_1 < x_1 + 1 \leqq x_2 < \cdots \leqq x_{m-1} < x_{m-1} + 1 \leqq x_m < x_m + 1 \leqq 2^n - 2.$$

Thus

$$m + 1 \leqq x_m + 1 \leqq 2^n - 2,$$
$$m \leqq 2^n - 3.$$

Thus Lemma 7.7 is proved.

From Lemma 7.7 it follows immediately that $\mathfrak{B}$ is weakly $(2^n - 1)$-stable. In particular, $\mathfrak{B}$ is weakly $(2^n - 1)$-stable over N_1. Next we show that $\mathfrak{B}$ is not weakly $(2^n - 2)$-stable over N_1. By 7.2.1 it suffices to show that there are $p, r \in W(X)$ with $l(r) = 2^n - 3$ and an $x \in X$ such that

$$g\big(f(N_1, pr), x\big) \neq g\big(f(N_1, r), x\big).$$

This inequality holds by the definition of g if and only if

$$f(N_1, pr) \neq f(N_1, r).$$

Let r be the word $1\,2\,3 \ldots 2^n - 3$, and p an arbitrary word from $W(X)$ with $l(p) \geqq 2^n - 2$. Then $f(N_1, p) = Z$ (by Lemma 7.7) and

$$f(N_1, pr) = f(Z, r) = Z \neq N_{2^n-2} = f(N_1, r),$$

hence $\mathfrak{B}$ is not weakly $(2^n - 2)$-stable over N_1.

The graph represented in Fig. 20 describes the transition function f of $\mathfrak{B}$ for $n = 3$, $N_1 = \{1\}$, $N_2 = \{2\}$, $N_3 = \{3\}$, $N_4 = \{1, 2\}$, $N_5 = \{1, 3\}$, $N_6 = \{2, 3\}$, $N_7 = \{1, 2, 3\}$; $X = \{1, 2, 3, 4, 5, 6\}$.

Now we extend the domain of definition of the relation $\underset{1}{-}$ considered in the proof of Theorem 7.5 in such a way that sets of states M, M' of eventually different ND-automata $\mathfrak{B}$, $\mathfrak{B}'$ are in this relation if and only if the set of output signals y, which can appear as the last signal (terminal signal) of an output word put out in response to the non empty input word px, does not depend on whether px is fed into $\mathfrak{B}$ with M as initial set or whether it is fed into $\mathfrak{B}'$ with M' as initial set. Since here only the terminal letters of the output words are considered we call this relation *terminal equivalence*.

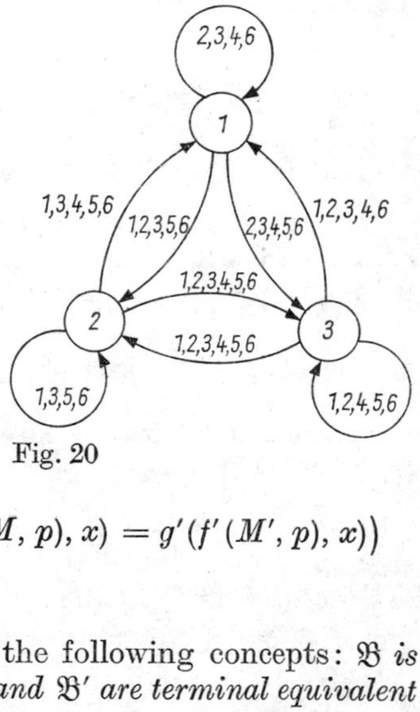

Fig. 20

Definition 7.2. Let $\mathfrak{B} = [X, Y, Z, h]$, $\mathfrak{B}' = [X, Y', Z', h']$ be ND-automata with the same input alphabet. Two states $z \in Z$, $z' \in Z'$ (or two sets of states $M \subseteq Z$, $M' \subseteq Z'$) are called *terminal equivalent*, written $z \underset{f}{\sim} z'$ (or $M \underset{f}{\sim} M'$) if

$$g\big(f(z, p), x\big) = g'\big(f'(z', p), x\big) \quad \big(\text{or } g(f(M, p), x) = g'(f'(M', p), x)\big)$$

for all $p \in W(X$, $x \in X)$.

Analogously to definition 2.1, we can introduce the following concepts: $\mathfrak{B}$ *is terminal equivalently embedded into* $\mathfrak{B}'$ ($\mathfrak{B} \underset{f}{\subsetneq} \mathfrak{B}'$), $\mathfrak{B}$ *and* $\mathfrak{B}'$ *are terminal equivalent* ($\mathfrak{B} \underset{f}{\sim} \mathfrak{B}'$), $\mathfrak{B}$ *is weakly terminal equivalently embedded into* $\mathfrak{B}'$ ($\mathfrak{B} \underset{f}{\lessapprox} \mathfrak{B}'$), *and* $\mathfrak{B}$, $\mathfrak{B}'$ *are weakly terminal equivalent* ($\mathfrak{B} \underset{f}{\approx} \mathfrak{B}'$).

Corollary 7.8.

1. If two states, sets of states or ND-automata are (weakly) equivalent, then they are (weakly) terminal equivalent.

2. If $\mathfrak{B} \underset{f}{\sim} \mathfrak{B}'$, then $\mathfrak{B} \underset{f}{\approx} \mathfrak{B}'$.

3. $\mathfrak{B} \lesseqqgtr_f \mathfrak{B}'$ if and only if for each state z of $\mathfrak{B}$ there is a set M' of states of $\mathfrak{B}'$ with $\{z\} \underset{f}{\sim} M'$.

4. For every ND-automaton $\mathfrak{B} = [X, Y, Z, h]$, the ND-Mealy automaton $\mathfrak{B}_M = [X, Y, Z, f, g]$ (with the transition and output functions of $\mathfrak{B}$) is terminal equivalent to $\mathfrak{B}$.

5. The states $z \in Z$, $z' \in Z'$ (or the sets of states $M \subseteq Z$, $M' \subseteq Z'$) are terminal equivalent if and only if for all $x \in X$

$$g(z, x) = g'(z', x) \quad \text{and} \quad f(z, x) \underset{f}{\sim} f'(z', x)$$

$$(\text{or } g(M, x) = g'(M', x) \quad \text{and} \quad f(M, x) \underset{f}{\sim} f'(M', x))$$

6. If $\mathfrak{B}$ is homogeneous with respect to M, and $\mathfrak{B}'$ is homogeneous with respect to M', then $M \sim M'$ if and only if $M \underset{f}{\sim} M'$.

7. (Strongly) homogeneous ND-automata are (weakly) equivalent if and only if they are (weakly) terminal equivalent.

Propositions 7.8.6 and 7.8.7 show that for homogeneous, and in particular for deterministic ND-automata, equivalence and terminal equivalence coincide. Therefore, in the theory of deterministic automata there is no need to define terminal equivalence.

Theorem 7.9. *The ND-automaton* $\mathfrak{B} = [X, Y, Z, h]$ *is weakly k-stable over* M $(\emptyset \neq M \subseteq Z)$ *if and only if for arbitrary* $N, N' \in \mathfrak{Z}_M$ *and all* $r \in W(X)$ *with* $l(r) \geqq k - 1$ *the sets* $f(N, r), f(N', r)$ *are terminal equivalent.*

Proof: Lemma 7.5c implies that $\mathfrak{B}$ is weakly k-stable over M if and only if $N \underset{k}{-} N'$ for all $N, N' \in \mathfrak{Z}_M$, which, by Lemma 7.5a, holds if and only if for all $N, N' \in \mathfrak{Z}_M$, $r \in W(X)$ with $l(r) \geqq k - 1$ and every $x \in X$, the equality

$$g(f(N, r), x) = g(f(N', r), x)$$

is satisfied. This is the case however if and only if for all $r \in W(X)$ with $l(r) \geqq k - 1$ the sets $f(N, r), f(N', r)$ are terminal equivalent.

Theorem 7.10. *Let* $\mathfrak{B} = [X, Y, Z, h]$ *be weakly k-stable over M. Then for every* $p \in W(X)$ *with* $l(p) \geqq k - 1$ *there is a* $p' \in W(X)$ *with* $l(p') \leqq k - 1$ *such that* $f(M, p) \underset{f}{\sim} f(M, p')$.

The proof is indirect, i.e., we assume that there is a $p' \in W(X)$ with $l(p') \geqq k - 1$ such that for all $p'' \in W(X)$ with $l(p'') \leqq k - 1$ the sets $f(M, p'), f(M, p'')$ are not terminal equivalent. Let $p' = x_1 \ldots x_n$ and $p''' = x_{n-k+2} \ldots x_n$ be the final segment of p' consisting of the last $k - 1$ letters of p', further let $q = x_1 \ldots x_{n-k+1}$. Then

$$f(M, qp''') \underset{f}{\not\sim} f(M, p'''),$$

hence there are $s \in W(X)$, $x \in X$ such that

$$g(f(M, qp'''s), x) \neq g(f(M, p'''s), x).$$

On the other hand, since $\mathfrak{B}$ is weakly k-stable over M, for each $p \in W(X)$ (in particular for $p = q$), $r \in W(X)$ with $l(r) \geqq k - 1$ (in particular for $r = p'''s$), $x \in X$ we have

$$g(f(M, pr), x) = g(f(M, r), x).$$

This contradiction shows that Theorem 7.10 is true.

Corollary 7.11. If $\mathfrak{B}$ is X-finite and weakly k-stable over M, then there are only finitely many equivalence classes of the relation $\underset{f}{\sim}$ on $\mathfrak{Z}_M$.

From Lemma 7.5c we also obtain

Corollary 7.12. If $\mathfrak{B}$ is k-stable over M, then for $N, N' \in \mathfrak{Z}_M$

$$N \underset{f}{\sim} N' \leftrightarrow \forall p \forall x (p \in W(X) \wedge l(p) \leqq k - 2 \wedge x \in X \rightarrow g(f(N, p), x) = g(f(N', p), x)).$$

Theorem 7.13. *Let $\mathfrak{B} = [X, Y, Z, h]$ be a Z-finite ND-automaton with $n > 0$ states. Two states $z, z' \in Z$ (or sets of states $M, M' \subseteq Z$) of $\mathfrak{B}$ are terminal equivalent if and only if for all $x \in X$ and $p \in W(X)$ with $l(p) \leqq 2^n - 3$*

$$g(f(z, p), x) = g(f(z', p), x) \quad \big(\text{or } g(f(M, p), x) = g(f(M', p), x)\big)$$

Proof: Let us again consider the equivalence relations $\underset{i}{—}$ defined in the proof of Theorem 7.5, however this time as a relation on the set $\mathfrak{P}^*(Z)$. In the proofs of Lemmas 7.5a and 7.5b we did not use the fact that the automaton under consideration was stable. Therefore these lemmas imply that the partition $\mathfrak{K}^{2^n - 1}$ belonging to the relation $\underset{2^n - 1}{—}$ contains exactly one class, since $\mathfrak{K}^1$ contains at most $2^n - 1$ classes. Consequently, for all $N, N' \in \mathfrak{P}^*(Z)$

$$N \underset{2^n - 1}{—} N',$$

i.e., for all $N, N' \in \mathfrak{P}^*(Z)$

$$\forall p \forall x \big(x \in X \wedge p \in W(X) \wedge l(p) \geqq 2^n - 2 \\ \rightarrow g(f(N, p), x) = g(f(N', p), x)\big).$$

This immediately implies our proposition.

From Theorem 7.13, which is an analogon of Theorem 2.9, it follows that the terminal equivalence of states or sets of states is decidable for finite ND-automata, i.e., for any two sets of states we can decide in a finite number of steps whether they are terminal equivalent or not. This implies that the equivalence classes of the relation $\underset{f}{\sim}$ can be constructed algorithmically for an arbitrary finite ND-automaton. Therefore it is sensible to deal with the terminal reduction of ND-automata, i.e., with the construction of an ND-automaton $\mathfrak{B}_f$, which is terminal equivalent to a given ND-automaton $\mathfrak{B}$ and in which two different states are no longer terminal equivalent.

Definition 7.3. Let $\mathfrak{B} = [X, Y, Z, h]$ be an arbitrary ND-automaton.
(7.3.1) $\mathfrak{B}$ is called *terminal reduced* if for $z, z' \in Z$, $z \underset{f}{\sim} z'$ implies $z = z'$.

(7.3.2) $\mathfrak{B}'$ is called a *terminal reduct of* $\mathfrak{B}$, if $\mathfrak{B}'$ is terminal reduced and terminal equivalent to $\mathfrak{B}$.

Similarly to Definition 2.4, we can introduce the concepts of being *terminal minimal*, of a *terminal minim*, of being *strongly terminal reduced*, of a *strong terminal reduct*.

Corollary 7.14.

1. Every strongly terminal reduced ND-automaton is strongly reduced and terminal minimal. Every terminal minimal ND-automaton is minimal and terminal reduced, every terminal reduced ND-automaton is reduced.

2. For a finite ND-automaton $\mathfrak{B}$ it is decidable whether $\mathfrak{B}$ is terminal reduced, terminal minimal or strongly terminal reduced.

The ND-automaton $\mathfrak{B}_2$ (cf. Fig. 14, page 158) is terminal reduced, but not terminal minimal, since it is not minimal. The ND-automaton $\mathfrak{B}_7$ (cf. Fig. 16, page 168) is terminal minimal, as can be easily shown, but not strongly terminal reduced, since $\mathfrak{B}_7$ is not strongly reduced.

From 7.8.6 and 7.8.7 we obtain

Corollary 7.15.

1. If $\mathfrak{B}$ is a homogeneous (or strongly homogeneous) ND-automaton, then $\mathfrak{B}'$ is a reduct (or a minim) of $\mathfrak{B}$, if and only if $\mathfrak{B}'$ is a terminal reduct (or a terminal minim) of $\mathfrak{B}$.

2. A deterministic ND-automaton is reduced if and only if it is terminal reduced.

Next we show how a terminal reduct of a given ND-automaton can be constructed.

Theorem 7.16. *Every ND-automaton* $\mathfrak{B} = [X, Y, Z, h]$ *has a terminal reduct.*

Proof: For $z \in Z$ let $[z] = \{z' \mid z' \in Z \wedge z' \underset{f}{\sim} z\}$, and for $M \subseteq Z$ let $\mathfrak{K}_M = \{[z] \mid z \in M\}$. We define the functions $\bar{f}$ and $\bar{g}$ on $\mathfrak{K}_Z \times X$ as follows:

$$\left.\begin{aligned} \bar{f}([z], x) &\underset{\text{Df}}{=} \{[z'] \mid z' \in f([z], x)\}, \\ \bar{g}([z], x) &\underset{\text{Df}}{=} g(z, x) \end{aligned}\right\} \text{ for } [z] \in \mathfrak{K}_Z,\ x \in X.$$

It is clear that the definition of $\bar{g}$ is independent of the representative z of the class $[z]$. The system $\overline{\mathfrak{B}}_f = [X, Y, \mathfrak{K}_Z, \bar{f}, \bar{g}]$ is an ND-Mealy automaton.

Lemma 7.16a. *For all* $M \subseteq Z$, *the sets of states* M *and* $\bigcup \mathfrak{K}_M$ *of the ND-automaton* $\mathfrak{B}$ *are terminal equivalent.*

Proof: Obviously, $M \subseteq \bigcup \mathfrak{K}_M$, i.e., for all $p \in W(X)$, $x \in X$ we have $g(f(M, p), x) \subseteq g(f(\bigcup K_M, p), x)$. If for certain M, p, x the last mentioned sets were different, then there would exist a $y \in g(f(\bigcup \mathfrak{K}_M, p), x)$ with $y \notin g(f(M, p), x)$ and a $z^* \in \bigcup \mathfrak{K}_M$ with $y \in g(f(z^*, p), x)$. However, for each

$z \in \dot{\bigcup} \mathfrak{K}_M$ there is a terminal equivalent state z' in M, i.e., we have $y \in g(f(z^*, p), x) = g(f(z', p), x) \subseteq g(f(M, p), x)$ which is in contradiction to $y \notin g(f(M, p), x)$.

Lemma 7.16b. *For all* $M \subseteq Z$, $x \in X$ *we have* $\mathfrak{K}_{f(\bigcup \mathfrak{K}_M, x)} = \bar{f}(\mathfrak{K}_M, x)$.

Proof: For an arbitrary equivalence class $\mathfrak{z} \in \mathfrak{K}_Z$

$$\begin{aligned}
\mathfrak{z} \in \mathfrak{K}_{f(\bigcup \mathfrak{K}_M, x)} &\leftrightarrow \exists z(\mathfrak{z} = [z] \wedge z \in f(\bigcup \mathfrak{K}_M, x)) \\
&\leftrightarrow \exists z(\mathfrak{z} = [z] \wedge \exists z_1(z_1 \in M \wedge z \in f([z_1], x))) \\
&\leftrightarrow \exists z(\mathfrak{z} = [z] \wedge \exists z_1([z_1] \in \mathfrak{K}_M \wedge [z] \in \bar{f}([z_1], x))) \\
&\leftrightarrow \exists z(\mathfrak{z} = [z] \wedge [z] \in \bar{f}(\mathfrak{K}_M, x)) \\
&\leftrightarrow \mathfrak{z} \in \bar{f}(\mathfrak{K}_M, x).
\end{aligned}$$

Now we prove by induction on p that for all $M \subseteq Z$, $p \in W(X)$ and $x \in X$

$$g(f(M, p), x) = \bar{g}(\bar{f}(\mathfrak{K}_M, p), x).$$

The initial step $p = e$ is trivial by Lemma 7.16a. The induction step is taken from p to $x_1 p$ for $x_1 \in X$:

$$\begin{aligned}
g(f(M, x_1 p), x) &= g(f(\bigcup \mathfrak{K}_M, x_1 p), x) && \text{(Lemma 7.16a)} \\
&= g(f(f(\bigcup \mathfrak{K}_M, x_1), p), x) \\
&= \bar{g}(\bar{f}(\mathfrak{K}_{f(\bigcup \mathfrak{K}_M, x_1)}, p), x) && \text{(induction hypothesis)} \\
&= \bar{g}(\bar{f}(\bar{f}(\mathfrak{K}_M, x_1), p), x) && \text{(Lemma 7.16b)} \\
&= \bar{g}(\bar{f}(\mathfrak{K}_M, x_1 p), x),
\end{aligned}$$

which was to be shown.

In particular we have shown that for all $z \in Z$ the state z of $\mathfrak{B}$ and the state $[z]$ of $\overline{\mathfrak{B}}_f$ are terminal equivalent. This implies that $\mathfrak{B} \underset{f}{\sim} \overline{\mathfrak{B}}_f$ and that $\overline{\mathfrak{B}}_f$ is terminal reduced. Hence $\overline{\mathfrak{B}}_f$ is a terminal reduct of $\mathfrak{B}$.

Similarly to Theorems 2.14, 2.16 and 2.17 we can prove

Theorem 7.17.

1. *All terminal reducts of the same ND-automaton have the same number of states.*

2. *If* $\mathfrak{B}$ *is terminal reduced, and terminal equivalent to a terminal minimal ND-automaton, then* $\mathfrak{B}$ *is terminal minimal.*

3. *If* $\mathfrak{B}$ *is terminal reduced and terminal equivalent to a strongly terminal reduced ND-automaton, then* $\mathfrak{B}$ *is strongly terminal reduced.*

4. *Weakly-terminal equivalent and terminal minimal ND-automata are terminal equivalent.*

5. *All terminal minims and all strong terminal reducts of the same ND-automaton are pairwise terminal equivalent and have the same number of states.*

6. *The ND-automaton* $\mathfrak{B}$ *has a strong terminal reduct if and only if* $\mathfrak{B}$ *has a terminal minim and every terminal minim of* $\mathfrak{B}$ *is strongly terminal reduced.*

The ND-automaton $\mathfrak{B}_4$ considered in § 2 yields us an example of a (terminal reduced) ND-automaton with no terminal minims. In what follows we consider the construction and the existence of minims in the terminal sense.

Theorem 7.18. *Let* $\mathfrak{B} = [X, Y, Z, h]$ *be a terminal reduced ND-automaton and* $Z_f^* \underset{\mathrm{Df}}{=} \{z \mid \exists M (M \subseteq Z \wedge M \underset{f}{\sim} \{z\} \wedge M \neq \{z\})\}$. $\mathfrak{B}$ *has a terminal minim if and only if for each* $z \in Z_f^*$ *there is a set* $M_z \subseteq Z$ *with* $M_z \underset{f}{\sim} \{z\}$ *and* $M_z \cap Z_f^* = \emptyset$.

Proof: The necessity of the given condition can be proved in the same way as the corresponding part of the proof of Theorem 2.18. Now we show that if this condition holds, then $\mathfrak{B}$ has a terminal minim. Let

$$f'(z', x) \underset{\mathrm{Df}}{=} \left(f(z', x) \setminus Z_f^*\right) \cup \bigcup_{z^* \in Z_f^* \cap f(z', x)} M_{z^*},$$
$$g'(z', x) \underset{\mathrm{Df}}{=} g(z', x).$$

$\mathfrak{B}' = [X, Y, Z', f', g']$ is an ND-Mealy automaton. Now we show that $\mathfrak{B}'$ is terminal reduced and weakly terminal equivalent to $\mathfrak{B}$.

Lemma 7.18a. *For all* $N' \subseteq Z'$, $p \in W(X)$, $x \in X$

$$g\left(f(N', p), x\right) = g'\left(f'(N', p), x\right).$$

By the definition of g', $g'\left(f'(N', p), x\right) = g\left(f'(N', p), x\right)$. On the other hand, the sets $f'(N', p)$, $f(N', p)$ of states of $\mathfrak{B}$ are terminal equivalent as follows from the definition of f'. Thus we have

$$g'\left(f'(N', p), x\right) = g\left(f'(N', p), x\right) = g\left(f(N', p), x\right).$$

Consequently, for each state $z' \in Z'$ of $\mathfrak{B}'$ there is a terminal equivalent state of $\mathfrak{B}$, namely z' itself. If $z \in Z$, then for $z \in Z'$ the set $\{z\}$ and for $z \in Z_f^*$ the set M_z is a set of states of $\mathfrak{B}'$ equivalent to z, i.e., $\mathfrak{B} \underset{f}{\approx} \mathfrak{B}'$. Since $\mathfrak{B}$ is terminal reduced, so is $\mathfrak{B}'$. Suppose $N' \subseteq Z'$, $z' \in Z'$ are such that the sets N', $\{z'\}$ of states of $\mathfrak{B}'$ are terminal equivalent. Then by Lemma 7.18a, N' and $\{z'\}$ are also terminal equivalent as sets of states of $\mathfrak{B}$. Now, if $N' \neq \{z'\}$ held, then z' would belong to Z_f^*. However, $z' \in Z' = Z \setminus Z_f^*$, hence $N' = \{z'\}$, and $\mathfrak{B}'$ is a terminal minim of $\mathfrak{B}$.

Propositions 2.19 to 2.21 can also be easily transferred to the case of terminal equivalence.

Theorem 7.19. *Let* $\mathfrak{B} = [X, Y, Z, h]$ *be an arbitrary ND-automaton.*

1. *If the condition*

$$\exists z\left(z \in Z \wedge \exists N (N \subseteq Z \wedge N \underset{f}{\sim} \{z\} \wedge N \setminus \{z\} \neq \emptyset)\right.$$
$$\left.\wedge \forall M (M \subseteq Z \wedge M \underset{f}{\sim} \{z\} \rightarrow z \in M)\right) \qquad (\overline{\mathrm{F}})$$

is satisfied by $\mathfrak{B}$, *then* $\mathfrak{B}$ *has no terminal minims.*

2. *If $\mathfrak{B}$ is terminal reduced, and the set*

$$Z_f^{**} \underset{\text{Df}}{=} \{z \mid \exists M (M \subseteq Z \wedge M \underset{f}{\sim} \{z\} \wedge z \notin M)\}$$

is finite, furthermore $\mathfrak{B}$ satisfies the condition

$$\forall z \big(z \in Z \to \forall N (N \subseteq Z \wedge N \underset{f}{\sim} \{z\} \to N = \{z\}) \vee \exists M (M \subseteq Z \wedge M \underset{f}{\sim} \{z\} \wedge z \notin M)\big), \qquad \text{(F)}$$

then $\mathfrak{B}$ has a terminal minim.

3. *If $\mathfrak{B}$ is terminal reduced and Z-finite, then $\mathfrak{B}$ has a terminal minim if and only if it satisfies condition* (F).

4. *Deterministic ND-automata are terminal minimal if and only if they are terminal reduced.*

The ND-automaton $\mathfrak{B}_8$ given in § 2, is an example of an ND-automaton satisfying condition (F) but having no terminal minims; $\mathfrak{B}_9$ shows that there are deterministic ND-automata which are not strongly terminal reduced.

§ 8. Events

In this concluding section we shall deal with the representability and generability of events in non-deterministic automata. We shall be motivated by the same objectives as in the investigation of the representability of events in deterministic automata. These are, the consideration of their classifying behaviour on one hand and the application of automata for deciding upon sets of words, on the other. Thus we shall investigate the external classifying behaviour of ND-automata (representability by an output signal), then relate this to the internal classifying behaviour (representability by a set of states) and characterize the class of events representable in finite ND-automata.

In addition to the representability of events, we shall also consider several kinds of generating events. The latter are motivated by considerations of mathematical linguistics.

In mathematical linguistics, by *acceptive grammar* we mean a mechanism which in finitely many steps decides upon an arbitrary finite "string" of words belonging to the "vocabulary" of the natural or artificial language under consideration, whether it is a "sentence" of this language or not. This means that the string satisfies certain syntactic criteria. Consider the (artificial) language of the regular terms. Its vocabulary consists of symbols, namely the symbol **0** for the impossible event, the symbol $\boldsymbol{x}$ for each member x of the alphabet X under consideration, the symbols $\vee$, $\circ$, $\langle\ \rangle$ for the operations of union, product and closure on events, and the technical symbols (,). An acceptive grammar for the language of regular terms is a mechanism which in finitely many steps decides upon an arbitrary sequence constructed from the above symbols whether it is a regular term or not. An acceptive grammar for ALGOL decides upon an arbitrary sequence of symbols belonging to the vocabulary of ALGOL whether it is a syntactically correct ALGOL program or not.

A *generative grammar* for a given language is a system which generates the sentences of this language and only these. In mathematical linguistics one often has the additional condition that together with every sentence generated by the grammar, a "structural description" of the sentence is also provided. This condition will not be required here.

Clearly, deterministic and non-deterministic automata can be used as grammars. A (perhaps initial) deterministic or non-deterministic automaton is an acceptive grammar for a certain language with vocabulary V if the input alphabet of this automaton is the set V and it puts out a certain output signal y or enters a state belonging to a certain set M if and only if it receives a word over V which is a sentence of the given language. In other words, if this language considered as an event over V is represented in the given automaton by y or M respectively. Since in a deterministic initial automaton to each input word there corresponds exactly one output word, it is difficult to use deterministic automata as generative grammars. A non-deterministic automaton with the set V as output alphabet however can be considered as a generative grammar for a language with vocabulary V, if in response to the input of an arbitrary word over its input alphabet a sentence of the language is put out (generated) if and only if meanwhile it enters into a state belonging to a given set. In this case, the given language is the event generated by the set M in this automaton. We are especially interested in events which can be generated in finite ND-automata.

First we turn to the investigation of the *representability* of events in non-deterministic automata.

Definition 8.1. An event $E \subseteq W(X)$ over the set X is said to *be represented* in the weakly initial ND-automaton $\mathfrak{B} = [X, Y, Z, h, M_1]$ *by the output signal* $y \in Y$ if an arbitrary word $p \in W(X)$ belongs to E if and only if there is a word $q \in V_{\mathfrak{B}}(M_1, p)$ which ends on y.

The fact that in the above definition X is required to be the input alphabet of $\mathfrak{B}$ does not imply any loss of generality, since if X is properly contained in the input alphabet of $\mathfrak{B}$, E remains an event over the input alphabet.

From Theorems 4.1 and 6.1 we obtain

Corollary 8.1. An event is representable in a (finite) weakly initial ND-automaton by an output signal if and only if it is representable in an initial (finite) ND-automaton by an output signal.

Therefore in what follows we always consider initial ND-automata. Let $\mathfrak{B} = [X, Y, Z, h, z_1]$ be an arbitrary initial ND-automaton, $y \in Y$ an output signal. If E is the event represented in $\mathfrak{B}$ by y, then for arbitrary $p \in W(X)$

$$p \in E \leftrightarrow \exists q\big(q \in W(Y) \wedge qy \in v_{\mathfrak{B}}(z_1, p)\big).$$

This obviously implies $e \notin E$. Therefore it suffices to require that the above equivalence be valid for all non-empty words $p \in W(X) \setminus \{e\}$. The following relation was established in § 7:

$$\exists q(q \in W(Y) \wedge qy \in v_{\mathfrak{B}}(z_1, px)) \leftrightarrow y \in g(f(z_1, p), x).$$

Thus the event E is represented in $\mathfrak{B}$ by y if and only if for $p \in W(X)$, $x \in X$

$$px \in E \leftrightarrow y \in g(f(z_1, p), x).$$

Indeed, we can assume that $\mathfrak{B}$ is an initial ND-Moore automaton, say $\mathfrak{B} = [X, Y, Z, f, m, z_1]$ and put $M_y = \{z \mid y \in m(z) \wedge z \in Z\}$, then

$$\begin{aligned} px \in E &\leftrightarrow y \in m(f(f(z_1, p), x)), \\ &\leftrightarrow f(z_1, px) \cap M_y \neq \emptyset. \end{aligned}$$

This way, the external reaction, i.e., the output of y, is reduced to an internal property of states. Accordingly, we define the representability of events by sets of states (properties of states).

Definition 8.2. The event $E \subseteq W(X)$ over X is said to be *represented* in the initial ND-automaton $\mathfrak{B} = [X, Y, Z, h, z_1]$ *by the set* $M \subseteq Z$ if for all $p \in W(X)$

$$p \in E \leftrightarrow f(z_1, p) \cap M \neq \emptyset.$$

The connection between the representability by an output signal and by a set of states, which is known in the theory of deterministic automata, remains valid in the theory of ND-automata.

Corollary 8.2.

1. Let $\mathfrak{B} = [X, Y, Z, f, m, z_1]$ be an ND-Moore automaton, $y \in Y$ and E the event represented by y in $\mathfrak{B}$, further let $M_y = \{z \mid z \in Z \wedge y \in m(z)\}$. Then if E' is the event represented in $\mathfrak{B}$ by M_y,

$$E' = \begin{cases} E \cup \{e\}, & \text{if } \quad y \in m(z_1), \\ E & \text{otherwise.} \end{cases}$$

2. Let $\mathfrak{B} = [X, Y, Z, h, z_1]$ be an initial ND-automaton, $M \subseteq Z$, and E the event represented in $\mathfrak{B}$ by M. For $z \in Z$ we put

$$m(z) \underset{\mathrm{Df}}{=} \begin{cases} \{0\}, & \text{if } \quad z \in M, \\ \{1\} & \text{otherwise.} \end{cases}$$

Then for the event E' represented in the ND-Moore automaton $\mathfrak{B}' = [X, \{0, 1\}, Z, f, m, z_1]$ by the output signal 0,

$$E' = E \setminus \{e\} = \begin{cases} E, & \text{if } \quad z_1 \notin M, \\ E \setminus \{e\} & \text{otherwise.} \end{cases}$$

In what follows we shall always use that definition of representability which is more convenient in the given situation. In a general characterization of the representable events, Definition 8.2 is obviously more advantageous, since it only requires the knowledge of X, Z, f and z_1, hence as in the theory of deterministic automata, it enables us to operate with "outputless automata". However, if we investigate the representability in automata with special external properties, (such as e.g., stability), then we shall use Definition 8.1.

Definition 8.3. An ND-automaton $\mathfrak{B} = [X, Y, Z, h]$ is called an *outputless ND-automaton* if $Y = Z$ and for all $z, z' \in Z$, $x \in X$, $y \in Y$

$$[y, z'] \in h(z, x) \to y = z'.$$

Thus an outputless ND-automaton is an ND-Moore automaton with a deterministic marking function m such that $m(z) = \{z\}$ for all $z \in Z$. Clearly for each deterministic automaton $\mathfrak{A} = [X, Z, \delta]$ there is an outputless ND-automaton $\mathfrak{B}$ such that $\mathfrak{A} = Det(\mathfrak{B})$, namely $\mathfrak{B} = [X, Z, f]$, where $f(z, x) = \{\delta(z, x)\}$ for all $z \in Z$, $x \in X$. Thus we obtain

Theorem 8.3.

1. *Every event can be represented in a suitable outputless ND-automaton.*
2. *Every regular event can be represented in a finite outputless ND-automaton.*

Now we prove the converse of 8.3.2.

Theorem 8.4 (Rabin, Scott [2]). *Every event representable in a finite ND-automaton is regular.*

Proof: Let $\mathfrak{B} = [X, Z, f, z_1]$ be a finite initial ND-automaton in which the event E is represented by the set M. Furthermore, let

$$\mathfrak{Z} \underset{\mathrm{Df}}{=} \{N \mid \exists p (p \in W(X) \wedge N = f(z_1, p))\},$$

$$\mathfrak{M} \underset{\mathrm{Df}}{=} \{N \mid N \in \mathfrak{Z} \wedge N \cap M \neq \emptyset\},$$

finally, for $N \in \mathfrak{Z}$, $x \in X$

$$\delta(N, x) \underset{\mathrm{Df}}{=} f(N, x).$$

$\mathfrak{A} = [X, \mathfrak{Z}, \delta, \{z_1\}]$ is an initial deterministic automaton[1]) which is finite, since $\mathfrak{B}$ is. Obviously, for all $p \in W(X)$ we have

$$\delta(\{z_1\}, p) = f(z_1, p).$$

Hence, for all $p \in W(X)$

$$\begin{aligned} p \in E &\leftrightarrow f(z_1, p) \cap M \neq \emptyset \\ &\leftrightarrow \delta(\{z_1\}, p) \cap M \neq \emptyset \\ &\leftrightarrow \delta(\{z_1\}, p) \in \mathfrak{M}, \end{aligned}$$

---

[1]) The automaton $\mathfrak{A}$ is known in the literature as the "determinization" of the outputless ND-automaton $\mathfrak{B}$, cf. Lyubich [2].

i.e., E is represented in the finite deterministic automaton $\mathfrak{A}$ by the set of states $\mathfrak{M}$ and thus is regular.

Let $\mathfrak{B} = [X, Y, Z, h, z_1]$ be an initial ND-automaton and $y \in Y$. We have shown above that E is represented in $\mathfrak{B}$ by y if and only if for all $p \in W(X)$, $x \in X$

$$px \in E \leftrightarrow y \in g\big(f(z_1, p), x\big).$$

From this we can easily deduce

Corollary 8.5. The states z_1, z_1' of the ND-automaton $\mathfrak{B} = [X, Y, Z, h]$ are terminal equivalent if and only if for arbitrary $y \in Y$ in the initial ND-automata $[X, Y, Z, h, z_1]$ and $[X, Y, Z, h, z_1']$, the same event is represented by y.

Now we shall investigate the properties of the event E, represented by y in an automaton $\mathfrak{B}$ which is weakly k-stable over z_1. In this case, for all $p, r \in W(X)$ with $l(r) \geqq k - 1$, and $x \in X$

$$g\big(f(z_1, pr), x\big) = g\big(f(z_1, r), x\big).$$

This implies

$$prx \in E \leftrightarrow rx \in E.$$

Let us put $E' = \{p \mid p \in E \wedge l(p) < k\}$ and $E'' = \{p \mid p \in E \wedge l(p) = k\}$, then

$$E = E' \cup W(X) \cdot E''.$$

Thus the event E is weakly k-definite (cf. Part I, Theorem 8.8.1), i.e., it is representable in a deterministic weakly $(k+1)$-definite initial automaton.

Conversely, if for all $y \in Y$ the event E_y represented by y in the ND-automaton $\mathfrak{B} = [X, Y, Z, h, z_1]$ is weakly k-definite, then for all $y \in Y$, $p, r \in W(X)$, $x \in X$ with $l(r) = k - 1$

$$prx \in E_y \leftrightarrow rx \in E_y$$

or

$$y \in g\big(f(z_1, pr), x\big) \leftrightarrow y \in g\big(f(z_1, r), x\big),$$

and $\mathfrak{B}$ is weakly k-stable over z_1. From this we obtain

Theorem 8.6. *The ND-automaton* $\mathfrak{B} = [X, Y, Z, h]$ *is weakly* k*-stable over* $z_1 \in Z$ *if and only if for all* $y \in Y$ *the event* E_y *represented by* y *in* $[X, Y, Z, h, z_1]$ *is weakly* k*-definite.*

Since every definite event E can already be represented in an initial deterministic automaton which is stable over its initial state (and which is finite if X is), we have the following result.

Theorem 8.7. *In initial ND-automata which are stable over their initial states, exactly the definite events are representable.*

Our earlier considerations about the representability of events in non-initial deterministic automata can also be easily transferred to the case of ND-automata.

In deterministic automata, only a relatively small number of events E can be represented by a singleton consisting of a state. Namely, this is the case if and only if E is a equivalence class by the relation $\underset{E}{\sim}$ (cf. I. 6.2). The structure of such events was investigated by SALOMAA [1], and BODNARCHUK [1], among others. To conclude these considerations on the representability of events, we shall show that if we do not admit the empty word as a member of an event, every event is representable in an ND-automaton by means of a singleton.

Theorem 8.8. *Every (regular) event not containing the empty word can be represented in a (finite) initial ND-automaton by means of a singleton.*

Proof: Let E be an event over X and $\mathfrak{A} = [X, Z, \delta, z_1]$ a deterministic initial automaton in which E is represented by the set $M \subseteq Z$. If E is regular, than $\mathfrak{A}$ can be chosen finite. Furthermore let $z^*, z^{**} \notin Z$, $z^* \neq z^{**}$. For $z \in Z^* \underset{\mathrm{Df}}{=} Z \cup \{z^*, z^{**}\}$, $x \in X$ we define

$$f(z, x) = \begin{cases} \{z^{**}\}, & \text{if } z \in \{z^*, z^{**}\}, \\ \{\delta(z, x), z^*\}, & \text{if } \delta(z, x) \in M \wedge z \in Z, \\ \{\delta(z, x)\}, & \text{if } \delta(z, x) \notin M \wedge z \in Z. \end{cases}$$

From this definition we obtain that $f(z_1, p)$ contains the state z^* if and only if $\delta(z_1, p) \in M$ or in other words the event E is represented in $\mathfrak{B} = [X, Z^*, f, z_1]$ by $\{z^*\}$.

Next we investigate several kinds of generating events in ND-automata. In accordance with our introductory remarks, we give the following

Definition 8.4. We say that the event $E \subseteq W(Y)$ is *generated* in the weakly initial ND-automaton $\mathfrak{B} = [X, Y, Z, h, M_1]$ *by the set* $N \subseteq Z$ if for all $q \in W(Y)$

$$q \in E \leftrightarrow \exists p\big(p \in W(X) \wedge h_q(M_1, p) \cap N \neq \emptyset\big).$$

Theorem 8.9. *An event can be generated if and only if it can be generated in an initial autonomous ND-automaton.*

Proof: Suppose the event $E \subseteq W(Y)$ is generated by $N \subseteq Z$ in $\mathfrak{B} = [X, Y, Z, h, M_1]$, furthermore let $z_1^* \notin Z$, $Z^* \underset{\mathrm{Df}}{=} Z \cup \{z_1^*\}$,

$$N^* \underset{\mathrm{Df}}{=} \begin{cases} N \cup \{z_1^*\}, & \text{if } M_1 \cap N \neq \emptyset, \\ N & \text{otherwise,} \end{cases}$$

and for $z \in Z^*$

$$h^*(z, 0) \underset{\mathrm{Df}}{=} \begin{cases} \bigcup\limits_{x \in X} h(z, x), & \text{if } z \in Z, \\ \bigcup\limits_{z \in M_1} \bigcup\limits_{x \in X} h(z, x), & \text{if } z = z_1^*. \end{cases}$$

Then $\mathfrak{B}^* = [\{0\}, Y, Z^*, h^*, z_1^*]$ is an initial autonomous ND-automaton with $N^* \subseteq Z^*$. We claim that E is generated in $\mathfrak{B}^*$ by N^*.

$e \in E$ holds if and only if $h_e(M_1, e) \cap N = M_1 \cap N \neq \emptyset$, i.e., if $N^* = N = \{z_1^*\}$ or $N^* \cap h_e(z_1^*, e) \neq \emptyset$. Thus for $q = e$ the equivalence of Definition 8.4 is valid.

Suppose now $q = y_1 \dots y_n$ is an arbitrary non-empty word from $W(Y)$. Then, by the definition of h_q and Definition 8.4,

$$q \in E \leftrightarrow \exists x_1 \dots \exists x_n \left(\bigwedge_{i=1}^{n} x_i \in X \wedge h_{y_1 \dots y_n}(M_1, x_1 \dots x_n) \cap N \neq \emptyset \right)$$
$$\leftrightarrow \exists z_1 \dots \exists z_{n+1} \exists x_1 \dots \exists x_n \Big(z_1 \in M_1 \wedge z_{n+1} \in N$$
$$\wedge \bigwedge_{i=1}^{n} x_i \in X \wedge z_{i+1} \in Z \wedge [y_i, z_{i+1}] \in h(z_i, x_i) \Big).$$

For $\nu = 1, \dots, n$

$$[y_\nu, z_{\nu+1}] \in h^*(z_\nu, 0) \leftrightarrow \exists x_\nu (x_\nu \in X \wedge [y_\nu, z_{\nu+1}] \in h(z_\nu, x_\nu));$$
$$[y_\nu, z_{\nu+1}] \in h^*(z_\nu, 0) \rightarrow z_{\nu+1} \in Z;$$

furthermore

$$h^*(z_1^*, 0) = \bigcup_{z_1 \in M_1} h^*(z_1, 0).$$

Thus we have

$$q \in E \leftrightarrow \exists z_1 \exists z_2 \dots \exists z_{n+1} \left(z_1 \in M_1 \wedge \bigwedge_{i=1}^{n} z_{i+1} \in Z \wedge [y_i, z_{i+1}] \in h^*(z_i, 0) \wedge z_{n+1} \in N \right)$$
$$\leftrightarrow \exists z_2 \dots \exists z_{n+1} \left([y_1, z_2] \in h^*(z_1^*, 0) \wedge \bigwedge_{i=2}^{n} [y_i, z_{i+1}] \in h^*(z_i, 0) \wedge z_{n+1} \in N \right)$$
$$\leftrightarrow h^*_{y_1 \dots y_n}(z_1^*, 0^n) \cap N \neq \emptyset.$$

By the definition of h^*, $\mathfrak{B}^*$ is in its initial state z_1 only in step 1, hence (for $n \geqq 1$)

$$h_q^*(z_1^*, 0^n) \cap N \neq \emptyset \leftrightarrow h_q^*(z_1^*, 0^n) \cap N^* \neq \emptyset.$$

This shows that E is indeed generated in $\mathfrak{B}^*$ by N^*.

Theorem 8.10.

1. *Every event can be generated.*
2. *An event can be generated in a finite ND-automaton if and only if it is regular.*

Proof: Let E be an arbitrary event over Y. Then there is an initial deterministic automaton $\mathfrak{A} = [Y, Z, \delta, z_1]$ and a set M such that E is represented in $\mathfrak{A}$ by M. If E is regular, then $\mathfrak{A}$ can be chosen finite. Let us put $\mathfrak{B} = [\{0\}, Y, Z, h, z_1]$ where for $z \in Z$

$$h(z, 0) = \{[y, z'] \mid y \in Y \wedge z' \in Z \wedge \delta(z, y) = z'\}$$

for all $z \in Z$, we have $h(z, 0) \neq \emptyset$, hence $\mathfrak{B}$ is an initial autonomous ND-automaton which is finite if E is regular. We show that E is generated in $\mathfrak{B}$ by M. Indeed,

$$\begin{aligned} e \in E &\leftrightarrow \delta(z_1, e) \in M \\ &\leftrightarrow z_1 \in M \\ &\leftrightarrow h_e(z_1, e) \subseteq M \\ &\leftrightarrow \exists p\big(p \in W(\{0\}) \wedge h_e(z_1, p) \cap M \neq \emptyset\big), \end{aligned}$$

and for all $q = y_1 \ldots y_n \in W(Y) \setminus \{e\}$

$$\begin{aligned} q \in E &\leftrightarrow \delta(z_1, q) \in M \\ &\leftrightarrow \exists z_2 \ldots \exists z_{n+1} \left(\bigwedge_{i=1}^{n} z_{i+1} = \delta(z_i, y_i) \wedge z_{n+1} \in M \right) \\ &\leftrightarrow \exists z_2 \ldots \exists z_{n+1} \left(\bigwedge_{i=1}^{n} [y_i, z_{i+1}] \in h(z_i, 0) \wedge z_{n+1} \in M \right) \\ &\leftrightarrow h_q(z_1, 0^n) \cap M \neq \emptyset \\ &\leftrightarrow \exists p\big(p \in W(\{0\}) \wedge h_q(z_1, p) \cap M \neq \emptyset\big). \end{aligned}$$

Thus Proposition 8.10.1 is verified, and for 8.10.2 it remains only to show that every event generated in a finite ND-automaton is regular.

Suppose $E \subseteq W(Y)$ is generated in $\mathfrak{B} = [\{0\}, Y, Z, h, z_1]$ by $M \subseteq Z$, further let $z^* \notin Z$, $Z^* \underset{\mathrm{Df}}{=} \{z^*\} \cup Z$, and for $z \in Z^*$, $y \in Y$

$$f^*(z, y) \underset{\mathrm{Df}}{=} \begin{cases} \{z' \mid [y, z'] \in h(z, 0)\}, & \text{if } h_y(z, 0) \neq \emptyset \text{ and } z \in Z, \\ \{z^*\} & \text{otherwise.} \end{cases}$$

Here, $\mathfrak{B}^* = [Y, Z^*, f^*, z_1]$ is an outputless initial ND-automaton which is finite if $\mathfrak{B}$ is. We show that E is represented in $\mathfrak{B}^*$ by M. First of all

$$\begin{aligned} e \in E &\leftrightarrow h_e(z_1, e) \cap M \neq \emptyset \\ &\leftrightarrow z_1 \in M \\ &\leftrightarrow f^*(z_1, e) \cap M \neq \emptyset. \end{aligned}$$

For all $q = y_1 \ldots y_n \in W(X) \setminus \{e\}$

$$\begin{aligned} q \in E &\leftrightarrow h_q(z_1, 0^n) \cap M \neq \emptyset \\ &\leftrightarrow \exists z_2 \ldots \exists z_{n+1} \left(\bigwedge_{i=1}^{n} [y_i, z_{i+1}] \in h(z_i, 0) \wedge z_{n+1} \in M \right) \\ &\leftrightarrow \exists z_2 \ldots \exists z_{n+1} \left(\bigwedge_{i=1}^{n} z_{i+1} \in f^*(z_i, y_i) \wedge z_{i+1} \in Z \wedge z_{n+1} \in M \right) \\ &\leftrightarrow f^*(z_1, q) \cap M \neq \emptyset, \end{aligned}$$

which was to be shown. Theorem 8.4 implies that E is regular provided $\mathfrak{B}$ (and thus $\mathfrak{B}^*$) is.

Now we define another kind of generating, in which the requirements on the generating ND-automaton are greater in that we have to be able to see directly from its output whether a sentence was generated, without first checking any property of its states. To achieve this, we provide the automaton with a special output signal y^*, which appears in its output if and only if the string generated so far (the output word) including y^* is *no longer* a sentence of the generated language.

This signal in general can not be omitted, since otherwise the ND-automaton could generate only such languages (events) in which every sentence could be extended to a new sentence by attaching a member of the vocabulary on the right. This means that for every word q belonging to this event there is an output signal $y \in Y$ such that qy also belongs to this event. This condition is certainly not satisfied for finite events or events whose members have a bounded length. We shall see later when the signal y^* can be omitted.

In what follows we assume $y^* \in Y$.

Definition 8.5. We say that the event $E \subseteq W(Y)$ is *produced* in the ND-automaton $\mathfrak{B} = [X, Y \cup \{y^*\}, Z, h]$ *by the set of states* $M \subseteq Z$ if

$$E = \bigcup_{p \in W(X)} v_{\mathfrak{B}}(M, p) \cap W(Y).$$

If $M = \{z\}$ is a singleton, then we refer to E *as the event produced by the state* z.

From Theorem 6.1 we obtain

Corollary 8.11. Every non-empty producible event can be produced by a state.

We recall that $Com(E)$, the completion of the event E, has been defined as follows:

$$Com(E) = \{q \mid \exists r (qr \in E)\} \cup \{e\}.$$

Theorem 8.12. *An event E is producible in a (finite) ND-automaton if and only if (E is regular and) $E = Com(E)$ or $E = \emptyset$.*

Proof: The impossible event can be produced in every ND-automaton by the empty set.

Suppose $\emptyset \neq E \subseteq W(Y)$ and E is produced in $\mathfrak{B} = [X, Y \cup \{y^*\}, Z, h]$ by z_1. For every $y_1 \dots y_n \in E$ $(n \geq 1)$ there is an $x_1 \dots x_n \in W(X)$ with $y_1 \dots y_n \in v_{\mathfrak{B}}(z_1, x_1 \dots x_n) \cap W(Y)$. This implies $y_1 \dots y_\nu \in v_{\mathfrak{B}}(z_1, x_1 \dots x_\nu) \cap W(Y)$ for $\nu = 0, 1, \dots, n$, i.e., the initial segments $e, y_1, y_1 y_2, \dots, y_1 \dots y_n$ of $y_1 \dots y_n$ also belong to E. That is, if $E \neq \emptyset$, then $E = Com(E)$.

Let $z^* \notin Z$, $Z^* \underset{\text{Df}}{=} \{z^*\} \cup Z$ and for $z \in Z^*$, $x \in X$

$$h^*(z, x) \underset{\text{Df}}{=} \begin{cases} (h(z, x) \setminus \{[y^*, z'] \mid z' \in Z\}) \cup \{[y^*, z^*]\}, & \text{if } z \in Z, \\ \{[y^*, z^*]\}, & \text{if } z = z^*. \end{cases}$$

$\mathfrak{B}^* = [X, Y \cup \{y^*\}, Z^*, h^*, z_1]$ is an initial ND-automaton which is finite if $\mathfrak{B}$ is. We show that E is generated in $\mathfrak{B}^*$ by Z.

Since $E \neq \emptyset$, the empty word e belongs to E, and as was required, $h_e(z_1, e) \cap Z \neq \emptyset$, because $z_1 \in Z$.

Let $q = y_1 \dots y_n \in W(Y \cup \{y^*\}) \setminus \{e\}$. Then

$$q \in E \leftrightarrow q \in W(Y) \wedge \exists p\big(p \in W(X) \wedge q \in v_{\mathfrak{B}}(z_1, p)\big)$$
$$\leftrightarrow \exists x_1 \dots \exists x_n \, \exists z_2 \dots \exists z_{n+1} \left(\bigwedge_{i=1}^{n} [y_i, z_{i+1}] \in h(z_i, x_i) \wedge y_i \in Y \wedge z_{i+1} \in Z \right).$$

For $y \in Y$, $z, z' \in Z$, $x \in X$ however

$$[y, z'] \in h(z, x) \leftrightarrow [y, z'] \in h^*(z, x).$$

Thus we obtain

$$q \in E \leftrightarrow \exists x_1 \dots \exists x_n \, \exists z_2 \dots \exists z_{n+1} \left(\bigwedge_{i=1}^{n} [y_i, z_{i+1}] \in h^*(z_i, x_i) \wedge x_i \in X \wedge y_i \in Y \wedge z_{i+1} \in Z \right).$$

Furthermore, by the definition of h^*, $z_{n+1} \in Z$ implies $z_1, \dots, z_n \in Z$ and thus $y_1, \dots, y_n \in Y$, since if $\mathfrak{B}^*$ puts out y^* then it always enters the state z^*. Therefore

$$q \in E \leftrightarrow \exists x_1 \dots \exists x_n \, \exists z_2 \dots \exists z_{n+1} \left(\bigwedge_{i=1}^{n} [y_i, z_{i+1}] \in h^*(z_i, x_i) \wedge x_i \in X \wedge z_{n+1} \in Z \right)$$
$$\leftrightarrow \exists p\big(p \in W(X) \wedge h_q^*(z_1, p) \cap Z \neq \emptyset\big),$$

which was to be shown.

Every non-empty event which is producible in a finite ND-automaton thus can be generated in a finite ND-automaton, and therefore is regular.

Suppose E is an arbitrary event over Y such that $E = Com(E)$. Then there is a deterministic automaton $\mathfrak{A} = [Y, Z, \delta, z_1]$ and a set $M \subseteq Z$ such that E is represented in $\mathfrak{A}$ by M. If E is regular, $\mathfrak{A}$ can be chosen finite. Moreover, since $E = Com(E)$, we can assume that $M = Z \setminus \{z^*\}$, and for all $q \in W(Y)$

$$\delta(z_1, q) \neq z^* \leftrightarrow q \in E.$$

Here, $z^* \neq z_1$, since $e \in Com(E) = E$. Now we construct from $\mathfrak{A}$ an ND-automaton $\mathfrak{B} = [\{0\}, Y \cup \{y^*\}, Z, h]$ by defining the function h as follows:

$$h(z, 0) = \{[y, z'] \mid z' = \delta(z, y) \wedge z' \neq z^*\} \cup \{[y^*, z^*]\}$$

for all $z \in Z$. $\mathfrak{B}$ is finite if $\mathfrak{A}$ is. We show that E is produced in $\mathfrak{B}$ by the state z_1.

Let $q = y_1 \dots y_n \in W(Y \cup \{y^*\})$ $(n \geqq 0)$. If $q \in E$, then the words $e, y_1, y_1 y_2, \dots, y_1 \dots y_n$ also belong to E. Consequently, z^* does not appear in the sequence $z_1 = \delta(z_1, e)$, $z_2 = \delta(z_1, y_1)$, $z_3 = \delta(z_2, y_2), \dots, z_{n+1} = \delta(z_n, y_n) = \delta(z_1, q)$. By the definition of h, the automaton $\mathfrak{B}$ can run through the sequence of states $z_1, \ldots, z_{n+1}$ and simultaneously put out the word q, i.e., $q \in v_{\mathfrak{B}}(z_1, 0^n)$. Conversely, suppose $q \in v_{\mathfrak{B}}(z_1, 0^n) \cap W(Y)$. Then if $\mathfrak{B}$ puts out the word q and meanwhile runs through the sequence of states $z_1, \ldots, z_{n+1}$, the state z^* does not appear in this sequence, since otherwise y^* would be put out at a transition to z^*.

Consequently $z_{n+1} \neq z^*$, and for $\nu = 1, \ldots, n$ we have $z_{n+1} = \delta(z_\nu, y_\nu)$, hence (by $\delta(z_1, q) = z_{n+1} \neq z^*$) $q \in E$.

Thus Theorem 8.12 is proved.

From Theorem 8.9 and the proof of Theorem 8.12 we obtain

Corollary 8.13. Every event producible in a (finite) ND-automaton can be produced in a (finite) autonomous ND-automaton.

Finally we investigate which events can be produced without using the output signal y^*. We call these events strongly producible.

Definition 8.6. The event $E \subseteq W(Y)$ over Y is said to be *strongly produced* in the ND-automaton $\mathfrak{B} = [X, Y, Z, h]$ *by the set of states* $M \subseteq Z$ if $E = \bigcup_{p \in W(X)} v_{\mathfrak{B}}(M, p)$.

Corollary 8.14.

1. An event over Y is strongly producible if and only if it is producible in an ND-automaton having the output alphabet Y.

2. A non-empty event E over Y is strongly producible if and only if there is a non-empty set X and a sequential ND-operator φ over $[X, Y]$ such that $E = \bigcup_{p \in W(X)} \varphi(p)$.

3. Every non-empty strongly producible event is strongly produced by a state.

4. Every strongly producible event is producible.

5. Every event strongly producible in a ($[Y, Z]$-finite) ND-automaton can be strongly produced and produced in an autonomous (finite) ND-automaton (and is regular).

6. In order for a sequential ND-operator φ over the finite alphabets X, Y to be generable in a finite ND-automaton, is necessary for the set $\bigcup_{p \in W(X)} \varphi(p)$ to be regular.

Thus among the non-empty producible events, exactly those which can be written in the form $\bigcup_{p \in W(X)} \varphi(p)$, where φ is a sequential ND-operator are strongly producible. This implies that a strongly producible event contains words of every possible length and thus is infinite if not empty. The claim that this necessary condition is also sufficient, as stated in STARKE [4], Theorem 15, is false. We shall clarify this by the following example: Let $E = \{1\} \cup \{0^n \mid n \geqq 0\}$, $\mathfrak{B}_{18} = [\{0\}, \{0, 1\} \cup \{y^*\}, \{1, 2, 3, 4\}, f, m]$, where $m(1) = m(2) = \{0\}$, $m(3) = \{1\}$, $m(4) = \{y^*\}$ and $f(1, 0) = \{2, 3\}$, $f(2, 0) = \{2\}$, $f(3, 0) = \{4\}$, $f(4, 0) = \{4\}$.

E contains words of every possible length and is generated in $\mathfrak{B}_{18}$ by the state 1. However, E is not strongly producible since for an arbitrary sequential ND-operator φ over $[\{0\}, \{0, 1\}]$ with $E = \bigcup_{n \geqq 0} \varphi(0^n)$, $1 \in E$, i.e., $1 \in \varphi(0)$ implies that for every $n \geqq 0$ there is an $s \in W(Y)$ with $1s \in \varphi(00^n)$. Thus 10 or 11 would have to belong to $\varphi(00)$, i.e., to E, which is not the case.

PART III

STOCHASTIC AUTOMATA

The strictly deterministic way of functioning of ordinary abstract automata cannot in general be realized by concrete technical systems which exist in practice. On the other hand, this determinacy often leads to difficulties in the mathematical description of concrete technical or natural systems in terms of automata theory. In addition to the question of how reliable a system is when constructed from a large number of more or less reliable elements, (cf. e.g. MULLIN [1], NEUMANN [1]), there was an early interest in investigating abstract stochastic systems. Research in this field was stimulated by the fact that deterministic automata are not suitable for modelling even the simplest forms of behaviour, such as the acquisition of a conditioned reflex. For instance, when creating a conditioned reflex in an animal there is a transitory phase in which there is only a certain probability that the animal would give a specified response to a given impulse. In this phase, the animal's behaviour can be adequately modelled only by means of a stochastic automaton[1]). Therefore, in order to develop an abstract theory of learning automata, it is necessary to first produce a systematic development of the theory of stochastic automata (cf. BUSH, MOSTELLER [1]).

The investigation of stochastic automata with the aim of developing an abstract theory of these systems similar to that of deterministic automata, began between 1961—1965 in the USA (CARLYLE [1], [2], RABIN [1]), in the USSR (SHREJDER [2], BUCHARAIEV [1], [2], TSERTSVADZE [1], [2]), and in the GDR (STARKE [3]) independently. It is interesting to point out that BUCHARAIEV, CARLYLE and STARKE arrived at the same definition of the concept of stochastic automata.

We shall consider systems working on a discrete time-scale, that is pulse-wise with states, input signals and output signals, in the same way as deterministic abstract automata. Thus in every step exactly one signal is received, exactly one signal is emitted, and exactly one state occurs. However, similarly to non-deterministic automata, in a given situation $[z, x]$ the external and internal reactions of the system are not uniquely determined, but for every imaginable reaction, i.e., every pair $[y, z']$, there is only a certain probability that in the situation $[z, x]$ the system would react with $[y, z']$, i.e., that it would put out y and meanwhile enter the state z'. We can easily verify that it does not imply any loss of generality

[1]) Cf. e.g., S. N. BRAINES, A. V. NAPALKOV, and W. B. SVECHINSKI, Neurocybernetics, Berlin 1964.

if we assume that this probability only depends on the situation $[z, x]$ and not on the number of the step t in which this situation occurs, or on the past history of this situation, i.e., on the situations which occured earlier.

§ 1. Fundamental Concepts

Let A be an at most countable set. A *discrete probability measure* (or shortly PM), P, over the set A is a probability function over the space of events $\mathfrak{P}(A)$, i.e., a normed measure on $\mathfrak{P}(A)$. Thus P is a discrete PM over A if and only if the following conditions are satisfied:

(K1) $P(E) \geqq 0$ for all $E \in \mathfrak{P}(A)$;

(K2) $P\left(\bigcup_{i=1}^{\infty} E_i\right) = \sum_{i=1}^{\infty} P(E_i)$, if $E_i \cap E_j = \emptyset$ for $i \neq j$ and $E_i \in \mathfrak{P}(A)$,

(K3) $P(A) = 1$.

The definition of a PM can be extended to arbitrary sets A as follows. Suppose A^* is an at most countable subset of A, and P is a discrete PM on A^*. Then we can extend P so that it is defined for each $E \subseteq P(A)$ by means of the following formula:

$$P(E) = \sum_{a \in E \cap A^*} P(\{a\}).$$

In what follows we shall write $P(a)$ instead of $P(\{a\})$ and $\sum_{a \in E} P(a)$ instead of $\sum_{a \in E \cap A^*} P(\{a\})$.

Definition 1.1. $\mathfrak{C} = [X, Y, Z, H]$ is called a *stochastic automaton* (abbreviated *S-automaton*) if

a) X, Y, Z, are arbitrary non-empty sets and

b) H is a function defined on $Z \times X$ each of whose values $H[z, x]$ is a discrete probability measure over $Y \times Z$.

Interpretation: The elements $x \in X$ are called *input signals* of $\mathfrak{C}$, and X itself the *input alphabet* of $\mathfrak{C}$. The members $y \in Y$ are the *output signals* of $\mathfrak{C}$, and Y itself the *output alphabet* of $\mathfrak{C}$. Finally, the elements $z \in Z$ are called the *states* of $\mathfrak{C}$. The stochastic automaton $\mathfrak{C}$ functions on a discrete time scale in a countably infinite number of steps $t = 1, 2, \ldots$ In each step t, $\mathfrak{C}$ receives exactly one input signal, puts out exactly one output signal and has exactly one state. If z is the state of $\mathfrak{C}$ in step t and x is the input signal received in step t, then for each subset $A \subseteq Y \times Z$ the value $H[z, x](A)$ of the discrete PM $H[z, x]$ on the set A is the probability that in step t the signal y would be put out, that in step $t+1$ the state of $\mathfrak{C}$ would be z' and $[y, z'] \in A$.

According to the above convention we shall write $H[z, x](y, z')$ instead of $H[z, x](\{[y, z']\})$.

First we define several fundamental functions and properties of S-automata and then we turn to the description of the behaviour of an S-automaton which occurs by feeding into it a finite sequence of input signals.

Definition 1.2. Let $\mathfrak{C} = [X, Y, Z, H]$ be an arbitrary S-automaton.

(1.2.1) The *transition function* F of $\mathfrak{C}$ is the function defined on $Z \times X$, whose values are discrete PM's over Z specified by the following formula:

$$F[z, x](Z') \underset{\mathrm{Df}}{=} H[z, x](Y \times Z')$$

for $Z' \subseteq Z$.

(1.2.2) The equality

$$G[z, x](Y') \underset{\mathrm{Df}}{=} H[z, x](Y' \times Z)$$

defines a function G on $Z \times X$ whose values are discrete PM's over Y. We refer to G as the *output function* of $\mathfrak{C}$.

(1.2.3) (Carlyle [4]) $\mathfrak{C}$ is said to be *observable* if there is a partial function δ from $Z \times X \times Y$ into Z such that for all $z, z' \in Z$, $x \in X$, $y \in Y$, $H[z, x](y, z')$ is different from 0 if and only if $\delta(z, x, y)$ is defined and $z' = \delta(z, x, y)$.

(1.2.4) $\mathfrak{C}$ is said to be *Z-deterministic* if for every $z \in Z$, $x \in X$ there is exactly one $z' \in Z$ with $F[z, x](z') \neq 0$ (and thus $F[z, x](z') = 1$).

(1.2.5) $\mathfrak{C}$ is said to be *Y-deterministic* if for every $z \in Z$, $x \in X$ there is exactly one $y \in Y$ with $G[z, x](y) \neq 0$.

(1.2.6) $\mathfrak{C}$ is said to be *deterministic* if it is both Z-deterministic and Y-deterministic.

(1.2.7) $\mathfrak{C}$ is called *X-finite*, *Y-finite* or *Z-finite* respectively if the corresponding set is finite. Similarly we can define *[X, Z]-finiteness*, *[Y, Z]-finiteness*, etc. *[X, Y, Z]-finite* automata are simply called *finite*.

(1.2.8) $\mathfrak{C}$ is called *autonomous* if X is a singleton.

(1.2.9) Every discrete PM $\mathfrak{z}$ over Z is called a *random state* of $\mathfrak{C}$.

(1.2.10) $\mathfrak{C}$ is said to be *initial* (or *weakly initial*) if a state $z \in Z$ (or a random state $\mathfrak{z}$ of $\mathfrak{C}$) is prescribed as an initial state. Initial (or weakly initial) automata will be denoted by $[X, Y, Z, H, z]$ (or $[X, Y, Z, H, \mathfrak{z}]$).

(1.2.11) $\mathfrak{C}$ is called a *subautomaton of* $\mathfrak{C}' = [X', Y', Z', H']$ if $X \subseteq X'$, $Y \subseteq Y'$, $Z \subseteq Z'$ and H is the restriction of H' to $Z \times X \subseteq Z' \times X'$.

(1.2.12) A discrete PM α over A is called *deterministic* if there is an $a \in A$ with $\alpha(a) = 1$.

The interpretation of Definition 1.1 implies that if in step t, $\mathfrak{C}$ is in the situation $[z, x]$, then $F[z, x](Z')$ is the probability that in step $t + 1$ the state of $\mathfrak{C}$ belongs to the set Z', and $G[z, x](Y')$ is the probability that in step t a signal belonging to the set Y' is emitted.

For an observable S-automaton which is in the situation $[z, x]$ in step t, and puts out the signal y in this step, the state of the S-automaton in step $t + 1$ can be computed, namely it is $z' = \delta(z, x, y)$.

For an S-automaton $\mathfrak{C} = [X, Y, Z, H]$ it is "natural" that in a given step t the state of $\mathfrak{C}$ is unknown, and only the probability that in this step $\mathfrak{C}$ has the state z is known. This way, we obtain a discrete PM $\mathfrak{z}$ over Z, whose value $\mathfrak{z}(z)$ is the above mentioned probability. Thus if $Z' \subseteq Z$, the value $\mathfrak{z}(Z')$ is the probability that in step t the state z_t of $\mathfrak{C}$ belongs to the set Z'. That is why every discrete PM over Z is called a random state of $\mathfrak{C}$.

Corollary 1.1.

1. Every Z-deterministic S-automaton is observable.

2. An S-automaton $\mathfrak{C} = [X, Y, Z, H]$ is deterministic if and only if for all $z \in Z$, $x \in X$ the discrete PM $H[z, x]$ is deterministic.

3. If $\mathfrak{C} = [X, Y, Z, h]$ is a subautomaton of $\mathfrak{C}' = [X', Y', Z', H']$ then for all $z \in Z$, $x \in X$, $y' \in Y'$, $z'' \in Z''$

$$H'[z, x](y', z'') = 0, \quad \text{if} \quad y' \in Y' \setminus Y \quad \text{or} \quad z'' \in Z' \setminus Z.$$

4. If $\mathfrak{C} = [X, Y, Z, H]$ is observable, then there is exactly one function δ from $Z \times X \times Y$ into Z such that for all $z, z' \in Z$, $x \in X$, $y \in Y$ the following condition is satisfied:

$$H[z, x](y, z') \neq 0 \leftrightarrow [z, x, y] \in Dom(\delta) \wedge \delta(z, x, y) = z',$$

where $Dom(\delta)$ denotes the domain (of definition) of the mapping δ. Thus we have

$$H[z, x](y, z') = \begin{cases} G[z, x](y), & \text{if } [z, x, y] \in Dom(\delta) \wedge \delta(z, x, y) = z', \\ 0 & \text{otherwise.} \end{cases}$$

5. An observable S-automaton is Z-deterministic if and only if δ does not depend on y.

In the introduction to the second part of this book we mentioned that a nondeterministic automaton $\mathfrak{B}$ can be assigned to every stochastic automaton $\mathfrak{C}$ so that something is possible in $\mathfrak{B}$ if and only if it can be carried out in $\mathfrak{C}$ with a positive probability. Moreover, it is obvious that an ordinary deterministic automaton can be canonically assigned to each deterministic stochastic automaton. This can also be obtained as the value of the mapping *Det* (defined in Part II, § 1) on the ND-automaton which is assigned to this deterministic S-automaton.

Definition 1.3.

(1.3.1) If $\mathfrak{C} = [X, Y, Z, H]$ is an S-automaton, then let $\mathfrak{B} = ND(\mathfrak{C})$ be defined as the ND-automaton $[X, Y, Z, h]$ where for $z \in Z$, $x \in X$ we put

$$h(z, x) = \{[y, z'] \mid H[z, x](y, z') > 0\}.$$

(1.3.2) If α is a discrete PM over A, then we define $ND(\alpha) = \{a \mid \alpha(a) > 0\}$.

(1.3.3) If β is a function which assigns to each $a \in A$ a discrete PM $\beta[\alpha]$ over B then $ND(\beta)$ denotes a singlevalued mapping of A into $\mathfrak{P}^*(B)$ such that

$$ND(\beta)(a) = \{b \mid \beta[a](b) > 0\} \quad \bigl(= ND(\beta[a])\bigr).$$

Corollary 1.2. Let $\mathfrak{C} = [X, Y, Z, H]$ be an arbitrary S-automaton.

1. $ND(\mathfrak{C}) = [X, Y, Z, ND(H)]$.

2. If f and g respectively are the transition and output functions of the ND-automaton $ND(\mathfrak{C})$, then $f = ND(F)$ and $g = ND(G)$.

3. If $\mathfrak{C}$ is observable, Z-deterministic, Y-deterministic, or deterministic, then $ND(\mathfrak{C})$ also has the corresponding property.

4. If $\mathfrak{C}$ is a deterministic stochastic automaton, with probability 1, then the deterministic automaton $\mathfrak{A} = Det\,(ND(\mathfrak{C})) = [X, Y, Z, Det\,(ND(F)), Det\,(ND(G))]$ does the same in every situation, as $\mathfrak{C}$.

5. For each deterministic automaton $\mathfrak{A}$, there is exactly one deterministic stochastic automaton $\mathfrak{C}$ with $\mathfrak{A} = Det\,(ND(\mathfrak{C}))$.

6. If $\mathfrak{C}$ is a subautomaton of $\mathfrak{C}'$, then $ND(\mathfrak{C})$ is a subautomaton of $ND(\mathfrak{C})$.

As we remarked in the introduction of Part II, there are ND-automata $\mathfrak{B}$ such that for no S-automaton $\mathfrak{C}$ do we have $\mathfrak{B} = ND(\mathfrak{C})$.

By Definition 1.1 and its interpretation, the stepwise external and internal behaviour of every S-automaton $\mathfrak{C} = [X, Y, Z, H]$ is specified. Now we extend the domain (of definition) of the function H in such a way that the extended function, which we also denote by H, describes the behaviour of $\mathfrak{C}$ "in large" arising when arbitrary finite sequences of input signals are fed into $\mathfrak{C}$.

For $z_1 \in Z$, $p \in W(X)$, $q \in W(Y)$, $r \in W(Z)$

$$H[z_1, p](q, r) \underset{\mathrm{Df}}{=} \begin{cases} 1, & \text{if } p = q = r = e; \\ \prod_{i=1}^{n} H[z_i, x_i](y_i, z_{i+1}), & \text{if } p = x_1 \dots x_n, \\ & \quad q = y_1 \dots y_n,\ n \geqq 1,\ r = z_2 \dots z_{n+1}; \\ 0 & \text{otherwise.} \end{cases}$$

Obviously, the number $H[z_1, p](q, r)$ is the probability that (for arbitrary $t \geqq 0$) the S-automaton $\mathfrak{C}$ puts out the word q in the course of the steps $t + 1, \dots, t + l(p)$ and meanwhile, for any $i = 1, \dots, l(p)$ in step $t + i + 1$, $\mathfrak{C}$ is in that state which occupies the ith place of the word r, provided that the state of $\mathfrak{C}$ in step $t + 1$ is z_1, and in the course of the steps $t + 1, \dots, t + l(p)$ the word p is fed into $\mathfrak{C}$. Since $H[z_i, x_i]$ can have non-zero values for at most countably many pairs $[y_i, z_{i+1}]$, for arbitrary $z \in Z$, $p \in W(X)$ there are at most countably many pairs $[q, r]$ with $H[z, p](q, r) \neq 0$. All these are contained in the set $Y^{l(p)} \times Z^{l(p)}$. Thus for $A \subseteq W(Y) \times W(Z)$, $z \in Z$, $p \in W(X)$ we can put

$$H[z, p](A) \underset{\mathrm{Df}}{=} \sum_{[q,r] \in A} H[z, p](q, r).$$

Thus H is extended to a function defined on $Z \times W(X)$, whose values are discrete PM's over $W(Y) \times W(Z)$.

Let $\mathfrak{Z}_Z$ be the set of all discrete PM's over Z, i.e., the set of all random states of $\mathfrak{C}$. We shall extend the domain of H once from the set $Z \times W(X)$ to $\mathfrak{Z}_Z \times W(X)$ in the following way. For $\mathfrak{z} \in \mathfrak{Z}_Z$, $p \in W(X)$, $A \subseteq W(Y) \times W(Z)$ let

$$H[\mathfrak{z}, p](A) \underset{\mathrm{Df}}{=} \sum_{z \in Z} \mathfrak{z}(z) \cdot H[z, p](A).$$

Thus H is a function defined on $\mathfrak{Z}_Z \times W(X)$, whose values are discrete PM's over $W(Y) \times W(Z)$. Here, the number $H[z, p](A)$ is the probability that the pair $[q, r]$ consisting of the word q given out by $\mathfrak{C}$ in the course of the steps

$t+1, \ldots, t+l(p)$ and the word r constructed from the states of $\mathfrak{C}$ in the steps $t+2, \ldots, t+l(p)+1$ belongs to A, provided that in step $t+1$ the state of $\mathfrak{C}$ is z with probability $\mathfrak{z}(z)$, and in the course of the steps $t+1, \ldots, t+l(p)$ the word p is fed into $\mathfrak{C}$.

The extension of the function H enables us to give a global description of the external and internal behaviour of the S-automaton $\mathfrak{C}$. However, we are often only interested in the following special questions: into which state and with what probability does $\mathfrak{C}$ enter, if beginning from a random state $\mathfrak{z}$ the word p is processed in $\mathfrak{C}$, or which word and with what probability is put out when the word p is fed into $\mathfrak{C}$, and at the beginning the state of $\mathfrak{C}$ is z with probability $\mathfrak{z}(z)$. To answer these questions we shall extend the domain of definition of the function F, and define a function $V_{\mathfrak{C}}$ which describes the global external behaviour of the S-automaton $\mathfrak{C}$.

In order to save parentheses, we agree that the symbol $\times$ separates more strongly than $\cdot$. For instance, $A \times B \cdot C$ should be read as $A \times (B \cdot C)$.

For $\mathfrak{z} \in \mathfrak{Z}_Z$, $p \in W(X)$, $Z' \subseteq Z$, let

$$F[\mathfrak{z}, p](Z') \underset{\mathrm{Df}}{=} \begin{cases} \mathfrak{z}(Z'), & \text{if} \quad p = e, \\ H[\mathfrak{z}, p]\big(W(Y) \times W(Z) \cdot Z'\big), & \text{if} \quad p \neq e. \end{cases}$$

For $\mathfrak{z} \in \mathfrak{Z}_Z$, $p \in W(X)$, $Q \subseteq W(Y)$, let

$$V_{\mathfrak{C}}[\mathfrak{z}, p](Q) \underset{\mathrm{Df}}{=} H[\mathfrak{z}, p]\big(Q \times W(Z)\big).$$

It is clear how both these definitions should be interpreted. Obviously, $F[\mathfrak{z}, p](Z')$ is the probability that the state of $\mathfrak{C}$ in step $t+l(p)$ belongs to the set Z', provided that in step t, $\mathfrak{C}$ has the random state $\mathfrak{z}$, and in the course of the steps $t, \ldots, t+l(p)-1$ the word p is fed into $\mathfrak{C}$.

The number $V_{\mathfrak{C}}[\mathfrak{z}, p](Q)$ is the probability that under the same conditions as above, in the course of the steps $t, \ldots, t+l(p)-1$, a word q belonging to the set Q is put out by $\mathfrak{C}$.

Obviously, for each $z \in Z$ there exists exactly one random state of $\mathfrak{C}$ whose value for z is equal to 1. This (deterministic) random state is denoted by δ_z; Clearly, for arbitrary $z, z' \in Z$

$$\delta_z(z') = \begin{cases} 1, & \text{if} \quad z = z', \\ 0 & \text{otherwise}. \end{cases}$$

Finally, we also extend the functions F and $V_{\mathfrak{C}}$ to $Z \times W(X)$ by putting:

For all $z \in Z$, $p \in W(X)$,

$$F[z, p] \underset{\mathrm{Df}}{=} F[\delta_z, p],$$

$$V_{\mathfrak{C}}[z, p] \underset{\mathrm{Df}}{=} V_{\mathfrak{C}}[\delta_z, p].$$

Finally, for $\mathfrak{z} \in \mathfrak{Z}_Z$, $x \in X$, $Y' \subseteq Y$

$$G[\mathfrak{z}, x](Y') \underset{\mathrm{Df}}{=} \sum_{z \in Z} \mathfrak{z}(z) \cdot G[z, x](Y').$$

There are several important consequences to the above definitions:

Corollary 1.3. Let $\mathfrak{C} = [X, Y, Z, H]$ be an S-automaton, $z \in Z$, $\mathfrak{z} \in \mathfrak{Z}_Z$, $p \in W(X)$.

1. For all $A \subseteq W(Y) \times W(Z)$ we have

$$H[\mathfrak{z}, p](A) = H[\mathfrak{z}, p](A \cap (Y^{l(p)} \times Z^{l(p)})).$$

2. For all $Q \subseteq W(Y)$ we have

$$V_{\mathfrak{C}}[\mathfrak{z}, p](Q) = V_{\mathfrak{C}}[\mathfrak{z}, p](Q \cap Y^{l(p)}).$$

3. $V_{\mathfrak{C}}[\mathfrak{z}, e](e) = 1$.

4. For all $z' \in Z$ we have

$$F[z, p](z') = \begin{cases} 1, & \text{if } p = e \text{ and } z = z', \\ H[z, p](Y^{l(p)} \times Z^{l(p)-1} \cdot \{z'\}), & \text{if } p \neq e. \end{cases}$$

As for the connection with the functions $f, g, v_{\mathfrak{B}}$ considered in the theory of non-deterministic automata, we can easily verify the following

Corollary 1.4. Let $\mathfrak{C} = [X, Y, Z, H]$ be an S-automaton and $\mathfrak{B} = [X, Y, Z, h] = ND(\mathfrak{C})$, then for $\mathfrak{z} \in \mathfrak{Z}_Z$, $z \in Z$, $x \in X$, $p \in W(X)$

1. $ND(F[\mathfrak{z}, p]) \quad = f(ND(\mathfrak{z}), p)$,
2. $ND(G[\mathfrak{z}, x]) \quad = g(ND(\mathfrak{z}), x)$,
3. $ND(V_{\mathfrak{C}}[\mathfrak{z}, p]) = v_{\mathfrak{B}}(ND(\mathfrak{z}), p)$.

To facilitate certain induction proofs, in the next theorem we verify certain "induction formulas" for the functions H, F and $V_{\mathfrak{C}}$.

Theorem 1.5. *Let $\mathfrak{C} = [X, Y, Z, H]$ be an S-automaton and $\mathfrak{z}$ a random state of $\mathfrak{C}$, furthermore, $p, r \in W(X)$ with $p \neq e$. Then we have:*

1. *For all $Q' \subseteq Y^{l(p)}$, $Q \subseteq W(Y)$, $R' \subseteq Z^{l(p)-1}$, $R \subseteq W(Z)$, $Z' \subseteq Z$,*

$$H[\mathfrak{z}, pr](Q' \cdot Q \times R' \cdot Z' \cdot R)$$
$$= \sum_{z' \in Z'} H[\mathfrak{z}, p](Q' \times R' \cdot \{z'\}) \cdot H[z', r](Q \times R).$$

2. *For all $Z' \subseteq Z$,*

$$F[\mathfrak{z}, pr](Z') = \sum_{z'' \in Z} F[\mathfrak{z}, p](z'') \cdot F[z'', r](Z').$$

3. *For all $Q' \subseteq Y^{l(p)}$, $Q \subseteq W(Y)$,*

$$V_{\mathfrak{C}}[\mathfrak{z}, pr](Q' \cdot Q) = \sum_{z'' \in Z} H[\mathfrak{z}, p](Q' \times W(Z) \cdot \{z''\})\, V_{\mathfrak{C}}[z'', r](Q).$$

Proof: Clearly all three propositions are valid for $r = e$. Suppose $p = x_1 \ldots x_n$ $(n \geq 1)$ and $r = x_{n+1} \ldots x_{n+k}$ $(k \geq 1)$. Then for $Q' \subseteq Y^n$, $Q \subseteq W(Y)$,

$R' \subseteq Z^{n-1}$, $R \subseteq W(Z)$, $Z' \subseteq Z$

$$H[\mathfrak{z}, pr](Q' \cdot Q \times R' \cdot Z' \cdot R) = \sum_{\substack{z_1 \in Z, q' \in Q' \\ q \in Q, w' \in R' \\ z' \in Z', w \in R}} \mathfrak{z}(z_1) \cdot H[z_1, pr](q'q, w'z'w)$$

$$= \sum_{\substack{z_1 \in Z, y_1 \ldots y_n \in Q' \\ y_{n+1} \ldots y_{n+k} \in Q \\ z_2 \ldots z_n \in R', z_{n+1} \in Z' \\ z_{n+2} \ldots z_{n+k+1} \in R}} \mathfrak{z}(z_1) \prod_{i=1}^{n+k} H[z_i, x_i](y_i, z_{i+1})$$

$$= \sum_{z_1 \in Z} \mathfrak{z}(z_1) \sum_{z_{n+1} \in Z'} \left(\sum_{\substack{y_1 \ldots y_n \in Q' \\ z_2 \ldots z_n \in R'}} \prod_{i=1}^{n} H[z_i, x_i](y_i, z_{i+1}) \right)$$

$$\cdot \left(\sum_{\substack{y_{n+1} \ldots y_{n+k} \in Q \\ z_{n+2} \ldots z_{n+k+1} \in R}} \prod_{i=n+1}^{n+k} H[z_i, x_i](y_i, z_{i+1}) \right)$$

$$= \sum_{z_1 \in Z} \mathfrak{z}(z_1) \sum_{z_{n+1} \in Z'} H[z_1, p](Q' \times R' \cdot \{z_{n+1}\}) H[z_{n+1}, r](Q \times R)$$

$$= \sum_{z' \in Z'} H[\mathfrak{z}, p](Q' \times R' \cdot \{z'\}) \cdot H[z', r](Q \times R).$$

Thus Proposition 1.5.1 is proved. For $Z' \subseteq Z$ we have

$$\begin{aligned} F[\mathfrak{z}, pr](Z') &= H[\mathfrak{z}, pr]\big(W(Y) \times W(Z) \cdot Z'\big) \\ &= H[\mathfrak{z}, pr](Y^{n+k} \times Z^{n+k-1} \cdot Z') \\ &= H[\mathfrak{z}, pr](Y^n \cdot Y^k \times Z^{n-1} \cdot Z \cdot Z^{k-1} \cdot Z') \\ &= \sum_{z'' \in Z} H[\mathfrak{z}, p](Y \times Z^{n-1} \cdot \{z''\}) H[z'', r](Y^k \times Z^{k-1} \cdot Z') \\ &= \sum_{z'' \in Z} F[\mathfrak{z}, p](z'') \cdot F[z'', r](Z'), \end{aligned}$$

and thus 1.5.2 is verified. Finally for $Q' \subseteq Y^n$, $Q \subseteq W(Y)$

$$\begin{aligned} V_{\mathfrak{C}}[\mathfrak{z}, pr](Q' \cdot Q) &= H[\mathfrak{z}, pr](Q' \cdot Q \times Z^{n-1} \cdot Z \cdot Z^k) \\ &= \sum_{z'' \in Z} H[\mathfrak{z}, p](Q' \times Z^{n-1} \cdot \{z''\}) H[z'', r](Q \times Z^k) \\ &= \sum_{z'' \in Z} H[\mathfrak{z}, p]\big(Q' \times W(Z) \cdot \{z''\}\big) V_{\mathfrak{C}}[z'', r](Q). \end{aligned}$$

Thus Theorem 1.5 is proved.

Remark: Clearly, Proposition 1.5.3:

$$V_{\mathfrak{C}}[\mathfrak{z}, pr](Q' \cdot Q) = \sum_{z'' \in Z} H[\mathfrak{z}, p]\big(Q' \times W(Z) \cdot \{z''\}\big) V_{\mathfrak{C}}[z'', r](Q)$$

can be transferred to the non-deterministic automaton $\mathfrak{B} = ND(\mathfrak{C})$ in the form

$$v_{\mathfrak{B}}(M, pr) = \bigcup_{z'' \in Z} h_{z''}(M, p) v_{\mathfrak{B}}(z'', r)$$

where $M = ND(\mathfrak{z}) \subseteq Z$. However, this does not yield us a proof of the above equality for arbitrary ND-automata, since there exists an ND-automaton $\mathfrak{B}$ and a set M of its states such that for each S-automaton $\mathfrak{C}$ with $\mathfrak{B} = ND(\mathfrak{C})$ and every random state $\mathfrak{z}$ of $\mathfrak{C}$, $M \neq ND(\mathfrak{z})$.

We define two fundamental types of stochastic automata, namely *stochastic Mealy* and *stochastic Moore automata*.

Definition 1.4. Let $\mathfrak{C} = [X, Y, Z, H]$ be an S-automaton.

(1.4.1) $\mathfrak{C}$ is called a *stochastic Mealy-automaton* if for all $z \in Z$, $x \in X$, $Y' \subseteq Y$, $Z' \subseteq Z$

$$H[z, x](Y' \times Z') = G[z, x](Y') \cdot F[z, x](Z').$$

(1.4.2) $\mathfrak{C}$ is called a *stochastic Moore automaton* if there is a function M defined on Z (a *marking function*), whose values $M[z]$ are discrete PM's over Y such that for all $z \in Z$, $x \in X$, $Z' \subseteq Z$, $Y' \subseteq Y$

$$H[z, x](Y' \times Z') = \sum_{z' \in Z'} F[z, x](z') \cdot M[z'](Y').$$

Interpretation: For a stochastic Mealy automaton, the random process by whose realization is determined the signal y put out by the automaton, and its next state z', decomposes into two independent random processes described by F and G respectively. The probability that a Mealy automaton $\mathfrak{C}$ in step $t+1$ enters a certain state z, is thus independent of the output signal of $\mathfrak{C}$ in step t, and the probability that in step t the output signal of $\mathfrak{C}$ is y, is independent of the state of $\mathfrak{C}$ in step $t+1$.

For an arbitrary stochastic Moore automaton $\mathfrak{C}$, the probability that in step t $\mathfrak{C}$ puts out a certain signal y, does not depend explicitely on the situation $[z_t, x_t]$ occuring in step t, but only on the state into which $\mathfrak{C}$ enters in step $t+1$. If the Moore automaton $\mathfrak{C}$ has the state z in step $t+1$, then in step t the signal y was put out with probability $M[z](y)$, independently of the situation occuring in step t.

Remark: The function M is in general not uniquely determined. This is the case if and only if there is a $z'' \in Z$ such that $F[z,x](z'') = 0$ for all $[z,x] \in Z \times X$. For such a state z'', the value of M can be specified arbitrarily without affecting the external or internal behaviour of the stochastic Moore automaton. Therefore, in what follows, we specify a member $y^* \in Y$ and put $M[z] = \delta_{y^*}$ for all of the above mentioned "critical" states z. Hence, in what follows, we shall refer to *the* marking function M of $\mathfrak{C}$, and denote a stochastic Moore automaton by $\mathfrak{C} = [X, Y, Z, F, M]$. Stochastic Mealy automata will be denoted by $\mathfrak{C} = [X, Y, Z, F, G]$.

Corollary 1.6. Let $\mathfrak{C} = [X, Y, Z, H]$ be an S-automaton.

1. $\mathfrak{C}$ is an S-Mealy automaton, if and only if for all $z, z' \in Z,\ x \in X,\ y \in Y$,

$$H[z, x](y, z') = F[z, x](z') G[z, x](y).$$

2. $\mathfrak{C}$ is an S-Moore automaton if and only if for all $z' \in Z,\ y \in Y$ the quotient $\dfrac{H[z, x](y, z')}{F[z, x](z')}$ $(= M[z'](y))$ is independent of $[z, x] \in Z \times X$, provided $F[z, x](z') > 0$.

3. If $\mathfrak{C}$ is an S-Mealy (Moore) automaton, then $\mathfrak{B} = ND(\mathfrak{C})$ is an ND-Mealy (Moore) automaton.

4. If $\mathfrak{C}$ is an S-Mealy automaton, then for all $z \in Z,\ x \in X,\ y \in Y,\ p \in W(X),\ q \in W(Y)$

$$\begin{aligned} V_{\mathfrak{C}}[z, xp](yq) &= G[z, x](y) \sum_{z' \in Z} F[z, x](z')\, V_{\mathfrak{C}}[z', p](q) \\ &= G[z, x](y)\, V_{\mathfrak{C}}[F[z, x], p](q). \end{aligned}$$

5. If $\mathfrak{C}$ is an S-Moore automaton, then for $z \in Z_Z,\ x \in X,\ y \in Y,\ p \in W(X),\ q \in W(Y)$

$$V_{\mathfrak{C}}[\mathfrak{z}, xp](yq) = \sum_{z' \in Z} F[\mathfrak{z}, x](z')\, M[z'](y)\, V_{\mathfrak{C}}[z', p](q).$$

Theorem 1.7. *An S-Mealy automaton $\mathfrak{C} = [X, Y, Z, F, G]$ is observable if and only if it is Z-deterministic.*

Proof: Since every Z-deterministic S-automaton is observable, it suffices to show that if $\mathfrak{C}$ is observable, it is also Z-deterministic. Let δ be the partial function from the set $Z \times X \times Y$ into Z belonging to $\mathfrak{C}$, for which

$$\begin{aligned} &F[z, x](z') \cdot G[z, x](y) > 0 \\ &\leftrightarrow [z, x, y] \in Dom(\delta) \wedge \delta(z, x, y) = z'. \end{aligned}$$

Furthermore let $[z, x] \in Z \times X$ and $z', z'' \in Z$ with $F[z, x](z') > 0$ and $F[z, x](z'') > 0$. Since $G[z, x]$ is a discrete PM over Y, there is a $y_0 \in Y$ with $G[z, x](y_0) > 0$. Consequently,

$$F[z, x](z') G[z, x](y_0) > 0,\quad F[z, x](z'') G[z, x](y_0) > 0,$$

hence $[z, x, y_0] \in Dom(\delta)$ and $z' = \delta(z, x, y_0) = z''$. Thus for $[z, x]$ there is exactly one state $z' \in Z$ with $F[z, x](z') > 0$, that is, $\mathfrak{C}$ is Z-deterministic.

Theorem 1.8. *If $\mathfrak{C} = [X, Y, Z, H]$ is a Z-deterministic or Y-deterministic S-automaton, then $\mathfrak{C}$ is a Z-deterministic or Y-deterministic S-Mealy automaton.*

Proof: Suppose $\mathfrak{C}$ is Z-deterministic: then for every $z \in Z,\ x \in X$ there is exactly one $z' \in Z$ with $F[z, x](z') > 0$. Put $\delta = Det\big(ND(F)\big)$, i.e., δ is a function defined on $Z \times X$ whose values belong to Z and $F[z, x](z') > 0$ holds if and only if $z' = \delta(z, x)$. Consequently, $H[z, x](y, z')$ can only be different from 0 if $z' = \delta(z, x)$. For all $z \in Z,\ x \in X,\ y \in Y$

$$G[z, x](y) = H[z, x](\{y\} \times Z) = H[z, x]\big(y, \delta(z, x)\big).$$

Hence for all $z, z' \in Z,\ x \in X,\ y \in Y$

$$H[z,x](y,z') = \left\{\begin{matrix} 0, & \text{if} \quad z' \neq \delta(z,x) \\ H[z,x]\big(y, \delta(z,x)\big) & \text{otherwise} \end{matrix}\right\}$$
$$= F[z,x](z') \cdot G[z,x](y),$$

which was to be shown. The proof of the case in which $\mathfrak{C}$ is Y-deterministic runs on similar lines.

Corollary 1.9. If $\mathfrak{C} = [X, Y, Z, F, M]$ is a Z-deterministic S-Moore automaton, then for all $z \in Z,\ x \in X,\ Y' \subseteq Y$

$$G[z,x](Y') = M[Det(ND(F[z,x]))](Y').$$

Just as for deterministic and non-deterministic automata, we can assign a graph to each S-automaton in a uniquely determined way.

Definition 1.5. Let $\mathfrak{C} = [X, Y, Z, H]$ be an S-automaton. The *graph* $\mathfrak{G}_{\mathfrak{C}}$ *of* $\mathfrak{C}$ is the system $[P, K, \alpha]$ where

$$P \underset{\mathrm{Df}}{=} Z,$$
$$K \underset{\mathrm{Df}}{=} \{[z, x, y, z', H[z,x](y,z')] \mid z, z' \in Z \wedge x \in X \wedge y \in Y \wedge H[z,x](y,z') > 0\}$$

and for $k = [z, x, y, z', \lambda] \in K \subseteq Z \times X \times Y \times Z \times \langle 0, 1\rangle$

$$\alpha(k) \underset{\mathrm{Df}}{=} [z, z'].$$

In a graphic representation of the graph of a (finite) S-automaton, only the figures x, y, λ are indicated at the edge $[z, x, y, z', \lambda]$, since it is clear from the representation from which vertice to which vertice the edge runs.

Definition 1.5 will be illustrated by the example (due to Even [4]) of the S-automaton $\mathfrak{C}_1$, with which we shall also deal in the next section. The ND-automaton $\mathfrak{B}_7 = ND(\mathfrak{C}_1)$ was already mentioned in Part II, § 2.

The function H_1 of $\mathfrak{C}_1 \underset{\mathrm{Df}}{=} [\{0,1\}, \{A,B,C\}, \{1,2,3,4,5\}, H_1]$ is given in the next six tables, where the entry of the table $T(x,y)$ in row i, column j $(1 \leq i,j \leq 5)$ is the probability $H_1[i,x](y,j)$. The graph $\mathfrak{G}_{\mathfrak{C}_1}$ is represented in Fig. 21.

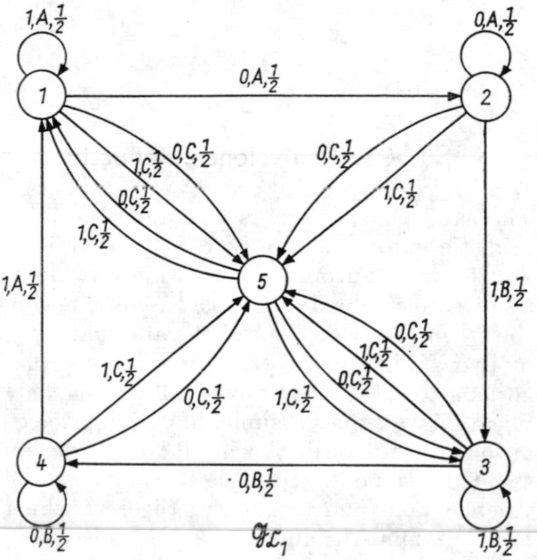

Fig. 21

$T(0, A)$	1	2	3	4	5
1	0	$\frac{1}{2}$	0	0	0
2	0	$\frac{1}{2}$	0	0	0
3	0	0	0	0	0
4	0	0	0	0	0
5	0	0	0	0	0

$T(0, B)$	1	2	3	4	5
1	0	0	0	0	0
2	0	0	0	0	0
3	0	0	0	$\frac{1}{2}$	0
4	0	0	0	$\frac{1}{2}$	0
5	0	0	0	0	0

$T(0, C)$	1	2	3	4	5
1	0	0	0	0	$\frac{1}{2}$
2	0	0	0	0	$\frac{1}{2}$
3	0	0	0	0	$\frac{1}{2}$
4	0	0	0	0	$\frac{1}{2}$
5	$\frac{1}{2}$	0	$\frac{1}{2}$	0	0

$T(1, A)$	1	2	3	4	5
1	$\frac{1}{2}$	0	0	0	0
2	0	0	0	0	0
3	0	0	0	0	0
4	$\frac{1}{2}$	0	0	0	0
5	0	0	0	0	0

$T(1, B)$	1	2	3	4	5
1	0	0	0	0	0
2	0	0	$\frac{1}{2}$	0	0
3	0	0	$\frac{1}{2}$	0	0
4	0	0	0	0	0
5	0	0	0	0	0

$T(1, C)$	1	2	3	4	5
1	0	0	0	0	$\frac{1}{2}$
2	0	0	0	0	$\frac{1}{2}$
3	0	0	0	0	$\frac{1}{2}$
4	0	0	0	0	$\frac{1}{2}$
5	$\frac{1}{2}$	0	$\frac{1}{2}$	0	0

§ 2. Equivalence, Reduction and Minimization

The same considerations which, in the theories of deterministic and non-deterministic automata, motivated the definition of the equivalence between states and between automata, and which we do not want to repeat here, can also be applied to stochastic automata. Now, however, we must take into consideration the stochastic behaviour of the automata, and we can only say that the behaviour of two automata are the same if the probabilities of the different external reactions to the same impulse also coincide. In order to avoid unnecessary complications, we shall assume, in defining the equivalence, that in the corresponding automata, not only the input alphabet, but also the output alphabets are the same. It would be possible to omit this condition from the definition of equivalence, and then to prove a theorem which is an analogon of Theorem 2.2, for non-deterministic automata. For this, however, in the definition of the equivalence certain additional conditions should be included which would imply that every signal y not contained in the intersection $Y \cap Y'$ of both output alphabets, can only be put out by both automata with probability zero.

Definition 2.1. Let $\mathfrak{C}, \mathfrak{C}'$ be S-automata with the input alphabet X, the output alphabet Y and the sets of states Z and Z'.

(2.1.1) If $\mathfrak{z}$ is a random state of $\mathfrak{C}$, $\mathfrak{z}'$ a random state of $\mathfrak{C}'$, then $\mathfrak{z}$ and $\mathfrak{z}'$ are called *equivalent* (notation: $\mathfrak{z} \sim \mathfrak{z}'$) if for all $p \in W(X)$, $q \in W(Y)$

$$V_{\mathfrak{C}}[\mathfrak{z}, p](q) = V_{\mathfrak{C}'}[\mathfrak{z}', p](q).$$

If $\delta_z \sim \mathfrak{z}'$, then we say that the state z is *equivalent to the random state* $\mathfrak{z}'$ and we write $z \sim \mathfrak{z}'$. Similarly, if $\delta_z \sim \delta_{z}'$, then z, z' are called equivalent (written: $z' \sim z$).

(2.1.2) $\mathfrak{C}$ is called *eqxivalently embedded into* $\mathfrak{C}'$ (notation: $\mathfrak{C} \subsetneqq \mathfrak{C}'$), if for each state z of $\mathfrak{C}$ there is an equivalent state z' of $\mathfrak{C}'$.

(2.1.3) $\mathfrak{C}, \mathfrak{C}'$ are called *equivalent* (notation: $\mathfrak{C} \sim \mathfrak{C}'$) if either is equivalently embedded into the other.

(2.1.4) $\mathfrak{C}$ is said to be *weakly equivalently embedded into* $\mathfrak{C}'$ (notation: $\mathfrak{C} \lessapprox \mathfrak{C}'$) if for each random state $\mathfrak{z}$ of $\mathfrak{C}$, there is an equivalent random state $\mathfrak{z}'$ of $\mathfrak{C}'$.

(2.1.5) $\mathfrak{C}, \mathfrak{C}'$ are called *weakly equivalent* (notation: $\mathfrak{C} \approx \mathfrak{C}'$) if $\mathfrak{C} \lessapprox \mathfrak{C}'$ and $\mathfrak{C}' \lessapprox \mathfrak{C}$.

Corollary 2.1.

1. The relations $\sim$, $\approx$ are equivalence relations.
2. The relations $\subsetneqq$, $\lessapprox$ are reflexive and transitive.
3. If $\mathfrak{z} \in Z_Z$, $\mathfrak{z}' \in \mathfrak{Z}_{Z'}$, then $\mathfrak{z} \sim \mathfrak{z}'$ if and only if for all $p \in W(X)$ the discrete PM's $V_{\mathfrak{C}}[\mathfrak{z}, p]$ and $V_{\mathfrak{C}'}[\mathfrak{z}', p]$ are identical.
4. If z, z' and $\mathfrak{z}, \mathfrak{z}'$ are equivalent states and random states respectively of the stochastic automata $\mathfrak{C}$ and $\mathfrak{C}'$, then z, z' and $ND(\mathfrak{z}), ND(\mathfrak{z}')$ are equivalent states and equivalent sets of states respectively of the ND-automata $ND(\mathfrak{C}), ND(\mathfrak{C}')$.
5. If $\mathfrak{C} \subsetneqq \mathfrak{C}'$ or $\mathfrak{C} \lessapprox \mathfrak{C}'$, then $ND(\mathfrak{C}) \subsetneqq ND(\mathfrak{C}')$ or $ND(\mathfrak{C}) \lessapprox ND(\mathfrak{C}')$.
6. If $\mathfrak{C} \sim \mathfrak{C}'$ or $\mathfrak{C} \approx \mathfrak{C}'$, then $ND(\mathfrak{C}) \sim ND(\mathfrak{C}')$ or $ND(\mathfrak{C}) \sim ND(\mathfrak{C}')$.

The converses of Propositions 2.1.4 to 2.1.6 are obviously false. Now we show that the equivalence of stochastic automata implies their weak equivalence. To do this we first prove a criterion for the weakly equivalent embeddability of $\mathfrak{C}$ into $\mathfrak{C}'$.

Theorem 2.2. *The S-automaton $\mathfrak{C} = [X, Y, Z, H]$ is weakly equivalently embedded into the S-automaton $\mathfrak{C}' = [X, Y, Z', H']$ if and only if for each state $z \in Z$ of $\mathfrak{C}$ (i.e., for each deterministic random state $\delta_z \in \mathfrak{Z}_Z$) there is an equivalent random state $\mathfrak{z}_z' \in \mathfrak{Z}_{Z'}$ of $\mathfrak{C}'$.*

Proof: Let $\mathfrak{z} \in \mathfrak{Z}_Z$ be an arbitrary random state of $\mathfrak{C}$. According to our hypothesis, for each $z \in Z$ there is a random state $\mathfrak{z}_z' \in \mathfrak{Z}_{Z'}$, with $z \sim \mathfrak{z}_z'$. For $z' \in Z'$ we put

$$\mathfrak{z}'(z') = \sum_{z \in Z} \mathfrak{z}(z) \cdot \mathfrak{z}_z'(z').$$

Obviously, this way we define a discrete PM over Z', that is a random state of $\mathfrak{C}'$, since for all $z' \in Z'$, $\mathfrak{z}'(z') \geqq 0$, and $\mathfrak{z}'(Z') = \sum_{z \in Z, z' \in Z'} \mathfrak{z}(z) \cdot \mathfrak{z}'_z(z')$ is equal to 1. We show that $\mathfrak{z}'$ is equivalent to $\mathfrak{z}$. For $p \in W(X)$, $q \in W(Y)$

$$\begin{aligned} V_{\mathfrak{C}'}[\mathfrak{z}', p](q) &= \sum_{z' \in Z'} \sum_{z \in Z} \mathfrak{z}(z) \cdot \mathfrak{z}'_z(z') \cdot V_{\mathfrak{C}}[z', p](q) \\ &= \sum_{z \in Z} \mathfrak{z}(z) \cdot V_{\mathfrak{C}'}[\mathfrak{z}'_z, p](q) \\ &= \sum_{z \in Z} \mathfrak{z}(z) \cdot V_{\mathfrak{C}}[z, p](q) = V_{\mathfrak{C}}[\mathfrak{z}, p](q). \end{aligned}$$

If for each $z \in Z$ there is a $\mathfrak{z}'_z \in \mathfrak{Z}_{Z'}$, with $z \sim \mathfrak{z}'_z$ then as we have just seen, $\mathfrak{C}$ is weakly equivalently embedded into $\mathfrak{C}'$. The converse is trivial.

Corollary 2.3.
1. If $\mathfrak{C} \subseteq \mathfrak{C}'$, then $\mathfrak{C} \lessapprox \mathfrak{C}'$.
2. If $\mathfrak{C} \sim \mathfrak{C}'$, then $\mathfrak{C} \approx \mathfrak{C}'$.

For stochastic automata too, $\mathfrak{C}' \lessapprox \mathfrak{C}$ does not necessarily imply the existence of a sub-automaton $\mathfrak{C}^*$ of $\mathfrak{C}$ which is equivalent to $\mathfrak{C}'$. As an example, consider the S-automata $\mathfrak{C}_2 = [\{0, 1\}, \{0, 1\}, \{a, b\}, H_2]$, $\mathfrak{C}_3 = [\{0, 1\}, \{0, 1\}, \{1, 2, 3\}, H_3]$ which were given by CARLYLE [2] and whose graphs are represented in Fig. 22. Let $\mathfrak{z}'$ be the random state of $\mathfrak{C}_2$ for which $\mathfrak{z}'(a) = \mathfrak{z}'(b) = 1/2$. We claim that $1 \sim a$, $2 \sim b$ and $3 \sim \mathfrak{z}'$. We show by induction on p that

$$V_{\mathfrak{C}_3}[1, p] = V_{\mathfrak{C}_2}[a, p], \quad V_{\mathfrak{C}_3}[2, p] = V_{\mathfrak{C}_2}[b, p], \quad V_{\mathfrak{C}_3}[3, p] = V_{\mathfrak{C}_2}[\mathfrak{z}', p].$$

The initial step $p = e$ is trivial. The step from p to xp: Case I: $x = 0$. Then for $q \neq e$

$$V_{\mathfrak{C}_3}[1, 0p](q) = \begin{cases} \frac{1}{5} V_{\mathfrak{C}_3}[1, p](q') + \frac{1}{5} V_{\mathfrak{C}_3}[2, p](q') + \frac{1}{5} V_{\mathfrak{C}_3}[3, p](q'), & \text{if } q = 0q', \\ \frac{2}{5} V_{\mathfrak{C}_3}[1, p](q'), & \text{if } q = 1q', \end{cases}$$

$$= \begin{cases} \frac{1}{5} V_{\mathfrak{C}_2}[a, p](q') + \frac{1}{5} V_{\mathfrak{C}_2}[b, p](q') \\ \qquad + \frac{1}{5}\left(\frac{1}{2} V_{\mathfrak{C}_2}[a, p](q') + \frac{1}{2} V_{\mathfrak{C}_2}[b, p](q')\right), & \text{if } q = 0q', \\ \frac{2}{5} V_{\mathfrak{C}_2}[a, p](q'), & \text{if } q = 1q', \end{cases}$$

$$= \begin{cases} \frac{3}{10} V_{\mathfrak{C}_2}[a, p](q') + \frac{3}{10} V_{\mathfrak{C}_2}[b, p](q'), & \text{if } q = 0q', \\ \frac{2}{5} V_{\mathfrak{C}_2}[a, p](q'), & \text{if } q = 1q' \end{cases}$$

$$= V_{\mathfrak{C}_2}[a, 0p](q).$$

$$
\begin{aligned}
V_{\mathfrak{C}_3}[2,0p](q) &= \begin{cases} \frac{1}{5}V_{\mathfrak{C}_3}[1,p](q') + \frac{1}{5}V_{\mathfrak{C}_3}[2,p](q') + \frac{1}{5}V_{\mathfrak{C}_3}[3,p](q'), & \text{if } q=0q', \\ \frac{1}{10}V_{\mathfrak{C}_3}[1,p](q') + \frac{3}{10}V_{\mathfrak{C}_3}[2,p](q'), & \text{if } q=1q', \end{cases} \\
&= \begin{cases} \frac{3}{10}V_{\mathfrak{C}_2}[a,p](q') + \frac{3}{10}V_{\mathfrak{C}_2}[b,p](q'), & \text{if } q=0q', \\ \frac{1}{10}V_{\mathfrak{C}_2}[a,p](q') + \frac{3}{10}V_{\mathfrak{C}_2}[b,p](q'), & \text{if } q=1q', \end{cases} \\
&= V_{\mathfrak{C}_2}[b,0p](q).
\end{aligned}
$$

$$
\begin{aligned}
V_{\mathfrak{C}_3}[3,0p](q) &= \begin{cases} \frac{1}{5}V_{\mathfrak{C}_3}[1,p](q') + \frac{1}{5}V_{\mathfrak{C}_3}[2,p](q') + \frac{1}{5}V_{\mathfrak{C}_3}[3,p](q'), & \text{if } q=0q', \\ \frac{1}{5}V_{\mathfrak{C}_3}[1,p](q') + \frac{1}{10}V_{\mathfrak{C}_3}[2,p](q') + \frac{1}{10}V_{\mathfrak{C}_3}[3,p](q'), & \text{if } q=1q', \end{cases} \\
&= \begin{cases} \frac{3}{10}V_{\mathfrak{C}_2}[a,p](q') + \frac{3}{10}V_{\mathfrak{C}_2}[b,p](q'), & \text{if } q=0q', \\ \frac{1}{4}V_{\mathfrak{C}_2}[a,p](q') + \frac{3}{20}V_{\mathfrak{C}_2}[b,p](q'), & \text{if } q=1q', \end{cases} \\
&= \frac{1}{2}\cdot\begin{cases} \frac{3}{5}V_{\mathfrak{C}_2}[a,p](q') + \frac{3}{5}V_{\mathfrak{C}_2}[b,p](q'), & \text{if } q=0q', \\ \frac{1}{2}V_{\mathfrak{C}_2}[a,p](q') + \frac{3}{10}V_{\mathfrak{C}_2}[b,p](q'), & \text{if } q=1q', \end{cases} \\
&= \frac{1}{2}V_{\mathfrak{C}_2}[a,0p](q) + \frac{1}{2}V_{\mathfrak{C}_2}[b,0p](q).
\end{aligned}
$$

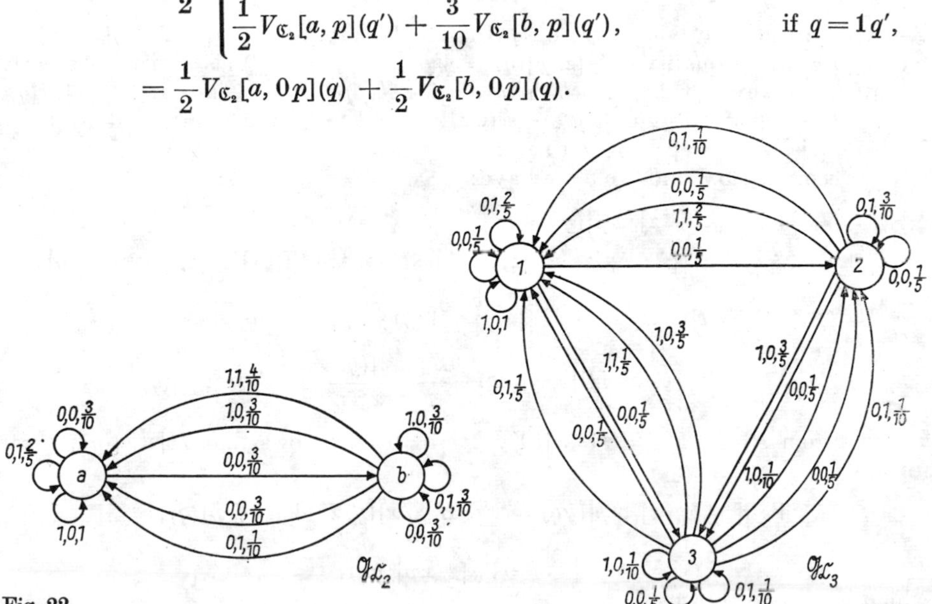

Fig. 22

We can proceed analogously in Case II: $x = 1$. Thus we have shown that $\mathfrak{C}_2 \subsetneq \mathfrak{C}_3$ and $\mathfrak{C}_2 \approx \mathfrak{C}_3$. Furthermore, $G_3[1, 1](0) = 1$, $G_3[2, 1](0) = 3/5$ and $G_3[3, 1](0) = 4/5$. Thus, the states 1, 2, 3 of $\mathfrak{C}_3$ are pairwise inequivalent and the state 3 is not equivalent either to a or to b. Consequently, the S-automata $\mathfrak{C}_2, \mathfrak{C}_3$ are not equivalent (i.e., the converse of 2.3 is not valid). Obviously, no subautomaton of $\mathfrak{C}_3$ is equivalent to $\mathfrak{C}_2$.

Theorem 2.4. *For every S-automaton $\mathfrak{C} = [X, Y, Z, H]$ there is an equivalent S-Moore automaton $\mathfrak{C}'$ which is Z-deterministic or $[X, Z]$-finite if $\mathfrak{C}$ is Z-deterministic or $[X, Z]$-finite, and an equivalent S-Moore automaton $\mathfrak{C}''$ which is $[Y, Z]$-finite if $\mathfrak{C}$ is $[Y, Z]$-finite, and whose marking function's values are only deterministic discrete PM's over Y.*

Proof: Let $Z' = Z \times X \times Z$ and for all $[z, x, z^*]$, $[z_1, x_1, z_1^*] \in Z'$, $x' \in X$, $y \in Y$

$$F'\big[[z,x,z^*],x'\big]([z_1,x_1,z_1^*]) \underset{\mathrm{Df}}{=} \begin{cases} F[z_1, x_1](z_1^*), & \text{if } z^* = z_1 \text{ and } x' = x_1,\\ 0 & \text{otherwise;}\end{cases}$$

$$M'\big[[z,x,z^*]\big](y) \underset{\mathrm{Df}}{=} \begin{cases} \dfrac{H[z,x](y,z^*)}{F[z,x](z^*)}, & \text{if } F[z,x](z^*) > 0,\\ \delta_{y^*}(y) & \text{otherwise,}\end{cases}$$

where $y^* \in Y$ is fixed. We can easily verify that $\mathfrak{C}' = [X, Y, Z', F', M']$ is an S-Moore automaton. We show that for all $z, z^* \in Z$, $x \in X$ the state $[z, x, z^*]$ of $\mathfrak{C}'$ is equivalent to the state z^* of $\mathfrak{C}$, which will prove the first part of Theorem 2.4.

First we prove by induction on p that for all $z_0, z \in Z$, $x_0 \in X$, $p \in W(X)$, $q \in W(Y)$, the equality $V_{\mathfrak{C}}[z, p](q) = V_{\mathfrak{C}'}\big[[z_0, x_0, z], p\big](q)$ is satisfied. Clearly it suffices to prove this for words p, q with $l(p) = l(q)$, since if $l(p) \neq l(q)$, then both sides of this equality are trivially equal to zero. The initial step $p = e$ is also trivial. The step from p to xp:

By Theorem 1.5.3 and 1.6.5 we have:

$$\begin{aligned} &V_{\mathfrak{C}'}\big[[z_0, x_0, z], xp\big](yq)\\ &= \sum_{z^* \in Z} F'\big[[z_0, x_0, z], x\big]([z, x, z^*])\, M'\big[[z, x, z^*]\big](y)\, V_{\mathfrak{C}'}\big[[z, x, z^*], p\big](q),\\ &= \sum_{z^* \in Z} F[z, x](z^*) \cdot M'\big[[z, x, z^*]\big](y) \cdot V_{\mathfrak{C}}[z^*, p](q)\\ &= \sum_{z^* \in Z \wedge F[z,x](z^*) > 0} F[z, x](z^*) \cdot \frac{H[z, x](y, z^*)}{F[z, x](z^*)} \cdot V_{\mathfrak{C}}[z^*, p](q). \end{aligned}$$

Since from $F[z,x](z^*) = H[z,x](Y \times \{z^*\}) = 0$, it follows that $H[z,x](y,z^*) = 0$ for all $y \in Y$ we have

$$\begin{aligned} V_{\mathfrak{C}'}\big[[z_0, x_0, z], xp\big](yq) &= \sum_{z^* \in Z} H[z, x](y, z^*)\, V_{\mathfrak{C}}[z^*, p](q),\\ &= V_{\mathfrak{C}}[z, xp](yq), \end{aligned}$$

which was to be shown.

To prove the second part of Theorem 2.4, we consider the system

$\mathfrak{C}'' = [X, Y, Z'', F'', M'']$, where $Z'' = Y \times Z$ and for $[y, z], [y', z'] \in Z''$, $x \in X$, $y'' \in Y$

$$F''\big[[y, z], x\big]([y', z']) = H[z, x](y', z'),$$

$$M''\big[[y, z]\big](y'') = \begin{cases} 1, & \text{if } \; y'' = y, \\ 0 & \text{otherwise}. \end{cases}$$

We can show as above without any difficulty that for all $y \in Y$, $z \in Z$, the state $[y, z]$ of the S-automaton $\mathfrak{C}''$ is equivalent to the state z of $\mathfrak{C}$. Thus Theorem 2.4 is proved.

The corresponding statement for S-Mealy automata is not true. In § 4 we shall give an S-automaton which cannot be equivalently embedded into any S-Mealy automaton.

Let $\mathfrak{C} = [X, Y, Z, H]$ be an S-automaton, $\mathfrak{z} \in \mathfrak{Z}_Z$ a random state of $\mathfrak{C}$, $p \in W(X)$, $Q \subseteq Y^{l(p)}$ with $V_{\mathfrak{C}}[\mathfrak{z}, p](Q) > 0$. For $z \in Z$ we put

$$\mathfrak{C}[\mathfrak{z}, p, Q](z) \underset{\mathrm{Df}}{=} \begin{cases} \mathfrak{z}(z), & \text{if } \; p = e \\ & \text{(consequently } \; Q = \{e\}), \\ \dfrac{H[\mathfrak{z}, p]\big(Q \times W(Z) \cdot \{z\}\big)}{V_{\mathfrak{C}}[\mathfrak{z}, p](Q)}, & \text{if } \; p \neq e. \end{cases}$$

For arbitrary $z \in Z$ we have $\mathfrak{C}[\mathfrak{z}, p, Q](z) > 0$, and obviously there are at most countably many $z \in Z$ with $\mathfrak{C}[\mathfrak{z}, p, Q](z) > 0$. Furthermore if $p \neq e$

$$\sum_{z \in Z} \mathfrak{C}[\mathfrak{z}, p, Q](z) = \frac{H[\mathfrak{z}, p]\big(Q \times W(Z) \cdot Z\big)}{V_{\mathfrak{C}}[\mathfrak{z}, p](Q)} = 1,$$

and if $p = e$ then

$$\sum_{z \in Z} \mathfrak{C}[\mathfrak{z}, e, \{e\}](z) = \mathfrak{z}(Z) = 1.$$

Thus the mapping $\mathfrak{C}[\mathfrak{z}, p, Q]$ defines a random state of $\mathfrak{C}$, with which we shall identify it. If $Q = \{q\}$ is a singleton, then we write $\mathfrak{C}[\mathfrak{z}, p, q]$ instead of $\mathfrak{C}[\mathfrak{z}, p, \{q\}]$, and if $\mathfrak{z} = \delta_z$ is deterministic, then we write $\mathfrak{C}[z, p, Q]$ instead of $\mathfrak{C}[\delta_z, p, Q]$. Thus e.g., $\mathfrak{C}[z, e, e] = \delta_z$.

Theorem 2.5. *Let* $\mathfrak{C} = [X, Y, Z, H]$ *be an S-automaton,* $\mathfrak{z} \in \mathfrak{Z}_Z$, $p \in W(X)$, $x \in X$, $Q \subseteq W(Y)$. *Then*

$$V_{\mathfrak{C}}[\mathfrak{z}, px](QY) = V_{\mathfrak{C}}[\mathfrak{z}, p](Q).$$

Proof: If $p = e$, then

$$V_{\mathfrak{C}}[\mathfrak{z}, px](QY) = V_{\mathfrak{C}}[\mathfrak{z}, x](QY) = \begin{cases} V_{\mathfrak{C}}[\mathfrak{z}, x](Y), & \text{if} \quad e \in Q, \\ 0 & \text{otherwise} \end{cases}$$
$$= \begin{cases} 1, & \text{if} \quad e \in Q, \\ 0 & \text{otherwise} \end{cases}$$
$$= V_{\mathfrak{C}}[\mathfrak{z}, e](Q) = V_{\mathfrak{C}}[\mathfrak{z}, p](Q)$$

and for $p \neq e$ (by 1.5.3)

$$V_{\mathfrak{C}}[\mathfrak{z}, px](QY) = \sum_{z^* \in Z} H[\mathfrak{z}, p]\big(Q \times W(Z) \cdot \{z^*\}\big)\, V_{\mathfrak{C}}[z^*, x](Y)$$
$$= \sum_{z^* \in Z} H[\mathfrak{z}, p](Q \times Z^{l(p)-1} \cdot \{z^*\})$$
$$= H[\mathfrak{z}, p](Q \times Z^{l(p)}) = V_{\mathfrak{C}}[\mathfrak{z}, p](Q).$$

Corollary 2.6. For all $p, r \in W(X)$, $Q \subseteq Y^{l(p)}$, $S \subseteq W(Y)$, $\mathfrak{z} \in \mathfrak{Z}_Z$

$$V_{\mathfrak{C}}[\mathfrak{z}, p](Q) \geqq V_{\mathfrak{C}}[\mathfrak{z}, pr](Q \cdot S).$$

Theorem 2.7. *Let* $\mathfrak{C} = [X, Y, Z, H]$ *be an S-automaton,* $\mathfrak{z} \in \mathfrak{Z}_Z$, $p \in W(X)$ *and* $Q \subseteq Y^{l(p)}$ *with* $V_{\mathfrak{C}}[\mathfrak{z}, p](Q) > 0$. *Then for every* $r \in W(X)$, $s \in W(Y)$

$$V_{\mathfrak{C}}\big[\mathfrak{C}[\mathfrak{z}, p, Q], r\big](s) = \frac{V_{\mathfrak{C}}[\mathfrak{z}, pr](Q \cdot \{s\})}{V_{\mathfrak{C}}[\mathfrak{z}, p](Q)}.$$

Proof: For $p = e$ $\big(l(p) = 0\big)$ we have $Q = \{e\}$, $\mathfrak{C}[\mathfrak{z}, e, e] = \mathfrak{z}$, and the above equality is trivial. For $p \neq e$ the equation will be verified by induction on r. The initial step $r = e$ is trivial, as well as the case in which $l(r) \neq l(s)$. The induction step is taken from r to xr for $x \in X$. For $y \in Y$, $z \in Z$

$$H\big[\mathfrak{C}[\mathfrak{z}, p, Q], x\big](y, z) = \sum_{z' \in Z} \frac{H[\mathfrak{z}, p](Q \times Z^{l(p)-1} \cdot \{z'\})}{V_{\mathfrak{C}}[\mathfrak{z}, p](Q)} H[z', x](y, z)$$
$$= \frac{H[\mathfrak{z}, px](Q \cdot \{y\} \times Z^{l(p)} \cdot \{z\})}{V_{\mathfrak{C}}[\mathfrak{z}, p](Q)},$$

then

$$V_{\mathfrak{C}}\big[\mathfrak{C}[\mathfrak{z}, p, Q], xr\big](ys) = \sum_{z \in Z} H\big[\mathfrak{C}[\mathfrak{z}, p, Q], x\big](y, z) \cdot V_{\mathfrak{C}}[z, r](s)$$
$$= \frac{\sum_{z \in Z} H[\mathfrak{z}, px](Q \cdot \{y\} \times Z^{l(p)} \cdot \{z\}) \cdot V_{\mathfrak{C}}[z, r](s)}{V_{\mathfrak{C}}[\mathfrak{z}, p](Q)}.$$

If $V_{\mathfrak{C}}[\mathfrak{C}[\mathfrak{z}, p, Q], x](y) = 0$, then $V_{\mathfrak{C}}\big[\mathfrak{C}[\mathfrak{z}, p, Q], xr\big](ys) = 0$ for every $r \in W(X)$, $s \in W(Y)$ by 2.6. Thus for all $z \in Z$

$$H[\mathfrak{z}, px](Q \cdot \{y\} \times Z^{l(p)} \cdot \{z\}) = 0$$

and consequently $V_{\mathfrak{C}}[\mathfrak{z}, px](Q \cdot \{y\}) = 0$, hence $V_{\mathfrak{C}}[\mathfrak{z}, pxr](Q \cdot \{ys\}) = 0$ for arbitrary $r \in W(X)$, $s \in W(Y)$, i.e., in this case we have

$$V_{\mathfrak{C}}\left[\mathfrak{C}[\mathfrak{z}, p, Q], xr\right](ys) = \frac{V_{\mathfrak{C}}[\mathfrak{z}, pxr](Q \cdot \{ys\})}{V_{\mathfrak{C}}[\mathfrak{z}, p](Q)} \ (= 0).$$

Suppose $V_{\mathfrak{C}}\left[\mathfrak{C}[\mathfrak{z}, p, Q], x\right](y) > 0$. Then $V_{\mathfrak{C}}\left[\mathfrak{C}[\mathfrak{z}, p, Q], xr\right](\{y\} \cdot Y^{l(r)}) > 0$ (cf. 2.5). Thus there is an $s' \in Y^{l(r)}$ with $V_{\mathfrak{C}}\left[\mathfrak{C}[\mathfrak{z}, p, Q], xr\right](ys') > 0$. Consequently, there is a $z \in Z$ with $H[\mathfrak{z}, px](Q \cdot \{y\} \times Z^{l(p)} \cdot \{z\}) > 0$. Thus in every case we have $V_{\mathfrak{C}}[\mathfrak{z}, px](Q \cdot \{y\}) > 0$. In this case we obtain:

$$\begin{aligned} &V_{\mathfrak{C}}\left[\mathfrak{C}[\mathfrak{z}, p, Q], xr\right](ys) \\ &= \frac{V_{\mathfrak{C}}[\mathfrak{z}, px](Q \cdot \{y\})}{V_{\mathfrak{C}}[\mathfrak{z}, p](Q)} \cdot \sum_{z' \in Z} \frac{H[\mathfrak{z}, px](Q \cdot \{y\} \times Z^{l(p)} \cdot \{z'\})}{V_{\mathfrak{C}}[\mathfrak{z}, px](Q \cdot \{y\})} \cdot V_{\mathfrak{C}}[z', r](s) \\ &= \frac{V_{\mathfrak{C}}[\mathfrak{z}, px](Q \cdot \{y\})}{V_{\mathfrak{C}}[\mathfrak{z}, p](Q)} \cdot V_{\mathfrak{C}}\left[\mathfrak{C}[\mathfrak{z}, px, Q \cdot \{y\}], r\right](s) \end{aligned}$$

and by the induction hypothesis

$$\begin{aligned} V_{\mathfrak{C}}\left[\mathfrak{C}[\mathfrak{z}, p, Q], xr\right](ys) &= \frac{V_{\mathfrak{C}}[\mathfrak{z}, px](Q \cdot \{y\})}{V_{\mathfrak{C}}[\mathfrak{z}, p](Q)} \cdot \frac{V_{\mathfrak{C}}[\mathfrak{z}, pxr](Q \cdot \{ys\})}{V_{\mathfrak{C}}[\mathfrak{z}, px](Q \cdot \{y\})} \\ &= \frac{V_{\mathfrak{C}}[\mathfrak{z}, pxr](Q \cdot \{ys\})}{V_{\mathfrak{C}}[\mathfrak{z}, p](Q)}, \end{aligned}$$

which was to be shown.

Corollary 2.8. Let $\mathfrak{C} = [X, Y, Z, H]$ be an S-automaton and $\mathfrak{z}$ a random state of $\mathfrak{C}$. Then for $p, r \in W(X)$ we have:

1. If $q \in W(Y)$ with $V_{\mathfrak{C}}[\mathfrak{z}, p](q) > 0$, $s \in W(Y)$ arbitrary, then $V_{\mathfrak{C}}[\mathfrak{z}, pr](qs) = V_{\mathfrak{C}}[\mathfrak{z}, p](q) \cdot V_{\mathfrak{C}}[\mathfrak{C}[\mathfrak{z}, p, q], r](s)$.
2. If $Q \subseteq Y^{l(p)}$ with $V_{\mathfrak{C}}[\mathfrak{z}, p](Q) > 0$ and $S \subseteq W(Y)$ arbitrary, then $V_{\mathfrak{C}}[\mathfrak{z}, pr](Q \cdot S) = V_{\mathfrak{C}}[\mathfrak{z}, p](Q) \cdot V_{\mathfrak{C}}[\mathfrak{C}[\mathfrak{z}, p, Q], r](S)$.
3. If $Q \subseteq Y^{l(p)}$ with $V_{\mathfrak{C}}[\mathfrak{z}, p](Q) > 0$, $S \subseteq Y^{l(r)}$ with $V_{\mathfrak{C}}[\mathfrak{C}[\mathfrak{z}, p, Q], r](S) > 0$, then the random states $\mathfrak{C}[\mathfrak{C}[\mathfrak{z}, p, Q], r, S]$, $\mathfrak{C}[\mathfrak{z}, pr, QS]$ exist and coincide.

Proposition 2.8.3 can be proved for $p \neq e$, $r \neq e$ as follows:

$$\begin{aligned} \mathfrak{C}[\mathfrak{z}, pr, QS](z) &= \frac{H[\mathfrak{z}, pr](Q \cdot S \times Z^{l(pr)-1} \cdot \{z\})}{V_{\mathfrak{C}}[\mathfrak{z}, pr](QS)} \\ &= \sum_{z' \in Z} \frac{H[\mathfrak{z}, p](Q \times Z^{l(p)-1} \cdot \{z'\})}{V_{\mathfrak{C}}[\mathfrak{z}, p](Q)} \cdot \frac{H[z', r](S \times Z^{l(r)-1} \cdot \{z\})}{V_{\mathfrak{C}}[\mathfrak{C}[\mathfrak{z}, p, Q], r](S)} \\ &= \sum_{z' \in Z} \mathfrak{C}[\mathfrak{z}, p, Q](z') \cdot \frac{H[z', r](S \times Z^{l(r)-1} \cdot \{z\})}{V_{\mathfrak{C}}[\mathfrak{C}[\mathfrak{z}, p, Q], r](S)} \\ &= \mathfrak{C}[\mathfrak{C}[\mathfrak{z}, p, Q], r, S](z). \end{aligned}$$

If $p = e$ or $r = e$ then 2.8.3 is trivial.

Theorem 2.9. *Let* $\mathfrak{C} = [X, Y, Z, H]$, $\mathfrak{C}' = [X, Y, Z', H']$ *be S-automata, furthermore let* $\mathfrak{z} \in \mathfrak{Z}_Z$ *and* $\mathfrak{z}' \in \mathfrak{Z}_{Z'}$.

1. *If* $\mathfrak{z} \sim \mathfrak{z}'$ *then for all* $p \in W(X)$, $Q \subseteq Y^{l(p)}$ *with* $V_{\mathfrak{C}}[\mathfrak{z}, p](Q) > 0$ $\mathfrak{C}[\mathfrak{z}, p, Q] \sim \mathfrak{C}'[\mathfrak{z}', p, Q]$.

2. *If* $n \geqq 0$ *is arbitrary and* $V_{\mathfrak{C}}[\mathfrak{z}, p](q) = V_{\mathfrak{C}'}[\mathfrak{z}', p](q)$ *for all* $p \in X^n$, $q \in W(Y)$ *and* $\mathfrak{C}[\mathfrak{z}, p, q] \sim \mathfrak{C}'[\mathfrak{z}', p, q]$ *for all* $p \in X^n, q \in Y^n$ *with* $V_{\mathfrak{C}}[\mathfrak{z}, p](q) > 0$, *then* $\mathfrak{z} \sim \mathfrak{z}'$.

3. *If* $\mathfrak{z} \sim \mathfrak{z}'$, *then* $F[\mathfrak{z}, p] \sim F'[\mathfrak{z}', p]$ *for every* $p \in W(X)$.

Proof: Since $V_{\mathfrak{C}}[\mathfrak{z}, p](Q) = V_{\mathfrak{C}'}[\mathfrak{z}', p](Q)$ the existence of $\mathfrak{C}[\mathfrak{z}, p, Q]$ implies that of $\mathfrak{C}'[\mathfrak{z}', p, Q]$, if $\mathfrak{z} \sim \mathfrak{z}'$. It follows immediately from Proposition 2.8 that $\mathfrak{C}[\mathfrak{z}, p, Q] \sim \mathfrak{C}'[\mathfrak{z}', p, Q]$. Thus Proposition 2.9.1 is valid.

Proposition 2.9.2 is trivial for $n = 0$. Suppose $n > 0$. Then we have to show that

$$V_{\mathfrak{C}}[\mathfrak{z}, r](s) = V_{\mathfrak{C}'}[\mathfrak{z}', r](s)$$

is satisfied for all $r \in W(X)$, $s \in Y^{l(r)}$.

If $r \in W(X)$ with $l(r) \leqq n$, then using 2.5, this equality follows from the assumption

$$\forall p \, \forall q \big(p \in X^n \wedge q \in Y^n \to V_{\mathfrak{C}}[\mathfrak{z}, p](q) = V_{\mathfrak{C}'}[\mathfrak{z}', p](q)\big).$$

Indeed, if $l(r) = m < n$, and $x \in X$, then from 2.5 we obtain by induction that

$$V_{\mathfrak{C}}[\mathfrak{z}, rx^k](\{s\} \cdot Y^k) = V_{\mathfrak{C}}[\mathfrak{z}, r](s)$$

and thus

$$\begin{aligned} V_{\mathfrak{C}}[\mathfrak{z}, r](s) &= V_{\mathfrak{C}}[\mathfrak{z}, rx^{n-m}](\{s\} \cdot Y^{n-m}) = \sum_{q \in Y^{n-m}} V_{\mathfrak{C}}[\mathfrak{z}, rx^{n-m}](sq) \\ &= \sum_{q \in Y^{n-m}} V_{\mathfrak{C}'}[\mathfrak{z}', rx^{n-m}](sq) \\ &= V_{\mathfrak{C}'}[\mathfrak{z}', r](s). \end{aligned}$$

If $r \in W(X)$ and $l(r) > n$, then let $r = pr'$ with $l(p) = n$, furthermore $s = qs'$ where $l(q) = n$. Then by the hypothesis, $V_{\mathfrak{C}}[z, p](q) > 0$ implies $\mathfrak{C}[\mathfrak{z}, p, q] \sim \mathfrak{C}'[\mathfrak{z}', p, q]$, and using 2.8.1 we obtain

$$\begin{aligned} V_{\mathfrak{C}}[\mathfrak{z}, r](s) &= V_{\mathfrak{C}}[\mathfrak{z}, pr'](qs') = V_{\mathfrak{C}}[\mathfrak{z}, p](q) \, V_{\mathfrak{C}}\big[\mathfrak{C}[\mathfrak{z}, p, q], r'\big](s') \\ &= V_{\mathfrak{C}'}[\mathfrak{z}', p](q) \, V_{\mathfrak{C}'}\big[\mathfrak{C}'[\mathfrak{z}', p, q], r'\big](s') = V_{\mathfrak{C}'}[\mathfrak{z}', pr'](qs') \\ &= V_{\mathfrak{C}'}[\mathfrak{z}', r](s). \end{aligned}$$

On the other hand, if $V_{\mathfrak{C}}[\mathfrak{z}, p](q) = 0 = V_{\mathfrak{C}'}[\mathfrak{z}', p](q)$, then by 2.6, the equalities $V_{\mathfrak{C}}[\mathfrak{z}, pr'](qs') = 0$ and $V_{\mathfrak{C}'}[\mathfrak{z}', pr'](qs') = 0$, are satisfied and thus

$$V_{\mathfrak{C}}[\mathfrak{z}, r](s) = V_{\mathfrak{C}'}[\mathfrak{z}', r](s) = 0.$$

This proves 2.9.2.

Proposition 2.9.3 is trivial for $p = e$. If $p \neq e$, then we have

$$\begin{aligned} V_{\mathfrak{C}}\left[F[\mathfrak{z}, p], r\right](s) &= \sum_{z^* \in Z} F[\mathfrak{z}, p](z^*)\, V_{\mathfrak{C}}[z^*, r](s) \\ &= \sum_{z^* \in Z} H[\mathfrak{z}, p](Y^{l(p)} \times Z^{l(p)-1} \cdot \{z^*\})\, V_{\mathfrak{C}}[z^*, r](s) \\ &= V_{\mathfrak{C}}[\mathfrak{z}, pr](Y^{l(p)} \cdot \{s\}) \\ &= V_{\mathfrak{C}'}[\mathfrak{z}', pr](Y^{l(p)} \cdot \{s\}) \\ &= V_{\mathfrak{C}'}\left[F'[\mathfrak{z}', p], r\right](s). \end{aligned}$$

This proves Theorem 2.9.

Remark: Propositions 2.5 to 2.9 are obviously also valid for states $z \in Z$ and $z' \in Z'$ instead of the random states $\mathfrak{z} \in \mathfrak{Z}_Z$ and $\mathfrak{z}' \in \mathfrak{Z}^0_{Z'}$.

Theorem 2.10. *For each S-automaton $\mathfrak{C} = [X, Y, Z, H]$ there is an observable S-automaton $\mathfrak{C}^* = [X, Y, Z^*, H^*]$ into which $\mathfrak{C}$ is equivalently embedded and which is weakly equivalent to $\mathfrak{C}$.*

Proof: We put $Z^* \underset{\mathrm{Df}}{=} \{\mathfrak{C}[z, p, q] \mid z \in Z \wedge p \in W(X) \wedge q \in W(Y) \wedge V_{\mathfrak{C}}[z, p](q) > 0\}$ and for all $z^* = \mathfrak{C}[z, p, q] \in Z^*$, $x \in X$, $y \in Y$ let

$$\delta^*(\mathfrak{C}[z, p, q], x, y) \underset{\mathrm{Df}}{=} \begin{cases} \mathfrak{C}[z, px, qy], & \text{if } V_{\mathfrak{C}}[z, px](qy) > 0, \\ \text{not defined otherwise.} \end{cases}$$

To justify this definition, we have to show that for all $z, z' \in Z$, $p, r \in W(X)$, $q, s \in W(Y)$ with $V_{\mathfrak{C}}[z, p](q) > 0$ and $V_{\mathfrak{C}}[z', r](s) > 0$ and for all $x \in X$, $y \in Y$ the following assertion holds:

If $\mathfrak{C}[z, p, q] = \mathfrak{C}[z', r, s]$ then $\mathfrak{C}[z, px, qy]$ exists if and only if $\mathfrak{C}[z', rx, sy]$ does, and if both these random states exist, they are identical.

By 2.8.1 we have

$$\begin{aligned} V_{\mathfrak{C}}[z, px](qy) > 0 &\leftrightarrow V_{\mathfrak{C}}\left[\mathfrak{C}[z, p, q], x\right](y) > 0 \\ &\leftrightarrow V_{\mathfrak{C}}\left[\mathfrak{C}[z', r, s], x\right](y) > 0 \\ &\leftrightarrow V_{\mathfrak{C}}[z', rx](sy) > 0; \end{aligned}$$

hence $\mathfrak{C}[z, px, qy]$ exists if and only if $\mathfrak{C}[z', rx, sy]$ does. If both these random states exist, then

$$V_{\mathfrak{C}}\left[\mathfrak{C}[z, p, q], x\right](y) = V_{\mathfrak{C}}\left[\mathfrak{C}[z', r, s], x\right](y) > 0,$$

and by 2.8.3 we obtain

$$\begin{aligned} \mathfrak{C}[z, px, qy] &= \mathfrak{C}\left[\mathfrak{C}[z, p, q], x, y\right] \\ &= \mathfrak{C}\left[\mathfrak{C}[z', r, s], x, y\right] = \mathfrak{C}[z', rx, sy]. \end{aligned}$$

Finally we put, for $z^* = \mathfrak{C}[z, p, q] \in Z^*$, $x \in X$, $y \in Y$, $z^{**} \in Z^*$

$$H^*\big[\mathfrak{C}[z, p, q], x\big](y, z^{**}) = \begin{cases} G\big[\mathfrak{C}[z, p, q], x\big](y), & \text{if } \mathfrak{C}[z, px, qy] \text{ exists and } z^{**} = \mathfrak{C}[z, px, qy] \\ 0 & \text{otherwise.} \end{cases}$$

Obviously, $\mathfrak{C}^* = [X, Y, Z^*, H^*]$ is an observable S-automaton. We show by induction on r that for all $z^* = \mathfrak{C}[z, p, q] \in Z^*$, $s \in W(Y)$

$$V_{\mathfrak{C}^*}\big[\mathfrak{C}[z, p, q], r\big](s) = V_{\mathfrak{C}}\big[\mathfrak{C}[z, p, q], r\big](s),$$

i.e., for all $z^* \in Z^*$, the random state z^* of $\mathfrak{C}$ is equivalent to the state z^* of $\mathfrak{C}^*$. According to this, for $z \in Z$, $\delta_z = \mathfrak{C}[z, e, e]$ is an equivalent state of $\mathfrak{C}^*$, hence $\mathfrak{C} \subsetneq \mathfrak{C}^*$ and $\mathfrak{C} \approx \mathfrak{C}^*$.

The initial step $r = e$ is trivial. The induction step is taken from r to xr for $x \in X$. We distinguish two cases:

I. $V_{\mathfrak{C}}[z, px](qy) = 0$.

Then

$$V_{\mathfrak{C}}\big[\mathfrak{C}[z, p, q], x\big](y) = \frac{V_{\mathfrak{C}}[z, px](qy)}{V_{\mathfrak{C}}[z, p](q)} = 0,$$

$$V_{\mathfrak{C}}\big[\mathfrak{C}[z, p, q], xr\big](ys) = 0,$$

and $\mathfrak{C}[z, px, qy]$ does not exist. Further,

$$V_{\mathfrak{C}^*}\big[\mathfrak{C}[z, p, q], x\big](y) = \sum_{z^* \in Z^*} H^*\big[\mathfrak{C}[z, p, q], x\big](y, z^*) = 0,$$

since $\delta^*(\mathfrak{C}[z, p, q], x, y)$ is not defined (because $\mathfrak{C}[z, px, qy]$ is not). Consequently, in this case

$$V_{\mathfrak{C}}\big[\mathfrak{C}[z, p, q], xr\big](ys) = 0 = V_{\mathfrak{C}^*}\big[\mathfrak{C}[z, p, q], xr\big](ys).$$

II. $V_{\mathfrak{C}}[z, px](qy) > 0$.

Then $\mathfrak{C}[z, px, qy]$ exists and we have

$$\begin{aligned} V_{\mathfrak{C}}\big[\mathfrak{C}[z, p, q], xr\big](ys) &= \frac{V_{\mathfrak{C}}[z, pxr](qys)}{V_{\mathfrak{C}}[z, p](q)} \\ &= \frac{V_{\mathfrak{C}}[z, px](qy)}{V_{\mathfrak{C}}[z, p](q)} \cdot V_{\mathfrak{C}}\big[\mathfrak{C}[z, px, qy], r\big](s) \\ &= V_{\mathfrak{C}}\big[\mathfrak{C}[z, p, q], x\big](y) \cdot V_{\mathfrak{C}}\big[\mathfrak{C}[z, px, qy], r\big](s) \\ &= G\big[\mathfrak{C}[z, p, q], x\big](y) \cdot V_{\mathfrak{C}^*}\big[\mathfrak{C}[z, px, qy], r\big](s) \\ &= \sum_{z^* \in Z^*} H^*\big[\mathfrak{C}[z, p, q], x\big](y, z^*) \cdot V_{\mathfrak{C}^*}[z^*, r](s) \\ &= V_{\mathfrak{C}^*}\big[\mathfrak{C}[z, p, q], xr\big](ys). \end{aligned}$$

Thus Theorem 2.10 is proved.

The observable S-automaton $\mathfrak{C}^*$ which, by Theorem 2.10, belongs to $\mathfrak{C}$, is in general infinite, even if $\mathfrak{C}$ is finite. As an example we consider the S-automaton $\mathfrak{C}_2$ and the state b. It is easy to verify by induction on n that for all $n \geqq 0$

$$V_{\mathfrak{C}_2}[b, 1^n](0^n) = \frac{3^n}{10^n} \cdot \frac{4}{7} + \frac{3}{7},$$

$$\mathfrak{C}_2[b, 1^n, 0^n](b) = \frac{\frac{3^n}{10^n}}{\frac{3^n}{10^n} \cdot \frac{4}{7} + \frac{3}{7}}$$

and thus $\mathfrak{C}_2[b, 1^n, 0^n] = \mathfrak{C}_2[b, 1^m, 0^m]$ if and only if $n = m$. Thus, for $\mathfrak{C}_2$, Z^* is infinite.

Furthermore, it is easy to show that $\mathfrak{C}_2[b, 1^n, 0^n] \sim \mathfrak{C}_2[b, 1^m, 0^m]$ if and only if $n = m$. This follows from a consideration of the equality

$$V_{\mathfrak{C}_2}\big[\mathfrak{C}_2[b, 1^n, 0^n], 1\big](1) = V_{\mathfrak{C}_2}\big[\mathfrak{C}_2[b, 1^m, 0^m], 1\big](1).$$

If $\mathfrak{C}_2$ is equivalently embedded into an S-automaton $\mathfrak{C}^{**} = [X, Y, Z^{**}, H^{**}]$ and $b \sim z^{**}$ ($z^{**} \in Z^{**}$) then $\mathfrak{C}_2[b, 1^n, 0^n] \sim \mathfrak{C}^{**}[z^{**}, 1^n, 0^n]$ for all n. Since $\mathfrak{C}^{**}$ is observable, $\mathfrak{C}^{**}[z^{**}, 1^n, 0^n]$ is deterministic, consequently $\mathfrak{C}^{**}$ has infinitely many states.

Thus there are finite S-automata which cannot be equivalently embedded into any Z-finite observable S-automaton.

Next we prove a criterion for the equivalence of random states of $[Y, Z]$-finite S-automata. This will be enable us to obtain an algorithmic procedure for deciding whether given random states of finite S-automata are equivalent.

Theorem 2.11 (Carlyle [2]). *Let $\mathfrak{C} = [X, Y, Z, H]$ be a $[Y, Z]$-finite S-automaton, $\mathrm{Card}(Z) = n$ and $\mathfrak{z}, \mathfrak{z}' \in \mathfrak{Z}_Z$. The random states $\mathfrak{z}, \mathfrak{z}'$ are equivalent if and only if for all $p \in W(X)$ with $l(p) = n - 1$*

$$V_{\mathfrak{C}}[\mathfrak{z}, p] = V_{\mathfrak{C}}[\mathfrak{z}', p].$$

Proof: For any fixed pair $[p, q] \in W(X) \times W(Y)$ the function $V_{\mathfrak{C}}$ induces a single-valued mapping which assigns the number $V_{\mathfrak{C}}[z, p](q)$ to each $z \in Z$. We denote this function by $V_{\mathfrak{C}}[., p](q)$. Similarly we can define, for fixed $x \in X$, $y \in Y$, $z^* \in Z$ the function $H[., x](y, z^*)$ on the set Z. If B is any set of real-valued functions defined on the set Z, then we denote by $L(B)$ the linear space (over the field of real numbers) spanned by the functions belonging to the set B. Let

$$D \underset{\mathrm{Df}}{=} L(\{\delta_z \mid z \in Z\}).$$

Thus, D is the space of all real-valued functions defined on Z, (which is isomorphic to the n-dimensional Euclidean space E_n) and thus its dimension is

$dim(D) = Card(Z) = n$. Let $\mathfrak{z}, \mathfrak{z}' \in \mathfrak{Z}_Z$ be arbitrary. We define a functional $\psi_{\mathfrak{z},\mathfrak{z}'}$ on D as follows:

$$\psi_{\mathfrak{z},\mathfrak{z}'}(d) = \sum_{z^* \in Z} \left(\mathfrak{z}(z^*) - \mathfrak{z}'(z^*)\right) d(z^*).$$

Obviously, $\psi_{\mathfrak{z},\mathfrak{z}'}$ is a linear functional and for arbitrary $p \in W(X), q \in W(Y)$

$$\begin{aligned}\psi_{\mathfrak{z},\mathfrak{z}'}\left(V_{\mathfrak{C}}[.,p](q)\right) &= \sum_{z^* \in Z} \left(\mathfrak{z}(z^*) - \mathfrak{z}'(z^*)\right) V_{\mathfrak{C}}[z^*, p](q) \\ &= V_{\mathfrak{C}}[\mathfrak{z}, p](q) - V_{\mathfrak{C}}[\mathfrak{z}', p](q).\end{aligned}$$

For $k = 0, 1, \ldots$ we put

$$L_k \underset{\text{Df}}{=} L\left(\{V_{\mathfrak{C}}[.,p](q) \mid p \in X^k \wedge q \in Y^k\}\right)$$

and

$$L \underset{\text{Df}}{=} L\left(\{V_{\mathfrak{C}}[.,p](q) \mid p \in W(X) \wedge q \in W(Y) \wedge l(p) = l(q)\}\right).$$

Thus the random states $\mathfrak{z}, \mathfrak{z}'$ are equivalent if and only if the functional $\psi_{\mathfrak{z},\mathfrak{z}'}$ is identically zero on the set L. Furthermore, we have the following obvious result:

Lemma 2.11a. *For all* $p \in X^k$, $V_{\mathfrak{C}}[z, p] = V_{\mathfrak{C}}[z', p]$ *if and only if the functional* $\psi_{\mathfrak{z},\mathfrak{z}'}$ *vanishes on* L_k.

We claim:

Lemma 2.11b. *For each* k, L_k *is a subspace of* L_{k+1}.

Proof: It suffices to show that the functions $V_{\mathfrak{C}}[.,p](q) \in L_k$ (i.e., with $p \in X^k$, $q \in Y^k$) can be written as linear combinations with real coefficients of certain functions $V_{\mathfrak{C}}[.,p'](q')$ with $p' \in X^{k+1}$, $q' \in Y^{k+1}$. By 2.8

$$V_{\mathfrak{C}}[z, p](q) = \sum_{y \in Y} V_{\mathfrak{C}}[z, px](qy)$$

for arbitrary fixed $x \in X$. Since Y is finite,

$$V_{\mathfrak{C}}[.,p](q) = \sum_{y \in Y} 1 \cdot V_{\mathfrak{C}}[.,px](qy)$$

is a linear combination of the required type for arbitrary $x \in X$.

Lemma 2.11c. *If* $L_k = L_{k+1}$, *then* $L_k = L_{k+j}$ *for all* $j = 0, 1, \ldots$

Proof: It suffices to show that $L_k = L_{k+1}$ implies $L_{k+1} = L_{k+2}$. Since by Lemma 2.11b L_{k+1} is a subspace of L_{k+2}, we only have to show that every generator $V_{\mathfrak{C}}[.,p](q)$ of L_{k+2} (i.e., where $p \in X^{k+2}$, $q \in Y^{k+2}$) belongs to the space L_{k+1}. Let $p = xp' \in X^{k+2}$, $q = yq' \in Y^{k+2}$.

Then

$$V_{\mathfrak{C}}[.,p](q) = V_{\mathfrak{C}}[.,xp'](yq') = \sum_{z^* \in Z} H[.,x](y, z^*) V_{\mathfrak{C}}[z^*, p'](q').$$

The function $V_{\mathfrak{C}}[\cdot, p'](q')$ is a member of $L_{k+1} = L_k$. Thus there are a natural number $m \geqq 1$, real numbers $\alpha_1, \ldots, \alpha_m$ and words $p_1, \ldots, p_m \in X^k$, $q_1, \ldots, q_m \in Y^k$ such that

$$V_{\mathfrak{C}}[\cdot, p'](q') = \sum_{\mu=1}^{m} \alpha_\mu \cdot V_{\mathfrak{C}}[\cdot, p_\mu](q_\mu).$$

Thus we obtain

$$\begin{aligned} V_{\mathfrak{C}}[\cdot, p](q) &= \sum_{\mu=1}^{m} \alpha_\mu \sum_{z^* \in Z} H[\cdot, x](y, z^*) \cdot V_{\mathfrak{C}}[z^*, p_\mu](q_\mu) \\ &= \sum_{\mu=1}^{m} \alpha_\mu \cdot V_{\mathfrak{C}}[\cdot, x p_\mu](y q_\mu), \end{aligned}$$

i.e., $V_{\mathfrak{C}}[\cdot, p](q)$ is a linear combination of certain functions from L_{k+1} and thus belongs to L_{k+1}.

We denote by $\mathbf{1}$ the constant function on Z whose value is 1. Lemma 2.11b implies

$$\begin{aligned} &L(\{\mathbf{1}\}) = L_0 \subseteq L_1 \subseteq \cdots \subseteq L_{n-1} \subseteq L_n \subseteq \cdots \subseteq L \subseteq D, \\ &1 = \mathit{dim}\,(L_0) \leqq \mathit{dim}\,(L_1) \leqq \cdots \leqq \mathit{dim}\,(L_{n-1}) \leqq \mathit{dim}\,(L_n) \leqq \cdots \\ &\qquad \leqq \mathit{dim}\,(L) \leqq n. \end{aligned}$$

If $L_i = L_{i+1}$, then by Lemma 2.11c we have $L_i = L_{i+j}$ for every $j = 0, 1, 2, \ldots$ and if i^* is the smallest i with $L_i = L_{i+1}$, then

$$\begin{aligned} &L_0 \subset L_1 \subset \cdots \subset L_{i^*-1} \subset L_{i^*} = L_{i^*+1} = \cdots = L \subseteq D, \\ &1 < \mathit{dim}\,(L_1) < \cdots < \mathit{dim}\,(L_{i^*-1}) < \mathit{dim}\,(L_{i^*}) = \mathit{dim}\,(L) \leqq n. \end{aligned}$$

Thus $\mathit{dim}\,(L_{i^*}) > i^*$, i.e., $i^* \leqq n - 1$. Therefore the random states $\mathfrak{z}, \mathfrak{z}'$ are equivalent if and only if $\psi_{\mathfrak{z},\mathfrak{z}'}$ vanishes on L_{i^*} i.e., if and only if for all $p \in X^{n-1}$

$$V_{\mathfrak{C}}[\mathfrak{z}, p] = V_{\mathfrak{C}}[\mathfrak{z}', p].$$

Thus Theorem 2.11 is proved.

Remark: If we compare Theorem 2.11 with the corresponding result on nondeterministic automata (Part II, Theorem 2.9), we see that the equivalence of the random states $\mathfrak{z}, \mathfrak{z}'$ of a stochastic automaton $\mathfrak{C}$ is a much stronger requirement than the equivalence of the corresponding sets of states $ND(\mathfrak{z})$, $ND(\mathfrak{z}')$ in $ND(\mathfrak{C})$.

The upper bound $n - 1$ for i^* cannot be further improved. Indeed, this bound is already the best possible for deterministic automata. It is easy to construct (deterministic) S-automata from these deterministic automata, in which there are two inequivalent states z, z' such that for all $p \in W(X)$ with $l(p) \leqq n - 2$ we have $V_{\mathfrak{C}}[\delta_z, p] = V_{\mathfrak{C}}[\delta_{z'}, p]$.

Corollary 2.12. The equivalence of states and random states of finite S-automata is (algorithmically) decidable.

If $\mathfrak{C} = [X, Y, Z, H]$, $\mathfrak{C}' = [X, Y, Z', H']$ are S-automata with the same input alphabet, the same output alphabet and (without loss of generality) disjoint sets of states, then similarly as in the theory of deterministic automata, we can define their *direct sum* $\mathfrak{C} + \mathfrak{C}'$ as follows: $\mathfrak{C} + \mathfrak{C}' = [X, Y, Z' \cup Z, H^+]$, where for $x \in X$, $z^*, z^{**} \in Z \cup Z'$,

$$H^+[z^*, x](y, z^{**}) \underset{\mathrm{Df}}{=} \begin{cases} H[z^*, x](y, z^{**}), & \text{if} \quad z^*, z^{**} \in Z, \\ H'[z^*, x](y, z^{**}), & \text{if} \quad z^*, z^{**} \in Z', \\ 0 & \text{otherwise} \end{cases}$$

This immediately implies the following theorem:

Theorem 2.13.

1. *If* $\mathfrak{C} = [X, Y, Z, H]$, $\mathfrak{C}' = [X, Y, Z', H']$ *are* $[Y, Z]$*-finite S-automata with* $n = \mathit{Card}\,(Z)$, $n' = \mathit{Card}\,(Z')$, *then the random states* $\mathfrak{z} \in \mathfrak{Z}_Z$, $\mathfrak{z}' \in \mathfrak{Z}_{Z'}$ *are equivalent if and only if* $V_{\mathfrak{C}}[\mathfrak{z}, p] = V_{\mathfrak{C}'}[\mathfrak{z}', p]$ *for all* $p \in X^{n+n'-1}$.
2. *For finite S-automata the relations* $\sim$, $\subsetneqq$ *are decidable.*

In the second part of this section we shall deal with problems arising in the investigation of equivalent or weakly equivalent simplification of S-automata. Our aim is to construct for an arbitrary given S-automaton an equivalent S-automaton in which any two states are pairwise inequivalent, and moreover from each such reduced automaton to eliminate those states which are equivalent to some (non-deterministic) random states.

Definition 2.2. Let $\mathfrak{C} = [X, Y, Z, H]$ be an arbitrary S-automaton.

(2.2.1) $\mathfrak{C}$ is said to be *reduced* if for $z, z' \in Z$, $z \sim z'$ implies $z = z'$.

(2.2.2) An S-automaton $\mathfrak{C}'$ is called a *reduct of* $\mathfrak{C}$ if $\mathfrak{C}'$ is reduced and equivalent to $\mathfrak{C}$.

(2.2.3) $\mathfrak{C}$ is called *minimal*, if for arbitrary $z \in Z$, $\mathfrak{z} \in \mathfrak{Z}_Z$, $z \sim \mathfrak{z}$ implies $\mathfrak{z} = \delta_z$.

(2.2.4) $\mathfrak{C}'$ is called a *minim of* $\mathfrak{C}$ if it is minimal and weakly equivalent to $\mathfrak{C}$.

(2.2.5) $\mathfrak{C}$ is said to be *strongly reduced* if for arbitrary $\mathfrak{z}, \mathfrak{z}' \in \mathfrak{Z}_z$, $\mathfrak{z} \sim \mathfrak{z}'$ implies $\mathfrak{z} = \mathfrak{z}'$.

(2.2.6) An S-automaton $\mathfrak{C}'$ is called a *strong reduct of* $\mathfrak{C}$ if it is strongly reduced and weakly equivalent to $\mathfrak{C}$.

Corollary 2.14.

1. Every strongly reduced S-automaton is minimal. Every minimal S-automaton is reduced.
2. Every strong reduct of $\mathfrak{C}$ is a minim of $\mathfrak{C}$.
3. For finite S-automata, the property of being reduced is decidable.
4. For finite S-automata $\mathfrak{C}$, $\mathfrak{C}'$, it is decidable whether $\mathfrak{C}'$ is a reduct of $\mathfrak{C}$.

The converses of propositions 2.14.1 and 2.14.2 are not valid. The S-automaton $\mathfrak{C}_3$ described above is reduced but not minimal, since $3 \sim \mathfrak{z}$, where $\mathfrak{z}(1) = \mathfrak{z}(2) = 1/2$, $\mathfrak{z}(3) = 0$. As we shall see, the S-automaton $\mathfrak{C}_1$ considered in the first section is minimal. However, $\mathfrak{C}_1$ is not strongly reduced, since the random states $\mathfrak{z}_1$ and $\mathfrak{z}_2$ defined below are equivalent.

$$\mathfrak{z}_1(1) = \mathfrak{z}_1(2) = \frac{1}{2}, \quad \mathfrak{z}_1(3) = \mathfrak{z}_1(4) = \mathfrak{z}_1(5) = 0,$$

$$\mathfrak{z}_2(1) = \mathfrak{z}_2(2) = \mathfrak{z}_2(3) = \mathfrak{z}_2(4) = \frac{1}{4}, \quad \mathfrak{z}_2(5) = 0.$$

This latter assertion can be proved in the same way as $\mathfrak{C}_2 \subsetneqq \mathfrak{C}_3$ and $\mathfrak{C}_2 \approx \mathfrak{C}_3$ were proved above.

Theorem 2.15.

1. [Even [4]). *Minimality is a decidable property of finite S-automata.*
2. *If $\mathfrak{C}$ is a finite S-automaton, then it is decidable whether it is strongly reduced.*

Proof: Let $\mathfrak{C} = [X, Y, Z, H]$ be a finite S-automaton with $Z = \{z_0, z_1, \ldots, z_n\}$, $n \geqq 1$. (Every S-automaton with $Card\,(Z) = 1$ is obviously minimal and strongly reduced.)

The automaton $\mathfrak{C}$ is not minimal if and only if there is a state $z \in Z$ and a random state $\mathfrak{z} \in \mathfrak{Z}_Z$ such that $\mathfrak{z} \neq \delta_z$ and $\mathfrak{z} \sim z$. Thus in order to decide whether $\mathfrak{C}$ is minimal, it suffices for each $j = 0, \ldots, n$ to decide whether there is a $\mathfrak{z}_j \in \mathfrak{Z}_Z$ with $\mathfrak{z}_j \sim z_j$ and $\mathfrak{z}_j(z_j) \neq 1$. As shall be shown in the proof of Theorem 2.20, such a $\mathfrak{z}_j$ exists if and only if there is a $\mathfrak{z}_j'$ with $\mathfrak{z}_j' \sim \mathfrak{z}_j \sim z_j$ and $\mathfrak{z}_j'(z_j) = 0$. Then we consider the space L defined in the proof of Carlyle's Theorem (Theorem 2.11), and the space $L_n = L(\{V_{\mathfrak{C}}[\cdot, p](q) \mid p \in X^n \wedge q \in Y^n\})$.

By Theorem 2.11, we have $L = L_n$ because $Card\,(Z) = n + 1$. Thus certain words $p_0, \ldots, p_{m-1} \in W(X)$, $q_0, \ldots, q_{m-1} \in W(Y)$ can be chosen so that

$$B = \{V_{\mathfrak{C}}[\cdot, p_0](q_0), \ldots, V_{\mathfrak{C}}[\cdot, p_{m-1}](q_{m-1})\}$$

is a basis of L, since L_n has a finite number of generators. Obviously, $m = dim\,(L) \leqq n + 1$. Since $L_0 \subseteq L$, we can assume without any loss of generality that $p_0 = q_0 = e$.

Now $\mathfrak{z}_j \sim z_j$ is satisfied if and only if $\psi_{\mathfrak{z}_j \delta_{z_j}}$ vanishes on the space L, i.e., if and only if $\psi_{\mathfrak{z}_j \delta_{z_j}}$ vanishes on the set B. Thus $\mathfrak{z}_j \sim z_j$ if and only if for all $i = 0, \ldots, m - 1$

$$\sum_{z^* \in Z} \big(\delta_{z_j}(z^*) - \mathfrak{z}_j(z^*)\big)\, V_{\mathfrak{C}}[z^*, p_i](q_i) = 0$$

and thus $\big($by $\mathfrak{z}_j(z_j) = 0\big)$ if and only if for all $i = 0, 1, \ldots, m - 1$

$$V_{\mathfrak{C}}[z_j, p_i](q_i) = V_{\mathfrak{C}}[\mathfrak{z}_j, p_i](q_i).$$

Consequently, there exists a random state $\mathfrak{z}_j$ equivalent to z_j and satisfying $\mathfrak{z}_j(z_j) = 0$ if and only if the $j+1$st column of the matrix

$$H_{\mathfrak{C}} = \begin{pmatrix} V_{\mathfrak{C}}[z_0, p_0](q_0) & \dots & V_{\mathfrak{C}}[z_j, p_0](q_0) & \dots & V_{\mathfrak{C}}[z_n, p_0](q_0) \\ \vdots & & \vdots & & \vdots \\ V_{\mathfrak{C}}[z_0, p_{m-1}](q_{m-1}) & \dots & V_{\mathfrak{C}}[z_j, p_{m-1}](q_{m-1}) & \dots & V_{\mathfrak{C}}[z_n, p_{m-1})(q_{m-1}) \end{pmatrix}$$

is a convex linear combination of its other columns, where "convex" means that all coefficients of the linear combination are non-negative and their sum is equal to one.

Thus to decide whether $\mathfrak{C}$ is minimal, it suffices to decide for all $j = 0, \dots, n$ whether the $j+1$st column of $H_{\mathfrak{C}}$ is a convex linear combination of the remaining columns.

Now we show that this question is indeed decidable. We can assume that $j = 0$. Since $p_0 = q_0 = e$, $V_{\mathfrak{C}}[z, e](e) = 1$ we obtain the following system of linear equations for the coefficients $\alpha_1, \dots, \alpha_n$ of the desired linear combination.

$$\begin{pmatrix} 1 & \dots & 1 \\ V_{\mathfrak{C}}[z_1, p_1](q_1) & \dots & V_{\mathfrak{C}}[z_n, p_1](q_1) \\ \vdots & & \vdots \\ V_{\mathfrak{C}}[z_1, p_{m-1}](q_{m-1}) & \dots & V_{\mathfrak{C}}[z_n, p_{m-1}](q_{m-1}) \end{pmatrix} \begin{pmatrix} \alpha_1 \\ \vdots \\ \alpha_n \end{pmatrix} = \begin{pmatrix} 1 \\ V_{\mathfrak{C}}[z_0, p_1](q_1) \\ \vdots \\ V_{\mathfrak{C}}[z_0, p_{m-1}](q_{m-1}) \end{pmatrix}.$$

Next we have to decide whether this system has a solution $\alpha_1, \dots, \alpha_n$ where $\alpha_i \geqq 0$ for each i. To achieve this, we formulate this as a linear optimization problem.

We shall use the following abbreviations:

$$a_{\nu,\mu} = V_{\mathfrak{C}}[z_\nu, p_\mu](q_\mu)$$

for $\nu = 0, \dots, n$; $\mu = 1, \dots, m-1$, and consider the following optimisation problem:

$$\alpha_i \geqq 0 \text{ for } i = 1, \dots, n, n+1, \dots, n+m-1;$$

$$\begin{pmatrix} 1 & 1 & \dots 1 & 0 & 0 \dots 0 \\ a_{1,1} & a_{2,1} & \dots a_{n,1} & 1 & 0 \dots 0 \\ a_{1,2} & a_{2,2} & \dots a_{n,2} & 0 & 1 \dots 0 \\ \vdots & \vdots & \vdots & \vdots & \vdots \\ a_{1,m-1} & a_{2,m-1} & \dots a_{n,m-1} & 0 & 0 \dots 1 \end{pmatrix} \begin{pmatrix} \alpha_1 \\ \vdots \\ \alpha_n \\ \vdots \\ \alpha_{n+m-1} \end{pmatrix} = \begin{pmatrix} 1 \\ a_{0,1} \\ \vdots \\ a_{0,m-1} \end{pmatrix},$$

$$C = \sum_{i=1}^{m-1} \alpha_{n+i} \to \text{Minimum}.$$

Using the methods developped in the theory of linear optimization[1]) one can decide algorithmically whether this problem has a solution, and if it does, obtain it. Obviously, this optimization problem has a solution with $C_{min} = 0$ if and only if the above system of linear equations has a solution in $\alpha_1, \ldots, \alpha_n$ with $\alpha_i \geqq 0$ for all i. Since it is decidable whether the optimization problem has a solution with $C_{min} = 0$, it is also decidable whether $\mathfrak{C}$ is minimal, and thus 2.15.1 is proved.

The S-automaton $\mathfrak{C}$ is not strongly reduced if and only if there are random states $\mathfrak{z}, \mathfrak{z}' \in \mathfrak{Z}_Z$ with $\mathfrak{z} \neq \mathfrak{z}'$ and $\mathfrak{z} \sim \mathfrak{z}'$. Let us consider the system of equations

$$\sum_{i=0}^{n} \alpha_i \cdot a_{i\mu} = 0 \qquad (\mu = 0, 1, \ldots, m-1), \tag{*}$$

where in particular we have the equation

$$\sum_{i=0}^{n} \alpha_i = 0$$

(for $\mu = 0$). This system of equations has a non-trivial solution if and only if $m < n + 1$ or $m = n + 1$ and the determinant of the matrix $(a_{\nu\mu})$ vanishes. Since B is a basis, the latter possibility cannot occur.

Let $\alpha_0, \ldots, \alpha_n$ be a non-trivial solution of (*). From $\sum_{i=0}^{n} \alpha_i = 0$ we obtain

$$\sum_{\alpha_i > 0} \alpha_i = -\sum_{\alpha_i < 0} \alpha_i .$$

We put

$$A = \sum_{\alpha_i > 0} \alpha_i ,$$

$$\mathfrak{z}(z_i) = \begin{cases} \dfrac{\alpha_i}{A}, & \text{if} \quad \alpha_i > 0, \\ 0 & \text{otherwise} \end{cases} \qquad \mathfrak{z}'(z_i) = \begin{cases} \dfrac{-\alpha_i}{A}, & \text{if} \quad \alpha_i < 0, \\ 0 & \text{otherwise.} \end{cases}$$

Then $\sum_{i=0}^{n} \mathfrak{z}(z_i) = 1 = \sum_{i=0}^{n} \mathfrak{z}'(z_i)$, $\mathfrak{z}(z_i) \geqq 0$, $\mathfrak{z}'(z_i) \geqq 0$ for $i = 0, \ldots, n$ and $\mathfrak{z}(z_i) - \mathfrak{z}'(z_i) = \frac{1}{A}\alpha_i$. If $\alpha_0, \ldots, \alpha_n$ is a solution of (*), then so is $\frac{1}{A}\alpha_0, \ldots, \frac{1}{A}\alpha_n$, hence

$$\sum_{z^* \in Z} \big(\mathfrak{z}(z^*) - \mathfrak{z}'(z^*)\big)\, V_{\mathfrak{C}}[z^*, p_\mu](q_\mu) = 0 \qquad (\mu = 0, 1, \ldots, m-1).$$

Consequently, $\psi_{\mathfrak{z},\mathfrak{z}'}$ vanishes on B, i.e., $\mathfrak{z}, \mathfrak{z}'$ are different but equivalent random states of $\mathfrak{C}$. Thus the S-automaton $\mathfrak{C}$ is strongly reduced if and only if $m = dim\,(L) = Card\,(Z) = n + 1$. In particular we obtain that the problem whether $\mathfrak{C}$ is strongly reduced, is decidable. Thus Theorem 2.15 is proved.

---

[1]) See e.g. J. Piehler: Einführung in die lineare Optimierung, 3. Aufl., Leipzig 1969, or B. Krekó: Lehrbuch der linearen Optimierung, 3. Aufl., Berlin 1968.

Now we show that $\mathfrak{C}_1$ is minimal. Since $\mathfrak{C}_1$ is not strongly reduced, we have *dim* $(L) \leqq 4$. The functions

$$V_{\mathfrak{C}_1}[z, e](e) = 1 \text{ for } z \in \{1, 2, \ldots, 5\}; \; V_{\mathfrak{C}_1}[z, 0](A) = \begin{cases} \frac{1}{2}, \text{ if } z = 1, \\ \frac{1}{2}, \text{ if } z = 2, \\ 0, \text{ if } z = 3, \\ 0, \text{ if } z = 4, \\ 0, \text{ if } z = 5; \end{cases}$$

$$V_{\mathfrak{C}_1}[z, 0](B) = \begin{cases} 0, \text{ if } z = 1, \\ 0, \text{ if } z = 2, \\ \frac{1}{2}, \text{ if } z = 3, \\ \frac{1}{2}, \text{ if } z = 4, \\ 0, \text{ if } z = 5; \end{cases}$$

$$V_{\mathfrak{C}_1}[z, 1](A) = \begin{cases} \frac{1}{2}, \text{ if } z = 1, \\ 0, \text{ if } z = 2, \\ 0, \text{ if } z = 3, \\ \frac{1}{2}, \text{ if } z = 4, \\ 0, \text{ if } z = 5, \end{cases}$$

are linearly independent and thus constitute a basis for L. Thus a matrix $H_{\mathfrak{C}_1}$ for the automaton $\mathfrak{C}_1$ is

$$\begin{pmatrix} 1 & 1 & 1 & 1 & 1 \\ \frac{1}{2} & \frac{1}{2} & 0 & 0 & 0 \\ 0 & 0 & \frac{1}{2} & \frac{1}{2} & 0 \\ \frac{1}{2} & 0 & 0 & \frac{1}{2} & 0 \end{pmatrix}.$$

There is a random state equivalent to the state 1 if and only if the following system of equations

$$\begin{pmatrix} 1 & 1 & 1 & 1 \\ \frac{1}{2} & 0 & 0 & 0 \\ 0 & \frac{1}{2} & \frac{1}{2} & 0 \\ 0 & 0 & \frac{1}{2} & 0 \end{pmatrix} \begin{pmatrix} x_2 \\ x_3 \\ x_4 \\ x_5 \end{pmatrix} = \begin{pmatrix} 1 \\ \frac{1}{2} \\ 0 \\ \frac{1}{2} \end{pmatrix}$$

has a convex solution. This system has exactly one solution, namely $(x_2, x_3, x_4, x_5) = (1, -1, 1, 0)$ which is not convex. For the state 2 we obtain the system of equations

$$\begin{pmatrix} 1 & 1 & 1 & 1 \\ \frac{1}{2} & 0 & 0 & 0 \\ 0 & \frac{1}{2} & \frac{1}{2} & 0 \\ \frac{1}{2} & 0 & \frac{1}{2} & 0 \end{pmatrix} \cdot \begin{pmatrix} x_1 \\ x_3 \\ x_4 \\ x_5 \end{pmatrix} = \begin{pmatrix} 1 \\ \frac{1}{2} \\ 0 \\ 0 \end{pmatrix},$$

whose only solution is $(x_1, x_3, x_4, x_5) = (1, 1, -1, 0)$ and this is not convex. Similarly we obtain that the corresponding systems of equations belonging to the states 3 and 4 have exactly one non-convex solution, while the system

$$\begin{pmatrix} 1 & 1 & 1 & 1 \\ \frac{1}{2} & \frac{1}{2} & 0 & 0 \\ 0 & 0 & \frac{1}{2} & \frac{1}{2} \\ \frac{1}{2} & 0 & 0 & \frac{1}{2} \end{pmatrix} \cdot \begin{pmatrix} x_1 \\ x_2 \\ x_3 \\ x_4 \end{pmatrix} = \begin{pmatrix} 1 \\ 0 \\ 0 \\ 0 \end{pmatrix},$$

which we encounter when trying to decide whether there is a random state equivalent to 5 has no solution at all.

Theorem 2.16. *Let* $\mathfrak{C} = [X, Y, Z, H]$ *be an S-automaton.*

1. *All reducts of* $\mathfrak{C}$ *have the same number of states.*

2. *If* $\mathfrak{C}$ *is reduced and equivalent to a minimal S-automaton, then it is minimal.*

3. *If* $\mathfrak{C}$ *is minimal, and equivalent to a strongly reduced S-automaton, then it is strongly reduced.*

The proof of 2.16.1 can be carried out in exactly the same way as the proof of the corresponding assertion on deterministic automata (cf. Part I, Theorem 2.11). Suppose $\mathfrak{C}^* = [X, Y, Z^*, H^*]$ is a minimal and thus reduced S-automaton which is equivalent to $\mathfrak{C}$. Then there is a one-to-one mapping ζ of Z onto Z^* which assigns to each $z \in Z$ that $z^* = \zeta(z)$ which is equivalent to z. Assume $z \in Z$, $\mathfrak{z} \in Z_Z$ and $z \sim \mathfrak{z}$. We denote by $\mathfrak{z}^\zeta$ the random state of $\mathfrak{C}^*$ defined as follows:

$$\mathfrak{z}^\zeta(z^*) = \mathfrak{z}\big(\zeta^{-1}(z^*)\big).$$

Since $z^* \sim \zeta^{-1}(z^*)$ for all $z^* \in Z^*$, we have

$$\zeta(z) \sim z \sim \mathfrak{z} \sim \mathfrak{z}^\zeta,$$

and the minimality of $\mathfrak{C}$ implies $\mathfrak{z}^\zeta = \delta_{\zeta(z)}$. By the definition of $\mathfrak{z}^\zeta$ we obtain $\mathfrak{z} = \delta_z$, which was to be shown.

If $\mathfrak{C}^*$ is even strongly reduced, and $\mathfrak{z}_1, \mathfrak{z}_2 \in \mathfrak{Z}_Z$ with $\mathfrak{z}_1 \sim \mathfrak{z}_2$, then in the same way we obtain $\mathfrak{z}_1^\zeta \sim \mathfrak{z}_1 \sim \mathfrak{z}_2 \sim \mathfrak{z}_2^\zeta$, hence $\mathfrak{z}_1^\zeta = \mathfrak{z}_2^\zeta$ and thus $\mathfrak{z}_1(z) = \mathfrak{z}_1^\zeta\big(\zeta(z)\big) = \mathfrak{z}_2^\zeta\big(\zeta(z)\big) = \mathfrak{z}_2(z)$ for all $z \in Z$.

Thus Theorem 2.16 is proved.

Theorem 2.17. *Let* $\mathfrak{C} = [X, Y, Z, H]$ *be an arbitrary S-automaton.*

1. (Nawrotzki [1], Carlyle [2]). *There exists a reduct* $\overline{\mathfrak{C}}$ *of* $\mathfrak{C}$. *If* $\mathfrak{C}$ *is finite, then* $\overline{\mathfrak{C}}$ *can be constructed algorithmically.*

2. *If* $\mathfrak{C}$ *is observable, or Z-deterministic, then* $\overline{\mathfrak{C}}$ *can be chosen observable or Z-deterministic.*

3. *If* $\mathfrak{C}$ *is an S-Mealy automaton, then it has a reduct which is also an S-Mealy automaton.*

Proof: For $z \in Z$ we denote by $[z]$ the equivalence class of the relation $\sim$ over Z containing the state z. If $\mathfrak{C}$ is finite, then the (finitely many) classes $[z]$ can be constructed algorithmically by Theorem 2.11.

We put

$$\bar{Z} \underset{\mathrm{Df}}{=} \{[z] \mid z \in Z\},$$

and for each $[z] \in \bar{Z}$ we choose an arbitrary discrete PM $P_{[z]}$ over $[z]$. For $[z], [z'] \in \bar{Z}$, $x \in X$, $y \in Y$ let

$$\bar{H}\big[[z], x\big](y, [z']) \underset{\mathrm{Df}}{=} \sum_{z'' \in [z]} P_{[z]}(z'')\, H[z'', x](\{y\} \times [z']).$$

Obviously, $\bar{H}\big[[z], x\big](y, [z']) \geqq 0$ and $\bar{H}\big[[z], x\big](y, [z']) > 0$ for at most countably many $\big[y, [z']\big] \in Y \times \bar{Z}$. Furthermore,

$$\begin{aligned}\bar{H}\big[[z], x\big](Y \times \bar{Z}) &= \sum_{z'' \in [z]} P_{[z]}(z'') \sum_{[z'] \in \bar{Z}} \sum_{y \in Y} H[z'', x](\{y\} \times [z'])\\ &= \sum_{z'' \in [z]} P_{[z]}(z'')\, H[z'', x](Y \times Z) = 1,\end{aligned}$$

thus $\bar{\mathfrak{C}} = [X, Y, \bar{Z}, \bar{H}]$ is an S-automaton. We shall show by induction on p that for all $z \in Z$, $p \in W(X)$, $q \in W(Y)$

$$V_{\mathfrak{C}}[z, p](q) = V_{\bar{\mathfrak{C}}}\big[[z], p\big](q).$$

The initial step $p = e$ is trivial. The step from p to xp:

$$\begin{aligned}V_{\bar{\mathfrak{C}}}\big[[z], xp\big](yq) &= \sum_{[z'] \in \bar{Z}} \bar{H}\big[[z], x\big](y, [z'])\, V_{\bar{\mathfrak{C}}}\big[[z'], p\big](q)\\ &= \sum_{[z'] \in \bar{Z}} \sum_{z'' \in [z]} P_{[z]}(z'')\, H[z'', x](\{y\} \times [z'])\, V_{\bar{\mathfrak{C}}}\big[[z'], p\big](q).\end{aligned}$$

By the induction hypothesis, $V_{\bar{\mathfrak{C}}}\big[[z'], p\big](q) = V_{\mathfrak{C}}[z_1', p](q)$ for all $z_1' \in [z']$. Thus

$$\begin{aligned}&V_{\bar{\mathfrak{C}}}\big[[z], xp\big](yq)\\ &= \sum_{z'' \in [z]} P_{[z]}(z'') \sum_{[z'] \in \bar{Z}} \sum_{z_1' \in [z']} H[z'', x](y, z_1')\, V_{\mathfrak{C}}[z_1', p](q)\\ &= \sum_{z'' \in [z]} P_{[z]}(z'')\, V_{\mathfrak{C}}[z'', xp](yq)\\ &= \Big(\sum_{z'' \in [z]} P_{[z]}(z'')\Big)\, V_{\mathfrak{C}}[z, xp](yq) = V_{\mathfrak{C}}[z, xp](yq),\end{aligned}$$

since every $z'' \in [z]$ is equivalent to z. Thus for every state z of $\mathfrak{C}$, $[z]$ is an equivalent state of $\bar{\mathfrak{C}}$ and conversely, therefore $\mathfrak{C} \sim \bar{\mathfrak{C}}$. $[z_1] \sim [z_2]$ implies $z_1 \sim z_2$ hence $[z_1] = [z_2]$, consequently $\bar{\mathfrak{C}}$ is reduced. This proves 2.17.1.

If $\mathfrak{C}$ is observable, then in order to obtain an observable reduct, we have to choose $P_{[z]}$ deterministic. For $[z] \in \bar{Z}$ let $\varrho([z])$ be that member of $[z]$ for which $P_{[z]}(\varrho([z])) = 1$, consequently for $[z], [z'] \in \bar{Z}$, $x \in X$, $y \in Y$

$$\bar{H}_\varrho[[z], x](y, [z']) = H[\varrho([z]), x](\{y\} \times [z']).$$

Thus $\bar{\mathfrak{C}}_\varrho = [X, Y, \bar{Z}, \bar{H}_\varrho]$ is a reduct of $\mathfrak{C}$. If δ is the function belonging to the S-automaton $\mathfrak{C}$ such that

$$H[z, x](y, z') > 0 \leftrightarrow [z, x, y] \in Vb(\delta) \wedge z' = \delta(z, x, y),$$

then for $[z] \in \bar{Z}$, $x \in X$, $y \in Y$, we put

$$\bar{\delta}([z], x, y) \underset{\mathrm{Df}}{=} \begin{cases} [\delta(\varrho([z]), x, y)], & \text{if } [\varrho([z]), x, y] \in Vb(\delta), \\ \text{not defined otherwise.} \end{cases}$$

Here

$$\begin{aligned} \bar{H}_\varrho[[z], x](y, [z']) > 0 &\leftrightarrow H[\varrho([z]), x](\{y\} \times [z']) > 0 \\ &\leftrightarrow \exists z''(z'' \in [z'] \wedge H[\varrho([z]), x](y, z'') > 0) \\ &\leftrightarrow \exists z''(z'' \in [z'] \wedge [\varrho([z]), x, y] \in Vb(\delta) \\ &\qquad \wedge z'' = \delta(\varrho([z]), x, y)) \\ &\leftrightarrow [[z], x, y] \in Vb(\bar{\delta}) \wedge [z'] = \bar{\delta}([z], x, y), \end{aligned}$$

hence $\bar{\mathfrak{C}}_\varrho$ is observable.

If $\mathfrak{C}$ is even Z-deterministic, then $\bar{\mathfrak{C}}_\varrho$ is also Z-deterministic, since for arbitrary $[z], [z'] \in \bar{Z}$, $x \in X$

$$\bar{F}_\varrho[[z], x]([z']) = \bar{H}_\varrho[[z], x](Y \times \{[z']\}) = F[\varrho([z]), x]([z']) \in \{0, 1\}.$$

Thus 2.17.2 is proved. If $\mathfrak{C}$ is an S-Mealy automaton, then

$$\begin{aligned} \bar{F}_\varrho[[z], x]([z']) &= F[\varrho([z]), x]([z']), \\ \bar{G}_\varrho[[z], x](y) &= G[\varrho([z]), x](y), \end{aligned}$$

and

$$\begin{aligned} \bar{H}_\varrho[[z], x](y, [z']) &= H[\varrho([z]), x](\{y\} \times [z']) \\ &= F[\varrho([z]), x]([z'])\, G[\varrho([z]), x](y) \\ &= \bar{F}_\varrho[[z], x]([z'])\, \bar{G}_\varrho[[z], x](y), \end{aligned}$$

hence $\bar{\mathfrak{C}}_\varrho$ is also an S-Mealy automaton.

Thus Theorem 2.17 is proved.

It follows from 2.16 that the number of classes in $\bar{Z} = Z/\sim$ is the minimum number of states that can be found among the S-automata equivalent to $\mathfrak{C}$. However, this number can be further decreased in the same way as for ND-automata if we replace equivalence by weak equivalence.[1])

[1]) Ott [1], [2], and Paz [6] have shown that there is a minimal finite S-automaton $\mathfrak{C}$ for which there is an S-automaton $\mathfrak{C}'$ with fewer states and $\mathfrak{C} \lneqq \mathfrak{C}'$. Every such $\mathfrak{C}$ is not strongly reduced, however this condition is not sufficient.

Theorem 2.18. *Let* $\mathfrak{C} = [X, Y, \bar{Z}, H]$ *be an S-automaton.*

1. *Every minim* $\mathfrak{C}'$ *of* $\mathfrak{C}$ *is equivalently embedded into* $\mathfrak{C}$.
2. *Weakly equivalent minimal S-automata are equivalent.*

Proof: Proposition 2.18.2 follows immediately from 2.18.1. We have to show that for each state $z' \in Z'$ of $\mathfrak{C}' = [X, Y, Z', H']$ there is an equivalent state $z \in Z$ of $\mathfrak{C}$.

For every $z' \in Z'$ we fix a random state $\mathfrak{z}_{z'} \in \mathfrak{Z}_Z$ of $\mathfrak{C}$ with $z' \sim \mathfrak{z}_{z'}$ and for every $z \in Z$ we choose a random state $\mathfrak{z}'_z \in \mathfrak{Z}_{Z'}$ of $\mathfrak{C}'$ with $z \sim \mathfrak{z}'_z$. This is possible because $\mathfrak{C}$ and $\mathfrak{C}'$ are weakly equivalent. Let $z' \in Z'$ be arbitrary. Then for all $p \in W(X)$, $q \in W(Y)$

$$V_{\mathfrak{C}'}[z', p](q) = V_{\mathfrak{C}}[\mathfrak{z}_{z'}, p](q) = \sum_{z \in Z} \mathfrak{z}_{z'}(z) \cdot V_{\mathfrak{C}}[z, p](q)$$
$$= \sum_{z \in Z} \mathfrak{z}_{z'}(z) \sum_{z'' \in Z'} \mathfrak{z}'_z(z'') \cdot V_{\mathfrak{C}'}[z'', p](q).$$

We put for $z'' \in Z'$

$$\mathfrak{z}^*_{z'}(z'') = \sum_{z \in Z} \mathfrak{z}_{z'}(z) \cdot \mathfrak{z}'_z(z''),$$

hence $\mathfrak{z}^*_{z'}$ is a random state of $\mathfrak{C}'$ which is equivalent to the state z' of $\mathfrak{C}'$. Indeed, for all $p \in W(X)$, $q \in W(X)$

$$V_{\mathfrak{C}'}[z', p](q) = \sum_{z'' \in Z'} \mathfrak{z}^*_{z'}(z'') \cdot V_{\mathfrak{C}'}[z'', p](q) = V_{\mathfrak{C}'}[\mathfrak{z}^*_{z'}, p](q).$$

Consequently, $\mathfrak{z}^*_{z'} = \delta_{z'}$, i.e., we obtain the following equalities:

$$\sum_{z \in Z} \mathfrak{z}_{z'}(z) \cdot \mathfrak{z}'_z(z') = 1 \quad \text{und} \quad \sum_{z \in Z} \mathfrak{z}_{z'}(z) = 1.$$

Hence for every $z \in Z$ with $\mathfrak{z}_{z'}(z) > 0$, we have $\mathfrak{z}'_z(z') = 1$, and thus $\mathfrak{z}'_z = \delta_{z'}$. Since there is at least one $z \in Z$ with $\mathfrak{z}_{z'}(z) > 0$, there is also a $z \in Z$ with $z \sim \mathfrak{z}'_z = \delta_{z'} \sim z'$, which was to be shown.

From 2.18 and 2.16 be obtain

Corollary 2.19. Let $\mathfrak{C}$ be an S-automaton.

1. All minims and strong reducts of $\mathfrak{C}$ are pairwise equivalent and have the same number of states.
2. Every strong reduct of $\mathfrak{C}$ can be equivalently embedded into $\mathfrak{C}$.
3. If $\mathfrak{C}$ has a minim which is not strongly reduced, then $\mathfrak{C}$ has no strong reduct.
4. $\mathfrak{C}$ has a strong reduct if and only if it has a minim and all of its minims are strongly reduced.

Now we show that every reduced S-automaton satisfying a certain finiteness condition (in particular every Z-finite S-automaton) has a minim.

Theorem 2.20. *Suppose* $\mathfrak{C} = [X, Y, Z, H]$ *is a reduced S-automaton such that the set* Z_0 *of its states* $z \in Z$, *for which there is an equivalent non-deterministic random state* $\mathfrak{z} \in \mathfrak{Z}_Z$, *is finite. Then* $\mathfrak{C}$ *has a minim. If* $\mathfrak{C}$ *is finite, then a minim of* $\mathfrak{C}$ *can be constructed algorithmically.*

Proof: If $Z_0 = \emptyset$, then $\mathfrak{C}$ itself is minimal. By 2.15.1 for finite S-automata it is decidable whether $Z_0 = \emptyset$. If $\mathfrak{C}$ is finite, then so is Z_0, and for each $z \in Z_0$ a random state $\mathfrak{z}_z$ with $z \sim \mathfrak{z}_z$ and $\mathfrak{z}_z \neq \delta_z$ can be constructed applying the algorithmic procedure given in the proof of 2.15.1. (It suffices to require $\mathfrak{z}_z \neq \delta_z$, since $\mathfrak{z}_z \sim \delta_{z'}$ implies $z \sim \mathfrak{z}_z \sim \delta_{z'} \sim z'$, and since $\mathfrak{C}$ is reduced, $z = z'$.) Suppose $Z_0 = \{z_1, \ldots, z_k\}$, and for $i = 1, \ldots, k$ let $\mathfrak{z}_i$ be a random state of $\mathfrak{C}$ with $z_i \sim \mathfrak{z}_i$ and $\mathfrak{z}_i \neq \delta_{z_i}$. First we construct step by step random states $\mathfrak{z}_i^*$ with $\mathfrak{z}_i^* \sim z_i$ and $\mathfrak{z}_i^*(Z_0) = 0$ for $i = 1, \ldots, k$.

1st Step: We have $\mathfrak{z}_1(z_1) \neq 1$.

For $z \in Z$ let

$$\mathfrak{z}_1^1(z) = \begin{cases} \dfrac{\mathfrak{z}_1(z)}{1 - \mathfrak{z}_1(z_1)}, & \text{if } z \neq z_1, \\ 0, & \text{if } z = z_1. \end{cases}$$

Obviously, $\mathfrak{z}_1^1$ is a random state of $\mathfrak{C}$ with $\mathfrak{z}_1^1(z_1) = 0$ and

$$\begin{aligned} V_{\mathfrak{C}}[\mathfrak{z}_1^1, p](q) &= \frac{1}{1 - \mathfrak{z}_1(z_1)} \sum_{z \in Z \setminus \{z_1\}} \mathfrak{z}_1(z) \cdot V_{\mathfrak{C}}[z, p](q) \\ &= \frac{1}{1 - \mathfrak{z}_1(z_1)} \big(V_{\mathfrak{C}}[\mathfrak{z}_1, p](q) - \mathfrak{z}_1(z_1) \cdot V_{\mathfrak{C}}[z_1, p](q)\big) \\ &= \frac{1}{1 - \mathfrak{z}_1(z_1)} \big(V_{\mathfrak{C}}[z_1, p](q) - \mathfrak{z}_1(z_1) \cdot V_{\mathfrak{C}}[z_1, p](q)\big) \\ &= V_{\mathfrak{C}}[z_1, p](q); \end{aligned}$$

therefore $\mathfrak{z}_1^1 \sim z_1$. Since $\mathfrak{z}_1^1(z_1) = 0$, $\mathfrak{z}_1$ is not deterministic. For $j = 2, \ldots, k$ and $z \in Z$ we set

$$\mathfrak{z}_j^1(z) - \begin{cases} \mathfrak{z}_j(z) + \mathfrak{z}_j(z_1) \cdot \mathfrak{z}_1^1(z), & \text{if } z \neq z_1, \\ 0, & \text{if } z = z_1. \end{cases}$$

It is easy to verify that $\mathfrak{z}_j^1$ is a random state of $\mathfrak{C}$ with $z_j \sim \mathfrak{z}_j^1$ and $\mathfrak{z}_j^1(z_1) = 0$. We claim that $\mathfrak{z}_j^1$ is not deterministic. Indeed, if $\mathfrak{z}_j^1$ were deterministic, (for $j \geqq 2$) then $\mathfrak{z}_j^1 = \delta_{z_j}$ would be satisfied, and

$$\mathfrak{z}_j(z) + \mathfrak{z}_j(z_1) \cdot \mathfrak{z}_1^1(z) = 0 \tag{*}$$

would hold for all $z \neq z_1, z_j$. We have $\mathfrak{z}_j(z_1) \neq 0$, since otherwise $\mathfrak{z}_j^1 = \mathfrak{z}_j$ and $\mathfrak{z}_j$ is deterministic, which is in contradiction to $\mathfrak{z}_j \neq \delta_{z_j}$. From $\mathfrak{z}_j(z_1) > 0$ and (*) it follows that $\mathfrak{z}_1^1(z) = 0$ for all $z \neq z_j$, i.e., $\mathfrak{z}_1^1 = \delta_{z_j}$ and $z_1 \sim z_j$, which is impossible because $\mathfrak{C}$ is reduced.

mth Step ($m \geqq 2$): Suppose that in the $m-1$st step we constructed the non-deterministic random states $\mathfrak{z}_1^{m-1}, \ldots, \mathfrak{z}_k^{m-1} \in \mathfrak{Z}_Z$ with $\mathfrak{z}_j^{m-1} \sim z_j$ and $\mathfrak{z}_j^{m-1}(z_i) = 0$ for $i = 1, \ldots, m-1$.

Then we put, for $z \in Z$

$$\mathfrak{z}_m^m(z) = \begin{cases} \dfrac{\mathfrak{z}_m^{m-1}(z)}{1 - \mathfrak{z}_m^{m-1}(z_m)}, & \text{if } z \neq z_m, \\ 0 & \text{otherwise,} \end{cases}$$

and for $j \in \{1, \ldots, k\}$ and $j \neq m$, $z \in Z$

$$\mathfrak{z}_j^m(z) = \begin{cases} \mathfrak{z}_j^{m-1}(z) + \mathfrak{z}_j^{m-1}(z_m) \cdot \mathfrak{z}_m^m(z), & \text{if } z \neq z_m, \\ 0 & \text{otherwise.} \end{cases}$$

Just as in the first step, we can show that for all $j = 1, \ldots, k$ we have $\mathfrak{z}_j^m \in \mathfrak{Z}_Z$ and $\mathfrak{z}_j^m \sim z_j$. Since $\mathfrak{z}_m^m \sim z_m$, $\mathfrak{z}_m^m(z_m) = 0$, $\mathfrak{z}_m^m$ is not deterministic, because $\mathfrak{z}_m^m = \delta_z$ would imply $z \neq z_m$ and $z \sim z_m$, which is impossible because $\mathfrak{C}$ is reduced. For $j \neq m$, $\mathfrak{z}_j^m$ is not deterministic, because $\mathfrak{z}_j^{m-1}$ and $\mathfrak{z}_m^m$ are not. Furthermore, $\mathfrak{z}_m^m(\{z_1, \ldots, z_m\}) = \mathfrak{z}_m^m(\{z_1, \ldots, z_{m-1}\}) + \mathfrak{z}_m^m(z_m) = 0$, since $\mathfrak{z}_m^{m-1}(\{z_1, \ldots, z_{m-1}\}) = 0$. Consequently, $\mathfrak{z}_j^m(\{z_1, \ldots, z_m\}) = 0$. Thus we have obtained non-deterministic random states $\mathfrak{z}_j^m \in \mathfrak{Z}_Z$ with $\mathfrak{z}_j^m \sim z_j$ and $\mathfrak{z}_j^m(\{z_1, \ldots, z_m\}) = 0$.

We continue this procedure until the random states $\mathfrak{z}_1^k, \ldots, z_k^k$ are constructed, and these obviously satisfy our requirements. For every $z_j \in Z_0$, $\mathfrak{z}_j^k \in \mathfrak{Z}_Z$ is a random state of $\mathfrak{C}$ equivalent to $\mathfrak{z}_j$ such that $\mathfrak{z}_j^k(Z_0) = 0$.

The existence of the random states $\mathfrak{z}_j^k$ implies $Z \setminus Z_0 \neq \emptyset$. For $z \in Z$ we put

$$\mathfrak{z}_z \underset{\mathrm{Df}}{=} \begin{cases} \delta_z, & \text{if } z \in Z \setminus Z_0, \\ \mathfrak{z}_j^k, & \text{if } z = z_j \in Z_0. \end{cases}$$

Since $\mathfrak{z}_z(Z_0) = 0$ for each $z \in Z$, the restrictions of these functions to the set $\mathfrak{P}(Z \setminus Z_0)$ are discrete probability measures over $Z \setminus Z_0$.

Let $\mathfrak{C}' = [X, Y, Z', H']$, where $Z' = Z \setminus Z_0$, and for $z', z'' \in Z'$, $x \in X$, $y \in Y$

$$H'[z', x](y, z'') \underset{\mathrm{Df}}{=} \sum_{z \in Z} H[z', x](y, z) \cdot \mathfrak{z}_z(z'').$$

We have $Z' \neq \emptyset$, $H'[z', x](y, z'') \geqq 0$ and for all $z' \in Z', x \in X$

$$\sum_{y \in Y, z'' \in Z'} H'[z', x](y, z'') = \sum_{y \in Y, z \in Z} H[z', x](y, z) \sum_{z'' \in Z'} \mathfrak{z}_z(z'') = 1.$$

Thus $\mathfrak{C}'$ is an S-automaton. We shall prove by induction on p that for all $p \in W(X)$, $z' \in Z'$

$$V_{\mathfrak{C}'}[z', p] = V_{\mathfrak{C}}[z', p].$$

For $p = e$, this is trivial. The induction step is taken from p to xp. For all $yq \in W(Y) \setminus \{e\}$, $z' \in Z'$

$$\begin{aligned} V_{\mathfrak{C}'}[z', xp](yq) &= \sum_{z'' \in Z'} H'[z', x](y, z'') \cdot V_{\mathfrak{C}'}[z'', p](q) \\ &= \sum_{z \in Z} H[z', x](y, z) \cdot \sum_{z'' \in Z'} \mathfrak{z}_z(z'')\, V_{\mathfrak{C}'}[z'', p](q). \end{aligned}$$

By the induction hypothesis, $V_{\mathfrak{C}'}[z'', p] = V_{\mathfrak{C}}[z'', p]$ for $z'' \in Z'$; further $\mathfrak{z}_z(z'') = 0$ for $z'' \in Z \setminus Z' = Z_0$. Thus,

$$\begin{aligned} V_{\mathfrak{C}'}[z', xp](yq) &= \sum_{z \in Z} H[z', x](y, z) \sum_{z'' \in Z} \mathfrak{z}_z(z'')\, V_{\mathfrak{C}}[z'', p](q) \\ &= \sum_{z \in Z} H[z', x](y, z) \cdot V_{\mathfrak{C}}[\mathfrak{z}_z, p](q), \end{aligned}$$

and by $\mathfrak{z}_z \sim z$ for $z \in Z$ we obtain

$$V_{\mathfrak{C}'}[z', xp](yq) = \sum_{z \in Z} H[z', x](y, z)\, V_{\mathfrak{C}}[z, p](q) = V_{\mathfrak{C}}[z', xp](yq),$$

hence $V_{\mathfrak{C}'}[z', xp] = V_{\mathfrak{C}}[z', xp]$. For every state z' of $\mathfrak{C}'$ we have thus found that z' is an equivalent state of $\mathfrak{C}$. On the other hand, for all $z \in Z$ the restriction of $\mathfrak{z}_z$ to Z' is a random state of $\mathfrak{C}'$ equivalent to z. Consequently, $\mathfrak{C}$ and $\mathfrak{C}'$ are weakly equivalent.

Suppose $z' \in Z'$, $z' \in \mathfrak{Z}_{Z'}$ and $z' \sim \mathfrak{z}'$. We define a random state $\mathfrak{z}^*$ of $\mathfrak{C}$ as follows:

$$\mathfrak{z}^*(z) = \begin{cases} \mathfrak{z}'(z) & \text{if } z \in Z', \\ 0 & \text{otherwise.} \end{cases}$$

Obviously, $\mathfrak{z}^*$ is equivalent to the state z' of $\mathfrak{C}$. Since $z' \notin Z_0$, $\mathfrak{z}^*$ must be deterministic, and since $\mathfrak{C}$ is reduced, we have $\mathfrak{z}^*(z') = 1$, i.e., $\mathfrak{z}'(z') = 1$ ($\mathfrak{z}' = \delta_{z'}$), which was to be shown. Thus $\mathfrak{C}'$ is a minim of $\mathfrak{C}$.

Corollary 2.21.

1. (Bacon [1]). For every finite S-automaton, a minim can be algorithmically constructed.
2. The relations $\approx$ and $\lessapprox$ are decidable for finite S-automata.

Proposition 2.21.2 follows from the fact that finite S-automata are weakly equivalent if and only if their minims coincide, i.e., if and only if their minims constructed by 2.20 are equivalent. By 2.13.2, it is decidable whether these minims are equivalent. Moreover, $\mathfrak{C} \lessapprox \mathfrak{C}'$ holds if and only if $\mathfrak{C} + \mathfrak{C}' \approx \mathfrak{C}'$ (where $\mathfrak{C} + \mathfrak{C}'$ is the direct sum of the S-automata $\mathfrak{C}$, $\mathfrak{C}'$, defined above), as can be easily seen using 2.2. Thus, the relation $\lessapprox$ is also decidable for finite S-automata.

It is not known whether there are S-automata (with infinitely many states) which have no minims. The requirement that Z_0 be finite is obviously not necessary for the existence of a minim. From the proof of Theorem 2.20 and 2.18.1 we obtain

Corollary 2.22. A reduced S-automaton $\mathfrak{C} = [X, Y, Z, H]$ has a minim if and only if for every $z \in Z_0 = \{z \mid z \in Z \wedge \exists \mathfrak{z}(\mathfrak{z} \in \mathfrak{Z}_Z \wedge \mathfrak{z} \sim z \wedge \mathfrak{z} \neq \delta_z)\}$ there is a random state $\mathfrak{z}_z \in \mathfrak{Z}_Z$ with $\mathfrak{z}_z \sim z$ and $\mathfrak{z}_z(Z_0) = 0$.

Theorem 2.23 (Even [4]). *A deterministic S-automaton is reduced if and only if it is minimal.*

Proof: Let $\mathfrak{C} = [X, Y, Z, H]$ be a reduced *deterministic* S-automaton, $z \in Z$ and $\mathfrak{z} \in Z_Z$ with $z \sim \mathfrak{z}$. Since $\mathfrak{C}$ is deterministic, for all $z' \in Z$, $p \in W(X)$ $V_{\mathfrak{C}}[z', p]$ is a deterministic discrete PM. Let $\lambda = Det(ND(V_{\mathfrak{C}}))$. Then for $p \in W(X)$

$$1 = V_{\mathfrak{C}}[z, p](\lambda(z, p)) = \sum_{z' \in Z} \mathfrak{z}(z')\, V_{\mathfrak{C}}[z', p](\lambda(z, p)),$$

i.e., for all $z' \in Z$ with $\mathfrak{z}(z') > 0$ and arbitrary $p \in W(X)$

$$V_{\mathfrak{C}}[z', p](\lambda(z, p)) = 1.$$

Thus all these z' are equivalent to z. Since $\mathfrak{C}$ is reduced, it follows that $1 = \mathfrak{z}(Z) = \mathfrak{z}(z)$. Thus $\mathfrak{C}$ is minimal.

Even's Theorem is not valid for Z-deterministic automata. As an example, we consider the autonomous S-automaton $\mathfrak{C}_4 = [\{x\}, \{0, 1\}, \{1, 2, 3\}, H_4]$, whose graph is represented in Fig. 23. $\mathfrak{C}_4$ is obviously Z-deterministic and reduced, however for $p \in W(\{x\})$, $q \in W(\{0, 1\})$

$$V_{\mathfrak{C}_4}[3, p](q) = \frac{1}{2} V_{\mathfrak{C}_4}[1, p](q) + \frac{1}{2} V_{\mathfrak{C}_4}[2, p](q),$$

as can be easily computed. Thus $\mathfrak{C}_4$ is not minimal.

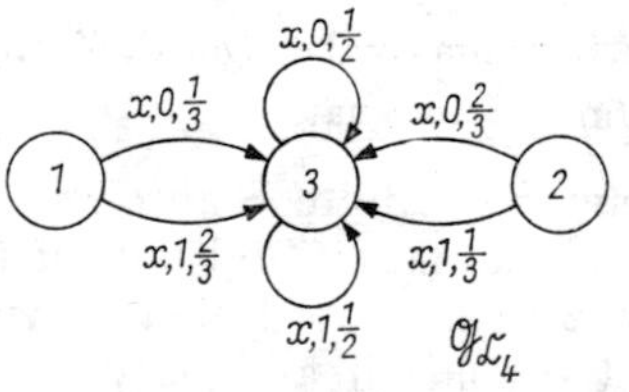

Abb. 23

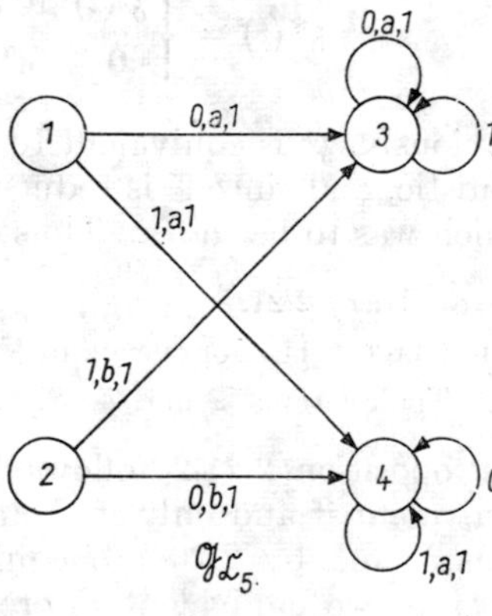

Abb. 24

There exist reduced deterministic S-automata which are not strongly reduced. As an example[1]) we consider the S-automaton $\mathfrak{C}_5 = [\{0, 1\}, \{a, b\}, \{1, 2, 3, 4\}, H_5]$,

[1]) The example is due to H.-D. Burkhard.

whose graph is represented in Fig. 24. Obviously, $\mathfrak{C}_5$ is reduced. On the other hand,

$$\frac{1}{2} V_{\mathfrak{C}_5}[1, xp](yq) + \frac{1}{2} V_{\mathfrak{C}_5}[2, xp](yq)$$

$$= \begin{cases} \frac{1}{2} V_{\mathfrak{C}_5}[3, p](q), & \text{if } x = 0,\ y = a \\ & \text{or } x = 1,\ y = b, \\ \frac{1}{2} V_{\mathfrak{C}_5}[4, p](q), & \text{if } x = 1,\ y = a \\ & \text{or } x = 0,\ y = b, \end{cases}$$

$$= \frac{1}{2} V_{\mathfrak{C}_5}[3, xp](yq) + \frac{1}{2} V_{\mathfrak{C}_5}[4, xp](yq),$$

consequently the random states $\mathfrak{z}_1$, $\mathfrak{z}_2$ of $\mathfrak{C}_5$, where

$$\mathfrak{z}_1(1) = \mathfrak{z}_1(2) = \frac{1}{2}, \quad \mathfrak{z}_1(3) = \mathfrak{z}_1(4) = 0, \quad \mathfrak{z}_2(1) = \mathfrak{z}_2(2) = 0,$$

$$\mathfrak{z}_2(3) = \mathfrak{z}_2(4) = \frac{1}{2}$$

are equivalent. Therefore $\mathfrak{C}_5$ is not strongly reduced.

Corollary 2.24.

1. Let $\mathfrak{C}$ be a deterministic S-automaton and $\mathfrak{C}'$ an arbitrary reduced S-automaton. Then no state of $\mathfrak{C}$ is equivalent to a non-deterministic random state of $\mathfrak{C}'$.

2. Deterministic S-automata are equivalent if and only if they are weakly equivalent.

To conclude this section, we establish one more connection between the reducedness properties of an S-automaton $\mathfrak{C}$ and those of ND$(\mathfrak{C})$.

Theorem 2.25. *Let* $\mathfrak{C} = [X, Y, Z, H]$ *be an S-automaton. If the nondeterministic automaton* $ND(\mathfrak{C})$ *is reduced, or minimal, or strongly reduced, then so is* $\mathfrak{C}$.

Proof: Since for $z, z' \in Z$, $\mathfrak{z} \in Z_Z$, $z \sim z'$ (in $\mathfrak{C}$) or $z \sim \mathfrak{z}$ (in $\mathfrak{C}$) imply that $z \sim z'$ (in $ND(\mathfrak{C})$) or $z \sim ND(\mathfrak{z})$ (in $ND(\mathfrak{C})$), the first two assertions are trivial.

Suppose $ND(\mathfrak{C})$ is strongly reduced, and $\mathfrak{z}, \mathfrak{z}' \in \mathfrak{Z}_Z$ with $\mathfrak{z} \sim \mathfrak{z}'$. We assume that $\mathfrak{z} \neq \mathfrak{z}'$.

Since $\mathfrak{z} \sim \mathfrak{z}'$, for all $p \in W(X)$, $q \in W(Y)$

$$\sum_{z \in Z} \left(\mathfrak{z}(z) - \mathfrak{z}'(z)\right) \cdot V_{\mathfrak{C}}[z, p](q) = 0.$$

Let $Z_1 = \{z \mid \mathfrak{z}(z) - \mathfrak{z}'(z) > 0\}$ and $Z_2 = \{z \mid \mathfrak{z}(z) - \mathfrak{z}'(z) < 0\}$ and for $z \in Z$

$$a_1(z) = \begin{cases} \mathfrak{z}(z) - \mathfrak{z}'(z), & \text{if } z \in Z_1, \\ 0 & \text{otherwise}; \end{cases}$$

$$a_2(z) = \begin{cases} \mathfrak{z}'(z) - \mathfrak{z}(z), & \text{if } z \in Z_2, \\ 0 & \text{otherwise}. \end{cases}$$

Therefore,

$$0 = \sum_{z \in Z} \left(\mathfrak{z}(z) - \mathfrak{z}'(z)\right) = \sum_{z \in Z} \left(a_1(z) - a_2(z)\right) = \sum_{z \in Z_1} a_1(z) - \sum_{z \in Z_2} a_2(z)$$

$$= \sum_{z \in Z} a_1(z) - \sum_{z \in Z} a_2(z),$$

consequently,

$$A \underset{\mathrm{Df}}{=} \sum_{z \in Z} a_1(z) = \sum_{z \in Z} a_2(z).$$

Since $\mathfrak{z} \neq \mathfrak{z}'$, $Z_1, Z_2 \neq \emptyset$ and $A > 0$, and the mappings

$$\mathfrak{z}_1(z) = \frac{a_1(z)}{A}, \quad \mathfrak{z}_2(z) = \frac{a_2(z)}{A}$$

are random states of $\mathfrak{C}$ with $Z_1 = ND(\mathfrak{z}_1)$, $Z_2 = ND(\mathfrak{z}_2)$. For all $p \in W(X)$, $q \in W(Y)$,

$$\sum_{z \in Z} \mathfrak{z}_1(z)\, V_{\mathfrak{C}}[z, p](q) = \sum_{z \in Z_1} \frac{\mathfrak{z}(z) - \mathfrak{z}'(z)}{A}\, V_{\mathfrak{C}}[z, p](q)$$

$$= \frac{1}{A} \left(\sum_{z \in Z} \left(\mathfrak{z}(z) - \mathfrak{z}'(z)\right) V_{\mathfrak{C}}[z, p]\,(q) - \sum_{z \in Z_2} \left(\mathfrak{z}(z) - \mathfrak{z}'(z)\right) V_{\mathfrak{C}}[z, p](q)\right)$$

$$= \frac{1}{A} \sum_{z \in Z_2} \left(\mathfrak{z}'(z) - \mathfrak{z}(z)\right) V_{\mathfrak{C}}[z, p](q) = \sum_{z \in Z} \mathfrak{z}_2(z)\, V_{\mathfrak{C}}[z, p](q).$$

Thus we have $\mathfrak{z}_1 \sim \mathfrak{z}_2$, hence $ND(\mathfrak{z}_1) \sim ND(\mathfrak{z}_2)$, i.e., $Z_1 = ND(\mathfrak{z}_1) = ND(\mathfrak{z}_2) = Z_2$, since $ND(\mathfrak{C})$ is strongly reduced. However, $Z_1 = Z_2$ contradicts $Z_1 \cap Z_2 = \emptyset$, $Z_1 \neq \emptyset$. Thus Theorem 2.25 is proved.

§ 3. Homomorphisms

In this section we shall define two concepts of homomorphisms and investigate the invariance of certain structural properties of S-automata under homomorphisms of both types. One of the two concepts appears to be an adequate counterpart to the homomorphisms defined for deterministic automata, in that every such homomorphism of a deterministic S-automaton $\mathfrak{C}$ onto another deterministic S-automaton $\mathfrak{C}'$ is a homomorphism of $ND(\mathfrak{C})$ onto $ND(\mathfrak{C}')$ (in the sense of the theory of ND-automata) and thus a homomorphism of $Det\left(ND(\mathfrak{C})\right)$ onto $Det\left(ND(\mathfrak{C}')\right)$ (in the sense of the theory of deterministic automata). It turns out that several important theorems known from the theory of deterministic automata are not valid for S-automata. Thus, e.g., there are S-automata which cannot be Z-homomorphically mapped onto any of their reducts.

Definition 3.1. Let $\mathfrak{C} = [X, Y, Z, H]$, $\mathfrak{C}' = [X', Y', Z', H']$ be S-automata and ξ, η, ζ be single-valued mappings of X onto X', Y onto Y' and Z onto Z' respectively.
(3.1.1) The triple $[\xi, \eta, \zeta]$ is called *a strong homomorphism of* $\mathfrak{C}$ *onto* $\mathfrak{C}'$ if for all $z, z^* \in Z$, $x \in X$, $y \in Y$,

$$H[z, x](y, z^*) = H'[\zeta(z), \xi(x)]\big(\eta(y), \zeta(z^*)\big).$$

(3.1.2) (Bucharaiev [3]). $[\xi, \eta, \zeta]$ is called a *homomorphism of* $\mathfrak{C}$ *onto* $\mathfrak{C}'$ if for all $z \in Z$, $x \in X$, $y' \in Y'$, $z' \in Z'$

$$H'[\zeta(z), \xi(x)](y', z') = \sum_{\eta(y)=y', \zeta(z^*)=z'} H[z, x](y, z^*)$$

If the mappings $[\xi, \eta, \zeta]$ are also one-to-one, then we refer to an *isomorphism of* $\mathfrak{C}$ *onto* $\mathfrak{C}'$.

If $X = X'$, $Y = Y'$ and ξ, η are the corresponding identity mappings I_X, I_Y, and $[I_X, I_Y, \zeta]$ is a (strong) homomorphism of $\mathfrak{C}$ onto $\mathfrak{C}'$, then $[I_X, I_Y, \zeta]$ is called a *(strong) Z-homomorphism of* $\mathfrak{C}$ *onto* $\mathfrak{C}'$. The concepts of *Z-isomorphism*, *(strong)* $[X, Z]$*-homomorphism*, etc. are defined analogously.

Corollary 3.1.

1. Every strong homomorphism (isomorphism) of an S-automaton $\mathfrak{C}$ onto an S-automaton $\mathfrak{C}'$ is a strong homomorphism (isomorphism) of $ND(\mathfrak{C})$ onto $ND(\mathfrak{C}')$.

2. Every homomorphism of an S-automaton $\mathfrak{C}$ onto an S-automaton $\mathfrak{C}'$ is a homomorphism of $ND(\mathfrak{C})$ onto $ND(\mathfrak{C}')$.

3. If $\mathfrak{C}, \mathfrak{C}'$ are deterministic S-automata, then $[\xi, \eta, \zeta]$ is a homomorphism of $\mathfrak{C}$ onto $\mathfrak{C}'$ if and only if $[\xi, \eta, \zeta]$ is a homomorphism of $Det(ND(\mathfrak{C}))$ onto $Det(ND(\mathfrak{C}'))$.

Theorem 3.2. *Let $[\xi, \eta, \zeta]$ be a strong homomorphism of $\mathfrak{C}$ onto $\mathfrak{C}'$. Then for all $y_1, y_2 \in Y$, $z_1, z_2 \in Z$ with $Card(\{y_1, y_2\}) \cdot Card(\{z_1, z_2\}) \geqq 2$, we have:*
If $\eta(y_1) = \eta(y_2)$ and $\zeta(z_1) = \zeta(z_2)$, then $H[z, x](\{y_1, y_2\} \times \{z_1, z_2\}) = 0$ for all $z \in Z$, $x \in X$.

The proof is carried out indirectly, supposing that there are $y_1, y_2 \in Y$, $z, z_1, z_2 \in Z$, $x \in X$ with $y_1 \neq y_2$ and $H[z, x](y_1, z_1) > 0$. (If $y_1 = y_2$, then $z_1 \neq z_2$ and the proof goes analogously.) For $i = 1, 2$

$$H[z, x](y_2, z_i) = H'[\zeta(z), \xi(x)]\big(\eta(y_2), \zeta(z_i)\big) = H[z, x](y_1, z_1) > 0$$

hence

$$1 = \sum_{y \in Y, z^* \in Z} H[z, x](y, z^*) = \sum_{y \in Y, z^* \in Z} H'[\zeta(z), \xi(x)]\big(\eta(y), \zeta(z^*)\big)$$
$$> \sum_{y' \in Y', z' \in Z'} H'[\zeta(z), \xi(x)](y', z') = 1,$$

which is a contradiction.

The domains (of definition) of the mappings ξ, η, ζ can be extended in the same way as in the theory of ND-automata (cf. Part II, § 3, page 178). In particular for $y \in Y$, $z \in Z$

$$\eta\zeta(y, z) \underset{\mathrm{Df}}{=} [\eta(y), \zeta(z)].$$

From Theorem 3.2 we immediately obtain

Corollary 3.3. If $[\xi, \eta, \zeta]$ is a strong homomorphism of $\mathfrak{C}$ onto $\mathfrak{C}'$, then for all $z \in Z$, $x \in X$:

1. $\eta\zeta$ is a one-to-one mapping of $ND(H[z, x])$ onto $ND(H'[\zeta(z), \xi(x)])$.
2. ζ is a one-to-one mapping of $ND(F[z, x])$ onto $ND(F'[\zeta(z), \xi(x)])$.
3. η is a one-to-one mapping of $ND(G[z, x])$ onto $ND(G'[\zeta(z), \xi(x)])$.
4. For all $z^* \in Z$, $F[z, x](z^*) = F'[\zeta(z), \xi(x)](\zeta(z^*))$.
5. For all $y \in Y$, $G[z, x](y) = G'[\zeta(z), \xi(x)](\eta(y))$.
6. $[\xi, \eta, \zeta]$ is a homomorphism of $\mathfrak{C}$ onto $\mathfrak{C}'$.

Theorem 3.4. *Let $[\xi, \eta, \zeta]$ be a strong homomorphism of $\mathfrak{C}$ onto $\mathfrak{C}'$.*

1. *$\mathfrak{C}$ is an S-Mealy automaton if and only if $\mathfrak{C}'$ is.*
2. *$\mathfrak{C}$ is Z-deterministic (or Y-deterministic) if and only if $\mathfrak{C}'$ is.*
3. *$\mathfrak{C}$ is observable if and only if $\mathfrak{C}'$ is.*

Proof: Propositions 3.4.1 and 3.4.2 can be easily verified and therefore we omit their proofs. Suppose $\mathfrak{C} = [X, Y, Z, H]$ is observable and δ is the function from $Z \times X \times Y$ into Z, belonging to $\mathfrak{C}$. For $\mathfrak{C}' = [X', Y', Z', H']$ we put, for $z' \in Z'$, $x' \in X'$, $y' \in Y'$,

$$\delta'(z', x', y') = \begin{cases} z'', & \text{if there is a } [z, x, y] \in Dom(\delta) \text{ with} \\ & \zeta(z) = z',\ \xi(x) = x',\ \eta(y) = y' \text{ and} \\ & \zeta(\delta(z, x, y)) = z'', \\ \text{not defined otherwise.} & \end{cases}$$

To prove that δ' is a single-valued mapping from $Z' \times X' \times Y'$ into Z' we show that for $z_1, z_2 \in Z$, $x_1, x_2 \in X$, $y_1, y_2 \in Y$ with $[z_1, x_1, y_1]$, $[z_2, x_2, y_2] \in Dom(\delta)$ and $\zeta(z_1) = \zeta(z_2)$, $\xi(x_1) = \xi(x_2)$, $\eta(y_1) = \eta(y_2)$

$$\zeta(\delta(z_1, x_1, y_1)) = \zeta(\delta(z_2, x_2, y_2)).$$

Suppose this is not true. Then $\delta(z_1, x_1, y_1) \neq \delta(z_2, x_2, y_2)$ and we obtain

$$\begin{aligned} 0 &= H[z_1, x_1](y_1, \delta(z_2, x_2, y_2)) = H'[\zeta(z_1), \xi(x_1)](\eta(y_1), \zeta(\delta(z_2, x_2, y_2))) \\ &= H'[\zeta(z_2), \xi(x_2)](\eta(y_2), \zeta(\delta(z_2, x_2, y_2))) \\ &= H[z_2, x_2](y_2, \delta(z_2, x_2, y_2)) > 0, \end{aligned}$$

which is a contradiction. Therefore the mapping δ' is single-valued. Moreover for $z', z'' \in Z'$, $x' \in X'$, $y' \in Y'$

$$\begin{aligned} H'[z', x'](y', z'') > 0 &\leftrightarrow \exists z \exists z^* \exists x \exists y (H[z, x](y, z^*) > 0 \wedge \zeta(z) = z' \\ &\qquad \wedge \zeta(z^*) = z'' \wedge \xi(x) = x' \wedge \eta(y) = y') \\ &\leftrightarrow \exists z \exists z^* \exists x \exists y ([z, x, y] \in Dom(\delta) \wedge z^* = \delta(z, x, y) \\ &\qquad \wedge \zeta(z) = z' \wedge \zeta(z^*) = z'' \wedge \xi(x) = x' \\ &\qquad \wedge \eta(y) = y') \\ &\leftrightarrow [z', x', y'] \in Dom(\delta') \wedge z'' = \delta'(z', x', y'). \end{aligned}$$

Thus the S-automaton $\mathfrak{C}'$ is also observable.

Conversely, if $\mathfrak{C}'$ is observable and δ' is its function from $Z' \times X' \times Y'$ into Z', then for $z \in Z$, $x \in X$, $y \in Y$ we put

$$\delta(z, x, y) = \begin{cases} z^*, & \text{if } [\zeta(z), \xi(x), \eta(y)] \in Dom(\delta') \text{ and} \\ & \quad \delta'(\zeta(z), \xi(x), \eta(y)) = \zeta(z^*), \\ \text{not defined otherwise.} \end{cases}$$

Theorem 3.2 implies that δ is single-valued, because if $z^*, z^{**} \in Z$ with $z^* \neq z^{**}$ and $\zeta(z^*) = \zeta(z^{**}) = \delta'(\zeta(z), \xi(x), \eta(y))$ held, then

$$H[z,x](\{y\} \times \{z^*, z^{**}\}) = 2 \cdot H'[\zeta(z), \xi(x)](\eta(y), \delta'(\zeta(z), \xi(x), \eta(y))) > 0,$$

would be satisfied, which is in contradiction to 3.2. Obviously,

$$H[z, x](y, z^*) > 0 \leftrightarrow [z, x, y] \in Dom(\delta) \wedge \delta(z, x, y) = z^*,$$

hence $\mathfrak{C}$ is observable.

Theorem 3.5. *If $[\xi, \eta, \zeta]$ is a strong homomorphism of $\mathfrak{C}$ onto $\mathfrak{C}'$, then $\mathfrak{C}$ is an S-Moore automaton if and only if $\mathfrak{C}'$ is.*

Proof: Let $\mathfrak{C}' = [X', Y', Z', F', M']$ and put for $z \in Z$, $y \in Y$

$$M[z](y) = M'[\zeta(z)](\eta(y)).$$

We obtain for $z, z^* \in Z$, $x \in X$, $y \in Y$

$$\begin{aligned} H[z, x](y, z^*) &= F'[\zeta(z), \xi(x)](\zeta(z^*)) \cdot M'[\zeta(z^*)](\eta(y)) \\ &= F[z, x](z^*) M[z^*](y); \end{aligned}$$

hence $\mathfrak{C}$ is an S-Moore automaton.

Conversely, let $\mathfrak{C} = [X, Y, Z, F, M]$ be an S-Moore automaton,

$$Z'' \underset{\text{Df}}{=} \bigcup_{z' \in Z', x' \in X'} ND(F'[z', x']),$$

and for $z' \in Z'$, $y' \in Y'$

$$M'[z'](y') \underset{\text{Df}}{=} \begin{cases} M[z](y), & \text{if } z' \in Z'' \text{ and } \eta\zeta(y, z) = [y', z'], \\ \psi(y'), & \text{if } z' \notin Z'', \end{cases}$$

where ψ is an arbitrary discrete PM over Y'. To justify this definition we show that for all $z' \in Z''$, $\zeta(z_1) = \zeta(z_2) = z'$ and $\eta(y_1) = \eta(y_2) = y'$ imply $M[z_1](y_1) = M[z_2](y_2)$. Since $z' \in Z''$, there are $z'' \in Z'$, $x' \in X'$ with $F'[z'', x'](z') > 0$. Suppose $z^* \in Z$, $x \in X$ with $\zeta(z^*) = z''$, $\xi(x) = x'$. Then

$$F[z^*, x](z_1) = F'[z'', x'](z') = F[z^*, x](z_2) > 0,$$

hence

$$M[z_1](y_1) = \frac{H[z^*, x](y_1, z_1)}{F[z^*, x](z_1)} = \frac{H'[z'', x'](y', z')}{F'[z'', x'](z')}$$

$$= \frac{H[z^*, x](y_2, z_2)}{F[z^*, x](z_2)} = M[z_2](y_2).$$

Thus we obtain for $z', z'' \in Z'$, $x' \in X'$, $y' \in Y'$

$$H'[z'', x'](y', z') = \begin{cases} 0, & \text{if } F'[z'', x'](z') = 0, \\ H[z^*, x](y, z), & \text{if } \zeta(z^*) = z'',\ \zeta(z) = z', \\ & \xi(x) = x',\ \eta(y) = y' \text{ and } F'[z'', x'](z') > 0; \end{cases}$$

$$= \begin{cases} 0, & \text{if } F'[z'', x'](z') = 0, \\ F[z^*, x](z) M[z](y), & \text{if } \zeta(z^*) = z'', \zeta(z) = z', \\ & \xi(x) = x', \eta(y) = y' \text{ and } F'[z'', x'](z') > 0; \end{cases}$$

$$= F'[z'', x'](z') M'[z'](y').$$

Thus Theorem 3.5 is proved.

Now we deduce several consequences of Definition (3.1.2).

Corollary 3.6. Let $\chi = [\xi, \eta, \zeta]$ be a homomorphism of $\mathfrak{C}$ onto $\mathfrak{C}'$. Then for $z \in Z$, $x \in X$, $y' \in Y'$, $z' \in Z'$

1. $G'[\zeta(z), \xi(x)](y') = \sum_{\eta(y) = y'} G[z, x](y)$.
2. $F'[\zeta(z), \xi(x)](z') = \sum_{\zeta(z^*) = z'} F[z, x](z^*)$.
3. If $\mathfrak{C}$ is an S-Mealy automaton, so is $\mathfrak{C}'$.
4. If $\mathfrak{C}$ is Z-deterministic (or Y-deterministic), so is $\mathfrak{C}'$.
5. If χ is an $[X, Z]$-homomorphism (or $[X, Y]$-homomorphism) of $\mathfrak{C}$ onto $\mathfrak{C}'$, then $\mathfrak{C}$ is Y-deterministic (Z-deterministic) if and only if $\mathfrak{C}'$ has this property.

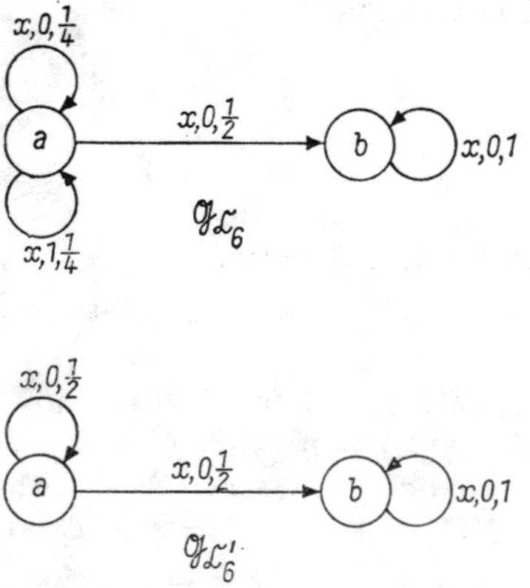

Fig. 25

The converse of 3.6.3 is not true, as is shown by the S-automata $\mathfrak{C}_6 = [\{x\}, \{0, 1\}, \{a, b\}, H_6]$, and $\mathfrak{C}_6' = [\{x\}, \{0\}, \{a, b\}, H_6]$, whose graphs are represented in Fig. 25. Obviously, $\mathfrak{C}_6$ is not an S-Mealy automaton, because

$$H_6[a, x](0, b) = \frac{1}{2} \neq G_6[a, x](0) F_6[a, x](b)$$

$$= \frac{3}{4} \cdot \frac{1}{2}$$

while $\mathfrak{C}_6'$ is Y-deterministic, and thus is an S-Mealy automaton. Nevertheless $[I_{\{x\}}, \eta, I_{\{a, b\}}]$ with $\eta(0) = \eta(1) = 0$ is a homomorphism of $\mathfrak{C}_6$ onto $\mathfrak{C}_6'$ as can be easily seen. We can also see from this example that the Y-determinedness of a homomorphic image of $\mathfrak{C}$ does not imply that of $\mathfrak{C}$. A corresponding statement is valid for Z-determinedness, as is shown by the following example. Consider the S-automata

$$\mathfrak{C}_7 = [\{x\}, \{0, 1\}, \{a, b\}, H_7], \quad \mathfrak{C}_8 = [\{x\}, \{0, 1\}, \{c\}, H_8]$$

with $H_7[z, x](y, z') = \frac{1}{2}$, if $[y, z'] \in \{[0, a], [1, b]\}$ for $z \in \{a, b\}$;

$H_8[c, x](y, c) = \frac{1}{2}$ for $y = \{0, 1\}$.

Obviously, $[I_{\{x\}}, I_{\{0,1\}}, \zeta]$ with $\zeta(a) = \zeta(b) = c$ is a Z-homomorphism of $\mathfrak{C}_7$ onto $\mathfrak{C}_8$. Here, $\mathfrak{C}_7$ is an S-Moore automaton, while $\mathfrak{C}_8$ is not. Thus, the homomorphic image of an S-Moore automaton is in general not an S-Moore automaton. The converse of this is also false, as is shown by the above example of the automata $\mathfrak{C}_6$ and $\mathfrak{C}_6'$; $\mathfrak{C}_6'$ is an S-Moore automaton, however $\mathfrak{C}_6$ is not.

If Z is a discrete PM over Z, and ζ a single-valued mapping of Z onto Z', then for $z' \in Z'$ we put

$$\zeta(\mathfrak{z})(z') \underset{\mathrm{Df}}{=} \sum_{\zeta(z)=z'} \mathfrak{z}(z).$$

Theorem 3.7. *If* $[\xi, \eta, \zeta]$ *is a homomorphism of* $\mathfrak{C} = [X, Y, Z, H]$ *onto* $\mathfrak{C}' = [X', Y', Z', H']$ *then for all* $\mathfrak{z} \in \mathfrak{Z}_Z$, $p \in W(X)$, $q' \in W(Y')$

$$V_{\mathfrak{C}'}[\zeta(\mathfrak{z}), \xi(p)](q') = \sum_{\eta(q)=q'} V_{\mathfrak{C}}[\mathfrak{z}, p](q).$$

Proof: We shall prove this equality by induction on p, where the initial step is trivial. Obviously, for $l(p) \neq l(q')$ the equality is always satisfied. The step from p to xp:

$$\begin{aligned} V_{\mathfrak{C}'}[\zeta(\mathfrak{z}), \xi(xp)](y'q') &= \sum_{z' \in Z'} \zeta(\mathfrak{z})(z') \cdot V_{\mathfrak{C}'}[z', \xi(xp)](y'q') \\ &= \sum_{z' \in Z'} \sum_{\zeta(z)=z'} \mathfrak{z}(z)\, V_{\mathfrak{C}'}[z', \xi(xp)](y'q') \\ &= \sum_{z \in Z} \mathfrak{z}(z) \sum_{z'' \in Z'} H'[\zeta(z), \xi(x)](y', z'')\, V_{\mathfrak{C}'}[z'', \xi(p)](q') \\ &= \sum_{z \in Z} \mathfrak{z}(z) \sum_{z'' \in Z'} \sum_{\zeta(z^*)=z''} \sum_{\eta(y)=y'} H[z, x](y, z^*)\, V_{\mathfrak{C}'}[z'', \xi(p)](q') \\ &= \sum_{\eta(y)=y'} \sum_{z \in Z} \mathfrak{z}(z) \sum_{z^* \in Z} H[z, x](y, z^*) \cdot V_{\mathfrak{C}'}[\zeta(z^*), \xi(p)](q') \\ &= \sum_{\eta(y)=y'} \sum_{z^* \in Z} H[\mathfrak{z}, x](y, z^*) \sum_{\eta(q)=q'} V_{\mathfrak{C}}[z^*, p](q) \\ &= \sum_{\eta(yq)=y'q'} V_{\mathfrak{C}}[\mathfrak{z}, xp](yq). \end{aligned}$$

Thus Theorem 3.7 is proved.

Corollary 3.8. If $\mathfrak{C} = [X, Y, Z, H]$, $\mathfrak{C}' = [X, Y, Z', H']$ and $[I_X, I_Y, \zeta]$ is a Z-homomorphism of $\mathfrak{C}$ onto $\mathfrak{C}'$, then for every $\mathfrak{z} \in \mathfrak{Z}_Z$, $\mathfrak{z} \sim \zeta(\mathfrak{z})$ and for $z \in Z$, $z \sim \zeta(z)$, consequently, the S-automata $\mathfrak{C}$ and $\mathfrak{C}'$ are equivalent.

Similarly as for the proof of Theorem 3.7, we can show without difficulty.

Theorem 3.9. *If* $[\xi, \eta, \zeta]$ *is a strong homomorphism of* $\mathfrak{C} = [X, Y, Z, H]$ *onto* $\mathfrak{C}' = [X', Y', Z', H']$ *then for all* $\mathfrak{z} \in Z_Z$, $p \in W(X)$, $q \in W(Y)$

$$V_{\mathfrak{C}}[\mathfrak{z}, p](q) = V_{\mathfrak{C}'}[\zeta(\mathfrak{z}), \xi(p)](\eta(q)).$$

Corollary 3.10. If $[\xi, \eta, \zeta]$ is a strong homomorphism of $\mathfrak{C}$ onto $\mathfrak{C}'$, then we have

1. If for $q_1, q_2 \in W(Y)$, $q_1 \neq q_2$ the equality $\eta(q_1) = \eta(q_2)$ is satisfied, then for all $\mathfrak{z} \in \mathfrak{Z}_Z$, $p \in W(X)$ $V_{\mathfrak{C}}[\mathfrak{z}, p](q_1) = V_{\mathfrak{C}}[\mathfrak{z}, p](q_2) = 0$.

2. For arbitrary $\mathfrak{z} \in \mathfrak{Z}_Z$, $p \in W(X)$, η is a single-valued mapping of the set $ND(V_{\mathfrak{C}}[\mathfrak{z}, p])$ onto the set $ND(V_{\mathfrak{C}}[\zeta(\mathfrak{z}), \xi(p)])$.

3. For $\mathfrak{z} \in \mathfrak{Z}_Z$, $p \in W(X)$, $Q \subseteq W(Y)$ is $V_{\mathfrak{C}}[\mathfrak{z}, p](Q) = V_{\mathfrak{C}'}[\zeta(\mathfrak{z}), \xi(p)](\eta(Q))$.

It follows from 3.9 that an S-automaton $\mathfrak{C}$ cannot in general be mapped Z-homomorphically onto any of its minims or strong reducts, since these S-automata are in general not equivalent to $\mathfrak{C}$.[1])

It is easy to verify that in general there is no strong homomorphism of an S-automaton $\mathfrak{C}$ onto one of its reducts. Let us consider the S-automata $\mathfrak{C}_9 = [\{x\}, \{1\}, \{a, b\}, H_9]$, $\mathfrak{C}_{10} = [\{x\}, \{1\}, \{c\}, H_{10}]$, where $H_9[a, x](1, a) = H_9[b, x](1, b) = H_{10}[c, x](1, c) = 1$. Obviously, $\mathfrak{C}_9$ is Z-isomorphic to the direct sum $\mathfrak{C}_{10} + \mathfrak{C}_{10}$. Consequently, $\mathfrak{C}_9 \sim \mathfrak{C}_{10}$ and $\mathfrak{C}_{10}$ is trivially reduced, $\mathfrak{C}_{10}$ is up to Z-isomorphisms the unique reduct of $\mathfrak{C}_9$ ($\mathfrak{C}_{10}$ is strongly reduced, cf. Theorem 3.13). Clearly, there is no strong homormophism of $\mathfrak{C}_9$ onto $\mathfrak{C}_{10}$ but only a homomorphism.

If $\mathfrak{C}$ is an S-automaton and $\mathfrak{C}'$ a reduct of $\mathfrak{C}$, then in general there is no Z-homomorphism of $\mathfrak{C}$ onto $\mathfrak{C}'$ since there are S-automata which have several pairwise non-Z-isomorphic reducts (and even non Z-isomorphic minims). However if there is a Z-homomorphism of $\mathfrak{C}$ onto $\mathfrak{C}'$, it is uniquely determined, namely it is the mapping ζ which assigns to every state z of $\mathfrak{C}$ that state z' of $\mathfrak{C}'$ which is equivalent to z.

As an example for equivalent but not Z-isomorphic minimal S-automata, we consider (following Even [4]) the S-automaton $\mathfrak{C}_1 = [\{0, 1\}, \{A, B, C\}, \{1, 2, 3, 4, 5\}, H_1]$ defined in § 1 (Fig. 21, page 251) and the S-automaton $\mathfrak{C}_1' = [\{0, 1\}, \{A, B, C\}, \{1, 2, 3, 4, 5\}, H_1']$, where

$$H_1'[i, x](y, j) = \begin{cases} H_1[i, x](y, j), & \text{if } i \neq 5,\ x \in \{0, 1\},\ y \in \{A, B, C\},\ j \in \{1, \ldots, 5\}, \\ \dfrac{1}{4}, & \text{if } i = 5,\ j \neq 5,\ y = C,\ x \in \{0, 1\}, \\ 0 & \text{otherwise}. \end{cases}$$

[1]) In the paper Starke [12] the concept of a "weak" homomorphism is introduced such a way that an S-automaton is in general only weakly equivalent with its weak homomorphic images.

For $i = 1, \ldots, 5$

$$\mathfrak{C}_1[5, 0, C](i) = \mathfrak{C}_1[5, 1, C](i) = \begin{cases} \frac{1}{2}, & \text{if } i \in \{1, 3\}, \\ 0 & \text{otherwise} \end{cases}$$

$$= H_1[5, 0](C, i) = H_1[5, 1](C, i).$$

We have shown above that the random states $\mathfrak{z}_1, \mathfrak{z}_2$ where $\mathfrak{z}_1 = \mathfrak{C}_1[5, 1, C]$ and $\mathfrak{z}_2 = \mathfrak{C}_1'[5, 0, C] = \mathfrak{C}_1'[5, 1, C]$ are equivalent. Consequently, for $i = 1, \ldots, 5$ the state i of $\mathfrak{C}_1$ is equivalent to the state i of $\mathfrak{C}_1'$, hence $\mathfrak{C}_1 \sim \mathfrak{C}_1'$ and thus $\mathfrak{C}_1'$ is also minimal. The S-automata $\mathfrak{C}_1, \mathfrak{C}_1'$ are thus equivalent and minimal (hence also reduced), but not Z-isomorphic.

Therefore, the best assertion which we can expect to be valid for an S-automaton $\mathfrak{C}$ is the following:

There exists a reduct $\mathfrak{C}'$ of $\mathfrak{C}$ onto which $\mathfrak{C}$ can be mapped Z-homomorphically.

Let $\mathfrak{C} = [X, Y, Z, H]$ be an S-automaton and $\mathfrak{C}' = [X, Y, Z', H']$ a reduct of $\mathfrak{C}$, furthermore $[I_X, I_Y, \zeta]$ a Z-homomorphism of $\mathfrak{C}$ onto $\mathfrak{C}'$. Then by 3.8 for $z_1, z_2 \in Z$

$$\zeta(z_1) = \zeta(z_2) \leftrightarrow z_1 \sim z_2,$$

and for $z' \in Z'$ $\zeta^{-1}(z') = \{z \mid z \in Z \wedge \zeta(z) = z'\}$ is an equivalence class from $\bar{Z} = Z/\sim$. For $z_1 \in Z,\ x \in X,\ y \in Y,\ z' \in Z'$,

$$H'[\zeta(z_1), x](y, z') = \sum_{\zeta(z^*)=z'} H[z_1, x](y, z^*) = H[z_1, x]\big(\{y\} \times \zeta^{-1}(z')\big),$$

thus we obtain

$$\left.\begin{array}{l} \text{For all } z_1, z_2 \in Z,\ x \in X,\ y \in Y,\ [z] \in \bar{Z} \text{ with } z_1 \sim z_2, \\ H[z_1, x](\{y\} \times [z]) = H[z_2, x](\{y\} \times [z]). \end{array}\right\} \text{(R)}.$$

Conversely, if $\mathfrak{C}$ satisfies condition (R) then the definition

$$\bar{H}[[z], x](y, [z']) \underset{\mathrm{Df}}{=} H[z, x](\{y\} \times [z']) \text{ for } [z], [z'] \in \bar{Z},\ x \in X,\ y \in Y$$

is justified and $\bar{\mathfrak{C}} = [X, Y, Z, H]$ is a reduct of $\mathfrak{C}$. Indeed it follows from (R) that the construction of a reduct of $\mathfrak{C}$ which was carried out in the proof of Theorem 2.17 is independent of the choice of the discrete PM's $P_{[z]}$ and always leads us to the S-automaton $\bar{\mathfrak{C}}$. Obviously, the mapping ζ with $\zeta(z) = [z]$ for $z \in Z$ is a single-valued mapping of Z onto $\bar{Z}$ such that $[I_X, I_Y, \zeta]$ is a Z-homomorphism of $\mathfrak{C}$ onto $\bar{\mathfrak{C}}$. Thus we obtain

Theorem 3.11. *An S-automaton $\mathfrak{C}$ has a reduct onto which it can be Z-homomorphically mapped if and only if $\mathfrak{C}$ satisfies condition* (R).

Theorem 3.12. *Every observable S-automaton satisfies condition* (R).

Proof: Let $\mathfrak{C} = [X, Y, Z, H]$ be observable and δ the corresponding function, furthermore $z_1, z_2 \in Z,\ x \in X,\ y \in Y,\ [z] \in \bar{Z}$ and $z_1 \sim z_2$. Then $G[z_1, x](y) = G[z_2, x](y)$. If $G[z_1, x](y) = 0$, then $H[z_1, x](\{y\} \times Z) = 0$, consequently,

$$H[z_1, x](\{y\} \times [z]) = 0 = H[z_2, x](\{y\} \times [z]).$$

However if $G[z_1, x](y) > 0$, then $[z_1, x, y]$, $[z_2, x, y] \in Dom(\delta)$, and by $z_1 \sim z_2$,

$$\delta_{\delta(z_1, x, y)} = \mathfrak{C}[z_1, x, y] \sim \mathfrak{C}[z_2, x, y] = \delta_{\delta(z_2, x, y)},$$

hence, $\delta(z_1, x, y) \sim \delta(z_2, x, y)$, i.e.,

$$\delta(z_1, x, y) \in [z] \leftrightarrow \delta(z_2, x, y) \in [z]$$

and

$$H[z_1, x](\{y\} \times [z]) = \begin{cases} G[z_1, x](y), & \text{if } \delta(z_1, x, y) \in [z], \\ 0 & \text{otherwise} \end{cases}$$

$$= \begin{cases} G[z_2, x](y), & \text{if } \delta(z_2, x, y) \in [z], \\ 0 & \text{otherwise} \end{cases}$$

$$= H[z_2, x](\{y\} \times [z]).$$

In particular every Z-deterministic S-automaton satisfies condition (R). However this statement is not true for all S-automata. Consider the S-Mealy automaton

$$\mathfrak{C}_{11} = [\{x\}, \{0, 1\}, \{1, \ldots, 6\}, F_{11}, G_{11}]$$

where

$$F_{11}[1, x](z') = F_{11}[2, x](z') = F_{11}[3, x](z') = 1, \quad \text{if } z' = 3,$$

$$F_{11}[4, x](z') = F_{11}[5, x](z') = 1, \quad \text{if } z' = 6,$$

$$F_{11}[6, x](z') = \frac{1}{2}, \quad \text{if } z' \in \{4, 5\},$$

$$G_{11}[1, x](y) = G_{11}[4, x](y) = \begin{cases} \frac{1}{3}, & \text{if } y = 0, \\ \frac{2}{3}, & \text{if } y = 1, \end{cases}$$

$$G_{11}[2, x](y) = G_{11}[5, x](y) = 1 - G_{11}[1, x](y) \quad \text{for } y \in \{0, 1\},$$

$$G_{11}[3, x](y) = G_{11}[6, x](y) = \frac{1}{2} \quad \text{for } y \in \{0, 1\}.$$

The S-automaton $\mathfrak{C}_4$ considered in § 2 (Fig. 23, page 278) is obviously a subautomaton of $\mathfrak{C}_{11}$. We have shown above that the random state $\mathfrak{z}'$ of $\mathfrak{C}_4$ (or $\mathfrak{C}_{11}$) with $\mathfrak{z}'(1) = \mathfrak{z}'(2) = 1/2$ is equivalent to the state 3 of $\mathfrak{C}_4$ (or $\mathfrak{C}_{11}$). This immediately implies that the states 1 and 4, 2 and 5, 3 and 6 of $\mathfrak{C}_{11}$ are respectively equivalent. Hence $3 \sim 6$, $[1] = \{1, 4\}$ and

$$H_{11}[3, x](\{0\} \times [1]) = 0,$$

$$H_{11}[6, x](\{0\} \times [1]) = G_{11}[6, x](0) \cdot F_{11}[6, x]([1]) = \frac{1}{2} \cdot \frac{1}{2} = \frac{1}{4} \neq 0.$$

Therefore, the S-automaton $\mathfrak{C}_{11}$ does not satisfy condition (R), consequently, it cannot be mapped Z-homomorphically onto any of its reducts (for instance $\mathfrak{C}_4$).

Theorem 3.13. *All strong reducts of the same S-automaton are pairwise Z-isomorphic.*

Proof: Since all strong reducts of the same S-automaton are pairwise equivalent, it suffices to show that equivalent strongly reduced S-automata $\mathfrak{C} = [X, Y, Z, H]$, $\mathfrak{C}' = [X, Y, Z', H']$ are Z-isomorphic. Let ζ be the one-to-one mapping of Z onto Z' for which $z \sim \zeta(z)$ for all $z \in Z$, furthermore let $z, z^* \in Z$, $x \in X$, $y \in Y$.

If $G[z, x](y) = 0$, then $G'[\zeta(z), x](y) = 0$ (by $z \sim \zeta(z)$) and

$$H[z, x](y, z^*) = 0 = H'[\zeta(z), x](y, \zeta(z^*)).$$

If $G[z, x](y) = G'[\zeta(z), x](y) > 0$ then the two random states $\mathfrak{C}[z, x, y]$ and $\mathfrak{C}'[\zeta(z), x, y]$ exist and are equivalent, moreover $\zeta(\mathfrak{C}[z, x, y])$ is a random state of $\mathfrak{C}'$ equivalent to $\mathfrak{C}[z, x, y]$. Since $\mathfrak{C}'$ is strongly reduced, we obtain

$$\zeta(\mathfrak{C}[z, x, y]) = \mathfrak{C}'[\zeta(z), x, y]$$

and thus

$$\begin{aligned} H'[\zeta(z), x](y, \zeta(z^*)) &= G'[\zeta(z), x](y) \cdot \mathfrak{C}'[\zeta(z), x, y](\zeta(z^*)) \\ &= G[z, x](y) \cdot \zeta(\mathfrak{C}[z, x, y])(\zeta(z^*)) \\ &= G[z, x](y) \cdot \mathfrak{C}[z, x, y](z^*) \quad \text{(since } \zeta \text{ is one-to-one)} \\ &= H[z, x](y, z^*), \end{aligned}$$

i.e., $[I_X, I_Y, \zeta]$ is a Z-isomorphism of $\mathfrak{C}$ onto $\mathfrak{C}'$.

Theorem 3.14. *Let $\mathfrak{M}(\mathfrak{C})$ be the set of all observable S-automata equivalent to a given observable S-automaton $\mathfrak{C} = [X, Y, Z, H]$. Then there is an up to Z-isomorphisms uniquely determined, reduced, observable S-automaton $\overline{\mathfrak{C}}$ in $\mathfrak{M}(\mathfrak{C})$. Every automaton from $\mathfrak{M}(\mathfrak{C})$ can be Z-homomorphically mapped onto $\overline{\mathfrak{C}}$.*

Proof: By Theorem 2.17.2, $\mathfrak{C}$ has an observable reduct $\overline{\mathfrak{C}} = [X, Y, \bar{Z}, \bar{H}]$. Suppose $\mathfrak{C}' = [X, Y, Z', H'] \in \mathfrak{M}(\mathfrak{C})$. Then $\overline{\mathfrak{C}} \sim \mathfrak{C}'$ and $\overline{\mathfrak{C}}$ is a reduct of $\mathfrak{C}'$. For $z' \in Z'$ let us denote by $\zeta(z')$ that state $\bar{z}$ of $\overline{\mathfrak{C}}$ which is equivalent to z'. Then ζ is a single-valued mapping of Z' onto Z and for every $z' \in Z'$, $x \in X$, $y \in Y$ we have

a) $G'[z', x](y) = \bar{G}[\zeta(z'), x](y)$,

b) $[z', x, y] \in Dom(\delta') \leftrightarrow [\zeta(z'), x, y] \in Dom(\bar{\delta})$.

If $[z', x, y] \in Dom(\delta')$, then $G'[z', x](y) > 0$, $\mathfrak{C}'[z', x, y]$ exists, and by $z' \sim \zeta(z')$

$$\delta'(z', x, y) \sim \mathfrak{C}'[z', x, y] \sim \overline{\mathfrak{C}}[\zeta(z'), x, y] \sim \bar{\delta}(\zeta(z'), x, y).$$

Thus we have for all $[z', x, y] \in Dom(\delta')$

$$\zeta(\delta'(z', x, y)) = \bar{\delta}(\zeta(z'), x, y).$$

Consequently, for $\bar{z} \in \bar{Z}$, $x \in X$, $y \in Y$, $z' \in Z'$

$$\bar{H}[\zeta(z'), x](y, \bar{z}) = \begin{cases} \bar{G}[\zeta(z'), x](y), & \text{if } [\zeta(z'), x, y] \in Dom(\bar{\delta}) \\ & \text{and } \bar{z} = \bar{\delta}(\zeta(z'), x, y), \\ 0 & \text{otherwise} \end{cases}$$

$$= \begin{cases} G'[z', x](y), & \text{if } [z', x, y] \in Dom(\delta') \\ & \text{and } \bar{z} = \zeta(\delta'(z', x, y)), \\ 0 & \text{otherwise} \end{cases}$$

$$= \sum_{\zeta(z^*) = \bar{z}} H'[z', x](y, z^*).$$

Therefore the triple $[I_X, I_Y, \zeta]$ is a Z-homomorphism of $\mathfrak{C}'$ onto $\bar{\mathfrak{C}}$. We have yet to show that every S-automaton $\bar{\bar{\mathfrak{C}}} \in \mathfrak{M}(\mathfrak{C})$ which is reduced, is Z-isomorphic to $\bar{\mathfrak{C}}$. As we have shown, there exists a Z-homomorphism $[I_X, I_Y, \zeta]$ of $\bar{\bar{\mathfrak{C}}}$ onto $\bar{\mathfrak{C}}$. By 3.8 we see that for $\bar{\bar{z}} \in \bar{\bar{Z}}$, $\zeta(\bar{\bar{z}}) \sim \bar{\bar{z}}$, which implies that ζ is one-to-one, hence $[I_X, I_Y, \zeta]$ is a Z-isomorphism.

Besides the observable reducts of an observable S-automaton in general there also exist other, non-observable reducts. As an example we consider the Z-deterministic automaton $\mathfrak{C}_4 = [\{x\}, \{0, 1\}, \{1, 2, 3\}, F_4, G_4]$ which was already considered in § 2 (cf. Fig. 23, page 278) and the non observable S-Mealy automaton $\mathfrak{C}_4' = [\{x\}, \{0, 1\}, \{1, 2, 3\}, F_4', G_4]$, where

$$F_4'[i, x](j) = \begin{cases} F_4[i, x](j) & \text{for } i = 1, 2, \quad j = 1, 2, 3, \\ \frac{1}{2} & \text{for } i = 3 \text{ and } j = 1, 2, \\ 0 & \text{otherwise.} \end{cases}$$

It is easy to see that the automata $\mathfrak{C}_4$, $\mathfrak{C}_4'$ are equivalent and reduced. Thus $\mathfrak{C}_4'$ is a non-observable reduct of $\mathfrak{C}_4$.

§ 4. Stochastic Operators

In this and the following sections we shall deal with the external forms of behaviour of stochastic automata, i.e., with the input-output relations established by S-automata. It is clear that only in the special case of deterministic stochastic automata we can restrict ourselves to functions assigning to every input word a (uniquely determined) output word. In the general case, the input-output relation generated by the state z of the stochastic automaton is a mapping which assigns to every input word $p \in W(X)$ a discrete probability measure over the set $W(Y)$. Such mappings will be called stochastic operators.

Definition 4.1. Let X, Y be non-empty sets. A mapping Φ is called a *stochastic operator* (shortly: *S-operator*) *over* $[X, Y]$ if it is defined on $W(X)$ and its values are discrete probability measures over $W(Y)$. We denote by Φ_p the value of Φ taken on the word $p \in W(X)$.

Corollary 4.1. Suppose Φ is an S-operator over $[X, Y]$.

1. $ND(\Phi)$ is a non-deterministic operator over $[X, Y]$.
2. For every $p \in W(X)$, the set $ND(\Phi_p)$ is at most countably infinite.

Definition 4.2. Let Φ be an S-operator over $[X, Y]$, and $\mathfrak{C}' = [X', Y', Z', H']$ an S-automaton, furthermore $\mathfrak{z}' \in \mathfrak{Z}_Z$. Φ is said to be *generated by* $\mathfrak{z}'$ *in* $\mathfrak{C}'$ if $X \subseteq X'$, $Y \subseteq Y'$ and for all $p \in W(X)$, $Q \subseteq W(Y)$

$$\Phi_p(Q) = V_{\mathfrak{C}'}[\mathfrak{z}', p](Q).$$

If $\mathfrak{z}' = \delta_{z'}$ (for $z' \in Z'$), then Φ is called the S-operator *generated by the state* z' *in* $\mathfrak{C}'$.

Theorem 4.2. *If the S-operator Φ over $[X, Y]$ can be generated (in a Z-finite S-automaton), then Φ can also be generated in a (Z-finite) S-automaton with the input alphabet X and the output alphabet Y by means of a state.*

Proof: Suppose Φ is generated by $\mathfrak{z}'$ in $\mathfrak{C}' = [X', Y', Z', H']$. Furthermore let

$$Z = \{z' \mid z' \in Z' \wedge \exists p(p \in W(X) \wedge F'[\mathfrak{z}', p](z') > 0)\}.$$

Then for $z \in Z$, $x \in X$

$$H'[z, x](Y \times Z) = 1,$$

since $H'[z, x](y', z') > 0$ implies $y' \in Y$ and $z' \in Z$, as we shall now see. Let $p = x_1 \ldots x_n$ be a word such that $F'[\mathfrak{z}', p](z) > 0$. Then

$$\begin{aligned} F'[\mathfrak{z}', px](z') &= \sum_{z'' \in Z'} F'[\mathfrak{z}', p](z'') F'[z'', x](z') \\ &\geqq F'[\mathfrak{z}', p](z) \cdot \sum_{y'' \in Y'} H'[z, x](y'', z') \\ &\geqq F'[\mathfrak{z}', p](z) \cdot H'[z, x](y', z') > 0; \end{aligned}$$

hence $z' \in Z$. Moreover

$$\begin{aligned} 1 = \Phi_{px}(W(Y)) &= V_{\mathfrak{C}'}[\mathfrak{z}', px](W(Y)) = V_{\mathfrak{C}'}[\mathfrak{z}', px](Y^{n+1}) \\ &\leqq V_{\mathfrak{C}'}[\mathfrak{z}', px]((Y')^n \cdot Y) \leqq V_{\mathfrak{C}'}[\mathfrak{z}', px](W(Y')) = 1, \end{aligned}$$

hence

$$1 = V_{\mathfrak{C}'}[\mathfrak{z}', px]((Y')^n \cdot Y) = \sum_{z'' \in Z'} F'[\mathfrak{z}', p](z'') H'[z'', x](Y \times Z').$$

Now we have $\sum_{z'' \in Z'} F'[\mathfrak{z}', p](z'') = 1$, and for all $z'' \in Z'$,

$$0 \leqq F'[\mathfrak{z}', p](z'') \leqq 1, \qquad 0 \leqq H'[z'', x](Y \times Z') \leqq 1.$$

Therefore, if $z'' \in Z'$ then

$$F'[\mathfrak{z}', p](z'') > 0 \rightarrow H'[z'', x](Y \times Z') = 1,$$

and by $F'[\mathfrak{z}', p](z) > 0$ we obtain $H'[z, x](Y \times Z') = 1$, hence $y' \in Y$.
Now we put for $z, z^* \in Z$, $x \in X$, $y \in Y$

$$H[z, x](y, z^*) \underset{\mathrm{Df}}{=} H'[z, x](y, z^*), \qquad \mathfrak{z}(z) \underset{\mathrm{Df}}{=} \mathfrak{z}'(z).$$

Here, $\mathfrak{C} = [X, Y, Z, H]$ is an S-automaton and $\mathfrak{z}$ is a random state of $\mathfrak{C}$. For arbitrary $p \in W(X)$, $q \in W(Y)$

$$V_{\mathfrak{C}'}[\mathfrak{z}', p](q) = V_{\mathfrak{C}}[\mathfrak{z}, p](q),$$

as can be easily seen, and consequently Φ is generated in $\mathfrak{C}$ by the random state $\mathfrak{z}$.
Suppose $z_1^* \notin Z$, $Z^* = Z \cup \{z_1^*\}$ and for $z^*, z^{**} \in Z^*$, $x \in X$, $y \in Y$

$$H^*[z^*, x](y, z^{**}) \underset{\mathrm{Df}}{=} \begin{cases} H[z^*, x](y, z^{**}), & \text{if } z^*, z^{**} \in Z, \\ H[\mathfrak{z}, x](y, z^{**}), & \text{if } z^* = z_1^*, \quad z^{**} \in Z, \\ 0 & \text{otherwise.} \end{cases}$$

Obviously, $\mathfrak{C}^* = [X, Y, Z^*, H^*]$ is an S-automaton which cannot enter the state z_1^* from any other state and in which the S-operator Φ is generated by the state z_1^*. If $\mathfrak{C}'$ is Z-finite, then (by $Z \subseteq Z'$) $\mathfrak{C}$ is also Z-finite and so is $\mathfrak{C}^*$. This proves Theorem 4.2.

Definition 4.3. An S-operator Φ over $[X, Y]$ is called *sequential* if for all $p \in W(X)$, $x \in X$, $Q \subseteq W(Y)$ we have:
(4.3a) $Q \cap Y^{l(p)} = \emptyset \rightarrow \Phi_p(Q) = 0$,
(4.3b) $\Phi_{px}(Q \cdot Y) = \Phi_p(Q)$.

Corollary 4.3. Let Φ be an S-operator over $[X, Y]$.
1. Φ is sequential if and only if for all $p \in W(X)$, $q \in W(Y)$, $x \in X$: If $l(p) \neq l(q)$, then $\Phi_p(q) = 0$ and $\sum_{y \in Y} \Phi_{px}(qy) = \Phi_p(q)$.
2. If Φ is sequential, $p, r \in W(X)$, $q, s \in W(Y)$ and $l(p) = l(q)$, then $\Phi_p(q) \geqq \Phi_{pr}(qs)$.
3. If Φ can be generated, then it is sequential.

Theorem 4.4. *If Φ is a sequential S-operator over $[X, Y]$ then $ND(\Phi)$ is a sequential ND-operator over $[X, Y]$.*

Proof: Let $\varphi = ND(\Phi)$, hence $\varphi(p) = \{q \mid \Phi_p(q) > 0\}$ for all $p \in W(X)$. Clearly, from 4.3a it follows that φ satisfies condition 4.2.1 (Part II, § 4), that is $q \in \varphi(p)$ always implies $l(p) = l(q)$. If $p \in W(X)$, $x \in X$ and $q \in \varphi(p)$, i.e., $0 < \Phi_p(q) = \sum_{y \in Y} \Phi_{px}(qy)$, then there is a $y \in Y$ with $\Phi_{px}(qy) > 0$, i. e.

$qy \in \varphi(px)$, from which, by induction on r, we obtain

$$\forall p\, \forall q\, \forall r\, \big(pr \in W(X) \wedge q \in \varphi(p) \to \exists s(qs \in \varphi(pr)\big).$$

This means that condition 4.2.2 is satisfied for φ. If $qs \in \varphi(pr)$ and $l(p) = l(q)$, i.e., $0 < \Phi_{pr}(qs) \leqq \Phi_p(q)$, then $q \in \varphi(p)$, and thus φ is in fact a sequential ND-operator.

Corollary 4.5. If Φ is a deterministic S-operator over $[X, Y]$, then it is sequential if and only if $Det(ND(\Phi))$ is a sequential function over $[X, Y]$ (cf. Part I, § 4), i.e., if it satisfies the automata conditions.

To show that every sequential S-operator can be generated, we shall define the states of sequential S-operators in analogy to the concept of a state of a sequential ND-operator.

Definition 4.4 Let Φ be a sequential S-operator over $[X, Y]$, $p \in W(X)$, $Q \subseteq Y^{l(p)}$ with $\Phi_p(Q) > 0$. Then the mapping $\Phi^{p,Q}$ defined for $r \in W(X)$ in the following way

$$\Phi_r^{p,Q}(S) = \frac{\Phi_{pr}(Q \cdot S)}{\Phi_p(Q)}$$

is called the *state* of the sequential S-operator Φ *belonging to the pair* $[p, Q]$. If $Q = \{q\}$ is a singleton, then we write $\Phi^{p,q}$ instead of $\Phi^{p,\{q\}}$ and $\Phi^{p,q}$ is called a *proper state* of Φ.

Theorem 4.6. *If Φ is a sequential S-operator over $[X, Y]$ then every state of Φ is a sequential S-operator.*

Proof: Let $p \in W(X)$, $Q \subseteq Y^{l(p)}$ with $\Phi_p(Q) > 0$. If $r \in W(X)$, $S \subseteq W(Y)$ with $S \cap Y^{l(r)} = \emptyset$, then $Q \cdot S \cap Y^{l(p)+l(r)} = \emptyset$, consequently $\Phi_r^{p,Q}(S) = 0$. Further,

$$\Phi_{rx}^{p,Q}(S \cdot Y) = \frac{\Phi_{prx}(Q \cdot S \cdot Y)}{\Phi_p(Q)} = \frac{\Phi_{pr}(Q \cdot S)}{\Phi_p(Q)} = \Phi_r^{p,Q}(S).$$

It is also clear that $\Phi_r^{p,Q}$ is a discrete PM over $W(Y)$.

Theorem 4.7. *An S-operator Φ over $[X, Y]$ is generable if and only if it is sequential.*

Proof: By 4.3.3 it suffices to show that Φ can be generated if it is sequential. Let us put $Z_\Phi \underset{\mathrm{Df}}{=} \{\Phi^{p,q} \mid p \in W(X) \wedge \Phi_p(q) > 0\}$ and for $\Phi^{p,q} \in Z_\Phi$, $x \in X$, $y \in Y$, $z' \in Z_\Phi$

$$H_\Phi[\Phi^{p,q}, x](y, z') \underset{\mathrm{Df}}{=} \begin{cases} \Phi_x^{p,q}(y), & \text{if } z' = \Phi^{px,qy}, \\ 0 & \text{otherwise.} \end{cases}$$

This definition is justified since from $\Phi^{p,q} = \Phi^{r,s}$, $\Phi^{p,q}_x(y) > 0$ it follows that for all $u \in W(X)$, $v \in W(Y)$

$$\Phi^{px,qy}_u(v) = \frac{\Phi_{pxu}(qyv)}{\Phi_{px}(qy)} = \frac{\Phi^{p,q}_{xu}(yv) \cdot \Phi_p(q)}{\Phi^{p,q}_x(y) \cdot \Phi_p(q)}$$

$$= \frac{\Phi^{r,s}_{xu}(yv)}{\Phi^{r,s}_x(y)} = \Phi^{rx,sy}_u(v),$$

i.e., $\Phi^{px,qy} = \Phi^{rx,sy}$.

Now we have

$$H_\Phi[\Phi^{p,q}, x](Y \times Z_\Phi) = \Phi^{p,q}_x(Y) = 1;$$

thus $\mathfrak{C}_\Phi = [X, Y, Z_\Phi, H_\Phi]$ is an *observable* S-automaton. We claim that for all $p \in W(X)$, $q \in W(Y)$ with $\Phi_p(q) > 0$ the state $\Phi^{p,q}$ of $\mathfrak{C}_\Phi$ generates in $\mathfrak{C}_\Phi$ the S-operator $\Phi^{p,q}$. To prove this, it suffices to show that for all $r \in W(X)$, $s \in W(Y)$

$$\Phi^{p,q}_r(s) = V_{\mathfrak{C}_\Phi}[\Phi^{p,q}, r](s),$$

which is trivial if $r = e$ or if $l(r) \neq l(s)$. We prove this equality by induction on r.

The step from r to xr for $x \in X$:

$$V_{\mathfrak{C}_\Phi}[\Phi^{p,q}, xr](ys) = \sum_{z' \in Z_\Phi} H_\Phi[\Phi^{p,q}, x](y, z') V_{\mathfrak{C}_\Phi}[z', r](s).$$

Here $H_\Phi[\Phi^{p,q}, x](y, z') > 0$ can only hold if $z' = \Phi^{px,qy}$.

The latter state exists if and only if $\Phi_{px}(qy) > 0$. If $\Phi_{px}(qy) = 0$, then $\Phi_{pxr}(qys) = 0$ and $V_{\mathfrak{C}_\Phi}[\Phi^{p,q}, xr](ys) = 0$. Thus we obtain

$$V_{\mathfrak{C}_\Phi}[\Phi^{p,q}, xr](ys) = 0 = \Phi_{pxr}(qys) = \frac{\Phi_{pxr}(qys)}{\Phi_p(q)} = \Phi^{p,q}_{xr}(ys).$$

If $\Phi_{px}(qy) > 0$, then

$$V_{\mathfrak{C}_\Phi}[\Phi^{p,q}, xr](ys) = \Phi^{p,q}_x(y) \cdot V_{\mathfrak{C}_\Phi}[\Phi^{px,qy}, r](s) = \frac{\Phi_{px}(qy)}{\Phi_p(q)} \cdot \Phi^{px,qy}_r(s)$$

$$= \frac{\Phi_{pxr}(qys)}{\Phi_p(q)} = \Phi^{p,q}_{xr}(ys),$$

which was to be shown. Consequently, the S-operator Φ is generated in $\mathfrak{C}_\Phi$ by the state $\Phi = \Phi^{e,e}$. Moreover, $\mathfrak{C}_\Phi$ is observable and reduced.

Corollary 4.8.

1. Every generable S-operator can be generated by a state.

2. Every sequential S-operator Φ can be generated in an observable S-automaton which has the same number of states as that of the proper states of Φ.

Theorem 4.9. *If the S-operator Φ over $[X, Y]$ is generated in the S-automaton $\mathfrak{C} = [X, Y, Z, H]$ by the random state $\mathfrak{z} \in \mathfrak{Z}_Z$, then for each $p \in W(X)$, $Q \subseteq Y^{l(p)}$ with $\Phi_p(Q) > 0$, the state $\Phi^{p,Q}$ of Φ is generated in $\mathfrak{C}$ by the random state $\mathfrak{C}[\mathfrak{z}, p, Q]$.*

Proof: By 2.7, for $r \in W(X)$, $s \in W(Y)$

$$V_{\mathfrak{C}}[\mathfrak{C}[\mathfrak{z}, p, Q], r](s) = \frac{V_{\mathfrak{C}}[\mathfrak{z}, pr](Q \cdot \{s\})}{V_{\mathfrak{C}}[\mathfrak{z}, p](Q)}$$

$$= \frac{\Phi_{pr}(Q \cdot \{s\})}{\Phi_p(Q)} = \Phi_r^{p,Q}(s).$$

Corollary 4.10. Let Φ be a sequential S-operator over $[X, Y]$.

1. If Φ is generated by a state of an observable S-automaton $\mathfrak{C}$, then every proper state $\Phi^{p,q}$ of Φ is generated by a state of $\mathfrak{C}$.

2. Φ can be generated by a state of a Z-finite, observable S-automaton, if and only if Φ only has finitely many proper states.

Thus, the finiteness of the set Z_Φ is sufficient for the generability of a sequential S-operator Φ in a Z-finite S-automaton. However this condition is not necessary, since otherwise every Z-finite S-automaton could be equivalently embedded into a Z-finite observable S-automaton.

It is easy to show that the sequential S-operator Φ generated by the state 1 in the S-Moore automaton $\mathfrak{C}_{12} = [\{0, 1\}, \{0, 1\}, \{1, 2, 3, 4\}, F_{12}, M_{12}]$ has infinitely many different proper states of the form $\Phi^{0^n, 0^n}$ ($n \in \boldsymbol{nz}$). In what follows, $0 < \varepsilon < 1$ is arbitrary and

$$F_{12}[1, 0](z') = \begin{cases} \varepsilon, & \text{if } z' = 1, \\ 1-\varepsilon, & \text{if } z' = 2, \\ 0 & \text{otherwise}; \end{cases}$$

$$F_{12}[1, 1](4) = F_{12}[2, 0](2) = F_{12}[2, 1](3)$$
$$= F_{12}[3, x](4) = F_{12}[4, x](4) = 1$$

for $x \in \{0, 1\}$ and

$$M_{12}[1](0) = M_{12}[2](0) = M_{12}[3](1) = M_{12}[4](0) = 1$$

(cf. Starke [6]).

Before characterizing the S-operators which can be generated in Z-finite S-automata, we shall make some remarks about the generability of S-operators in S-Mealy automata.

Theorem 4.11. *Suppose the S-operator Φ over $[X, Y]$ is generated in the S-Mealy automaton $\mathfrak{C} = [X, Y, Z, F, G]$ by a state z. Then for all $p \in W(X)$, $q \in W(Y)$ and $x \in X$ the quotient $\dfrac{\Phi_{xp}(yq)}{\Phi_x(y)}$ is independent of y, provided $\Phi_x(y) > 0$.*

Proof: Let $\Phi_x(y) = G[z, x](y) > 0$. Then

$$\frac{\Phi_{xp}(yq)}{\Phi_x(y)} = \frac{G[z, x](y)\, V_{\mathfrak{C}}[F[z, x], p](q)}{G[z, x](y)} = V_{\mathfrak{C}}[F[z, x], p](q).$$

Let us consider the S-Moore automaton $\mathfrak{C}_{13} = [\{x\}, \{0, 1\}, \{a, b\}, F_{13}, M_{13}]$:

$$F_{13}[a, x](z') = \begin{cases} \frac{3}{4}, & \text{if } z' = a, \\ \frac{1}{4}, & \text{if } z' = b, \end{cases} \qquad F_{13}[b, x](z') = \frac{1}{2} \text{ for } z' \in \{a, b\},$$

$$M_{13}[a](y) = \begin{cases} \frac{1}{3}, & \text{if } y = 0, \\ \frac{2}{3}, & \text{if } y = 1, \end{cases} \qquad M_{13}[b](y) = 1 - M_{13}[a](y).$$

If Φ is the S-operator over $[\{x\}, \{0, 1\}]$ generated by the state a in $\mathfrak{C}_{13}$ then

$$\Phi_x(0) = \frac{5}{12}, \quad \Phi_{xx}(00) = \frac{3}{16}, \quad \Phi_x(1) = \frac{7}{12}, \quad \Phi_{xx}(10) = \frac{1}{4}.$$

Consequently,

$$\frac{\Phi_{xx}(00)}{\Phi_x(0)} = \frac{9}{20} \neq \frac{9}{21} = \frac{\Phi_{xx}(10)}{\Phi_x(1)},$$

hence the S-operator Φ cannot be generated by a state in any S-Mealy automaton and thus $\mathfrak{C}_{13}$ cannot be equivalently embedded into any S-Mealy automaton. Nevertheless, Φ can be generated by a random state in an S-Mealy automaton, since the input alphabet of Φ is a singleton.

Theorem 4.12. *Let Φ be a sequential S-operator over* $[\{x\}, Y]$.

1. *If Φ has the property given in Theorem 4.11, then it can be generated in an S-Mealy automaton by a state.*

2. *Φ can be generated by a random state in an autonomous S-Mealy automaton.*

Proof: If $\Phi^{p,q}$ is a state of the S-operator Φ over $[\{x\}, Y]$, then $l(p) = l(q)$, hence $p = x^{l(q)}$. Therefore, we denote the proper states of Φ by Φ^q. Let $y^* \in Y$ be chosen such that $\Phi_x(y^*) > 0$. Then

$$Z \underset{\mathrm{Df}}{=} \{[\Phi^q, y] \mid q \in W(Y) \wedge y \in Y \wedge \Phi_{x^{l(q)}}(q) > 0 \wedge \Phi^q_x(y) > 0\},$$

$$z^* \notin Z \text{ and } Z^* \underset{\mathrm{Df}}{=} Z \cup \{z^*\},$$

furthermore for $z = [\Phi^q, y'] \in Z$,

$$F\big[[\Phi^q, y'], x\big](z') \underset{\mathrm{Df}}{=} \begin{cases} \Phi_x^{qy'}(y), & \text{if} \quad z' = [\Phi^{qy'}, y], \quad y \in Y, \\ 0 & \text{otherwise,} \end{cases}$$

$$F[z^*, x](z') \underset{\mathrm{Df}}{=} \begin{cases} \Phi_x^{y^*}(y), & \text{if} \quad z' = [\Phi^{y^*}, y], \quad y \in Y, \\ 0 & \text{otherwise,} \end{cases}$$

$$G\big[[\Phi^q, y'], x\big](y) \underset{\mathrm{Df}}{=} \begin{cases} 1, & \text{if} \quad y = y', \\ 0 & \text{otherwise.} \end{cases}$$

$$G[z^*, x](y) \underset{\mathrm{Df}}{=} \Phi_x(y).$$

$\mathfrak{C} = [\{x\}, Y, Z^*, F, G]$ is an autonomous S-Mealy automaton. Finally let us put for all $q \in W(Y)$ with $\Phi_{x^{l(q)}}(q) > 0$

$$\mathfrak{z}_q(z) \underset{\mathrm{Df}}{=} \begin{cases} \Phi_x^q(y), & \text{if} \quad z = [\Phi^q, y], \\ 0 & \text{otherwise,} \end{cases}$$

First we show that for all such q the random state $\mathfrak{z}_q$ generates the state Φ^q of Φ in $\mathfrak{C}$, i.e., we prove (by induction on r) that for all $q, s \in W(Y)$ with $l(q) = n$, $\Phi_{x^n}(q) > 0$, $r \in W(\{x\})$,

$$V_{\mathfrak{C}}[\mathfrak{z}_q, r](s) = \Phi_r^q(s).$$

In the step from r to xr, that is in the proof of the equality

$$\sum_{z \in Z^*} \mathfrak{z}_q(z) \cdot V_{\mathfrak{C}}[z, xr](ys) = \Phi_{xr}^q(ys),$$

we distinguish two cases.

I. $\Phi_x^q(y) = 0$.

Then $\Phi_{xr}^q(ys) = 0$ and

$$\sum_{z \in Z^*} \mathfrak{z}_q(z) \cdot V_{\mathfrak{C}}[z, xr](ys)$$
$$= \sum_{y' \in Y} \Phi_x^q(y') \cdot G\big[[\Phi^q, y'], x\big](y)\, V_{\mathfrak{C}}\big[F[[\Phi^q, y'], x], r\big](s) = 0 = \Phi_{xr}^q(ys);$$

since $G\big[[\Phi^q, y'], x\big](y) > 0$ holds if and only if $y = y'$ and $\Phi_x^q(y) = 0$.

II. $\Phi_x^q(y) > 0$.

Then Φ^{qy} exists, and we obtain

$$V_{\mathfrak{C}}[\mathfrak{z}_q, xr](ys) = \Phi_x^q(y) \cdot V_{\mathfrak{C}}\big[F[[\Phi^q, y], x], r\big](s).$$

For $z \in Z^*$

$$F\big[[\Phi^q, y], x\big](z) = \begin{cases} \Phi_x^{qy}(y'), & \text{if} \quad z = [\Phi^{qy}, y'], \quad y' \in Y, \\ 0 & \text{otherwise} \end{cases}$$
$$= \mathfrak{z}_{qy}(z).$$

Hence by the induction hypothesis

$$V_{\mathfrak{C}}\big[F[[\Phi^q, y], x], r\big](s) = V_{\mathfrak{C}}[\mathfrak{z}_{qy}, r](s) = \Phi_x^{qy}(s)$$

and

$$V_{\mathfrak{C}}[\mathfrak{z}_q, xr](ys) = \Phi_x^q(y) \cdot \Phi_r^{qy}(s) = \Phi_{xr}^q(ys),$$

which was to be shown.

Thus the S-operator Φ is generated in $\mathfrak{C}$ by the random state $\mathfrak{z}_e$ and 4.12.2 is proved. Lastly we show that if the quotient $\dfrac{\Phi_{xp}(yq)}{\Phi_x(y)}$ does not depend on y whenever $\Phi_x(y) > 0$, then Φ is generated in $\mathfrak{C}$ by z^*.

For $y \in Y$

$$V_{\mathfrak{C}}[z^*, x](y) = G[z^*, x](y) = \Phi_x(y),$$

and for $xp \in W(\{x\})$, $yq \in W(Y)$ we have

$$V_{\mathfrak{C}}[z^*, xp](yq) = G[z^*, x](y)\, V_{\mathfrak{C}}\big[F[z^*, x], p\big](q).$$

If $\Phi_x(y) = 0$, then $G[z^*, x](y) = 0$ and

$$\Phi_{xp}(yq) = 0 = V_{\mathfrak{C}}[z^*, xp](yq).$$

Let $\Phi_x(y) > 0$. Then

$$F[z^*, x](z') = \left\{\begin{matrix} \Phi_x^{y^*}(y), & \text{if} \quad z' = [\Phi^{y^*}, y], \quad y \in Y, \\ 0 & \text{otherwise} \end{matrix}\right\} = \mathfrak{z}_{y^*}(z');$$

thus we obtain

$$V_{\mathfrak{C}}[z^*, xp](yq) = \Phi_x(y) \cdot \Phi_p^{y^*}(q) = \Phi_x(y) \cdot \frac{\Phi_{xp}(y^*q)}{\Phi_x(y^*)}$$
$$= \Phi_x(y)\, \frac{\Phi_{xp}(yq)}{\Phi_x(y)} \quad \big(\text{by } \Phi_x(y) > 0\big)$$
$$= \Phi_{xp}(yq),$$

which was to be shown. Thus Theorem 4.12 is proved.

This yields us a characterization of the S-operators which can be generated by a state or a random state in an autonomous S-Mealy automaton. The general question is still unsolved. The condition given by Bucharaiev in [3] (Theorem 6) is sufficient (it characterizes the homogenous S-operators), but not necessary as he erroneously claims.

Corollary 4.13. A sequential S-operator Φ over $[\{x\}, Y]$ can be generated by a state in an S-Mealy automaton with a deterministic output function if and only if there is a $y \in Y$ with $\Phi_x(y) = 1$ and Φ satisfies the condition of Theorem 4.11.

In order to characterize the S-operators which can be generated in Z-finite S-automata, first we have to investigate a larger class of mappings which we call *pseudo-stochastic operators*.

Definition 4.5. A mapping Ψ which assigns to each $p \in W(X)$ a real-valued function Ψ_p defined on $\mathfrak{P}(W(Y))$, is called a *pseudo-stochastic operator* (shortly: *PS-operator*) over $[X, Y]$ if for all $p \in W(X)$ the following conditions are satisfied:

(1) $0 \leqq \Psi_p(Q)$ for all $Q \subseteq W(Y)$;

(2) $\Psi_p\left(\bigcup_{i=0}^{\infty} Q_i\right) = \sum_{i=0}^{\infty} \Psi_p(Q_i)$, if $Q_i \subseteq W(Y)$ for all $i \in \boldsymbol{nz}$ and from $i \neq j$, $Q_i \cap Q_j = \emptyset$ follows;

(3) $\Psi_p(W(Y)) = \Psi_p(ND(\Psi_p))$ and $\Psi_p(W(Y))$ is finite.

Obviously, every S-operator over $[X, Y]$ is a PS-operator over $[X, Y]$, but the converse is false. It follows from condition (3) that for PS-operators as well, for every $p \in W(X)$ the set $ND(\Psi_p) \subseteq W(Y)$ is at most countable. In what follows we are especially concerned with the class of those PS-operators for which $\Psi_p(W(Y)) \leqq 1$ holds for all $p \in W(X)$. Among these we shall distinguish certain PS-operators to be defined below, and which we call *generable*. After giving a general characterization of this concept of generability, we shall turn to the problem of describing those PS-operators which can be generated in a Z-finite S-automaton. Here we shall also obtain a characterization of the set of all S-operators which are generable in a Z-finite S-automaton.

The description of PS-operators generable in a Z-finite S-automaton is analogous to the theory of regular events. We shall define certain operations on PS-operators, the application of which we must restrict, however, to ensure that, applying them to PS-operators which can be generated in Z-finite S-automata, the result is again such a PS-operator. In order to avoid unnecessary complications, in the definition of these operations we shall not require that $\Psi_p(W(Y)) \leqq 1$ for all $p \in W(X)$.

Definition 4.6. A PS-operator Ψ over $[X, Y]$ is said to be *generated in the S-automaton* $\mathfrak{C} = [X, Y, Z, H]$ *by* $[\mathfrak{z}, N]$, where $\mathfrak{z}$ is a random state of $\mathfrak{C}$ and N is a subset of Z, if for all $p \in W(X)$, $q \in W(Y)$

$$\Psi_p(q) = \begin{cases} \mathfrak{z}(N), & \text{if } p = q = e, \\ H[\mathfrak{z}, p](\{q\} \times Z^{l(p)-1} \cdot N), & \text{if } p \neq e, \\ 0 & \text{otherwise.} \end{cases}$$

Theorem 4.14. *A PS-operator Ψ over $[X, Y]$ can be generated if and only if there is a sequential S-operator Φ over $[X, Y]$ such that for all $p \in W(X)$, $q \in W(Y)$*

$$\Phi_p(q) \geqq \Psi_p(q).$$

Proof: If Ψ is generated in the S-automaton $\mathfrak{C} = [X, Y, Z, H]$ by $[\mathfrak{z}, N]$, then the S-operator Φ defined by

$$\Phi_p(q) = V_{\mathfrak{C}}[\mathfrak{z}, p](q) \quad \text{for} \quad p \in W(X),\ q \in W(Y)$$

satisfies our requirements. Indeed, $\Psi_e(q) = 0$ if $q \neq e$ and

$$\Psi_e(e) = \mathfrak{z}(N) \leqq 1 = \Phi_e(e)$$

and for $p \in W(X) \setminus \{e\}$, $q \in W(Y)$,

$$\Psi_p(q) = H[\mathfrak{z}, p](\{q\} \times Z^{l(p)-1} \cdot N) \leqq H[\mathfrak{z}, p](\{q\} \times Z^{l(p)-1} \cdot Z) = \Phi_p(q).$$

Conversely, let Φ be a sequential S-operator over $[X, Y]$ with $\Psi_p(q) \leqq \Phi_p(q)$, and $\mathfrak{C} = [X, Y, Z, H]$ be an S-automaton in which Φ is generated by the state z_1. Then we put

$$Z' = \{[z, p, q, i] \mid z \in Z \wedge p \in W(X) \wedge q \in Y^{l(p)} \wedge i \in \{0, 1\}\}$$

and for $[z, p, q, i] \in Z'$, $x \in X$, $y \in Y$, $z'' \in Z'$

$$H'[[z, p, q, i], x](y, z'') \underset{\text{Df}}{=} \begin{cases} H[z, x](y, z^*)\dfrac{\Psi_{px}(qy)}{\Phi_{px}(qy)}, & \text{if} \\ \qquad z'' = [z^*, px, qy, 1] \text{ and } \Phi_{px}(qy) > 0, \\ H[z, x](y, z^*)\left(1 - \dfrac{\Psi_{px}(qy)}{\Phi_{px}(qy)}\right), & \text{if} \\ \qquad z'' = [z^*, px, qy, 0] \text{ and } \Phi_{px}(qy) > 0, \\ H[z, x](y, z^*), \text{ if } \Phi_{px}(qy) = 0 \text{ and} \\ \qquad z'' = [z^*, px, qy, 0], \\ 0 \qquad \text{otherwise.} \end{cases}$$

It is easy to verify that $\mathfrak{C}' = [X, Y, Z', H']$ is an S-automaton (by $\Psi_p(q) \leqq \Phi_p(q)$ we have $\dfrac{\Psi_p(q)}{\Phi_p(q)} \leqq 1$). For $z' \in Z'$ we set

$$\mathfrak{z}(z') \underset{\text{Df}}{=} \begin{cases} \Psi_e(e), & \text{if} \quad z' = [z_1, e, e, 1], \\ 1 - \Psi_e(e), & \text{if} \quad z' = [z_1, e, e, 0], \\ 0 & \text{otherwise.} \end{cases}$$

Finally we put

$$N \underset{\text{Df}}{=} \{[z, p, q, 1] \mid z \in Z \wedge p \in W(X) \wedge q \in Y^{l(p)}\}.$$

We shall show by induction on p that for all $p \in W(X)$, $q \in W(Y)$ with $\Phi_p(q) > 0, l(p) = n \geqq 1$, $z' \in Z'$, the following relation holds.

$$H'[\mathfrak{z}, p]\big(\{q\} \times (Z')^{n-1} \cdot \{z'\}\big)$$
$$= \begin{cases} H[z_1, p](\{q\} \times Z^{n-1} \cdot \{z^*\}) \dfrac{\Psi_p(q)}{\Phi_p(q)}, & \text{if } z' = [z^*, p, q, 1], \\ H[z_1, p](\{q\} \times Z^{n-1} \cdot \{z^*\}) \left(1 - \dfrac{\Psi_p(q)}{\Phi_p(q)}\right), & \text{if } z' = [z^*, p, q, 0], \\ 0 & \text{otherwise.} \end{cases}$$

For $p = x$, this is satisfied by the definition of H' and $\mathfrak{z}$. The induction step is taken from p to px. Since $\Phi_{px}(q) > 0$, q is of the form $q'y$ where $\Phi_p(q') > 0$. Let $n = l(p)$. Then

$$H'[\mathfrak{z}, px]\big(\{q'y\} \times (Z')^n \cdot \{z'\}\big)$$
$$= \sum_{z'' \in Z'} H'[\mathfrak{z}, p]\big(\{q'\} \times (Z')^{n-1} \cdot \{z''\}\big) H'[z'', x](y, z')$$
$$= \sum_{z^* \in Z} H[z_1, p](\{q'\} \times Z^{n-1} \cdot \{z^*\}) \cdot 1 \cdot H'\big[[z^*, p, q, 1], x\big](y, z')$$
$$= \begin{cases} H[z_1, px](\{q'y\} \times Z^n \cdot \{z^{**}\}) \dfrac{\Psi_{px}(q'y)}{\Phi_{px}(q'y)}, & \text{if } z' = [z^{**}, px, q'y, 1], \\ H[z_1, px](\{q'y\} \times Z^n \cdot \{z^{**}\}) \left(1 - \dfrac{\Psi_{px}(q'y)}{\Phi_{px}(q'y)}\right), & \text{if } z' = [z^{**}, px, q'y, 0], \\ 0 & \text{otherwise.} \end{cases}$$

For $p \neq e$, $l(p) = n$

$$1 = \sum_{q \in W(Y)} H'[\mathfrak{z}, p]\big(\{q\} \times (Z')^n\big) \geqq \sum_{q \in W(Y),\, \Phi_p(q) > 0} H'[\mathfrak{z}, p]\big(\{q\} \times (Z')^n\big)$$
$$\geqq \sum_{\Phi_p(q) > 0} \sum_{z^* \in Z} \sum_{i \in \{0,1\}} H'[\mathfrak{z}, p]\big(\{q\} \times (Z')^{n-1} \cdot \{[z^*, p, q, i]\}\big)$$
$$= \sum_{\Phi_p(q) > 0} H[z_1, p](\{q\} \times Z^n) = \sum_{\Phi_p(q) > 0} \Phi_p(q) = 1.$$

Hence if $p \in W(X) \setminus \{e\}$, $q \in W(Y)$ with $\Phi_p(q) = 0$ (i. e., $\Psi_p(q) = 0$)

$$H'[\mathfrak{z}, p]\big(\{q\} \times (Z')^{l(p)-1} \cdot N\big) \leqq H'[\mathfrak{z}, p]\big(\{q\} \times (Z')^{l(p)}\big) = 0 = \Psi_p(q)$$

and if $\Phi_p(q) > 0$

$$H'[\mathfrak{z}, p]\big(\{q\} \times (Z')^{l(p)-1} \cdot N\big) = \sum_{z^* \in Z} H[z_1, p](\{q\} \times Z^{l(p)-1} \cdot \{z^*\}) \frac{\Psi_p(q)}{\Phi_p(q)}$$
$$= \Phi_p(q) \frac{\Psi_p(q)}{\Phi_p(q)} = \Psi_p(q).$$

Finally we have $\Psi_e(q) = 0$ for $q \neq e$ and

$$\mathfrak{z}(N) = \mathfrak{z}([z_1, e, e, 1]) = \Psi_e(e).$$

Thus Ψ is generated in $\mathfrak{C}'$ by $[\mathfrak{z}, N]$.

Remark: If for a PS-operator Ψ over $[X, Y]$ there exists an S-operator Φ over $[X, Y]$ with the properties given in 4.14 and which is generable in a Z-finite S-automaton, it might happen that there is no Z-finite S-automaton in which Ψ could be generated. As an example, we consider the PS-operator Ψ over $[\{x\}, \{y\}]$ defined as follows:

$$\Psi_p(q) = \begin{cases} 1, & \text{if } \ l(p) = l(q) \ \text{ is a square number,} \\ 0 & \text{otherwise.} \end{cases}$$

Ψ is generable, since the S-operator Φ over $[\{x\}, \{y\}]$ with

$$\Phi_p(q) = \begin{cases} 1, & \text{if } \ l(p) = l(q), \\ 0 & \text{otherwise} \end{cases}$$

satisfies the condition of 4.14. Φ can be generated in an S-automaton with exactly one state, while Ψ cannot be generated in any Z-finite S-automaton, as will become clear later.

Definition 4.6. Let Ψ be a PS-operator over $[X, Y]$.

(4.6.1) Ψ is called an *elementary operator over* $[X, Y]$ if $\Psi_p(q) > 0$ implies $l(p) = l(q) = 1$.

(4.6.2) Ψ is called *regular* if it can be generated in a Z-finite S-automaton.

Theorem 4.15. *A PS-operator Ψ over $[X, Y]$ is regular if and only if the PS-operators Ψ^0, Ψ^1 with*

$$\Psi^0_e(e) = 0, \quad \Psi^1_e(e) = 1, \quad \Psi^0_p(q) = \Psi^1_p(q) = \Psi_p(q)$$

(for all $p \in W(X) \setminus \{e\}$, $q \in W(Y)$) can be generated in Z-finite S-automata by deterministic random states (and sets of states).

Proof: Let Ψ be regular and $\mathfrak{C} = [X, Y, Z, H]$ a Z-finite S-automaton, furthermore $\mathfrak{z} \in \mathfrak{Z}_Z$ and $N \subseteq Z$ such that Ψ is generated in $\mathfrak{C}$ by $[\mathfrak{z}, N]$. Let us choose a $z_0 \notin Z$ and put $Z' = Z \cup \{z_0\}$, $N^0 = N$, $N^1 = N \cup \{z_0\}$ and for $z', z'' \in Z'$, $x \in X$, $y \in Y$,

$$H'[z', x](y, z'') \underset{\mathrm{Df}}{=} \begin{cases} H[z', x](y, z''), & \text{if } \ z', z'' \in Z, \\ H[\mathfrak{z}, x](y, z''), & \text{if } \ z' = z_0 \text{ and } z'' \in Z, \\ 0 & \text{otherwise.} \end{cases}$$

Obviously, Ψ^0 and Ψ^1 are generated in the S-automaton $\mathfrak{C}' = [X, Y, Z', H']$ by $[\delta_{z_0}, N^0]$ and $[\delta_{z_1}, N^1]$, respectively.

Conversely, suppose Ψ^1 is generated in $\mathfrak{C} = [X, Y, Z, H]$ by $[\delta_{z_1}, N]$. As above we choose a $z_0 \notin Z$ and construct $\mathfrak{C}' = [X, Y, Z \cup \{z_0\}, H']$. Since $\Psi_e^1(e) = 1$, we have $\delta_{z_1}(N) = 1$, hence $z_1 \in N$. We put for $z' \in Z \cup \{z_0\}$

$$\mathfrak{z}(z') = \begin{cases} \Psi_e(e), & \text{if } z' = z_1, \\ 1 - \Psi_e(e), & \text{if } z' = z_0, \\ 0 & \text{otherwise.} \end{cases}$$

Obviously, $\Psi_e(e) = z(N)$ (since $z_0 \notin N$), and Ψ is generated in $\mathfrak{C}'$ by $[\mathfrak{z}, N]$.

Thus in order to characterize the regular PS-operators over $[X, Y]$ it suffices to give a criterion for the regularity of a PS-operator Ψ over $[X, Y]$ such that $\Psi_e(e) \in \{0, 1\}$.

Now we define certain operations on the set of all PS-operators over a given pair $[X, Y]$ such that by means of these operations every regular PS-operator with $\Psi(e) \in \{0, 1\}$ can be obtained from elementary operators. However, we shall see that these operations, when applied to regular elementary operators, can also lead to non-regular PS-operators. (An elementary operator Ψ is regular if and only if $\Psi_x(Y) \leqq 1$ for all $x \in X$.) This means that these operations can only be performed under certain restrictions, which will be given in the definitions of *standard terms and regular codes.*

Definition 4.7. Let Ψ, Ψ' be arbitrary PS-operators over $[X, Y]$. Then we define, for $p \in W(X)$, $Q \subseteq W(Y)$:

(4.7.1) the *addition* $[\Psi + \Psi']$ *of* Ψ, Ψ' by

$$[\Psi + \Psi']_p(Q) \underset{\mathrm{Df}}{=} \sum_{q \in Q} \mathit{min}\left(1, \Psi_p(q) + \Psi'_p(q)\right);$$

(4.7.2) the *multiplikation* $[\Psi \cdot \Psi']$ *of* Ψ *by* Ψ', by

$$[\Psi \cdot \Psi']_p(Q) \underset{\mathrm{Df}}{=} \sum_{y_1 \ldots y_n \in Q \cap Y^n} \mathit{min}\left(1, \sum_{i=0}^{n} \Psi_{x_1 \ldots x_i}(y_1 \cdots y_i) \cdot \Psi'_{x_{i+1} \ldots x_n}(y_{i+1} \cdots y_n)\right)$$

(where $p = x_1 \ldots x_n$) and

(4.7.3) the *iteration* $\langle\Psi\rangle$ *of* Ψ by

$$\langle\Psi\rangle_p(Q) \underset{\mathrm{Df}}{=} \sum_{q \in Q} \langle\Psi\rangle_p(q),$$

where

$$\langle\Psi\rangle_p(q) = \begin{cases} 1, & \text{if } p = q = e, \\ \mathit{min}\left(1, \sum_{m=1}^{n} \sum_{0 = l_0 < l_1 < \cdots < l_m = n} \prod_{i=0}^{m-1} \Psi_{x_{l_i+1} \ldots x_{l_{i+1}}}(y_{l_i+1} \cdots y_{l_{i+1}})\right), \\ \quad \text{if } p = x_1 \ldots x_n,\ q = y_1 \cdots y_n,\ n > 0, \\ 0 & \text{otherwise.} \end{cases}$$

Theorem 4.16. *If Ψ, Ψ' are PS-operators over $[X, Y]$, then the mappings $[\Psi + \Psi']$, $[\Psi \cdot \Psi']$, $\langle\Psi\rangle$ are also PS-operators over $[X, Y]$.*

Proof: It is clear that conditions (1) and (2) of definition 4.5 are satisfied. Thus we have only to show that the values $[\Psi + \Psi']_p(W(Y))$, $[\Psi \cdot \Psi']_p(W(Y))$ and $\langle\Psi\rangle_p(W(Y))$ are finite for all $p \in W(X)$.

We have

$$[\Psi + \Psi']_p(W(Y)) \leqq \sum_{q \in W(Y)} \Psi_p(q) + \Psi'_p(q) = \Psi_p(W(Y)) + \Psi'_p(W(Y)),$$

which is finite and for $p = x_1 \dots x_n$

$$\begin{aligned}
&[\Psi \cdot \Psi']_p(W(Y)) \\
&\leqq \sum_{y_1 \dots y_n \in Y^n} \sum_{i=0}^{n} \Psi_{x_1 \dots x_i}(y_1 \cdots y_i) \cdot \Psi'_{x_{i+1} \dots x_n}(y_{i+1} \cdots y_n) \\
&= \sum_{i=0}^{n} \sum_{y_1 \dots y_i \in Y^i} \Psi_{x_1 \dots x_i}(y_1 \cdots y_i) \sum_{y_{i+1} \dots y_n \in Y^{n-i}} \Psi'_{x_{i+1} \dots x_n}(y_{i+1} \cdots y_n) \\
&\leqq \sum_{i=0}^{n} \Psi_{x_1 \dots x_i}(W(Y)) \cdot \Psi'_{x_{i+1} \dots x_n}(W(Y)),
\end{aligned}$$

which is also finite. Finally one shows that for $p = x_1 \dots x_n$, $n \geqq 1$

$$\langle\Psi\rangle_p(W(Y)) \leqq \sum_{m=1}^{n} \sum_{0 = l_0 < l_1 < \dots < l_m = n} \prod_{i=0}^{m-1} \Psi_{x_{l_i+1} \dots x_{l_{i+1}}}(W(Y)),$$

which is again finite, and $\langle\Psi\rangle_e(W(Y)) = 1$ by definition.

This proves Theorem 4.16.

Let NZ be a notational system for the set of natural numbers, e.g., the set of all decimal representations of natural numbers. For the number $j \in \boldsymbol{nz}$ we denote by $\boldsymbol{j}$ the symbol representing it. A regular term T over $\boldsymbol{nz}$ is a sequence of symbols consisting of certain symbols $\boldsymbol{j} \in NZ$, the symbols $\vee$, $\circ$, $\langle\ \rangle$ and the technical symbols (,) constructed according to the usual rules. We put $Val(\boldsymbol{j}) = \{j\}$ (in particular $Val(\boldsymbol{0}) = \{0\} \neq \emptyset$) and the symbols $\vee$, $\circ$, $\langle\ \rangle$ are interpreted as usual so that for every regular term over $\boldsymbol{nz}$ the set of words $Val(T) \subseteq W(\boldsymbol{nz})$ is defined. Furthermore, if T is a regular term over $\boldsymbol{nz}$, we define the sets $I(T)$, $A(T)$, $E(T)$ and the function f^T as follows:

$$\begin{aligned}
I(T) &= \{j \mid j \in \boldsymbol{nz} \wedge \exists p \exists r(p, r \in W(\boldsymbol{nz}) \wedge pjr \in Val(T))\}, \\
A(T) &= \{j \mid j \in \boldsymbol{nz} \wedge \exists p(p \in W(\boldsymbol{nz}) \wedge jp \in Val(T))\}, \\
E(T) &= \{j \mid j \in \boldsymbol{nz} \wedge \exists p(p \in W(\boldsymbol{nz}) \wedge pj \in Val(T))\}, \\
f^T(i) &= \{j \mid j \in \boldsymbol{nz} \wedge \exists p \exists r(p, r \in W(\boldsymbol{nz}) \wedge pijr \in Val(T))\}.
\end{aligned}$$

Moreover, we introduce the following definitions:

$$Ed(T) = \{p \mid p \neq e \wedge \exists r (r, rp \in Val(T))\},$$
$$Ad(T) = \{p \mid p \neq e \wedge \exists r (pr, r \in Val(T))\},$$
$$Di(T) = \{p \mid p \neq e \wedge \exists r \exists s (r \neq e \wedge r, rp \in Val(T) \wedge ps, s \in Val(\langle T \rangle))\}$$

and for all $n \geqq 0$,

$$W_n(T) = \{p \mid p \in Val(T) \wedge l(p) = n\}.$$

Definition 4.8. (*Standard term*)

(A) If $\boldsymbol{j} \in NZ$, then $\boldsymbol{j}$ is a standard term.

(I) If T and T' are standard terms and

a) $Val(T) \cap Val(T') = \emptyset$, then $(T \vee T')$ is a standard term;

b) $Ed(T) \cap Ad(T') = \emptyset$, then $(T \circ T')$ is a standard term;

c) $Di(T) = \emptyset$, then $\langle T \rangle$ is a standard term.

A sequence of symbols is a standard term if it can be constructed using (A) and (I) in finitely many steps.

Corollary 4.17. Every standard term is a regular term over $\boldsymbol{nz}$ and over $I(T)$. The converse is false.

Theorem 4.18. *It is decidable whether a sequence of symbols T is a standard term.*

Proof: Obviously it suffices to show that for every regular term T over $\boldsymbol{nz}$ the sets $Ed(T)$, $Ad(T)$ and $Di(T)$ are regular events $(\subseteq W(I(T)))$ because the intersection of regular events is again regular, and it is decidable whether a given regular event is empty or not.

Every regular term T over $\boldsymbol{nz}$ is also a regular term over the finite set $I(T)$ and it is trivial that $Val(T)$ is a regular event. Suppose $Val(T)$ is represented in a finite initial deterministic automaton $\mathfrak{A} = [I(T), Z, \delta, z_1]$ by the set N. Then for every word $r \in W(I(T))$ there is a word $r' \in W(I(T))$ with $l(r') < Card(Z)$ and

$$\delta(z_1, r) = \delta(z_1, r').$$

Consequently, there is an r with $r, rp \in Val(T)$ if and only if there is an r' with $l(r') < Card(Z)$ and $r', r'p \in Val(T)$. Therefore

$$Ed(T) = \bigcup_{m=0}^{Card(Z)} \bigcup_{r \in W_m(T)} \{p \mid p \neq e \wedge rp \in Val(T)\}$$

is a finite union of regular events. Indeed, the set of words $\{p \mid rp \in Val(T)\}$ is represented by the set N in the finite automaton $\mathfrak{A}_r = [I(T), Z, \delta, \delta(z_1, r)]$ and thus is regular; furthermore we have

$$\{p \mid p \neq e \wedge rp \in Val(T)\} = \{p \mid rp \in Val(T)\} \setminus \{e\}.$$

If the event E is regular, then so is $E^* = \{p^* \mid p \in E\}$, where p^* denotes the inverse of the word p. Thus $(Val(T))^*$ is also regular, and consequently, if T_1 is a regular term with $Val(T_1) = (Val(T))^*$, then for $p \in W(I(T))$

$$\begin{aligned} p \in Ed(T_1) &\leftrightarrow p \neq e \wedge \exists r(r, rp \in Val(T_1)) \\ &\leftrightarrow p \neq e \wedge \exists r(r^*, (rp)^* \in Val(T)) \\ &\leftrightarrow p^* \neq e \wedge \exists r^*(r^*, p^* r^* \in Val(T)) \\ &\leftrightarrow p^* \in Ad(T) \\ &\leftrightarrow p \in (Ad(T))^*. \end{aligned}$$

Hence $Ad(T) = (Ed(T_1))^*$ is a regular event. Finally

$$\begin{aligned} Di(T) = \{p \mid p \neq e \wedge \exists r(r \neq e \wedge r, rp \in Val(T)) \\ \wedge \exists s(s, ps \in Val(\langle T \rangle))\}. \end{aligned}$$

Let T' be a regular term such that $Val(T') = Val(T) \setminus \{e\}$. Then we have

$$Di(T) = \{p \mid p \in Ed(T') \wedge p \in Ad(\langle T \rangle)\} = Ed(T') \cap Ad(\langle T \rangle).$$

Since the sets $Ed(T')$ and $Ad(\langle T \rangle)$ are regular, so is $Di(T)$, which proves Theorem 4.18.

If by means of a function B which we call a *code*, we assign elementary operators to the number symbols appearing in a given regular term T over $\boldsymbol{nz}$, then this term will describe the construction of a PS-operator from these elementary operators by means of the operations of addition, multiplication and iteration. This construction is clarified by the following definition:

Definition 4.9.

(4.9.1) Every function B mapping the set NZ into the set of all elementary operators over $[X, Y]$ is called an $[X, Y]$-*code*. The image of the number $\boldsymbol{j}$ under B will be denoted by $B^{\boldsymbol{j}}$.

(4.9.2) If T is a regular term over $\boldsymbol{nz}$ and B is an $[X, Y]$-code, then the PS-operator $\mathfrak{W}[T, B]$ described by T and B is given by the following inductive definition:

(A) If $T = \boldsymbol{j}$, then $\mathfrak{W}[T, B] = B^{\boldsymbol{j}}$.

$$\text{(I)} \qquad \mathfrak{W}[T, B] = \begin{cases} \mathfrak{W}[T_1, B] + \mathfrak{W}[T_2, B], & \text{if } T \equiv (T_1 \vee T_2), \\ \mathfrak{W}[T_1, B] \cdot \mathfrak{W}[T_2, B], & \text{if } T \equiv (T_1 \circ T_2), \\ \langle \mathfrak{W}[T_1, B] \rangle, & \text{if } T \equiv \langle T_1 \rangle. \end{cases}$$

(4.9.3) An $[X, Y]$-code B is called *regular for the regular term T over $\boldsymbol{nz}$* if for all $x \in X$,

$$\sum_{\boldsymbol{j} \in A(T)} B_x^{\boldsymbol{j}}(Y) \leqq 1,$$

and for all $i \in I(T)$,

$$\sum_{\boldsymbol{j} \in f^T(i)} B_x^{\boldsymbol{j}}(Y) \leqq 1.$$

Corollary 4.19.

1. If X and Y are finite sets, then it is decidable whether B is regular for T.
2. A code B can only be regular for T if for all $j \in I(T)$, $B^{\boldsymbol{j}}$ is a regular elementary operator.

After these preliminaries the characterization theorem can be formulated as follows:

Theorem 4.20 (Küstner [1]). *A PS-operator Ψ over $[X, Y]$ with $\Psi_e(e) \in \{0, 1\}$ is regular if and only if there is a standard term T and an $[X, Y]$-code B which is regular for T such that $\mathfrak{W}[T, B] = \Psi$.*

Proof: First we shall deal with the *analysis*, that is we show that for every PS-operator Ψ with $\Psi_e(e) \in \{0, 1\}$ which can be generated in a Z-finite S-automaton, there is a standard term and a code with the above mentioned properties.

Suppose the PS-operator Ψ is generated in $\mathfrak{C} = [X, Y, Z, H]$ by $[\mathfrak{z}, N]$ and $Card(Z) = m$. Without any loss of generality we can assume that $Z = \{1, \ldots, m\}$ and $\mathfrak{z} = \delta_1$. Thus

$$\Psi_p(q) = \begin{cases} 1, & \text{if } p = q = e \text{ and } 1 \in N, \\ H[1, p](\{q\} \times Z^{l(p)-1} \cdot N), & \text{if } l(p) = l(q) > 0, \\ 0 & \text{otherwise.} \end{cases}$$

If $N = \emptyset$ then $\Psi_p(q) = 0$ for all $p \in W(X)$, $q \in W(Y)$. This PS-operator will be denoted by Λ. $\mathbf{0}$ is a standard term and B with

$$B^{\boldsymbol{j}} = \Lambda \qquad \text{for all } \boldsymbol{j} \in NZ$$

is a regular $[X, Y]$-code for $\mathbf{0}$ such that $\mathfrak{W}[\mathbf{0}, B] = \Psi$. Suppose $N \neq \emptyset$. For $k \in nz$ with $0 \leq k \leq m$ let

$$[k] \underset{\mathrm{Df}}{=} \begin{cases} \{1, 2, \ldots, k\}, & \text{if } k \geqq 1, \\ \emptyset, & \text{if } k = 0. \end{cases}$$

Then we define for $i, j \in Z$, $k \in Z \cup \{0\}$ the PS-operator $[\Psi^k_{i,j}]$ by

$$[\Psi^k_{i,j}]_p(q) = \begin{cases} 0, & \text{if } p = q = e \text{ or } l(p) \neq l(q), \\ H[i, p](\{q\} \times [k]^{l(p)-1} \cdot \{j\}), & \text{if } l(p) = l(q) > 0, \end{cases}$$

for all $p \in W(X)$, $q \in W(Y)$.

Since $\emptyset^l$ is non-empty if and only if $l = 0$, the PS-operators $[\Psi^0_{i,j}]$ are elementary.

Next we show that for every $i, j \in Z$, $k \in Z \cup \{0\}$ there is a standard term $T^k_{i,j}$ and a code B which is regular for all $T^k_{i,j}$ such that $\mathfrak{W}[T^k_{i,j}, B] = [\Psi^k_{i,j}]$.

Let α be a one-to-one mapping of $Z \times Z$ into $\boldsymbol{nz} \setminus \{0\}$. We denote by (i, j) the value of α taken on the pair $[i, j] \in Z \times Z$, and the corresponding number symbol from NZ is denoted by $(\boldsymbol{i}, \boldsymbol{j})$. For a word $p = i_1 i_2 \ldots i_n \in W(Z)$ with $l(p) = n \geqq 2$ we put

$$(\boldsymbol{p}) \underset{\text{Df}}{=} (\boldsymbol{i_1}, \boldsymbol{i_2})(\boldsymbol{i_2}, \boldsymbol{i_3}) \ldots (\boldsymbol{i_{n-1}}, \boldsymbol{i_n}) \qquad \big(\in W(\boldsymbol{nz})\big).$$

For all $i, j \in Z$, $k \in Z \cup \{0\}$ we define by induction on k a regular term $T^k_{i,j}$ over $\boldsymbol{nz}$ such that

$$T^0_{i,j} \equiv (\boldsymbol{i}, \boldsymbol{j}),$$

$$T^k_{i,j} \equiv \big(T^{k-1}_{i,j} \vee (T^{k-1}_{i,k} \circ (\langle T^{k-1}_{k,k} \rangle \circ T^{k-1}_{k,j}))\big).$$

Lemma 4.20.1. *For all* $i, j \in Z$, $k \in Z \cup \{0\}$, $T^k_{i,j}$ *is a standard term and* $e \notin Val(T^k_{i,j}) = \{(\boldsymbol{ipj}) \mid p \in W([k])\}$.

The proof is carried out by induction on k. The initial step is $k = 0$. Then $T^0_{i,j} = (\boldsymbol{i}, \boldsymbol{j}) \in NZ$ and thus is a standard term, moreover

$$Val(T^0_{i,j}) = \{(i, j)\} = \{(\boldsymbol{ipj}) \mid p \in W(\emptyset)\} = \{(\boldsymbol{ipj}) \mid p \in W([0])\}.$$

The induction step is taken from $k - 1$ to k $(k \in Z)$.

Then

$$\begin{aligned} Val(T^k_{i,j}) &= Val(T^{k-1}_{i,j}) \cup Val(T^{k-1}_{i,k}) \cdot \langle Val(T^{k-1}_{k,k}) \rangle \cdot Val(T^{k-1}_{k,j}) \\ &= \{(\boldsymbol{ipj}) \mid p \in W([k-1])\} \cup \{(\boldsymbol{irk}) \mid r \in W([k-1])\} \\ &\quad \cdot \langle \{(\boldsymbol{ksk}) \mid s \in W([k-1])\} \rangle \{(\boldsymbol{kqj}) \mid q \in W([k-1])\} \\ &= \{(\boldsymbol{ipj}) \mid p \in W([k-1])\} \cup \{(\boldsymbol{ipj}) \mid p \in W([k]) \setminus W([k-1])\} \\ &= \{(\boldsymbol{ipj}) \mid p \in W([k])\}. \end{aligned}$$

This proves the assertion about $Val(T^k_{i,j})$. Simultaneously we have

$$Val(T^{k-1}_{i,j}) \cap Val\big(T^{k-1}_{i,k} \circ (\langle T^{k-1}_{k,k} \rangle \circ T^{k-1}_{k,j})\big) = \emptyset.$$

It suffices to show that $\left(T^{k-1}_{i,k} \circ (\langle T^{k-1}_{k,k}\rangle \circ T^{k-1}_{k,j})\right)$ is a standard term. This follows from the following assertions:

(1) $Di(T^{k-1}_{k,k}) = \emptyset$,

(2) $Ed(\langle T^{k-1}_{k,k}\rangle) \cap Ad(T^{k-1}_{k,j}) = \emptyset$,

(3) $Ed(T^{k-1}_{i,k}) \cap Ad(\langle T^{k-1}_{k,k}\rangle \circ T^{k-1}_{k,j}) = \emptyset$.

Suppose $p \in Di(T^{k-1}_{k,k})$; then $p \neq e$, and there are words r, s with $r \neq e$, $r, rp \in Val(T^{k-1}_{k,k})$ and $ps, s \in \langle Val(T^{k-1}_{k,k})\rangle$. Since $l(rp) \geqq 2$ and $rp \in Val(T^{k-1}_{k,k})$ we have $k \geqq 2$, because $Val(T^{0}_{k,k}) = \{(k, k)\}$. Let $l = l(rp) - 1$. Then $rp \in W_{l+1}(T^{k-1}_{k,k})$. Hence there are numbers $i_1, \ldots, i_l \in [k-1]$ with $rp = (ki_1 \ldots i_l k) = (k, i_1)(i_1, i_2) \ldots (i_l, k)$. Since $p, r \neq e$ and $r \in Val(T^{k-1}_{k,k})$ there is an n with $1 \leqq n \leqq l$ such that $i_n = k$, which is in contradiction to $i_1, \ldots, i_l \in [k-1]$. Thus $Di(T^{k-1}_{k,k}) = \emptyset$. Now we show that $Ad(T^{k-1}_{k,j}) = \emptyset$, which implies (2). Let us suppose that $p \in Ad(T^{k-1}_{k,j})$. Then $p \neq e$, and there is an r with $pr, r \in Val(T^{k-1}_{k,j}) = \{(ksj) \mid s \in W([k-1])\}$. Consequently, $r \neq e$ and $l(pr) \geqq 2$, $k \neq 1$, and for $l = l(pr) - 1 \geqq 1$ we have $pr \in W_{l+1}(T^{k-1}_{k,j})$; therefore there are numbers $i_1, \ldots, i_l \in [k-1]$ with $pr = (k, i_1)(i_1, i_2) \ldots (i_l, j)$. On the other hand, $p, r \neq e$ and $r \in W_{l(r)}(T^{k-1}_{k,j})$, hence $r = (k, j)$, if $l(r) = 1$, i.e., $i_l = k$ which is in contradiction to $i_l \in [k-1]$, or $n = l(r) - 1 \geqq 1$, and there are numbers $j_1, \ldots, j_n \in [k-1]$ with $r = (k, j_1) \ldots (j_n, j)$, which implies $n < l$ and $i_{l-n} = k$, in contradiction to $i_{l-n} \in [k-1]$.

Similarly we can show that $Ed(T^{k-1}_{i,k}) = \emptyset$, which implies (3). Thus Lemma 4.20.1 is proved.

For $n \in \boldsymbol{nz}$ let

$$B^n \underset{\text{Df}}{=} \begin{cases} [\Psi^0_{i,j}], & \text{if } \boldsymbol{n} = (\boldsymbol{i}, \boldsymbol{j}),^{1)} \\ \Lambda & \text{otherwise.} \end{cases}$$

We claim that B is an $[X, Y]$-code which is regular for all $T^k_{i,j}$. By Lemma 4.20.1 we have

$$A(T^k_{i,j}) \subseteq \{(i, l) \mid l \in Z\};$$

hence for all $x \in X$

$$\sum_{n \in A(T^k_{i,j})} B^n_x(Y) \leqq \sum_{l \in Z} B^{(i,l)}_x(Y)$$
$$= \sum_{l \in Z} [\Psi^0_{i,l}]_x(Y) = H[i, x](Y \times Z) = 1,$$

and thus condition a) of Definition (4.9.3) is satisfied. Furthermore, for $i', j' \in Z$,

$$f^{T^k_{i,j}}\left((i', j')\right) \subseteq \{(j', l) \mid l \in Z\},$$

---

[1]) That is $\alpha^{-1}(n)$ is defined and $\alpha^{-1}(n) = [i, j] \in Z \times Z$.

that is for all $x \in X,\ i', j' \in Z$,

$$\sum_{n \in f^{T^k_{i,j}}((i', j'))} B^n_x(Y) \leqq \sum_{l \in Z} B^{(j',l)}_x(Y)$$
$$= \sum_{l \in Z} [\Psi^0_{j',l}]_x(Y) = H[j', x](Y \times Z) = 1,$$

hence B is regular for $T^k_{i,j}$.

Lemma 4.20.2. *For all* $i, j \in Z,\ k \in Z \cup \{0\},\ \mathfrak{W}[T^k_{i,j}, B] = [\Psi^k_{i,j}]$.

The proof is carried out by induction on k. The initial step $k = 0$ is trivial by the definition of B. The induction step is taken from $k - 1$ to k (for $k \in Z$). By Definition (4.9.2) and the induction hypothesis

$$\begin{aligned}\mathfrak{W}[T^k_{i,j}, B] &= \mathfrak{W}[T^{k-1}_{i,j}, B] \\ &\quad + \big(\mathfrak{W}[T^{k-1}_{i,k}, B] \cdot (\langle \mathfrak{W}[T^{k-1}_{k,k}, B]\rangle \cdot \mathfrak{W}[T^{k-1}_{k,j}, B])\big) \\ &= [\Psi^{k-1}_{i,j}] + \big([\Psi^{k-1}_{i,k}] \cdot (\langle[\Psi^{k-1}_{k,k}]\rangle \cdot [\Psi^{k-1}_{k,j}])\big).\end{aligned}$$

It remains to show that for all $p \in W(X),\ q \in W(Y)$,

$$\big([\Psi^{k-1}_{i,j}] + ([\Psi^{k-1}_{i,k}] \cdot (\langle[\Psi^{k-1}_{k,k}]\rangle \cdot [\Psi^{k-1}_{k,j}]))\big)_p(q) = [\Psi^k_{i,j}]_p(q).$$

This equality is trivial for all p, q with $l(p) \neq l(q)$.

Now

$$\langle[\Psi^{k-1}_{k,k}]\rangle_e(e) = 1,$$

and for $r = x_1 \ldots x_n \in W(X),\ s = y_1 \ldots y_n \in W(Y)$ with $l(r) = l(s) = n \geqq 1$

$$\begin{aligned}&\langle[\Psi^{k-1}_{k,k}]\rangle_r(s) \\ &= \min\left(1, \sum_{\nu=1}^{n} \sum_{0=l_0<l_1<\cdots<l_\nu=n} \prod_{i=0}^{\nu-1} [\Psi^{k-1}_{k,k}]_{x_{l_i+1}\cdots x_{l_{i+1}}}(y_{l_i+1}\cdots y_{l_{i+1}})\right).\end{aligned}$$

We have

$$\begin{aligned}&\prod_{i=0}^{\nu-1} [\Psi^{k-1}_{k,k}]_{x_{l_i+1}\cdots x_{l_{i+1}}}(y_{l_i+1} \cdots y_{l_{i+1}}) \\ &= \prod_{i=0}^{\nu-1} H[k, x_{l_i+1} \ldots x_{l_{i+1}}](\{y_{l_i+1} \ldots y_{l_{i+1}}\} \times [k-1]^{(l_{i+1}-l_i)} \cdot \{k\}) \\ &= H[k, r](\{s\} \times [k-1]^{(l_1-l_0-1)} \cdot \{k\} \cdot \ldots \cdot [k-1]^{(l_\nu-l_{\nu-1}-1)} \cdot \{k\}).\end{aligned}$$

Therefore

$$\begin{aligned}\langle[\Psi^{k-1}_{k,k}]\rangle_r(s) &= \min\big(1, H[k, r](\{s\} \times [k]^{n-1} \cdot \{k\})\big) \\ &= H[k, r](\{s\} \times [k]^{n-1} \cdot \{k\}).\end{aligned}$$

Furthermore

$$(\langle[\Psi^{k-1}_{k,k}]\rangle \cdot [\Psi^{k-1}_{k,j}])_e(e) = 0$$

by $[\Psi^{k-1}_{k,j}]_e(e) = 0$, and for $r = x_1 \ldots x_n$, $s = y_1 \ldots y_n$, $n \geqq 1$,

$$\begin{aligned}
&(\langle[\Psi^{k-1}_{k,k}]\rangle \cdot [\Psi^{k-1}_{k,j}])_r(s) \\
&= \min\left(1, \sum_{i=0}^{n} \langle[\Psi^{k-1}_{k,k}]\rangle_{x_1\ldots x_i}(y_1 \ldots y_i) \cdot [\Psi^{k-1}_{k,j}]_{x_{i+1}\ldots x_n}(y_{i+1} \ldots y_n)\right) \\
&= \min\Big(1, [\Psi^{k-1}_{k,j}]_r(s) \\
&\qquad + \sum_{i=1}^{n-1} \langle[\Psi^{k-1}_{k,k}]\rangle_{x_1\ldots x_i}(y_1 \ldots y_i)\, [\Psi^{k-1}_{k,j}]_{x_{i+1}\ldots x_n}(y_{i+1} \ldots y_n)\Big) \\
&= \min\Big(1, H[k, r](\{s\} \times [k-1]^{n-1} \cdot \{j\}) \\
&\qquad + \sum_{i=1}^{n-1} H[k, x_1 \ldots x_i](\{y_1 \ldots y_i\} \times [k]^{n-1} \cdot \{k\}) \\
&\qquad \cdot H[k, x_{i+1} \ldots x_n](\{y_{i+1} \ldots y_n\} \times [k-1]^{n-i-1} \cdot \{j\})\Big) \\
&= \min\big(1, H[k, r](\{s\} \times [k-1]^{n-1} \cdot \{j\}) \\
&\qquad + H[k, r]\big(\{s\} \times ([k]^{n-1} \setminus [k-1]^{n-1}) \cdot \{j\}\big)\big) \\
&= H[k, r](\{s\} \times [k]^{n-1} \cdot \{j\}).
\end{aligned}$$

Thus we obtain

$$\big([\Psi^{k-1}_{i,k}] \cdot (\langle[\Psi^{k-1}_{k,k}]\rangle \cdot [\Psi^{k-1}_{k,j}])\big)_e(e) = 0$$

and for $p = x_1 \ldots x_n$, $q = y_1 \ldots y_n$, $n \geqq 1$

$$\begin{aligned}
&\big([\Psi^{k-1}_{i,k}] \cdot (\langle[\Psi^{k-1}_{k,k}]\rangle \cdot [\Psi^{k-1}_{k,j}])\big)_p(q) \\
&= \min\left(1, \sum_{\nu=0}^{n} [\Psi^{k-1}_{i,k}]_{x_1\ldots x_\nu}(y_1 \ldots y_\nu) \cdot (\langle[\Psi^{k-1}_{k,k}]\rangle \cdot [\Psi^{k-1}_{k,j}])_{x_{\nu+1}\ldots x_n}(y_{\nu+1} \ldots y_n)\right) \\
&= \min\Big(1, \sum_{\nu=1}^{n-1} H[i, x_1 \ldots x_\nu](\{y_1 \ldots y_\nu\} \times [k-1]^{\nu-1} \cdot \{k\}) \\
&\qquad \cdot H[k, x_{\nu+1} \ldots x_n](\{y_{\nu+1} \ldots y_n\} \times [k]^{n-\nu-1} \cdot \{j\})\Big) \\
&= H[i, p]\big(\{q\} \times ([k]^{n-1} \setminus [k-1]^{n-1}) \cdot \{j\}\big).
\end{aligned}$$

Thus for all $p \in W(X)$, $q \in W(Y)$ we obtain

$$\begin{aligned}
&\big([\Psi^{k-1}_{i,j}] + ([\Psi^{k-1}_{i,k}] \cdot (\langle[\Psi^{k-1}_{k,k}]\rangle \cdot [\Psi^{k-1}_{k,j}]))\big)_p(q) \\
&= \begin{cases} \min\big(1, H[i, p](\{q\} \times [k-1]^{n-1} \cdot \{j\}) \\ \qquad + H[i, p]\big(\{q\} \times ([k]^{n-1} \setminus [k-1]^{n-1}) \cdot \{j\}\big)\big), \\ \qquad \text{if } l(p) = l(q) = n > 0, \\ 0 \quad \text{otherwise} \end{cases} \\
&= \begin{cases} H[i, p](\{q\} \times [k]^{n-1} \cdot \{j\}), & \text{if } l(p) = l(q) = n > 0, \\ 0 & \text{otherwise} \end{cases} \\
&= [\Psi^{k}_{i,j}]_p(q).
\end{aligned}$$

This proves Lemma 4.20.2.

Suppose $N = \{j_1, \ldots, j_n\}$ with $n \geqq 1$, $1 \leqq j_1 < j_2 < \cdots < j_n \leqq m$ and

$$T \equiv \left(T^m_{1,j_1} \vee (\ldots \vee (T^m_{1,j_{n-1}} \vee T^m_{1,j_n}) \ldots)\right).$$

By Lemma 4.20.1, T is a standard term,

$$A(T) = \bigcup_{i=1}^{n} A(T^m_{1,j_i}) \subseteq \{(1, l) \mid l \in Z\}$$

and for $i, j \in Z$

$$f^T\big((i, j)\big) \subseteq \bigcup_{\nu=1}^{n} f^{T^m_{1,j_\nu}}\big((i, j)\big) \subseteq \{(j, l) \mid l \in Z\},$$

from which we obtain as above that B is regular for T.

For $p \in W(X)$, $q \in W(Y)$ we have

$$\mathfrak{W}[T, B]_p(q) = min\left(1, \sum_{\nu=1}^{n} [\Psi^m_{1,j_\nu}]_p(q)\right).$$

Thus

$$\mathfrak{W}[T, B]_e(q) = 0 \qquad \text{for all } q \in W(Y),$$

and for $p \in W(X) \setminus \{e\}$,

$$\mathfrak{W}[T, B]_p(q) = min\left(1, \sum_{\nu=1}^{n} H[1, p](\{q\} \times Z^{l(p)-1} \cdot \{j_\nu\})\right)$$

$$= H[1, p](\{q\} \times Z^{l(p)-1} \cdot N) = \Psi_p(q).$$

If $\Psi_e(e) = 0$, then T is a standard term and B is an $[X, Y]$-code regular for T of the desired type.

If $\Psi_e(e) = 1$ then we consider the term $T' \equiv (\langle 0 \rangle \vee T)$. Since $0 \notin I(T)$ and $\langle 0 \rangle$ is a standard term, so is T'. Furthermore, (since $(i, j) \neq 0$ for $i, j \in Z$) $B^0 = \Lambda$. Consequently B is regular for T' and

$$\mathfrak{W}[T', B]_p(q) = \begin{cases} 1, & \text{if } p = q = e, \\ \Psi_p(q), & \text{if } p \neq e, \end{cases} = \Psi_p(q)$$

for all $p \in W(X)$, $q \in W(Y)$.

Now we turn to the *synthesis problem*, that is, we want to give a procedure which enables us to construct, for every standard term T and every code B regular for T, an S-automaton $\mathfrak{C}$, a state z_1 and a set N in such a way that the PS-operator $\mathfrak{W}[T, B]$ is generated in $\mathfrak{C}$ by $[\delta_{z_1}, N]$.

Lemma 4.20.3. *If T, T' are standard terms, then:*

a) *if $Ed(T) \cap Ad(T') = \emptyset$, then for all $n \geqq 1$ the system of sets*

$$\{W_i(T) \cdot W_{n-i}(T') \mid 0 \leqq i \leqq n \wedge W_i(T) \cdot W_{n-i}(T') \neq \emptyset\}$$

is a partition of the set $W_n(T \circ T')$.

b) *If* $Di(T) = \emptyset$, *then for all* $n \geqq 1$ *the system of sets*

$$\{W_{l_1}(T) \cdot \ldots \cdot W_{l_m}(T) \mid m \leqq n \wedge \bigwedge_{\mu=1}^{m} l_\mu \geqq 1 \wedge \sum_{\mu=1}^{m} l_\mu = n \wedge W_{l_1}(T) \cdot \ldots \cdot W_{l_m}(T) \neq \emptyset\}$$

is a partition of the set $W_n(\langle T \rangle)$.

Proof: Ad a). It suffices to show that the existence of numbers i, j, n with $0 \leqq i < j \leqq n$ and $W_i(T) \cdot W_{n-i}(T') \cap W_j(T) \cdot W_{n-j}(T') \neq \emptyset$ implies $Ed(T) \cap Ad(T') \neq \emptyset$. If $k_1 \ldots k_n \in W_i(T) \cdot W_{n-i}(T') \cap W_j(T) \cdot W_{n-j}(T')$, then $r = k_1 \ldots k_i \in W_i(T)$, hence $r \in Val(T)$, $s = k_{j+1} \ldots k_n \in W_{n-j}(T')$, and $s \in Val(T')$, and for $p = k_{i+1} \ldots k_j$, by $i < j$, we have

$$p \neq e, \; rp \in Val(T), \; ps \in Val(T').$$

Since $p \neq e$, $rp, r \in Val(T)$, we have $p \in Ed(T)$ and since $p \neq e$, $ps, s \in Val(T')$, $p \in Ad(T')$ and thus $Ed(T) \cap Ad(T') \neq \emptyset$.

Ad b). We only have to show that the existence of numbers $n, m, m', l_1, \ldots, l_m, l'_1, \ldots, l'_{m'} \geqq 1$ with $[l_1, \ldots, l_m] \neq [l'_1, \ldots, l'_{m'}]$,

$$\sum_{\mu=1}^{m} l_\mu = n = \sum_{\mu=1}^{m'} l'_\mu$$

and

$$W_{l_1}(T) \cdot \ldots \cdot W_{l_m}(T) \cap W_{l'_1}(T) \cdot \ldots \cdot W_{l'_{m'}}(T) \neq \emptyset,$$

implies $Di(T) \neq \emptyset$. If there are such numbers, there also are words $p_1, \ldots, p_m$, $p'_1, \ldots, p'_{m'} \in Val(T) \setminus \{e\}$ with $[p_1, \ldots, p_m] \neq [p'_1, \ldots, p'_{m'}]$, but $p_1 \ldots p_m = p'_1 \ldots p'_{m'}$. Let i be the minimal index such that $p_i \neq p'_i$. We can assume that $l(p_i) < l(p'_i)$. Obviously, for this i we have $i \leqq m$. There are words r, q with

$$p_i r = p'_i, \; rq = p_{i+1} \ldots p_m.$$

Here, $r \neq e$ since $l(p_i) < l(p'_i)$. If $i = m$, then $q = e$, otherwise $q = p'_{i+1} \ldots p'_{m'}$. Therefore

$$q \in Val(\langle T \rangle), \quad rq \in Val(\langle T \rangle),$$

$$p_i \in Val(T), \quad p_i r = p'_i \in Val(T), \quad p_i \neq e;$$

hence $r \in Di(T)$, and thus $Di(T) \neq \emptyset$. This proves Lemma 4.20.3.

For a standard term T let us denote by $l(T)$ the number of those places in T where symbols for natural numbers appear, and let $\hat{T}$ be the regular term which is obtained from T by affixing as lower indices $0, 1 \ldots, l(T) - 1$ in this order from left to right to the corresponding number symbols in T. In calculating the values these indices are indicated, e.g., $Val(\mathbf{1} \circ \mathbf{1}) = \{\mathbf{11}\}$, but $Val(\widehat{\mathbf{1} \circ \mathbf{1}}) = Val(\mathbf{1}_0 \circ \mathbf{1}_1) = \{\mathbf{1}_0\mathbf{1}_1\}$. Obviously, $Val(\hat{T}) \subseteq W(I(\hat{T}))$.

For a standard term T and $j \in \boldsymbol{nz}$ we put

$$I_j(\hat{T}) = \{j_0, j_1, \ldots\} \cap I(\hat{T}),$$

$$A_j(\hat{T}) = I_j(\hat{T}) \cap A(\hat{T}),$$

$$E_j(\hat{T}) = I_j(\hat{T}) \cap E(\hat{T}),$$

$$f_j^{\hat{T}}(z) = I_j(\hat{T}) \cap \bigcup_{k_\nu \in z} f^{\hat{T}}(k_\nu) \qquad \text{for } z \subseteq \{k_\nu \mid k, \nu \in \boldsymbol{nz}\}.$$

Then $j, j' \in \boldsymbol{nz}$ with $j \neq j'$ imply $I_j(\hat{T}) \cap I_{j'}(\hat{T}) = \emptyset$. Finally, for a standard term T, we define the set $Z(T)$ as the smallest system of sets such that

(A) for every $j \in A(T)$, the set $A_j(\hat{T})$ belongs to $Z(T)$ and

(I) if a set z belongs to $Z(T)$, then for every $j \in I(T)$ the set $f_j^{\hat{T}}(z)$ also belongs to $Z(T)$, provided it is not empty.

From these definitions we immediately obtain

Corollary 4.20.4. If T is a standard term, then

a) $j \in A(T)$ if and only if $A_j(\hat{T}) \neq \emptyset$.

b) If $A_j(\hat{T}) \cap A_k(\hat{T}) \neq \emptyset$, then $j = k$.

c) For every $z \in Z(T)$ there is exactly one $j \in I(T)$ with $z \subseteq I_j(\hat{T})$.

d) $Z(T)$ is a finite system of finite sets.

e) If $z \in Z(T)$ and $f_k^{\hat{T}}(z) \cap f_j^{\hat{T}}(z) \neq \emptyset$ then $j = k$.

For a standard term T we put

$$N(T) \underset{\mathrm{Df}}{=} \{z \mid z \in Z(T) \wedge z \cap E(\hat{T}) \neq \emptyset\}$$

and for $j^1 \ldots j^n \in Val(T)$, $n \geqq 1$

$$\delta^T(j^1 \ldots j^n) \underset{\mathrm{Df}}{=} z_2 z_3 \ldots z_{n+1},$$

where $z_2 = A_{j^1}(\hat{T})$ and $z_{i+1} = f_{j^i}^{\hat{T}}(z_i)$ for $i = 2, \ldots, n$.

Lemma 4.20.5. *If T is a standard term, $n \geqq 1$, $j^1 \ldots j^n$, $k^1 \ldots k^n \in Val(T)$ $j^1 \ldots j^n \neq k^1 \ldots k^n$ and $\delta^T(j^1 \ldots j^n) = z_2 \ldots z_{n+1}$, then*

a) $z_{i+1} \in Z(T)$ *for* $i = 1, \ldots, n$,

b) $z_{i+1} \in I_{j^i}(\hat{T})$ *for* $i = 1, \ldots, n$,

c) $z_{n+1} \in N(T)$,

d) $\delta^T(j^1 \ldots j^n) \neq \delta^T(k^1 \ldots k^n)$.

Proof: Since $j^1 \ldots j^n \in Val(T)$, there are numbers (indices) $i_1, \ldots, i_n$ such that $j_{i_1}^1 \ldots j_{i_n}^n \in Val(\hat{T})$ from which it follows (cf. Part I, Lemma 6.16) that

$$j_{i_1}^1 \in A(\hat{T}) \wedge \bigwedge_{\nu=1}^{n-1} j_{i_{\nu+1}}^{\nu+1} \in f^{\hat{T}}(j_{i_\nu}^\nu) \wedge j_{i_n}^n \in E(\hat{T}).$$

Hence $j^1_{i_1} \in A_{j^1}(\hat{T}) = z_2 \neq \emptyset$, i.e., $z_2 \in Z(T)$, and for $\nu = 1, \ldots, n-1$

$$j^{\nu+1}_{i_{\nu+1}} \in f^{\hat{T}}_{j^{\nu+1}}(j^\nu_{i_\nu}) \subseteq f^{\hat{T}}_{j^{\nu+1}}(z_{\nu+1}) = z_{\nu+2},$$

i.e., $z_{\nu+2} \neq \emptyset$ and consequently $z_{\nu+2} \in Z(T)$. Furthermore, $j^n_{i_n} \in z_{n+1} \cap E(T)$, hence $z_{n+1} \in N(\hat{T})$. Let l be the smallest number such that $j^l \neq k^l$ and $\delta^T(k^1 \ldots k^n) = z'_2 \ldots z'_{n+1}$. If $l = 1$, then we have $z_2 = A_{j^1}(\hat{T})$, $z'_2 = A_{k^1}(\hat{T})$, hence $z_2 \cap z'_2 = \emptyset$ by 4.20.4, i.e., $z_2 \neq z'_2$ and consequently, d) holds. If $l \geqq 2$, then $e \neq j^1 \ldots j^{l-1} = k^1 \ldots k^{l-1}$, hence $z_l = z'_l$ and $z_{l+1} = f^{\hat{T}}_{j^l}(z_l) \neq f^{\hat{T}}_{k^l}(z_l) = z'_{l+1}$ by $j^l \neq k^l$ and 4.20.4. This proves Lemma 4.20.5.

Lemma 4.20.6. *Let T be a standard term and B an $[X, Y]$-code regular for T. Then*

$$\mathfrak{W}[T, B]_e(e) = \begin{cases} 1, & \text{if } e \in Val(T), \\ 0 & \text{otherwise} \end{cases}$$

and for all $p = x_1 \ldots x_n \in W(X) \setminus \{e\}$, $q = y_1 \ldots y_n \in W(Y) \setminus \{e\}$

$$\mathfrak{W}[T, B]_p(q) = \sum_{j^1 \ldots j^n \in W_n(T)} \prod_{i=1}^n B^{j^i}_{x_i}(y_i).$$

Proof: For $n \geqq 1$, $x_1 \ldots x_n \in W(X)$, $y_1 \ldots y_n \in W(Y)$

$$\sum_{j^1 \ldots j^n \in W_n(T)} \prod_{i=1}^n B^{j^i}_{x_i}(y_i)$$

$$= \sum_{j^1 \in A(T)} B^{j^1}_{x_1}(y_1) \sum_{j^2 \in f^T(j^1)} B^{j^2}_{x_2}(y_2) \ldots \sum_{j^n \in f^T(j^{n-1}) \cap E(T)} B^{j^n}_{x_n}(y_n)$$

$$\leqq \sum_{j^1 \in A(T)} B^{j^1}_{x_1}(y_1) \sum_{j^2 \in f^T(j^1)} B^{j^2}_{x_2}(y_2) \ldots \sum_{j^n \in f^T(j^{n-1})} B^{j^n}_{x_n}(y_n).$$

Since B is regular for T, the last sum of this chain cannot exceed 1, and thus

$$\sum_{j^1 \ldots j^n \in W_n(T)} \prod_{i=1}^n B^{j^i}_{x_i}(y_i) \leqq 1. \qquad (*)$$

We prove the lemma by induction on T. The initial step $T \equiv j$ is trivial.

Induction step:

I. $T \equiv (T_1 \vee T_2)$.

Since T is a standard term, both T_1 and T_2 are standard terms with $Val(T_1) \cap Val(T_2) = \emptyset$, hence for all $n \geqq 0$ $W_n(T_1) \cap W_n(T_2) = \emptyset$. Obviously, every $[X, Y]$-code which is regular for T is also regular for T_1 and T_2. This implies that for $p = x_1 \ldots x_n \in W(X) \setminus \{e\}$, $q = y_1 \ldots y_n \in W(Y) \setminus \{e\}$ by the induction hypothesis and (*),

$$\begin{aligned}&\sum_{j^1\cdots j^n\in W_n(T)}\prod_{i=1}^{n} B_{x_i}^{j^i}(y_i)\\ &= \sum_{j^1\cdots j^n\in W_n(T_1)}\prod_{i=1}^{n} B_{x_i}^{j^i}(y_i) + \sum_{j^1\cdots j^n\in W_n(T_2)}\prod_{i=1}^{n} B_{x_i}^{j^i}(y_i)\\ &= \mathfrak{W}[T_1, B]_p(q) + \mathfrak{W}[T_2, B]_p(q)\\ &= min\bigl(1, \mathfrak{W}[T_1, B]_p(q) + \mathfrak{W}[T_2, B]_p(q)\bigr)\\ &= \mathfrak{W}[T, B]_p(q).\end{aligned}$$

Furthermore,

$$\begin{aligned}\mathfrak{W}[T, B]_e(e) &= \begin{cases}1, & \text{if } e\in Val(T_1)\cup Val(T_2),\\ 0 & \text{otherwise}\end{cases}\\ &= \begin{cases}1, & \text{if } e\in Val(T),\\ 0 & \text{otherwise.}\end{cases}\end{aligned}$$

II. $T \equiv (T_1 \circ T_2)$.

Here, T_1 and T_2 are standard terms, with $Ed(T_1) \cap Ad(T_2) = \emptyset$, i.e., for $n \geqq 1$, $0 \leqq i < j \leqq n$ we have $W_i(T_1)\,W_{k-i}(T_2) \cap W_j(T_1)\,W_{n-j}(T_1) = \emptyset$. Since B is regular for T, it is also regular for T_1, and for all $x \in X$, by $f^{T_2}(i) \subseteq f^T(i)$ for $i \in I(T_2)$, we have

$$\sum_{j\in f^{T_2}(i)} B_x^j(Y) \leqq 1.$$

Thus it suffices to show that condition a) of Definition (4.9.3) is satisfied for T_2 in order to show that B is also regular for T_2. This is trivial if $e \in Val(T_1)$ since then $A(T_2) \subseteq A(T)$.

If $e \notin Val(T_1)$, then $A(T_2) = f^T(i)$ for every $i \in E(T_1)$. Since T_1 is a standard term, $E(T_1) \neq \emptyset$ and for $x \in X$

$$\sum_{j\in A(T_2)} B_x^j(Y) = \sum_{j\in f^T(i)} B_x^j(Y) \leqq 1$$

for arbitrary $i \in E(T_1)$. Hence B is regular for both T_1 and T_2. 4.20.3, the induction hypothesis and (*) imply, for $n \geqq 1$,

$$\begin{aligned}&\sum_{j^1\cdots j^n\in W_n(T)}\prod_{i=1}^{n} B_{x_i}^{j^i}(y_i)\\ &= \mathfrak{W}[T_1, B]_e(e)\cdot \sum_{j^1\cdots j^n\in W_n(T_2)}\prod_{i=1}^{n} B_{x_i}^{j^i}(y_i)\\ &\quad + \sum_{\nu=1}^{n-1}\ \sum_{j^1\cdots j^\nu\in W_\nu(T_1)}\ \sum_{j^{\nu+1}\cdots j^n\in W_{n-\nu}(T_2)}\prod_{i=1}^{n} B_{x_i}^{j^i}(y_i)\\ &\quad + \mathfrak{W}[T_2, B]_e(e)\cdot \sum_{j^1\cdots j^n\in W_n(T_1)}\prod_{i=1}^{n} B_{x_i}^{j^i}(y_i)\\ &= \sum_{\nu=0}^{n} \mathfrak{W}[T_1, B]_{x_1\cdots x_\nu}(y_1\cdots y_\nu)\,\mathfrak{W}[T_2, B]_{x_{\nu+1}\cdots x_n}(y_{\nu+1}\cdots y_n)\\ &= \mathfrak{W}[T, B]_{x_1\cdots x_n}(y_1\cdots y_n).\end{aligned}$$

Furthermore,

$$\mathfrak{W}[T, B]_e(e) = \begin{cases} 1, & \text{if } e \in Val(T_1) \text{ and } e \in Val(T_2), \\ 0 & \text{otherwise} \end{cases}$$

$$= \begin{cases} 1, & \text{if } e \in Val(T), \\ 0 & \text{otherwise.} \end{cases}$$

III. $T \equiv \langle T_1 \rangle$.

Since T is a standard term, so is T_1 and $Di(T_1) = \emptyset$. Every $\lfloor X, Y \rfloor$-code which is regular for T is obviously also regular for T_1. Hence, by 4.20.3, the induction hypothesis, and (*) if $n \geqq 1$, then

$$W_n(T) = \bigcup_{m=1}^{n} \bigcup_{0=l_0<l_1<\cdots<l_m=n} W_{l_1-l_0}(T_1)\, W_{l_2-l_1}(T_1) \ldots W_{l_m-l_{m-1}}(T_1)$$

and

$$\sum_{j^1\ldots j^n \in W_n(T)} \prod_{i=1}^{n} B_{x_i}^{j^i}(y_i)$$

$$= \sum_{m=1}^{n} \sum_{0=l_0<\cdots<l_m=n} \prod_{\mu=0}^{m-1} \sum_{j^{l_\mu+1}\ldots j^{l_{\mu+1}} \in W_{l_{\mu+1}-l_\mu}(T_1)} \prod_{i=l_\mu+1}^{l_{\mu+1}} B_{x_i}^{j^i}(y_i)$$

$$= \sum_{m=1}^{n} \sum_{0=l_0<\cdots<l_m=n} \prod_{\mu=0}^{m-1} \mathfrak{W}[T_1, B]_{x_{l_\mu+1}\cdots x_{l_{\mu+1}}}(y_{l_\mu+1} \ldots y_{l_{\mu+1}})$$

$$= \mathfrak{W}[\langle T_1 \rangle, B]_{x_1\cdots x_n}(y_1 \ldots y_n) = \mathfrak{W}[T, B]_{x_1\cdots x_n}(y_1 \ldots y_n).$$

Furthermore, $e \in Val(T)$ and $\mathfrak{W}[T, B]_e(e) = 1$. Thus Lemma 4.20.6 is proved.

Now we construct the desired S-automaton. Let T be a standard term, B an $[X, Y]$-code regular for T and $\Psi = \mathfrak{W}[T, B]$ the PS-operator over $[X, Y]$ described by T and B. We choose two different elements $z_0, z_1 \notin Z(T)$ and put

$$Z = Z(T) \cup \{z_0, z_1\}$$

where, for all $z, z' \in Z$, $x \in X$, $y \in Y$ and a fixed $y_0 \in Y$,

$$H[z, x](y, z') = \begin{cases} B_x^j(y), & \text{if } z = z_1,\ j \in A(T) \text{ and } z' = A_j(\hat{T}) \\ & \quad \text{or } z \in Z(T),\ f_j^T(\hat{z}) \neq \emptyset \text{ and } z' = f_j^{\hat{T}}(z); \\ 1 - \sum_{j \in A(T)} B_x^j(Y), & \text{if } z = z_1,\ z' = z_0 \text{ and } y = y_0, \\ 1 - \sum_{j \in f^T(k)} B_x^j(Y), & \text{if } z \in Z(T),\ z \subseteq I_k(\hat{T}),\ z' = z_0 \\ & \quad \text{and } y = y_0, \\ 1, & \text{if } z = z' = z_0 \text{ and } y = y_0, \\ 0 & \text{otherwise.} \end{cases}$$

This definition is justified by Corollary 4.20.4. Since B is regular for T, we have $0 \leqq H[z, x](y, z') \leqq 1$ for all $z, z' \in Z$, $x \in X$, $y \in Y$. Thus for arbitrary $x \in X$

$$H[z_1, x](Y \times Z) = \sum_{j \in A(T)} H[z_1, x]\big(Y \times \{A_j(\hat{T})\}\big) + H[z_1, x](Y \times \{z_0\})$$
$$= \sum_{j \in A(T)} B_x^j(Y) + \Big(1 - \sum_{j \in A(T)} B_x^j(Y)\Big) = 1.$$

By 4.20.4, for each $z \in Z(T)$ there is exactly one $k \in I(T)$ with $z \subseteq I_k(\hat{T})$, therefore z is of the form $\{k_{i_1}, \ldots, k_{i_n}\}$ with $n \geqq 1$. We have $f_j^{\hat{T}}(z) \neq \emptyset$ if and only if there is an index ν with $j_\nu \in f^T(z)$ which holds if and only if $j \in f^T(k)$. Thus for $z \in Z(T)$ with $z \subseteq I_k(\hat{T})$ and every $x \in X$

$$H[z, x](Y \times Z) = H[z, x]\big(Y \times Z(T)\big) + H[z, x](Y \times \{z_0\})$$
$$= \sum_{j \in f^T(k)} B_x^j(Y) + \Big(1 - \sum_{j \in f^T(k)} B_x^j(Y)\Big) = 1.$$

is satisfied.

Consequently, the system $\mathfrak{C} = [X, Y, Z, H]$ is an S-automaton. We claim that the PS-operator Ψ generated in $\mathfrak{C}$ by $[\delta_{z_1}, N(T)]$ or $[\delta_{z_1}, N(T) \cup \{z_1\}]$, depending on whether $\Psi_e(e) = 0$ $\big($i.e., $e \notin Val(T)\big)$ or $\Psi_e(e) = 1$ (i.e., $e \in Val(T)$). For this it obviously suffices to show that for all $n \geqq 1$, $p = x_1 \ldots x_n \in W(X)$, $q = y_1 \ldots y_n \in W(Y)$

$$\Psi_p(q) = H[z_1, p]\big(\{q\} \times Z^{n-1} \cdot N(T)\big)$$

since $\Psi_p(q) = \mathfrak{W}[T, B]_p(q) = 0$ if $l(p) \neq l(q)$ and since $\mathfrak{C}$ cannot enter the state z_1 from any other state with positive probability. On the other hand, since $\mathfrak{C}$ cannot go from the state z_0 into any other state with a positive probability, we have

$$H[z_1, p]\big(\{q\} \times Z^{n-1} \cdot N(T)\big) = H[z_1, p]\big(\{q\} \times (Z(T))^{n-1} \cdot N(T)\big).$$

Let $z_2 \ldots z_{n+1} \in \big(Z(T)\big)^{n-1} \cdot N(T)$ with $H[z_1, x_1 \ldots x_n](y_1 \ldots y_n, z_2 \ldots z_{n+1}) > 0$.

Then, $H[z_1, x_1](y_1, z_2) > 0$ and $z_2 \in Z(T)$. Consequently, there is a $j^1 \in A(T)$ with $z_2 = A_{j^1}(\hat{T})$, $z_2 \subseteq I_{j^1}(\hat{T})$. For $i = 2, \ldots n$, $H[z_i, x_i](y_i, z_{i+1}) > 0$ and $z_{i+1} \in Z(T)$. Thus there is a j^i with $f_{j^i}^{\hat{T}}(z_i) \neq \emptyset$ and $z_{i+1} = f_{j^i}^{\hat{T}}(z_i)$, $z_{i+1} \subseteq I_{j^i}(\hat{T})$, and for the word $j^1 \ldots j^n$ we have $z_2 \ldots z_{n+1} = \delta^T(j^1 \ldots j^n)$. Furthermore, $z_{n+1} \cap E(\hat{T}) \neq \emptyset$, because $z_{n+1} \in N(T)$. By $z_{n+1} \subseteq I_{j^n}(\hat{T})$ there is an index i_n such that $j_{i_n}^n \in z_{n+1} \cap E(\hat{T})$, i.e., $j_{i_n}^n \in E(\hat{T})$ and $j_{i_n}^n \in z_{n+1} = f_{j^n}^{\hat{T}}(z_n)$. Consequently, $\big($since $z_n \subseteq I_{j^{n-1}}(\hat{T})\big)$ there is an i_{n-1} with $j_{i_n}^n \in f^{\hat{T}}\binom{n-1}{i_{n-1}}$ and $j_{i_{n-1}}^{n-1} \in z_n$. We can continue this process until we obtain an i_2 with $j_{i_2}^2 \in f^{\hat{T}}(z_2) = f^{\hat{T}}\big(A_{j^1}(\hat{T})\big)$. Therefore, there is an index i_1 with $j_{i_1}^1 \in A(\hat{T})$, $j_{i_2}^2 \in f^{\hat{T}}(j_{i_1}^1)$. For the numbers $i_1, \ldots, i_n$ we have

$$j_{i_1}^1 \in A(\hat{T}) \wedge \bigwedge_{\nu=1}^{n-1} j_{i_{\nu+1}}^{\nu+1} \in f^{\hat{T}}(j_{i_\nu}^\nu) \wedge j_{i_n}^n \in E(\hat{T}),$$

which implies (cf. Part I, Lemma 6.16, page 61), that $j^1_{i_1} \dots j^n_{i_n} \in Val(\hat{T})$, i.e. $j^1 \dots j^n \in Val(T)$. For every sequence $z_2 \dots z_{n+1} \in (Z(T))^{n-1} N(T)$ with

$$H[z_1, x_1 \dots x_n](y_1 \dots y_n, z_2 \dots z_{n+1}) > 0$$

we can thus find a word $j^1 \dots j^n \in Val(T)$ such that $z_2 \dots z_{n+1} = \delta^T(j^1 \dots j^n)$. By Lemma 4.20.5, δ^T establishes a one-to-one mapping of the set $W_n(T)$ into $(Z(T))^{n-1} \cdot N(T)$ for $n \geqq 1$. Thus

$$\begin{aligned} &H[z_1, x_1 \dots x_n](\{y_1 \dots y_n\} \times (Z(T))^{n-1} \cdot N(T)) \\ &= \sum_{j^1 \dots j^n \in W_n(T)} H[z_1, x_1 \dots x_n](y_1 \dots y_n, \delta^T(j^1 \dots j^n)). \end{aligned}$$

If $H[z_1, x_1 \dots x_n](y_1 \dots y_n, \delta^T(j^1 \dots j^n)) > 0$, then by the definition of H,

$$\begin{aligned} &H[z_1, x_1 \dots x_n](y_1 \dots y_n, \delta^T(j^1 \dots j^n)) \\ &= H[z_1, x_1](y_1, A_{j^1}(\hat{T})) \cdot H[A_{j^1}(\hat{T}), x_2](y_2, f^{\hat{T}}_{j^2}(A_{j^1}(\hat{T}))) \cdot \\ &\dots \cdot H[f^{\hat{T}}_{j^{n-1}}(\dots f^{\hat{T}}_{j^2}(A_{j^1}(\hat{T})) \dots), x_n](y_n, f^{\hat{T}}_{j^n}(f^{\hat{T}}_{j^{n-1}}(\dots f^{\hat{T}}_{j^2}(A_{j^1}(\hat{T})) \dots))) \\ &= \prod_{i=1}^{n} B^{j^i}_{x_i}(y_i). \end{aligned}$$

Hence by Lemma 4.20.6,

$$\begin{aligned} &H[z_1, x_1 \dots x_n](\{y_1 \dots y_n\} \times Z^{n-1} \cdot N(T)) \\ &= \sum_{j^1 \dots j^n \in W_n(T)} \prod_{i=1}^{n} B^{j^i}_{x_i}(y_i) = \mathfrak{W}[T, B]_{x_1 \dots x_n}(y_1 \dots y_n) \\ &= \Psi_{x_1 \dots x_n}(y_1 \dots y_n). \end{aligned}$$

This proves Theorem 4.20.

It follows from Theorem 4.20, that for every regular stochastic operator Φ over $[X, Y]$ (i.e., which can be generated in a Z-finite S-automaton), there is a standard term T and an $[X, Y]$-code B regular for T such that $\mathfrak{W}[T, B] = \Phi$ $(\Phi_e(e) = 1 \in \{0, 1\})$. Conversely, if a stochastic operator Φ over $[X, Y]$ is described by a standard term T and a code B regular for T (i.e., $\mathfrak{W}[T, B] = \Phi$), then Φ is regular. We obtain from 4.20 the existence of a Z-finite S-automaton $\mathfrak{C} = [X, Y, Z, H]$, of a state z_1, and of a set N with $z_1 \in N$ such that for $p \in W(X) \setminus \{e\}$, $q \in W(Y)$

$$\Phi_p(q) = H[z_1, p](\{q\} \times Z^{n-1} \cdot N).$$

For all $p \in W(X) \setminus \{e\}$ with $l(p) = n \geqq 1$

$$1 = \Phi_p(W(Y)) = H[z_1, p](W(Y) \times Z^{n-1} \cdot N) = F[z_1, p](N),$$

hence $F[z_1, p](Z \setminus N) = 0$ and

$$H[z_1, p]\big(\{q\} \times Z^{n-1} \cdot (Z \setminus N)\big) = 0$$

for all $p \in W(X) \setminus \{e\}$ with $l(p) = n$, $q \in W(Y)$, i.e.,

$$\Phi_p(q) = H[z_1, p](\{q\} \times Z^{n-1} \cdot N) = H[z_1, p](\{q\} \times Z^n) = V_{\mathfrak{C}}[z_1, p](q).$$

Thus we obtain

Theorem 4.21. *A stochastic operator Φ over $[X, Y]$ can be generated in a Z-finite S-automaton if and only if there is a standard term T and an $[X, Y]$-code B regular for T with $\mathfrak{W}[T, B] = \Phi$.*

If we compare our result with the corresponding result developed in the theory of regular events, we find it unsatisfactory because we were not able to find such operations on the PS-operators for which the class of regular PS-operators is the smallest set of PS-operators containing all regular elementary operators and closed under these operations. We shall show later (cf. § 9), that the class of regular PS-operators is not closed under either addition or iteration.

A further criterion for the regularity of an S-operator has been found by Arbib [6]. Unfortunately, this result is not illuminating from the point of view of the structure of the regularity property.

Theorem 4.22 (Arbib [6]). *A sequential S-operator over $[X, Y]$ is regular if and only if there is a finite set $\{\Phi_1, \ldots, \Phi_n\}$ of sequential S-operators such that Φ and every $\Phi_i^{x,y}$ of an S-operator Φ_i $\big(x \in X,\ y \in X,\ [\Phi_i]_x(y) > 0\big)$ from this set can be represented as a convex linear combination of the S-operators $\Phi_1, \ldots, \Phi_n$.*[1])

Proof: I. Let Φ be regular and $\mathfrak{C} = [X, Y, Z, H]$ a Z-finite S-automaton with $Z = \{1, 2, \ldots, n\}$ in which Φ is generated by the random state $\mathfrak{z} \in \mathfrak{Z}_Z$. Then the S-operators Φ_i with

$$[\Phi_i]_p(q) \underset{\text{Df}}{=} V_{\mathfrak{C}}[i, p](q) \qquad \big(\text{for } p \in W(X),\ q \in W(Y)\big)$$

for $i = 1, \ldots, n$ satisfy our requirements, since

$$\Phi_p(q) = \sum_{i=1}^{n} \mathfrak{z}(i)[\Phi_i]_p(q)$$

$$[\Phi_i^{x,y}]_p(q) = \sum_{j=1}^{n} \mathfrak{C}[i, x, y](j)[\Phi_j]_p(q)$$

$$(\text{for } 1 \leqq i \leqq n,\ x \in X,\ y \in Y \text{ with } [\Phi_i]_x(y) > 0)$$

are convex linear combinations of the desired type.

---

[1]) The S-operator Φ is written as a convex linear combination of the Φ_i if for some non-negative real numbers $\lambda_1, \ldots, \lambda_n$ with $\sum_{i=1}^{n} \lambda_i = 1$ and all $p \in W(X)$, $q \in W(Y)$

$$\Phi_p(q) = \sum_{i=1}^{n} \lambda_i [\Phi_i]_p(q).$$

II. Conversely, if $\Phi_1, \ldots, \Phi_n$ are S-operators with the above properties, such that

$$\Phi_p(q) = \sum_{j=1}^{n} \lambda_j [\Phi_j]_p(q)$$

and for $i = 1, \ldots, n,\ x \in X,\ y \in Y$ with $[\Phi_i]_x(y) > 0$

$$[\Phi_i^{x,y}]_p(q) = \sum_{j=1}^{n} \lambda_j^{i,x,y} [\Phi_j]_p(q)$$

are convex linear combinations, then we put

$$Z \underset{\text{Df}}{=} \{1, 2, \ldots, n\}$$

and for $i, j \in Z,\ x \in X,\ y \in Y$

$$H[i, x](y, j) \underset{\text{Df}}{=} \begin{cases} [\Phi_i]_x(y) \cdot \lambda_j^{i,x,y}, & \text{if } [\Phi_i]_x(y) > 0, \\ 0, & \text{otherwise.} \end{cases}$$

Here

$$H[i, x](Y \times Z) = \sum_{y \in Y,\, [\Phi_i]_x(y) > 0} [\Phi_i]_x(y) \sum_{j=1}^{n} \lambda_j^{i,x,y} = 1$$

since $\sum_{j=1}^{n} \lambda_j^{i,x,y} = 1$. Because of the convexity of these linear combinations, we obtain an S-automaton $\mathfrak{C} = [X, Y, Z, H]$. In $\mathfrak{C}$ the state i generates the S-operator Φ_i, i.e.,

$$V_{\mathfrak{C}}[i, p](q) = [\Phi_i]_p(q).$$

We prove this by induction on p where the initial step $p = e$ is trivial. The step from p to xp:

$$\begin{aligned} V_{\mathfrak{C}}[i, xp](yq) &= \sum_{j=1}^{n} H[i, x](y, j)\, V_{\mathfrak{C}}[j, p](q) \\ &= \begin{cases} \sum_{j=1}^{n} [\Phi_i]_x(y) \lambda_j^{i,x,y} [\Phi_j]_p(q), & \text{if } [\Phi_i]_x(y) > 0, \\ 0, & \text{otherwise} \end{cases} \\ &= \begin{cases} [\Phi_i]_x(y) [\Phi_i^{x,y}]_p(q), & \text{if } [\Phi_i]_x(y) > 0, \\ 0, & \text{otherwise} \end{cases} \\ &= [\Phi_i]_{xp}(yq). \end{aligned}$$

Now the random state $\mathfrak{z}$ of $\mathfrak{C}$ with $\mathfrak{z}(i) \underset{\text{Df}}{=} \lambda_i$ $(i = 1, \ldots, n)$ generates in $\mathfrak{C}$ the S-operator Φ; indeed

$$\begin{aligned} \Phi_p(q) &= \sum_{j=1}^{n} \lambda_j [\Phi_j]_p(\delta) \\ &= \sum_{j=1}^{n} \lambda_j V_{\mathfrak{C}}[j, p](q) = V_{\mathfrak{C}}[\mathfrak{z}, p](q). \end{aligned}$$

Hence the S-operator Φ is generated in a Z-finite S-automaton and is regular.

§ 5. Homogeneity

In this section we shall deal with a special class of S-automata and with those S-operators which can be generated in the automata of this class. We shall see that in this class the efficiency of Mealyautomata is indistinguishable from that of Moore automata, or the general type of automata. The class of homogeneous S-automata contains all Z-deterministic S-automata, and every homogeneous S-automaton can be equivalently embedded into a Z-deterministic one. However, there are Z-finite, homogeneous S-automata which cannot be equivalently embedded into any Z-finite, Z-deterministic S-automata.

Definition 5.1. Let $\mathfrak{C} = [X, Y, Z, H]$ be an S-automaton, $\mathfrak{z} \in \mathfrak{Z}_Z$ a random state of $\mathfrak{C}$.

(5.1.1) $\mathfrak{C}$ is called *homogeneous with respect to* $\mathfrak{z}$ if for all $p \in W(X)$, $x \in X$, $z \in W(Y)$ with $V_{\mathfrak{C}}[\mathfrak{z}, p](q) > 0$, $y \in Y$ the following condition is satisfied:

$$V_{\mathfrak{C}}[\mathfrak{z}, px]\big(W(Y) \cdot \{y\}\big) = \frac{V_{\mathfrak{C}}[\mathfrak{z}, px](qy)}{V_{\mathfrak{C}}[\mathfrak{z}, p](q)}.$$

(5.1.2) If $\mathfrak{z} = \delta_z$ is deterministic, then $\mathfrak{C}$ is called *homogeneous with respect to the state* z.

(5.1.3) $\mathfrak{C}$ is said to be *homogeneous* if it is homogeneous with respect to every state $z \in Z$.

(5.1.4) $\mathfrak{C}$ is called *strongly homogeneous* if it is homogeneous with respect to every random state $\mathfrak{z} \in \mathfrak{Z}_Z$.

If in step t the S-automaton $\mathfrak{C}$ has the state z with the probability $\mathfrak{z}(z)$ and in the course of the steps $t, \ldots, t + l(p)$ the word px is fed into $\mathfrak{C}$ then

$$V_{\mathfrak{C}}[\mathfrak{z}, px](Y^{l(p)} \cdot \{y\}) = V_{\mathfrak{C}}[\mathfrak{z}, px]\big(W(Y) \cdot \{y\}\big)$$

is the probability that in step $t + l(p)$ the signal y is put out by $\mathfrak{C}$ and

$$\frac{V_{\mathfrak{C}}[\mathfrak{z}, px](qy)}{V_{\mathfrak{C}}[\mathfrak{z}, p](q)}$$

is the probability that in step $t + l(p)$ $\mathfrak{C}$ puts out the signal y, provided that in the course of the steps $i, \ldots, t + l(p) - 1$ the word q has been put out. Thus, $\mathfrak{C}$ is homogeneous with respect to $\mathfrak{z}$ if and only if for all $p \in W(X)$, $x \in X$, $y \in Y$ the probability that in step $t + l(p)$ $\mathfrak{C}$ puts out the signal y under the condition that in the course of the steps $t, \ldots, t + l(p) - 1$ the word q is put out, is independent of q as long as this conditional probability exists (i.e., $V_{\mathfrak{C}}[\mathfrak{z}, p](q) > 0$).

Corollary 5.1.

1. $\mathfrak{C}$ is homogeneous with respect to $\mathfrak{z}$ if and only if for all $p \in W(X)$, $x \in X$, $y \in Y$ the quotient

$$\frac{V_{\mathfrak{C}}[\mathfrak{z}, px]\,(qy)}{V_{\mathfrak{C}}[\mathfrak{z}, p]\,(q)}$$

does not depend on q provided $V_{\mathfrak{C}}[\mathfrak{z}, p](q) > 0$.

2. Every strongly homogeneous S-automaton is homogeneous.

3. If $\mathfrak{C}$ is homogeneous with respect to $\mathfrak{z}$, or homogeneous or strongly homogeneous, then $ND(\mathfrak{C})$ is homogeneous with respect to $ND(\mathfrak{z})$ or homogeneous, or strongly homogeneous respectively.

Clearly, there are homogeneous S-automata which are not strongly homogeneous. As an example we consider the deterministic autonomous S-automaton $\mathfrak{C}_{14} = [\{x\}, \{0, 1\}, \{a, b\}, H_{14}]$ whose graph is represented in Fig. 26. If $\mathfrak{z}$ is an arbitrary random state of $\mathfrak{C}_{14}$, with $\mathfrak{z}(a), \mathfrak{z}(b) \neq 0$, then

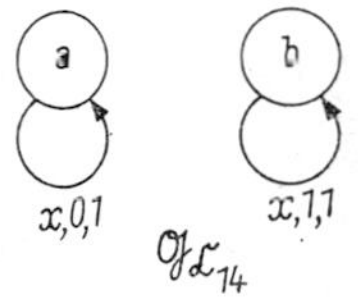

Fig. 26

$$\frac{V_{\mathfrak{C}_{14}}[\mathfrak{z}, xx](01)}{V_{\mathfrak{C}_{14}}[\mathfrak{z}, x](0)} = \frac{0}{\mathfrak{z}(a)} \neq 1 = \frac{\mathfrak{z}(b)}{\mathfrak{z}(b)} = \frac{V_{\mathfrak{C}_{14}}[\mathfrak{z}, xx](11)}{V_{\mathfrak{C}_{14}}[\mathfrak{z}, x](1)};$$

hence $\mathfrak{C}_{14}$ is not strongly homogeneous. That $\mathfrak{C}_{14}$ is homogeneous follows from Theorem 5.6, to be proved later.

Theorem 5.2. *Let* $\mathfrak{C} = [X, Y, Z, H]$ *be an S-automaton,* $\mathfrak{z} \in \mathfrak{Z}_Z$.

1. $\mathfrak{C}$ *is homogeneous with respect to* $\mathfrak{z}$ *if and only if for all* $p \in W(X)$, $x \in X$, $q \in W(Y)$, $y \in Y$ *the following equation is satisfied:*

$$V_{\mathfrak{C}}[\mathfrak{z}, px](qy) = V_{\mathfrak{C}}[\mathfrak{z}, p](q)\, G\big[F[\mathfrak{z}, p], x\big](y).$$

2. $\mathfrak{C}$ *is homogeneous with respect to* $\mathfrak{z}$ *if and only if for all* $p, r \in W(X)$, $q, s \in W(Y)$ *with* $l(r) = l(s)$ $\big($*or* $l(p) = l(q)\big)$

$$V_{\mathfrak{C}}[\mathfrak{z}, pr](qs) = V_{\mathfrak{C}}[\mathfrak{z}, p](q)\, V_{\mathfrak{C}}\big[F[\mathfrak{z}, p], r\big](s).$$

3. $\mathfrak{C}$ *is homogeneous with respect to* $\mathfrak{z}$ *if and only if for all* $p \in W(X)$, $q \in W(Y)$ *with* $V_{\mathfrak{C}}[\mathfrak{z}, p](q) > 0$

$$\mathfrak{C}[\mathfrak{z}, p, q] \sim F[\mathfrak{z}, p].$$

Proof: Ad 5.2.1. If $V_{\mathfrak{C}}[\mathfrak{z}, p](q) = 0$, then we also have $V_{\mathfrak{C}}[\mathfrak{z}, px](qy) = 0$, and then the above equality is trivial. Suppose $V_{\mathfrak{C}}[\mathfrak{z}, p](q) > 0$. Then

$$\frac{V_{\mathfrak{C}}[\mathfrak{z}, px](qy)}{V_{\mathfrak{C}}[\mathfrak{z}, p](q)} = V_{\mathfrak{C}}[\mathfrak{z}, px]\big(W(Y) \cdot \{y\}\big) = V_{\mathfrak{C}}[\mathfrak{z}, px](Y^{l(p)} \cdot \{y\}).$$

We shall show by induction on p that

$$V_{\mathfrak{C}}[\mathfrak{z}, px](Y^{l(p)} \cdot \{y\}) = G\big[F[\mathfrak{z}, p], x\big](y).$$

The initial step $p = e$ is trivial. The step from p to $x'p$:

$$
\begin{aligned}
&V_{\mathfrak{C}}[\mathfrak{z}, x'px](Y^{l(p)+1} \cdot \{y\}) \\
&= \sum_{z' \in Z} H[\mathfrak{z}, x'](Y \times \{z'\}) \cdot V_{\mathfrak{C}}[z', px](Y^{l(p)} \cdot \{y\}) \\
&= \sum_{z' \in Z} F[\mathfrak{z}, x'](z') \cdot G\big[F[z', p], x\big](y) \\
&= G\big[F[\mathfrak{z}, x'p], x\big](y).
\end{aligned}
$$

This proves 5.2.1. Proposition 5.2.3 follows from 5.2.2 and 2.7, while 5.2.2 can easily be proved by induction on r and using 5.2.1.

Corollary 5.3. Let $\mathfrak{C} = [X, Y, Z, H]$ be an S-automaton, $\mathfrak{z} \in \mathfrak{Z}_Z$.

1. $\mathfrak{C}$ is homogeneous with respect to $\mathfrak{z}$ if and only if for all $n \geqq 0$, $x_1, x_2, \ldots, x_n \in X$, $y_1, y_2, \ldots, y_n \in Y$

$$
\begin{aligned}
&V_{\mathfrak{C}}[\mathfrak{z}, x_1 \ldots x_n](y_1 \ldots y_n) \\
&= G[\mathfrak{z}, x_1](y_1) G\big[F[\mathfrak{z}, x_1], x_2\big](y_2) \ldots G\big[F[\mathfrak{z}, x_1 \ldots x_{n-1}], x_n\big](y_n).
\end{aligned}
$$

2. If $\mathfrak{C}$ is homogeneous with respect to $\mathfrak{z}$, $\mathfrak{C}' = [X, Y, Z', H']$, $\mathfrak{z}' \in \mathfrak{Z}_{Z'}$ and $\mathfrak{C}'$ is homogeneous with respect to $\mathfrak{z}'$, then $\mathfrak{z}$ and $\mathfrak{z}'$ are equivalent if and only if $G[\mathfrak{z}, x] = G'[\mathfrak{z}', x]$ and $F[\mathfrak{z}, x] \sim F'[\mathfrak{z}', x]$ for all $x \in X$.

3. $\mathfrak{C}$ is homogeneous with respect to $\mathfrak{z}$ if and only if for all $p \in W(X)$, $x \in X$, $Q \subseteq W(Y)$ with $V_{\mathfrak{C}}[\mathfrak{z}, p](Q) > 0$, $Y' \subseteq Y$

$$V_{\mathfrak{C}}[\mathfrak{z}, px](W(Y) \cdot Y') = \frac{V_{\mathfrak{C}}[\mathfrak{z}, px](Q \cdot Y')}{V_{\mathfrak{C}}[\mathfrak{z}, p](Q)}.$$

4. $\mathfrak{C}$ is homogeneous with respect to $\mathfrak{z}$ if and only if for all $pr \in W(X)$, $Q \subseteq W(Y)$, $S \subseteq Y^{l(r)}$

$$V_{\mathfrak{C}}[\mathfrak{z}, pr](Q \cdot S) = V_{\mathfrak{C}}[\mathfrak{z}, p](Q) \cdot V_{\mathfrak{C}}\big[F[\mathfrak{z}, p], r\big](S).$$

5. $\mathfrak{C}$ is homogeneous with respect to $\mathfrak{z}$ if and only if $\mathfrak{C}[\mathfrak{z}, p, Q] \sim F[\mathfrak{z}, p]$ for all $p \in W(X)$, $Q \subseteq Y^{l(p)}$ with $V_{\mathfrak{C}}[\mathfrak{z}, p](Q) > 0$.

6. If $\mathfrak{C}' = [X, Y, Z', H']$ is an S-automaton, $\mathfrak{z}' \in \mathfrak{Z}_{Z'}$ and $\mathfrak{z} \sim \mathfrak{z}'$, then $\mathfrak{C}$ is homogeneous with respect to $\mathfrak{z}$ if and only if $\mathfrak{C}'$ is homogeneous with respect to $\mathfrak{z}'$.

7. If $\mathfrak{C} \sim \mathfrak{C}'$, then $\mathfrak{C}$ is homogeneous if and only if $\mathfrak{C}'$ is.

8. If $\mathfrak{C} \approx \mathfrak{C}'$, then $\mathfrak{C}$ is strongly homogeneous if and only if $\mathfrak{C}'$ is.

9. Every homogeneous S-automaton is equivalent to a homogeneous S-Moore automaton with a deterministic marking function.

10. Every reduct, minim or strong reduct of a homogeneous S-automaton is again homogeneous.

11. Every minim or strong reduct of a strongly homogeneous S-automaton is strongly homogeneous.

Theorem 5.4. *Every (strongly) homogeneous S-automaton is equivalent to a (strongly) homogeneous S-Mealy automaton.*

Proof: Let $\mathfrak{C} = [X, Y, Z, H]$ be an S-automaton and $\mathfrak{C}_M = [X, Y, Z, F, G]$ be that S-Mealy automaton whose transition and output functions coincide with those of $\mathfrak{C}$.

If $\mathfrak{C}$ is homogeneous, then for all $z \in Z$, the state z of $\mathfrak{C}$ is equivalent to the state z of $\mathfrak{C}_M$. Indeed, for all $x \in X$, $y \in Y$

$$V_{\mathfrak{C}}[z, x](y) = G[z, x](y) = V_{\mathfrak{C}_M}[z, x](y),$$

and for $G[z, x](y) > 0$,

$$\mathfrak{C}[z, x, y] \sim F[z, x] = \mathfrak{C}_M[z, x, y],$$

which, by Theorem 2.9.2, implies our assertion. If $\mathfrak{C}$ is homogeneous, then $\mathfrak{C} \sim \mathfrak{C}_M$, hence $\mathfrak{C}_M$ is also homogeneous. If $\mathfrak{C}$ is strongly homogeneous, then it is also homogeneous, consequently, $\mathfrak{C} \sim \mathfrak{C}_M$ hence also $\mathfrak{C} \approx \mathfrak{C}_M$ and therefore $\mathfrak{C}_M$ is strongly homogeneous.

The following example shows that there are non-homogeneous S-Mealy automata.

Let $\mathfrak{C}_{15} = [\{x\}, \{0, 1\}, \{a, b\}, F_{15}, G_{15}]$ be the Mealy automaton with

$$F_{15}[a, x](z) = \begin{cases} \frac{3}{4}, & \text{if } z = a, \\ \frac{1}{4}, & \text{if } z = b, \end{cases} \qquad F_{15}[b, x](z) = \frac{1}{2} \text{ for } z \in \{a, b\},$$

$$G_{15}[a, x](y) = \begin{cases} \frac{1}{3}, & \text{if } y = 0, \\ \frac{2}{3}, & \text{if } y = 1, \end{cases} \qquad G_{15}[b, x](y) = 1 - G_{15}[a, x](y).$$

It is easy to verify that the following relations hold:

$$V_{\mathfrak{C}_{15}}[a, xx](00) = \frac{5}{36}, \qquad V_{\mathfrak{C}_{15}}[b, xx](00) = \frac{1}{3},$$

$$V_{\mathfrak{C}_{15}}[a, xxx](000) = \frac{1}{16},$$

$$V_{\mathfrak{C}_{15}}[a, xx](10) = \frac{5}{18}, \qquad V_{\mathfrak{C}_{15}}[b, xx](10) = \frac{1}{6},$$

$$V_{\mathfrak{C}_{15}}[a, xxx](110) = \frac{1}{6},$$

$$V_{\mathfrak{C}_{15}}[a, xx](11) = \frac{7}{8}.$$

We obtain

$$\frac{V_{\mathfrak{C}_{15}}[a, xxx](000)}{V_{\mathfrak{C}_{15}}[a, xx](00)} = \frac{9}{20} + \frac{9}{21} = \frac{V_{\mathfrak{C}_{15}}[a, xxx](110)}{V_{\mathfrak{C}_{15}}[a, xx](11)},$$

i.e., $\mathfrak{C}_{15}$ is not homogeneous with respect to a.

Theorem 5.5. *If* $\mathfrak{C} = [X, Y, Z, H]$ *is homogeneous with respect to* $\mathfrak{z} \in \mathfrak{Z}_Z$, *then it is also homogeneous with respect to every random state* $\mathfrak{C}[\mathfrak{z}, p, Q]$ *if* $p \in W(X)$, $Q \subseteq Y^{l(p)}$ *and* $V_{\mathfrak{C}}[\mathfrak{z}, p](Q) > 0$.

Proof: We have

$$\begin{aligned} & V_{\mathfrak{C}}\big[\mathfrak{C}[\mathfrak{z}, p, Q], rx\big](sy) \\ & = \frac{V_{\mathfrak{C}}[\mathfrak{z}, prx](Q \cdot \{sy\})}{V_{\mathfrak{C}}[\mathfrak{z}, p](Q)} \\ & = \frac{V_{\mathfrak{C}}[\mathfrak{z}, pr](Q \cdot \{s\}) \cdot V_{\mathfrak{C}}[F[\mathfrak{z}, pr], x](y)}{V_{\mathfrak{C}}[\mathfrak{z}, p](Q)} \\ & = \frac{V_{\mathfrak{C}}[\mathfrak{z}, p](Q)}{V_{\mathfrak{C}}[\mathfrak{z}, p](Q)} \cdot V_{\mathfrak{C}}\big[\mathfrak{C}[\mathfrak{z}, p, Q], r\big](s)\, V_{\mathfrak{C}}\big[F[\mathfrak{z}, pr], x\big](y) \\ & = V_{\mathfrak{C}}\big[\mathfrak{C}[\mathfrak{z}, p, Q], r\big](s)\, V_{\mathfrak{C}}\big[F[F[\mathfrak{z}, p], r], x\big](y) \\ & = V_{\mathfrak{C}}\big[\mathfrak{C}[\mathfrak{z}, p, Q], r\big](s)\, V_{\mathfrak{C}}\big[F[\mathfrak{C}[\mathfrak{z}, p, Q], r], x\big](y), \end{aligned}$$

because $F[\mathfrak{z}, p] \sim \mathfrak{C}[\mathfrak{z}, p, Q]$ and $\mathfrak{z} \sim \mathfrak{z}'$ implies $F[\mathfrak{z}, p] \sim F[\mathfrak{z}', p]$ (cf. 2.9).

Theorem 5.6. *Every Z-deterministic S-automaton is homogeneous.*

Proof: If $\mathfrak{C} = [X, Y, Z, H]$ is Z-deterministic, and $\delta = Det\big(ND(F)\big)$, then for $z \in Z$, $p, r \in W(X)$, $q, s \in W(Y)$ with $l(r) = l(s)$

$$\begin{aligned} V_{\mathfrak{C}}[z, pr](qs) &= V_{\mathfrak{C}}[z, p](q)\, V_{\mathfrak{C}}[\delta(z, p), r](s) \\ &= V_{\mathfrak{C}}[z, p](q)\, V_{\mathfrak{C}}\big[F[z, p], r\big](s), \end{aligned}$$

.e., $\mathfrak{C}$ is homogeneous.

Every observable S-Mealy automaton is Z-deterministic, hence homogeneous. There are S-Mealy automata, namely the non-homogeneous ones, which cannot be equivalently embedded into any observable S-Mealy automata. This makes it difficult to find a criterion for the generability of an S-operator in an S-Mealy automaton.

Theorem 5.7. *If* $\mathfrak{C} = [X, Y, Z, H]$ *is reduced, homogeneous and observable, then it is Z-deterministic.*

Proof: Let δ be the function from $Z \times X \times Y$ into Z, which belongs to $\mathfrak{C}$ by definition 1.2.3; furthermore $z \in Z$, $x \in X$. Then for $y, y' \in Y$ with $G[z, x](y) > 0$, $G[z, x](y') > 0$

$$\delta_{\delta(z,x,y)} = \mathfrak{C}[z, x, y] \sim F[z, x] \sim \mathfrak{C}[z, x, y'] = \delta_{\delta(z,x,y')}.$$

Since $\mathfrak{C}$ is reduced, we obtain $\delta(z, x, y) = \delta(z, x, y')$ for all $z \in Z$, $x \in X$, $y, y' \in Y$ with $[z, x, y], [z, x, y'] \in Dom(\delta)_0$. Hence the function δ does not depend on y and by 1.2.5 this means that $\mathfrak{C}$ is Z-deterministic.

Corollary 5.8.

1. Every observable homogeneous S-automaton has a Z-deterministic reduct.

2. For every homogeneous S-automaton $\mathfrak{C}$ there is an observable homogeneous S-automaton $\mathfrak{C}^*$ with $\mathfrak{C} \subsetneq \mathfrak{C}^*$ and $\mathfrak{C} \approx \mathfrak{C}^*$.

3. An S-automaton $\mathfrak{C}$ is homogeneous if and only if it is equivalently embedded into a Z-deterministic S-automaton which is weakly equivalent to $\mathfrak{C}$.

Proposition 5.8.1 is trivial, while 5.8.2 is implied by the proof of Theorem 2.10 as follows: The states of $\mathfrak{C}^*$ are the random states $\mathfrak{C}[z, p, q]$ (where $V_{\mathfrak{C}}[z, p](q) > 0$) of $\mathfrak{C}$. The state $\mathfrak{C}[z, p, q]$ of $\mathfrak{C}^*$ is equivalent to the random state $\mathfrak{C}[z, p, q]$ of $\mathfrak{C}$. By 5.5, $\mathfrak{C}$ is homogeneous with respect to $\mathfrak{C}[z, p, q]$ hence $\mathfrak{C}^*$ is homogeneous with respect to its state $\mathfrak{C}[z, p, q]$ and thus $\mathfrak{C}^*$ is homogeneous. By 2.17, $\mathfrak{C}^*$ has an observable reduct $\overline{\mathfrak{C}^*}$, which by 5.3.7 is homogeneous and by 5.7 is Z-deterministic. $\mathfrak{C} \subsetneq \mathfrak{C}^* \sim \overline{\mathfrak{C}^*}$ implies $\mathfrak{C} \subsetneq \overline{\mathfrak{C}^*}$ and $\mathfrak{C} \approx \mathfrak{C}^* \sim \overline{\mathfrak{C}^*}$ implies $\mathfrak{C} \approx \overline{\mathfrak{C}^*}$. Thus by 5.6 we have 5.8.3.

Theorem 5.9. *Let* $\mathfrak{C} = [X, Y, Z, H]$, $\mathfrak{C}' = [X', Y', Z', H']$ *be S-automata and* $[\xi, \eta, \zeta]$ *be a homomorphism of* $\mathfrak{C}$ *onto* $\mathfrak{C}'$.

1. *If* $\mathfrak{C}$ *is homogeneous with respect to* $\mathfrak{z}$, *then* $\mathfrak{C}'$ *is homogeneous with respect to* $\zeta(\mathfrak{z})$.

2. *If* $\mathfrak{C}$ *is homogeneous, or strongly homogeneous, so is* $\mathfrak{C}'$.

Proof: Let $\mathfrak{z}' \in \mathfrak{Z}_{Z'}$, $p' \in W(X')$, $x' \in X'$, further $\mathfrak{z} \in \mathfrak{Z}_Z$, $p \in W(X)$, $x \in X$ with $\zeta(\mathfrak{z}) = \mathfrak{z}'$, $\xi(px) = p'x'$. For every $q' \in W(Y')$, we put

$$\eta^{-1}(q') = \{q \mid q \in W(Y) \wedge \eta(q) = q'\}.$$

Hence,

$$\begin{aligned} V_{\mathfrak{C}'}[\mathfrak{z}', p'](q') &= V_{\mathfrak{C}'}[\zeta(\mathfrak{z}), \xi(p)](q') \\ &= \sum_{\eta(q)=q'} V_{\mathfrak{C}}[\mathfrak{z}, p](q) = V_{\mathfrak{C}}[\mathfrak{z}, p]\big(\eta^{-1}(q')\big). \end{aligned}$$

For all $q' \in W(Y')$ with $V_{\mathfrak{C}'}|[\mathfrak{z}', p'](q') > 0$ by 5.3.3 the quotient

$$\frac{V_{\mathfrak{C}'}[\mathfrak{z}', p'x'](q'y')}{V_{\mathfrak{C}'}[\mathfrak{z}', p'](q')} = \frac{V_{\mathfrak{C}}[\mathfrak{z}, px]\big(\eta^{-1}(q'y')\big)}{V_{\mathfrak{C}}[\mathfrak{z}, p]\big(\eta^{-1}(q')\big)} = V_{\mathfrak{C}}[F[\mathfrak{z}, p], x]\big(\eta^{-1}(y')\big)$$

is independent of q', i.e., $\mathfrak{C}'$ is homogeneous with respect to $\zeta(\mathfrak{z})$. This immediately implies both 5.9.1 and 5.9.2.

Corollary 5.10. Let $\mathfrak{C}, \mathfrak{C}'$ be S-automata and $\chi = [\xi, \eta, \zeta]$ be a homomorphism of $\mathfrak{C}$ onto $\mathfrak{C}'$. If the mapping η is one-to-one or χ is a strong homomorphism of $\mathfrak{C}$ onto $\mathfrak{C}'$, then $\mathfrak{C}$ is homogeneous with respect to $\mathfrak{z} \in \mathfrak{Z}_Z$, or homogeneous, or strongly homogeneous if and only if $\mathfrak{C}'$ is homogeneous with respect to $\zeta(\mathfrak{z})$, or homogeneous, or strongly homogeneous.

Definition 5.2. A sequential S-operator Φ over $[X, Y]$ is called *homogeneous* if for all $p \in W(X)$, $x \in X$, $y \in Y$ the quotient $\dfrac{\Phi_{px}(qy)}{\Phi_p(q)}$ is independent of $q \in W(Y)$ provided $\Phi_p(q) > 0$.

Corollary 5.11.

1. If Φ is the sequential S-operator generated in $\mathfrak{C} = [X, Y, Z, H]$ by $\mathfrak{z}$ then Φ is homogeneous if and only if $\mathfrak{C}$ is homogeneous with respect to $\mathfrak{z}$.

2. An S-automaton $\mathfrak{C}$ is homogeneous (or strongly homogeneous) if and only if every S-operator which can be generated by a state (or by a random state) in $\mathfrak{C}$ is homogeneous.

From Theorems 5.2, 5.3, 5.5, 5.8, 5.11 we immediately obtain

Theorem 5.12. *If Φ is a sequential S-operator over $[X, Y]$ then the following assertions are equivalent:*

1. *Φ is homogeneous.*

2. *For all $p \in W(X)$, $x \in X$, $Y' \subseteq Y$ the quotient $\dfrac{\Phi_{px}(Q \cdot Y')}{\Phi_p(Q)}$ is independent of $Q \subseteq Q(Y)$ provided $\Phi_p(Q) > 0$.*

3. *For all $p, r \in W(X)$, $Q \subseteq W(Y)$, $S \subseteq Y^{l(r)}$ we have: the quotient $\dfrac{\Phi_{px}(Q \cdot S)}{\Phi_p(Q)}$ is independent of Q provided $\Phi_p(Q) > 0$.*

4. *For all $p, r \in W(X)$, $Q \subseteq Y^{l(p)}$ with $\Phi_p(Q) > 0$, $S \subseteq Y^{l(r)}$,*

$$\Phi_{pr}(W(Y) \cdot S) = \frac{\Phi_{pr}(Q \cdot S)}{\Phi_p(Q)}.$$

5. *All the states of Φ are homogeneous.*

6. *For all $p \in W(X)$, $Q \subseteq Y^{l(p)}$ with $\Phi_p(Q) > 0$ we have $\Phi^{p,Q} = \Phi^{p,ND(\Phi_p)}$.*

7. *Φ can be generated in a Z-deterministic S-automaton.*

Thus a homogeneous S-operator has finitely many proper states if and only if it has finitely many states. If a homogeneous S-operator has only finitely many proper states, then obviously it can be generated in a Z-finite and Z-deterministic S-automaton. Indeed, the state $\Phi^{p,Q}$ or $\Phi^{p,q}$ is essentially only dependent on p, hence the transition function given in the construction for proving 4.7 is deterministic: $F_\Phi[\Phi^p, x](\Phi^{px}) = 1$. However, there are homogeneous S-operators which can be generated in Z-finite S-automata but have infinitely many states. As an example we choose the S-operator Φ over $[\{0, 1\}, \{0, 1\}]$ which is generated in the automaton $\mathfrak{C}_{12}$ by the state 1 (cf. page 295). We have seen that Φ has infinitely many states. If we show that Φ is homogeneous, this will also imply that $\mathfrak{C}_{12}$ is homogeneous, because the subautomaton of $\mathfrak{C}_{12}$ with the set of states $\{2, 3, 4\}$ is obviously Z-deterministic. We show that for all $p \in W(\{0, 1\})$, $x \in \{0, 1\}$, $y \in \{0, 1\}$, the quotient $\dfrac{\Phi_{px}(qy)}{\Phi_p(q)}$ does not depend on $q \in W(\{0, 1\})$ provided $\Phi_p(q) > 0$. We distinguish two cases:

I. $p = 0^m$, $m \geqq 0$.

Then $q = 0^m$ is the only word with $\Phi_p(q) > 0$, hence the quotient trivially has the required property.

2. $p = 0^n 1 r$, $n \geqq 0$, $r \in W(\{0, 1\})$.

If $n = 0$, then $q = 0^{l(r)+1}$ is the only word with $\Phi_p(q) > 0$ and the quotient obviously has the required property. If $n \geqq 1$, then $0^n 10^{l(r)}$ and $0^{n+1+l(r)}$ are all the words $q \in W(\{0, 1\}$, with $\Phi_p(q) > 0$. We have to show that for $x, y \in \{0,1\}$, $n \geqq 1$

$$\frac{\Phi_{0^n 1rx}(0^n 10^{l(r)} y)}{\Phi_{0^n 1r}(0^n 10^{l(r)})} = \frac{\Phi_{0^n 1rx}(0^{n+1+l(r)} y)}{\Phi_{0^n 1r}(0^{n+1+l(r)})}.$$

We have

$$\frac{\Phi_{0^n 1rx}(0^n 10^{l(r)} y)}{\Phi_{0^n 1r}(0^n 10^{l(r)})} = \frac{1}{1-\varepsilon^n} \cdot \begin{cases} 1-\varepsilon^n, & \text{if } y = 0, \\ 0 & \text{otherwise} \end{cases}.$$

$$= \begin{cases} 1, & \text{if } y = 0, \\ 0 & \text{otherwise} \end{cases}$$

$$= \frac{1}{\varepsilon^n} \cdot \left\{ \begin{matrix} \varepsilon^n, & \text{if } y = 0, \\ 0 & \text{otherwise} \end{matrix} \right\} = \frac{\Phi_{0^n 1rx}(0^{n+1+l(r)} y)}{\Phi_{0^n 1r}(0^{n+1+l(r)})}.$$

Theorem 5.13. *Let Φ be a homogeneous S-operator over $[X, Y]$ and for $p \in W(X)$ we put*

$$E_p \underset{\mathrm{Df}}{=} \{r \mid r \in W(X) \wedge \forall x \forall y (x \in X \wedge y \in Y \to \Phi_x^p(y) = \Phi_x^r(y))\}.$$

Then the following assertions are equivalent.

(1) *Φ can be generated in a Z-finite, Z-deterministic S-automaton by means of a state.*

(2) *The system of events $\mathfrak{E}^\Phi = \{E_p \mid p \in W(X)\}$ can be represented in a Z-finite, deterministic automaton.*

(3) *Φ has only finitely many states.*

Proof: The equivalence (1) $\leftrightarrow$ (3) can be easily verified if we observe that the states $\Phi^{p,Q}$ only depend on p.

Let Φ be generated in the Z-finite, Z-deterministic S-automaton $[X, Y, Z, H]$ by the state z^* and let $\delta = Det(ND(F))$. Then $\mathfrak{A} = [X, Z, \delta, z^*]$ is an initial Z-finite, deterministic outputless automaton in which, for every $p \in W(X)$ the event E_p is represented by the set

$$Z_p \underset{\mathrm{Df}}{=} \{z \mid z \in Z \wedge \forall x \forall y (x \in X \wedge y \in Y \to G[z, x](y) = \Phi_x^p(y))\}.$$

This can be shown as follows:

For $p, r \in W(X)$

$$r \in E_p \leftrightarrow \forall x \forall y (x \in X \wedge y \in Y \to \Phi_x^p(y) = \Phi_x^r(y)),$$

and for $x \in X$, $y \in Y$,

$$\Phi_x^r(y) = \frac{\Phi_{rx}(ND(\Phi_r) \cdot \{y\})}{\Phi_r(ND(\Phi_r))} = \Phi_{rx}(ND(\Phi_r) \cdot \{y\})$$

$$= V_{\mathfrak{C}}[z^*, rx](W(Y) \cdot \{y\}) = G[\delta(z^*, r), x](y),$$

hence

$$r \in E_p \leftrightarrow \forall x \forall y \big(x \in X \wedge y \in Y \rightarrow G[\delta(z^*, r), x](y) = \Phi_x^p(y)\big)$$
$$\leftrightarrow \delta(z^*, r) \in Z_p.$$

The system $\mathfrak{E}^\Phi$ is thus represented in $\mathfrak{A} = [X, Z, \delta, z^*]$ and consequently $\mathfrak{E}^\Phi$ is a finite system of events over the (possibly infinite) set X.

Suppose now that $\mathfrak{E}^\Phi$ is represented in the Z-finite, deterministic initial automaton $\mathfrak{A} = [X, Z, \delta, z^*]$. We can assume that $\mathfrak{A}$ is connected from the state z^*. If $p \in W(X)$ we choose $Z_p \subseteq Z$ such that E_p is represented in $\mathfrak{A}$ by Z_p. Then, for $p, r \in W(X)$ we have

a) $Z_p \cap Z_r \neq \emptyset \leftrightarrow Z_p = Z_r$,

b) $\bigcup_{p \in W(X)} Z_p = Z$.

This follows immediately from the fact that $E_p \cap E_r \neq \emptyset$ implies $E_p = E_r$, that $\mathfrak{A}$ is connected from the state z^* and $\bigcup_{p \in W(X)} E_p = W(X)$. By a) and b) the following definition is justified:

For $z \in Z$, $x \in X$, $y \in Y$,

$$G[z, x](y) = \Phi_x^p(y), \quad \text{if} \quad z \in Z_p.$$

Let F be that (stochastic) transition function for which $Det\big(ND(F)\big) = \delta$. Then $\mathfrak{C} = [X, Y, Z, F, G]$ is a Z-deterministic Z-finite S-automaton in which the state z^* generates the S-operator Φ. Indeed, for $x_1, \ldots, x_n \in X$, $y_1, \ldots, y_n \in Y$

$$V_{\mathfrak{C}}[z^*, x_1 \ldots x_n](y_1 \ldots y_n)$$
$$= G[z^*, x_1](y_1) \cdot G[\delta(z^*, x_1), x_2](y_2) \ldots G[\delta(z^*, x_1 \ldots x_{n-1}), x_n](y_n),$$

and for $i = 0, 1, \ldots, n-1$

$$x_1 \ldots x_i \in E_{x_1 \ldots x_i}, \quad \text{hence} \quad \delta(z^*, x_1 \ldots x_i) \in Z_{x_1 \ldots x_i}, \quad \text{i.e.,}$$
$$G[\delta(z^*, x_1 \ldots x_i), x](y) = \Phi_x^{x_1 \ldots x_i}(y).$$

Thus we obtain

$$V_{\mathfrak{C}}[z^*, x_1 \ldots x_n](y_1 \ldots y_n) = \Phi_{x_1}^e(y_1) \cdot \Phi_{x_2}^{x_1}(y_2) \ldots \Phi_{x_n}^{x_1 \ldots x_{n-1}}(y_n)$$
$$= \Phi_{x_1 \ldots x_n}(y_1 \ldots y_n).$$

This proves Theorem 5.13.

Theorem 5.14. *A (homogeneous) S-operator Φ can be generated in a Z-deterministic, Z-finite S-automaton if and only if it can be generated by a state in a Z-deterministic, Z-finite S-automaton.*

Proof: Suppose that Φ is generated by $\mathfrak{z}$ in $\mathfrak{C} = [X, Y, Z, F, G]$ where Z is finite, F is deterministic, and $Det\big(ND(F)\big) = \delta$. For every $p \in W(X)$ the state Φ^p of Φ is then generated in $\mathfrak{C}$ by the random state $F[\mathfrak{z}, p]$. Let

$$Z^* = \{\mathfrak{z}^* \mid \mathfrak{z}^* \in \mathfrak{Z}_Z \wedge \exists p(p \in W(X) \wedge \mathfrak{z}^* = F[\mathfrak{z}, p])\},$$

furthermore for $\mathfrak{z}^* = F[\mathfrak{z}, p] \in Z^*$, $x \in X$, $y \in Y$

$$F^*[\mathfrak{z}^*, x](\mathfrak{z}^{**}) = \begin{cases} 1, & \text{if } \mathfrak{z}^{**} = F[\mathfrak{z}, px], \\ 0 & \text{otherwise} \end{cases}$$

$$G^*[\mathfrak{z}^*, x](y) = G[\mathfrak{z}^*, x](y) \quad \big(= G[F[\mathfrak{z}, p], x](y)\big).$$

Since Φ is homogeneous, the state $F[\mathfrak{z}, p] \in Z^*$ generates the S-operator Φ_p in $\mathfrak{C}^* = [X, Y, Z^*, F^*, G^*]$, hence in particular Φ is generated in $\mathfrak{C}^*$ by the state $\mathfrak{z}$ of $\mathfrak{C}^*$. It remains to show that Z^* is finite when Z is. Now for $p \subset W(X)$, $z' \in Z$

$$F[\mathfrak{z}, p](z') = \sum_{z \in Z} \mathfrak{z}(z) \cdot F[z, p](z') = \sum_{\substack{z \in Z \\ \delta(z,p)=z'}} \mathfrak{z}(z).$$

Every word $p \in W(X)$ induces a single-valued mapping δ_p of Z into itself $\big(\delta_p(z) = \delta(z, p)\big)$, and every single-valued mapping ζ of Z into itself induces a random state $\mathfrak{z}_\zeta$ such that

$$\mathfrak{z}_\zeta(z') = \sum_{\zeta(z)=z'} \mathfrak{z}(z).$$

Consequently, there are at most as many members of Z^* as there are single-valued mappings of Z into itself. Since Z is finite, this indeed implies that Z^* also is $\big(\mathit{Card}\,(Z^*) \leqq (\mathit{Card}\,(Z))^{\mathit{Card}(Z)}\big)$.

Thus exactly those S-operators can be generated in Z-deterministic, Z-finite S-automata which are homogeneous and have only a finite number of states.

§ 6. Closure Operations for Stochastic Automata

For every S-automaton $\mathfrak{C}$ we can construct S-automata $\hat{\mathfrak{C}}$ and $\bar{\mathfrak{C}}$ which, in a certain sense, are the closures of the automaton $\mathfrak{C}$. $\hat{\mathfrak{C}}$ and $\bar{\mathfrak{C}}$ are closed under the generability of S-operators. Exactly those S-operators can be generated in $\bar{\mathfrak{C}}$ (and even by a state) which can be generated in $\mathfrak{C}$ by a random state while in $\hat{\mathfrak{C}}$ exactly those S-operators can be generated (even by a state) which are either generated by a state in $\mathfrak{C}$ or are states of such S-operators. The S-automaton $\bar{\mathfrak{C}}$ which we call the closure of $\mathfrak{C}$, has as its states the random states of $\mathfrak{C}$ while $\hat{\mathfrak{C}}$, the realizable closure of $\mathfrak{C}$, has as its states all $\mathfrak{C}$-realizable random states. With regard to the $\mathfrak{C}$-realizability of random states we shall consider a further equivalence concept between S-automata. We shall investigate to what extent the properties of an S-automaton $\mathfrak{C}$ are preserved by its closures $\hat{\mathfrak{C}}$, $\bar{\mathfrak{C}}$ as well as the connections between $\mathfrak{C}$, $\hat{\mathfrak{C}}$, $\bar{\mathfrak{C}}$ on one hand, and $\hat{\mathfrak{C}}$, $\hat{\hat{\mathfrak{C}}}$, $\bar{\mathfrak{C}}$, $\bar{\bar{\mathfrak{C}}}$ on the other.

Definition 6.1. Let $\mathfrak{C} = [X, Y, Z, H]$ be an S-automaton.
(6.1.1) A random state $\mathfrak{z}$ of $\mathfrak{C}$ is called *$\mathfrak{C}$-realizable* if there are $z \in Z$, $p \in W(X)$, $Q \subseteq Y^{l(p)}$ with $V_{\mathfrak{C}}[z, p](Q) > 0$ such that $\mathfrak{z} = \mathfrak{C}[z, p, Q]$.

(6.1.2) The S-automaton $\mathfrak{C}$ is called *realizable equivalently embedded into* $\mathfrak{C}' = [X, Y, Z', H']$ (notation: $\mathfrak{C} \underset{r}{\subsetneq} \mathfrak{C}'$), if for every $\mathfrak{C}$-realizable random state of $\mathfrak{C}$ there is an equivalent $\mathfrak{C}'$-realizable random state of $\mathfrak{C}'$.

(6.1.3) We call $\mathfrak{C}$ *realizable equivalent* to the S-automaton $\mathfrak{C}' = [X, Y, Z', H']$ (notation: $\mathfrak{C} \underset{r}{\sim} \mathfrak{C}'$), if $\mathfrak{C} \underset{r}{\subsetneq} \mathfrak{C}'$ and $\mathfrak{C}' \underset{r}{\subsetneq} \mathfrak{C}$.

Theorem 6.1. *Let* $\mathfrak{C} = [X, Y, Z, H]$, $\mathfrak{C}' = [X, Y, Z', H']$ *be S-automata.*

1. *If $\mathfrak{z}$ is $\mathfrak{C}$-realizable,* ($\mathfrak{z} = \mathfrak{C}[z, p, Q]$), $r \in W(X)$, $S \subseteq Y^{l(r)}$ *with* $V_{\mathfrak{C}}[\mathfrak{z}, r](S) > 0$, *then* $\mathfrak{C}[\mathfrak{z}, r, S]$ *is also (and* $\mathfrak{C}[\mathfrak{z}, r, S] = \mathfrak{C}[z, pr, QS]$).
2. $\mathfrak{C} \subsetneq \mathfrak{C}' \rightarrow \mathfrak{C} \underset{r}{\subsetneq} \mathfrak{C}'$,
3. $\mathfrak{C} \underset{r}{\subsetneq} \mathfrak{C}' \rightarrow \mathfrak{C} \lesssim \mathfrak{C}'$,
4. $\mathfrak{C} \sim \mathfrak{C}' \rightarrow \mathfrak{C} \underset{r}{\sim} \mathfrak{C}'$,
5. $\mathfrak{C} \underset{r}{\sim} \mathfrak{C}' \rightarrow \mathfrak{C} \approx \mathfrak{C}'$.
6. *$\mathfrak{C}$ is Z-deterministic if and only if every $\mathfrak{C}$-realizable random state is deterministic.*

Proof: Proposition 6.1.1 follows immediately from 2.8.3.
If $\mathfrak{z} = \mathfrak{C}[z, p, Q]$ is a $\mathfrak{C}$-realizable random state of $\mathfrak{C}$, furthermore z' is a state of $\mathfrak{C}'$ equivalent to z, then $\mathfrak{C}'[z', p, Q]$ exists and by Theorem 2.9 is equivalent to $\mathfrak{C}[z, p, Q]$. This implies 6.1.2 and 6.1.4. Suppose now $\mathfrak{z} \in \mathfrak{Z}_Z$ and for $z \in Z$ let $\mathfrak{z}'_z$ be a ($\mathfrak{C}'$-realizable) random state of $\mathfrak{C}'$ which is equivalent to $\delta_z = \mathfrak{C}[z, e, e]$. Then $\mathfrak{z}' \in \mathfrak{Z}_{Z'}$ if for $z' \in Z'$ we put

$$\mathfrak{z}'(z') = \sum_{z \in Z} \mathfrak{z}(z) \cdot \mathfrak{z}'_z(z'),$$

is a random state of $\mathfrak{C}'$ which is equivalent to $\mathfrak{z}$. Indeed, for $p \in W(X)$, $q \in W(Y)$

$$V_{\mathfrak{C}}[\mathfrak{z}, p](q) = \sum_{z \in Z} \mathfrak{z}(z) \cdot V_{\mathfrak{C}}[z, p](q) = \sum_{z \in Z} \mathfrak{z}(z) \cdot V_{\mathfrak{C}'}[\mathfrak{z}'_z, p](q) = V_{\mathfrak{C}'}[\mathfrak{z}', p](q).$$

This shows that Propositions 6.1.3 and 6.1.5 are valid. Assume that $\mathfrak{C}$ is Z-deterministic and $\delta = Det\big(ND(F)\big)$, furthermore $z \in Z$, $p \in W(X)$ with $l(p) > 0$, $Q \subseteq Y^{l(p)}$. Then we have for $z' \in Z$

$$H[z, p](Q \times Z^{l(p)-1} \cdot \{z'\}) = \begin{cases} V_{\mathfrak{C}}[z, p](Q), & \text{if } z' = \delta(z, p), \\ 0 & \text{otherwise}, \end{cases}$$

hence if $V_{\mathfrak{C}}[z, p](Q) > 0$,

$$\mathfrak{C}[z, p, Q](z') = \frac{H[z, p](Q \times Z^{l(p)-1} \cdot \{z'\})}{V_{\mathfrak{C}}[z, p](Q)} = \begin{cases} 1, & \text{if } z' = \delta(z, p), \\ 0 & \text{otherwise}. \end{cases}$$

Thus if $\mathfrak{C}$ is Z-deterministic, then every $\mathfrak{C}$-realizable random state is deterministic. Conversely, if this is the case then for $z \in Z$, $x \in X$, the random state $\mathfrak{C}[z, x, Y]$ is deterministic, hence for $z' \in Z$

$$\begin{aligned} F[z, x](z') &= H[z, x](Y \times \{z'\}) = \frac{H[z, x](Y \times \{z'\})}{V_{\mathfrak{C}}[z, x](Y)} \\ &= \mathfrak{C}[z, x, Y](z') \in \{0, 1\}, \end{aligned}$$

i.e. $F[z, x]$ is deterministic, and thus $\mathfrak{C}$ is Z-deterministic. This proves Theorem 6.1.

Let $\mathfrak{C} = [X, Y, Z, H]$ be an S-automaton. We denote by $\mathfrak{R}_{\mathfrak{C}}$ the set of all $\mathfrak{C}$-realizable random states of $\mathfrak{C}$ and by $\mathfrak{D}_Z$, the set of all δ_z for $z \in Z$. Obviously, $\mathfrak{D}_Z \subseteq \mathfrak{R}_{\mathfrak{C}} \subseteq \mathfrak{Z}_Z$. For $\mathfrak{z}, \mathfrak{z}' \in Z_Z$, $x \in X$, $y \in Y$ we put

$$\tilde{H}[\mathfrak{z}, x](y, \mathfrak{z}') = \begin{cases} \sum\limits_{z \in Z} \mathfrak{z}(z) \cdot H[z, x](y, z'), & \text{if } \mathfrak{z}' = \delta_{z'}, \\ 0 & \text{otherwise}. \end{cases}$$

Thus for all $\mathfrak{z} \in \mathfrak{Z}_Z$, $x \in X$ we have defined a discrete PM over $Y \times \mathfrak{Z}_Z$ which can have a non-zero value only for such pairs $[y, z'] \in Y \times \mathfrak{Z}_Z$ for which $[y, z'] \in Y \times \mathfrak{D}_Z$. Therefore, $\tilde{H}$ can be restricted to the sets $\mathfrak{R}_{\mathfrak{C}} \times X$ and $\mathfrak{D}_Z \times X$. The respective restrictions will be denoted by $\hat{H}$ and H_d. Thus we have defined for every S-automaton $\mathfrak{C} = [X, Y, Z, H]$ the S-automata

$$\tilde{\mathfrak{C}} = [X, Y, \mathfrak{Z}_Z, \tilde{H}], \quad \hat{\mathfrak{C}} = [X, Y, \mathfrak{R}_{\mathfrak{C}}, \hat{H}], \mathfrak{C}_d = [X, Y, \mathfrak{D}_Z, H_d].$$

Obviously, $\mathfrak{C}$ and $\mathfrak{C}_d$ are always Z-isomorphic. $\tilde{\mathfrak{C}}$ is called the *closure of* $\mathfrak{C}$, and $\hat{\mathfrak{C}}$ the *realizable closure of* $\mathfrak{C}$. This terminology will be justified by the following theorems.

Theorem 6.2. *Let* $\mathfrak{C} = [X, Y, Z, H]$, $\mathfrak{C}' = [X, Y, Z', H']$ *be S-automata.*

1. $\mathfrak{C} \subsetneq \tilde{\mathfrak{C}} \wedge \mathfrak{C} \approx \tilde{\mathfrak{C}}$,

2. $\mathfrak{C} \subsetneq \mathfrak{C}' \rightarrow \tilde{\mathfrak{C}} \subsetneq \tilde{\mathfrak{C}}'$, $\quad \mathfrak{C} \underset{\approx}{\subsetneq} \mathfrak{C}' \leftrightarrow \tilde{\mathfrak{C}} \subsetneq \tilde{\mathfrak{C}}'$,

3. $\tilde{\mathfrak{C}} \sim \tilde{\tilde{\mathfrak{C}}}$.

Proof: By the definition of $\tilde{H}$, for all $\mathfrak{z} \in \mathfrak{Z}_Z$, $p \in W(X)$, $q \in W(Y)$

$$V_{\mathfrak{C}}[\mathfrak{z}, p](q) = \sum_{z' \in Z} \mathfrak{z}(z') \cdot V_{\mathfrak{C}}[z', p](q) = V_{\tilde{\mathfrak{C}}}[\mathfrak{z}, p](q),$$

hence 6.2.1 is true. $\mathfrak{C} \subsetneq \mathfrak{C}'$ implies $\mathfrak{C} \underset{\approx}{\subsetneq} \mathfrak{C}'$ and the latter holds obviously if and only if $\tilde{\mathfrak{C}} \subsetneq \tilde{\mathfrak{C}}'$. 6.2.3 is an immediate consequence of the following theorem.

Theorem 6.3. *There is a strong Z-homomorphism of* $\tilde{\mathfrak{E}}$ *onto* $\mathfrak{E}$.

Proof: For $\tilde{\mathfrak{z}} \in \mathfrak{Z}_{\mathfrak{Z}_Z}$, $z \in Z$ let

$$\tilde{\zeta}(\tilde{\mathfrak{z}})(z) \underset{\mathrm{Df}}{=} \sum_{\mathfrak{z} \in \mathfrak{Z}_Z} \tilde{\mathfrak{z}}(\mathfrak{z}) \cdot \mathfrak{z}(z).$$

$\tilde{\zeta}(\tilde{\mathfrak{z}})$ is a random state of $\mathfrak{E}$. In particular, if $\mathfrak{z} \in \mathfrak{Z}_Z$, then $\tilde{\zeta}(\delta_{\mathfrak{z}}) = \mathfrak{z}$. Consequently, $\tilde{\zeta}$ is a single-valued mapping of $\mathfrak{Z}_{\mathfrak{Z}_Z}$, the set of states of $\tilde{\tilde{\mathfrak{E}}}$, onto $\mathfrak{Z}_Z$, the set of states of $\tilde{\mathfrak{E}}$. Furthermore, for $\tilde{\mathfrak{z}} \in \mathfrak{Z}_{\mathfrak{Z}_Z}$, $z^* \in Z$

$$\tilde{\mathfrak{z}} = \delta_{\delta_{z^*}} \leftrightarrow \tilde{\zeta}(\tilde{\mathfrak{z}}) = \delta_{z^*}.$$

Here the implication from left to right is obvious. Let

$$\sum_{\mathfrak{z} \in \mathfrak{Z}_Z} \tilde{\mathfrak{z}}(\mathfrak{z}) \cdot \mathfrak{z}(z^*) = \delta_{z^*}(z^*) = 1.$$

Then $\sum_{\mathfrak{z} \in \mathfrak{Z}_Z} \tilde{\mathfrak{z}}(\mathfrak{z}) = 1$, and for $\mathfrak{z} \in \mathfrak{Z}_Z, 0 \leqq \tilde{\mathfrak{z}}(\mathfrak{z}) \leqq 1$, $0 \leqq \mathfrak{z}(z^*) \leqq 1$. Thus for all $\mathfrak{z} \in \mathfrak{Z}_Z$

$$\tilde{\mathfrak{z}}(\mathfrak{z}) > 0 \rightarrow \mathfrak{z}(z^*) = 1.$$

Hence if $\tilde{\mathfrak{z}}(\mathfrak{z}) > 0$, then $\mathfrak{z} = \delta_{z^*}$, i.e., $\tilde{\mathfrak{z}}(\delta_{z^*}) = 1$, i.e., $\tilde{\mathfrak{z}} = \delta_{\delta_{z^*}}$. Suppose $\tilde{\mathfrak{z}}_1, \tilde{\mathfrak{z}} \in \mathfrak{Z}_{\mathfrak{Z}_Z}$, $x \in X$, $y \in Y$ are arbitrary. Then

$$\begin{aligned}
\tilde{\tilde{H}}[\tilde{\mathfrak{z}}_1, x](y, \tilde{\mathfrak{z}}) &= \begin{cases} \sum_{\mathfrak{z} \in \mathfrak{Z}_Z} \tilde{\mathfrak{z}}_1(\mathfrak{z}) \cdot \tilde{H}[\mathfrak{z}, x](y, \mathfrak{z}'), & \text{if } \tilde{\mathfrak{z}} = \delta_{\mathfrak{z}'}, \\ 0 & \text{otherwise} \end{cases} \\
&= \begin{cases} \sum_{\mathfrak{z} \in \mathfrak{Z}_Z} \tilde{\mathfrak{z}}_1(\mathfrak{z}) \cdot \sum_{z \in Z} \mathfrak{z}(z) H[z, x](y, z^*), & \text{if } \tilde{\mathfrak{z}} = \delta_{\delta_{z^*}}, \\ 0 & \text{otherwise} \end{cases} \\
&= \begin{cases} \tilde{H}[\tilde{\zeta}(\tilde{\mathfrak{z}}_1), x](y, \delta_{z^*}), & \text{if } \tilde{\zeta}(\tilde{\mathfrak{z}}) = \delta_{z^*}, \\ 0 & \text{otherwise} \end{cases} \\
&= \tilde{H}[\tilde{\zeta}(\tilde{\mathfrak{z}}_1), x]\big(y, \tilde{\zeta}(\tilde{\mathfrak{z}})\big).
\end{aligned}$$

This proves Theorem 6.3.

Corollary 6.4. An S-operator Φ can be generated (by a random state) in an S-automaton $\mathfrak{E}$ if and only if Φ can be generated in $\tilde{\mathfrak{E}}$ by a state.

Theorem 6.5. *Let* $\mathfrak{E} = [X, Y, Z, H]$, $\mathfrak{E}' = [X, Y, Z', H']$ *be S-automata.*

1. $\mathfrak{E} \subsetneqq \tilde{\mathfrak{E}} \;\wedge\; \mathfrak{E} \underset{r}{\sim} \tilde{\mathfrak{E}} \;\wedge\; \mathfrak{E} \approx \tilde{\mathfrak{E}}$,
2. $\mathfrak{E} \subsetneqq \mathfrak{E}' \rightarrow \tilde{\mathfrak{E}} \subsetneqq \tilde{\mathfrak{E}}'$ *and* $\mathfrak{E} \underset{r}{\subsetneqq} \mathfrak{E}' \leftrightarrow \tilde{\mathfrak{E}} \subsetneqq \tilde{\mathfrak{E}}'$,
3. $\tilde{\mathfrak{E}} \sim \hat{\tilde{\mathfrak{E}}}$.

Proof: Obviously, $\tilde{\mathfrak{E}}_d$ is a subautomaton of $\tilde{\mathfrak{E}}$ and Z-isomorphic to $\mathfrak{E}$. Consequently, $\mathfrak{E} \subsetneqq \tilde{\mathfrak{E}}$ and thus (by 6.1.2) we have $\mathfrak{E} \underset{r}{\subsetneqq} \tilde{\mathfrak{E}}$. Let $\mathfrak{z} = \tilde{\mathfrak{E}}[z, p, Q]$ be a $\hat{\mathfrak{C}}$-realizable random state of $\hat{\mathfrak{C}}$ such that $\mathfrak{z} \in \mathfrak{R}_{\mathfrak{C}}$, $p \in W(X)$, $Q \subseteq Y^{l(p)}$ and $V_{\hat{\mathfrak{C}}}[\mathfrak{z}, p](Q) > 0$. Further $\mathfrak{z} = \mathfrak{C}[z, r, S]$ for $z \in Z$, $r \in W(X)$, $S \subseteq Y^{l(r)}$ with $V_{\hat{\mathfrak{C}}}[z, r](S) > 0$. Now

$$V_{\hat{\mathfrak{C}}}[\mathfrak{z}, p](Q) = V_{\mathfrak{C}}\big[\mathfrak{C}[z, r, S], p\big](Q) > 0,$$

hence the random state $\mathfrak{C}[z, rp, SQ]$ exists and is trivially $\mathfrak{C}$-realizable. The state $\mathfrak{z}$ of $\hat{\mathfrak{C}}$ is equivalent to the random state $\mathfrak{z}$ of $\mathfrak{C}$, hence the random states $\hat{\mathfrak{z}} = \hat{\mathfrak{C}}[\mathfrak{z}, p, Q]$ and $\mathfrak{C}[\mathfrak{z}, p, Q] = \mathfrak{C}[z, rp, SQ]$ are also equivalent (cf. 2.8.3 and 2.9). Consequently, $\hat{\mathfrak{C}} \underset{r}{\subseteq} \mathfrak{C}$, hence $\hat{\mathfrak{C}} \underset{r}{\sim} \mathfrak{C}$, which by 6.1.5 also implies $\hat{\mathfrak{C}} \approx \mathfrak{C}$.

Proposition 6.5.2 can be easily verified (using 6.1.2). Instead of 6.5.3, we shall show below that there is a Z-homomorphism of $\hat{\hat{\mathfrak{C}}}$ onto $\hat{\mathfrak{C}}$.

Theorem 6.7. *There is a strong S-homomorphism of* $\hat{\hat{\mathfrak{C}}}$ *onto* $\hat{\mathfrak{C}}$.

To prove this we shall need the following

Lemma 6.7a. *For every nondeterministic* $\hat{\mathfrak{C}}$*-realizable random state* $\hat{\mathfrak{z}}$ *of* $\hat{\mathfrak{C}}$ *there exists exactly one* $\mathfrak{C}$*-realizable random state* $\mathfrak{z}^* \in \mathfrak{R}_{\mathfrak{C}}$ *such that for all* $z \in Z$

$$\hat{\mathfrak{z}}(\delta_z) = \mathfrak{z}^*(z).$$

Proof: Let $\hat{\mathfrak{z}} = \hat{\mathfrak{C}}[\mathfrak{z}', p, Q]$, where $\mathfrak{z}' \in \mathfrak{R}_{\mathfrak{C}}$, $p \in W(X)$, $Q \in Y^{l(p)}$ and $V_{\hat{\mathfrak{C}}}[\mathfrak{z}', p](Q) > 0$. Since $\hat{\mathfrak{z}}$ is not deterministic, $p \neq e$. (Otherwise we would have $\hat{\mathfrak{z}} = \delta_{\mathfrak{z}'}$.) For $z \in Z$

$$\hat{\mathfrak{z}}(\delta_z) = \frac{\hat{H}[\mathfrak{z}', p](Q \times \mathfrak{R}_{\mathfrak{C}}^{l(p)-1} \cdot \{\delta_z\})}{V_{\hat{\mathfrak{C}}}[\mathfrak{z}', p](Q)}$$

$$= \frac{H[\mathfrak{z}', p](Q \times Z^{l(p)-1} \cdot \{z\})}{V_{\mathfrak{C}}[\mathfrak{z}', p](Q)} = \mathfrak{C}[\mathfrak{z}', p, Q](z),$$

thus $\mathfrak{z}^* = \mathfrak{C}[\mathfrak{z}', p, Q]$ satisfies our requirements. Since $\mathfrak{C}[\mathfrak{z}', p, Q](Z) = \hat{\mathfrak{C}}[\mathfrak{z}', p, Q](\mathfrak{D}_Z) = 1$, we have $\hat{\mathfrak{C}}[\mathfrak{z}', p, Q](\mathfrak{z}'') = 0$, if $\mathfrak{z}'' \notin \mathfrak{D}_Z$. We define the mapping $\hat{\zeta}$ on the states $\hat{\mathfrak{z}}$ of $\hat{\hat{\mathfrak{C}}}$ as follows:

$$\hat{\zeta}(\hat{\mathfrak{z}}) = \begin{cases} \mathfrak{z}, & \text{if } \hat{\mathfrak{z}} = \delta_{\mathfrak{z}} \text{ is deterministic,} \\ \mathfrak{z}^*, & \text{if } \hat{\mathfrak{z}} \text{ is not deterministic, where } \mathfrak{z}^* \text{ is chosen} \\ & \text{according to 6.7a.} \end{cases}$$

Clearly, ζ is a single-valued mapping of $\mathfrak{R}_{\hat{\mathfrak{C}}}$ onto $\mathfrak{R}_{\mathfrak{C}}$.

Let $\hat{\mathfrak{z}}_1, \hat{\mathfrak{z}} \in \mathfrak{R}_{\hat{\mathfrak{C}}}$, $x \in X$, $y \in Y$. We distinguish two cases.

I. $\hat{\mathfrak{z}}$ is not deterministic.

Then $\hat{H}[\hat{\mathfrak{z}}_1, x](y, \hat{\mathfrak{z}}) = 0$, and there are $\mathfrak{z}, \mathfrak{z}' \in \mathfrak{R}_{\mathfrak{C}}$ with $\mathfrak{z} \neq \mathfrak{z}'$ and $\hat{\mathfrak{z}}(\mathfrak{z}) \cdot \hat{\mathfrak{z}}(\mathfrak{z}') > 0$. On the other hand, by 6.7a, $\hat{\mathfrak{z}}(\mathfrak{z}) > 0$ can only be satisfied if $\mathfrak{z} \in \mathfrak{D}_Z$. Therefore, we have states $z, z' \in Z$ with $\hat{\mathfrak{z}}(\delta_z) \cdot \hat{\mathfrak{z}}(\delta_{z'}) > 0$ and $z \neq z'$. Consequently, $\hat{\zeta}(\hat{\mathfrak{z}})(z) \cdot \hat{\zeta}(\hat{\mathfrak{z}})(z') > 0$ is not deterministic and $\hat{H}[\hat{\zeta}(\hat{\mathfrak{z}}_1), x]\big(y, \hat{\zeta}(\hat{\mathfrak{z}})\big) = 0 = \hat{H}[\hat{\mathfrak{z}}_1, x](y, \hat{\mathfrak{z}})$.

II. $\hat{\mathfrak{z}}$ is deterministic.

Let $\hat{\mathfrak{z}} = \delta_{\mathfrak{z}'}$, $\mathfrak{z}' \in \mathfrak{R}_{\mathfrak{C}}$. Then

$$\hat{\hat{H}}[\hat{\mathfrak{z}}_1, x](y, \hat{\mathfrak{z}}) = \sum_{\mathfrak{z} \in \mathfrak{R}_{\mathfrak{C}}} \hat{\mathfrak{z}}_1(\mathfrak{z}) \cdot \hat{H}[\mathfrak{z}, x](y, \mathfrak{z}')$$

$$= \begin{cases} \hat{H}[\mathfrak{z}_1, x](y, \mathfrak{z}'), & \text{if } \hat{\mathfrak{z}}_1 = \delta_{\mathfrak{z}_1} \text{ for a } \mathfrak{z}_1 \in \mathfrak{R}_{\mathfrak{C}}, \\ \sum_{z \in Z} \hat{\mathfrak{z}}_1(\delta_z) \hat{H}[\delta_z, x](y, \mathfrak{z}') & \text{otherwise} \end{cases}$$

$$= \hat{H}[\hat{\zeta}(\hat{\mathfrak{z}}_1), x]\big(y, \hat{\zeta}(\hat{\mathfrak{z}})\big).$$

Hence $[I_X, I_Y, \hat{\zeta}]$ is a strong Z-homomorphism of $\hat{\hat{\mathfrak{C}}}$ onto $\hat{\mathfrak{C}}$. We can similarly prove

Theorem 6.8. *There exists a strong Z-homomorphism of* $\hat{\hat{\mathfrak{C}}}$ *onto* $\hat{\mathfrak{C}}$.

Theorem 6.9.

1. If $\mathfrak{C}$ *is Z-deterministic, then* $\mathfrak{C}$ *and* $\hat{\mathfrak{C}}$ *are Z-isomorphic.*
2. $\mathfrak{C}$ *is Z-deterministic, if and only if* $\hat{\mathfrak{C}}$ *is.*
3. *If* $\mathfrak{C}$ *is Z-finite, and* $\mathfrak{C}$ *and* $\hat{\mathfrak{C}}$ *are Z-isomorphic, then both* $\mathfrak{C}$ *and* $\hat{\mathfrak{C}}$ *are Z-deterministic.*
4. $\mathfrak{C}$ *is homogeneous if and only if* $\hat{\mathfrak{C}}$ *is.*
5. $\mathfrak{C}$ *is strongly homogeneous if and only if* $\hat{\hat{\mathfrak{C}}}$ *is homogeneous.*

Proof: If $\mathfrak{C}$ is Z-deterministic, then by 6.1.6, every $\mathfrak{C}$-realizable random state is deterministic, hence $\mathfrak{R}_{\mathfrak{C}} = \mathfrak{D}_Z$. Then $[I_X, I_Y, \xi]$, where $\zeta(z) = \delta_z$ for $z \in Z$, is a Z-isomorphism of $\mathfrak{C}$ onto $\hat{\mathfrak{C}}$.

From 6.9.1 and 3.4.2 it follows that if $\mathfrak{C}$ is Z-deterministic, so is $\hat{\mathfrak{C}}$.

Conversely, if $\hat{\mathfrak{C}}$ is Z-deterministic, then for all $z \in Z$, $x \in X$, $\mathfrak{z} \in \mathfrak{R}_{\mathfrak{C}}$

$$\hat{F}[\delta_z, x](\mathfrak{z}) = \left\{ \begin{array}{ll} F[z, x](z'), & \text{if } \mathfrak{z} = \delta_{z'}, \\ 0 & \text{otherwise}, \end{array} \right\} \in \{0, 1\};$$

hence $F[z, x]$ is deterministic, i.e., $\mathfrak{C}$ is Z-deterministic.

If there exists a Z-isomorphism of $\mathfrak{C}$ onto $\hat{\mathfrak{C}}$, and Z is finite, then $\mathfrak{D}_Z = \mathfrak{R}_{\mathfrak{C}}$. Thus for $z \in Z$, $x \in X$, the random state $\mathfrak{C}[z, x, Y] = F[z, x]$ is deterministic. Therefore $\mathfrak{C}$ and by 6.9.2 also $\hat{\mathfrak{C}}$ is Z-deterministic.

The automaton $\mathfrak{C}$ is homogeneous if and only if it is homogeneous with resepct to every member of $\mathfrak{R}_{\mathfrak{C}}$ i.e., if and only if $\hat{\mathfrak{C}}$ is homogeneous. We can just as easily verify 6.9.5.

Proposition 6.9.3 is no longer valid if we drop the assumption that Z is finite. This can be illustrated by the example of the automaton $\mathfrak{C}_{16} = [\{x\}, \{y\}, \boldsymbol{nz}, H_{16}]$, where for $k, l \in \boldsymbol{nz}$

$$H_{16}[k, x](y, l) = \begin{cases} \frac{1}{2}, & \text{if } k \geqq 2,\ l \in \{0, 1\}, \\ 1, & \text{if } k = l \in \{0, 1\}, \\ 0 & \text{otherwise.} \end{cases}$$

Obviously, $\mathfrak{R}_{\mathfrak{C}_{16}} = \{\delta_i \mid i \in \boldsymbol{nz}\} \cup \{\mathfrak{z}_0\}$ with

$$\mathfrak{z}_0(k) = \begin{cases} \frac{1}{2}, & \text{if} \quad k \in \{0, 1\}, \\ 0 & \text{otherwise.} \end{cases}$$

Let, for $i \in \boldsymbol{nz}$

$$\zeta(i) = \begin{cases} \delta_i, & \text{if} \quad i \in \{0, 1\}, \\ \mathfrak{z}_0, & \text{if} \quad i = 2, \\ \delta_{i-1}, & \text{if} \quad i \geqq 3. \end{cases}$$

ζ is a one-to-one mapping of $\boldsymbol{nz}$ onto $\mathfrak{R}_{\mathfrak{C}_{16}}$. We shall show that for all $k, l \in \boldsymbol{nz}$

$$H_{16}[k, x](y, l) = \hat{H}_{16}[\zeta(k), x]\big(y, \zeta(l)\big),$$

i.e., that $[I_{\{x\}}, I_{\{y\}}, \zeta]$ is a Z-isomorphism of $\mathfrak{C}_{16}$ onto $\hat{\mathfrak{C}}_{16}$, although $\mathfrak{C}_{16}$ is not Z-deterministic. In the proof we distinguish two cases:

I. $l \in \{0, 1\}$.

$$\hat{H}_{16}[\zeta(k), x]\big(y, \zeta(l)\big) = \sum_{i \in \boldsymbol{nz}} \zeta(k)(i) H_{16}[i, x](y, l)$$

$$= \begin{cases} 1, & \text{if} \quad k = l, k \in \{0, 1\}, \\ \frac{1}{2} H_{16}[0, x](y, l) + \frac{1}{2} H_{16}[1, x](y, l), & \text{if} \quad k = 2, \\ H_{16}[k-1, x](y, l), & \text{if} \quad k > 2, \\ 0 & \text{otherwise} \end{cases}$$

$$= \begin{cases} \frac{1}{2}, & \text{if} \quad k \geqq 2, \ l \in \{0, 1\}, \\ 1, & \text{if} \quad k = l \in \{0, 1\}, \\ 0 & \text{otherwise} \end{cases}$$

$$= H_{16}[k, x](y, l).$$

II. $l \geqq 2$.

$$\hat{H}_{16}[\zeta(k), x]\big(y, \zeta(l)\big) = \begin{cases} 0, & \text{if} \quad l = 2, \\ \sum_{i \in \boldsymbol{nz}} \zeta(k)(i) H_{16}[i, x](y, l-1), & \text{if} \quad l > 2, \end{cases}$$

$$= 0 = H_{16}[k, x](y, l).$$

In contrast, we prove the following

Theorem 6.10. *If $\mathfrak{C}$ is reduced and Z-isomorphic to $\hat{\mathfrak{C}}$, then $\mathfrak{C}$ is Z-deterministic.*

Proof: It suffices to show that $\mathfrak{R}_{\mathfrak{C}} = \mathfrak{D}_Z$. Let $[I_X, I_Y, \zeta]$ be a Z-isomorphism of $\mathfrak{C}$ onto $\hat{\mathfrak{C}}$, furthermore $\mathfrak{z} \in R_{\mathfrak{C}}$. Then there is a $z \in Z$ with $\zeta(z) = \mathfrak{z}$ and a

$z^* \in Z$ with $\zeta(z^*) = \delta_z$. Consequently, $z \sim \mathfrak{z}$, $z^* \sim \delta_z$ and by $\delta_z \sim z$, hence $z^* \sim z$. Since $\mathfrak{C}$ is reduced, this implies $z^* = z$ and hence $\delta_z = \zeta(z^*) = \zeta(z) = \mathfrak{z}$. Therefore, every $\mathfrak{z} \in \mathfrak{R}_{\mathfrak{C}}$ is deterministic, and thus $\mathfrak{R}_{\mathfrak{C}} = \mathfrak{D}_Z$.

Theorem 6.11.

1. *$\mathfrak{C}$ is an S-Moore automaton if and only if $\hat{\mathfrak{C}}$ and $\tilde{\mathfrak{C}}$ are.*
2. *If $\hat{\mathfrak{C}}$ or $\tilde{\mathfrak{C}}$ is a S-Mealy automaton, then so is $\mathfrak{C}$.*
3. *If $\hat{\mathfrak{C}}$ or $\tilde{\mathfrak{C}}$ is Y-deterministic, then so is $\mathfrak{C}$.*
4. *If $\hat{\mathfrak{C}}$ or $\tilde{\mathfrak{C}}$ is observable, then so is $\mathfrak{C}$.*

Proof: If $\mathfrak{C} = [X, Y, Z, F, M]$ is a Moore automaton, then for $\mathfrak{z} \in \mathfrak{Z}_Z$

$$\tilde{M}[\mathfrak{z}] \underset{\text{Df}}{=} \begin{cases} M[z], & \text{if } \mathfrak{z} = \delta_z, \\ \Psi & \text{otherwise,} \end{cases}$$

where Ψ is an arbitrary discrete PM over Y. Obviously,

$$\tilde{F}[\mathfrak{z}, x](\mathfrak{z}') = \begin{cases} F[\mathfrak{z}, x](z'), & \text{if } \mathfrak{z}' = \delta_{z'}, \\ 0 & \text{otherwise,} \end{cases}$$

and consequently,

$$\tilde{H}[\mathfrak{z}, x](y, \mathfrak{z}') = \begin{cases} \sum_{z \in Z} \mathfrak{z}(z) \cdot F[z, x](z') M[z'](y), & \text{if } \mathfrak{z}' = \delta_{z'}, \\ 0 & \text{otherwise} \end{cases}$$

$$= \begin{cases} \tilde{F}[\mathfrak{z}, x](\delta_{z'}) \tilde{M}[\delta_{z'}](y), & \text{if } \mathfrak{z}' = \delta_{z'}, \\ 0 & \text{otherwise} \end{cases}$$

$$= \tilde{F}[\mathfrak{z}, x](\mathfrak{z}') \tilde{M}[\mathfrak{z}'](y).$$

Thus $\tilde{\mathfrak{C}}$ and $\hat{\mathfrak{C}}$ (as a subautomaton of $\tilde{\mathfrak{C}}$) are also S-Moore automata.

Conversely, if $\hat{\mathfrak{C}}$ is a Moore automaton $[X, Y, R_{\mathfrak{C}}, \hat{F}, \hat{M}]$ then for $z \in Z$

$$M[z] \underset{\text{Df}}{=} \hat{M}[\delta_z],$$

and we obtain

$$H[z, x](y, z') = \hat{H}[\delta_z, x](y, \delta_{z'}) = \hat{F}[\delta_z, x](\delta_{z'}) \hat{M}[\delta_{z'}](y)$$
$$= F[z, x](z') M[z'](y);$$

hence $\mathfrak{C}$ is an S-Moore automaton. The proof of 6.11.2, 6.11.3 and 6.11.4 are carried out similarly, by applying

$$\hat{G}[\delta_z, x](y) = G[z, x](y).$$

If $\mathfrak{C}$ is an S-Mealy automaton, then in general, $\tilde{\mathfrak{C}}$ is not. Otherwise, every S-operator, which can be generated by a random state in an S-Mealy automaton $\mathfrak{C}$, could also be generated by a state in an S-Mealy automaton (namely in $\tilde{\mathfrak{C}}$) which is in contradiction to 4.11 and 4.12. The fact that $\hat{\mathfrak{C}}$ does not have to be an S-Mealy automaton either, can be clarified by the following example. Consider $\mathfrak{C}_{17} = [\{x\}, \{0, 1\}, \{a, b\}, F_{17}, G_{17}]$ where

$$F_{17}[a, x](z') = \frac{1}{2}, \qquad F_{17}[b, x](z') = \begin{cases} \frac{1}{3}, & \text{if } z' = a, \\ \frac{2}{3}, & \text{if } z' = b, \end{cases}$$

$$G_{17}[a,x](y) = \begin{cases} \frac{1}{3}, & \text{if } y = 0, \\ \frac{2}{3}, & \text{if } y = 1, \end{cases} \qquad G_{17}[b,x](y) = \begin{cases} \frac{2}{3}, & \text{if } y = 0, \\ \frac{1}{3}, & \text{if } y = 1. \end{cases}$$

Here,

$$\mathfrak{C}_{17}[a, xx, 00](z') = \begin{cases} \frac{7}{18}, & \text{if } z' = a, \\ \frac{11}{18}, & \text{if } z' = b, \end{cases}$$

further,

$$\hat{H}_{17}\big[\mathfrak{C}_{17}[a, xx, 00], x\big](0, \delta_a) = \frac{5 \cdot 13}{2^2 \cdot 3^4},$$

$$\hat{F}_{17}\big[\mathfrak{C}_{17}[a, xx, 00], x\big](\delta_a) = \frac{43}{2^2 \cdot 3^3},$$

$$\hat{G}_{17}\big[\mathfrak{C}_{17}[a, xx, 00], x\big](0) = \frac{29}{2 \cdot 3^3}.$$

Obviously,

$$\hat{H}_{17}\big[\mathfrak{C}_{17}[a, xx, 00], x\big](0, \delta_a) \neq \hat{F}_{17}\big[\mathfrak{C}_{17}[a, xx, 00], x\big](\delta_a) \cdot \hat{G}_{17}\big[\mathfrak{C}_{17}[a, xx, 00], x\big](0);$$

hence $\hat{\mathfrak{C}}_{17}$ is not an S-Mealy automaton. That $\hat{\mathfrak{C}}$ or $\tilde{\mathfrak{C}}$ do not have to be Y-deterministic when $\mathfrak{C}$ is, is obvious. Just as easily, we can show that the converse of 6.11.4 is false.

Theorem 6.12. *Let* $\mathfrak{C} = [X, Y, Z, H]$, $\mathfrak{C}' = [X', Y', Z', H']$ *be S-automata.*

1. *If there is a strong homomorphism of* $\mathfrak{C}$ *onto* $\mathfrak{C}'$, *then there also exist strong homomorphisms of* $\tilde{\mathfrak{C}}$ *onto* $\tilde{\mathfrak{C}}'$ *and of* $\hat{\mathfrak{C}}$ *onto* $\hat{\mathfrak{C}}'$.

2. *If there is a homomorphism of* $\mathfrak{C}$ *onto* $\mathfrak{C}'$, *then there exists a homomorphism of* $\tilde{\mathfrak{C}}$ *onto* $\tilde{\mathfrak{C}}'$.

3. *If there is an* $[X, Z]$*-homomorphism of* $\mathfrak{C}$ *onto* $\mathfrak{C}'$, *then there is an* $[X, Z]$*-homomorphism of* $\hat{\mathfrak{C}}$ *onto* $\hat{\mathfrak{C}}'$.

Proof: Let $[\xi, \eta, \zeta]$ be a strong homomorphism of $\mathfrak{C}$ onto $\mathfrak{C}'$. For $\mathfrak{z} \in \mathfrak{Z}_Z$, $z' \in Z'$ we put

$$\tilde{\zeta}(\mathfrak{z})(z') = \sum_{z \in Z} \mathfrak{z}(z) \cdot \delta_{\zeta(z)}(z').$$

Clearly, $\tilde{\zeta}$ is a single-valued mapping of $\mathfrak{Z}_Z$ onto $\mathfrak{Z}_{Z'}$ which assigns to every element of $\mathfrak{D}_Z$ an element of $\mathfrak{D}_{Z'}$. We claim that for all $\mathfrak{z}, \mathfrak{z}^* \in \mathfrak{Z}_Z$, $x \in X$, $y \in Y$ the following relation is satisfied:

$$\tilde{H}[\mathfrak{z}, x](y, \mathfrak{z}^*) = \tilde{H}'[\tilde{\zeta}(\mathfrak{z}), \xi(x)]\big(\eta(y), \tilde{\zeta}(\mathfrak{z}^*)\big).$$

In the proof we distinguish two cases:

I. $\mathfrak{z}^*$ is deterministic.

Let $z^* \in Z$ with $\mathfrak{z}^* = \delta_{z^*}$. Then $\tilde{\zeta}(z^*) = \delta_{\zeta(z^*)}$ and we obtain

$$\begin{aligned} H[\mathfrak{z}, x](y, \delta_{z^*}) &= \sum_{z \in Z} \mathfrak{z}(z) \cdot H[z, x](y, z^*) \\ &= \sum_{z \in Z} \mathfrak{z}(z) \cdot H'[\zeta(z), \xi(x)]\big(\eta(y), \zeta(z^*)\big) \\ &= \sum_{z \in Z} \mathfrak{z}(z) \sum_{z' \in Z'} \delta_{\zeta(z)}(z') H'[z', \xi(x)]\big(\eta(y), \zeta(z^*)\big) \\ &= \sum_{z' \in Z'} \tilde{\zeta}(\mathfrak{z})(z') H'[z', \xi(x)]\big(\eta(y), \zeta(z^*)\big) \\ &= \tilde{H}'[\tilde{\zeta}(\mathfrak{z}), \xi(x)]\big(\eta(y), \tilde{\zeta}(\mathfrak{z}^*)\big). \end{aligned}$$

II. $\mathfrak{z}^*$ is not deterministic.

Then the left hand side of our equation is equal to zero. Suppose that

$$\tilde{H}'[\tilde{\zeta}(\mathfrak{z}), \xi(x)]\big(\eta(y), \tilde{\zeta}(\mathfrak{z}^*)\big) > 0.$$

Then $\zeta(\mathfrak{z}^*)$ is deterministic. Let $\zeta(\mathfrak{z}^*) = \delta_{z'} \in \mathfrak{D}_{Z'}$. Then

$$1 = \tilde{\zeta}(\mathfrak{z}^*)(z') = \sum_{z \in Z, z' = \zeta(z)} \mathfrak{z}^*(z).$$

We have $\sum_{z'' \in Z'} \tilde{\zeta}(\mathfrak{z})(z'') H'[z'', \xi(x)]\big(\eta(y), z'\big) > 0$; thus there is a $z'' \in Z'$ with $\tilde{\zeta}(\mathfrak{z})(z'') > 0$ and $H'[z'', \xi(x)]\big(\eta(y), z'\big) > 0$; further there exist states $z^*, z_1, z_2 \in Z$ with

$$\begin{aligned} &z_1 \neq z_2, \ \mathfrak{z}^*(z_1) > 0, \ \mathfrak{z}^*(z_2) > 0, \ \zeta(z_1) = z' = \zeta(z_2), \ \zeta(z^*) = z'', \\ &H[z^*, x](y, z_1) = H'[z'', \xi(x)]\big(\eta(y), z'\big) > 0, \\ &H[z^*, x](y, z_2) = H'[z'', \xi(x)]\big(\eta(y), z'\big) > 0, \end{aligned}$$

which is in contradiction to Theorem 3.2. Thus the left hand side of our equality must also be 0. Consequently, this equality is always satisfied and therefore $[\xi, \eta, \tilde{\zeta}]$ is a strong homomorphism of $\tilde{\mathfrak{C}}$ onto $\tilde{\mathfrak{C}}'$.

Now we show that the mapping $\hat{\zeta}$ maps the set $\mathfrak{R}_{\mathfrak{C}}$ onto $\mathfrak{R}_{\mathfrak{C}'}$ and therefore $[\xi, \eta, \hat{\zeta}]$ is a strong homomorphism of $\hat{\mathfrak{C}}$ onto $\mathfrak{C}'$ where $\hat{\zeta}$ denotes the restriction of $\hat{\zeta}$ onto $\mathfrak{R}_{\mathfrak{C}}$. It suffices to show that for

$$z_1 \in Z, \ p \in W(X), \ Q \subseteq Y^{l(p)} \text{ with } V_{\mathfrak{C}}[z_1, p](Q) > 0$$

$$\hat{\zeta}(\mathfrak{C}[z, p, Q]) = \mathfrak{C}'[\zeta(z), \xi(p), \eta(Q)].$$

If $p = e$ this is trivial. Let $p = x_1 \ldots x_n \in W(X)$, $q = y_1 \ldots y_n \in W(Y)$, $n \geqq 1$.

Then for $z' \in Z'$

$$\sum_{\zeta(z^*)=z'} H[z_1, p](\{q\} \times Z^{n-1} \cdot \{z^*\})$$
$$= \sum_{\substack{z_2, \ldots, z_n \in Z \\ \zeta(z^*)=z'}} \left(\prod_{i=1}^{n-1} H[z_i, x_i](y_i, z_{i+1}) \right) \cdot H[z_n, x_n](y_n, z^*).$$

By 3.2 $H[z_n, x_n](y_n, z^*) > 0$ can only be satisfied if z^* is the single element of Z, which is mapped by ζ onto z'. Therefore,

$$H[z_n, x_n](y_n, z^*) = H'[\zeta(z_n), \xi(x_n)](\eta(y_n), z'),$$

and for $i = 1, \ldots, n-1$, $H[z_i, x_i](y_i, z_{i+1}) > 0$ can only hold if z_{i+1} is the single element of Z which is mapped by ζ onto $\zeta(z_{i+1})$. Thence

$$H[z_i, x_i](y_i, z_{i+1}) = H'[\zeta(z_i), \xi(x_i)](\eta(y_i), \zeta(z_{i+1})).$$

Thus we obtain

$$\sum_{\zeta(z^*)=z'} H[z_1, p](\{q\} \times Z^{n-1} \cdot \{z^*\}) = H'[\zeta(z_1), \xi(p)](\{\eta(q)\} \times W(Z') \cdot \{z'\}).$$

Obviously,

$$\sum_{q \in Q} H'[\zeta(z_1), \xi(p)](\{\eta(q)\} \times W(Z') \cdot \{z'\})$$
$$\geqq \sum_{q' \in \eta(Q)} H'[\zeta(z_1), \xi(p)](\{q'\} \times W(Z') \cdot \{z'\}).$$

Suppose that the left hand side of this inequality is bigger than the right hand side. Then by 3.9 we would have

$$\begin{aligned} V_{\mathfrak{C}'}[\zeta(z_1), \xi(p)](\eta(Q)) &= \sum_{z' \in Z'} \sum_{q' \in \eta(Q)} H'[\zeta(z_1), \xi(p)](\{q'\} \times W(Z') \cdot \{z'\}) \\ &< \sum_{z' \in Z'} \sum_{q \in Q} H'[\zeta(z_1), \xi(p)](\{\eta(q)\} \times W(Z') \cdot \{z'\}) \\ &= \sum_{q \in Q} V_{\mathfrak{C}'}[\zeta(z_1), \xi(p)](\eta(q)) = \sum_{q \in Q} V_{\mathfrak{C}}[z_1, p](q) \\ &= V_{\mathfrak{C}}[z_1, p](Q), \end{aligned}$$

which is in contradiction to 3.10.3. Thus for $z' \in Z'$

$$\tilde{\xi}(\mathfrak{C}[z_1, p, Q])(z') = \frac{\sum_{\zeta(z^*)=z'} H[z_1, p](Q \times W(Z) \cdot \{z^*\})}{V_{\mathfrak{C}}[z_1, p](Q)}$$

$$= \frac{H'[\zeta(z_1), \xi(p)](\eta(Q) \times W(Z') \cdot \{z'\})}{V_{\mathfrak{C}'}[\zeta(z_1), \xi(p)](\eta(Q))}$$

$$= \mathfrak{C}'[\zeta(z_1), \xi(p), \eta(Q)](z'),$$

which was to be shown. This proves 6.12.1.

Suppose $[\xi, \eta, \zeta]$ is a homormophism of $\mathfrak{C}$ onto $\mathfrak{C}'$. We define $\tilde{\zeta}$ as above, and show that $[\xi, \eta, \tilde{\zeta}]$ is a homomorphism of $\tilde{\mathfrak{C}}$ onto $\tilde{\mathfrak{C}}'$.

Let $\mathfrak{z} \in \mathfrak{Z}_Z$, $x \in X$, $y' \in Y'$, $\mathfrak{z}' \in \mathfrak{Z}_{Z'}$. We claim that

$$\tilde{H}'[\tilde{\zeta}(\mathfrak{z}), \xi(x)](y', \mathfrak{z}') = \sum_{\substack{\eta(y)=y' \\ \tilde{\zeta}(\mathfrak{z}^*)=\mathfrak{z}'}} \tilde{H}[\mathfrak{z}, x](y, \mathfrak{z}^*)$$

Case I. $\mathfrak{z}'$ is deterministic, $\mathfrak{z}' = \delta_{z'}$.

Then

$$\tilde{H}'[\tilde{\zeta}(\mathfrak{z}), \xi(x)](y', \mathfrak{z}') = \sum_{z'' \in Z'} \sum_{z \in Z} \mathfrak{z}(z)\, \delta_{\zeta(z)}(z'')\, H'[z'', \xi(x)](y', z').$$

$$= \sum_{z \in Z} \mathfrak{z}(z) \cdot H'[\zeta(z), \xi(x)](y', z')$$

$$= \sum_{\eta(y)=y'} \sum_{\zeta(z^*)=z'} \tilde{H}[\mathfrak{z}, x](y, \delta_{z^*}).$$

Now we have $\zeta(z^*) = z'$ if and only if $\tilde{\zeta}(\delta_{z^*}) = \delta_{z'}$ and for $\mathfrak{z}^* \in \mathfrak{Z}_Z \setminus \mathfrak{D}'_Z$ $\tilde{H}[\mathfrak{z}, x](y, \mathfrak{z}^*) = 0$, also if $\tilde{\zeta}(\mathfrak{z}^*) = \delta_{z'} = \mathfrak{z}'$. Thus for a deterministic $\mathfrak{z}'$

$$\tilde{H}'[\tilde{\zeta}(\mathfrak{z}), \xi(x)](y', \mathfrak{z}') = \sum_{\substack{\eta(y)=y' \\ \tilde{\zeta}(\mathfrak{z}^*)=\mathfrak{z}'}} \tilde{H}[\mathfrak{z}, x](y, \mathfrak{z}^*).$$

Case II. $\mathfrak{z}'$ is not deterministic.

Then the left hand side of the last equality is zero. All random states $\mathfrak{z}^* \in \mathfrak{Z}_Z$ with $\tilde{\zeta}(\mathfrak{z}^*) = \mathfrak{z}'$ are non-deterministic, because $\tilde{\zeta}$ maps the set $\mathfrak{D}_Z$ onto $\mathfrak{D}_{Z'}$. Consequently, the left hand side of the equality under consideration must also be zero. Therefore, $[\xi, \eta, \tilde{\zeta}]$ is a homomorphism of $\tilde{\mathfrak{C}}$ onto $\tilde{\mathfrak{C}}'$ and thus 6.12.2 is proved.

Finally let $[\xi, I_Y, \zeta]$ be an $[X, Z]$-homomorphism of $\mathfrak{C}$ onto $\mathfrak{C}'$. It suffices to show that $\tilde{\zeta}$ maps the set $\mathfrak{R}_{\mathfrak{C}}$ onto $\mathfrak{R}_{\mathfrak{C}'}$ and for this it is enough to show that for $z \in Z$, $p \in W(X) \setminus \{e\}$, $Q \subseteq Y^{l(p)}$, $z' \in Z'$,

$$\sum_{\zeta(z^*)=z'} H[z, p](Q \times Z^{l(p)-1} \cdot \{z^*\}) = H'[\zeta(z), \xi(p)](Q \times (Z')^{l(p)-1} \cdot \{z'\}).$$

Now, if $p = x_1 \dots x_n \quad (n \geqq 1)$

$$\sum_{\zeta(z^*)=z'} H[z, p](Q \times Z^{l(p)-1} \cdot \{z\})$$
$$= \sum_{y_1 \cdots y_n \in Q} \sum_{z_2 \in Z} H[z, x_1](y_1, z_2) \dots$$
$$\sum_{z_n \in Z} H[z_{n-1}, x_{n-1}](y_{n-1}, z_n) \cdot \sum_{\zeta(z^*)=z'} H[z_n, x_n](y_n, z^*).$$

Then,

$$\sum_{\zeta(z^*)=z'} H[z_n, x_n](y_n, z^*) = H'[\zeta(z_n), \xi(x_n)](y_n, z'),$$

hence,

$$\sum_{z_n \in Z} H[z_{n-1}, x_{n-1}](y_{n-1}, z_n) H'[\zeta(z_n), \xi(x_n)](y_n, z')$$
$$= \sum_{z' \in Z'} \sum_{\zeta(z_n)=z_n'} H[z_{n-1}, x_{n-1}](y_{n-1}, z_n) H'[z_n', \xi(x_n)](y_n, z')$$
$$= \sum_{z_n' \in Z'} H'[\zeta(z_{n-1}), \xi(x_{n-1})](y_{n-1}, z_n') H'[z_n', \xi(x_n)](y_n, z').$$

We can continue in this way and obtain

$$\sum_{\zeta(z^*)=z'} H[z, p](Q \times Z^{l(p)-1} \cdot \{z^*\})$$
$$= \sum_{y_1 \dots y_n \in Q} H'[\zeta(z), \xi(p)]\big(\{y_1 \dots y_n\} \times (Z')^{l(p)-1} \cdot \{z'\}\big)$$
$$= H'[\zeta(z), \xi(p)]\big(Q \times W(Z') \cdot \{z'\}\big),$$

which was to be shown. This proves Theorem 6.12.

The existence of a homomorphism of $\mathfrak{C}$ onto $\mathfrak{C}'$ does not in general imply that there is a homomorphism of $\hat{\mathfrak{C}}$ onto $\hat{\mathfrak{C}}'$. We consider as an example the S-automata $\mathfrak{C}_6 = [\{x\}, \{0, 1\}, \{a, b\}, H_6]$, $\mathfrak{C}_6' = [\{x\}, \{0\}, \{a, b\}, H_6']$ introduced on page 284 (Fig. 25). As we have seen in § 3, there exists a Y-homomorphism of $\mathfrak{C}_6$ onto $\mathfrak{C}_6'$. The random state $\mathfrak{z}_0$ with $\mathfrak{z}_0(a) = \frac{1}{3}$, $\mathfrak{z}_0(b) = \frac{2}{3}$ is $\mathfrak{C}_6$-realizable ($z_0 = \mathfrak{C}_6[a, x, 0]$). In $\mathfrak{C}_6'$, exactly the random states $\delta_a, \delta_b, \mathfrak{z}^\nu$, with $\mathfrak{z}^\nu(a) = \frac{1}{2^\nu}$, $\mathfrak{z}^\nu(b) = 1 - \frac{1}{2^\nu}$ for $\nu = 1, 2, \dots,$ are realizable. Assume that $[\xi, \eta, \hat{\zeta}]$ is a homomorphism of $\hat{\mathfrak{C}}_6$ onto $\hat{\mathfrak{C}}_6'$. Then $\xi = I_{\{x\}}$ and $\eta(0) = \eta(1) = 0$.

$\hat{\zeta}$ maps $\mathfrak{R}_{\mathfrak{C}_6}$ onto $\mathfrak{R}_{\mathfrak{C}_6'}$. Since $\delta_a \in \mathfrak{R}_{\mathfrak{C}_6'}$, there exists a $\mathfrak{z}_a^* \in R_{\mathfrak{C}_6}$ with $\hat{\zeta}(\mathfrak{z}_a^*) = \delta_a$. Here, if $z \in \{a, b\}$

$$\hat{H}_6'[\delta_a, x](0, \delta_z) = H_6'[a, x](0, z) > 0,$$

hence for $z \in \{a, b\}$

$$0 < \sum_{\substack{\eta(y)=0 \\ \hat{\zeta}(\mathfrak{z}^*)=\delta_z}} \hat{H}_6[\mathfrak{z}_a^*, x](y, \mathfrak{z}^*) = \sum_{\hat{\zeta}(\delta_{z'})=\delta_z} \hat{H}_6[\mathfrak{z}_a^*, x](\{0, 1\} \times \{\delta_{z'}\}).$$

For every $z \in \{a, b\}$ thus there is a $z' \in \{a, b\}$ such that $\hat{\zeta}(\delta_{z'}) = \delta_z$. Suppose that $\hat{\zeta}(\delta_b) = \delta_a$. Then

$$\hat{H}'_6[\hat{\zeta}(\delta_b), x](0, \delta_a) = \hat{H}'_6[\delta_a, x](0, \delta_a) = H'_6[a, x](0, a) = \frac{1}{2},$$

hence

$$\frac{1}{2} = \sum_{\hat{\zeta}(\delta_{z'})=\delta_a} \hat{H}_6[\delta_b, x](\{0, 1\} \times \{\delta_{z'}\}) \geqq H_6[b, x](\{0, 1\} \times \{b\}) = 1,$$

i.e., we obtain a contradiction. Consequently $\hat{\zeta}(\delta_a) = \delta_a$ and $\hat{\zeta}(\delta_b) = \delta_b$.

Suppose $\mathfrak{z}^* \in \mathfrak{R}_{\mathfrak{C}'_6}$ with $\hat{\zeta}(\mathfrak{z}_0) = \mathfrak{z}^*$. Then on one hand

$$\hat{H}'_6[\mathfrak{z}^*, x](0, \delta_a) = \mathfrak{z}^*(a) \cdot H'_6[a, x](0, a) + \mathfrak{z}^*(b)\, H'_6[b, x](0, a) = \frac{\mathfrak{z}^*(a)}{2},$$

and on the other

$$\begin{aligned} \hat{H}'_6[\mathfrak{z}^*, x](0, \delta_a) &= \sum_{\hat{\zeta}(\mathfrak{z})=\delta_a} \hat{H}_6[\mathfrak{z}_0, x](\{0, 1\} \times \{\mathfrak{z}\}) \\ &= \hat{H}_6[\mathfrak{z}_0, x](\{0, 1\} \times \{\delta_a\}) \\ &= \mathfrak{z}_0(a) \cdot F_6[a, x](a) + \mathfrak{z}_0(b) \cdot F_6[b, x](a) \\ &= \frac{1}{3} \cdot \frac{1}{2}. \end{aligned}$$

Hence $\mathfrak{z}^*(a) = \frac{1}{3}$, which contradicts the fact that for every member $\mathfrak{z}$ of $\mathfrak{R}_{\mathfrak{C}'_6}$

$$\mathfrak{z}(a) \in \left\{0, 1, \frac{1}{2}, \frac{1}{4}, \frac{1}{8}, \ldots\right\}.$$

Thus there is no homomorphism of $\mathfrak{C}_6$ onto $\mathfrak{C}'_6$.

§ 7. Stability and Terminal Equivalence

In this section the results obtained in the investigation of certain stability properties of non-deterministic automata will be transferred to stochastic automata. An S-automaton will be called stable if there is a positive natural number k such that the behaviour of the S-automaton in step $t + k$ or in the following steps is not affected by the input signals of the automaton received in the course of the steps $1, \ldots, t$. It turns out that for every stable S-automaton $\mathfrak{C}$ the *ND*-automaton $ND(\mathfrak{C})$ is stable in the sense of the theory of *ND*-automata. Further, we define an equivalence relation for S-automata which corresponds to the terminal equivalence between non-deterministic automata, and investigate the corresponding problems of reduction. The basic definitions 7.1 and 7.2 are due to FISCHER, LINDNER, THIELE [1].

Definition 7.1. Let $\mathfrak{C} = [X, Y, Z, H]$ be an S-automaton, $\mathfrak{z} \in \mathfrak{Z}_Z$ a random state of $\mathfrak{C}$ and k a positive natural number.

(7.1.1) $\mathfrak{C}$ is called *weakly k-stable over $\mathfrak{z}$* if for all $x \in X$, $pr \in W(X)$ with $l(r) = k - 1$ we have $G[F[\mathfrak{z}, pr], x] = G[F[\mathfrak{z}, r], x]$. If $\mathfrak{z} = \delta_z$ (for $z \in Z$), then we say that $\mathfrak{C}$ is weakly k-stable over z.

(7.1.2) $\mathfrak{C}$ is called *weakly k-stable* if it is weakly k-stable over every state $\mathfrak{z}$ of $\mathfrak{C}$.

(7.1.3) $\mathfrak{C}$ is called *k-stable (over $\mathfrak{z}$)* if it is weakly k-stable (over $\mathfrak{z}$) and either $k = 1$ or $\mathfrak{C}$ is not weakly $(k-1)$ stable (over $\mathfrak{z}$).

(7.1.4) $\mathfrak{C}$ is said to be *stable (over $\mathfrak{z}$)* if there is a positive natural number k such that $\mathfrak{C}$ is k-stable (over $\mathfrak{z}$).

Corollary 7.1. If the S-automaton $\mathfrak{C} = [X, Y, Z, H]$ is weakly k-stable over $\mathfrak{z} \in \mathfrak{Z}_Z$, then the non-deterministic automaton $\mathfrak{B} = ND(\mathfrak{C})$ is weakly k-stable over $M = ND(\mathfrak{z})$.

Theorem 7.2. *If $\mathfrak{C} = [X, Y, Z, H]$ is an S-automaton, and $\mathfrak{z} \in \mathfrak{Z}_Z$, then the following assertions are pairwise equivalent.*

(1) *$\mathfrak{C}$ is weakly k-stable over $\mathfrak{z}$.*

(2) *For all $j \geqq 0$, $\mathfrak{C}$ is weakly $(k+j)$-stable over $\mathfrak{z}$.*

(3) *For all $p, r \in W(X)$, $x \in X$ with $l(r) \geqq k - 1$,*

$$G[F[\mathfrak{z}, pr], x] = G[F[\mathfrak{z}, r], x].$$

(4) *For all $p, r, u \in W(X)$, $x \in X$ with $l(r) \geqq k - 1$,*

$$G[F[\mathfrak{z}, pr], x] = G[F[\mathfrak{z}, ur], x].$$

(5) *For all $\mathfrak{z}', \mathfrak{z}'' \in \{F[\mathfrak{z}, p] \mid p \in W(X)\}$, $r \in W(X)$ with $l(r) \geqq k - 1$, $x \in X$,*

$$G[F[\mathfrak{z}', r], x] = G[F[\mathfrak{z}'', r], x].$$

(6) *For all $p \in W(X)$, $\mathfrak{C}$ is weakly k-stable over $F[\mathfrak{z}, p]$.*

Proof: Obviously, it suffices to show that (1) implies (2). So assume $p, r \in W(X)$ with $l(r) = k + j - 1$, $j \geqq 0$ and $x \in X$. Furthermore, let $r = r'r''$ with $l(r'') = k - 1$, hence $l(r') = j$. Then

$$\begin{aligned} G[F[\mathfrak{z}, pr], x] &= G[F[\mathfrak{z}, pr'r''], x] = G[F[\mathfrak{z}, r''], x] \\ &= G[F[\mathfrak{z}, r'r''], x] = G[F[\mathfrak{z}, r], x], \end{aligned}$$

which was to be shown.

Theorem 7.3. *Let $\mathfrak{C} = [X, Y, Z, H]$, $\mathfrak{C}' = [X', Y', Z', H']$ be S-automata and $\mathfrak{z}$ a random state of $\mathfrak{C}$.*

1. *If $[\xi, \eta, \zeta]$ is a homomorphism of $\mathfrak{C}$ onto $\mathfrak{C}'$, and $\mathfrak{C}$ is weakly k-stable over $\mathfrak{z}$, then $\mathfrak{C}'$ is weakly k-stable over $\zeta(\mathfrak{z})$.*

2. *If* $[\xi, \eta, \zeta]$ *is a strong homomorphism of* $\mathfrak{C}$ *onto* $\mathfrak{C}'$, *then* $\mathfrak{C}$ *is weakly* k*-stable over* $\mathfrak{z}$ *(or stable) if and only if* $\mathfrak{C}'$ *is weakly* k*-stable over* $\zeta(\mathfrak{z})$ *(or stable).*

Proof: We have shown in § 5 (page 323) that the following lemma is valid:

Lemma 7.4. *For every S-automaton* $\mathfrak{C}$ *and any* $p \in W(X)$, $x \in X$, $y \in Y$, $\mathfrak{z} \in \mathfrak{Z}_Z$, $G[F[\mathfrak{z}, p], x](y) = V_{\mathfrak{C}}[\mathfrak{z}, px]\big(W(Y) \cdot \{y\}\big)$.

Now if $\mathfrak{C}$ is weakly k-stable over $\mathfrak{z} \in \mathfrak{Z}_Z$, $p'r' \in W(X')$, $x' \in X'$ with $l(r') \geqq k-1$, further $pr \in W(X)$, $x \in X$ with $\xi(pr) = p'r'$, $\xi(r) = r'$, $\xi(x) = x'$ and $y' \in Y'$, then we have

$$\begin{aligned} G'\big[F'[\zeta(\mathfrak{z}), p'r'], x'\big](y') &= V_{\mathfrak{C}'}[\zeta(\mathfrak{z}), \xi(prx)]\big(W(Y') \cdot \{y'\}\big) && \text{(by 7.4)} \\ &= \sum_{q' \in W(Y')} V_{\mathfrak{C}'}[\zeta(\mathfrak{z}), \xi(prx)](q'y') \\ &= \sum_{q' \in W(Y')} \sum_{\eta(qy) = q'y'} V_{\mathfrak{C}}[\mathfrak{z}, prx](qy) && \text{(cf. 3.7)} \\ &= \sum_{\eta(y) = y'} V_{\mathfrak{C}}[\mathfrak{z}, prx]\big(W(Y) \cdot \{y\}\big), \end{aligned}$$

and because $\mathfrak{C}$ is weakly k-stable over $\mathfrak{z}$, we obtain (by 7.4)

$$\begin{aligned} G'\big[F'[\zeta(\mathfrak{z}), p'r'], x'\big](y') &= \sum_{\eta(y) = y'} V_{\mathfrak{C}}[\mathfrak{z}, rx]\big(W(Y) \cdot \{y\}\big) \\ &= V_{\mathfrak{C}'}[\zeta(\mathfrak{z}), r'x']\big(W(Y') \cdot \{y'\}\big) \\ &= G'\big[F'[\zeta(\mathfrak{z}), r'], x'\big](y'), \end{aligned}$$

hence $\mathfrak{C}'$ is weakly k-stable over $\zeta(\mathfrak{z})$.

Since every strong homomorphism is a homomorphism, to prove 7.3.2 it suffices to show that $\mathfrak{C}$ is weakly k-stable over $\mathfrak{z}$ when $\mathfrak{C}'$ is weakly k-stable over $\zeta(\mathfrak{z})$. This can be easily proved in the same way as above, using Propositions 7.4, 3.9, and 3.10. Since the extension of the function ζ to the set $\mathfrak{Z}_Z$ is a single-valued mapping of $\mathfrak{Z}_Z$ onto $\mathfrak{Z}_{Z'}$, this proves Theorem 7.3.

Remark: Let $\mathfrak{C} = [X, Y, Z, H]$ be an arbitrary S-automaton and $\mathfrak{C}' = [X, \{0\}, Z, H']$ where

$$H'[z, x](0, z') = H[z, x](Y \times \{z'\}) \big(= F[z, x](z')\big).$$

Obviously, $[I_X, \eta, I_Y]$ with $\eta(y) = 0$ for all $y \in Y$, is a homomorphism of $\mathfrak{C}$ onto $\mathfrak{C}'$ and $\mathfrak{C}'$ is 1-stable, because for all $\mathfrak{z} \in \mathfrak{Z}_Z$, $x \in X$ we have $G'[\mathfrak{z}, x](0) = 1$. Since obviously there are S-automata which are not 1-stable (e.g., the deterministic S-automaton which corresponds to the deterministic automaton $\mathfrak{A}_3^3$ of Part I, § 8), the converse of 7.3.1 is false.

From 7.4 (using 6.2.1 and 6.5.1) we obtain:

Corollary 7.5. Let $\mathfrak{C}, \mathfrak{C}'$ be S-automata with the same input and output alphabets, $\mathfrak{z}$ (or $\mathfrak{z}'$) a random state of $\mathfrak{C}$ (or $\mathfrak{C}'$).

1. If $\mathfrak{z} \sim \mathfrak{z}'$, then $\mathfrak{C}$ is weakly k-stable over $\mathfrak{z}$ if and only if $\mathfrak{C}'$ is weakly k-stable over $\mathfrak{z}'$.
2. If $\mathfrak{C} \approx \mathfrak{C}'$, then $\mathfrak{C}$ is stable if and only if $\mathfrak{C}'$ is.
3. $\mathfrak{C}$ is weakly k-stable over $\mathfrak{z}$, if and only if $\tilde{\mathfrak{C}}$ is weakly k-stable over its state $\mathfrak{z}$.
4. $\mathfrak{C}$ is stable if and only if $\tilde{\mathfrak{C}}$ and $\hat{\mathfrak{C}}$ are.

Theorem 7.6. *If* $\mathfrak{C} = [X, Y, Z, H]$ *is weakly k-stable over* $\mathfrak{z}$, *and homogeneous with respect to every random state of the form* $F[\mathfrak{z}, u]$ *for* $u \in W(X)$ *with* $l(u) \geqq k-1$, *then* $F[\mathfrak{z}, pr] \sim F[\mathfrak{z}, r]$ *for all* $p, r \in W(X)$ *with* $l(r) \geqq k-1$.

To prove this we first show by induction on w that for all $w \in W(X)$, $q \in Y^{l(w)}$

$$V_{\mathfrak{C}}[F[\mathfrak{z}, pr], w](q) = V_{\mathfrak{C}}[F[\mathfrak{z}, r], w](q).$$

For $w = e$ this is trivial. The step from w to xw:

$$V_{\mathfrak{C}}[F[\mathfrak{z}, pr], xw](yq) = G[F[\mathfrak{z}, pr], x](y)\; V_{\mathfrak{C}}[F[\mathfrak{z}, prx], w](q),$$

because $l(pr) \geqq k-1$, and thus $\mathfrak{C}$ is homogeneous with respect to $F[\mathfrak{z}, pr]$ (cf. 5.2.2). By the induction hypothesis,

$$V_{\mathfrak{C}}[F[\mathfrak{z}, prx], w](q) = V_{\mathfrak{C}}[F[\mathfrak{z}, rx], w](q);$$

since $l(rx) \geqq k-1$, and because $\mathfrak{C}$ is weakly k-stable over $\mathfrak{z}$ we obtain

$$\begin{aligned} V_{\mathfrak{C}}[F[\mathfrak{z}, pr], xw](yq) &= G[F[\mathfrak{z}, r], x](y)\; V_{\mathfrak{C}}[F[\mathfrak{z}, rx], w](q) \\ &= V_{\mathfrak{C}}[F[\mathfrak{z}, r], xw](yq), \end{aligned}$$

since $\mathfrak{C}$ is homogeneous with respect to $F[\mathfrak{z}, r]$.

Theorem 7.7. *If the Z-finite S-automaton* $\mathfrak{C} = [X, Y, Z, H]$ *with* $Card(Z) = n$ *is stable over the random state* $\mathfrak{z}_0 \in \mathfrak{Z}_Z$, *then* $\mathfrak{C}$ *is also weakly n-stable over* $\mathfrak{z}_0$.

Proof: We shall proceed analogously as in the proof of Carlyle's theorem (Theorem 2.11) and consider for $p \in W(X)$, $x \in X$, $y \in Y$ the functions $G[F[.,p], x](y)$, which map the set Z into the set of real numbers. For $i = 0, 1, \dots$ let

$$L'_i = L(\{G[F[.,p], x](y) \mid p \in W(X) \wedge l(p) \geqq i \wedge x \in X \wedge y \in Y\}).$$

Here, obviously

$$L'_0 \supseteq L'_1 \supseteq \cdots \supseteq L'_i \supseteq L'_{i+1} \supseteq \cdots.$$

Furthermore, if $i \in \boldsymbol{n z}$ then $L'_{i+1} = L'_{i+2}$ is implied by $L'_i = L'_{i+1}$.

To prove this let $G[F[.,p], x](y)$ be an arbitrary generator of L'_{i+1}. If $l(p) \geqq i+2$, then $G[F[.,p], x](y) \in L'_{i+2}$. For $p = x'p'$ with $l(p) = i+1$ for $z \in Z$,

$$G[F[z, x'p'], x](y) = \sum_{z^* \in Z} F[z, x'](z^*)\; G[F[z^*, p'], x](y).$$

Since $l(p') = i$ with $G[F[., p'], x](y) \in L'_i = L'_{i+1}$, hence there are words $p_1, \ldots, p_m \in W(X)$ with $l(p_\mu) \geqq i + 1$ for $\mu = 1, \ldots, m$, and furthermore letters $x_1, \ldots, x_m \in X$, $y_1, \ldots, y_m \in Y$ and numbers $\alpha_1, \ldots, \alpha_m$ with

$$G[F[., p'], x](y) = \sum_{\mu=1}^{m} \alpha_\mu \cdot G[F[., p_\mu], x_\mu](y_\mu);$$

hence

$$G[F[., x'p'], x](y) = \sum_{\mu=1}^{m} \alpha_\mu G[F[., x'p_\mu], x_\mu](y_\mu).$$

Since $l(p_\mu) \geqq i + 1$, the functions $G[F[., x'p_\mu], x_\mu](y_\mu)$ belong to L'_{i+2}, hence $G[F[., p], x](y) \in L'_{i+2}$, i.e. $L'_{i+1} \subseteq L'_{i+2}$, and by $L'_{i+2} \subseteq L'_{i+1}$ we have $L'_{i+1} = L'_{i+2}$.

Let i_0 be the smallest number such that $L'_{i_0} = L'_{i_0+1}$. Then we have

$$L'_0 \supset L'_1 \supset \cdots \supset L'_{i_0-1} \supset L'_{i_0} = L'_{i_0+1} = \cdots,$$

$$n \geqq dim\,(L'_0) > dim\,(L'_1) > \cdots > dim\,(L'_{i_0}) > 0,$$

i.e., $i_0 \leqq n - 1$.

Suppose $\mathfrak{C}$ is k-stable over $\mathfrak{z}_0$ and $\langle\mathfrak{z}_0\rangle = \{F(\mathfrak{z}_0, p] \mid p \in W(X)\}$, further for $\mathfrak{z}', \mathfrak{z}'' \in \langle\mathfrak{z}_0\rangle$, $d \in L'_0$

$$\overline{\varphi}_{\mathfrak{z}',\mathfrak{z}''}(d) \underset{\mathrm{Df}}{=} \sum_{z \in Z} \big(\mathfrak{z}'(z) - \mathfrak{z}''(z)\big)\, d(z);$$

thus $\overline{\varphi}_{\mathfrak{z}',\mathfrak{z}''}$ is a linear functional operating on all the spaces L'_i.

$\mathfrak{C}$ is k-stable over $\mathfrak{z}_0$ if and only if for all $\mathfrak{z}', \mathfrak{z}'' \in \langle\mathfrak{z}_0\rangle$, $p \in W(X)$ with $l(p) \geqq k - 1$, $x \in X$, $y \in Y$,

$$G[F[\mathfrak{z}', p], x](y) = G[F[\mathfrak{z}'', p], x](y),$$

.e., $\overline{\varphi}_{\mathfrak{z}',\mathfrak{z}''}\big(G[F[., p], x](y)\big) = 0$, and there are $p' \in X^{k-2}$, $\mathfrak{z}'_0, \mathfrak{z}''_0 \in \langle\mathfrak{z}_0\rangle$, $x' \in X$, $y' \in Y$ with $\overline{\varphi}_{\mathfrak{z}'_0,\mathfrak{z}''_0}\big(G[F[., p'], x'](y')\big) \neq 0$. If $\mathfrak{C}$ is k-stable over $\mathfrak{z}_0$, then for every $\mathfrak{z}, \mathfrak{z}' \in \langle\mathfrak{z}_0\rangle$ the functional $\overline{\varphi}_{\mathfrak{z},\mathfrak{z}'}$ vanishes on the space L'_{k-1} and there are random states $\mathfrak{z}'_0, \mathfrak{z}''_0 \in \langle\mathfrak{z}_0\rangle$ such that $\overline{\varphi}_{\mathfrak{z}'_0,\mathfrak{z}''_0}$ does not vanish on L'_{k-2}. Consequently, $L'_{k-1} \subset L'_{k-2}$, i.e., $k - 1 \leqq i_0 \leqq n - 1$, and thus $k \leqq n$ which was to be shown.

The upper bound n given in Theorem 7.7 cannot be improved as follows from 7.1, because there are already deterministic automata with n states which are not $(n - 1)$-stable (cf. Part I, § 8, Theorem 8.4, and the following example).

Similarly as in our investigations in the theory of non-deterministic automata, we define the terminal equivalence for stochastic automata and consider the corresponding problems of reduction.

Definition 7.2. Let $\mathfrak{C} = [X, Y, Z, H]$, $\mathfrak{C}' = [X, Y, Z', H']$ be S-automata, with the same input and output alphabets. The random states $\mathfrak{z} \in \mathfrak{Z}_Z$, $\mathfrak{z}' \in Z_Z$ are called *terminal equivalent* ($\mathfrak{z} \underset{f}{\sim} \mathfrak{z}'$) if $G[F[\mathfrak{z}, p], x] = G'[F'[\mathfrak{z}', p], x]$ for al

$p \in W(X)$, $x \in X$. If $\mathfrak{z} = \delta_z$ or $\mathfrak{z}' = \delta_{z'}$ (for $z \in Z$, $z' \in Z'$) then the state z is said to be terminal equivalent to $\mathfrak{z}'$, or $\mathfrak{z}$ is said to be *terminal equivalent to the state* z'. In analogy to Definition 2.1 we introduce the concepts "$\mathfrak{C}$ is terminal equivalently embedded into $\mathfrak{C}'$ ($\mathfrak{C} \underset{f}{\subseteq} \mathfrak{C}'$)", "$\mathfrak{C}$ and $\mathfrak{C}'$ are terminal equivalent ($\mathfrak{C} \underset{f}{\sim} \mathfrak{C}'$)", "$\mathfrak{C}$ is weakly terminal equivalently embedded into $\mathfrak{C}'$ ($\mathfrak{C} \underset{f}{\subseteq\!\!\approx} \mathfrak{C}'$)", "$\mathfrak{C}$ and $\mathfrak{C}'$ are weakly terminal equivalent ($\mathfrak{C} \underset{f}{\approx} \mathfrak{C}'$)".

Corollary 7.8.

1. The relations $\underset{f}{\sim}$, $\underset{f}{\approx}$ are equivalence relations.
2. Equivalence implies terminal equivalence for states, random states and S-automata.
3. Weak equivalence implies weak terminal equivalence.
4. If $\mathfrak{C}$ is (weakly) equivalently embedded into $\mathfrak{C}'$ then $\mathfrak{C}$ is (weakly) terminal equivalently embedded into $\mathfrak{C}'$.
5. If $\mathfrak{C}$ is weakly k-stable over $\mathfrak{z}$, then for $\mathfrak{z}', \mathfrak{z}'' \in \langle \mathfrak{z} \rangle$

$$\mathfrak{z}' \underset{f}{\sim} \mathfrak{z}'' \leftrightarrow \forall p \forall x (p \in W(X) \wedge x \in X \wedge l(p) \leq k - 2 \\ \rightarrow G[F[\mathfrak{z}', p], x] = G[F[\mathfrak{z}'', p], x]).$$

6. If the random states $\mathfrak{z}, \mathfrak{z}'$ of the S-automata $\mathfrak{C}, \mathfrak{C}'$ respectively are terminal equivalent, then the sets of states $ND(\mathfrak{z})$, $ND(\mathfrak{z}')$ of the ND-automata $ND(\mathfrak{C})$, $ND(\mathfrak{C}')$ are terminal equivalent in the sense of the theory of ND-automata.
7. For every S-automaton $\mathfrak{C} = [X, Y, Z, H]$, $\mathfrak{C}_M = [X, Y, Z, F, G]$ is a terminal equivalent S-Mealy automaton.
8. If $\mathfrak{C}$ or $\mathfrak{C}'$ is homogeneous with respect to $\mathfrak{z}$ or $\mathfrak{z}'$ respectively, and $z \underset{f}{\sim} \mathfrak{z}'$ then $\mathfrak{z} \sim \mathfrak{z}'$.
9. Homogeneous (or strongly homogeneous) S-automata are equivalent (or weakly equivalent) if and only if they are terminal equivalent (or weakly terminal equivalent).

Thus equivalence and terminal equivalence coincide for homogeneous S-automata or their states. This is why in the theory of deterministic automata terminal equivalence is not defined explicitely. Similarly as for Theorem 2.2 we can prove

Theorem 7.9.

1. $\mathfrak{C} \underset{f}{\subseteq\!\!\approx} \mathfrak{C}'$ *if and only if for every state z of Z there is a random state $\mathfrak{z}'$ of $\mathfrak{C}'$ such that* $z \underset{f}{\sim} \mathfrak{z}'$.
2. *If* $\mathfrak{C} \underset{f}{\subseteq} \mathfrak{C}'$ *then* $\mathfrak{C} \underset{f}{\subseteq\!\!\approx} \mathfrak{C}'$.
3. *If* $\mathfrak{C} \underset{f}{\sim} \mathfrak{C}'$ *then* $\mathfrak{C} \underset{f}{\approx} \mathfrak{C}'$.

Theorem 7.10. *The random states $\mathfrak{z}, \mathfrak{z}'$ of the S-automata $\mathfrak{C}, \mathfrak{C}'$ with the same input alphabet X are terminal equivalent if and only if* $G[\mathfrak{z}, x] = G'[\mathfrak{z}', x]$ *and* $F[\mathfrak{z}, x] \underset{f}{\sim} F'[\mathfrak{z}', x]$ *for all* $x \in X$.

Proof: We have $\mathfrak{z} \underset{f}{\sim} \mathfrak{z}'$ if and only if for all $x, x_1 \in X$, $p \in W(X)$

$$G[\mathfrak{z}, x] = G'[\mathfrak{z}', x] \text{ and } G[F[\mathfrak{z}, xp], x_1] = G'[F'[\mathfrak{z}', xp], x_1],$$

i.e., if and only if for all $x \in X$ the equality $G[\mathfrak{z}, x] = G'[\mathfrak{z}', x]$ is satisfied and for all $x \in X$, $p \in W(X)$ and for every $x_1 \in X$

$$G[F[F[\mathfrak{z}, x], p], x_1] = G'[F'[F'[\mathfrak{z}', x], p], x_1],$$

which immediately implies 7.10.

Theorem 7.11. *Let $\mathfrak{C} = [X, Y, Z, H]$ be an S-automaton.*

1. *$\mathfrak{C}$ is weakly k-stable over $\mathfrak{z} \in \mathfrak{Z}_Z$ if and only if for all $\mathfrak{z}', \mathfrak{z}'' \in \langle\mathfrak{z}\rangle$ and every $r \in W(X)$ with $l(r) \geqq k-1$ the random states $F[\mathfrak{z}', r], F[\mathfrak{z}'', x]$ are terminal equivalent.*

2. *If $\mathfrak{C}$ is weakly k-stable over $\mathfrak{z}$, then for every $p \in W(X)$ with $l(p) \geqq k-1$ there is a $p' \in W(X)$ with $l(p') = k-1$ and $F[\mathfrak{z}, p] \underset{f}{\sim} F[\mathfrak{z}, p']$.*

3. *If X is finite, and $\mathfrak{C}$ is weakly k-stable over $\mathfrak{z}$, then the relation $\underset{f}{\sim}$ divides $\langle\mathfrak{z}\rangle$ into finitely many equivalence classes only.*

Proof: By 7.2, $\mathfrak{C}$ is weakly k-stable over $\mathfrak{z}$ if and only if for all $\mathfrak{z}', \mathfrak{z}'' \in \langle\mathfrak{z}\rangle$, $x \in X$, $r \in W(X)$ with $l(r) \geqq k-1$ the equality $G[F[\mathfrak{z}', r], x] = G[F[\mathfrak{z}'', r], x]$ is satisfied. This holds however if and only if for all $\mathfrak{z}', \mathfrak{z}'' \in \langle\mathfrak{z}\rangle$, $x \in X$, $p, r \in W(X)$ with $l(r) \geqq k-1$,

$$\begin{aligned} G[F[\mathfrak{z}', rp], x] &= G[F[F[\mathfrak{z}', r], p], x] = G[F[F[\mathfrak{z}'', r], p], x] \\ &= G[F[\mathfrak{z}'', rp], x], \end{aligned}$$

which implies 7.11.1.

To prove 7.11.2, let $p = x_1 \dots x_m \in W(X)$ with $m \geqq k$, furthermore $p'' = x_1 \dots x_{m-k+1}$ and $p' = x_{m-k+2} \dots x_m$. Thus $p = p''p'$ and $l(p') = k-1$. We have $\mathfrak{z}' \underset{\mathrm{Df}}{=} F[\mathfrak{z}, p''] \in \langle\mathfrak{z}\rangle$, $\mathfrak{z} \in \langle\mathfrak{z}\rangle$; hence by $l(p') = k-1$ and 7.11.1 the random states $F[\mathfrak{z}', p'] = F[\mathfrak{z}, p]$ and $F[\mathfrak{z}, p']$ are terminal equivalent, which was to be shown. Proposition 7.11.3 follows immediately from 7.11.2.

Theorem 7.12. *Let $\mathfrak{C} = [X, Y, Z, H]$ be a Z-finite S-automaton with $Card(Z) = n \geqq 2$. Then for $\mathfrak{z}, \mathfrak{z}' \in \mathfrak{Z}_Z$,*

$$\begin{aligned} \mathfrak{z} \underset{f}{\sim} \mathfrak{z}' \leftrightarrow \forall p \forall x (p \in W(X) \wedge x \in X \wedge l(p) \leqq n-2 \\ \rightarrow G[F[\mathfrak{z}, p], x] = G[F[\mathfrak{z}', p], x]). \end{aligned}$$

Proof: As in the proof of 7.7, we consider the functions $G[F[., p], x](y)$ and put for $k \geqq 0$,

$$L_k'' = L(\{G[F[., p], x](y) \mid p \in W(X) \wedge l(p) \leqq k \wedge x \in X \wedge y \in Y\}).$$

For all $k \geqq 0$, L_k'' is a subspace of L_{k+1}'', and the following can be easily shown:

If $L_k'' = L_{k+1}''$, then $L_{k+1}'' = L_{k+2}''$.

Let j_0 be the smallest number j such that $L_j'' = L_{j+1}''$. Then

$$\begin{aligned} L_0'' \subset L_1'' \subset \cdots \subset L_{j_0}'' = L_{j_0+1}'' = L_0' \\ = L(\{G[F[., p], x](y) \mid p \in W(X) \wedge x \in X \wedge y \in Y\}). \end{aligned}$$

Trivially, $dim(L_0'') \geqq 1$. Next we show

Lemma 7.12a. *If* $dim(L_0'') = 1$ *then all* $\mathfrak{z}, \mathfrak{z}' \in \mathfrak{Z}_Z$ *are pairwise terminal equivalent.*

Since $L_0'' = L(\{G[., x](y) \mid x \in X \wedge y \in Y\})$, if $dim(L_0'') = 1$ then for every $x \in X$, $y, y' \in Y$ there is a real number $\alpha(x, y, y')$ with

$$G[., x](y') = \alpha(x, y, y')\, G[., x](y).$$

Therefore, for all $z \in Z$, $x \in X$, $y \in Y$,

$$G[z, x](Y) = 1 = G[z, x](y) \cdot \sum_{y' \in Y} \alpha(x, y, y'),$$

hence $G[z, x](y) = \left(\sum_{y' \in Y} \alpha(x, y, y')\right)^{-1}$. Thus if $dim(L_0'') = 1$, the output function G of $\mathfrak{C}$ does not depend on z, consequently, all states and random states are pairwise terminal equivalent.

If $dim(L_0'') = 1$, then our assertion is trivial. Thus assume $dim(L_0'') \geqq 2$. Then $\mathfrak{z}, \mathfrak{z}' \in \mathfrak{Z}_Z$ are terminal equivalent if and only if the linear functional $\overline{\varphi}_{\mathfrak{z},\mathfrak{z}'}$ defined in the proof of Theorem 7.7 is identically zero on $L_0' = L_{j_0}''$, hence if and only if

$$\forall p \forall x (p \in W(X) \wedge x \in X \wedge l(p) \leqq j_0 \rightarrow G[F[\mathfrak{z}, p], x] = G[F[\mathfrak{z}', p], x]).$$

Now we have

$$2 \leqq dim\,(L_0'') < dim\,(L_1'') < \cdots < dim\,(L_{j_0}'') \leqq n;$$

hence $j_0 + 2 \leqq n$, i.e., $j_0 \leqq n - 2$, which was to be shown.

Corollary 7.13. For finite S-automata, the relation $\underset{f}{\sim}$ between states and random states is decidable, furthermore, it is decidable whether for finite S-automata $\mathfrak{C}$, $\mathfrak{C}'$ the relation $\mathfrak{C} \underset{f}{\sim} \mathfrak{C}'$ holds or not.

In what follows, in analogy to the investigations carried out in § 2, we shall make some remarks on the "terminal equivalent" simplication of S-automata.

Definition 7.3. Let $\mathfrak{C} = [X, Y, Z, H]$ be an S-automaton.

(7.3.1) $\mathfrak{C}$ is called *terminal reduced* if for $z, z' \in Z$, $z \underset{f}{\sim} z'$ implies $z = z'$.[1])

(7.3.2) $\mathfrak{C}'$ is called a *terminal reduct of* $\mathfrak{C}$ if $\mathfrak{C}'$ is terminal reduced and terminal equivalent to $\mathfrak{C}$.

The concepts of *terminal minimality, terminal minim, strong terminal reducedness* and *strong terminal reduct* can be introduced similarly as in Definition 2.2.

---

[1]) In Fischer, Lindner, Thiele [1] terminal reducedness is defined in a different way.

Corollary 7.14.

1. Every strongly terminal reduced S-automaton is terminal minimal, every terminal minimal S-automaton is terminal reduced.

2. Every strong terminal reduct of $\mathfrak{C}$ is a terminal minim of $\mathfrak{C}$.

3. For finite S-automata the property of being terminal reduced is decidable.

4. If $\mathfrak{C}$ is terminal reduced, or terminal minimal, or strongly terminal reduced, then $\mathfrak{C}$ is reduced, or minimal, or strongly reduced respectively.

We have shown in § 2 that for finite S-automata $\mathfrak{C}$, it is decidable whether $\mathfrak{C}$ is minimal or strongly reduced. The proof of Theorem 2.15.1 can be transferred to our present case without serious difficulties. We have only to observe that in formulating the optimization problem the equality

$$\sum_{i=1}^{n} \alpha_i = 1$$

must be taken into consideration. Therefore, in transferring the proof of 2.15.2 we have to distinguish two cases, namely whether this equality is linearly independent of the other equations or not. Similarly the proof of Theorem 2.16 can also be transferred to the present case. Thus we obtain

Theorem 7.15.

1. *For finite S-automata $\mathfrak{C}$ it is decidable whether $\mathfrak{C}$ is terminal minimal or strongly terminal reduced.*

2. *All terminal reducts of the same S-automaton have the same number of states.*

3. *If $\mathfrak{C}$ is terminal reduced, $\mathfrak{C}'$ is terminal minimal and $\mathfrak{C} \underset{f}{\sim} \mathfrak{C}'$, then $\mathfrak{C}$ is terminal minimal.*

4. *If $\mathfrak{C}$ is terminal minimal, $\mathfrak{C}'$ is strongly terminal reduced, and $\mathfrak{C} \underset{f}{\sim} \mathfrak{C}'$, then $\mathfrak{C}$ is strongly terminal reduced.*

Theorem 7.16. *Every S-automaton $\mathfrak{C} = [X, Y, Z, H]$ has a terminal reduct $\overline{\mathfrak{C}}_f$. If $\mathfrak{C}$ is finite, then $\overline{\mathfrak{C}}_f$ can be constructed algorithmically.*

Proof: For $z \in Z$ let $[z] = \{z' \mid z' \in Z \wedge z' \underset{f}{\sim} z\}$, $\bar{Z}_f = \{[z] \mid z \in Z\}$, and ϱ be a choice function on $\bar{Z}_f$. For $\bar{z}, \bar{z}' \in \bar{Z}_f$, $x \in X$, $y \in Y$ we define

$$\bar{F}_f[\bar{z}, x](\bar{z}') \underset{\mathrm{Df}}{=} F[\varrho(\bar{z}), x](\bar{z}'); \quad \bar{G}_f[\bar{z}, x](y) \underset{\mathrm{Df}}{=} G[\varrho(\bar{z}), x](y).$$

Then $\overline{\mathfrak{C}}_f = [X, Y, \bar{Z}_f, \bar{F}_f, \bar{G}_f]$ is an S-Mealy automaton. We shall prove by induction on p that for all $[z] \in \bar{Z}_f$, $p \in W(X)$, $x \in X$, $y \in Y$

$$G\big[F[\varrho([z]), p], x\big](y) = \bar{G}_f\big[\bar{F}_f[[z], p], x\big](y).$$

For $p = e$ this equality is trivial. The step from p to $x_1 p$:

$$G\big[F[\varrho([z]), x_1 p], x\big](y) = \sum_{z' \in Z} F\big[\varrho([z]), x_1\big](z')\, G\big[F[z', p], x\big](y).$$

Since $\varrho([z']) \in [z']$, we have $z' \underset{f}{\sim} \varrho([z'])$, and we obtain

$$\begin{aligned} G\big[F[\varrho([z]), x_1 p], x\big](y) &= \sum_{z' \in Z} F\big[\varrho([z]), x_1\big](z')\, G\big[F[\varrho([z']), p], x\big](y) \\ &= \sum_{z' \in Z} F\big[\varrho([z]), x_1\big](z')\, \overline{G}_f\big[\overline{F}_f[[z'], p], x\big](y) \\ &= \sum_{\bar{z} \in \overline{Z}_f} \Big(\sum_{z' \in \bar{z}} F\big[\varrho([z]), x_1\big](z')\Big)\, \overline{G}_f\big[\overline{F}_f[\bar{z}, p], x\big](y) \\ &= \sum_{\bar{z} \in \overline{Z}_f} F\big[\varrho([z]), x_1\big](\bar{z})\, \overline{G}_f\big[\overline{F}_f[\bar{z}, p], x\big](y) \\ &= \sum_{\bar{z} \in \overline{Z}_f} \overline{F}_f\big[[z], x_1\big](\bar{z})\, \overline{G}_f\big[\overline{F}_f[\bar{z}, p], x\big](y) \\ &= \overline{G}_f\big[\overline{F}_f[[z], x_1 p], x\big](y). \end{aligned}$$

The automata $\mathfrak{C}$, $\overline{\mathfrak{C}}_f$ are thus terminal equivalent and $\overline{\mathfrak{C}}_f$ is terminal reduced, hence $\overline{\mathfrak{C}}_f$ is a terminal reduct of $\mathfrak{C}$.

Similarly as for 2.18 we can prove

Theorem 7.17.

1. *Every terminal minim $\mathfrak{C}'$ of an S-automaton $\mathfrak{C}$ is terminal equivalently embedded into $\mathfrak{C}$.*

2. *Weakly terminal equivalent and terminal minimal S-automata are terminal equivalent.*

3. *All terminal minims and strong terminal reducts of the same S-automata are pairwise terminal equivalent and have the same number of states.*

4. *An S-automaton $\mathfrak{C}$ has a strong terminal reduct if and only if $\mathfrak{C}$ has a terminal minim and all terminal minims of $\mathfrak{C}$ are strongly terminal reduced.*

It is easy to verify that Theorems 2.18 to 2.25 can be transferred without difficulty to the case of terminal equivalence. Therefore we shall not discuss them here.

§ 8. Stochastic Events

In the investigation of events over stochastic automata, we shall use two different approaches. The first one, due to Rabin [1] considers both stochastic and deterministic automata as instruments for deciding upon sets of words, or for classifying words over the input alphabet, but of course for stochastic automata there is no deterministic decision as to whether $p \in E$ or $p \notin E$, but only a decision concerning a certain probability of these relations. Thus, Rabin calls an event $E \subseteq W(X)$ c-represented in the weakly initial S-automaton $\mathfrak{C} = [X, Y, Z, H, \mathfrak{z}]$ by the set $N \subseteq Z$ (where $0 \leqq c \leqq 1$), if $E = \{p \mid p \in W(X) \wedge F[\mathfrak{z}, p](N) > c\}$.

This means that a word p belongs to the c-represented set of words if and only if the probability that the automaton $\mathfrak{C}$ "accepts" this word (i.e., enters into one of the states of the set N) exceeds c. We shall use this approach in the following section.

The second approach proposed by THIELE and first used in STARKE [3], [5], [6], aims at the adequate generalization of the concept of events in the theory of stochastic automata. Our starting point is the fact that to every set (in particular to every set of words) there corresponds a property, an attribute which can take exactly two truth values, which we shall denote by 1 and 0. For instance to the set of words $E \subseteq W(X)$ there corresponds the (one place and two valued) attribute φ_E which, for a word p takes the value 1 ("true") if and only if $p \in E$. If we drop the restriction that the range of the attribute φ_E has to be a set consisting of the two truth values, and admit all one place attributes whose range is contained in the closed interval $\langle 0, 1\rangle$ of the real numbers, (i.e. attributes from a so called probability logic), then we arrive at the concept of a stochastic event. Thus, a stochastic event φ is a single-valued mapping of $W(X)$ into the interval $\langle 0, 1\rangle$. The following considerations show that this generalization is indeed adequate. The definition of the representability of a set of words $E \subseteq W(X)$ in a deterministic automaton $\mathfrak{A} = [X, Z, \delta, z_0]$ by a set N requires that for all $p \in W(X)$, the two one-place and two-valued attributes $p \in E$ and $\delta(z_0, p) \in N$ take the same truth value. If we consider a stochastic automaton, then the attribute $\delta(z_0, p) \in N$ might in general take infinitely many values, this being the attribute $F[z_0, p](N)$. Accordingly, the attribute $p \in E$ should also be generalized to one which can take infinitely many values.

We shall say that a stochastic event φ over X is represented in the S-automaton $\mathfrak{C} = [X, Y, Z, H, \mathfrak{z}]$ by the set N if $\varphi(p) = F[\mathfrak{z}, p](N)$ for all $p \in W(X)$. Here we only need to know the transition function F of the automaton $\mathfrak{C}$, and therefore we define the concept of a "stochastic automaton without output". In addition to representability, we shall also investigate in this section two ways of generating stochastic events which are generalizations of the corresponding notions for non-deterministic automata. We shall also set up a connection between stochastic operators and systems of stochastic events.

Definition 8.1. Let X be a non-empty set.

(8.1.1) φ is called a *stochastic event over* X if it is a single-valued mapping of $W(X)$ into the interval $\langle 0, 1\rangle$.

(8.1.2) A stochastic event φ over X is called a *stochastic elementary event* if $\varphi(p) > 0$ implies $p \in X$.

(8.1.3) A non-empty system $\{\varphi_y \mid y \in Y\}$ of stochastic events over X is called a *spectrum of events over* $[X, Y]$ if

a) for every $p \in W(X) \setminus \{e\}$ there are at most countably many $y \in Y$ with $\varphi_y(p) > 0$ and in addition

$$\sum_{y \in Y} \varphi_y(p) = 1,$$

and b) for all $y \in Y$ we have $\varphi_y(e) = 0$.

Remark: Condition b) of Definition (8.1.3) serves only for norming. With its application, we can achieve that for every homogeneous S-operator there exists exactly one spectrum of events with certain properties (cf. Theorem 8.1).

Let Φ be an arbitrary sequential S-operator over $[X, Y]$. For $p \in W(X)$, $y \in Y$ we put

$$\varphi_y(p) = \begin{cases} 0, & \text{if } p = e, \\ \Phi_{rx}\big(W(Y) \cdot \{y\}\big), & \text{if } p = rx \neq e. \end{cases} \tag{*}$$

Since $\sum_{y \in Y} \varphi_y(rx) = \Phi_{rx}\big(W(Y) \cdot Y\big) = 1$, as can be easily seen, $\{\varphi_y \mid y \in Y\}$ is a spectrum of events over $[X, Y]$. This we call the *spectrum belonging to* Φ.

Conversely, if $\{\varphi_y \mid y \in Y\}$ is a spectrum of events over $[X, Y]$ then the formula

$$\Phi_p(q) = \begin{cases} 1, \text{ if } & p = q = e, \\ \varphi_{y_1}(x_1)\, \varphi_{y_2}(x_1 x_2) \ldots \varphi_{y_n}(x_1 \ldots x_n), & \\ \quad \text{if } & p = x_1 \ldots x_n \in W(X) \\ \quad \text{and } & q = y_1 \ldots y_n \in W(Y), \quad n \geqq 1, \\ 0 \quad \text{otherwise} & \end{cases} \tag{**}$$

defines a homogeneous S-operator Φ over $[X, Y]$, since for $p \in W(X)$, $x \in X$, $q \in W(Y)$, and $y \in Y$, (**) implies

$$\Phi_{px}(qy) = \Phi_p(q) \cdot \varphi_y(px).$$

Now we can easily prove

Theorem 8.1. (*) *and* (**) *establish a one-to-one correspondence between the homogeneous S-operators over* $[X, Y]$ *and the spectra of events over* $[X, Y]$.

Definition 8.2. Let φ be a stochastic event over X.

(8.2.1) We call φ *represented in the weakly initial S-automaton* $\mathfrak{C} = [X, Y, Z, H, \mathfrak{z}]$ *by the set of states* $N \subseteq Z$ if $\varphi(p) = F[\mathfrak{z}, p](N)$ for all $p \in W(X)$.

(8.2.2) The stochastic event φ is said to be *represented in* $\mathfrak{C} = [X, Y, Z, H, \mathfrak{z}]$ *by the output signal* $y \in Y$ if $\varphi(p) = V_{\mathfrak{C}}[\mathfrak{z}, p]\big(W(Y) \cdot \{y\}\big)$ for all $p \in W(X)$.

(8.2.3) φ is said to be *generated in the weakly initial autonomous S-automaton* $\mathfrak{C} = [\{x_0\}, X, Z, H, \mathfrak{z}]$ *by the set* $N \subseteq Z$ if

$$\varphi(p) = \begin{cases} \mathfrak{z}(N), & \text{if } p = e, \\ H[\mathfrak{z}, x_0^{l(p)}](\{p\} \times Z^{l(p)-1} \cdot N), & \text{if } p \in W(X) \setminus \{e\}. \end{cases}$$

(8.2.4) φ is said to be *produced in* $\mathfrak{C} = [\{x_0\}, X, Z, H, \mathfrak{z}]$ if $\varphi(p) = V_{\mathfrak{C}}[\mathfrak{z}, x_0^{l(p)}](p)$ for all $p \in W(X)$.

If the stochastic event φ is represented in $\mathfrak{C} = [X, Y, Z, H, \mathfrak{z}]$ by the output signal y then $\varphi(e) = 0$ and for $p \in W(X)$, $x \in X$

$$\varphi(px) = V_{\mathfrak{C}}[\mathfrak{z}, px]\big(W(Y) \cdot \{y\}\big) = G\big[F[\mathfrak{z}, p], x\big](y).$$

Without any loss of generality, we can assume that $\mathfrak{C}$ is an S-Moore automaton with a deterministic marking function M, moreover that $\mathfrak{z}$ is deterministic, $\mathfrak{z} = \delta_z$ and $M[z](y) = 0$. Then, by $N = \{z' \mid M[z'](y) = 1\}$ and $z \notin N$, we obtain that φ is represented in $\mathfrak{C} = [X, Y, Z, F, M, \delta_z]$ by the set N. Indeed

$$F[z, e](N) = 0 = \varphi(e),$$

and for $px \in W(X) \setminus \{e\}$,

$$\varphi(px) = G\big[F[\delta_z, p], x\big](y) = M\big[F[z, px]\big](y) = F[z, px](N).$$

Hence every stochastic event representable by an output signal (in a Z-finite S-automaton) can also be represented by a set of states (in a Z-finite S-automaton). Just as easily, we can see that if a stochastic event φ can be represented by a set of states (in a Z-finite S-automaton) then the stochastic event φ^0 where

$$\varphi^0(p) = \begin{cases} 0, & \text{if } p = e, \\ \varphi(p) & \text{otherwise} \end{cases}$$

can also be represented by an output signal (in a Z-finite S-automaton). Hence if we omit the values $\varphi(e)$, then Definitions 8.2.1 and 8.2.2 are equivalent. Similarly as in the theory of deterministic automata, in investigating the representability of stochastic events, we can restrict ourselves to automata without output.

Definition 8.3. An S-automaton $\mathfrak{C} = [X, Y, Z, H]$ is called an *S-automaton without output* (or an *outputless S-automaton*) if $\mathfrak{C}$ is an S-Moore automaton with $Y = Z$ and $M[z](z) = 1$ for all $z \in Z$.

Weakly initial or initial S-automata without output are denoted by $[X, Z, F, \mathfrak{z}]$ or $[X, Z, F, z]$ respectively.

Definition 8.4. A stochastic event φ over X is called *regular* if it can be represented by a set of states in a Z-finite S-automaton.

Theorem 8.2. *Let Φ be an S-operator over $[X, Y]$ and $\mathfrak{C} = [X, Y, Z, F, M]$ an S-Moore automaton with a deterministic marking function, in which Φ is generated by a state z_0. Then every member φ_y of the spectrum $\{\varphi_y \mid y \in Y\}$ of events over $[X, Y]$ belonging to Φ can be represented in the same S-automaton $\mathfrak{C}'$. If $\mathfrak{C}$ is Z-finite then $\mathfrak{C}'$ can also be chosen Z-finite.*

Proof: Let $z_{00} \notin Z$. For $z, z' \in Z' = Z \cup \{z_{00}\}$, $x \in X$ we put

$$F'[z, x](z') = \begin{cases} F[z, x](z'), & \text{if } z \in Z,\ z' \in Z, \\ F[z_0, x](z'), & \text{if } z = z_{00},\ z' \in Z, \\ 0 & \text{otherwise.} \end{cases}$$

Here, $\mathfrak{C}' = [X, Z', F', z_{00}]$ is an initial S-automaton without output such that for all $p \in W(X) \setminus \{e\}$, $N \subseteq Z \subset Z'$

$$F'[z_{00}, p](N) = F[z_0, p](N).$$

For $y \in Y$ we put $N_y = \{z \mid z \in Z \wedge M[z](y) = 1\}$. We claim that φ_y is represented in $\mathfrak{C}'$ by $N_y \subseteq Z \subseteq Z'$. We have

$$F'[z_{00}, e](N_y) = 0 = \varphi_y(e),$$

since $z_{00} \in N_y$, and for $px \in W(X) \setminus \{e\}$

$$\begin{aligned}\varphi_y(px) &= \Phi_{px}\big(W(Y)\cdot\{y\}\big) = V_{\mathfrak{C}}[z_0, px]\big(W(Y)\cdot\{y\}\big)\\ &= \sum_{z'\in Z} F[z_0, px](z')\, M[z'](y) = F[z_0, px](N_y)\\ &= F'[z_{00}, px](N_y).\end{aligned}$$

This proves Theorem 8.2.

Theorem 8.3.

1. *Every stochastic event is representable.*

2. *A stochastic event φ over X is regular if and only if the pseudo-stochastic operator Ψ^φ over $[X, \{y_0\}]$ defined below*

$$\Psi_p^\varphi(Q) = \left\{\begin{array}{ll}\varphi(p), & \textit{if}\quad y_0^{l(p)} \in Q,\\ 0 & \textit{otherwise}\end{array}\right\} \quad \textit{for}\quad p \in W(X),\ Q \subseteq W(\{y_0\})$$

is regular.

Remark: Obviously, Ψ^φ is uniquely determined by φ up to Y-isomorphisms.

Proof: Let φ be an arbitrary stochastic event over X. By Theorem 4.14, Ψ^φ is generable, because the stochastic operator Φ over $[X, \{y_0\}]$ with

$$\Phi_p(q) = \begin{cases}1, & \text{if}\quad p \in W(X),\quad q = y_0^{l(p)},\\ 0 & \text{otherwise}\end{cases}$$

is sequential, and $\Psi_p^\varphi(q) \leqq \Phi_p(q)$ for all $p \in W(X)$, $q \in W(\{y_0\})$, because $\varphi(p) \leqq 1$. Let Ψ^φ be generated in $\mathfrak{C} = [X, \{y_0\}, Z, H]$ by $[\mathfrak{z}, N]$. If Ψ^φ is regular, then we choose $\mathfrak{C}$ Z-finite. For $p \in W(X)$

$$\varphi(p) = \Psi_p^\varphi(y_0^{l(p)}) = \begin{cases}\mathfrak{z}(N), & \text{if}\quad p = e,\\ H[\mathfrak{z}, p](\{y_0^n\} \times Z^{n-1}\cdot N), & \text{if}\quad l(p) = n > 0.\end{cases}$$

Since the output alphabet of $\mathfrak{C}$ is a singleton, for $n = l(p) > 0$ we have

$$H[\mathfrak{z}, p](\{y_0^n\} \times Z^{n-1}\cdot N) = F[\mathfrak{z}, p](N),$$

i.e., for all $p \in W(X)$, $\varphi(p) = F[\mathfrak{z}, p](N)$. This means that φ is represented in the weakly initial (and for regular Ψ^φ also Z-finite) outputless S-automaton $\mathfrak{C}' = [X, Z, F, \mathfrak{z}]$ by N.

Conversely, if φ is represented in $[X, Z, F, \mathfrak{z}]$ by N, where Z is finite, then Ψ^φ is regular. Indeed, the PS-operator Ψ^φ is generated in the Z-finite S-automaton $[X, \{y_0\}, Z, H]$ by $[\mathfrak{z}, N]$ where for $z, z' \in Z$, $x \in X$

$$H[z, x](y_0, z') = F[z, x](z').$$

This proves Theorem 8.3.

If φ, φ' are stochastic events over X, then we define $\bar{\varphi}$, $\varphi \times \varphi'$ and $\varphi \bigtriangledown \varphi'$ for every $p \in W(X)$ as follows

$$\bar{\varphi}(p) \underset{\mathrm{Df}}{=} 1 - \varphi(p),$$

$$\varphi \times \varphi'(p) \underset{\mathrm{Df}}{=} \varphi(p) \cdot \varphi'(p),$$

$$\varphi \bigtriangledown \varphi'(p) \underset{\mathrm{Df}}{=} \overline{\bar{\varphi} \times \bar{\varphi}'}(p) = \varphi(p) + \varphi'(p) - \varphi(p)\,\varphi'(p).$$

If φ is represented in $\mathfrak{C} = [X, Z, F, z]$ by the set N, and φ' is represented in $\mathfrak{C}' = [X, Z', F', z']$ by N', then φ is represented in $\mathfrak{C}$ by $Z \setminus N$ and $\varphi \times \varphi'$ is represented in the S-automaton $\mathfrak{C} \times \mathfrak{C}' = [X, Z \times Z', F^*, \mathfrak{z}^*]$ by $N \times N'$, where for all $z, z^* \in Z$, $z', z'' \in Z'$, $x \in X$

$$F^*\big[[z, z'], x\big]([z^*, z'']) \underset{\mathrm{Df}}{=} F[z, x](z^*)\, F'[z', x](z''),$$

$$\mathfrak{z}^*([z, z']) \underset{\mathrm{Df}}{=} \mathfrak{z}(z)\, \mathfrak{z}'(z').$$

To prove this, one shows by easy induction on p that

$$F^*[\mathfrak{z}^*, p]([z, z']) = F[\mathfrak{z}, p](z)\, F'[\mathfrak{z}', p](z')$$

for all $p \in W(X)$, $z \in Z$, $z' \in Z'$. Thus we have

Theorem 8.4.

1. *A stochastic event* φ *is regular if and only if* $\bar{\varphi}$ *is.*
2. *If* φ, φ' *are regular, so are* $\varphi \times \varphi'$ *and* $\varphi \bigtriangledown \varphi'$.

Remark: The set of regular stochastic events is closed under the operations $^-$, $\times$, $\bigtriangledown$; however, it is not a lattice with respect to $\times$, $\bigtriangledown$ since in general $\varphi \times \varphi \neq \varphi$.

Consider an arbitrary stochastic event φ over X and define, for every $r \in W(\{x_0\})$ a totally additive measure $\tilde{\Psi}_r^\varphi$ on $\mathfrak{P}\big(W(X)\big)$ by

$$\tilde{\Psi}_r^\varphi(Q) \underset{\mathrm{Df}}{=} \sum_{p \in Q \cap X^{l(r)}} \varphi(p).$$

The (single-valued) mapping $\tilde{\Psi}^\varphi$ which assigns the measure $\tilde{\Psi}_r^\varphi$ to every $r \in W(\{x_0\})$ is obviously a PS-operator over $[\{x_0\}, X]$ if and only if the value $\tilde{\Psi}_r^\varphi\big(W(X)\big)$ is finite for all such r. Next we prove

Theorem 8.5. *A stochastic event φ over X can be generated in a (Z-finite) S-automaton if and only if the mapping $\tilde{\Psi}^{\varphi}$ is a PS-operator over $[\{x_0\}, X]$ which can be generated in a (Z-finite) S-automaton.*

Proof: Suppose the stochastic event φ is generated in $[\{x_0\}, X, Z, H, \mathfrak{z}]$ by the set $N \subseteq Z$. Then for $n \geqq 0$

$$\tilde{\Psi}^{\varphi}_{x_0^n}(W(X)) = \tilde{\Psi}^{\varphi}_{x_0^n}(X^n)$$

$$= \begin{cases} \varphi(e), & \text{if } n = 0, \\ \sum_{p \in X^n} \varphi(p), & \text{if } n > 0, \end{cases}$$

$$= \left.\begin{cases} \mathfrak{z}(N), & \text{if } n = 0, \\ H[\mathfrak{z}, x_0^n](X^n \times Z^{n-1} \cdot N), & \text{if } n > 0, \end{cases}\right\} \leqq 1.$$

Hence the mapping $\tilde{\Psi}^{\varphi}$ is a PS-operator over $[\{x_0\}, X]$. Also, it is easy to see that $\tilde{\Psi}^{\varphi}$ is generated in the S-automaton $[\{x_0\}, X, Z, H]$ by $[\mathfrak{z}, N]$. The converse is trivial.

The value $\varphi(e)$ (just as for PS-operators Ψ the value $\Psi_e(e)$) has no influence on whether φ can be represented or generated in a possibly Z-finite S-automaton. From Theorem 4.15 we obtain

Theorem 8.6. *A stochastic event φ over X is representable or generable in a (Z-finite) S-automaton if and only if the stochastic events φ^0, φ^1 with*

$$\varphi^0(e) = 0, \quad \varphi^1(e) = 1, \quad \varphi^0(p) = \varphi^1(p) = \varphi(p) \quad \textit{for} \quad p \in W(X) \setminus \{e\}$$

can be represented or generated in an initial (Z-finite) S-automaton.

Now we characterize the producibility of stochastic events and thus we obtain a criterion (as a corollary to Theorem 4.14) for when a stochastic event can be generated.

Theorem 8.7. *Let φ be a stochastic event over X.*

1. *φ is producible if and only if the following conditions are satisfied.*

$$\text{(E1)} \quad \sum_{p \in X^n} \varphi(p) = 1 \qquad \textit{for all} \quad n \in \boldsymbol{nz}.$$

$$\text{(E2)} \quad \sum_{x \in X} \varphi(px) = \varphi(p) \quad \textit{for all} \quad p \in W(X).$$

2. *φ can be produced in a Z-finite S-automaton if and only if it satisfies condition (E1) and can be generated in a Z-finite S-automaton.*

Proof: It follows from Definition (8.2.4) that φ is producible if and only if there is a sequential S-operator Φ over $[\{x_0\}, X]$ such that $\varphi(p) = \Phi_{x_0^{l(p)}}(p)$

for all $p \in W(X)$. Thus φ is producible if and only if the mapping Φ^{φ} defined by

$$\Phi^{\varphi}_{x_0^n}(p) = \begin{cases} \varphi(p), & \text{if } l(p) = n, \\ 0 & \text{otherwise,} \end{cases}$$

is a sequential S-operator, which is the case if and only if φ satisfies (E 1) and (E 2).

If φ is generated in $\mathfrak{C} = [\{x_0\}, X, Z, H, \mathfrak{z}]$ by the set N and (E 1) is satisfied, then $\varphi(p) = V_{\mathfrak{C}}[\mathfrak{z}, x_0^{l(p)}](p)$ for all $p \in W(X)$, as we shall now show. If $p = e$, then $\varphi(e) = 1$ by (E 1), since $X^0 = \{e\}$. Suppose $p \in W(X) \setminus \{e\}$, $l(p) = n > 0$. Then we have to show that

$$H[\mathfrak{z}, x_0^n]\big(\{p\} \times Z^{n-1}(Z \setminus N)\big) = 0.$$

Suppose this is not the case. Then from (E 1) we obtain

$$\begin{aligned} 1 = \sum_{r \in X^n} \varphi(r) &= H[\mathfrak{z}, x_0^n](X^n \times Z^{n-1} \cdot N) \\ &< H[\mathfrak{z}, x_0^n](X^n \times Z^{n-1} \cdot N) + H[\mathfrak{z}, x_0^n]\big(\{p\} \times Z^{n-1} \cdot (Z \setminus N)\big) \\ &\leqq H[\mathfrak{z}, x_0^n](X^n \times Z^{n-1} \cdot N) + H[\mathfrak{z}, x_0^n]\big(X^n \times Z^{n-1} \cdot (Z \setminus N)\big) = 1, \end{aligned}$$

which is a contradiction. Consequently, φ is produced in $\mathfrak{C}$.

Conversely, if φ is produced in $\mathfrak{C} = [\{x_0\}, X, Z, H, \mathfrak{z}]$ then φ is also generated in $\mathfrak{C}$ by the set Z. This proves Theorem 8.7.

Theorem 8.8. *A stochastic event φ over X can be generated if and only if there is a producible stochastic event φ' over X such that $\varphi(p) \leqq \varphi'(p)$ for all $p \in W(X)$.*

Proof: By 8.5, φ can be generated if and only if $\tilde{\Psi}^{\varphi}$ is a generable PS-operator over $[\{x_0\}, X]$ i.e., by 4.14, if and only if there is a sequential S-operator Φ over $[\{x_0\}, X]$ with

$$\Psi^{\varphi}_r(p) \leqq \Phi_r(p)$$

for all $r \in W(\{x_0\})$, $p \in W(X)$. To every sequential S-operator over $[\{x_0\}, X]$ there corresponds a uniquely determined stochastic event φ' with

$$\Phi_{x_0^{l(p)}}(p) = \varphi'(p)$$

for $p \in W(X)$. Since

$$\varphi(p) = \tilde{\Psi}^{\varphi}_{x_0^{l(p)}}(p) \leqq \Phi_{x_0^{l(p)}}(p) = \varphi'(p),$$

this proves Theorem 8.8.

Theorems 8.3 and 8.6, together with Theorem 4.20, characterize the sets of stochastic events which can be represented or generated in Z-finite S-automata.

However, it is possible to characterize the representability or generability of stochastic events in Z-finite S-automata (which corresponds to Theorem 4.20), without any reference to the regularity of PS-operators. For this it is necessary to transfer to stochastic events the operations of addition, multiplication and iteration, to define the notion of an event code and to define and clarify how a stochastic event, described by a regular term over $\boldsymbol{nz}$ and an event code, is constructed.

Definition 8.4. Let φ, φ' be stochastic events over X. The *addition* $[\varphi + \varphi']$ *of* φ *and* φ', the *multiplication* $[\varphi \cdot \varphi']$ *of* φ *by* φ', and the *iteration* $\langle\varphi\rangle$ *of* φ are defined for all $p \in W(X)$ as follows:

$$[\varphi + \varphi'](p) = min\left(1, \varphi(p) + \varphi'(p)\right),$$

$$[\varphi \cdot \varphi'](p) = min\left(1, \sum_{rs=p} \varphi(r) \cdot \varphi'(s)\right),$$

$$\langle\varphi\rangle(p) = \begin{cases} 1, & \text{if} \quad p = e, \\ min\left(1, \sum_{m=1}^{l(p)} \sum_{\substack{p_1,\ldots,p_m \neq e \\ p_1\ldots p_m = p}} \prod_{i=1}^{m} \varphi(p_i)\right), & \text{if} \quad p \neq e. \end{cases}$$

Corollary 8.9. Let φ, φ' be stochastic events over X.

1. $\Psi^{[\varphi+\varphi']} = [\Psi^{\varphi} + \Psi^{\varphi'}]$ and $\tilde{\Psi}^{[\varphi+\varphi']} = [\tilde{\Psi}^{\varphi} + \tilde{\Psi}^{\varphi'}]$,
2. $\Psi^{[\varphi\cdot\varphi']} = [\Psi^{\varphi} \cdot \Psi^{\varphi'}]$ and $\tilde{\Psi}^{[\varphi\cdot\varphi']} = [\tilde{\Psi}^{\varphi} \cdot \tilde{\Psi}^{\varphi'}]$,
3. $\Psi^{\langle\varphi\rangle} = \langle\Psi^{\varphi}\rangle$ and $\tilde{\Psi}^{\langle\varphi\rangle} = \langle\tilde{\Psi}^{\varphi}\rangle$.

Definition 8.5.

(8.5.1) A function β which assigns to every number symbol $\boldsymbol{j} \in NZ$ a stochastic elementary event $\beta^{\boldsymbol{j}}$ over X, is called an *event code over* X.

(8.5.2) If T is a regular term over $\boldsymbol{nz}$ and β is an event code over X, then the stochastic event $\mathfrak{E}(T, \beta)$ described by T and β is defined inductively as follows:

(A) $$\mathfrak{E}[\boldsymbol{j}, \beta] = \beta^{\boldsymbol{j}},$$

(I) $$\mathfrak{E}[T, \beta] = \begin{cases} \mathfrak{E}[T_1, \beta] + \mathfrak{E}[T_2, \beta], & \text{if} \quad T \equiv (T_1 \vee T_2), \\ \mathfrak{E}[T_1, \beta] \cdot \mathfrak{E}[T_2, \beta], & \text{if} \quad T \equiv (T_1 \circ T_2), \\ \langle\mathfrak{E}[T_1, \beta]\rangle, & \text{if} \quad T \equiv \langle T_1\rangle. \end{cases}$$

(8.5.3) Let T be a regular term over $\boldsymbol{nz}$ and β an event code over X. β is said to be *regular for* T, if for all $x \in X$

a) $$\sum_{\boldsymbol{j} \in A(T)} \beta^{\boldsymbol{j}}(x) \leq 1,$$

and for $i \in I(T)$

b) $$\sum_{j \in f^T(i)} \beta^j(x) \leqq 1.$$

β is called *strongly regular for T*, if

a') $$\sum_{x \in X} \sum_{j \in A(T)} \beta^j(x) \leqq 1,$$

and for all $i \in I(T)$

b') $$\sum_{x \in X} \sum_{j \in f^T(i)} \beta^j(x) \leqq 1.$$

Corollary 8.10. Let T be a regular term over $\boldsymbol{nz}$.

1. If B is a regular $[X, \{y_0\}]$-code for T then:

a) For every $j \in I(T)$ there exists exactly one stochastic elementary event φ^j over X with $B^j = \Psi^{\varphi^j}$.

b) Every event code β over X with $\beta^j = \varphi^j$ for all $j \in I(T)$ is regular for T.

c) $\mathfrak{W}[T, B] = \Psi^{\mathfrak{E}[T,\beta]}$ for all β satisfying b).

2. If B is a regular $[\{x_0\}, X]$-code for T then:

a) For every $j \in I(T)$ there is exactly one stochastic elementary event φ^j over X with $B^j = \tilde{\Psi}^{\varphi^j}$.

b) Every event code β over X with $\beta^j = \varphi^j$ for all $j \in I(T)$ is strongly regular for T.

c) $\mathfrak{W}[T, B] = \tilde{\Psi}^{\mathfrak{E}[T,\beta]}$ for all β satisfying b).

3. If β is a regular event code over X for T, then the $[X, \{y_0\}]$-code B defined by $B^j = \Psi^{\beta^j}$ for $\boldsymbol{j} \in NZ$ is regular for T and $\mathfrak{W}[T, B] = \Psi^{\mathfrak{E}[T,\beta]}$.

4. If β is a strongly regular event code over X for T then:

a) For $j \in I(T)$ $\tilde{\Psi}^{\beta^j}$ is a PS-operator over $[\{x_0\}, X]$.

b) Every $[\{x_0\}, X]$-code B with $B^j = \tilde{\Psi}^{\beta^j}$ for $j \in I(T)$ is regular for T.

c) $\mathfrak{W}[T, B] = \tilde{\Psi}^{\mathfrak{E}[T,\beta]}$ for all B satisfying b).

Thus from Theorem 4.20 we obtain

Theorem 8.11. *A stochastic event φ over X can be represented (or generated) in a Z-finite S-automaton if and only if there is a standard term T and an event code β which is regular (or strongly regular) for T such that for all $p \in W(X) \setminus \{e\}$*

$$\varphi(p) = \mathfrak{E}[T, \beta](p).$$

Since for an arbitrary standard term T, every strongly regular event code β for T is also regular for T, we have

Corollary 8.12. Every stochastic event generated in a Z-finite S-automaton is regular.

§ 9. Stochastic Events and Sets of Words

In this section, we shall deal with the other kind of representability of sets of words (events) in stochastic automata, using a definition due to Rabin. This notion of representability has been investigated in many papers, therefore we restrict ourselves here to the most important results.

Definition 9.1 (Rabin [1]). Let c be a real number with $0 \leqq c \leqq 1$, and $\mathfrak{C} = [X, Z, F, \mathfrak{z}]$ a weakly initial S-automaton without output. A set of words $E \subseteq W(X)$ is said to be *c-represented in* $\mathfrak{C}$ *by the set of states* $N \subseteq Z$ if for all $p \in W(X)$ the following relation holds:

$$p \in E \leftrightarrow F[\mathfrak{z}, p](N) > c.$$

Corollary 9.1. A set of words $E \subseteq W(X)$ can be c-represented (in a Z-finite S-automaton) if and only if there is a regular stochastic event φ over X such that

$$E = \{p \mid p \in W(X) \wedge \varphi(p) > c\}.$$

Thus only the empty set is 1-representable. Since for every set of words $E \subseteq W(X)$ there is a deterministic automaton in which E is representable, we obtain

Theorem 9.2. *Let* $0 \leqq c < 1$.

1. *Every set of words* $E \subseteq W(X)$ *is c-representable.*

2. *If E can be represented in a Z-finite, deterministic automaton, then it is c-representable in a Z-finite S-automaton.*

In particular, (if X is finite) every regular set of words over X can be c-represented in a Z-finite S-automaton where $0 \leqq c < 1$ is arbitrary. In what follows, we shall investigate the converse of 9.2.2, that is the question of when a set of words E which is c-representable in a Z-finite S-automaton can also be represented in a Z-finite deterministic automaton, which for finite X means that E is regular over X.

Theorem 9.3. *Every set of words which is* 0*-representable in a Z-finite S-automaton, is also representable in a Z-finite deterministic automaton.*

Proof: Suppose E is 0-represented in $\mathfrak{C} = [X, Z, F, \mathfrak{z}]$ by the set N, i.e.,

$$E = \{p \mid F[\mathfrak{z}, p](N) > 0\}.$$

Consider the non-deterministic automaton $\mathfrak{B} = ND(\mathfrak{C}) = [X, Z, f, M]$ where $f = ND(F)$, $M = ND(\mathfrak{z})$. Then

$$F[\mathfrak{z}', r](N') > 0 \leftrightarrow f(ND(\mathfrak{z}'), r) \cap N' \neq \emptyset$$

for $\mathfrak{z}' \in \mathfrak{Z}_Z$, $r \in W(X)$, $N' \subseteq Z$. Hence, E is represented in the Z-finite deterministic initial automaton $\mathfrak{A} = [X, \mathfrak{P}(Z), \delta, M]$, where for $N' \in \mathfrak{P}(Z)$, $x \in X$

$$\delta(N', x) = f(N', x) \quad \big(= \{z' \mid \exists z (z \in N' \wedge F[z, x](z') > 0)\}\big),$$

by the set $\mathfrak{N} = \{N' \mid N' \in \mathfrak{P}(Z) \wedge N' \cap N \neq \emptyset\}$ (cf. Part II, Proof of Theorem 8.4).

If φ is a stochastic event over X and c is a real number with $0 \leqq c \leqq 1$, then we put

$$E_{\varphi > c} = \{p \mid p \in W(X) \wedge \varphi(p) > c\},$$
$$E_{\varphi = c} = \{p \mid p \in W(X) \wedge \varphi(p) = c\},$$
$$E_{\varphi < c} = \{p \mid p \in W(X) \wedge \varphi(p) < c\}.$$

Corollary 9.4. If φ is a regular stochastic event over X, then the sets $E_{\varphi>0}$, $E_{\varphi=0}$, $E_{\varphi<1}$, $E_{\varphi=1}$ can be represented in Z-finite deterministic automata.

That $E_{\varphi=0}$ can be represented in a Z-finite deterministic automaton follows from $E_{\varphi=0} = W(X) \setminus E_{\varphi>0} = \overline{E}_{\varphi>0}$ and the proof of Theorem 6.9 in Part I. Furthermore $E_{\varphi<1} = E_{1-\varphi>0} = E_{\overline{\varphi}>0}$ and by 8.4 $\overline{\varphi}$ is also regular if φ is.

We consider for $m \in \boldsymbol{nz}$, $m \geqq 2$ the initial outputless S-automaton $\mathfrak{C}^m = [X, \{a, b\}, F^m, a]$, where $X = \{0, 1, \ldots, m-1\}$ and for $z, z' \in \{a, b\}$, $x \in X$

$$F^m[z, x](z') = \begin{cases} 1 - \dfrac{x}{m}, & \text{if} \quad z = z' = a, \\[2ex] \dfrac{x}{m}, & \text{if} \quad z = a,\ z' = b, \\[2ex] 1 - \dfrac{x+1}{m}, & \text{if} \quad z = b,\ z' = a, \\[2ex] \dfrac{x+1}{m}, & \text{if} \quad z = z' = b. \end{cases}$$

Let φ be the stochastic event represented in $\mathfrak{C}^m$ by the set $N = \{b\}$. Thus $\varphi(e) = 0$, and we claim that for $x_1 \ldots x_n \in W(X) \setminus \{e\}$

$$\varphi(x_1 \ldots x_n) = 0, x_n x_{n-1} \ldots x_1 \quad (m\text{-adic}),$$

i.e., that $0, x_n \ldots x_1$ is the m-adic expansion of the number $\varphi(x_1 \ldots x_n)$. We shall prove this by induction.

Initial step:

$$\varphi(x) = F^m[a, x](b) = \frac{x}{m} = 0, x \quad (m\text{-adic}).$$

Induction step: $p \to px$

$$\begin{aligned}\varphi(px) &= F^m[a, p](a) F^m[a, x](b) + F^m[a, p](b) F^m[b, x](b)\\ &= \big(1 - \varphi(p)\big) \cdot \frac{x}{m} + \varphi(p) \cdot \frac{x+1}{m}\\ &= \frac{x}{m} + \frac{\varphi(p)}{m}\\ &= 0, x + 0, 0p^* = 0, xp^* = 0, (px)^* \qquad (m\text{-adic})\end{aligned}$$

(where p^* denotes the inverse of the word p).

That is why we call φ the *m-adic stochastic event*. The set of all values of φ (the range of φ) is dense in the interval $\langle 0, 1 \rangle$. This implies

$$E_{\varphi > c} = E_{\varphi > c'} \leftrightarrow c = c',$$

for arbitrary real numbers c, c' with $0 \leqq c, c' \leqq 1$. Consequently, there are uncountably many sets of words which can be c-represented in $\mathfrak{C}^m$. But since there are only countably many regular sets of words over X, this implies that irregular sets of words can also be c-represented in $\mathfrak{C}^m$.

Theorem 9.5 (Rabin [1], Paz [2]). *If φ is the m-adic stochastic event, then for $0 \leqq c \leqq 1$ the set of words $E_{\varphi > c}$ is regular if and only if c is rational.*

Proof: If $c = 0$, or $c = 1$, this is trivial. If $0 < c < 1$ then for $p, q \in W(X)$ ($X = \{0, 1, \ldots, m-1\}$, $m \geqq 2$) we define the relation $\underset{c}{\sim}$ as follows:

$$p \underset{c}{\sim} q \leftrightarrow \forall r \big(r \in W(X) \to (pr \in E_{\varphi > c} \leftrightarrow qr \in E_{\varphi > c})\big).$$

By Nerode's Theorem (Part I, Theorem 6.2), $E_{\varphi > c}$ is regular if and only if the partition $W(X)/\underset{c}{\sim}$ is finite. So it suffices to show that $\underset{c}{\sim}$ is of finite rank if and only if c is rational.

Let v be a real number whose m-adic expansion is $v = 0, v_1 v_2 \ldots$ and u a number with the *finite* m-adic expansion $u = 0, u_1 \ldots u_k$. Then we put

$$u * v \underset{\text{Df}}{=} 0, u_1 \ldots u_k v_1 v_2 \ldots \qquad (m\text{-adic}),$$

hence $u * v = u + \dfrac{v}{m^k}$; furthermore for $i \in \boldsymbol{nz},\ i > 0$

$$r_i(v) = 0, v_i v_{i+1} \ldots, \qquad l_i(v) = 0, v_1 \ldots v_i,$$

and thus $v = l_i(v) * r_{i+1}(v)$.

The words $p, q \in W(X)$ belong to different equivalence classes of $\underset{c}{\sim}$ if and only if there is a word $r \in W(X)$ such that

$$\varphi(pr) > c \leftrightarrow \varphi(qr) \leqq c,$$

i. e.,

$$\varphi(r) * \varphi(p) > c \leftrightarrow \varphi(r) * \varphi(q) \leqq c.$$

Two real numbers $u = 0, u_1 u_2 \ldots$, $v = 0, v_1 v_2 \ldots$ are called *c-separable* if there is a number $w = 0, w_1 \ldots w_k$ (with finite m-adic expansion) such that

$$w * u > c \leftrightarrow w * v \leqq c.$$

Thus the words p, q belong to different equivalence classes of $\underset{c}{\sim}$ if and only if the numbers $\varphi(p), \varphi(q)$ are c-separable.

Suppose c is rational $(0 < c < 1)$. Then the m-adic expansion $c = 0, c_1 c_2 \ldots$ of c is either finite or periodic, consequently, there are only finitely many numbers $r_i(c)$. Let $d_1, \ldots, d_k$ with $d_1 < d_2 < \cdots < d_k$ be these numbers, and put $d_{k+1} = 1$.

Case I. The m-adic expansion $0, c_1 c_2 \ldots c_k$ of c is finite.

Then $d_k < d_{k+1}$ and $d_1 = 0$. We put

$$R_1 = \{0\},$$

$$R_j = \{v \mid d_{j-1} < v \leqq d_j\} \quad \text{for} \quad j = 2, \ldots, k+1.$$

Obviously, $\{R_j \mid 1 \leqq j \leqq k+1\}$ is a partition of the interval $\langle 0, 1\rangle$. We show that for $p, q \in W(X)$ the following relation holds:

$$p \underset{c}{\sim} q \leftrightarrow \exists j \big(1 \leqq j \leqq k+1 \wedge \varphi(p), \varphi(q) \in R_j\big),$$

which implies that $\underset{c}{\sim}$ is of finite rank over $W(X)$.

A. Let $\varphi(p), \varphi(q) \in R_j$.

If $\varphi(p) = 0$ then $j = 1$, consequently $\varphi(q) = 0 = \varphi(p)$ and the numbers $\varphi(p), \varphi(q)$ are not c-separable, i.e., $p \underset{c}{\sim} q$.

Let $\varphi(p) = u > 0$, $\varphi(q) = v > 0$. Then

$$d_{j-1} < u, \; v \leqq d_j,$$

and for every $w = 0, w_1 \ldots w_n$ (with finite m-adic expansion)

$$w * d_{j-1} < w * u, \; w * v \leqq w * d_j.$$

If $w * d_j \leqq c$, then $w * u$, $w * v \leqq c$.

If $w * d_j > c$, then we have

$$w = l_n(w * d_j) \geqq l_n(c).$$

If $w > l_n(c)$ then $w * d_{j-1} > c$, hence $c < w * d_{j-1} < w * u$, $w * v$, while if $w = l_n(c)$ then, by $w * d_j > c = l_n(c) * r_{n+1}(c)$, the inequality $d_j > r_{n+1}(c)$ is satisfied. Now among the numbers of the form $r_i(c)$ and smaller than d_j, d_{j-1} is closest to d_j. Hence $d_{j-1} \geqq r_{n+1}(c)$ and $w * d_{j-1} \geqq c$, i.e., $c < w * u$, $w * v$.

If $u, v > 0$, then for every $w = 0, w_1 \ldots w_n$, either $w * u$, $w * v \leqq c$ or $w * u$, $w * v > c$. Thus the numbers $u = \varphi(p)$, $v = \varphi(q)$ are not c-separable, and therefore $p \underset{c}{\sim} q$.

B. Suppose $1 \leqq i < j \leqq k+1$, $u = \varphi(p) \in R_i$, $v = \varphi(q) \in R_j$.

Then $u \leqq d_i$ (if, $u = 0$ then $u = 0 = d_1$) and $v > d_i$, hence $u < v$. Let n be chosen in such a way that $d_i = r_{n+1}(c)$, furthermore $w = l_n(c)$. Then $w * u \leqq w * d_i = l_n(c) * r_{n+1}(c) = c$ and $w * v > c$. Thus the numbers u, v are c-separable, i.e., we have $p \underset{c}{\not\sim} q$.

Case II. The m-adic expansion of c is infinite.

Then $d_k < d_{k+1} = 1$ and $d_1 > 0$, since otherwise c would have a finite m-adic expansion. We put

$$R'_1 = \{v \mid 0 \leqq v \leqq d_1\},$$
$$R'_j = \{v \mid d_{j-1} < v \leqq d_j\} \quad \text{for} \quad j = 2, \ldots, k+1$$

and show that for $p, q \in W(X)$ the following relation holds:

$$p \underset{c}{\sim} q \leftrightarrow \exists j \big(1 \leqq j \leqq k+1 \wedge \varphi(p), \varphi(q) \in R'_j\big).$$

Since $R_j = R'_j$ for $j \geqq 2$, we have only to show that $\varphi(p), \varphi(q) \in R_1$ implies $p \underset{c}{\sim} q$. If $\varphi(p), \varphi(q) > 0$ then we put $d_0 = 0$, and proceed as above. Thus we can assume that $u = \varphi(p) = 0$, $v = \varphi(q) > 0$, and we have to show that u and v are not c-separable.

Let $w = 0, w_1 \ldots w_n$ be arbitrary. If $w > c$, then $w * u$, $w * v > c$. If $w \leqq c$ then $w = l_n(w) \leqq l_n(c)$. Furthermore $v \leqq d_1 \leqq r_{n+1}(c)$, hence $w * v \leqq w * d_1 \leqq l_n(c) * r_{n+1}(c) = c$. Thus, by $w = w * u$, for every w with a finite m-adic expansion, either $w * u$, $w * v > c$ or $w * u$, $w * v \leqq c$, i.e., the numbers u, v are not c-separable.

Now we show that if c is irrational, then the equivalence relation $\underset{c}{\sim}$ is of infinite rank, or in other words, there are infinitely many real numbers with finite m-adic expansions which are pairwise c-separable.

Consider the sequence $\big(r_i(c)\big)_{i \in \boldsymbol{nz}}$. Since c is irrational, the set $\{r_i(c) \mid i \in \boldsymbol{nz}\}$ is infinite, and since it is bounded, it has a accumulation point. Therefore, there is a convergent and strictly monotone subsequence $(d_j)_{j \in \boldsymbol{nz}}$ of the sequence $\big(r_i(c)\big)$. Assume e.g., that (d_i) is strictly monotone increasing. Let $(u_i)_{i \in \boldsymbol{nz}}$ be a sequence of numbers with finite m-adic expansion such that for all $i \in \boldsymbol{nz}$

$$d_i < u_i < d_{i+1}.$$

Obviously, there exists such a sequence (u_i). If $i < j$, then $u_i < d_{i+1} < u_j$ and because $d_{i+1} \in \{r_j(c) \mid j \in \boldsymbol{nz}\}$, say $d_{i+1} = r_n(c)$, we have

$$l_{n-1}(c) * u_i < l_{n-1}(c) * r_n(c) = c < l_{n-1}(c) * u_j,$$

consequently u_i and u_j are c-separable $\big(\text{by } w = l_{n-1}(c)\big)$. This proves Theorem 9.5.

For the m-adic stochastic event φ and for every $0 \leqq c \leqq 1$ we have $Card(E_{\varphi=c}) \leqq 1$ and $E_{\varphi=c}$ is a singleton (i.e., it is non-empty) if and only if c has a finite m-adic expansion.

Corollary 9.6. Let φ denote the m-adic stochastic event; then every set $E_{\varphi=c}$ is regular, and for $0 \leqq c \leqq 1$ the set $E_{\varphi<c}$ is regular if and only if c is rational.

One can show the existence of autonomous Z-finite S-automata in which irregular sets of words (over a singleton) can be c-represented. Salomaa [4] has shown that in an autonomous Z-finite S-automaton, at most finitely many irregular sets of words can be c-represented and that in an autonomous S-automaton with two states, only regular sets of words can be c-represented. Both of these assertions are false for S-automata with at least two input signals, as follows from 9.5 in the case where $m = 2$. Paz [2] and Turakainen [1] gave autonomous S-automata with three states and a (rational) c such that the sets of words c-representable in these S-automata are all irregular. They also gave conditions under which the set of words c-represented in a given Z-finite autonomous S-automaton is regular for every c (with $0 \leqq c < 1$). Turakainen [1] in addition to this, establishes a criterion for the c-representability of an irregular set of words in an autonomous S-automaton with three states.

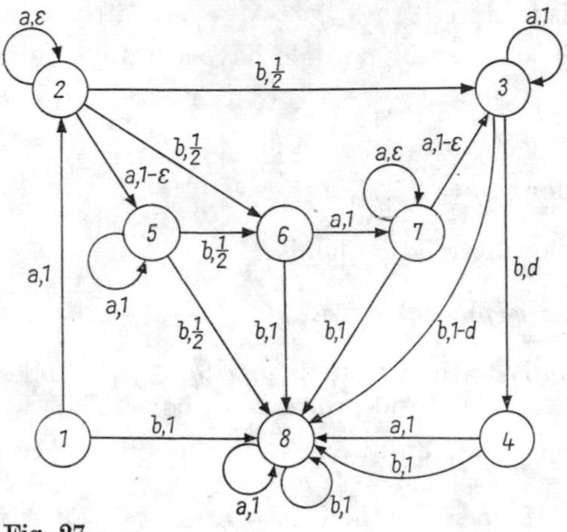

Fig. 27

Theorem 9.7. *For every c with* $0 < c < 1$ *there is a regular stochastic event* φ *over* $\{a, b\}$ *such that the sets* $E_{\varphi<c}$, $E_{\varphi=c}$, $E_{\varphi>c}$ *are irregular.*

Proof: Let us first consider the case in which $0 < c \leqq \frac{1}{2}$, and put $d = 2c$. Then $0 < d \leqq 1$ and for arbitrary ε with $0 < \varepsilon < 1$ let

$$\mathfrak{C}_\varepsilon = [\{a, b\}, \{1, 2, \ldots, 8\}, F_\varepsilon, 1]$$

be the initial S-automaton without output whose (transition) graph is expanted in Fig. 27. Furthermore let $N = \{4\}$ and φ be the stochastic event represented by N in $\mathfrak{C}_\varepsilon$.

One can see immediately that for $p \in W(\{a, b\})$ the following relations hold:

1. If $l(p) \leqq 2$, then $F_\varepsilon[1, p](4) = 0$.

2. If $p = bq$ or $p = ra$, then $F_\varepsilon[1, p](4) = 0$.

3. $F_\varepsilon[1, p](4) > 0$ can only be satisfied if the signal b occurs in p exactly twice.

Thus $F_\varepsilon[1, p](4) > 0$ implies $p = a^n b a^m b$ where $n \geqq 1$, and $m \geqq 0$.

Let $p = a^n b b$ $(n \geqq 1)$. Then

$$F_\varepsilon[1, p](4) = 1 \cdot \varepsilon^{n-1} \cdot \frac{1}{2} \cdot d = \varepsilon^{n-1} \cdot c.$$

Suppose $p = a^n b a^m b$ with $n, m \geqq 1$. Then

$$\begin{aligned}
F_\varepsilon[1,p](4) &= F_\varepsilon[2, a^{n-1} b a^m b](4) \\
&= \varepsilon^{n-1} \cdot F_\varepsilon[2, b a^m b](4) + (1 - \varepsilon^{n-1}) F_\varepsilon[5, b a^m b](4) \\
&= \varepsilon^{n-1} \cdot \frac{1}{2} \cdot F_\varepsilon[3, a^m b](4) + \varepsilon^{n-1} \cdot \frac{1}{2} F_\varepsilon[6, a^m b](4) \\
&\quad + (1 - \varepsilon^{n-1}) \cdot \frac{1}{2} F_\varepsilon[6, a^m b](4) \\
&= \frac{1}{2} \cdot \varepsilon^{n-1} \cdot F_\varepsilon[3, a^m b](4) + \frac{1}{2} F_\varepsilon[6, a^m b](4) \\
&= \frac{1}{2} \cdot \varepsilon^{n-1} \cdot F_\varepsilon[3, a^{m-1} b](4) + \frac{1}{2} \cdot F_\varepsilon[7, a^{m-1} b](4) \\
&= \frac{1}{2} \cdot \varepsilon^{n-1} \cdot F_\varepsilon[3, b](4) + \frac{1}{2} (1 - \varepsilon^{m-1}) F_\varepsilon[3, b](4) \\
&= (1 - \varepsilon^{m-1} + \varepsilon^{n-1}) \cdot c .
\end{aligned}$$

Thus for $p \in W(\{a, b\})$,

$$\varphi(p) = \begin{cases} \varepsilon^{n-1} \cdot c, & \text{if} \quad p = a^n b b, \qquad n \geqq 1, \\ (1 - \varepsilon^{m-1} + \varepsilon^{n-1}) c, & \text{if} \quad p = a^n b a^m b; \quad n, m \geqq 1, \\ 0 & \text{otherwise}. \end{cases}$$

Consequently,

$$\begin{aligned}
E_{\varphi > c} &= \{a^n b a^m b \mid 1 \leqq n < m\}, \\
E_{\varphi = c} &= \{a^n b a^n b \mid n \geqq 1\} \cup \{abb\}, \\
E_{\varphi < c} &= W(\{a, b\}) \setminus (E_{\varphi > c} \cup E_{\varphi = c}).
\end{aligned}$$

It is easy to verify that the sets of words $E_{\varphi > c}$, $E_{\varphi = c}$, and their union are irregular, which immediately implies that $E_{\varphi < c}$ is also irregular.

If $1/2 < c < 1$, then $0 < 1 - c < 1/2$. Using the above construction we can obtain a stochastic event φ' such that $E_{\varphi' < 1-c}$, $E_{\varphi' = 1-c}$ and $E_{\varphi' > 1-c}$ are irregular. If φ' is representable in a finite S-automaton, so is $\bar{\varphi}'$ and the sets

$$E_{\bar{\varphi}' > c} = E_{\varphi' < 1-c}, \qquad E_{\bar{\varphi}' = c} = E_{\varphi' = 1-c}, \qquad E_{\bar{\varphi}' < c} = E_{\varphi' > 1-c}$$

are irregular. This proves Theorem 9.7.

Now we shall consider a condition (due to Rabin [1]) sufficient for the c-representability of a set of words in a Z-finite S-automaton to imply its representability in a Z-finite deterministic automaton.

Definition 9.2. Let φ be a stochastic event over X and $0 \leqq c \leqq 1$.

(9.2.1) The number c is called *weakly isolated with respect to* φ if there is an $\varepsilon > 0$ such that either $\varphi(p) = c$ or $|\varphi(p) - c| \geqq \varepsilon$ for all $p \in W(X)$.

(9.2.2) The number c is called *isolated with respect to* φ if it is weakly isolated and $\varphi(p) \neq c$ for all $p \in W(X)$.

Corollary 9.8. The number c is weakly isolated with respect to φ if and only if c is not an accumulation point of the set $\{\varphi(p) \mid p \in W(X)\}$.

Theorem 9.9 (Rabin [1]). *If φ is a regular stochastic event over X and c is isolated with respect to φ, then the set $E_{\varphi>c}$ can be represented in a Z-finite, deterministic automaton; hence if X is finite, it is regular.*

Proof: We consider the (right invariant) equivalence relation $\underset{c}{\sim}$ over $W(X)$ defined in the proof of Theorem 9.5. From the proofs of Myhill's Theorem (Part I, Theorem 6.1) and Nerode's Theorem (Part I, Theorem 6.2) it follows that even if X is infinite, the finiteness of the partition $W(X)/\underset{c}{\sim}$ is sufficient for the existence of a Z-finite deterministic automaton in which the set of words $E_{\varphi>c}$ is representable.

Let $p_1, \ldots, p_k$ be a system of representatives for $W(X)/\underset{c}{\sim}$, that is for every $p \in W(X)$ there is exactly one i with $1 \leqq i \leqq k$ and $p \underset{c}{\sim} p_i$. Our assertion will be proved as soon as we can show that the ordinal k is a natural number.

For every i, j with $1 \leqq i < j \leqq k$ there is a $q \in W(X)$ with

$$(p_i q \in E_{\varphi>c} \wedge p_j q \notin E_{\varphi>c}) \vee (p_i q \notin E_{\varphi>c} \wedge p_j q \in E_{\varphi>c}),$$

i.e.,

$$\big(\varphi(p_i q) > c \wedge \varphi(p_j q) \leqq c\big) \vee \big(\varphi(p_i q) \leqq c \wedge \varphi(p_j q) > c\big).$$

Since c is isolated with respect to φ, $\varphi(r) \leqq c$ implies $\varphi(r) < c$. Let $\varepsilon > 0$ be a positive number whose existence is assured by Definition 9.2, and φ be represented in the S-automaton $[X, \{1, \ldots, n\}, F, z]$ by the set of states $N \subseteq \{1, \ldots, n\}$. For every i, j with $1 \leqq i < j \leqq k$ there is a $q \in W(X)$ with

$$2\varepsilon \leqq |\varphi(p_i q) - \varphi(p_j q)|.$$

Now

$$\begin{aligned}
&|\varphi(p_i q) - \varphi(p_j q)| \\
&= \Big|\sum_{\nu=1}^{n} F[\mathfrak{z}, p_i](\nu) F[\nu, q](N) - \sum_{\nu=1}^{n} F[\mathfrak{z}, p_j](\nu) F[\nu, q](N)\Big| \\
&= \Big|\sum_{\nu=1}^{n} \big(F[\mathfrak{z}, p_i](\nu) - F[\mathfrak{z}, p_j](\nu)\big) F[\nu, q](N)\Big| \\
&\leqq \sum_{\nu=1}^{n} |F[\mathfrak{z}, p_i](\nu) - F[\mathfrak{z}, p_j](\nu)|\, F[\nu, q](N) \\
&\leqq \sum_{\nu=1}^{n} |F[\mathfrak{z}, p_i](\nu) - F[\mathfrak{z}, p_j](\nu)|.
\end{aligned}$$

For all i, j with $1 \leqq i < j \leqq k$,

$$2\varepsilon \leqq \sum_{\nu=1}^{n} |F[\mathfrak{z}, p_i](\nu) - F[\mathfrak{z}, p_j](\nu)|. \qquad (*)$$

For arbitrary $p \in W(X)$, $[\xi_1, \ldots, \xi_n] = [F[\mathfrak{z}, p](1), \ldots, F[\mathfrak{z}, p](n)]$ is a point in the n-dimensional Euclidean space. Let us consider for $1 \leqq i \leqq k$

$$\sigma_i \underset{\mathrm{Df}}{=} \left\{[\xi_1, \ldots, \xi_n] \mid \sum_{\nu=1}^{n} \left(\xi_\nu - F[\mathfrak{z}, p_i](\nu)\right) = \varepsilon \wedge \bigwedge_{\nu=1}^{n} \xi_\nu \geqq F[\mathfrak{z}, p_i](\nu)\right\}.$$

For all i with $1 \leqq i \leqq k$, $[\xi_1, \ldots, \xi_n] \in \sigma_i$ we have

$$\sum_{\nu=1}^{n} \xi_\nu = \varepsilon + 1.$$

Thus every σ_i is an $(n-1)$-dimensional simplex, which can be translated into the simplex

$$\sigma \underset{\mathrm{Df}}{=} \left\{[\xi_1, \ldots, \xi_n] \mid \sum_{\nu=1}^{n} \xi_\nu = \varepsilon \wedge \bigwedge_{\nu=1}^{n} \xi_\nu \geqq 0\right\}$$

on the hyper plane

$$\xi_1 + \xi_2 + \cdots + \xi_n = \varepsilon.$$

Since the $(n-1)$-dimensional volumo V_{n-1} is invariant under translations, for all i with $1 \leqq i \leqq k$

$$V_{n-1}(\sigma_i) = V_{n-1}(\sigma) = K \cdot \varepsilon^{n-1},$$

where K is a constant (independent of ε). Obviously, for the $(n-1)$-dimensional simplex

$$\tau \underset{\mathrm{Df}}{=} \left\{[\xi_1, \ldots, \xi_n] \mid \sum_{\nu=1}^{n} \xi_\nu = 1 + \varepsilon \wedge \bigwedge_{\nu=1}^{n} \xi_\nu \geqq 0\right\}$$

we have

$$\tau \supseteq \sigma_i \qquad (1 \leqq i \leqq k).$$

A point $[\xi_1, \ldots, \xi_n] \in \sigma_i$ is in the interior of σ_i (in the topology of the hyperplane $\sum_{\nu=1}^{n} \xi_\nu = 1 + \varepsilon$), if and only if $\xi_\nu - F[z, p_i](\nu) > 0$ for all $\nu = 1, \ldots, n$. Thus if $i \neq j$, then the interiors of σ_i and σ_j are disjoint. Indeed, if $[\xi_1^*, \ldots, \xi_n^*]$ was an interior point of both σ_i and σ_j, then for all $\nu = 1, \ldots, n$ we would have

$$\xi_\nu^* - F[\mathfrak{z}, p_i](\nu) > 0, \qquad \xi_\nu^* - F[\mathfrak{z}, p_j](\nu) > 0,$$

hence

$$|F[\mathfrak{z}, p_i](\nu) - F[\mathfrak{z}, p_j](\nu)| < |F[\mathfrak{z}, p_i](\nu) - \xi_\nu^*| + |\xi_\nu^* - F[\mathfrak{z}, p_j](\nu)|$$

and consequently

$$\sum_{\nu=1}^{n} |F[\mathfrak{z}, p_i](\nu) - F[\mathfrak{z}, p_j](\nu)|$$

$$< \sum_{\nu=1}^{n} |F[\mathfrak{z}, p_i](\nu) - \xi_\nu^*| + \sum_{\nu=1}^{n} |\xi_\nu^* - F[\mathfrak{z}, p_j](\nu)| = 2\varepsilon,$$

which contradicts (∗). Since every σ_i is contained in τ, and the interiors of different simplices σ_i, σ_j $(i \neq j)$ are disjoint, we have

$$\sum_{\varkappa=1}^{k} V_{n-1}(\sigma_\varkappa) = k \cdot V_{n-1}(\sigma) \leqq V_{n-1}(\tau),$$

i.e.,

$$k \cdot K \cdot \varepsilon^{n-1} \leqq K \cdot (1 + \varepsilon)^{n-1},$$

hence

$$k \leqq \left(1 + \frac{1}{\varepsilon}\right)^{n-1}.$$

This proves Theorem 9.9.

Corollary 9.10. Let φ be a regular stochastic event and $0 \leqq c \leqq 1$.

1. If c is isolated with respect to φ, then $E_{\varphi=c} = \emptyset$ and the sets $E_{\varphi>c}$, $E_{\varphi<c} = W(X) \setminus E_{\varphi>c}$ can be represented in a Z-finite deterministic automaton.

2. If c is weakly isolated with respect to φ, then the sets $E_{\varphi>c}, E_{\varphi=c}, E_{\varphi<c}$ can be represented in Z-finite, deterministic automata.

Proposition 9.10.2 is trivial if $c = 0$, or $c = 1$. Suppose $0 < c < 1$. Since c is weakly isolated with respect to φ, there is an $\varepsilon > 0$ such that $c - \varepsilon \geqq 0$, $c + \varepsilon \leqq 1$, and there is no value of φ in the open intervals $(c - \varepsilon, c)$, $(c, c + \varepsilon)$. Then every $c' \in (c - \varepsilon, c)$, $c'' \in (c, c + \varepsilon)$ is isolated with respect to φ. Moreover

$$E_{\varphi>c} = E_{\varphi>c''}, \quad E_{\varphi<c} = E_{\varphi<c'}.$$

The converse of Proposition 9.9 is false, since for the m-adic stochastic event φ there is no c which is isolated (or weakly isolated) with respect to φ, but still for every rational c with $0 < c < 1$ the set $E_{\varphi>c}$ is regular.

A stochastic event φ has finitely many values if and only if every c with $0 \leqq c \leqq 1$ is weakly isolated with respect to φ. For such stochastic events, we have

Theorem 9.11. *If φ is a stochastic event over X, such that $\{\varphi(p) \mid p \in W(X)\}$ is finite, then φ is regular if and only if for all c with $0 \leqq c \leqq 1$ the set $E_{\varphi=c}$ can be represented in a Z-finite deterministic automaton.*

Proof: If φ is regular, then the sets $E_{\varphi=c}$ are representable in Z-finite deterministic automata, since every c with $0 \leqq c \leqq 1$ is weakly isolated with respect to φ.

Suppose $\{\varphi(p) \mid p \in W(X)\} = \{c_1, \ldots, c_n\}$. Then $\{E_{\varphi=c_\nu} \mid \nu = 1, \ldots, n\}$ is a partition of the set $W(X)$. For every $i = 1, \ldots, n$ let $\mathfrak{A}_i = [X, Z_i, \delta_i, z_i^0]$ be an initial deterministic Z-finite automaton and $N_i \subseteq Z_i$ such that $E_{\varphi=c_i}$ is represented in $\mathfrak{A}_i$ by N_i. Furthermore let

$$Z \underset{\mathrm{Df}}{=} Z_1 \times Z_2 \times \cdots \times Z_n$$

and for $[z^1, \ldots, z^n] \in Z$, $x \in X$

$$\delta([z^1, \ldots, z^n], x) \underset{\mathrm{Df}}{=} [\delta_1(z^1, x), \ldots, \delta_n(z^n, x)],$$

finally, for $i = 1, \ldots, n$

$$M_i \underset{\mathrm{Df}}{=} (Z_1 \setminus N_1) \times \cdots \times (Z_{i-1} \setminus N_{i-1}) \times N_i \times (Z_{i+1} \setminus N_{i+1}) \times \cdots \times (Z_n \setminus N_n).$$

We claim that for $i = 1, \ldots, n$ the set $E_{\varphi=c_i}$ is represented in the initial Z-finite deterministic automaton $\mathfrak{A} = [X, Z, \delta, [z_1^0, \ldots, z_n^0]]$ by M_i. Obviously, if $p \in W(X)$ then

$$\delta([z_1^0, \ldots, z_n^0], p) = [\delta_1(z_1^0, p), \ldots, \delta_n(z_n^0, p)],$$

hence $\delta([z_1^0, \ldots, z_n^0], p) \in M_i$ implies $\delta_i(z_i^0, p) \in N_i$, i.e., $p \in E_{\varphi=c_i}$. Conversely, if $p \in E_{\varphi=c_i}$, then

$$\delta_i(z_i^0, p) \in N_i$$

and for $j = 1, \ldots, n$, $j \neq i$ we have $p \notin E_{\varphi=c_j}$, i.e.,

$$\delta_j(z_j^0, p) \notin N_j, \quad \text{hence} \quad \delta_j(z_j^0, p) \in Z_j \setminus N_j;$$

and thus $\delta([z_1^0, \ldots, z_n^0], p) \in M_i$.

For $i \neq j$ obviously, $M_i \cap M_j = \emptyset$. Let

$$Z^* = \left(\bigcup_{i=1}^{n} M_i\right) \times \{0, 1\},$$

and for $[z, i], [z', j] \in Z^*$, $x \in X$

$$F[[z,i],x]([z',j]) = \begin{cases} c_\nu, & \text{if } z' = \delta(z,x) \wedge z' \in M_\nu \wedge j = 1, \\ 1 - c_\nu, & \text{if } z' = \delta(z,x) \wedge z' \in M_\nu \wedge j = 0, \\ 0 & \text{otherwise.} \end{cases}$$

further for $z_0 = [z_1^0, \dots, z_n^0]$ let

$$\mathfrak{z}([z, i]) = \begin{cases} \varphi(e), & \text{if } z = z_0 \wedge j = 1, \\ 1 - \varphi(e), & \text{if } z = z_0 \wedge j = 0, \\ 0 & \text{otherwise.} \end{cases}$$

It is easy to verify that for all $z \in \bigcup_{i=1}^{n} M_i$, $p \in W(X)$

$$F\big[[z, 0], p\big] = F\big[[z, 1], p\big],$$

and that $F\big[[z, i], p\big]([z', j]) > 0$ can only be satisfied if $z' = \delta(z, p)$. Obviously, $\mathfrak{C} = [X, Z^*, F, \mathfrak{z}]$ is a Z-finite weakly initial S-automaton. We claim that the stochastic event φ is represented in $\mathfrak{C}$ by the set of states $N = \left(\bigcup_{i=1}^{n} M_i\right) \times \{1\} \subseteq Z^*$, i.e., that

$$\varphi(p) = F[\mathfrak{z}, p](N)$$

for all $p \in W(X)$. The proof of this equality is trivial in the case where $p = e$. Suppose $px \in W(X) \setminus \{e\}$. Then

$$\begin{aligned} F[\mathfrak{z}, px](N) &= \varphi(e) F\big[[z_0, 1], px\big](N) + \big(1 - \varphi(e)\big) F\big[[z_0, 0], px\big](N) \\ &= F\big[[z_0, 1], px\big](N) \\ &= \sum_{[z, j] \in Z^*} F\big[[z_0, 1], p\big]([z, j]) F\big[[z, j], x\big](N) \\ &= F\big[[z_0, 1], p\big]\big([\delta(z_0, p), 0]\big) F\big[[\delta(z_0, p), 0], x\big](N) \\ &\quad + F\big[[z_0, 1], p\big]\big([\delta(z_0, p), 1]\big) F\big[[\delta(z_0, p), 1], x\big](N) \\ &= F\big[[\delta(z_0, p), 1], x\big]\left(\bigcup_{i=1}^{n} M_i \times \{1\}\right) \\ &= F\big[[\delta(z_0, p), 1], x\big]\big([\delta(z_0, px), 1]\big) \\ &= c_i, \quad \text{if} \quad \delta(z_0, px) \in M_i, \\ &= c_i, \quad \text{if} \quad px \in E_{\varphi = c_i}, \\ &= \varphi(px). \end{aligned}$$

This proves Theorem 9.11.

Now we show that the set of regular stochastic events φ over X is not closed under the addition and iteration of stochastic events, if X contains at least two elements. From this we can deduce an analogous result for the set of regular PS-operators.

Theorem 9.12. *If $Card(X) \geqq 2$, then there is a regular stochastic event φ over X such that $[\varphi + \varphi]$ is not regular, and there is a stochastic event φ' which can be generated in a Z-finite S-automaton (and which consequently is regular) and for which $\langle \varphi' \rangle$ is not regular.*

Proof: We can assume that $\{a, b\} \subseteq X (a \neq b)$. Consider the stochastic event φ over X for which

$$\varphi(p) = \begin{cases} \varepsilon^{n-1} \cdot \frac{1}{2}, & \text{if} \quad p = a^n b b; \qquad n \geqq 1, \\ (1 - \varepsilon^{m-1} + \varepsilon^{n-1}) \cdot \frac{1}{2}, & \text{if} \quad p = a^n b a^m b; \quad n, m \geqq 1, \\ 0 & \text{otherwise} \end{cases}$$

for all $p \in W(X)$, where ε is chosen arbitrarily with $0 < \varepsilon < 1$. It follows from the proof of Theorem 9.7 for $c = 1/2$ that φ is regular, since it is represented in the S-automaton $[X, \{1, \ldots, 8\}, F', 1]$ by the set $\{4\}$, where for $i, j \in \{1, \ldots, 8\}$, $x \in X$

$$F'[i, x](j) = \begin{cases} F_\varepsilon[i, x](j), & \text{if} \quad x \in \{a, b\}, \\ 1, & \text{if} \quad x \in X \setminus \{a, b\}, \quad j = 8, \\ 0 & \text{otherwise.} \end{cases}$$

We have

$$E_{\varphi = \frac{1}{2}} = \{a^n b a^n b \mid n \geqq 1\} \cup \{abb\}, \qquad E_{\varphi > \frac{1}{2}} = \{a^n b a^m b \mid 1 \leqq n < m\},$$

and these sets cannot be represented in any Z-finite deterministic automaton. Furthermore if $p \in W(X)$,

$$\begin{aligned} [\varphi + \varphi](p) = 1 &\leftrightarrow min\,(1, \varphi(p) + \varphi(p)) = 1 \\ &\leftrightarrow \varphi(p) \geqq \frac{1}{2} \\ &\leftrightarrow p \in \{a^n b a^m b \mid 1 \leqq n \leqq m\} \cup \{abb\}. \end{aligned}$$

The set $E_{[\varphi + \varphi] = 1}$ therefore cannot be represented in any Z-finite deterministic automaton, and by 9.4, $[\varphi + \varphi]$ is irregular.

To prove the second part of our assertion,[1]) we consider the standard term $T \equiv \langle \mathbf{1} \rangle$ and the event code β over X, for which $\beta^j(p) = 0$ for all $j \in \boldsymbol{nz} \setminus \{1\}$, $p \in W(X)$ and

$$\beta^1(p) = \begin{cases} \frac{1}{4}, & \text{if} \quad p = a, \\ \frac{1}{\sqrt{2}}, & \text{if} \quad p = b, \\ 0 & \text{otherwise.} \end{cases}$$

Obviously, β is strongly regular for T, hence $\varphi' = \mathfrak{E}[T, \beta] = \langle \beta \rangle$ is a stochastic event over X which can be generated in a Z-finite S-automaton. We claim that $\langle \varphi' \rangle = \langle\langle \beta \rangle\rangle$ is irregular. For this it suffices to show that $E_{\langle \varphi' \rangle = 1}$ is an irregular subset of $W(\{a, b\})$.

---

[1]) cf. KÜSTNER [1].

Since $Val(T) = \{1^k \mid k \geqq 0\}$, $\varphi'(e) = 1$, and for $p = x_1 \ldots x_n \in W(X)$,

$$\varphi'(p) = \prod_{i=1}^{n} \beta^1(x_i).$$

Thus $\langle\varphi'\rangle(e) = 1$ and for $p = x_1 \ldots x_n \in W(X)$, $n \geqq 1$

$$\begin{aligned}\langle\varphi'\rangle(p) &= min\left(1, \sum_{m=1}^{n} \sum_{\substack{p_1 \ldots p_m = p \\ p_1, \ldots, p_m \neq e}} \prod_{\mu=1}^{m} \varphi'(p_\mu)\right) \\ &= min\left(1, \sum_{m=1}^{n} \sum_{\substack{p_1 \ldots p_m = p \\ p_1, \ldots, p_m \neq e}} \prod_{\nu=1}^{n} \beta^1(x_\nu)\right) \\ &= min\left(1, 2^{n-1} \cdot \prod_{\nu=1}^{n} \beta^1(x_\nu)\right),\end{aligned}$$

since there are exactly 2^{n-1} different representations of the word $p = x_1 \ldots x_n$ as concatenations of some non-empty words $p_1, \ldots, p_m$. Let $A(p)$ and $B(p)$ denote the number of occurences in p of the signals a and b respectively, then for $p = x_1 \ldots x_n \in W(X) \setminus \{e\}$

$$\langle\varphi'\rangle(p) = 1 \leftrightarrow A(p) + B(p) = n \wedge 2^{n-1} \cdot \left(\beta^1(a)\right)^{A(p)} \cdot \left(\beta^1(b)\right)^{B(p)} \geqq 1.$$

The set $E_{\langle\varphi'\rangle=1}$ is therefore a subset of $W(\{a, b\})$. If $p \in W(\{a, b\})$ then by $A(p) + B(p) = n$,

$$2^{n-1} \cdot \left(\beta^1(a)\right)^{A(p)} \cdot \left(\beta^1(b)\right)^{B(p)} \geqq 1$$

if and only if

$$\left(2 \cdot \beta^1(a)\right)^{A(p)} \cdot \left(2 \cdot \beta^1(b)\right)^{B(p)} \geqq 2,$$

i.e.,

$$A(p) \cdot ld\left(\frac{1}{2}\right) + B(p) \cdot ld\left(\sqrt{2}\right) \geqq 1,$$

$$B(p) \geqq 2 \cdot A(p) + 2.$$

Therefore,

$$E_{\langle\varphi'\rangle=1} = \{e\} \cup \{p \mid p \in W(\{a, b\}) \wedge B(p) \geqq 2 \cdot A(p) + 2\}.$$

It is easy to see that this set is irregular.

Theorem 9.13. *If $Card(X) \geqq 2$, $Y \neq \emptyset$, then there are regular PS-operators Ψ, Ψ' over $[X, Y]$ such that the PS-operators $[\Psi + \Psi]$, $\langle\Psi'\rangle$ are irregular.*

Proof: Let $y \in Y_0$. Then for $p \in W(X)$, $q \in W(Y)$ we put

$$\Psi_p(q) = \begin{cases} \Psi_p^{\varphi}(q), & \text{if} \quad q \in W(\{y_0\}), \\ 0 & \text{otherwise} \end{cases}$$

and

$$\Psi'_p(q) = \begin{cases} \Psi_p^{\varphi'}(q), & \text{if} \quad q \in W(\{y_0\}), \\ 0 & \text{otherwise} \end{cases}$$

where φ, φ' are the regular stochastic events considered in the proof of 9.12. By 8.3.2, Ψ^{φ}, $\Psi^{\varphi'}$ are regular PS-operators hence obviously, Ψ and Ψ' are also regular. For instance if Ψ^{φ} is generated in $[X, \{y_0\}, Z, H]$ by $[\mathfrak{z}, N]$ then Ψ is generated in $[X, Y, Z, H']$ by $[\mathfrak{z}, N]$, where

$$H'[z, x](y, z') = \begin{cases} H[z, x](y_0, z'), & \text{if} \quad y = y_0, \\ 0 & \text{otherwise.} \end{cases}$$

By 8.9, $[\Psi^{\varphi} + \Psi^{\varphi}] = \Psi^{[\varphi+\varphi]}$ and $\langle \Psi^{\varphi'} \rangle = \Psi^{\langle \varphi' \rangle}$. $p \in W(X)$, $q \in W(Y)$

$$[\Psi + \Psi]_p(q) = \begin{cases} \Psi_p^{[\varphi+\varphi]}(q), & \text{if} \quad q \in W(\{y_0\}), \\ 0 & \text{otherwise,} \end{cases}$$

$$\langle \Psi' \rangle_p(q) = \begin{cases} \Psi_p^{\langle \varphi' \rangle}(q), & \text{if} \quad q \in W(\{y_0\}), \\ 0 & \text{otherwise.} \end{cases}$$

The PS-operators $\Psi^{[\varphi+\varphi]}$, $\Psi^{\langle \varphi' \rangle}$ (over $[X, \{y_0\}]$) are not regular, because otherwise $[\varphi + \varphi]$, $\langle \varphi' \rangle$ would be regular stochastic events. Therefore, the PS-operators $[\Psi + \Psi]$, $\langle \Psi' \rangle$ are not regular either. Indeed, if e.g., $\langle \Psi' \rangle$ were generated in the Z-finite S-automaton $[X, Y, Z, H]$ by $[\mathfrak{z}, N]$, then for all $p \in W(X) \setminus \{e\}$ we would have

$$\begin{aligned} \langle \varphi' \rangle(p) &= \Psi_p^{\langle \varphi' \rangle}(y_0^{l(p)}) = \langle \Psi' \rangle_p(y_0^{l(p)}) \\ &= \langle \Psi' \rangle_p(W(Y)) = H[\mathfrak{z}, p](W(Y) \times Z^{l(p)-1} \cdot N) \\ &= F[\mathfrak{z}, p](N), \end{aligned}$$

hence $\langle \varphi' \rangle$ would be generated in the Z-finite S-automaton $[X, Z, F, \mathfrak{z}]$ by the set N although $\langle \varphi' \rangle$ is not regular. This proves Theorem 9.13.

The example of the PS-operator $\tilde{\Psi}^{\varphi'}$ shows us that the iteration of regular PS-operators even over $[\{x_0\}, X]$ need not be regular.

We conclude our investigation by some remarks about definite stochastic events and the corresponding sets of words. It follows from the considerations which led us to the definition of events in the theory of stochastic automata, that the following definition of definite stochastic events is an adequate generalization of the concept of definite sets of words.

Definition 9.3. Let φ be a stochastic event over X and k a natural number.
(9.3.1) We call φ *weakly k-definite* if for all $pr \in W(X)$ with $l(r) \geqq k$, $\varphi(pr) = \varphi(r)$.
(9.3.2) φ is called *k-definite* if it is weakly k-definite and either $k = 0$ or φ is not weakly $(k-1)$-definite.

Corollary 9.14.
1. A stochastic event is 0-definite if and only if it is constant.
2. Every stochastic event can only be k-definite for at most one k.
3. Every stochastic event over X for which there is a real number c with $0 \leqq c \leqq 1$ such that $\varphi(p) = c$ for all $p \in W(X)$ with $l(p) \geqq k$ is weakly k-definite.
4. A stochastic event φ is weakly k-definite if and only if $\bar{\varphi}$ is.

Let φ be a weakly k-definite stochastic event over X. We put, for $p \in W(X)$

$$\varphi'_k(p) = \begin{cases} \varphi(p), & \text{if} \quad l(p) < k, \\ 0 & \text{otherwise,} \end{cases}$$

$$\varphi''_k(p) = \begin{cases} \varphi(p), & \text{if} \quad l(p) = k, \\ 0 & \text{otherwise.} \end{cases}$$

Let us denote by $\mathbf{1}$ the stochastic event over X for which

$$\mathbf{1}(p) = 1 \text{ for all } p \in W(X).$$

For $p, r \in W(X)$ with $l(r) = k$,

$$\begin{aligned}[\mathbf{1} \cdot \varphi''_k](pr) &= min\Big(1, \sum_{qs=pr} \mathbf{1}(q) \cdot \varphi''_k(s)\Big) \\ &= min\Big(1, \sum_{qs=pr} \varphi''_k(s)\Big) = \varphi''_k(r) = \varphi(pr),\end{aligned}$$

and if $l(p) < k$, then

$$[\mathbf{1} \cdot \varphi''_k](p) = 0.$$

For all $p \in W(X)$ thus we have

$$\begin{aligned}\varphi(p) &= \begin{cases} \varphi'_k(p), & \text{if} \quad l(p) < k, \\ \varphi''_k(r), & \text{if} \quad l(p) \geqq k,\ p = qr,\ l(r) = k, \end{cases} \\ &= \begin{cases} \varphi'_k(p), & \text{if} \quad l(p) < k, \\ [\mathbf{1} \circ \varphi''_k](p), & \text{if} \quad l(p) \geqq k, \end{cases} \\ &= \varphi'_k(p) + [\mathbf{1} \circ \varphi''_k](p) = [\varphi'_k + (\mathbf{1} \circ \varphi''_k)](p).\end{aligned}$$

Consequently we have

Theorem 9.15. *A stochastic event* φ *over* X *is weakly k-definite if and only if* $\varphi = [\varphi'_k + (1 \circ \varphi''_k)]$.

The connection between the stability of an automaton and the definiteness of the events representable by output signals in it, which is known from the theory of deterministic automata, is valid here too.

Theorem 9.16. *Let* $k \geqq 1$.

1. *An S-automaton* $\mathfrak{C} = [X, Y, Z, H]$ *is weakly k-stable over* $\mathfrak{z} \in \mathfrak{Z}_Z$ *if and only if every stochastic event representable by an output signal in the weakly initial S-automaton* $[X, Y, Z, H, \mathfrak{z}]$ *is weakly k-definite.*

2. *A stochastic event* φ *with* $\varphi(e) = 0$, *is weakly k-definite if and only if it can be represented by an output signal in an initial S-automaton which is weakly k-stable over its initial state.*

Proof: $\mathfrak{C}$ is weakly k-stable over $\mathfrak{z}$ if and only if for all $y \in Y$, $p, r \in W(X)$ with $l(r) \geqq k - 1$, $x \in X$

$$G\big[F[\mathfrak{z}, pr], x\big](y) = G\big[F[\mathfrak{z}, r], x\big](y).$$

If φ_y denotes the event represented by y in $[X, Y, Z, H, \mathfrak{z}]$ then $\varphi_y(e) = 0$ and for $rx \in W(X) \setminus \{e\}$

$$\varphi_y(rx) = V_{\mathfrak{C}}[\mathfrak{z}, rx]\big(W(Y) \cdot \{y\}\big) = G\big[F[\mathfrak{z}, r], x\big](y).$$

Therefore, $\mathfrak{C}$ is weakly k-stable over $\mathfrak{z}$ if and only if for all $y \in Y$, $p, r \in W(X)$ with $l(r) \geqq k - 1$, $x \in X$

$$\varphi_y(prx) = G\big[F[\mathfrak{z}, pr], x\big](y) = G\big[F[\mathfrak{z}, r], x\big](y) = \varphi_y(rx),$$

that is if φ_y is weakly k-definite.

It remains to show that every weakly k-definite stochastic event φ over X with $\varphi(e) = 0$ can be represented by an output signal in an initial S-automaton which is weakly k-stable over its initial state.

Let φ be represented in $[X, Z, F, z_1]$ by the set $N \subseteq Z$. We put $Y = \{0, 1\}$ and for $z \in Z$, $y \in Y$,

$$M[z](y) \underset{\text{Df}}{=} \begin{cases} 1, & \text{if} \quad (z \in N \wedge y = 0) \vee (z \notin N \wedge y = 1), \\ 0 & \text{otherwise.} \end{cases}$$

Here, $\mathfrak{C}' = [X, Y, Z, F, M, z_1]$ is an initial S-Moore automaton, for which

$$\begin{aligned} V_{\mathfrak{C}'}[z_1, px]\big(W(Y) \cdot \{0\}\big) &= G\big[F[z_1, p], x\big](0) \\ &= \sum_{z \in Z} F[z_1, px](z)\, M[z](0) \\ &= F[z_1, px](N) = \varphi(px) \end{aligned}$$

for all $px \in W(X) \setminus \{e\}$. Thus, in $\mathfrak{C}'$, φ is represented by the output signal 0. Furthermore for all $p, r \in W(X)$, $x \in X$ with $l(r) \geqq k - 1$

$$G[F[z_1, pr], x](0) = \varphi(prx) = \varphi(rx) = G[F[z_1, r], x](0),$$
$$G[F[z_1, pr], x](1) = \overline{\varphi}(prx) = \overline{\varphi}(rx) = G[F[z_1, r], x](1);$$

hence $\mathfrak{C}'$ is weakly k-stable over z_1.

Theorem 9.17. *Let φ be a stochastic event over X.*

1. *If φ is weakly k-definite, then for all c with $0 \leqq c \leqq 1$ the sets of words $E_{\varphi<c}$, $E_{\varphi=c}$, $E_{\varphi>c}$ are weakly k-definite.*

2. *If $E_{\varphi=c}$ is weakly k-definite for every c with $0 \leqq c \leqq 1$, then φ is weakly k-definite.*

3. *If the sets $E_{\varphi<c}$, $E_{\varphi>c}$ are weakly k-definite for all c with $0 \leqq c \leqq 1$ then φ is weakly k-definite.*

4. *If X is finite, and φ is weakly k-definite, then φ is regular.*

Proof: Propositions 9.17.1 and 9.17.2 can be easily verified. Proposition 9.17.3 follows immediately from 9.17.2 because $E_{\varphi=c} = W(X) \setminus (E_{\varphi>c} \cup E_{\varphi<c})$, and the weakly k-definite sets of words constitute a Boolean algebra with respect to the operations of intersection, union and relative complementation.

If X is finite, and φ is weakly k-definite, then

$$\{\varphi(p) \mid p \in W(X)\} = \{\varphi(p) \mid p \in W(X) \wedge 0 \leqq l(p) \leqq k\}$$

is a finite set, and all the sets $E_{\varphi=c}$ are regular, hence by 9.11, φ is also regular.

For infinite X, 9.17.4 is not valid, not even if φ has only finitely many values. As an example we consider the stochastic event φ^* over $\boldsymbol{nz}$ for which

$$\varphi^*(p) = \begin{cases} \frac{1}{2}, & \text{if} \quad p = ii,\ i \in \boldsymbol{nz}, \\ 0 & \text{otherwise.} \end{cases}$$

This stochastic event is weakly 3-definite, because $\varphi^*(p) = 0$ for all $p \in W(\boldsymbol{nz})$ with $l(p) \geqq 3$. However, $E_{\varphi^*>0} = \{ii \mid i \in \boldsymbol{nz}\}$, and this set cannot be represented in a Z-finite deterministic automaton (cf. Pohl [3]).

BIBLIOGRAPHY

AANDERAA, S.

[1] On the algebra of regular expressions. Appl. Math., Harvard Univ., Cambridge, Jan. 1965, 1–18.

AGASANDIAN, G. A.

[1] Automata with variable structure, DAN SSSR **174** (1967), No. 3, 529–530.

AIZERMAN, M. A.; GUSEV, L. A.; ROZONOER, L. I.; SMIRNOVA, I. M.; TAL, A. A.

[1] Algorithmic unsolvability of the recognition problem for the representability of recursive events in finite automata. Automatika i telemechanika, 1962, No. 11.

[2] Logik — Automaten — Algorithmen. Akademie-Verlag, Berlin/Oldenbourg-Verlag, München—Wien 1967.

AMAR, V.; PUTZOLU, G.

[1] Generalizations of regular events. Automata Theory, Academic Press Inc., New York—London 1966, 1–5.

ARBIB, M. A.

[1] Turing machines, finite automata and neural nets. J. ACM **8** (1961), No. 4.

[2] Brains, machines and mathematics. McGraw-Hill Book Co., New York 1964.

[3] Automata theory and control theory — a rapprochement. Automatica **3** (1966), No. 3–4, 161–189.

[4] Simple self-reproducing automata. Information and Control **9** (1966), 177 to 189.

[5] Tolerance automata. Kybernetika (Praha) **3** (1967), 223–233.

[6] Realization of stochastic systems. Ann. Math. Statistics **38** (1967), No. 3, 927 to 933.

[7] Automaton automorphisms. Information and Control **11** (1967), 147–154.

[8] The automata theory of semigroup embeddings. J. Australian Math. Soc. **8** (1968), part 3, 568–570.

[9] Theories of abstract automata. Prentice-Hall, Englewood Cliffs (N.J.) 1968.

[10] Algebraic theory of machines, languages, and semigroups. Academic Press, New York—London 1968.

ARBIB, M. A.; GIVE'ON, Y.

[1] Algebra automata I: Parallel programming as a prolegomena to the categorical approach. Information and Control **12** (1968), No. 4, 331–345.

ARDEN, D. N.

[1] Delayed logic and finite state machines. Theory of Computing Machine Design, Univ. of Michigan Press, Ann. Arbor 1960, 1–35.

ARESHIAN, G. L.; MARANDSHIAN, G. B.

[1] On certain problems of the theory of probabilistic automata. Tr. Vich. Centra AN Arm. SSR i Erev. Un. **2** (1964), 73–82.

Armstrong, D. B.
[1] A programmed algorithm for assigning internal codes to sequential machines. IRE Trans. Electr. Comp. EC—**11** (1962), No. 4, 466—472.
[2] On the efficient assignment of internal codes to sequential machines. IRE Trans. Electr. Comp. EC—**11** (1962), 611—622.
[3] Sequential circuits. Part A: Structural properties. IEEE Trans. Circuit Theory CT—**11** (1964), No. 1, 25—27.

Asser, G.
[1] Über eine Darstellung der rekursiven Wortfunktionen in endlichen Automaten. Z. Math. Logik Grundl. Math. **12** (1966), 1—12.

Atamov, F. A.
[1] On a method of synthesis concerning abstract finite asynchronous automata. Tr. Vich. Centra AN Aserb. SSR **3** (1965), 20—29.

Aufenkamp, D. D.
[1] Analysis of sequential machines II. IRE Trans. Electr. Comp. EC—**7** (1958), No. 4, 299—306.

Aufenkamp, D. D.; Hohn, F. E.
[1] Oriented graphs and sequential machines. Bell Labs. Reports, 30, 1954.
[2] Analysis of sequential machines. IRE Trans. Electr. Comp. EC—**6** (1957), No. 4, 276 to 285.

Aufenkamp, D. D.; Seshu, S.; Hohn, F. E.
[1] The theory of nets. IRE Trans. Electr. Comp. EC—**6** (1957), No. 3.

Bacon, G. C.
[1] Minimal-state stochastic finite-state systems. IEEE Trans. Circuit Theory CT—**11** (1964), 307—308.
[2] The decomposition of stochastic automata. Information and Control **7** (1964), 320 to 339.

Bar-Hillel, Y.
[1] Language and information. Addison-Wesley Publ. Comp., Reading (Mass.) 1964.

Bar-Hillel, Y.; Perles, M.; Shamir, E.
[1] On formal properties of simple phrase structure grammars. Z. f. Phonetik, Sprachwissenschaft u. Kommunikationsforschung **14** (1961), 143—172.

Barnes, B.
[1] Groups of automorphisms and sets of equivalence classes of input for automata. J. ACM **12** (1965), 561—565.

Barsdin, Ya. M.; Korshunov, A. D.
[1] On the diameter of reduced automata. Discrete analysis **9** (1967), 3—45.

Bartee, T. C.; Lebow, I. L.; Reed, I. S.
[1] Theory and design of digital machines. McGraw-Hill Book Co., New York 1962.

Bavel, Z.
[1] On the total length of an experiment I. Switching Circuit Theory and Logical Design, Inst. of Electric. and Electron. Engng., New York 1964, 234—248.
[2] On the structure and automorphisms of finite automata. Doctoral Diss., Univ. of Illinois, 1965.

Bavel, Z.; Muller, D. E.
[1] Reversebility in monadic algebras and automata. Switching Circuit Theory and Logic. Design (IEEE Conf. Rec.), New York 1965, 242—247.

Beatty, J. C.
[1] On some properties of the semigroup of a machine which are preserved under state minimization. Information and Control **11** (1967), 290—316.

Beatty, J. C.; Miller, R. E.
[1] Some theorems for incompletely specified sequential machines with application to state-minimization. Switching Circuit Theory and Logic. Design, New York 1963.
Bellman, R.
[1] Sequential machines, ambiguity and dynamic programming. J. ACM **7** (1960), No. 1, 24–28.
Bloch, A. S.
[1] Equivalent transformations of sequential machines. Automatika i telemechanika **21** (1960).
[2] Über Probleme, die mit sequentiellen Maschinen gelöst worden. Probl. d. Kybernetik **3**, Akademie-Verlag, Berlin 1963, 93–100.
Bodnarchuk, V. G.
[1] On events representable in finite automata by a single state. Ukr. Math. Journ. **14** (1962), 190–191.
[2] Automata and events. Ukr. Math. Journ. **14** (1962), 351–361.
[3] Systems of equations in the algebra of events. Journ. Vich. Math. i Math. Phys. **3** (1963), 1077–1088.
[4] Analysis of weightened graphs by solving systems of equations in the algebra of events. The theory of finite and probabilistic automata. Isd. Nauka, Moscow 1965, 246 to 249.
[5] The metric space of events. Cybernetics (Kiev), 1965, No. 1, 24–27; No. 4, 22–30.
Böhling, K. H.
[1] Netzwerke — Schaltwerke — Automaten. Ein Überblick über die synchrone Theorie. 2. Colloquium über Schaltkreis- und Schaltwerktheorie, ISNM Bd. 4, Birkhäuser-Verlag, Basel 1963, 82–106.
[2] Zur Strukturtheorie sequentieller Automaten. Forschungsber. d. Landes Nordrhein-Westfalen, No. 1279, 1964.
Booth, T. L.
[1] An analytical representation of signals in sequential networks. Proc. Symp. Mathematical Theory of Automata, Polytechnic Press of Brooklyn, 1963, 301–340.
[2] Nonlinear sequential networks. IEEE Trans. Circuit Theory CT–10 (1963), 279–281.
[3] Random input automata. Intern. Conf. on Microwaves, Circuit Theory and Information Theory, Tokyo (Japan) 1964.
[4] Random processes in sequential networks. Proc. of the IEEE Symp. on Signal Transmission and Processing, 1965, 19–25.
[5] Sequential machines and automata. J. Wiley & Sons, New York 1967.
Borodianskii, Yu. M.
[1] Experiments with finite Moore automata. Cybernetics (Kiev), 1965, No. 6, 18–27.
[2] Some remarks concerning methods of calculating the length of an experiment for a class of automata. The theory of automata, a seminar, No. 3 (1966), 32–35.
Bouchet, A.
[1] An algebraic method for minimizing the number of states in an incompletely specified sequential machine. IEEE Trans. on Comp. C–**17** (1968), No. 8, 795–798.
Brauer, W.
[1] Zu den Grundlagen einer Theorie topologischer sequentieller Systeme und Automaten. Berichte d. Ges. f. Mathematik u. Datenverarbeitung Nr. 31, Bonn 1970.
Brown, F. M.
[1] Code transformations in sequential machines. IEEE Trans. Electr. Comp. EC–14 (1965), 822.
Brown, R. R.
[1] Tape sets and automata. J. ACM **11** (1964), No. 1, 10–14.

CHAITIN, G. J.
[1] An improvement on an theorem by E. F. Moore. IEEE Trans. Electr. Comp. EC—14 (1965), 466—467.
CHANDRASEKARAN, B.; SHEN, D. W. C.
[1] On expediency and convergence in variable-structure automata. IEEE Trans. Systems Science and Cybernetics SSC—4 (1968), 52—60.
[2] Stochastic automata games. IEEE Trans. Systems Sci. and Cybernetics SSC—5 (1969), 145—149.
CHEN, I-NGO; SHENG, C. L.
[1] The decision problems of definite stochastic automata. SIAM J. Control 8 (1970), No. 1, 124—134.
CHENTSOV, V. M.
[1] On a method of synthesis of an autonomous stochastic automaton. Cybernetika, Izd. Nauk. Dumka 1967.
[2] Synthesis of a stochastic automaton. Probl. Synth. Digital Automata, Izd. Nauka, Moscow, 1967, 135—141.
CHI-HAU CHEN
[1] A note on sequential decision approach to pattern recognition and machine learning. Information and Control 9 (1966), 549—562.
CHIRKOV, M. K.
[1] On probabilistic, finite automata. Vich. Tech. i Vopr. Program. 3 (1965), 44—67.
[2] On the analysis of probabilistic automata. Vich. Tech. i Vopr. Program. 4 (1965), 100 to 103.
[3] Probabilistic automata and probabilistic mappings. Discr. Analysis 7 (1966), 61—70.
CHOMSKY, N.
[1] On certain formal properties of grammars. Information and Control 2 (1959), 133—167.
CHOMSKY, N.; MILLER, G. A.
[1] Finite state languages. Information and Control 1 (1958), 91—112.
CHU, J. T.
[1] Some methods for simplifying switching circuits using "don't care" conditions. J. ACM 8 (1961), 497—512.
CHURCH, A.
[1] Application of recursive arithmetic to the problem of circuit synthesis. Notes of the Summer Inst. of Symb. Logic, Cornell Univ. Ithaka, New York 1957, 3—50.
[2] Application of recursive arithmetic in the theory of computers and automata. Univ. of Michigan, Ann. Arbor 1959, 1—68.
[3] Logic, arithmetic and automata. Proc. Internat. Congr. Math. Stockholm 1962, 23—35.
CLAUS, V.
[1] Der Homomorphiebegriff bei stochastischen Automaten. Diplom-Arbeit, Inst. f. angew. Math. der Univ. d. Saarlandes, 1967.
COHN, M.
[1] Controllability in linear sequential circuits. IRE Trans. Circuit Theory CT—9 (1962), 74—78.
[2] Properties of linear machines. J. ACM 11 (1964), No. 3, 296—301.
[3] A theorem on linear automata. IEEE Trans. Electr. Comp. EC—13 (1964), 52.
COHN, M.; EVEN, S.
[1] Identification and minimization of linear machines. IEEE Trans. Electr. Comp. EC—14 (1965), 367—376.
COPI, I. M.; ELGOT, C. C.; WRIGHT, J. B.
[1] Realization of events by logical nets. J. ACM 5 (1958), 181—196.

COWAN, J. D.
[1] Synthesis of reliable automata from unreliable components. Automata Theory, Academic Press, New York—London 1966, 131—145.
ČULIK I, K.
[1] Some notes on finite-state languages and events represented by finite automata using labelled graphs. Časopis pro pest. Mat. 86 (1961), 43—55.
ČULIK II, K.
[1] Construction of the automaton mapping. Appl. Mat. 10 (1965), 459—468.
[2] Relace representovaně n-paskovymi automaty. Kybernetika (Praha) 3 (1967), 321—345.
CURTIS, H. A.
[1] Use of decomposition theory in the solution of the state assignment problem of sequential machines. J. ACM 10 (1963), 386—412.
[2] Polylinear sequential circuit realization of finite automata. IEEE Trans. on Computers C—17 (1968), No. 3, 251—259.
CUTLIP, W. F.
[1] Amendments to Zeigers cascade synthesis of finite-state machines. Information and Control 12 (1968), 499—507.
[2] On the cascade decomposition of prefix automata. IEEE Trans. on Computers C—17 (1968), No. 1, 94—95.

DALEN, D. VAN
[1] Fans generated by nondeterministic automata. Z. Math. Logik Grundl. Math. 14 (1968), 273—278.
DAUBER, P. S.
[1] An analysis of errors in finite automata. Information and Control 8 (1965), 295—303.
DAVIS, A. S.
[1] Markow chains as random input automata. Amer. Math. Monthly 68 (1961), 264 to 267.
DAVIS, W. A.
[1] Single shift register realizations for sequential machines. IEEE Trans. on Computers C—17 (1968), No. 5, 421—431.
[2] Sequential machines realizable with delay elements only. IEEE Trans. on Computers C—19 (1960), No. 4, 353—355.
DEBACKER, W.; VERBECK, L.
[1] Study of analog, digital and hybrid computers using automata theory. ICC Bulletin 5 (1966), 215—244.
DELEEUW, K.; MOORE, E. F.; SHANNON, C. E.; SHAPIRO, N.
[1] Computability by probabilistic machines. Automata Studies, Ann. Math. Studies 34, Princeton 1956, 183—212.
DERENNA E SOUZA, C.
[1] A note on embedding nonlinear machines. IEEE Trans. on Computers C—17 (1968), No. 9, 894—896.
[2] A theorem on the state reduction of synthesized stochastic machines. IEEE Trans. on Computers C—18 (1969), No. 5, 473—474.
DERENNA E SOUZA, C.; LEAKE, J. R.
[1] Relationships among distinct models and notions of equivalence for stochastic finite state systems. IEEE Trans. on Computers C—18 (1969), No. 7, 633—641.
DEUSSEN, P.
[1] Zur Synthese von Automaten. Colloquium über Schaltkreis- und Schaltwerktheorie, (Bonn 1960), ISNM Bd. 3, Birkhäuser Verlag, Basel—Stuttgart 1961, 96—113.
[2] On the algebraic theory of finite automata. ICC Bulletin 4 (1966), 231—264.

[3] Some results on the set of congruence relations in a finite strongly connected automaton. Computing **2** (1967), 57—81.

DOBREV, D.

[1] Weak and strong inversability of quasi-machines. C.R. Acad. Bulgare Sci. **17** (1964), 881—883.

DOLOTTA, T. A.; McCLUSKEY, E. J.

[1] The coding of internal states of sequential circuits. IEEE Trans. Electr. Comp. EC—**13** (1964), 549—562.

DÖRR, J.; HOTZ, G. (Eds.)

[1] Automatentheorie und formale Sprachen. Bericht einer Tagung des Math. Forschungsinstituts Oberwolfach im Oktober 1969, Mannheim 1970.

DUSCHSKI, W. A.

[1] Über charakteristische Experimente mit Automaten. Probl. d. Kybernetik **7**, Akademie-Verlag, Berlin 1966, 339—345.

EATON, J. H.; ZADEH, L. A.

[1] Optimal pursuit strategies in discrete-state probabilistic systems. J. Basic Engng., Ser. D 84, 1962, 23—29.

EGGAN, L. C.

[1] Transition graphs and the star-height of regular events. Michigan Math. J. **10** (1963), 385—397.

EILENBERG, S.; WRIGHT, J. B.

[1] Automata in general algebras. Information and Control **11** (1967), 452—470.

ELGOT, C. C.

[1] Lectures on switching and automata theory. Techn. Report, Univ. Michigan Res. Inst., 1959.

[2] Decision problems of finite automata design and related arithmetics. Trans. Amer. Math. Soc. **98** (1961), No. 4, 21—51.

ELGOT, C. C.; MEZEI, J. E.

[1] On finite relations defined by generalized automata. IBM J. Res. Dev. **9** (1965), 47—68.

ELGOT, C. C.; RUTLEDGE, J. D.

[1] Operations on finite automata. Switching Circuit Theory and Logic. Design (Conf. Rec.) New York 1962.

[2] Machine properties preserved under state minimization. Switching Circuit Theory and Logic. Design (Conf. Rec.), New York 1963.

[3] *RS*-Machines with almost blank tape. J. ACM **11** (1964), 313—337.

ELSPAS, B.

[1] The theory of autonomous linear sequential networks. IRE Trans. Circuit Theory CT—**6** (1959), No. 1, 45—50.

ENGELBERT, H.-J.

[1] Zur Reduktion stochastischer Automaten. Elektron. Informationsverarbeitung u. Kybernetik **4** (1968), No. 2, 81—92.

EVEN, S.

[1] Rational numbers and regular events. IEEE Trans. Electr. Comp. EC—**13** (1964), 740 to 741.

[2] Test for synchronizability of finite automata and variable length codes. IEEE Trans. Information Theory IT—**10** (1964), 185—189.

[3] On information lossless automata of finite order. IEEE Trans. Electr. Comp. EC—**14** (1965), No. 4, 561—569.

[4] Comments on the minimization of stochastic machines. IEEE Trans. Electr. Comp. EC—**14** (1965), 634—637.

EVEN, S.; MEYER, A. R.
[1] Test for planarity of a circuit given by an expression. IEEE Trans. Electr. Comp. EC—**15** (1966), 372.

FARR, E. H.
[1] Lattice properties of sequential machines. J. ACM **10** (1963), No. 3, 365—385.

FECHNER, J.
[1] Automatenspiele stochastischer Automaten. Diplom-Arbeit, Inst. Math. Logik Humboldt-Univ., Berlin 1965.

FEICHTINGER, G.
[1] Some results on the relation between automata and their automorphism groups. Computing **1** (1966), No. 4, 327—340.
[2] Beiträge zur Theorie abstrakter Automaten. elektronische datenverarbeitung 8 (1967), 361—366.
[3] Über isomorphe Unterautomaten in abstrakten Automaten. elektronische datenverarbeitung 8 (1967), 411—415.
[4] Über die Anzahl aller nichtisomorphen transitiven Automaten von Primzahlordnung. Elektron. Informationsverarb. u. Kybernetik **3** (1967), 275—282.
[5] Der Quotientenautomat nach einem direkten Faktor einer Automorphismengruppe. Computing **3** (1968), 1—8.
[6] Eine automatentheoretische Deutung des einelementigen Lernmodells der Stimulus Sampling Theorie. Grundlagenstudien aus Kybernetik und Geisteswissenschaft **9** (1968), No. 1, 13—20.
[7] Zur Theorie abstrakter stochastischer Automaten. Z. Wahrscheinlichkeitstheorie verw. Geb. **9** (1968), 341—356.
[8] Automatentheorie und dynamische Programmierung. Elektron. Informationsverarb. u. Kybernetik **4** (1968), No. 6, 347—352.
[9] Stochastische Automaten als Grundlage linearer Lernmodelle. To appear in Statistische Hefte.

FISCHER, K.; LINDNER, R.; THIELE, H.
[1] Stabile stochastische Automaten. Elektron. Informationsverarb. u. Kybernetik **3** (1967), 201—213.

FISCHER, P. C.
[1] Multi-tape and infinite automata — a survey. Commun. ACM **8** (1965), 799—805.

FITCH, F. B.
[1] Representation of sequential circuits in combinatory logic. Philosoph. Sci. **25** (1958), No. 4, 263—279.

FLECK, A. C.
[1] Isomorphism groups of automata. J. ACM **9** (1963), 469—476.
[2] On the automorphism group of an automaton. J. ACM **12** (1965), No. 4, 566 to 569.
[3] On the strong connectedness of the direct product. IEEE Trans. Electr. Comp. EC—**16** (1967), No. 1, 90.

FRANK, H.; YAU, S. S.
[1] Improving reliability of a sequential machine by error-correcting state assignments. IEEE Trans. Electr. Comp. EC—**15** (1966), 111.

FRANKLIN, J. N.
[1] Deterministic simulation of random processes. Math. of Computation **17** (1963), 28—59.

FREEMAN, H.
[1] Discrete-time systems. J. Wiley & Sons, New York 1965.

FREY, T.
[1] Über die Konstruktion nicht vollständiger Automaten. Acta Math. Acad. Scient. Hung. **15** (1964), 375–381.
[2] Über den Kalmárschen Begriff des Rechenautomaten. Colloq. Found. Math., Math. Machines and Appl. (Tihany 1962), Budapest 1965, 111–117.
FRIEDES, A.
[1] Critical pairs and set systems. IEEE Trans. Electr. Comp. EC–**15** (1966), 162.
FRIEDLAND, B.
[1] Linear modular sequential circuits. IRE Trans. Circuit Theory CT–**6** (1959), 61–68.
FRIEDMAN, A. D.
[1] Feedback in synchronous sequential circuits. IEEE Trans. Electr. Comp. EC–**15** (1966), 354–367.
[2] Feedback in asynchronous sequential circuits. IEEE Trans. Electr. Comp. EC–**15** (1966), 740.
FU, K. S.
[1] Stochastic automata as models of learning systems. In: Computer and Information Sci. II (Ed. J. T. TOU), Academic Press, New York–London 1967, 177–191.
FU, K. S.; MCLAREN, R. W.
[1] An application of stochastic automata to the synthesis of learning systems. Techn. Rept. TR EE 65–17, School of Electr. Engng., Purdue Univ. Michigan 1965.
FUJIMOTO, S.; FUKAO, T.
[1] The decomposition of probabilistic automata. Bull. Electrotechn. Lab. **30** (1966), No. 8, 688–698.
FUKUNAGA, K.
[1] A theory of nonlinear autonomous sequential nets using z transforms. IEEE Trans. Electr. Comp. EC–**13** (1964), No. 3, 310.

GAGLIARDI, R. M.
[1] State-identification in finite state systems having input–output noise. Joint Automat. Control Conf., Reusselaer Polytechn. Inst., Troy (N.Y.) 1965, 452–457.
GALLAIRE, H.; GRAY, J.; HARRISON, M. A.; HERMAN, G.
[1] Infinite linear sequential machines. J. Computer and System Sci. **2** (1968), No. 4, 381–419.
GAVRILOV, M. A.
[1] The present status of the theory of relay devices and finite automata. The theory of finite and probabilistic automata. Izd. Nauka, Moscow, 1965, 17–39.
GERACE, G. B.; GESTRI, G.
[1] State assignments for reducing the number of delay elements in sequential machines Information and Control **10** (1967), 223–253.
[2] Decomposition of synchronous sequential machines into synchronous and asynchronous submachines. Information and Control **11** (1967), 568–591.
[3] Decomposition of a synchronous machine into a asynchronous submachine driving a synchronous one. Information and Control **12** (1968), No. 5, 6, 538–548.
GHIRON, H.
[1] Rules to manipulate regular expressions of finite automata. IRE Trans. Electr. Comp. EC–**11** (1962), 574–575.
GILL, A.
[1] Comparison of finite state models. IRE Trans. Circuit Theory CT–**7** (1960), 178–179.
[2] A note on Moore's distinguishability theorem. IRE Trans. Electr. Comp. EC–**10** (1961), No. 2, 290–291.

[3] State-identification experiments in finite automata. Information and Control **4** (1961), No. 3, 132—154.
[4] Cascaded finite-state machines. IRE Trans. Electr. Comp. EC—**10** (1961), No. 3, 366 to 370.
[5] Introduction to the theory of finite-state machines. McGraw-Hill Book Comp., New York 1962.
[6] Synthesis of probability transformers. J. Franklin Inst. **274** (1962), 1—19.
[7] On an weight distribution problem with application to the design of stochastic generators. J. ACM **10** (1963), 110—121.
[8] Analysis of linear sequential switching circuits by confluence sets. IEEE Trans. Electr. Comp. EC—**13** (1964), No. 3, 226—231.
[9] On the bound to the memory of a sequential machine. IEEE Trans. Electr. Comp. EC—**14** (1965), No. 3, 464—466.
[10] Analysis and synthesis of stable linear sequential circuits. J. ACM **12** (1965), 141—149.
[11] Realization of input—output relations by sequential machines. J. ACM **13** (1966), 33 to 42.
[12] The reduced form of a linear automaton. Automata Theory, Academic Press Inc., New York—London 1966, 164—175.
[13] State graphs of autonomous linear automata. Automata Theory, Academic Press Inc., New York—London 1966, 176—180.
[14] On the series-to-parallel transformation of linear sequential circuits. IEEE Trans. Electr. Comp. EC—**15** (1966), 107.
[15] Linear sequential circuits — analysis, synthesis and application. McGraw-Hill Book Comp., New York 1967.

Ginsburg, S.
[1] On the length of the smallest uniform experiment which distinguishes the terminal state of the machine. J. ACM **5** (1958), 266—280.
[2] Synthesis of minimal-state sequential machines. IRE Trans. Electr. Comp. EC—8 (1959), No. 4, 441—448.
[3] On the reduction of superflous states in a sequential machine. J. ACM **6** (1959), No. 2, 259—282.
[4] A synthesis technique for minimal-state sequential machines. IRE Trans. Electr. Comp. EC—**8** (1959), No. 1, 13—24.
[5] A technique for the reduction of a given machine to a minimal-state machine. IRE Trans. Electr. Comp. EC—**8** (1959), 346—355.
[6] Connective properties preserved in minimal-state machines. J. ACM **7** (1960), No. 4, 311—325.
[7] Some remarks on abstract machines. Trans. Amer. Math. Soc. **96** (1960), 400—441.
[8] Set of tapes accepted by different types of automata. J. ACM **8** (1961), No. 1, 81—86.
[9] Compatibility of states of input independent machines. J. ACM **8** (1961), No. 3.
[10] An introduction to mathematical machine theory. Addison-Wesley Publ. Comp., Reading (Mass.), 1962.
[11] Examples of abstract machines. IRE Trans. Electr. Comp. EC—**11** (1962), 132—135.
[12] Abstract machines — a generalization of sequential machines. Mathematical Theory of Automata, Polytechnic Press, Brooklyn (N.J.) 1963, 125—138.
[13] The mathematical theory of context-free languages. McGraw-Hill Book Co., New York 1966.
[14] Two way balloon automata and AFL. J. ACM **17** (1970), No. 1, 3—13.

Ginsburg, S.; Greibach, S.
[1] Deterministic context-free languages. Information and Control **9** (1966), 620—648.

Ginsburg, S.; Harrison, M. A.
[1] On the elimination of endmarkers. Information and Control **12** (1968), 103—115.

GINSBURG, S.; HIBBARD, T. N.

[1] Solvability of machine mappings of regular sets to regular sets. J. ACM **11** (1964), No. 3, 302–312.

GINSBURG, S.; ROSE, G.

[1] A characterization of the automaton mappings. Canad. J. Math. **18** (1966), 381–388.

[2] Preservation of languages by transducers. Information and Control **9** (1966), 153 to 176.

[3] A note on preservation of languages by transducers. Information and Control **12** (1968), 549–552.

GINZBURG, A.

[1] About some properties of definite, reverse-definite and related automata. IEEE Trans. Electr. Comp. EC–**15** (1966), No. 5, 806–810.

[2] A procedure for checking equality of regular expressions. J. ACM **14** (1967), 355–362.

[3] Algebraic theory of automata. Academic Press, New York–London 1968.

GINZBURG, A.; YOELI, M.

[1] Products of automata and the problem of covering. Trans. Amer. Math. Soc. **116** (1965), 253–266.

GIVE'ON, Y.

[1] The theory of algebraic automata. I: Morphisms and regular systems. Techn. Inf. Univ. Michigan, Ann Arbor 1964.

GIVE'ON, Y.; ARBIB, M. A.

[1] Algebra automata II: The categorical framework for dynamic analysis. Information and Control **12** (1968), 346–370.

GLEBSKII, YU. V.

[1] Coding by means of finite automata. DAN SSSR **141** (1961), No. 5, 1054–1057.

[2] In endlichen Automaten realisierbare Wörter. Probl. d. Kybernetik **5**, Akademie-Verlag, Berlin 1965, 321–325.

GLEBSKII, YU. V.; DUCHICH, A. M.; KOGAN, M. I.; LIOGONSKII, M. M.; MARKOV, A. A.

[1] Algorithms obtained by repeated applications of finite automata. Prob. Cyb. **13** (1965), 241–244.

GLUSHKOV, V. M.

[1] On a method of analysis of abstract automata. DAN USSR 1960, No. 9, 1151–1154.

[2] On an algorithm of the synthesis of abstract automata. Ukr. Math. Journ. **12** (1960), No. 2, 147–156.

[3] Some problems of the synthesis of abstract automata. Vich. Math. i Math. Phys. **1** (1961), 371–411.

[4] Abstract automata and partitions of free semi-groups. DAN USSR **136** (1961), No. 4, 765–767.

[5] Synthesis of digital automata. Physmatgiz. Moscow 1962.

[6] Theorie der abstrakten Automaten. VEB Deutscher Verlag der Wissenschaften, Berlin 1963.

GORBOVITSKAIA, N. A.

[1] Equivalent transformations of certain types of automata. Prob. Cyb. **12** (1964), 5–28.

GRASSELLI, A.

[1] Minimal closed partitions for incompletely specified flow tables. IEEE Trans. Electr. Comp. EC–**15** (1966), No. 2, 245–249.

GRASSELLI, A.; LUCCIO, F. A.

[1] A method for minimizing the number of internal states in incompletely specified sequential machines. IEEE Trans. Electr. Comp. EC–**14** (1965), 350–359.

GRAY, J. N.; HARRISON, M. A.

[1] The theory of sequential relations. Information and Control **9** (1966), 435–468.

GRIFFITHS, T. V.
[1] The unsolvability of the equivalence problem for Λ-free nondeterministic generalized machines. J. ACM **15** (1968), No. 3, 409–413.
GRENANDER, U.
[1] Can we look inside an unreliable automaton? Res. Papers Statist., Festschrift J. NEYMAN, 1966, 107–123.
GRUEL, J.
[1] Ein Beitrag zum Thema „Minimalautomaten". Elektron. Informationsverarb. u. Kybernetik **4** (1968), 353–362.
GRZYMALA-BUSSE, J.
[1] Automorphisms of polyadic automata. J. ACM **16** (1969), No. 2, 208–219.
[2] On the periodic representation and the reducibility of periodic automata. J. ACM **16** (1969), No. 3, 432–441.
[3] On the automorphisms of infinite time varying automata. Bull. Acad. Polon. Sci. **18** (1970), No. 5, 261–266.
GUIAȘU, S.
[1] On codification in finite abstract random automata. Information and Control **12** (1968), 277–283.

HÄNDLER, W.
[1] Einfache diagnostische Experimente bei endlichen Automaten. 3. Colloquium über Automatentheorie, ISNM Bd. 6, Birkhäuser-Verlag, Basel–Stuttgart 1967, 56–75.
[2] Die Behandlung von Aufgaben der Kybernetik mit Hilfe der Automatentheorie. Fortschritte der Kybernetik, Oldenbourg-Verlag, München 1967, 29–42.
[3] Automatentheorie. Erscheint im Verlag W. de Gruyter, Berlin.
HARARY, F.; PALMER, E.
[1] Enumeration of finite automata. Information and Control **10** (1967), 499–508.
HARRISON, M. A.
[1] Introduction to switching and automata theory. McGraw-Hill Book Co., New York 1965.
[2] A census of finite automata. Canad. J. Math. **17** (1966), No. 1, 100–113.
[3] On the error correcting capacity of finite automata. Information and Control **8** (1965), 430–450.
[4] On asymptotic estimates in switching and automata theory. J. ACM **13** (1966), No. 1, 151–157.
[5] On equivalence of state-assignments. IEEE Trans. on Comp. C–**17** (1968), No. 1, 55–57.
HARTMANIS, J.
[1] Linear multivalued sequential coding networks. IRE Trans. Circuit Theory CT–**6** (1959), 69–74.
[2] Symbolic analysis of a decomposition of information processing machines. Information and Control **3** (1960), 154–178.
[3] On the state-assignment problem for sequential machines I. IRE Trans. Electr. Comp. EC–**10** (1961), No. 2, 157–165.
[4] Maximal autonomous clocks of sequential machines. IEEE Trans. Electr. Comp. EC–**11** (1962), 83–85.
[5] Loop-free structure of sequential machines. Information and Control **5** (1962), 25–43.
[6] The equivalence of sequential machine models. IEEE Trans. Electr. Comp. EC–**12** (1963), 18–19.
[7] Further results on the structure of sequential machines. J. ACM **10** (1963), 78–88.
[8] Two tests for the linearity of sequential machines. IEEE Trans. Electr. Comp. EC–**14** (1965), No. 6, 781–786.

[9] Minimal feedback realizations of sequential machines. IEEE Trans. Electr. Comp. EC—**15** (1966), No. 6, 931—933.
[10] On the complexity of undecidable problems in automata theory. J. ACM **16** (1969), No. 1, 160—167.

HARTMANIS, J.; DAVIS, W. A.
[1] Homomorphic images of linear sequential machines. J. Computer System Sciences **1** (1965), 155—156.

HARTMANIS, J.; STEARNS, R. E.
[1] Some dangers in state reduction of sequential machines. Information and Control **5** (1962), 252—260.
[2] A study of feedback and errors in sequential machines. IEEE Trans. Electr. Comp. EC—**12** (1963), 223—232.
[3] Pair algebra and its application to automata theory. Information and Control **7** (1964), 485—507.
[4] Algebraic structure theory of sequential machines. Prentice-Hall Inc., Englewood Cliffs (N.J.) 1966.
[5] Sets of numbers defined by finite automata. Amer. Math. Monthly **74** (1967), 539—542.

HAZELTINE, B.
[1] Regular expressions and variable length encodings. IEEE Trans. Information Theory IT—**9** (1963), No. 1, 48.

HELLER, A.
[1] Probabilistic automata and stochastic transformations. Math. System Theory **1** (1967), No. 3, 197—208.

HELLERMAN, L.; DUDA, W. S.; WINOGRAD, S.
[1] Continuity and realizability of sequence transformers. IEEE Trans. Electr. Comp. EC—**15** (1966), No. 4, 580.

HENNIE, F. C.
[1] Fault detecting experiments for sequential circuits. Switching Circuit Theory and Logic. Design, Inst. El. Electron. Engngs, New York 1964, 95—110.

HIBBARD, T. N.
[1] Least upper bounds on minimal terminal state experiments for two classes of sequential machines. J. ACM **8** (1961), No. 4, 601—612.

HOHN, F. E.
[1] States of sequential machines whose logical elements involve delay. Proc. 3rd Ann. Symp. Switching Circuit Theory and Logic. Design, New York 1963, 81—90.

HOŘEJŠ, J.
[1] Durch endliche Automaten definierte Abbildungen. Probl. d. Kybernetik **6**, Akademie-Verlag, Berlin 1966, 31—35.

HOTZ, G.
[1] Nichtsinguläre Schaltwerke. Z. angew. Math. u. Mech. **41** (1961), Sonderheft, 71—74.
[2] On the mathematical theory of linear sequential networks. Switching Theory in Space Technology, Stanford (Calif.) Univ. Press 1963, 11—19.
[3] Quasilineare Automaten. Computing **2** (1967), No. 2, 139—152.
[4] Transfer of propositions about automata to Chomsky languages. Computing **4** (1969), No. 1, 30—42.

HUFFMAN, D. A.
[1] The synthesis of sequential switching circuits. J. Franklin Inst. **257** (1954), 161—190, 275—303.
[2] Canonical forms for information-lossless finite-state logical machines. IRE Trans. Circuit Theory, Special Supplement CT—**6** (1959), 41—59.

[3] An algebra for periodically time-varying linear binary sequence transducers. Ann. Comp. Lab. Harvard Univ. **29** (1959), 189—203.
[4] The synthesis of linear sequential coding networks. Information Theory (Ed.: C. CHERRY) Academic Press Inc., New York 1961.

HUZINO, S.
[1] On some sequential machines and experiments. Mem. Fac. Sci., Kyusyu Univ., Ser. A, **12** (1958), 136—158.
[2] Reduction theorems on sequential machines and experiments. Mem. Fac. Sci., Kyusyu Univ., Ser. A, **12** (1958), 159—172.
[3] Theory of finite automata. Mem. Fac. Sci., Kyusyu Univ. Ser. A, **15** (1961), No. 2.
[4] Simulatability of finite automata by Shepherdson-Sturgis-machines. Mem. Fac. Sci., Kyusyu Univ., Ser. A, **20** (1966), No. 1, 1—15.

IBARRA, O. H.
[1] On the equivalence of finite state sequential machine models. IEEE Trans. Electr. Comp. EC—**16** (1967), No. 1.

INDERMARK, K.
[1] Zur Zustandsminimisierung nichtdeterministischer erkennender Automaten. Berichte d. Ges. f. Mathematik u. Datenverarbeitung Nr. 33, Bonn 1970.

ION ION, D.
[1] On the connection between the theory of algorithms and the abstract theory of automata. Rev. math. pures et appl. RPR **8** (1963), No. 4, 673—682.
[2] Un sistem de axiome pentru algebra evenimentelor. Studii se cercetari mat. Acad. RPR **17** (1965), No. 4, 599—606.

JEFFREY, R. C.
[1] Finite-state transformations. Information and Control **7** (1964), 45—54.

JOYCE, F.
[1] A decision procedure for computation of finite automata. J. ACM **9** (1962), 315—323.

JUMP, R. J.
[1] A note on the iterative decomposition of finite automata. Information and Control **15** (1969), 424—435.

KALMÁR, L.
[1] Algorithmische Sprachen und Programmierung von Rechenautomaten. Math. und physikalisch-technische Probleme der Kybernetik, Akademie-Verlag, Berlin 1963, 147—176.

KAMBAYASHI, Y.; YAJIMA, S.; OHBAYASHI, J.
[1] On finite memory sequential machines. IEEE Trans. on Computers C—**19** (1970), 254 to 270.

KAMEDA, T.
[1] Generalized transition matrix of a sequential machine and its applications. Information and Control **12** (1968), No. 3, 259—275.
[2] Some new useful concepts in automata theory. Proc. Hawaii Intern. Conf. on System Sci. 1968, 320—323.

KAMEDA, T.; WEINER, P.
[1] On the reduction of non-deterministic automata. To appear in IEEE Trans. on Computers.

KANDELAKI, N. P.; TSERVADZE, G. N.
[1] On the behaviour of certain classes of stochastic automata in a random environment. Automatika i telemechanika, 1966, No. 6, 115—119.

KAPHENGST, H.
[1] Implications of events and checking automata. Dop. AN URSR 1965, No. 5, 567—569.
[2] Axiomatizable classes of automata. Vopr. Teor. Cyb. Kiev, 1965, 6—30.
KAPITONOVA, YU. V.
[1] On a method of synthesis of abstract automata. Vich. Mat. i Tech. AN USSR, Kiev, 1962, 114—120.
[2] On the isomorphism of abstract automata. Cybernetika (Kiev), 1965, No. 3, 25—28, No. 5, 10—13.
KARATSUBA, A. A.
[1] Solution of a problem of the theory of finite automata. Usp. Mat. Nauk. **15** (1960), No. 3, 157—159.
KARP, R. M.
[1] Some techniques of state assignment for synchronous sequential machines. IEEE Trans. Electr. Comp. EC—**13** (1964), 507—518.
Correction: EC—**14** (1965), 61.
KASAMI, T.; TORII, K.; OZAKI, H.
[1] Generalized sequential machine mappings of finite state languages to finite state languages. Techn. Repts. Osaka Univ. **16** (1966), 71—88.
KASHYAP, R. L.
[1] Optimization of stochastic finite state systems. IEEE Trans. Automatic Control AC—**11** (1966), No. 4, 685—692.
KASNACHEIEV, V. I.
[1] Construction of tests for finite automata by means of the language of regular expressions. Probl. Synth. Digital automata. Izd. Nauka, Moscow, 1967, 145—150.
KAUTZ, W. H.
[1] Totally sequential switching circuits. Switching Theory in Space Technology, Stanford (Calif.) Univ. Press 1963, 20—46.
[2] Linear sequential switching circuits. Holden-Day, San Francisco 1965.
KEISTER, W.; RITCHIE, A. E.; WASHBURN, S.
[1] The design of switching circuits. New York 1951.
KFOURY, D. J.
[1] Synchronizing sequences for probabilistic automata. Studies in Appl. Math. **49** (1970), No. 1, 101—103.
KLEENE, S. C.
[1] Representation of events in nerve nets and finite automata. Automata Studies, Ann. Math. Studies **34**, Princeton 1956, 3—41.
KLOSS, B. M.; MALISHEV, V. A.
[1] A definition of the regularity of an automaton by means of its canonical equations. DAN SSSR **172** (1967), No. 3, 543—546.
KLUKOVITS, L.
[1] Some measure problems concerning the retrospective sequential functions. Acta Cybernetica **1** (1969), No. 1, 27—40.
KNAST, R.
[1] Linear probabilistic sequential machines. Information and Control **15** (1969), 111—129.
[2] Continuous-time probabilistic automata. Information and Control **15** (1969), 335 to 352.
[3] Representability of nonregular languages in finite probabilistic automata. Information and Control **16** (1970), 285—302.
KOBAYASHI, K.; SEKIGUCHI, S.
[1] On the class of predicates decidable by two-way multi-tape finite automata. J. ACM **13** (1966), No. 2, 236—261.

KOBRINSKI, N. E.; TRACHTENBROT, B. A.
[1] Einführung in die Theorie endlicher Automaten. Akademie-Verlag, Berlin 1967.
KOCHKARIEV, B. S.
[1] On the stability of probabilistic automata. Cybernetika, Kiev, 1968, No. 2, 24–30.
KOHAVI, Z.
[1] Minimizing of incompletely specified sequential switching circuits. US Gov. Research Rept. **38** (1963).
[2] Secondary state assignment for sequential machines. IEEE Trans. Electr. Comp. EC–**13** (1964), No. 3, 193–203.
[3] Reduction of the number of states in incompletely specified sequential machines. Electron. Letters **1** (1965), 209–210.
[4] Reduction of output dependence in sequential machines. IEEE Trans. Electr. Comp. EC–**14** (1965), No. 6, 932–934.
KOHAVI, Z.; SMITH, E. J.
[1] Decomposition of sequential machines. Switching Circuit Theory and Logic. Design (IEEE Conf. Rec.) New York 1965, 52–61.
KORSHUNOV, A. D.
[1] On asymptotic estimates for the number of reduced, finite automata. Discr. Analysis **6** (1966), 35–50.
[2] On asymptotic estimates for the number of finite automata. Cybernetika, Kiev, 1967, No. 2, 12–19.
KOSMIDIADI, V. A.
[1] On sets, solvable and enumerable, by automata. Probl. Logic, AN SSSR 1963, 102–115.
KOSMIDIAI, V. A.; CHERNIAVSKII, V. S.
[1] On the ordering of a set of automata. Vopr. Toer. Mat. Machine **2** (1962), 34–51.
KOVALENKO, I. N.
[1] A remark on the complexity of the representation of events in probabilistic and deterministic finite automata. Cybernetika, Kiev, 1965, No. 2.
KRAL, J.
[1] Set-theoretical operations on k-multiple languages. Kybernetika (Praha) **3** (1967), 315–320.
KRATKO, M. I.
[1] Algorithmic unsolvability of a problem in the theory of finite automata. Discr. Analysis **2** (1964), 37–41.
[2] Algorithmic unsolvability of the recognition problem for the completeness of finite automata. DAN SSSR **155** (1964), No. 1, 35–37.
[3] Formal Post calculus and finite automata. Probl. Cyb. **17** (1966), 41–65.
KRINSKII, V. I.
[1] An asymptotically optimal automaton with an exponential order of convergence. Biophysika **6** (1963), No. 6.
[2] On a construction of a sequence of automata and its behaviour in games. DAN SSSR **156** (1964), No. 6, 1312–1315.
KROHN, K. B.; MATEOSIAN, R.; RHODES, J. L.
[1] Complexity of ideals in finite semigroups and finite state machines. Math. Systems Theory **1** (1967), 59–66.
[2] Methods of the algebraic theory of machines. I. Decomposition theorem for generalized machines; properties preserved under series and parallel composition of machines. J. Computer and Systems Sci. **1** (1967), 55–85; Erratum: 373.
KROHN, K. B.; RHODES, J. L.
[1] Algebraic theory of machines. I. The main decomposition theorem. Techn. Rept. Dept. Math., Univ. Calif., Berkeley 1963.

[2] Algebraic theory of machines. Mathematical Theory of Automata. Polytechnic Press, Brooklyn (N.J.) 1963, 341–384.
[3] Algebraic theory of machines. I. Prime decomposition theorem for finite semigroups and machines. Trans. Amer. Math. Soc. **116** (1965), 450–464.
[4] Results on finite semigroups derived from the algebraic theory of machines. Proc. Nat. Acad. Sci. USA **53** (1965), 499–501.
[5] Complexity of finite semigroups and finite-state machines. In Arbib [10].

Krylov, V. Yu.
[1] On a stochastic automaton which is asymptotically optimal in a random environment. Automatika i telemechanika **24** (1963), No. 9.
[2] Representation of encoded, regular events in abstract finite automata. Ukr. Mat. Journ. **16** (1964), No. 3, 385–389.

Kudriavtsev, V. B.
[1] A completeness theorem for a class of automata without feedback. DAN SSSR **132** (1960), No. 2.
[2] Vollständigkeitstheoreme für eine Klasse von Automaten ohne Rückführungen. Probl. d. Kybernetik **8**, Akademie-Verlag, Berlin 1965, 105–136.

Kurmit, A. A.
[1] Solution of some problems in the theory of abstract finite automata by means of graph theory. Aut. i Vich. Tech. 1967, No. 1.
[2] Generalized inverse automata. Aut. i Vich. Tech. 1967, No. 3.
[3] Inversions of automata with respect to a regular event. Aut. i Vich. Tech. 1967, No. 4.

Kuroda, S. Y.
[1] Classes of languages and linear-bounded automata. Information and Control **7** (1964), 207–223.

Kusnietsov, O. P.
[1] On asynchronous logical networks. Probl. Pered. inf. **9** (1961), 103–115.
[2] Representation of regular events in asynchronous automata. Automatika i telemechanika **26** (1965), No. 6, 1086–1093.

Küstner, H.
[1] Analyse und Synthese von stochastischen Automaten. Diplomarbeit, Inst. f. Math. Logik d. Humboldt-Univ., Berlin 1968 (to appear in Elektron. Informationsverarb. u. Kybernetik).

Laemmel, A. E.
[1] Application of lattice-ordered semi-groups to codes and finite-state transducers. Mathematical Theory of Automata, Polytechnic Press, Brooklyn (N.J.) 1963, 241–256.

Landweber, P. S.
[1] Three theorems on phrase structure grammars of type 1. Information and Control **6** (1963), 131–136.

Larin, L. K.; Ossinskii, L. M.
[1] Economical coding of states of finite automata. Cybernetika, Kiev, 1966, No. 3.

Lavallee, P.
[1] Nonstable cycle and level sets for linear sequential machines. IEEE Trans. Electr. Comp. EC–**14** (1965), No. 6, 957–959.
[2] Some new group teoretic properties of singular linear sequential machines. IEEE Trans. Electr. Comp. EC–**14** (1965), 959.

Lazarev, V. G.; Piyl, E. I.
[1] A method of synthesis of finite automata. Automatika i telemechanika **22** (1961), No. 9, 1194–1201.

[2] Reduction of the number of states in a class of finite automata. DAN SSSR **143** (1962), No. 5, 1064—1066.
[3] Synthesis of asynchronous, finite automata. Izd. Nauka. Moscow, 1964.
[4] Minimication of the number of inner states in certain classes of finite automata. Theory of finite and probabilistic automata. Izd. Nauka, Moscow, 1965, 154—167.

LAZARIEV, V. G.; PIYL, E. I.; TURUTA, E. N.
[1] On the reliability of discrete automata. Cybernetika, Kiev, 1968, No. 1.

LEE, C. Y.
[1] Automata and finite automata. Bell System Techn. J. **39** (1960), No. 5, 1267—1295.

LETICHEVSKII, A. A.
[1] Completeness conditions for finite automata. Vich. Mat. i Mat. Phys. 1961, No. 4.
[2] On the synthesis of finite automata. DAN USSR **2** (1961) 139—141.
[3] Alphabet mappings and finite automata. Theory of finite and probabilistic automata. Izd. Nauka, Moscow 1965, 250—252.
[4] Equivalence of automata with a terminal state. Cybernetika, Kiev, 1966, No. 1, 1967, No. 1.

LEVIN, V. I.
[1] Definition of characteristics of probabilistic automata with feedback. Izv. AN SSSR Techn. Cyb. 1966, No. 3, 107—110.
[2] The operation method of investigating probabilistic automata. Automatika i Vich. Techn. 1967, No. 1.

LEVINE, E.
[1] On the characterizing parameters of a threshold function. IEEE Trans. on Comp. C—**17** (1968), No. 7, 696.

LEWIS, E. W.
[1] Stochastic sequential machines; theory and application. Ph. D. Thesis, Northwestern Univ. 1966.

LINDNER, R.
[1] Sequentielle Operatoren und ihre Anwendung beim Studium sequentieller (diskreter) Codierungen. Elektron. Informationsverarb. u. Kybernetik **4** (1968), 107—136, 151—172.

LIU, C. L.
[1] A property of partially specified automata. Information and Control **6** (1963), 169 to 176.
[2] Determination of the final state of an automaton whose initial state is unknown. IEEE Trans. Electr. Comp. EC—**12** (1963), 918—921.
[3] k-th order finite automaton. IEEE Trans. Electr. Comp. EC—**12** (1963), 470—475; EC—**13** (1964), 642.
[4] A state variable assignment method for asynchronous sequential switching circuits. J. ACM **10** (1963), No. 2, 209—216.
[5] A note on definite stochastic sequential machines. Information and Control **14** (1969), 407—421.
[6] Lattice functions, pair algebras and finite state machines. J. ACM **16** (1969), No. 3, 442—454.

LIUBICH, YU. I.
[1] On periodicity properties of events representable in finite automata. Ukr. Mat. Journ. 1964, No. 3, 396—402.
[2] Estimates for the optimal determinization of non-deterministic autonomous automata. Sib. Mat. Journ. **5** (1964), 337—355.

LIUBICH, YU. I.; LIFSHITS, E. M.
[1] An estimate for the weight of a regular event over a one letter alphabet. Sib. Mat. Journ. **6** (1965), 122—126.

LORENTS, A.
[1] Some questions of the constructive theory of finite probabilistic automata. Z. Math. Logik Grundl. Math. **14** (1968), 413–447.
LÖWENSTEIN, B. I.
[1] Self adjusting automata for decoding messages. DAN SSSR **141** (1961), No. 6, 1320 to 1323.
[2] On the inversion of finite automata. DAN SSSR **147** (1962), No. 6, 1300–1303..
[3] Decoding automata invariant under the initial state. Probl. Cyb. **12** (1964), 125 to 136.
[4] On self-adjusting automata. The theory of finite and probabilistic automata. Izd. Nauk, Moscow 1965, 150–153.
[5] Über einige Eigenschaften von Codierungen und von selbstkorrigierenden Automaten zur Decodierung von Nachrichten. Probl. d. Kybernetik **7**, Akademie-Verlag, Berlin 1966, 96–165.
[6] Zur Existenz stabiler Fortsetzungen partieller Automaten. Probl. d. Kybernetik **7**, Akademie-Verlag, Berlin 1966, 333–340.
LUCCIO, F.
[1] Reduction of the number of columns in flow table minimization. IEEE Trans. Electr. Comp. EC–**15** (1966), No. 5, 803.
[2] Extending the definition of prime compatibility classes of states in incomplete sequential machine reduction. IEEE Trans. on Computers C–**18** (1969), No. 6, 537 to 540.
LUNTS, A. G.
[1] Algebraic methods in the analysis and synthesis of contact schemes. Izv. AN SSSR ser. Math. **10** (1952), No. 5.
[2] The p-adic method in the theory of finite automata. Theory of finite and probabilistic automata. Izd. Nauka, Moscow, 1965, 224–229.
[3] The method of analysis of finite automata. DAN SSSR **160** (1965), No. 4, 778–780.
[4] The p-adic apparatus in the theory of finite automata. Probl. Cyb. **14** (1965), 17 to 30.
LUPANOV, O. B.
[1] On the principle of local coding and the realization of functions of certain classes by means of circuits from functional elements. DAN SSSR **140** (1961), No. 2.

MAKAROV, S. V.
[1] On the realization of stochastic matrices by finite automata. Vich. Syst. (Novosibirsk) **9** (1963), 65–70.
MARCUS, S.
[1] Gramatici şi automate finite. Bucuresti 1964.
MARKOW, A. A.
[1] Nicht rekurrente Codierung. Probl. d. Kybernetik **8**, Akademie-Verlag, Berlin 1965, 154–177.
MARTYNJUK, W. W.
[1] Über Beziehungen zwischen der Speicherkapazität und der Leistungsfähigkeit endlicher Automaten. Probl. d. Kybernetik **5**, Akademie-Verlag, Berlin 1964, 78–89.
MASSEY, J. L.
[1] Note on finite memory sequential machines. IEEE Trans. Electr. Comp. EC–**15** (1966), No. 4, 658–659.
MASSEY, J. L.; SAIN, M. K.
[1] Inverses of linear sequential circuits. IEEE Trans. on Computers C–**17** (1968), No. 4, 330–337.

McCluskey, E. J.
[1] A comparison of sequential and iterative circuits. Trans. AIEE 78 (Comm. and Electronics, No. 46) 1960, 1039—1044.
[2] Minimum state sequential circuits for a restricted class of incompletely specified flow tables. Bell System Techn. J. **41** (1962), No. 6.
[3] Reduction of feedback-loops in sequential circuits and carry leads in iterative networks. Information and Control **6** (1963), 99—118.
[4] Introduction to the theory of switching circuits. McGraw-Hill Book Co., New York 1965.
McCluskey, E. J.; Bartee, T. C.
[1] A survey of switching circuit theory. McGraw-Hill Book Comp., New York 1962.
McCluskey, E. J.; Unger, S. H.
[1] A note on the number of internal variable assignments for sequential switching circuits. IRE Trans. Electr. Comp. EC—**8** (1959), 439—440.
McNaughton, R.
[1] Symbolic logic and automata. Wright Air Dev. Div., Techn. Note 60. Cincinnati (Ohio) 1960.
[2] The theory of automata, a survey. Advances in Comp. **2**, Acad. Press, New York 1961, 379—421.
[3] Sequential circuits. Part B: Behavioral properties. IEEE Trans. Circuit Theory CT—**11** (1964), No. 1, 27—29.
[4] Testing and generating infinite sequences by a finite automaton. Information and Control **9** (1966), 521—530.
[5] The loop complexity of pure-group events. Information and Control **11** (1967), 167 to 176.
McNaughton, R.; Yamada, H.
[1] Regular expressions and state graphs for automata. IRE Trans. Electr. Comp. EC—**9** (1960), 39—47.
Mealy, G. H.
[1] A method for synthesizing sequential circuits. Bell System Techn. J. **34** (1955), 1045 to 1079.
Medvediev, O. V.
[1] Minimization of the number of states of a sequential machine under input sequences not containing two consecutive symbols which coincide. Automatika i telemechanika 1966, No. 5.
Medvediev, Yu. T.
[1] On a class of events representable in finite automata. "Automata" IL, Moscow 1956, 385—401.
Melikhov, A. N.; Bernstein, L. S.
[1] Sequential decomposition of abstract automata. Izv. AN SSSR, Techn. Cyb. 1968, No. 3, 44—53.
Melikhov, A. N.; Dvoriantsev, Yu. A.
[1] Set theoretic and algebraic operations on finite automata. Izv. AN SSSR, Techn. Cyb. 1967, No. 3, 118—125.
Meo, A. R.
[1] Determination of the *ps* maximal implicants of a switching function. IEEE Trans. Electr. Comp. EC—**14** (1965), No. 2, 830.
Meyer, A. R.
[1] A note on star-free events. J. ACM **16** (1969), No. 2, 220—225.
Mezei, J. E.
[1] Minimal characterizing experiments for finite memory automata. IRE Trans. Electr. Comp. EC—**10** (1961), No. 2, 288.

[2] Structures of monoids with applications to automata. Mathematical Theory of Automata, Polytechnic Press, Brooklyn (N.J.) 1963, 267—300.

Mezei, J.; Wright, J. B.

[1] Algebraic automata and context-free sets. Information and Control **11** (1967), 3—29.

Miller, R. E.

[1] Switching theory. Vol. I: Combinatorial circuits, Vol. II: Sequential circuits. J. Wiley & Sons, New York 1965.

Miller, R. E.; Winograd, S.

[1] On the number of transitions entering the states of a finite automaton. IEEE Trans. Electr. Comp. EC—**13** (1964), 463.

Minsky, M.; Papert, S.

[1] Unrecognizable sets of numbers. J. ACM **13** (1966), 281—286.

Mirkin, B. G.

[1] On dual automata. Cybernetika, Kiev, 1966, No. 1, 7—10.

[2] On the theory of multipe tape automata. Cybernetika, Kiev, 1966, No. 5, 12—18.

[3] On the recognition of the relative equivalence of states in sequential machines. Automatika i telemechanika 1967, No. 2, 133—136.

[4] Minimization of sequential machines with respect to regular and complete to the right events. Automatika i telemechanika 1967, No. 11, 149—153.

Mizumoto, M.; Toyoda, J.; Tanaka, K.

[1] Some considerations of fuzzy automata. J. Computer and Systems Sci. **3** (1969), 409 to 422.

Modrow, H. D.

[1] Über einen Automatentyp, der nicht-sequentielle Funktionen realisiert. Vortrag, Jahrestagung der Math. Ges. d. DDR, 13.—18. Febr. 1967 in Berlin. In: Eine Erweiterung der Theorie der determinierten abstrakten Automaten auf nicht-sequentielle Wortfunktionen. Dissertation, Humboldt-Univ., Berlin 1971.

Moisil, G. C.

[1] Algebraicka teorie automatů. Praha 1964.

Moore, E. F.

[1] Gedanken-experiments on sequential machines. Automata Studies, Ann. Math. Studies **34**, Princeton 1956, 129—153.

[2] Bibliographic comments on sequential machines. Sequential Machines, Addison-Wesley Publ. Comp., Reading (Mass.), 1964, 236—244.

Moshchenskii, V. A.

[1] On a problem in the theory of synthesis of finite automata. Izv. AN SSSR Techn. Cyb. 1966, No. 1, 70—78.

Muller, D. E.

[1] Infinite sequences and finite machines. Switching Circuit Theory and Logic. Design (IEEE Conf. Rec.) New York 1963, 3—16.

Mullin, A. A.

[1] Stochastic combinational relay switching circuits and reliability. IRE Trans. Circuit Theory CT—**6** (1959), 131—133.

Muroga, S.

[1] Preliminary study of the probabilistic behavior of a digital network with majority decision elements. RADC-TN-60-146 (1960).

Münteferiing, P.

[1] Über stabile und definite partielle Automaten. To appear in Elektron. Informationsverarb. u. Kybernetik.

[2] Transformation von partiellen Automaten. To appear in Elektron. Informationsverarb. u. Kybernetik.

Poage, J. F.; McCluskey, E. J.
[1] Derivation of optimum test sequences for sequential machines. Switching Circuit Theory and Logic. Design (IEEE Conf. Rec.) New York 1964, 121—132.
Pohl, H.-J.
[1] Theoretische Grundlagen der dynamischen Optimierung. Diplom-Arbeit, Inst. f. Math. Logik, Humboldt-Univ., Berlin 1965.
[2] Über die Reduzierung der Anzahl der Eingabesignale von Automaten. Z. Math. Logik Grundl. Math. **14** (1968), 93—96.
[3] Darstellbarkeit von Ereignissen in Z-endlichen Automaten. Z. Math. Logik Grundl. Math. **15** (1969), 93—95.
[4] Ein Ansatz zur Theorie topologischer Automaten. Dissertation, Humboldt-Univ., Berlin 1971.
Polyak, B. T.
[1] The problem of multistep choice. Vopr. Theor. Mat. Machin. Moscow **2** (1962), 156 to 173.
Ponomariev, V. A.
[1] On a construction of a finite automaton which is asymptotically optimal in a stationary, random environment. Biophysica **6** (1963), No. 6.
Pospielov, D. A.
[1] Probabilistic automata. Bibl. autom., Vol. **394**, Moscow 1970.
Pottosin, Yu. V.
[1] A comparative estimate for two algorithms minimizing the number of states of a discrete automaton. Autom. i Vich. Techn. 1967, No. 4.
Preparata, F. P.
[1] State logic relations for autonomous sequential networks. IEEE Trans. Electr. Comp. EC—**13** (1964), 542.
[2] On the realizibility of special classes of autonomous sequential networks. IEEE Trans. Electr. Comp. EC—**14** (1965), No. 6, 791—797; Correction: EC—**15** (1966), No. 3, 327.
Przymusinska, J.
[1] Pewne aspekty teorii automatow skonczonych w zastosowaniu do teorii sterowania. Arch. automat. i telemech. **10** (1965), 391—404.
Pu, A. T.
[1] Generalized decomposition of incomplete finite automata. Information and Control **13** (1968), 1—19.
Pugsley, J. H.
[1] Sequential functions and linear sequential machines. IEEE Trans. Electr. Comp. EC—**14** (1965), No. 3, 376—382.

Rabin, M. O.
[1] Probabilistic automata. Information and Control **6** (1963), 230—245.
[2] Lectures on classical and probabilistic automata. Automata Theory, Academic Press, New York—London 1966, 304—313.
[3] Mathematical theory of automata. Proc. Amer. Math. Soc. 1967.
Rabin, M. O.; Scott, D.
[1] Remarks on finite automata. Summaries Summer Inst. Symb. Logic (Cornell Univ. 1957) 1960, 106—112.
[2] Finite automata and their decision problems. IBM J. Res. Dev. **3** (1959), 114—125.
Radke, C. E.
[1] Enumeration of strongly connected sequential machines. Information and Control 8 (1965), 377—389.

[3] Minimisierungsprobleme in der Theorie der abstrakten Automaten. Dissertation, Humboldt-Univ., Berlin 1971.
Münteferinc, P.; Starke, P. H.
[1] Über reduzible Ereignisse. To appear in Elektron. Informationsverarb. u. Kybernetik.
Muroga, S.; Toda, I.
[1] Lower bound of the number of threshold functions. IEEE Trans. Electr. Comp. EC—**15** (1966), No. 4, 805.
Murray, F. J.
[1] Mechanisms and robots. J. ACM **2** (1955), 61—82.
Murskii, V. L.
[1] On the transformations of finite automata. Probl. cybern. **15** (1965), 101—116.
Myhill, J.
[1] Finite automata and representation of events. Wright Air Dev. Center Report, Dayton (Ohio) 1957.
[2] Linear bounded automata. Wright Air Dev. Div. Techn. Note 60—165, Cincinnati (Ohio) 1960.

Narasimhan, R.
[1] Minimizing incompletely specified sequential switching functions. IRE Trans. Electr. Comp. EC—**10** (1961), 531—532.
Naslin, P.
[1] Finite automata. Progr. Control Engng. **2**, Academic Press, New York 1964, 117—159.
[2] Circuits logiques et automatisme à sequences. 2-e ed., Dunod, Paris 1965.
Nasu, M.; Honda, N.
[1] Fuzzy events realized by finite probabilistic automata. Information and Control **12** (1968), 284—303.
[2] Mappings induced by PGSM-mappings and some recursively unsolvable problems of finite probabilistic automata. Information and Control **15** (1969), 250—273.
Nawrotzki, K.
[1] Eine Bemerkung zur Reduktion stochastischer Automaten. Elektron. Informationsverarb. u. Kybernetik **2** (1966), 191—193.
Neimark, Yu. I.; Grigorenko, V. P.; Rapoport, A. N.
[1] On the optimization of independent, deterministic and stochastic automata. Prikl. Mat. i Cyb. Gorkii, 1967, 148—166.
Nelson, R. J.
[1] Basic concepts of automata theory. Proc. of the ACM 20th Nat. Conf., Spartan Books, Washington (D.C.) 1965, 138—161.
[2] Introduction to automata. J. Wiley Sons Inc., New York—London—Sidney 1968.
Nepomniashchii, V. A.
[1] On algorithms realizable by repeated applications of finite automata. Discr. analysis **5** (1965), 77—82.
[2] On certain automata which can compute a basis for the recursively enumerable sets. Algebra i Logika Seminar 1966, No. 5, 69—83.
Nerode, A.
[1] Linear automaton transformations. Proc. Amer. Math. Soc. **9** (1958), 541—544.
Netherwood, D. S.
[1] Minimal sequential machines. IRE Trans. Electr. Comp. EC—8 (1959), 339—345.
Neuber, S.; Starke, P. H.
[1] Über Homomorphie und Reduktion bei nicht-deterministischen Automaten. Elektron. Informationsverarb. u. Kybernetik **3** (1967), 349—359.

NEUMANN, J. VON
[1] Probabilistics logic and the synthesis of reliable organisms from unreliable components. Automata Studies. Ann. Math. Studies **34**, Princeton 1956, 43—98.
NEUMANN, P. G.
[1] Error limiting codes using information-lossless sequential machines. IEEE Trans. Information Theory IT—**10** (1964), 108—115.
NEWBORN, M. M.
[1] Maximal memory binary input — binary output finite-memory sequential machines. IEEE Trans. on Computers C—**17** (1968), 67—71.
[2] A synthesis technique for binary input — binary output synchronous sequential Moore machines. IEEE Trans. on Computers C—**17** (1968), No. 7, 697—699.
NICHOLS, A. J.
[1] Modular synthesis of sequential machines. Switching Circuit Theory and Logic. Design (IEEE Conf. Rec.) New York 1965, 62—70.
NICHOLS, A. J.; BERNSTEIN, A. J.
[1] State assignments in combinational circuits. IEEE Trans. Electr. Comp. EC—**14** (1965), No. 3, 343.
NIEH, T. T.
[1] Orderings of stochastic sequential machines. D. Sc. Dissertation, Univ. of California, Berkeley 1968.
[2] Stochastic sequential machines with prescribed performance criteria. Information and Control **13** (1968), 99—113.
[3] On the uniqueness of minimal-state stochastic sequential machines. IEEE Trans. on Computers C—**19** (1970), 164—166.
NIEH, T. T.; CARLYLE, J. W.
[1] On the deterministic realization of stochastic finite-state machines. In: Proc. of the 2nd Ann. Princeton Conf. on Information Sci. and Systems, 1968.
NIEVERGELT, J.
[1] Partially ordered classes of finite automata. Switching Circuit Theory and Logic. Design (IEEE Conf. Rec.) New York 1965, 229—234.
NOVANSKY, R.
[1] Syntéza sekvenčnich obvodu s využitim obecnych pamětovych elementu. Kybernetika (Praha) **3** (1967), 234—251.
[2] Memory elements and partition pairs in the synthesis of sequential circuits. Kybernetika (Praha) **3** (1967), 377—397.

OEHMKE, R. H.
[1] On the structure of an automaton and its input semigroup. J. ACM **10** (1963), No. 4, 521—525.
OFMAN, YU. P.
[1] A universal automaton. Tr. Moscow Mat. Obsh. **14** (1965) 189—199.
ONICESCU, O.; GUIAŞU, S.
[1] Finite abstract random automata. Z. f. Wahrscheinlichkeitstheorie **3** (1965), 279—285.
OTT, E. H.
[1] Theory and application of stochastic sequential machines. Research Rept., Sperry Rand Res. Center, Sudbury (Mass.) 1966.
[2] Reconsider the state minimization problem for stochastic finite state systems. IEEE Conf. Rec. of the 7th Ann. Symp. on Switching Circuit and Automata Theory, 1966, 267 to 273.
OTT, G.; FEINSTEIN, N. F.
[1] Design of sequential machines from their regular expressions. J. ACM **8** (1961), 585—600.

OVERHEU, D. L.
[1] An abstract machine for symbolic computation. J. ACM **13** (1966), 444—468.

PAGE, C. V.
[1] Equivalences between probabilistic sequential machines. Techn. Rept., Univ. of Michigan, Ann. Arbor 1965.
[2] Equivalences between probabilistic and deterministic sequential machines. Information and Control **9** (1966), 469—520.
[3] Strong stability problems for probabilistic sequential machines. Information and Control **15** (1969), 487—509.
PAULL, M. C.; UNGER, S. H.
[1] Minimizing the number of states in incompletely specified sequential switching functions. IRE Trans. Electr. Comp. EC—8 (1959), 356—367.
PAZ, A.
[1] Homomorphisms between finite automata. Bull. Res. Council Israel, F **10** (1962), No. 3, 93—100.
[2] Some aspects of probabilistic automata. Information and Control **9** (1966), 26—60.
[3] Minimization theorems and techniques for sequential stochastic machines. Information and Control **11** (1967), 155—166.
[4] A finite set of $n \times n$ stochastic matrices generating all n-dimensional probability vectors whose coordinates have finite binary expansion. SIAM J. Control **5** (1967), 545 to 554.
[5] Fuzzy star functions, probabilistic automata, and their approximation by nonprobabilistic automata. J. Computer and System Sci. **1** (1967), 371—390.
[6] Homomorphisms between stochastic sequential machines and related topics. Math. Systems Theory **2** (1968), No. 3, 223—245.
[7] Regular in stochastic sequential machines. IEEE Trans. on Computers C—**19** (1970), 456—457.
[8] Introduction to probabilistic automata. Academic Press, New York—London 1971.
PAZ, A.; PELEG, B.
[1] Ultimate-definite and symmetric-definite events and automata. J. ACM **12** (1965), 399—410.
[2] On concatenative decompositions of regular events. IEEE Trans. on Computers C—**17** (1968), No. 3, 229—237.
PEDELTY, M. J.
[1] Temporally organized automata and an algebraic theory of machines. Comp. and Inform. Sci., Spartan Books, Washington (D.C.) 1964, 246—261.
PERLES, M.; RABIN, M. O.; SHAMIR, E.
[1] The theory of definite automata. IEEE Trans. Electr. Comp. EC—**12** (1963), No. 3, 233—243.
PETROSIAN, A. V.; SHUKURIAN, YU. G.
[1] On decompositions of automata. Tr. Vich. Centr. AN Arm. SSR **2** (1964), 51—60.
PFEIFFER, P. E.
[1] Sets, events and switching. McGraw-Hill Book Co., New York 1964.
PIYL, E. I.
[1] On coding inner states of finite automata. Izv. AN SSSR Tech. Cyb. 1965, No. 2, 58—65.
[2] Some problems of coding finite automata. Probl. Synth. digital automata. Izd. Nauka, 1967, 14—27.
PLESNEVICH, G. S.
[1] On events connected with a family of automata. Vich. Syst. **9** (1963) 44—64 (Novosibirsk).

RAMAMOORTHY, C. V.
[1] Connectivity considerations of graphs representing discrete sequential systems. IEEE Trans. Electr. Comp. EC—**14** (1965), No. 5, 724.
RANEY, G. N.
[1] Sequential functions. J. ACM **5** (1958), 177—180.
REDKO, V. N.
[1] On commutative closures of events. DAN URSR 1963, No. 9, 1156—1159.
[2] On the algebra of comutative events. Ukr. Mat. Journ. **16** (1964), No. 2, 185 to 195.
[3] On a defining collection of relations in the algebra of regular events. Ukr. Mat. Journ. **16** (1964), 120—126.
[4] On commutative automata. Theory of finite and probabilistic automata. Izd. Nauka Moscow, 1965, 253—256.
[5] On the connection of automata and semi-groups. Vop. Theor. Cyb. Kiev 1965, 183 to 190.
[6] On a class of compositions of automata. Theory of automata seminar. Izd. Nauk. dumka Kiev **1** (1966), 5—11.
REED, I. S.
[1] Some remarks on state reduction of asynchronous circuits by the Paull-Unger method. IEEE Trans. Electr. Comp. EC—**14** (1965), No. 2, 262.
REIFFEN, B.
[1] Sequential decoding for discrete input memoryless channels. IEEE Trans. Information Theory IT—**8** (1963), 208—221.
REIFFEN, B.; YUDKIN, H. L.
[1] On nonlinear binary sequential circuits and their inverses. IEEE Trans. Electr. Comp. EC—**15** (1966), No. 4, 586.
REUSCH, B.
[1] Lineare Automaten. B.I.-Hochschulskripten 708, Mannheim 1969.
REYNOLDS, B. G.
[1] Some results on cascade decomposition of automata. Information and Control **14** (1969), 478—489.
[2] General repetitive events and machines. IEEE Trans. on Computers C—**19** (1970), 167—169.
REYNOLDS, B. G.; CUTLIP, W. F.
[1] Synchronization and general repetitive machines with application to ultimate definite automata. J. ACM **16** (1969), No. 2, 226—234.
RITCHIE, R. W.
[1] Finite automata and sets of squares. J. ACM **10** (1963), 528—531.
ROSE, G. F.
[1] Output completeness in sequential machines. Proc. Amer. Math. Soc. **13** (1962), No. 4, 611—614.
ROSEN, R.
[1] Abstract biological systems as sequential machines. Bull. Math. Biophys. **26** (1964), 103—111, 239—246.
ROSENBERG, A. L.
[1] On n-tape finite state acceptors. Switching Circuit Theory and Logic. Design (IEEE Conf. Rec.) New York 1964, 76—81.
[2] On multi-head finite automata. IBM. J. Res. Dev. **10** (1966), 388—394.
ROSENKRANTZ, D. J.
[1] Synchronizing sequences for incompletely specified flow tables. IEEE Trans. Electr. Comp. EC—**15** (1966), No. 1, 104.

Salomaa, A.
[1] Theorems on the representation of events in Moore-automata. Ann. Univ. Turkuensis, Ser. A, I., 69, 1964.
[2] On the reducibility of events represented in automata. Ann. Acad. Sci. Fennicae, Ser. A, I., 353, 1964.
[3] Axiom systems for regular expressions of finite automata. Ann. Univ. Turkuensis, Ser. A, I, 75, 1964.
[4] On probabilistic automata with one input letter. Ann. Univ. Turkuensis, Ser. A., I., 85 (1965), 3–16.
[5] Two complete axiom systems for the algebra of regular events. J. ACM **13** (1966), 158 to 169.
[6] On m-adic probabilistic automata. Information and Control **10** (1967), 215–219.
[7] On events represented by probabilistic automata of different types. Canad. Math. J. **20** (1968), 242–251.
[8] Theory of automata. Pergamon Press 1968.
[9] On languages accepted by probabilistic and time-variant automata. In: Proc. of the 2nd Ann. Princeton Conf. on Information Sci. and Systems 1968.
[10] On finite automata with a time-variant structure. Information and Control **13** (1968), 85–98.
[11] On finite time-variant automata with monitors of different types. Ann. Univ. Turku, Ser. A. I., **118**: **3** (1968).
[12] On regular expressions and regular canonical systems. Math. Systems Theory **2** (1968), 341–355.
[13] Probabilistic and weighted grammars. Information and Control **15** (1969), 529 to 544.
Salomaa, A.; Tixier, V.
[1] Two complete axiom systems for the extended language of regular expressions. IEEE Trans. on Comp. C–**17** (1968), No. 7, 700.
Santos, E. S.
[1] Maximin automata. Information and Control **13** (1968), 363–377.
[2] Maximin sequential chains. J. Math. Anal. and Appl. **26** (1969), 28–38.
Santos, E. S.; Wee, W. G.
[1] General formulation of sequential machines. Information and Control **12** (1968), 5–10.
Schmitt, A.
[1] Theorie der nicht-deterministischen und unvollständigen Mealy-Automaten. Dissertation, Techn. Hochschule Hannover, Dez. 1966.
Schnorr, C.-P.
[1] Freie assoziative Systeme. Elektron. Informationsverarb. u. Kybernetik **3** (1967), 319 to 340.
Schützenberger, M. P.
[1] On the definition of family of automata. Information and Control **4** (1961), 245–270.
[2] Finite counting automata. Information and Control **5** (1962), 91–107.
[3] On context-free languages and push-down automata. Information and Control **6** (1963), 246–264.
[4] A remark on incompletely specified automata. Information and Control **8** (1965), 373–376.
[5] On the algebraic theory of automata. Proc. IFIP Congr. New York City 1965, Vol I, Washington–London 1965, 27–29.
Scott, D.
[1] Some definitorial suggestions for automata theory. J. Computer System Sci. **1** (1967), 187–212.

SESHU, S.
[1] Mathematical models for sequential machines. IRE Nat. Convent. Rec. 7, No. 2 (1959), 4–16.
SESHU, S.; FREEMAN, D. N.
[1] The diagnosis of asynchronous sequential switching systems. IRE Trans. Electr. Comp. EC–**11** (1962), 459–465.
SESHU, S.; MILLER, R. E.; METZE, G.
[1] Transition matrices of sequential machines. IRE Trans. Circuit Theory CT–**6** (1959), No. 1, 5–12.
SEKI, S.; HIROSE, K.
[1] A remark on the theory of automata. Comment. math. Univ. St. Pauli **11** (1963), No. 2, 115–119.
SEREBRIANII, A. U.
[1] On events representable in finite automata. Uspekhi Mat. Nauk. **20** (1965), No. 2, (122) 203–206.
SHEPHERDSON, J. C.
[1] The reduction of two-way automata to one-way automata. IBM J. Res. Dev. **3** (1959), 198–199.
SHISHKOV, D. B.
[1] Several questions on the analysis and synthesis of discrete automata. Dissertation. AN USSR Kiev 1967.
SHREIDER, YU. A.
[1] The problem of dynamic planning and automata. Probl. Cyb. **5** (1961), 31–47.
[2] Teaching models and control systems. "Stochastic models of Teaching". IL, Moscow 1962.
SHUKURIAN, YU. G.
[1] On the optimization of automata with a terminal state and without cycles. Cybernetika Kiev, 1967, No. 2, 27–35.
SIDELNIKOV, V. M.
[1] On the statistical properties of transformations established by finite automata. Cybernetika Kiev, 1965, No. 6, 1–14.
SIMON, J. M.
[1] A note on memory aspects of sequence transducers. IRE Trans. Circuit Theory CT–**6** (1959), 26–29.
SKLANSKY, J.
[1] Learning systems of automatic control. IEEE Trans. Automatic Control AC–**11** (1966), No. 1, 6–19.
SKORNJAKOW, L. A.
[1] Über eine Klasse von Automaten (Nervensystemen). Probl. d. Kybernetik **4**, Akademie-Verlag, Berlin 1964, 23–40.
SORKIN, J. I.
[1] Theorie der definierenden Relationen für Automaten. Probl. d. Kybernetik **6**, Akademie-Verlag, Berlin 1966, 57–90.
SOŮKUP, J.
[1] Non-deterministic behavior of deterministic computer. Kybernetika (Praha) **4** (1968), No. 1, 1–5.
SPIVAK, M. A.
[1] A new algorithm for the abstract synthesis of automata. Theory of automata, seminar, **3** (1963), 3–43 (Kiev).
[2] An approach to the theory of automata through the methods of the theory of relations. Probl. Cyb. **12** (1964), 69–98.

[3] On the method of analysis of abstract automata by means of equations in the algebra of events. Cybernetika Kiev, 1965, No. 1.
[4] An algorithm for the abstract synthesis of automata in the extended language of regular expressions. Izv. AN SSSR Rechn. Cyb. 1965, No. 1, 51—57.
[5] An algebraic characteristic of the calculating capacity of an automaton. Cybernetika Kiev, 1965, No. 4, 1—11.
[6] Representation of automata mappings by regular expressions. Cybernetika Kiev, 1965, No. 6, 15—17.
[7] Decomposition of a regular expression on the basis of its application. DAN SSSR **162** (1965), No. 3, 520—522.
[8] Some properties of the set of experiments on an automaton. Cybernetika Kiev, 1966, No. 6, 1—7.
[9] On the minimization of a Moore automaton. Cybernetica Kiev, 1967, No. 1, 5—6.
[10] On a remark by A. C. Fleck. Cybernetika Kiev, 1969, No. 2, 97—98.
[11] Synthesis of finite automata on the basis of their sets of experiments. Cybernetika Kiev, 1969, No. 5, 15—20.

Srinivasan, C. V.
[1] State diagrams of linear sequential machines. J. Franklin Inst. **273** (1962), No. 5, 383 to 418.

Stănciulescu, F. S.
[1] Einige Bemerkungen zur Sequenziallogik der endlichen Automaten. Z. Math. Logik Grundl. Math. **11** (1965), 57—60.
[2] Sequential logic and its application to the synthesis of finite automata. IEEE Trans. Electr. Comp. EC—**14** (1965), No. 6, 786.

Stănciulescu, F.; Oprescu, M. F. A.
[1] A mathematical model of finite random automata. IEEE Trans. on Comp. C—**17** (1968), No. 1, 27—31.

Starke, P. H.
[1] Über die Darstellbarkeit von Ereignissen in nicht-initialen Automaten. Z. Math. Logik Grundl. Math. **9** (1963), 315—319.
[2] Die Imitation endlicher Medwedjew-Automaten durch Nervennetze. Z. Math. Logik Grundl. Math. **11** (1965), 241—248.
[3] Theorie stochastischer Automaten. Elektron. Informationsverarb. u. Kybernetik **1** (1965), 5—32, 71—98.
[4] Einige Bemerkungen über nicht-deterministische Automaten. Elektron. Informationsverarb. u. Kybernetik **2** (1966), 61—82.
[5] Stochastische Ereignisse und Wortmengen. Z. Math. Logik Grundl. Math. **12** (1966), 61 to 68.
[6] Stochastische Ereignisse und stochastische Operatoren. Elektron. Informationsverarb. u. Kybernetik **2** (1966), 177—190.
[7] Theory of stochastic automata. Kybernetika (Praha) **2** (1966), 475—482.
[8] Eine Bemerkung über homogene Experimente. Elektron. Informationsverarb. u. Kybernetik **2** (1966), 257—259.
[9] Über Experimente an Automaten. Z. Math. Logik Grundl. Math. **13** (1967), 67—80.
[10] Hüllenoperationen für nicht-deterministische Automaten. Elektron. Informationsverarb. u. Kybernetik **3** (1967), 283—294.
[11] Die Reduktion von stochastischen Automaten. Elektron. Informationsverarb. u. Kybernetik **4** (1968), 93—99.
[12] Schwache Homomorphismen für stochastische Automaten. Z. Math. Logik Grundl. Math. **15** (1969), 421—429.

[13] Über die Minimalisierung von stochastischen Rabin-Automaten. Elektron. Informationsverarb. u. Kybernetik **5** (1969), 153—170.
[14] Über reguläre nicht-deterministische Operatoren. Elektron. Informationsverarb. u. Kybernetik **6** (1970), 229—237.
[15] Über Minima von nicht-deterministischen Automaten. Wiss. Z. Humboldt-Univ. Berlin, Math.-Nat. Reihe, **19** (1970), No. 6, 663—664.
[16] Einige Bemerkungen über asynchrone stochastische Automaten. Ann. Acad. Sci. Fennicae, Ser. A, I, No. 491 (1971).
[17] Über die Transformation zweiseitig unendlicher Folgen. To appear in Elektron. Informationsverarb. u. Kybernetik.
[18] Über die Experimentmengen determinierter Automaten. To appear in Elektron. Informationsverarb. u. Kybernetik.
[19] Über Automaten mit halbgeordnetem Ausgabealphabet. To appear in Wiss. Z. Humboldt-Univ. Berlin.
[20] Allgemeine Probleme und Methoden in der Automatentheorie. To appear in Wiss. Z. Humboldt-Univ. Berlin.

Starke, P. H.; Thiele, H.
[1] Zufällige Zustände in stochastischen Automaten. Elektron. Informationsverarb. u. Kybernetik **3** (1967), 25—37.
[2] On asynchronous stochastic automata. Information and Control **17** (1970), 265—293.

Stearns, R. E.; Hartmanis, J.
[1] On the state assignment problem for sequential machines II. IRE Trans. Electr. Comp. EC—**10** (1961), No. 4, 593—603.
[2] Regularity preserving modifications of regular expressions. Information and Control **6** (1963), 55—69.

Stefanok, V. L.
[1] An example concerning the problem of collective behaviour of two automata. Automatika i telemechanika **24** (1963), No. 6.

Sucheston, L.
[1] Note on mixing sequences of events. Acta Math. Acad. Scient. Hung. **11** (1960), 3—4.

Sunaga, T.
[1] Algebraic theory of the composition and decomposition of automata. RAAG Mem. Unifying Study Basic Probl. Engng. and Phys., Sci., Tokyo, **3** (1962), 495—510.
[2] An algebraic theory of the analysis and synthesis of automata. Mathematical Theory of Automata, Polytechnic Press, Brooklyn (N.J.) 1963, 385—414.

Tal, A. A
[1] Question language and the abstract synthesis of minimal sequential machines. Automatika i telemechanika **25** (1964), No. 6, 946—962.

Thatcher, J. W.; Wright, J. B.
[1] Generalized finite automata theory with application to a decision problem of second-order logic. Math. Systems Theory **2** (1968), No. 1, 57—81.

Thierrin, G.
[1] Permutation automata. Math. Systems Theory **2** (1968), No. 1, 83—90.

Tracey, J. H.
[1] Internal state assignment for asynchronous sequential machines. IEEE Trans. Electr. Comp. EC—**15** (1966), No. 4, 551—560.

Trauth, C. A.
[1] Group-type automata. J. ACM **13** (1966), 170—175.

Troshin, V. I.
[1] An algebraic way of minimizing incompletely specified sequential machines. Automatika i telemechanika 1965, No. 12, 2176—2181.
Tsertsvadze, G. N.
[1] Some properties and methods of the synthesis of stochastic automata. Automatika i telemechanika **14** (1963), No. 3, 341—352.
[2] Stochastic automata and the problem of constructing reliable automata from unreliable elements. Automatika i telemechanika **25** (1964), No. 2, 213—226, No. 4, 492—499.
Tsetlin, M. L.
[1] On the behaviour of finite automata in random environments. Automatika i telemechanika **22** (1961), No. 10, 1345.
[2] Some problems concerning the behaviour of finite automata, DAN SSSR **139** (1961), No. 4, 830.
[3] Über sequentielle Schaltungen. Probl. d. Kybernetik **1**, Akademie-Verlag, Berlin 1962.
[4] Finite automata and modelling the simplest forms of behaviour. Uspechi Mat. Nauk **18** (1963), No. 4, (112) 3—27.
[5] Remarks on the game of a finite automaton with a partner applying a mixed strategy. DAN SSSR **149** (1963) No. 1, 52.
Tsetlin, M. L.; Krilov, V. Yu.
[1] On games of automata. Automatika i telemechanika **24** (1963), No. 7.
[2] Examples of games of automata. DAN SSSR **149** (1963), No. 2, 284.
Turakainen, P.
[1] On nonregular events representable in probabilistic automata with one input letter. Ann. Univ. Turkuensis, Ser. A, I., **90** (1966), 3—14.
[2] On probabilistic automata and their generalizations. Ann. Acad. Sci. Fennicae, Ser. A, I., 429 (1968).

Unger, S. H.
[1] Flow table simplification — some usefull aids. IEEE Trans. Electr. Comp. EC—**14** (1965), No. 3, 472.

Vaisbord, E. M.; Rosenstein, G. Sh.
[1] On the life span of stochastic automata. Izv. AN SSSR, Tech. Cyb. 1965, No. 4, 52—59.
[2] On a method of constructing optimal environment for non-stable automata. Izv. AN SSSR, Tech. Cyb. 1966, No. 2, 45—48.
Varshavskii, V. I.
[1] Some problems in the theory of logical networks constructed from threshhold elements. Vopr. Theor. Mat. Machine **2** (1962), 52—106.
Varshavskii, V. I.; Gersht, A. M.
[1] The behaviour of continuous automata in random environments. Probl. Pered. Inf. **2** (1966), No. 3.
Varshavskii, V. I., Meleshina, M. V., Tsetlin, M. L.
[1] The behaviour of automata in periodic random environments, and the problem of synchronization in the presence of noise. Probl. Pered. Inf. **1** (1965), No. 1, 65—71.
Varshavskii, V. I.; Vorontsova, I. P.
[1] On the behaviour of stochastic automata with variable structure. Automatika i telemechanika **24** (1963), No. 3, 353.
Varshavskii, V. I.; Vorontsova, I. P.; Tsetlin, M. L.
[1] Teaching stochastic automata. Biological aspects of cybernetics. Izd. AN SSSR, Moscow 1962.

Vavilov, E. N., Shishkov, D. B.
[1] Analysis and synthesis of automata given by a system of functions of excitation and outputs. Cybernetika Kiev, 1967, No. 4, 1—8.
Verbeek, L. A. M.
[1] Reliable computation with unreliable circuitry. Proc. Bionics Symp., Wright Air Devel. Div., Techn. Report 60—600 (1960), 83—91.
[2] Pseudo-variety separability of subsets of a monoid with application to finite automata. Automata Theory, Academic Press, New York—London 1966, 325—332.
Vorontsova, I. P.
[1] Algorithms for changing the transition probabilities of stochastic automata. Probl. Pered. Inf. **1** (1965), No. 3, 122—126.

Wang, F. L.
[1] Isomorphic notations of switching circuits. IEEE Trans. Electr. Comp. EC—**14** (1965), No. 6, 952.
Warfield, J. N.
[1] Synthesis of switching circuits to yield prescribed probability relations. Switching Circuit Theory and Logic. Design (IEEE Conf. Rec.) New York 1965, 303—309.
Weeg, G. P.
[1] The structure of an automaton and its operation-preserving transformation group. J. ACM **9** (1962), No. 3, 345—349.
[2] The group and semi-group associated with automata. Mathematical Theory of Automata, Polytechnic Press, Brooklyn (N.J.) 1963, 257—266.
[3] The automorphism group of the direct product of strongly related automata. J. ACM **12** (1965), No. 2, 187—195.
Wing, O.; Demetriuos, P.
[1] Analysis of probabilistic networks. IEEE Trans. Commun. Technol. (formerly IEEE Trans. Comm. Systems) **12** (1964), No. 3, 38—40.
Winograd, S.
[1] Redundancy and complexity of logical elements. Information and Control **6** (1963), 177—194.
[2] Input-error-limiting automata. J. ACM **11** (1964), No. 3, 338—351.
Winograd, S.; Cowan, J. D.
[1] Reliable computation in the presence of noise. MIT-Press, Cambridge (Mass.) 1963.
Wolf, F.
[1] Untersuchungen über den Vorhersagefehler bei stochastischen Automaten. Arbeitsber. Inst. f. Math. Maschinen u. Datenverarb. Univ. Erlangen-Nürnberg **1** (1968), No. 6
Wolf, F.; Schmitt, A.
[1] Modelle lernender Automaten. elektronische datenverarb. Beiheft 8, 1966.

Yakubaitis, E. A.
[1] An asynchronous logical automaton. Autom. i Vich. Techn. 1967, No. 1.
[2] The operation of establishing new transitions in the graph of a finite automaton. Autom. i Vich. Techn. 1967, No. 2.
[3] Indication of redundancy of a transitory signal of an asynchronous, logical automaton. Aut. i Vich. Techn. 1967, No. 3.
[4] Equal transitory signals of an asynchronous, logical automaton. Aut. i Vich. Techn. 1967, No. 4.
Yamada, H.
[1] Disjunctively linear logical nets. IRE Trans. Electr. Comp. EC—**11** (1962), 623—639.

YANOV, YU. I.
[1] On the identical transformations of regular expressions. DAN SSSR **147** (1962), 327—330.
[2] On invariant operations over events. Probl. Cyb. **12** (1963), 253—258.
[3] On equivalent transformations of regular expressions. The theory of finite and probabilistic automata. Izd. Nauka, Moscow 1965, 230—231.
YAROVITSKII, N. V.
[1] The limit behaviour of a closed system of automata with a random output. Cybernetika Kiev, 1965, No. 1, 57—61. [35—43.
[2] Probabilistic automata modelling of discrete systems. Cybernetika Kiev, 1966, No. 5,
YAU, S. S.
[1] Autonomous clocks in sequential machines. IEEE Trans. Electr. Comp. EC—**14** (1965), No. 3, 467.
YAU, S. S.; WANG, K. S.
[1] Linearity of sequential machines. IEEE Trans. Electr. Comp. EC—**15** (1966), 337—354; Corrections: EC—**15**, No. 5, 749; No. 6, 926.
YERSHOVA, E. B.
[1] A method for optimal coding of inner states of a finite automaton. Probl. Pered. Inf. **17** (1964), 70—84.
YOELI, M.
[1] The cascade decomposition of sequential machines. IRE Trans. Electron. Comp. EC—**10** (1961), 587—592.
[2] Cascade-parallel decompositions of sequential machines. IEEE Trans. Electr. Comp. EC—**12** (1963), 322—324.
[3] Generalized cascade decompositions of automata. J. ACM **12** (1965), 411—422.
[4] Canonical representations of chain events. Information and Control **8** (1965), No. 2, 180—189.
YOELI, M.; GINZBURG, A.
[1] On homomorphic images of transition graphs. Israel Inst. Technology, Techn. Rept. No. 11, Haifa 1963.
ZAKREVSKII, A. D. [89—94.
[1] On the synthesis of sequential automata. Tr. Sibirsk Phys. Tech. Inst. Tomsk **40** (1961),
[2] Realisation of random events with a given probability. Tr. Sibirsk Phys. Tech. Inst. Tomsk. **47** (1965), 56—59.
ZADEH, L. A.
[1] Stochastic finite state systems in control theory. Proc. Symp. on Optimal Control and Nonlinear Systems, Fac. des Sciences de Paris 1963, 123—132.
ZANDER, H.-J.
[1] Zur Zustandsreduktion ungetakteter (asynchroner) Folgeschaltungen. Elektron. Informationsverarb. u. Kybernetik **4** (1968), 257—278, 285—300.
ZECH, K.-A.
[1] Homomorphe Dekomposition stochastischer und nicht-deterministischer Automaten. Elektron. Informationsverarb. u. Kybernetik **7** (1971), No. 5—6, 299—317.
[2] Eine Bemerkung zur Theorie stochastischer und nicht-deterministischer Nervennetze. Elektron. Informationsverarb. u. Kybernetik **7** (1971), No. 7.
[3] Eine Bemerkung über stochastische Wahrheitsfunktionen und ihre Anwendung in der Strukturtheorie endlicher stochastischer Automaten. Elektron. Informationsverarb. u. Kybernetik **7** (1971), No. 8.
ZEIGER, H. P.
[1] Cascade synthesis of finite-state machines. Information and Control **10** (1967), 419—433.
[2] Yet another proof of the cascade decomposition theorem for finite automata. Math. Systems Theory **1** (1967), 225—228.

INDEX